GENERAL MOTORS
LUMINA/GRAND PRIX/CUTLASS SUPREME/REGAL
1988-96 REPAIR MANUAL

CHILTON'S

Covers all U.S. and Canadian models of
Buick Regal, Chevrolet Lumina, Monte Carlo,
Oldsmobile Cutlass Supreme and Pontiac Grand Prix

by Christine L. Sheeky, S.A.E.

CHILTON *Automotive Books*

PUBLISHED BY **HAYNES NORTH AMERICA**, Inc.

Manufactured in USA
© 1996 Haynes North America, Inc.
ISBN 0-8019-8800-4
Library of Congress Catalog Card No. 96-84547
11 12 13 14 15 9876543210

Haynes Publishing Group
Sparkford Nr Yeovil
Somerset BA22 7JJ England

Haynes North America, Inc
861 Lawrence Drive
Newbury Park
California 91320 USA

ABCDE
FG

Contents

Contents

SAFETY NOTICE

Proper service and repair procedures are vital to the safe, reliable operation of all motor vehicles, as well as the personal safety of those performing repairs. This manual outlines procedures for servicing and repairing vehicles using safe, effective methods. The procedures contain many NOTES, CAUTIONS and WARNINGS which should be followed, along with standard procedures to eliminate the possibility of personal injury or improper service which could damage the vehicle or compromise its safety.

It is important to note that repair procedures and techniques, tools and parts for servicing motor vehicles, as well as the skill and experience of the individual performing the work vary widely. It is not possible to anticipate all of the conceivable ways or conditions under which vehicles may be serviced, or to provide cautions as to all possible hazards that may result. Standard and accepted safety precautions and equipment should be used when handling toxic or flammable fluids, and safety goggles or other protection should be used during cutting, grinding, chiseling, prying, or any other process that can cause material removal or projectiles.

Some procedures require the use of tools specially designed for a specific purpose. Before substituting another tool or procedure, you must be completely satisfied that neither your personal safety, nor the performance of the vehicle will be endangered.

Although information in this manual is based on industry sources and is complete as possible at the time of publication, the possibility exists that some car manufacturers made later changes which could not be included here. While striving for total accuracy, the authors or publishers cannot assume responsibility for any errors, changes or omissions that may occur in the compilation of this data.

PART NUMBERS

Part numbers listed in this reference are not recommendations by Haynes North America, Inc. for any product brand name. They are references that can be used with interchange manuals and aftermarket supplier catalogs to locate each brand supplier's discrete part number.

SPECIAL TOOLS

Special tools are recommended by the vehicle manufacturer to perform their specific job. Use has been kept to a minimum, but where absolutely necessary, they are referred to in the text by the part number of the tool manufacturer. These tools can be purchased, under the appropriate part number, from your local dealer or regional distributor, or an equivalent tool can be purchased locally from a tool supplier or parts outlet. Before substituting any tool for the one recommended, read the SAFETY NOTICE at the top of this page.

ACKNOWLEDGMENTS

Portions of materials contained herein have been reprinted with the permission of General Motors Corporation, Service Technology Group.

1

GENERAL INFORMATION AND MAINTENANCE

HOW TO USE THIS BOOK

This Chilton's Total Car Care manual for the Chevrolet Lumina and Monte Carlo, Buick Regal, Oldsmobile Cutlass Supreme, and Pontiac Grand Prix is intended to help you learn more about the inner workings of your vehicle while saving you money on its upkeep and operation.

The beginning of the book will likely be referred to the most, since that is where you will find information for maintenance and tune-up. The other sections deal with the more complex systems of your vehicle. Systems (from engine through brakes) are covered to the extent that the average do-it-yourselfer can attempt. This book will not explain such things as rebuilding a differential because the expertise required and the special tools necessary make this uneconomical. It will, however, give you detailed instructions to help you change your own brake pads and shoes, replace spark plugs, and perform many more jobs that can save you money and help avoid expensive problems.

A secondary purpose of this book is a reference for owners who want to understand their vehicle and/or their mechanics better.

Where to Begin

Before removing any bolts, read through the entire procedure. This will give you the overall view of what tools and supplies will be required. So read ahead and plan ahead. Each operation should be approached logically and all procedures thoroughly understood before attempting any work.

If repair of a component is not considered practical, we tell you how to remove the part and then how to install the new or rebuilt replacement. In this way, you at least save labor costs.

Avoiding Trouble

Many procedures in this book require you to "label and disconnect . . ." a group of lines, hoses or wires. Don't be think you can remember where everything goes—you won't. If you hook up vacuum or fuel lines incorrectly, the vehicle may run poorly, if at all. If you hook up electrical wiring incorrectly, you may instantly learn a very expensive lesson.

You don't need to know the proper name for each hose or line. A piece of masking tape on the hose and a piece on its fitting will allow you to assign your own label. As long as you remember your own code, the lines can be reconnected by matching your tags. Remember that tape will dissolve in gasoline or solvents; if a part is to be washed or cleaned, use another method of identification. A permanent felt-tipped marker or a metal scribe can be very handy for marking metal parts. Remove any tape or paper labels after assembly.

Maintenance or Repair?

Maintenance includes routine inspections, adjustments, and replacement of parts which show signs of normal wear. Maintenance compensates for wear or deterioration. Repair implies that something has broken or is not working. A need for a repair is often caused by lack of maintenance. for example: draining and refilling automatic transmission fluid is maintenance recommended at specific intervals. Failure to do this can shorten the life of the transmission/transaxle, requiring very expensive repairs. While no maintenance program can prevent items from eventually breaking or wearing out, a general rule is true: MAINTENANCE IS CHEAPER THAN REPAIR.

Two basic mechanic's rules should be mentioned here. First, whenever the left side of the vehicle or engine is referred to, it means the driver's side. Conversely, the right side of the vehicle means the passenger's side. Second, screws and bolts are removed by turning counterclockwise, and tightened by turning clockwise unless specifically noted.

Safety is always the most important rule. Constantly be aware of the dangers involved in working on an automobile and take the proper precautions. Please refer to the information in this section regarding SERVICING YOUR VEHICLE SAFELY and the SAFETY NOTICE on the acknowledgment page.

Avoiding the Most Common Mistakes

Pay attention to the instructions provided. There are 3 common mistakes in mechanical work:

1. Incorrect order of assembly, disassembly or adjustment. When taking something apart or putting it together, performing steps in the wrong order usually just costs you extra time; however, it CAN break something. Read the entire procedure before beginning. Perform everything in the order in which the instructions say you should, even if you can't see a reason for it. When you're taking apart something that is very intricate, you might want to draw a picture of how it looks when assembled in order to make sure you get everything back in its proper position. When making adjustments, perform them in the proper order. One adjustment possibly will affect another.

2. Overtorquing (or undertorquing). While it is more common for overtorquing to cause damage, undertorquing may allow a fastener to vibrate loose causing serious damage. Especially when dealing with aluminum parts, pay attention to torque specifications and utilize a torque wrench in assembly. If a torque figure is not available, remember that if you are using the right tool to perform the job, you will probably not have to strain yourself to get a fastener tight enough. The pitch of most threads is so slight that the tension you put on the wrench will be multiplied many times in actual force on what you are tightening.

There are many commercial products available for ensuring that fasteners won't come loose, even if they are not torqued just right (a very common brand is Loctite®). If you're worried about getting something together tight enough to hold, but loose enough to avoid mechanical damage during assembly, one of these products might offer substantial insurance. Before choosing a threadlocking compound, read the label on the package and make sure the product is compatible with the materials, fluids, etc. involved.

3. Crossthreading. This occurs when a part such as a bolt is screwed into a nut or casting at the wrong angle and forced. Crossthreading is more likely to occur if access is difficult. It helps to clean and lubricate fasteners, then to start threading the bolt, spark plug, etc. with your fingers. If you encounter resistance, unscrew the part and start over again at a different angle until it can be inserted and turned several times without much effort. Keep in mind that many parts have tapered threads, so that gentle turning will automatically bring the part you're threading to the proper angle. Don't put a wrench on the part until it's been tightened a couple of turns by hand. If you suddenly encounter resistance, and the part has not seated fully, don't force it. Pull it back out to make sure it's clean and threading properly.

Be sure to take your time and be patient, and always plan ahead. Allow yourself ample time to perform repairs and maintenance.

TOOLS AND EQUIPMENT

▶ See Figures 1 thru 15

Without the proper tools and equipment it is impossible to properly service your vehicle. It would be virtually impossible to catalog every tool that you would need to perform all of the operations in this book. It would be unwise for the amateur to rush out and buy an expensive set of tools on the theory that he/she may need one or more of them at some time.

The best approach is to proceed slowly, gathering a good quality set of those tools that are used most frequently. Don't be misled by the low cost of bargain tools. It is far better to spend a little more for better quality. Forged wrenches, 6 or 12-point sockets and fine tooth ratchets are by far preferable to their less expensive counterparts. As any good mechanic can tell you, there are few worse experiences than trying to work on a vehicle with bad tools.

Your monetary savings will be far outweighed by frustration and mangled knuckles.

Begin accumulating those tools that are used most frequently: those associated with routine maintenance and tune-up. In addition to the normal assortment of screwdrivers and pliers, you should have the following tools:

• Wrenches/sockets and combination open end/box end wrenches in sizes ⅛–¾ in. and/or 3mm–19mm ¹³⁄₁₆ in. or ⅝ in. spark plug socket (depending on plug type).

➡ If possible, buy various length socket drive extensions. Universal-joint and wobble extensions can be extremely useful, but be careful when using them, as they can change the amount of torque applied to the socket.

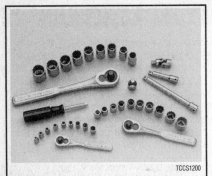

TCCS1200

Fig. 1 All but the most basic procedures will require an assortment of ratchets and sockets

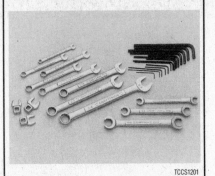

TCCS1201

Fig. 2 In addition to ratchets, a good set of wrenches and hex keys will be necessary

TCCS1202

Fig. 3 A hydraulic floor jack and a set of jackstands are essential for lifting and supporting the vehicle

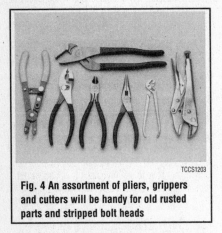

TCCS1203

Fig. 4 An assortment of pliers, grippers and cutters will be handy for old rusted parts and stripped bolt heads

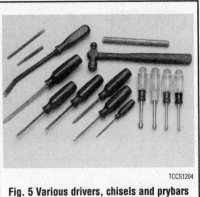

TCCS1204

Fig. 5 Various drivers, chisels and prybars are great tools to have in your toolbox

TCCS1205

Fig. 6 Many repairs will require the use of a torque wrench to assure the components are properly fastened

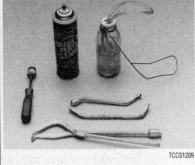

TCCS1209

Fig. 7 Although not always necessary, using specialized brake tools will save time

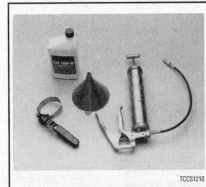

TCCS1210

Fig. 8 A few inexpensive lubrication tools will make maintenance easier

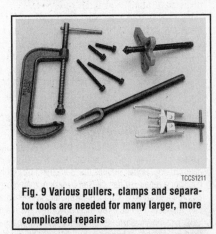

TCCS1211

Fig. 9 Various pullers, clamps and separator tools are needed for many larger, more complicated repairs

TCCS1212

Fig. 10 A variety of tools and gauges should be used for spark plug gapping and installation

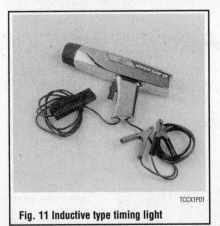

TCCX1P01

Fig. 11 Inductive type timing light

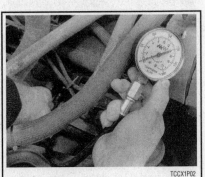

TCCX1P02

Fig. 12 A screw-in type compression gauge is recommended for compression testing

Fig. 13 A vacuum/pressure tester is necessary for many testing procedures

TCCX1P03

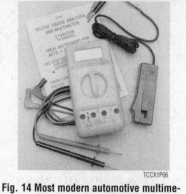

Fig. 14 Most modern automotive multimeters incorporate many helpful features

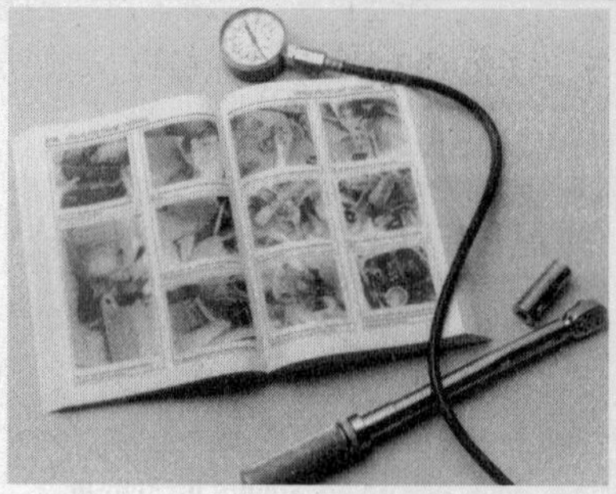

TCCX1P06

![Fig. 15]

Fig. 15 Proper information is vital, so always have a Chilton Total Car Care manual handy

TCCS1213

- Jackstands for support.
- Oil filter wrench.
- Spout or funnel for pouring fluids.
- Grease gun for chassis lubrication (unless your vehicle is not equipped with any grease fittings)
- Hydrometer for checking the battery (unless equipped with a sealed, maintenance-free battery).
- A container for draining oil and other fluids.
- Rags for wiping up the inevitable mess.

In addition to the above items there are several others that are not absolutely necessary, but handy to have around. These include an equivalent oil absorbent gravel, like cat litter, and the usual supply of lubricants, antifreeze and fluids. This is a basic list for routine maintenance, but only your personal needs and desire can accurately determine your list of tools.

After performing a few projects on the vehicle, you'll be amazed at the other tools and non-tools on your workbench. Some useful household items are: a large turkey baster or siphon, empty coffee cans and ice trays (to store parts), a ball of twine, electrical tape for wiring, small rolls of colored tape for tagging lines or hoses, markers and pens, a note pad, golf tees (for plugging vacuum lines), metal coat hangers or a roll of mechanic's wire (to hold things out of the way), dental pick or similar long, pointed probe, a strong magnet, and a small mirror (to see into recesses and under manifolds).

A more advanced set of tools, suitable for tune-up work, can be drawn up easily. While the tools are slightly more sophisticated, they need not be outrageously expensive. There are several inexpensive tach/dwell meters on the market that are every bit as good for the average mechanic as a professional model. Just be sure that it goes to a least 1200–1500 rpm on the tach scale and that it works on 4, 6 and 8-cylinder engines. The key to these purchases is to make them with an eye towards adaptability and wide range. A basic list of tune-up tools could include:

- Tach/dwell meter.
- Spark plug wrench and gapping tool.
- Feeler gauges for valve adjustment.
- Timing light.

The choice of a timing light should be made carefully. A light which works on the DC current supplied by the vehicle's battery is the best choice; it should have a xenon tube for brightness. On any vehicle with an electronic ignition system, a timing light with an inductive pickup that clamps around the No. 1 spark plug cable is preferred.

In addition to these basic tools, there are several other tools and gauges you may find useful. These include:

- Compression gauge. The screw-in type is slower to use, but eliminates the possibility of a faulty reading due to escaping pressure.
- Manifold vacuum gauge.
- 12V test light.
- A combination volt/ohmmeter.
- Induction Ammeter. This is used for determining whether or not there is current in a wire. These are handy for use if a wire is broken somewhere in a wiring harness.

As a final note, you will probably find a torque wrench necessary for all but the most basic work. The beam type models are perfectly adequate, although the newer click types (breakaway) are easier to use. The click type torque wrenches tend to be more expensive. Also keep in mind that all types of torque wrenches should be periodically checked and/or recalibrated. You will have to decide for yourself which better fits your pocketbook, and purpose.

Special Tools

Normally, the use of special factory tools is avoided for repair procedures, since these are not readily available for the do-it-yourself mechanic. When it is possible to perform the job with more commonly available tools, it will be pointed out, but occasionally, a special tool was designed to perform a specific function and should be used. Before substituting another tool, you should be convinced that neither your safety nor the performance of the vehicle will be compromised.

Special tools can usually be purchased from an automotive parts store or from your dealer. In some cases special tools may be available directly from the tool manufacturer.

SERVICING YOUR VEHICLE SAFELY

▶ See Figures 16, 17 and 18

It is virtually impossible to anticipate all of the hazards involved with automotive maintenance and service, but care and common sense will prevent most accidents.

The rules of safety for mechanics range from "don't smoke around gasoline," to "use the proper tool(s) for the job." The trick to avoiding injuries is to develop safe work habits and to take every possible precaution.

Do's

- Do keep a fire extinguisher and first aid kit handy.
- Do wear safety glasses or goggles when cutting, drilling, grinding or prying, even if you have 20–20 vision. If you wear glasses for the sake of vision, wear safety goggles over your regular glasses.
- Do shield your eyes whenever you work around the battery. Batteries contain sulfuric acid. In case of contact with, flush the area with water or a mixture of water and baking soda, then seek immediate medical attention.

- Do use safety stands (jackstands) for any undervehicle service. Jacks are for raising vehicles; jackstands are for making sure the vehicle stays raised until you want it to come down.
- Do use adequate ventilation when working with any chemicals or hazardous materials. Like carbon monoxide, the asbestos dust resulting from some brake lining wear can be hazardous in sufficient quantities.
- Do disconnect the negative battery cable when working on the electrical system. The secondary ignition system contains EXTREMELY HIGH VOLTAGE. In some cases it can even exceed 50,000 volts.
- Do follow manufacturer's directions whenever working with potentially hazardous materials. Most chemicals and fluids are poisonous.
- Do properly maintain your tools. Loose hammerheads, mushroomed punches and chisels, frayed or poorly grounded electrical cords, excessively worn screwdrivers, spread wrenches (open end), cracked sockets, slipping ratchets, or faulty droplight sockets can cause accidents.
- Likewise, keep your tools clean; a greasy wrench can slip off a bolt head, ruining the bolt and often harming your knuckles in the process.

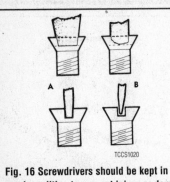

Fig. 16 Screwdrivers should be kept in good condition to prevent injury or damage which could result if the blade slips from the screw

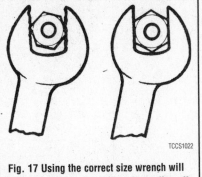

Fig. 17 Using the correct size wrench will help prevent the possibility of rounding off a nut

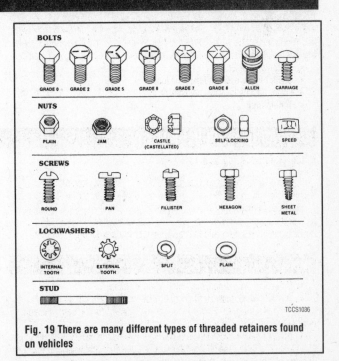

Fig. 18 NEVER work under a vehicle unless it is supported using safety stands (jackstands)

- Do use the proper size and type of tool for the job at hand. Do select a wrench or socket that fits the nut or bolt. The wrench or socket should sit straight, not cocked.
- Do, when possible, pull on a wrench handle rather than push on it, and adjust your stance to prevent a fall.
- Do be sure that adjustable wrenches are tightly closed on the nut or bolt and pulled so that the force is on the side of the fixed jaw.
- Do strike squarely with a hammer; avoid glancing blows.
- Do set the parking brake and block the drive wheels if the work requires a running engine.

Don'ts

- Don't run the engine in a garage or anywhere else without proper ventilation—EVER! Carbon monoxide is poisonous; it takes a long time to leave the human body and you can build up a deadly supply of it in your system by simply breathing in a little at a time. You may not realize you are slowly poisoning yourself. Always use power vents, windows, fans and/or open the garage door.
- Don't work around moving parts while wearing loose clothing. Short sleeves are much safer than long, loose sleeves. Hard-toed shoes with neoprene soles protect your toes and give a better grip on slippery surfaces. Watches and jewelry is not safe working around a vehicle. Long hair should be tied back under a hat or cap.
- Don't use pockets for toolboxes. A fall or bump can drive a screwdriver deep into your body. Even a rag hanging from your back pocket can wrap around a spinning shaft or fan.
- Don't smoke when working around gasoline, cleaning solvent or other flammable material.
- Don't smoke when working around the battery. When the battery is being charged, it gives off explosive hydrogen gas.
- Don't use gasoline to wash your hands; there are excellent soaps available. Gasoline contains dangerous additives which can enter the body through a cut or through your pores. Gasoline also removes all the natural oils from the skin so that bone dry hands will suck up oil and grease.
- Don't service the air conditioning system unless you are equipped with the necessary tools and training. When liquid or compressed gas refrigerant is released to atmospheric pressure it will absorb heat from whatever it contacts. This will chill or freeze anything it touches.
- Don't use screwdrivers for anything other than driving screws! A screwdriver used as an prying tool can snap when you least expect it, causing injuries. At the very least, you'll ruin a good screwdriver.
- Don't use an emergency jack (that little ratchet, scissors, or pantograph jack supplied with the vehicle) for anything other than changing a flat! These jacks are only intended for emergency use out on the road; they are NOT designed as a maintenance tool. If you are serious about maintaining your vehicle yourself, invest in a hydraulic floor jack of at least a 1½ ton capacity, and at least two sturdy jackstands.

FASTENERS, MEASUREMENTS AND CONVERSIONS

Bolts, Nuts and Other Threaded Retainers

▶ See Figures 19 and 20

Although there are a great variety of fasteners found in the modern car or truck, the most commonly used retainer is the threaded fastener (nuts, bolts, screws, studs, etc.). Most threaded retainers may be reused, provided that they are not damaged in use or during the repair. Some retainers (such as stretch bolts or torque prevailing nuts) are designed to deform when tightened or in use and should not be reinstalled.

Whenever possible, we will note any special retainers which should be replaced during a procedure. But you should always inspect the condition of a retainer when it is removed and replace any that show signs of damage. Check all threads for rust or corrosion which can increase the torque necessary to achieve the desired clamp load for which that fastener was originally selected. Additionally, be sure that the driver surface of the fastener has not been compromised by rounding or other damage. In some cases a driver surface may become only partially rounded, allowing the driver to catch in only one direction. In many of these occurrences, a fastener may be installed and tightened, but the driver would not be able to grip and loosen the fastener again.

If you must replace a fastener, whether due to design or damage, you must ALWAYS be sure to use the proper replacement. In all cases, a retainer of the same design, material and strength should be used. Markings on the heads of most bolts will help determine the proper strength of the fastener. The same material, thread and pitch must be selected to assure proper installation and safe operation of the vehicle afterwards.

Thread gauges are available to help measure a bolt or stud's thread. Most auto-

Fig. 19 There are many different types of threaded retainers found on vehicles

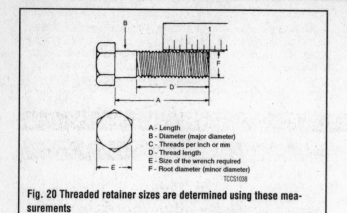

A - Length
B - Diameter (major diameter)
C - Threads per inch or mm
D - Thread length
E - Size of the wrench required
F - Root diameter (minor diameter)

TCCS1038

Fig. 20 Threaded retainer sizes are determined using these measurements

motive and hardware stores keep gauges available to help you select the proper size. In a pinch, you can use another nut or bolt for a thread gauge. If the bolt you are replacing is not too badly damaged, you can select a match by finding another bolt which will thread in its place. If you find a nut which threads properly onto the damaged bolt, then use that nut to help select the replacement bolt.

✻✻ WARNING

Be aware that when you find a bolt with damaged threads, you may also find the nut or drilled hole it was threaded into has also been damaged. If this is the case, you may have to drill and tap the hole, replace the nut or otherwise repair the threads. NEVER try to force a replacement bolt to fit into the damaged threads.

Torque

Torque is defined as the measurement of resistance to turning or rotating. It tends to twist a body about an axis of rotation. A common example of this would be tightening a threaded retainer such as a nut, bolt or screw. Measuring torque is one of the most common ways to help assure that a threaded retainer has been properly fastened.

When tightening a threaded fastener, torque is applied in three distinct areas, the head, the bearing surface and the clamp load. About 50 percent of the measured torque is used in overcoming bearing friction. This is the friction between the bearing surface of the bolt head, screw head or nut face and the base material or washer (the surface on which the fastener is rotating). Approximately 40 percent of the applied torque is used in overcoming thread friction. This leaves only about 10 percent of the applied torque to develop a useful clamp load (the force which holds a joint together). This means that friction can account for as much as 90 percent of the applied torque on a fastener.

TORQUE WRENCHES

♦ See Figure 21

In most applications, a torque wrench can be used to assure proper installation of a fastener. Torque wrenches come in various designs and most automotive supply stores will carry a variety to suit your needs. A torque wrench should be used any time we supply a specific torque value for a fastener. Again, the general rule of "if you are using the right tool for the job, you should not have to strain to tighten a fastener" applies here.

Beam Type

The beam type torque wrench is one of the most popular types. It consists of a pointer attached to the head that runs the length of the flexible beam (shaft) to a scale located near the handle. As the wrench is pulled, the beam bends and the pointer indicates the torque using the scale.

Click (Breakaway) Type

Another popular design of torque wrench is the click type. To use the click type wrench you pre-adjust it to a torque setting. Once the torque is reached, the wrench has a reflex signaling feature that causes a momentary breakaway of the torque wrench body, sending an impulse to the operator's hand.

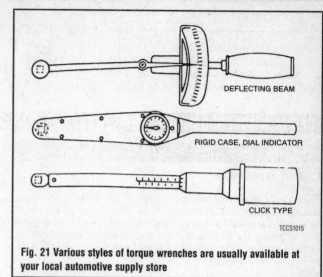

TCCS1015

Fig. 21 Various styles of torque wrenches are usually available at your local automotive supply store

Pivot Head Type

♦ See Figure 22

Some torque wrenches (usually of the click type) may be equipped with a pivot head which can allow it to be used in areas of limited access. BUT, it must be used properly. To hold a pivot head wrench, grasp the handle lightly, and as you pull on the handle, it should be floated on the pivot point. If the handle comes in contact with the yoke extension during the process of pulling, there is a very good chance the torque readings will be inaccurate because this could alter the wrench loading point. The design of the handle is usually such as to make it inconvenient to deliberately misuse the wrench.

➡️It should be mentioned that the use of any U-joint, wobble or extension will have an effect on the torque readings, no matter what type of wrench you are using. For the most accurate readings, install the socket directly on the wrench driver. If necessary, straight extensions (which hold a socket directly under the wrench driver) will have the least effect on the torque reading. Avoid any extension that alters the length of the wrench from the handle to the head/driving point (such as a crow's foot). U-joint or wobble extensions can greatly affect the readings; avoid their use at all times.

Rigid Case (Direct Reading)

A rigid case or direct reading torque wrench is equipped with a dial indicator to show torque values. One advantage of these wrenches is that they can be held at any position on the wrench without affecting accuracy. These wrenches are often preferred because they tend to be compact, easy to read and have a great degree of accuracy.

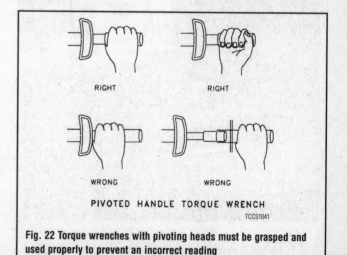

RIGHT   RIGHT

WRONG   WRONG

PIVOTED HANDLE TORQUE WRENCH

TCCS1041

Fig. 22 Torque wrenches with pivoting heads must be grasped and used properly to prevent an incorrect reading

TORQUE ANGLE METERS

Because the frictional characteristics of each fastener or threaded hole will vary, clamp loads which are based strictly on torque will vary as well. In most applications, this variance is not significant enough to cause worry. But, in certain applications, a manufacturer's engineers may determine that more precise clamp loads are necessary (such is the case with many aluminum cylinder heads). In these cases, a torque angle method of installation would be specified. When installing fasteners which are torque angle tightened, a predetermined seating torque and standard torque wrench are usually used first to remove any compliance from the joint. The fastener is then tightened the specified additional portion of a turn measured in degrees. A torque angle gauge (mechanical protractor) is used for these applications.

SERIAL NUMBER IDENTIFICATION

Vehicle

▶ See Figures 23 and 24

The Vehicle Identification Number (VIN) plate, which contains the Vehicle Identification Number (VIN), is located at the top rear of the instrument panel on the left side. It is visible from outside the vehicle on the lower left (driver's) side of the windshield. The VIN consists of 17 characters which represent codes supplying important information about your vehicle. Refer to the illustration of an example of VIN interpretation.

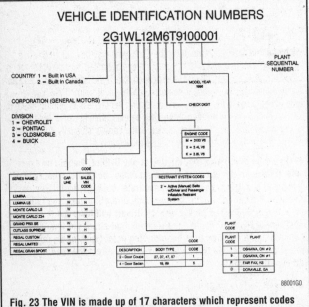

Fig. 23 The VIN is made up of 17 characters which represent codes supplying important information about your car

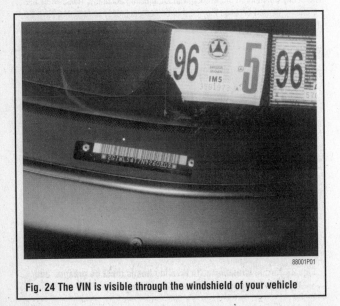

Fig. 24 The VIN is visible through the windshield of your vehicle

Engine

▶ See Figures 25 thru 30

The engine code is represented by the eighth character in the VIN and identifies the engine type, displacement, fuel system and manufacturing division.

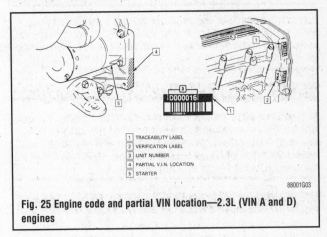

Fig. 25 Engine code and partial VIN location—2.3L (VIN A and D) engines

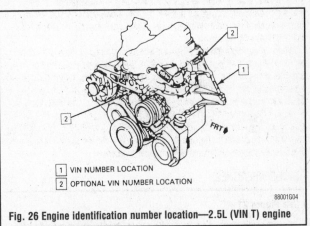

Fig. 26 Engine identification number location—2.5L (VIN T) engine

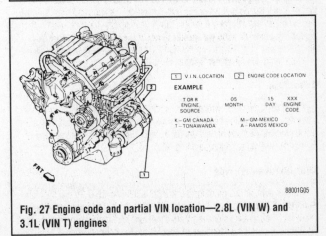

Fig. 27 Engine code and partial VIN location—2.8L (VIN W) and 3.1L (VIN T) engines

The engine identification code is either stamped onto the engine block or found on a label affixed to the engine. This code supplies information about the manufacturing plant location and time of manufacture. The location of the engine code is shown in the accompanying illustrations.

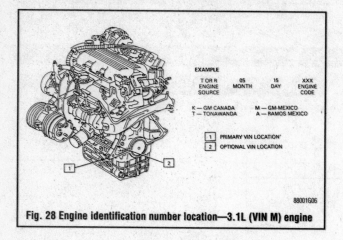

Fig. 28 Engine identification number location—3.1L (VIN M) engine

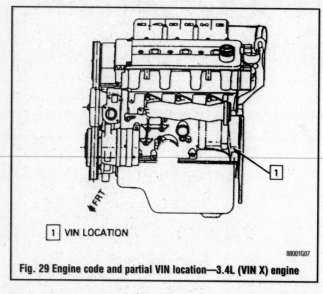

Fig. 29 Engine code and partial VIN location—3.4L (VIN X) engine

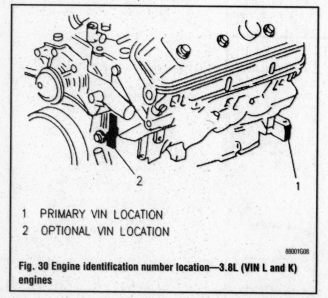

1   PRIMARY VIN LOCATION
2   OPTIONAL VIN LOCATION

Fig. 30 Engine identification number location—3.8L (VIN L and K) engines

Transaxle

▶ See Figures 31, 32, 33, 34 and 35

Similar to the engine identification code, the transaxle identification code supplies information about the transaxle such as the manufacturing plant, Julian date of manufacture, shift number and model. The location for the transaxle code is shown in the accompanying illustrations.

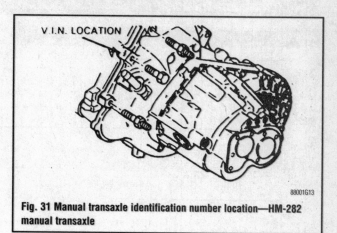

Fig. 31 Manual transaxle identification number location—HM-282 manual transaxle

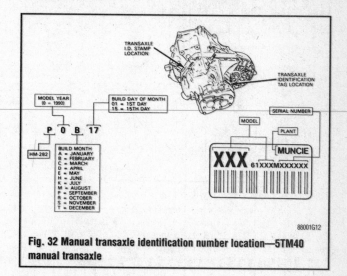

Fig. 32 Manual transaxle identification number location—5TM40 manual transaxle

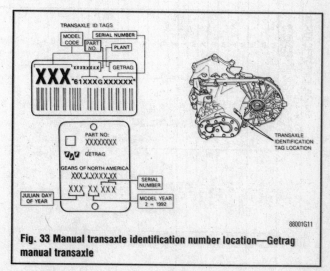

Fig. 33 Manual transaxle identification number location—Getrag manual transaxle

ENGINE IDENTIFICATION

Year	Model	Engine Displacement Liters (cc)	Engine Series (ID/VIN)	Fuel System	No. of Cylinders	Engine Type
1988	Cutlass Supreme	2.8 (2837)	W	MFI	6	OHV
	Grand Prix	2.8 (2837)	W	MFI	6	OHV
	Regal	2.8 (2837)	W	MFI	6	OHV
1989	Cutlass Supreme	2.8 (2837)	W	MFI	6	OHV
	Cutlass Supreme	3.1 (3135)	T	MFI	6	OHV
	Grand Prix	2.8 (2837)	W	MFI	6	OHV
	Grand Prix	3.1 (3135)	T	MFI	6	OHV
	Grand Prix	3.1 (3135)	V	MFI - Turbo	6	OHV
	Regal	2.8 (2837)	W	MFI	6	OHV
1990	Cutlass Supreme	2.3 (2260)	A	MFI	4	DOHC
	Cutlass Supreme	2.3 (2260)	D	MFI	4	DOHC
	Cutlass Supreme	3.1 (3135)	T	MFI	6	OHV
	Grand Prix	2.3 (2260)	D	MFI	4	DOHC
	Grand Prix	3.1 (3135)	T	MFI	6	OHV
	Grand Prix	3.1 (3135)	V	MFI - Turbo	6	OHV
	Lumina	2.5 (2471)	R	TFI	4	OHV
	Lumina	3.1 (3135)	T	MFI	6	OHV
1991	Cutlass Supreme	2.3 (2260)	D	MFI	4	DOHC
	Cutlass Supreme	3.1 (3135)	T	MFI	6	OHV
	Cutlass Supreme	3.4 (3350)	X	MFI	6	DOHC
	Grand Prix	3.1 (3135)	T	MFI	6	OHV
	Grand Prix	3.4 (3350)	X	MFI	6	DOHC
	Lumina	2.5 (2471)	R	TFI	4	OHV
	Lumina	3.1 (3135)	T	MFI	6	OHV
	Regal	3.1 (3135)	T	MFI	6	OHV
	Regal	3.8 (3791)	L	MFI	6	OHV
1992	Cutlass Supreme	3.1 (3135)	T	MFI	6	OHV
	Cutlass Supreme	3.4 (3350)	X	MFI	6	DOHC
	Grand Prix	3.1 (3135)	T	MFI	6	OHV
	Grand Prix	3.4 (3350)	X	MFI	6	DOHC
	Lumina	2.5 (2471)	R	TFI	4	OHV
	Lumina	3.1 (3135)	T	MFI	6	OHV
	Lumina	3.4 (3350)	X	MFI	6	DOHC
	Regal	3.1 (3135)	T	MFI	6	OHV
	Regal	3.8 (3791)	L	MFI	6	OHV

88001C02

ENGINE IDENTIFICATION

Year	Model	Engine Displacement Liters (cc)	Engine Series (ID/VIN)	Fuel System	No. of Cylinders	Engine Type
1993	Cutlass Supreme	3.1 (3135)	M	SFI	6	OHV
	Cutlass Supreme	3.1 (3135)	T	MFI	6	OHV
	Cutlass Supreme	3.4 (3350)	X	MFI	6	DOHC
	Grand Prix	3.1 (3135)	T	MFI	6	OHV
	Grand Prix	3.4 (3350)	X	MFI	6	DOHC
	Lumina	2.2 (2190)	4	MFI	4	OHV
	Lumina	3.1 (3135)	T	MFI	6	OHV
	Lumina	3.4 (3350)	X	MFI	6	DOHC
	Regal	3.1 (3135)	T	SFI	6	OHV
	Regal	3.8 (3791)	L	SFI	6	OHV
1994	Cutlass Supreme	3.1 (3135)	M	SFI	6	OHV
	Cutlass Supreme	3.4 (3350)	X	SFI	6	DOHC
	Grand Prix	3.1 (3135)	M	SFI	6	OHV
	Grand Prix	3.4 (3350)	X	MFI	6	DOHC
	Lumina	3.1 (3135)	M	SFI	6	OHV
	Lumina	3.4 (3350)	X	SFI	6	DOHC
	Regal	3.1 (3135)	M	SFI	6	OHV
	Regal	3.8 (3791)	L	SFI	6	OHV
1995	Cutlass Supreme	3.1 (3135)	M	SFI	6	OHV
	Cutlass Supreme	3.4 (3350)	X	SFI	6	DOHC
	Grand Prix	3.1 (3135)	M	SFI	6	OHV
	Grand Prix	3.4 (3350)	X	SFI	6	DOHC
	Lumina	3.1 (3135)	M	SFI	6	OHV
	Lumina	3.4 (3350)	X	SFI	6	DOHC
	Monte Carlo	3.1 (3135)	M	SFI	6	OHV
	Monte Carlo	3.4 (3350)	X	SFI	6	DOHC
	Regal	3.1 (3135)	M	SFI	6	OHV
	Regal	3.8 (3791)	L	SFI	6	OHV
1996	Cutlass Supreme	3.1 (3135)	M	SFI	6	OHV
	Cutlass Supreme	3.4 (3350)	X	SFI	6	DOHC
	Grand Prix	3.1 (3135)	M	SFI	6	OHV
	Grand Prix	3.4 (3350)	X	SFI	6	DOHC
	Lumina	3.1 (3135)	M	SFI	6	OHV
	Lumina	3.4 (3350)	X	SFI	6	DOHC
	Monte Carlo	3.1 (3135)	M	SFI	6	OHV
	Monte Carlo	3.4 (3350)	X	SFI	6	DOHC
	Regal	3.1 (3135)	M	SFI	6	OHV
	Regal	3.8 (3791)	K	SFI	6	OHV

88001C03

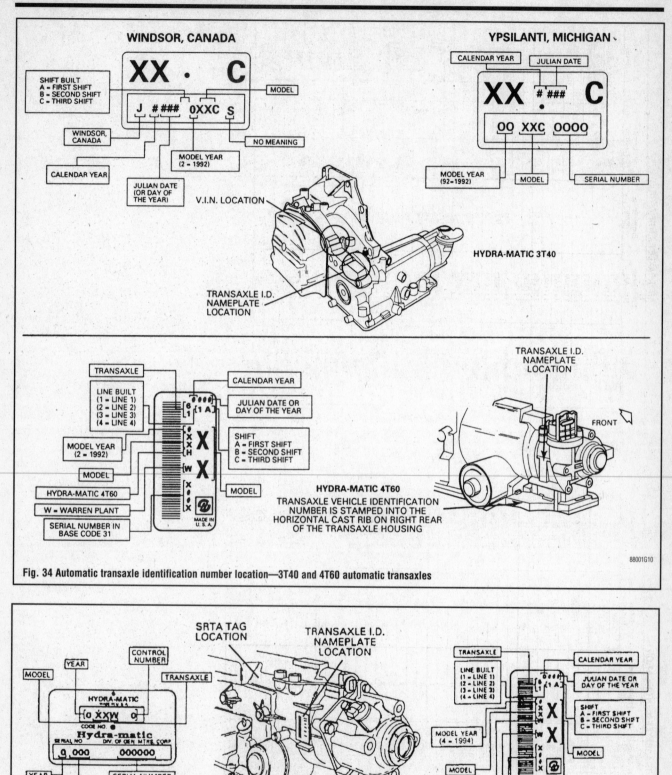

Fig. 34 Automatic transaxle identification number location—3T40 and 4T60 automatic transaxles

Fig. 35 Automatic transaxle identification number location—4T60-E automatic transaxle

TRANSAXLE IDENTIFICATION

Year	Model	Engine Displacement Liters (cc)	Engine Series (ID/VIN)	Manual Transaxle	Automatic Transaxle
1988	Grand Prix	2.8 (2835)	W	HM 282	440 T4
	Cutlass Supreme	2.8 (2835)	W	HM 282	440 T4
	Regal	2.8 (2835)	W	-	440 T4
1989	Grand Prix	2.8 (2835)	W	HM 282	440 T4
	Grand Prix	3.1 (3136)	T	HM 282	440 T4
	Cutlass Supreme	2.8 (2835)	W	HM 282	440 T4
	Cutlass Supreme	3.1 (3146)	T	-	440 T4
	Regal	2.8 (2835)	W	-	440 T4
1990	Lumina	2.5 (2475)	R	-	THM125/3T40
	Lumina	3.1 (3130)	T	-	440 T4/4T60
	Grand Prix	2.3 (2262)	D	-	THM125/3T40
	Grand Prix	3.1 (3136)	T	5TM40	440 T4/4T60
	Grand Prix	3.1 (3136)	V	-	440 T4/4T60
	Cutlass Supreme	2.3 (2261)	A	5TM40	-
	Cutlass Supreme	2.3 (2261)	D	-	THM125/3T40
	Cutlass Supreme	3.1 (3146)	T	-	440 T4/4T60
	Regal	3.1 (3146)	T	-	440 T4
1991	Lumina	2.5 (2475)	R	-	3T40
	Lumina	3.1 (3130)	X	Getrag 284	3T40 or 4T60
	Grand Prix	2.3 (2262)	D	-	3T40
	Grand Prix	3.1 (3136)	T	-	3T40 or 4T60
	Grand Prix	3.4 (3350)	X	Getrag 284	4T60-E
	Cutlass Supreme	2.3 (2261)	D	-	3T40
	Cutlass Supreme	3.1 (3146)	T	-	3T40 or 4T60
	Cutlass Supreme	3.4 (3392)	X	Getrag 284	4T60-E
	Regal	3.1 (3146)	T	-	440 T4
	Regal	3.8 (3785)	L	-	3T40
1992	Lumina	2.5 (2475)	R	-	3T40
	Lumina	3.1 (3130)	T	-	3T40 or 4T60-E
	Lumina	3.4 (3393)	X	Getrag 284	4T60-E
	Grand Prix	3.1 (3136)	T	-	3T40 or 4T60
	Grand Prix	3.4 (3350)	X	-	4T60-E
	Cutlass Supreme	3.1 (3146)	T	Getrag 284	3T40 or 4T60
	Cutlass Supreme	3.4 (3392)	X	-	4T60-E
	Regal	3.1 (3146)	T	-	440 T4/4T60
	Regal	3.8 (3785)	L	-	440 T4/4T60

88001C04

TRANSAXLE IDENTIFICATION

Year	Model	Engine Displacement Liters (cc)	Engine Series (ID/VIN)	Manual Transaxle	Automatic Transaxle
1993	Lumina	2.2 (2180)	4	-	3T40
	Lumina	3.1 (3130)	T	-	3T40 or 4T60-E
	Lumina	3.4 (3393)	X	Getrag	4T60-E
	Grand Prix	3.1 (3136)	T	-	3T40 or 4T60-E
	Grand Prix	3.4 (3350)	X	Getrag	4T60-E
	Cutlass Supreme	3.1 (3146)	T	-	3T40 or 4T60-E
	Cutlass Supreme	3.4 (3392)	X	Getrag	4T60-E
	Regal	3.1 (3146)	T	-	4T60-E
	Regal	3.8 (3785)	L	-	4T60-E
1994	Lumina	3.1 (3130)	T	-	4T60-E
	Lumina	3.4 (3393)	X	-	3T40 or 4T60-E
	Grand Prix	3.1 (3136)	M	-	4T60-E
	Grand Prix	3.4 (3350)	X	-	4T60-E
	Cutlass Supreme	3.1 (3130)	M	-	4T60-E
	Cutlass Supreme	3.4 (3392)	X	-	4T60-E
	Regal	3.1 (3130)	M	-	4T60-E
	Regal	3.8 (3785)	L	-	4T60-E
1995	Lumina	3.1 (3130)	M	-	3T40 or 4T60-E
	Lumina	3.4 (3393)	X	-	4T60-E
	Monte Carlo	3.1 (3130)	M	-	3T40 or 4T60-E
	Monte Carlo	3.4 (3393)	X	-	4T60-E
	Grand Prix	3.1 (3136)	M	-	3T40 or 4T60-E
	Grand Prix	3.4 (3350)	X	-	4T60-E
	Cutlass Supreme	3.1 (3130)	M	-	3T40 or 4T60-E
	Cutlass Supreme	3.4 (3392)	X	-	3T40 or 4T60-E
	Regal	3.8 (3785)	L	-	4T60-E
1996	Lumina	3.1 (3130)	M	-	4T60-E
	Lumina	3.4 (3350)	X	-	4T60-E
	Monte Carlo	3.1 (3130)	M	-	4T60-E
	Monte Carlo	3.4 (3350)	X	-	4T60-E
	Grand Prix	3.1 (3136)	M	-	4T60-E
	Grand Prix	3.4 (3350)	M	-	4T60-E
	Cutlass Supreme	3.1 (3130)	M	-	4T60-E
	Cutlass Supreme	3.4 (3350)	M	-	4T60-E
	Regal	3.1 (3130)	M	-	4T60-E
	Regal	3.8 (3785)	K	-	4T60-E

88001C05

ROUTINE MAINTENANCE

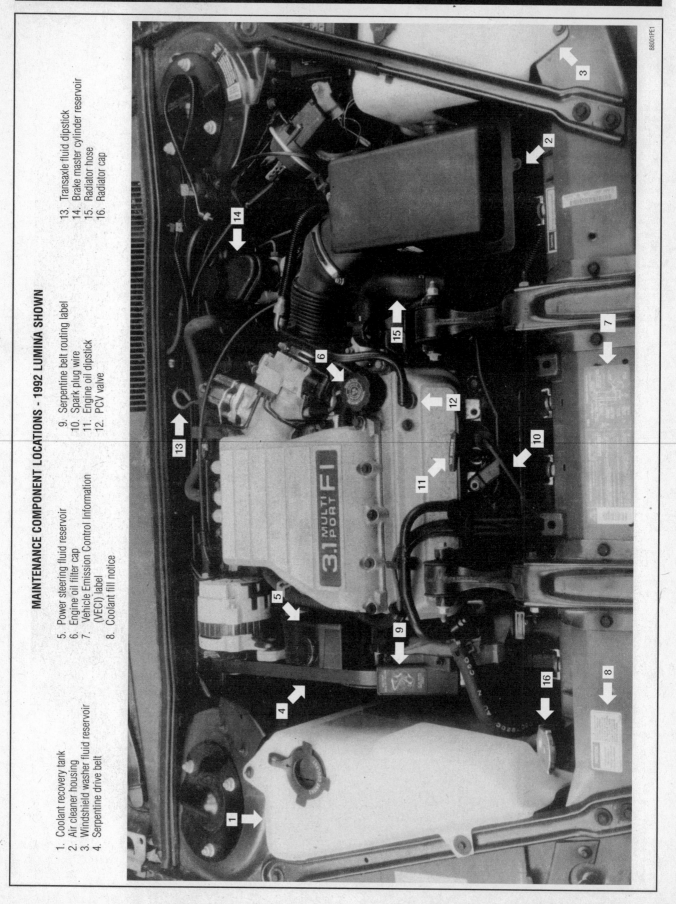

MAINTENANCE COMPONENT LOCATIONS - 1992 LUMINA SHOWN

1. Coolant recovery tank
2. Air cleaner housing
3. Windshield washer fluid reservoir
4. Serpentine drive belt
5. Power steering fluid reservoir
6. Engine oil filter cap
7. Vehicle Emission Control Information (VECI) label
8. Coolant fill notice
9. Serpentine belt routing label
10. Spark plug wire
11. Engine oil dipstick
12. PCV valve
13. Transaxle fluid dipstick
14. Brake master cylinder reservoir
15. Radiator hose
16. Radiator cap

MAINTENANCE COMPONENT LOCATIONS - 1996 LUMINA SHOWN

1. Radiator cap
2. Coolant notice label
3. Fan warning label
4. Vehicle Emission Control Information (VECI) label
5. Engine oil filler cap
6. Engine oil dipstick
7. Radiator hose
8. Windshield washer fluid reservoir
9. Air cleaner housing
10. Brake master cylinder fluid reservoir
11. Automatic transaxle fluid dipstick
12. Power steering pump fluid reservoir
13. Serpentine drive belt
14. Coolant recovery tank

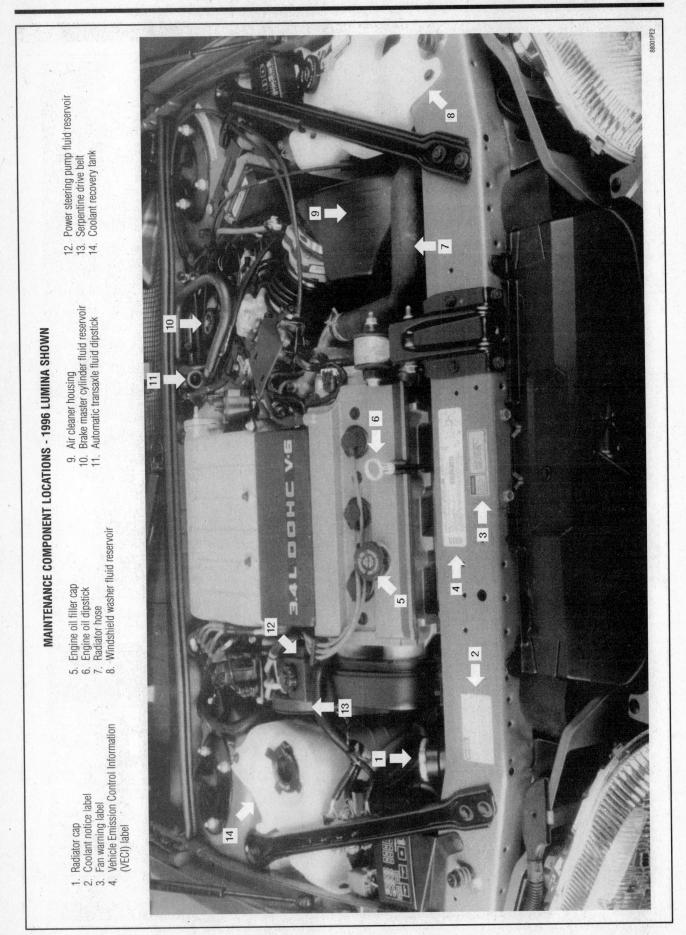

Proper maintenance and tune-up is the key to long and trouble-free vehicle life, and the work can yield its own rewards. Studies have shown that a properly tuned and maintained vehicle can achieve better gas mileage than an out-of-tune vehicle. As a conscientious owner and driver, set aside a Saturday morning, say once a month, to check or replace items which could cause major problems later. Keep your own personal log to jot down which services you performed, how much the parts cost you, the date, and the exact odometer reading at the time. Keep all receipts for such items as engine oil and filters, so that they may be referred to in case of related problems or to determine operating expenses. As a do-it-yourselfer, these receipts are the only proof you have that the required maintenance was performed. In the event of a warranty problem, these receipts will be invaluable.

The literature provided with your vehicle when it was originally delivered includes the factory recommended maintenance schedule. If you no longer have this literature, replacement copies are usually available from the dealer. A maintenance schedule is provided later in this section, in case you do not have the factory literature.

Air Cleaner

REMOVAL & INSTALLATION

♦ **See Figures 36 thru 42**

1. Unfasten the bolts/screws, wing nut(s) or retaining clips, then remove the air cleaner cover.

Fig. 36 On this 3.1L engine, unfasten the retaining screws . . .

Fig. 37 . . . then lift the lid and remove the air cleaner element

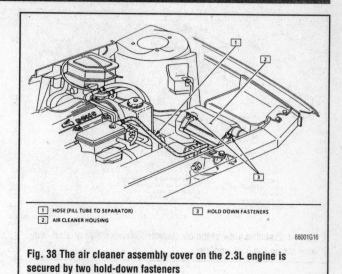

| 1 | HOSE (FILL TUBE TO SEPARATOR) | 3 | HOLD DOWN FASTENERS |
| 2 | AIR CLEANER HOUSING | | |

Fig. 38 The air cleaner assembly cover on the 2.3L engine is secured by two hold-down fasteners

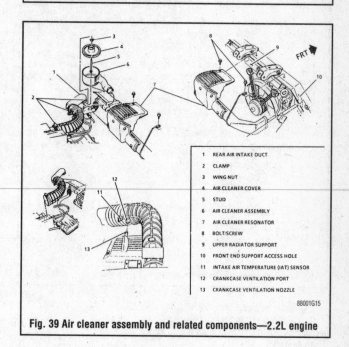

1	REAR AIR INTAKE DUCT
2	CLAMP
3	WING NUT
4	AIR CLEANER COVER
5	STUD
6	AIR CLEANER ASSEMBLY
7	AIR CLEANER RESONATOR
8	BOLT/SCREW
9	UPPER RADIATOR SUPPORT
10	FRONT END SUPPORT ACCESS HOLE
11	INTAKE AIR TEMPERATURE (IAT) SENSOR
12	CRANKCASE VENTILATION PORT
13	CRANKCASE VENTILATION NOZZLE

Fig. 39 Air cleaner assembly and related components—2.2L engine

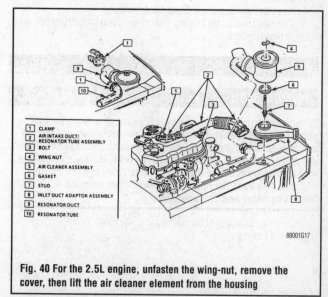

1	CLAMP
2	AIR INTAKE DUCT/ RESONATOR TUBE ASSEMBLY
3	BOLT
4	WING NUT
5	AIR CLEANER ASSEMBLY
6	GASKET
7	STUD
8	INLET DUCT ADAPTOR ASSEMBLY
9	RESONATOR DUCT
10	RESONATOR TUBE

Fig. 40 For the 2.5L engine, unfasten the wing-nut, remove the cover, then lift the air cleaner element from the housing

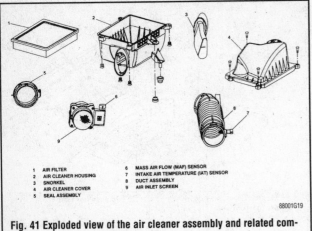

1 AIR FILTER
2 AIR CLEANER HOUSING
3 SNORKEL
4 AIR CLEANER COVER
5 SEAL ASSEMBLY
6 MASS AIR FLOW (MAF) SENSOR
7 INTAKE AIR TEMPERATURE (IAT) SENSOR
8 DUCT ASSEMBLY
9 AIR INLET SCREEN

88001G19

Fig. 41 Exploded view of the air cleaner assembly and related components on the 3.4L engine

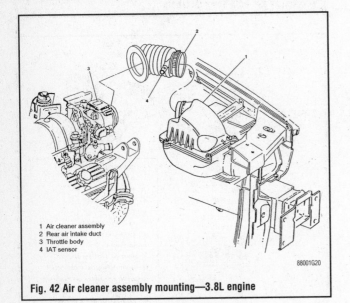

1 Air cleaner assembly
2 Rear air intake duct
3 Throttle body
4 IAT sensor

88001G20

Fig. 42 Air cleaner assembly mounting—3.8L engine

2. Lift the air cleaner element from the housing.

3. Clean the air cleaner housing to remove any remaining dirt. Inspect the element for dirt, dust and/or water and replace if necessary.

To install:

4. Position a new element in the air cleaner housing.

5. Place the cover on the housing, then secure using the bolts/screws, wing nut(s) or retaining clips.

Fuel Filter

✳✳ CAUTION

To reduce the risk of fire and personal injury, it is necessary to relieve the fuel system pressure before servicing any fuel system component. If this procedure is not performed, fuel may be sprayed out of the connection under pressure. Cover fuel hose connections with a shop towel before disconnecting to catch any residual fuel that may still be in the line. Always keep a dry chemical (Class B) fire extinguisher near the work area.

The fuel filter is located in the fuel feed line attached to the left frame rail, at the rear of the vehicle.

REMOVAL & INSTALLATION

▶ **See Figures 43, 44, 45, 46 and 47**

1. Relieve the fuel system pressure. For details regarding this procedure, please refer to

2. If not done already, disconnect the negative battery cable.

3. Raise and safely support the vehicle.

4. Clean both fuel feed pipe connections and the surrounding areas at the in-line fuel filter with a clean rag to avoid possible contamination of the fuel system.

5. Using a backup wrench, remove the fuel line fittings from the fuel filter.

6. Either separate the quick-connect fittings or remove the fuel filter mounting screws, then slide the fuel filter out of the mounting bracket.

7. Discard the fuel line O-rings and replace with new ones during installation.

To install:

8. Install new O-rings to the fuel line fittings.

9. Connect the fuel lines to the fuel filter.

88001P04

Fig. 43 Location of the fuel filter

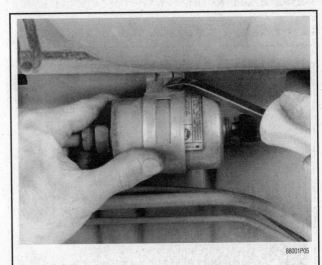

88001P05

Fig. 44 Unfasten the retaining bracket can make removal of the fuel filter easier

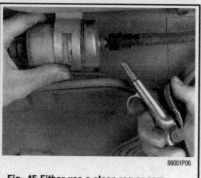

Fig. 45 Either use a clean rag or compressed air to clean the surrounding areas of the filter

Fig. 46 Use a backup wrench to disconnect the fuel line fittings from the filter

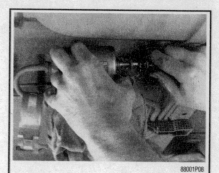

Fig. 47 Disengage the quick-connect fittings, then remove the filter from the vehicle

10. Position the filter in the mounting bracket, in the same position it was during removal. Using a backup wrench, tighten the fuel lines to 16 ft. lbs. (22 Nm).

11. Install the fuel filter mounting screws.

12. Carefully lower the vehicle. Install or tighten the fuel filler cap.

13. Connect the negative battery cable.

14. Start the engine and check for leaks.

PCV Valve

▶ See Figures 48 and 49

The PCV valve should be inspected every 30,000 miles (50,000 km) for proper operation. A rough idle or oil consumption may result from improper operation or vacuum leak. To maintain proper idle control, the PCV valve restricts the flow when the intake manifold vacuum is high. The system is designed to allow excess blow by gases to be vented into the intake manifold to be burned, reducing hydrocarbon emissions.

Vehicles equipped with the 2.3L (VIN D) engine, or the 1991 2.5L (VIN R), use a crankcase ventilation system that does not use a PCV valve. The 2.3L engine is equipped with an oil/air separator that does not require service. Should the oil/air separator become clogged, the unit must be replace. On the 1991 2.5L engine, the standard PCV valve is replaced with a constant bleed orifice. If the orifice becomes clogged, clear if possible or replace.

REMOVAL & INSTALLATION

Except 3.8L Engine

▶ See Figures 50, 51 and 52

1. Remove the PCV valve from the grommet in the valve (rocker arm) cover.
2. Disconnect the PCV valve from the breather hose.

To install:

3. Connect the new PCV valve into the breather hose.
4. Install the PCV valve into the grommet in the valve (rocker arm) cover.

3.8L Engine

1991–92 VEHICLES

▶ See Figure 53

1. Disconnect the negative battery cable.
2. Remove the cosmetic cover from the fuel rail and intake manifold.
3. While holding the access cover down with your finger to keep the spring from pushing the cover off, unfasten the cover retaining screws.
4. Lift the cover and gasket off slowly.
5. Remove the spring and valve, with the O-ring, from the intake manifold. Inspect the O-ring and replace if damaged.

To install:

6. Install the PCV valve and O-ring, then position the spring.
7. Position a new gasket, then install the cover and secure with the retaining screws.

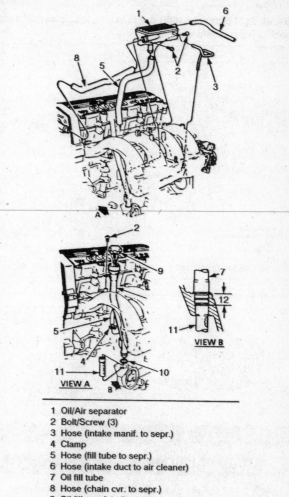

1 Oil/Air separator
2 Bolt/Screw (3)
3 Hose (intake manif. to sepr.)
4 Clamp
5 Hose (fill tube to sepr.)
6 Hose (intake duct to air cleaner)
7 Oil fill tube
8 Hose (chain cvr. to sepr.)
9 Oil fill cap & indicator asm.
10 O-ring seal
11 Oil level indicator guide,
   Holes in guide must face outboard 90° ± 5° degrees from center line of crankshaft.
   (In line with oil filter)
12 Position top of guide 18mm - 19mm
   (2 3/32" - 3/4") down from surface of block

Fig. 48 Vehicles with the 2.3L engine utilize a crankcase ventilation system which uses a oil/air separator instead of a conventional PCV valve

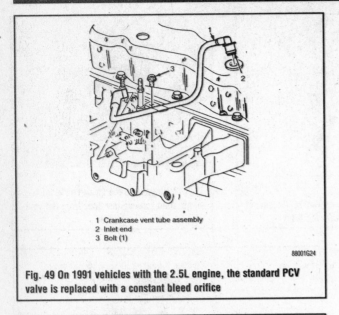

1 Crankcase vent tube assembly
2 Inlet end
3 Bolt (1)

88001G24

Fig. 49 On 1991 vehicles with the 2.5L engine, the standard PCV valve is replaced with a constant bleed orifice

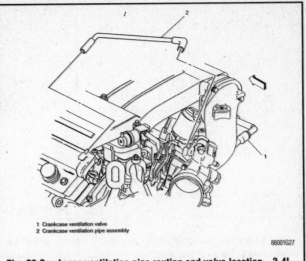

1 Crankcase ventilation valve
2 Crankcase ventilation pipe assembly

88001G27

Fig. 52 Crankcase ventilation pipe routing and valve location—3.4L engine

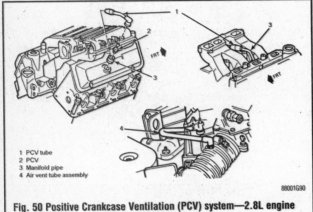

1 PCV tube
2 PCV
3 Manifold pipe
4 Air vent tube assembly

88001G90

Fig. 50 Positive Crankcase Ventilation (PCV) system—2.8L engine

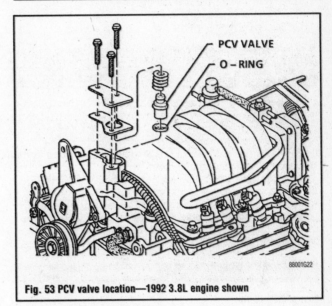

PCV VALVE
O–RING

88001G22

Fig. 53 PCV valve location—1992 3.8L engine shown

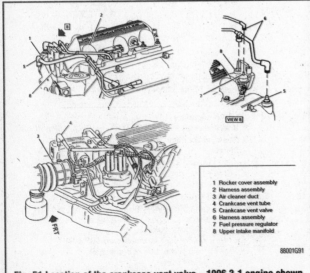

VIEW B

1 Rocker cover assembly
2 Harness assembly
3 Air cleaner duct
4 Crankcase vent tube
5 Crankcase vent valve
6 Harness assembly
7 Fuel pressure regulator
8 Upper intake manifold

88001G91

Fig. 51 Location of the crankcase vent valve—1996 3.1 engine shown

8. Install the cosmetic cover.
9. Connect the negative battery cable.

1993–96 VEHICLES

▶ See Figure 54

1. Disconnect the negative battery cable.
2. Remove the sight shield from the fuel rail and intake manifold.
3. For 1995–96 vehicles, remove the MAP sensor.
4. Using a 16mm socket, press the access cover down and rotate ¼ turn counterclockwise.
5. Lift the cover and O-ring off slowly.
6. Remove the spring and valve with the O-ring from the intake manifold. Inspect the O-ring for damage and replace if necessary.

To install:
7. Position the PCV valve and O-ring.
8. Install the spring.

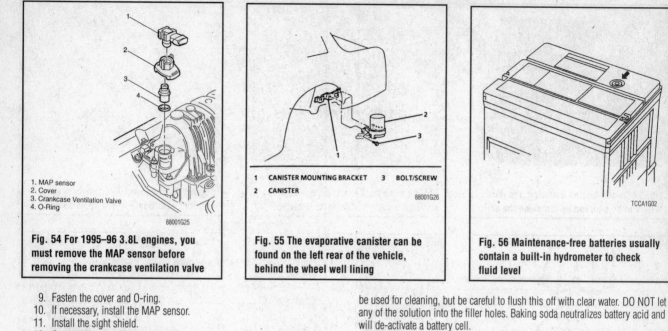

Fig. 54 For 1995–96 3.8L engines, you must remove the MAP sensor before removing the crankcase ventilation valve

1. MAP sensor
2. Cover
3. Crankcase Ventilation Valve
4. O-Ring

88001G25

Fig. 55 The evaporative canister can be found on the left rear of the vehicle, behind the wheel well lining

| 1 | CANISTER MOUNTING BRACKET | 3 | BOLT/SCREW |
| 2 | CANISTER | | |

88001G26

Fig. 56 Maintenance-free batteries usually contain a built-in hydrometer to check fluid level

TCCA1G02

9. Fasten the cover and O-ring.
10. If necessary, install the MAP sensor.
11. Install the sight shield.
12. Connect the negative battery cable.

Evaporative Canister

▶ See Figure 55

This system is designed to limit gasoline vapor, which normally escapes from the fuel tank and intake manifold, from discharging into the atmosphere. Vapor absorption is accomplished through the use of the charcoal canister and stores them until they can be removed and burned in the combustion process.

SERVICING

The evaporative canister does not require periodic service. Check the hoses and canister for cracks and/or other damage. For canister removal and installation procedures, please refer to Section 4 of this manual.

Battery

PRECAUTIONS

Always use caution when working on or near the battery. Never allow a tool to bridge the gap between the negative and positive battery terminals. Also, be careful not to allow a tool to provide a ground between the positive cable/terminal and any metal component on the vehicle. Either of these conditions will cause a short circuit, leading to sparks and possible personal injury.

Do not smoke or all open flames/sparks near a battery; the gases contained in the battery are very explosive and, if ignited, could cause severe injury or death.

All batteries, regardless of type, should be carefully secured by a battery hold-down device. If not, the terminals or casing may crack from stress during vehicle operation. A battery which is not secured may allow acid to leak, making it discharge faster. The acid can also eat away at components under the hood.

Always inspect the battery case for cracks, leakage and corrosion. A white corrosive substance on the battery case or on nearby components would indicate a leaking or cracked battery. If the battery is cracked, it should be replaced immediately.

GENERAL MAINTENANCE

Always keep the battery cables and terminals free of corrosion. Check and clean these components about once a year.

Keep the top of the battery clean, as a film of dirt can help discharge a battery that is not used for long periods. A solution of baking soda and water may be used for cleaning, but be careful to flush this off with clear water. DO NOT let any of the solution into the filler holes. Baking soda neutralizes battery acid and will de-activate a battery cell.

Batteries in vehicles which are not operated on a regular basis can fall victim to parasitic loads (small current drains which are constantly drawing current from the battery). Normal parasitic loads may drain a battery on a vehicle that is in storage and not used for 6–8 weeks. Vehicles that have additional accessories such as a phone or an alarm system may discharge a battery sooner. If the vehicle is to be stored for longer periods in a secure area and the alarm system is not necessary, the negative battery cable should be disconnected to protect the battery.

Remember that constantly deep cycling a battery (completely discharging and recharging it) will shorten battery life.

BATTERY FLUID

▶ See Figure 56

Check the battery electrolyte level at least once a month, or more often in hot weather or during periods of extended vehicle operation. On non-sealed batteries, the level can be checked either through the case (if translucent) or by removing the cell caps. The electrolyte level in each cell should be kept filled to the split ring inside each cell, or the line marked on the outside of the case.

If the level is low, add only distilled water through the opening until the level is correct. Each cell must be checked and filled individually. Distilled water should be used, because the chemicals and minerals found in most drinking water are harmful to the battery and could significantly shorten its life.

If water is added in freezing weather, the vehicle should be driven several miles to allow the water to mix with the electrolyte. Otherwise, the battery could freeze.

Although some maintenance-free batteries have removable cell caps, the electrolyte condition and level on all sealed maintenance-free batteries must be checked using the built-in hydrometer "eye." The exact type of eye will vary. But, most battery manufacturers, apply a sticker to the battery itself explaining the readings.

➡ **Although the readings from built-in hydrometers will vary, a green eye usually indicates a properly charged battery with sufficient fluid level. A dark eye is normally an indicator of a battery with sufficient fluid, but which is low in charge. A light or yellow eye usually indicates that electrolyte has dropped below the necessary level. In this last case, sealed batteries with an insufficient electrolyte must usually be discarded.**

Checking the Specific Gravity

▶ See Figures 57, 58 and 59

A hydrometer is required to check the specific gravity on all batteries that are not maintenance-free. On batteries that are maintenance-free, the specific gravity is checked by observing the built-in hydrometer "eye" on the top of the battery case.

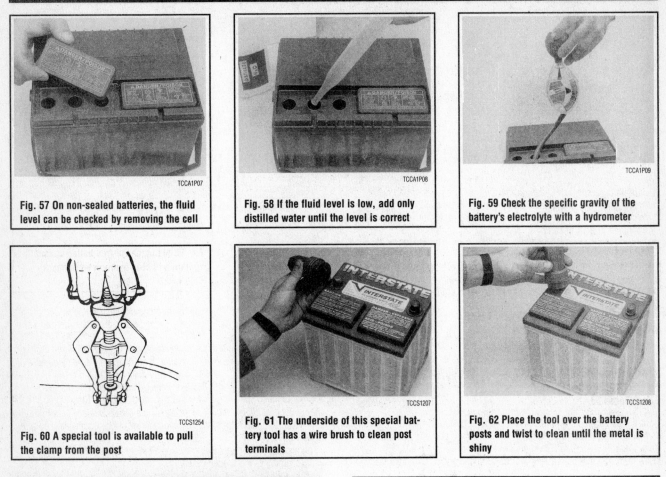

Fig. 57 On non-sealed batteries, the fluid level can be checked by removing the cell

Fig. 58 If the fluid level is low, add only distilled water until the level is correct

Fig. 59 Check the specific gravity of the battery's electrolyte with a hydrometer

Fig. 60 A special tool is available to pull the clamp from the post

Fig. 61 The underside of this special battery tool has a wire brush to clean post terminals

Fig. 62 Place the tool over the battery posts and twist to clean until the metal is shiny

✳✳ CAUTION

Battery electrolyte contains sulfuric acid. If you should splash any on your skin or in your eyes, flush the affected area with plenty of clear water. If it lands in your eyes, get medical help immediately.

The fluid (sulfuric acid solution) contained in the battery cells will tell you many things about the condition of the battery. Because the cell plates must be kept submerged below the fluid level in order to operate, the fluid level is extremely important. And, because the specific gravity of the acid is an indication of electrical charge, testing the fluid can be an aid in determining if the battery must be replaced. A battery in a vehicle with a properly operating charging system should require little maintenance, but careful, periodic inspection should reveal problems before they leave you stranded.

At least once a year, check the specific gravity of the battery. It should be between 1.20 and 1.26 on the gravity scale. Most auto stores carry a variety of inexpensive battery hydrometers. These can be used on any non-sealed battery to test the specific gravity in each cell.

The battery testing hydrometer has a squeeze bulb at one end and a nozzle at the other. Battery electrolyte is sucked into the hydrometer until the float is lifted from its seat. The specific gravity is then read by noting the position of the float. If gravity is low in one or more cells, the battery should be slowly charged and checked again to see if the gravity has come up. Generally, if after charging, the specific gravity between any two cells varies more than 50 points (0.50), the battery should be replaced, as it can no longer produce sufficient voltage to guarantee proper operation.

CABLES

♦ See Figures 60, 61, 62 and 63

Once a year (or as necessary), the battery terminals and the cable clamps should be cleaned. Loosen the clamps and remove the cables, negative cable first. On top post batteries, the use of a puller specially made for this purpose is

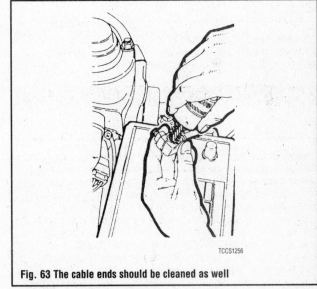

Fig. 63 The cable ends should be cleaned as well

recommended. These are inexpensive and available in most parts stores. Side terminal battery cables are secured with a small bolt.

Clean the cable clamps and the battery terminal with a wire brush, until all corrosion, grease, etc., is removed and the metal is shiny. It is especially important to clean the inside of the clamp thoroughly (an old knife is useful here), since a small deposit of oxidation there will prevent a sound connection and inhibit starting or charging. Special tools are available for cleaning these parts, one type for conventional top post batteries and another type for side terminal batteries. It is also a good idea to apply some dielectric grease to the terminal, as this will aid in the prevention of corrosion.

After the clamps and terminals are clean, reinstall the cables, negative cable last; DO NOT hammer the clamps onto battery posts. Tighten the clamps securely, but do not distort them. Give the clamps and terminals a thin external coating of grease after installation, to retard corrosion.

Check the cables at the same time that the terminals are cleaned. If the cable insulation is cracked or broken, or if the ends are frayed, the cable should be replaced with a new cable of the same length and gauge.

CHARGING

❊❊ CAUTION

The chemical reaction which takes place in all batteries generates explosive hydrogen gas. A spark can cause the battery to explode and splash acid. To avoid personal injury, be sure there is proper ventilation and take appropriate fire safety precautions when working with or near a battery.

A battery should be charged at a slow rate to keep the plates inside from getting too hot. However, if some maintenance-free batteries are allowed to discharge until they are almost "dead," they may have to be charged at a high rate to bring them back to "life." Always follow the charger manufacturer's instructions on charging the battery.

REPLACEMENT

When it becomes necessary to replace the battery, select one with an amperage rating equal to or greater than the battery originally installed. Deterioration and just plain aging of the battery cables, starter motor, and associated wires makes the battery's job harder in successive years. This makes it prudent to install a new battery with a greater capacity than the old.

Belts

INSPECTION

◗ **See Figures 64, 65, 66, 67 and 68**

Inspect the belts for signs of glazing or cracking. A glazed belt will be perfectly smooth from slippage, while a good belt will have a slight texture of fabric visible. Cracks will usually start at the inner edge of the belt and run outward. All worn or damaged drive belts should be replaced immediately. It is best to replace all drive belts at one time; as a preventive maintenance measure, during this service operation.

Once a year or at 12,000 miles (19,200km), the tension and condition of the drive belts should be checked, and, if necessary, adjusted. Loose accessory drive belts can lead to poor engine cooling and diminish alternator, power steering pump, air conditioning compressor or air pump output. A belt that is too tight places a severe strain on the water pump, alternator, power steering pump, compressor or air pump bearings. Inspection of the belt may reveal cracks in the belt ribs. The cracks will not impair belt performance and should not considered a problem requiring belt replacement. Belts should be replaced if sections of the belt ribs are missing or if the belt is outside the tensioners operating range. The material used in late-model drive belts is such that the belts do not show wear. Replace belts at least every three years.

A single serpentine belt is used to drive all engine accessories formerly driven by multiple drive belts. The accessories are rigidly mounted with the belt tension maintained automatically by a spring loaded tensioner (all engines except 2.8L and 3.1L engines with manual transaxles). The manual transaxle engines use a separate belt to drive the air pump.

The 2.3L QUAD 4 engine uses two drive belts, one to drive the power steering pump and the second to drive the A/C compressor and alternator. The power steering belt is not self-adjusting and has to be adjusted manually. The A/C and

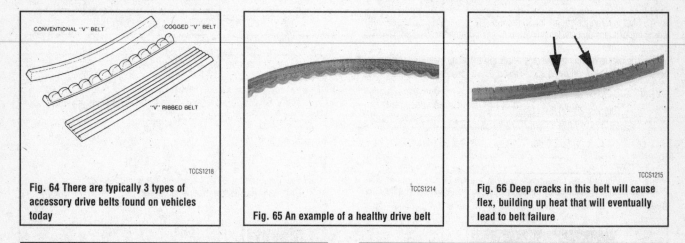

Fig. 64 There are typically 3 types of accessory drive belts found on vehicles today

Fig. 65 An example of a healthy drive belt

Fig. 66 Deep cracks in this belt will cause flex, building up heat that will eventually lead to belt failure

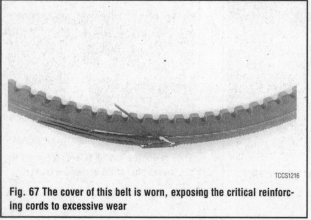

Fig. 67 The cover of this belt is worn, exposing the critical reinforcing cords to excessive wear

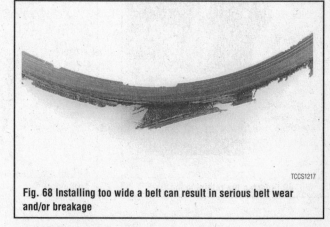

Fig. 68 Installing too wide a belt can result in serious belt wear and/or breakage

alternator belt is automatically adjusted by a spring loaded belt tensioner, requiring no periodic adjustment. QUAD 4 engine without air conditioning has an idler pulley in place of the compressor, consequently the A/C and non-A/C belts are the same.

TENSION MEASUREMENT

Vehicles Through 1992

1. Run the engine with all of the accessories off for until the engine is warmed up. Shut the engine **OFF**. Using a belt tension gauge No. J 23600-B or equivalent, placed halfway between the alternator and power steering pump, measure the belt tension. Note the reading.
2. With the accessories off, start the engine and allow to stabilize for 15 seconds. Turn the engine **OFF**. Using a 15mm socket or ½ in. breaker bar, apply clockwise force to the tensioner pulley bolt. Release the tension and record the tension.
3. Using the 15mm socket or breaker bar, apply counterclockwise force to the tensioner pulley bolt and raise the pulley to eliminate all tension. Slowly lower the pulley to the belt and take a tension reading without disturbing the belt tensioner position.
4. Average the three readings. If the average is not between 50–70 lbs. (225–315 N) and the belt is within the tensioner's operating range, replace the belt.

1993–96 Vehicles

1. Run the engine for 10 minutes.
2. Shut the engine **OFF**, then check the belt tension between any two pulleys using J 23600-B or equivalent belt tension gauge. Note the tension.
3. Start and run the engine for 30 seconds, then shut the engine **OFF** and check the belt tension between any two pulleys using the belt tension gauge. Note the tension.
4. Start and run the engine for 30 seconds, then shut the engine **OFF** and check the belt tension between any two pulleys using the belt tension gauge. Note the tension.
5. The belt tension is the average of the three readings taken. The tension should fall within the following specifications:
   - 1993–94 Vehicles: 105–125 lbs. (467–556 N)
   - 1995 Vehicles: 55–75 lbs. (245–356 N)
   - 1996 Vehicles: 30–50 lbs. (133–222 N)
6. Replace the drive belt tensioner if the belt tension is below the minimum specified and if the drive belt tensioner is within its operating range.

ADJUSTMENT

Belt tension is maintained by the automatic tensioner and is NOT adjustable except on the following:

2.8L and 3.1L Air Pump Belt

1. Loosen the air pump mounting bolts.
2. Using a suitable prybar, move the air pump until the belt deflection at the center of the longest span of the belt is about ¼ inch (6mm). Be careful not to damage the aluminum pump housing.
3. Tighten the air pump bolts.

2.3L Power Steering Belt

1. Place a belt tension gauge J36018 or equivalent onto the pump belt.
2. Loosen the two pump-to-rear bracket adjustment bolts.
3. Tighten the engine-to-front bracket bolts to 44 inch lbs. (5 Nm).
4. For the 2.3L (VIN D) engine, use a inch drive handle in the tab to move the pump to the proper adjustment lbs.
5. For the 2.3L (VIN A) engine, tighten the adjustment stud to the proper adjustment.
6. Adjust to 110 lbs.
7. Tighten the pump adjusting bolts.

REMOVAL & INSTALLATION

2.8L and 3.1L Air Pump Belt

1. Disconnect the negative battery cable.
2. Loosen the air pump.
3. Remove the worn belt.
To install:
4. Wrap the new belt around the pump.
5. Adjust the belt to specifications and tighten the pump mounting bolts.
6. Connect the negative battery cable.

2.3L Power Steering Belt

1. Disconnect the negative battery cable.
2. Loosen the adjustment bolts.
3. Remove the power steering belt from the pulley.
To install:
4. Route the belt around the pulley.
5. Adjust the belt to specifications, then tighten the adjustment bolts.
6. Connect the negative battery cable.

Serpentine Belt

▶ **See Figures 69 thru 78**

1. Remove the belt. Clean the accessory drive belt surfaces.
2. Disconnect the negative battery cable.

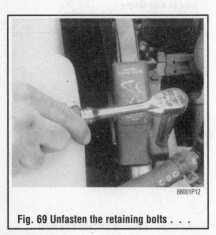

88001P12

Fig. 69 Unfasten the retaining bolts . . .

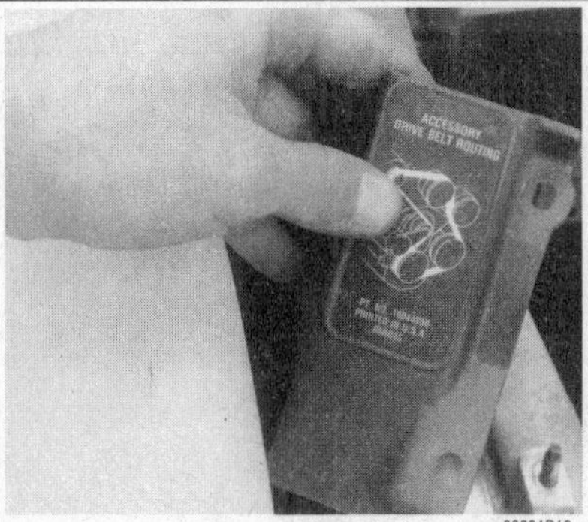

88001P13

Fig. 70 . . . then remove the serpentine belt guard

88001P10

Fig. 71 For the 1992 3.1L engine, use a ½ in. breaker bar to lift or rotate the tensioner . . .

3. Remove the belt guard or coolant recovery reservoir as required.

✳✳ CAUTION

To avoid personal injury when rotating the serpentine belt tensioner, use a tight fitting wrench that is at least 24 in. (61cm) long.

4. Take note of the belt's routing. Lift or rotate the tensioner using a suitable sized breaker bar in the square opening or box end wrench on the pulley nut. Loosen the pump-to-engine bracket bolts and adjusting stud to remove the power steering pump belt on the 2.3L QUAD 4 engines.
   To install:

➡**Be sure the belt is aligned into the proper grooves of the accessory drive pulleys.**

5. Lift the tensioner, and install the belt onto pulleys. Make sure the belt is routed properly.
6. Install the belt guard or reservoir.

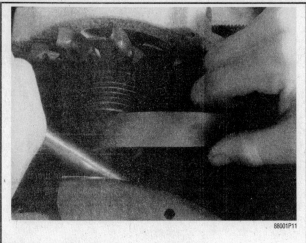

88001P11

Fig. 72 . . . then remove the serpentine belt

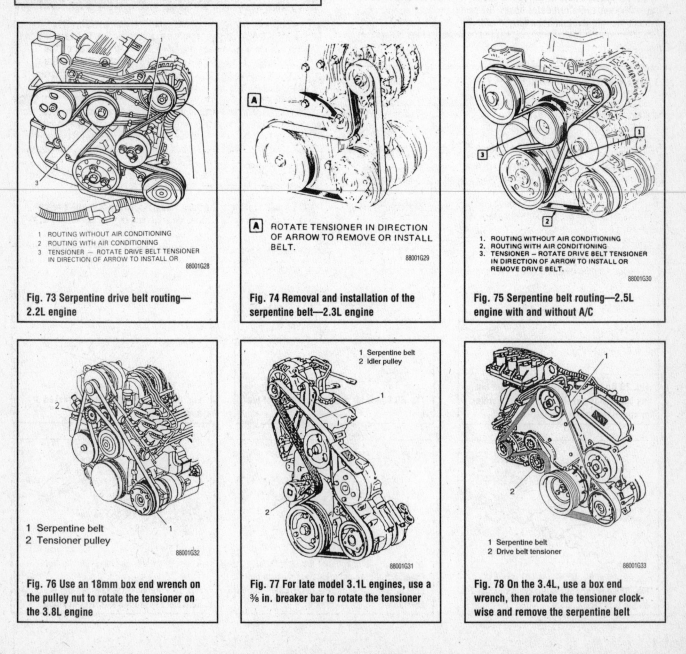

1 ROUTING WITHOUT AIR CONDITIONING
2 ROUTING WITH AIR CONDITIONING
3 TENSIONER — ROTATE DRIVE BELT TENSIONER IN DIRECTION OF ARROW TO INSTALL OR

88001G28

Fig. 73 Serpentine drive belt routing— 2.2L engine

A ROTATE TENSIONER IN DIRECTION OF ARROW TO REMOVE OR INSTALL BELT.

88001G29

Fig. 74 Removal and installation of the serpentine belt—2.3L engine

1. ROUTING WITHOUT AIR CONDITIONING
2. ROUTING WITH AIR CONDITIONING
3. TENSIONER — ROTATE DRIVE BELT TENSIONER IN DIRECTION OF ARROW TO INSTALL OR REMOVE DRIVE BELT.

88001G30

Fig. 75 Serpentine belt routing—2.5L engine with and without A/C

1 Serpentine belt
2 Tensioner pulley

88001G32

Fig. 76 Use an 18mm box end wrench on the pulley nut to rotate the tensioner on the 3.8L engine

1 Serpentine belt
2 Idler pulley

88001G31

Fig. 77 For late model 3.1L engines, use a ⅜ in. breaker bar to rotate the tensioner

1 Serpentine belt
2 Drive belt tensioner

88001G33

Fig. 78 On the 3.4L, use a box end wrench, then rotate the tensioner clockwise and remove the serpentine belt

Timing Belts

INSPECTION

➧ **See Figures 79 thru 84**

Vehicles equipped with the 3.4L (VIN X) engine are the only vehicles covered by this manual which utilize a timing belt. The timing belt should be inspected for cracks, wear and other damage at 60,000 miles (100,000 km) and then every 15,000 miles (25,000 km). Replace the belt and/or tensioner as needed.

For the timing belt removal and installation procedure, please refer to Section 3 of this manual.

Hoses

✻✻ CAUTION

On models equipped with an electric cooling fan, disconnect the negative battery cable or fan motor wiring harness connector before replacing any radiator/heater hose. The fan may come on even though the ignition has been turned OFF.

INSPECTION

➧ **See Figures 85, 86, 87 and 88**

Upper and lower radiator hoses along with the heater hoses should be checked for deterioration, leaks and loose hose clamps at least every 15,000 miles (24,000 km). It is also wise to check the hoses periodically in early spring and at the beginning of the fall or winter when you are performing other maintenance. A quick visual inspection could discover a weakened hose which might have left you stranded if it had remained unrepaired.

Whenever you are checking the hoses, make sure the engine and cooling system are cold. Visually inspect for cracking, rotting or collapsed hoses, and replace as necessary. Run your hand along the length of the hose. If a weak or swollen spot is noted when squeezing the hose wall, the hose should be replaced.

REMOVAL & INSTALLATION

1. Remove the radiator pressure cap.

✻✻ CAUTION

Never remove the pressure cap while the engine is running, or personal injury from scalding hot coolant or steam may result. If possible, wait until the engine has cooled to remove the pressure cap. If this is not possible, wrap a thick cloth around the pressure cap and turn it slowly to the stop. Step back while the pressure is released from the cooling system. When you are sure all the pressure has been released, use the cloth to turn and remove the cap.

2. Position a clean container under the radiator and/or engine draincock or plug, then open the drain and allow the cooling system to drain to an appropriate level. For some upper hoses, only a little coolant must be drained. To remove hoses positioned lower on the engine, such as a lower radiator hose, the entire cooling system must be emptied.

✻✻ CAUTION

When draining coolant, keep in mind that cats and dogs are attracted by ethylene glycol antifreeze, and are quite likely to drink any that is left in an uncovered container or in puddles on the ground. This will prove fatal in sufficient quantity. Always drain coolant into a sealable container. Coolant may be reused unless it is contaminated or several years old.

3. Loosen the hose clamps at each end of the hose requiring replacement. Clamps are usually either of the spring tension type (which require pliers to squeeze the tabs and loosen) or of the screw tension type (which require screw or hex drivers to loosen). Pull the clamps back on the hose away from the connection.
4. Twist, pull and slide the hose off the fitting, taking care not to damage the neck of the component from which the hose is being removed.

➡**If the hose is stuck at the connection, do not try to insert a screwdriver or other sharp tool under the hose end in an effort to free it, as**

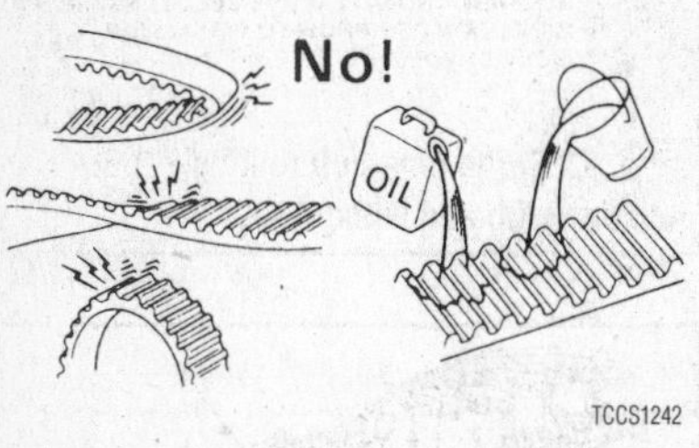

Fig. 79 Do not bend, twist or turn the timing belt inside out. Never allow oil, water or steam to contact the belt

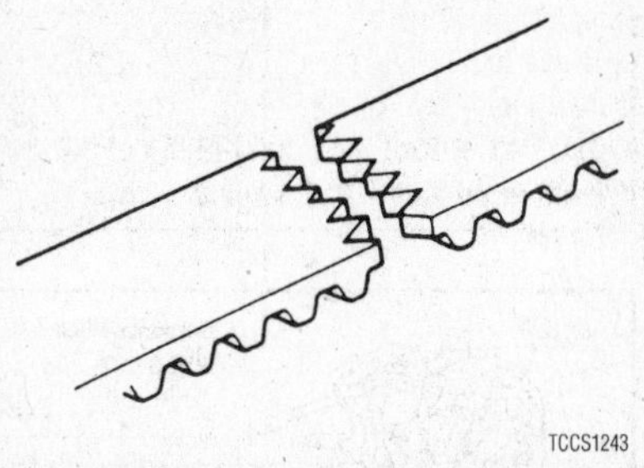

Fig. 80 Check for premature parting of the belt

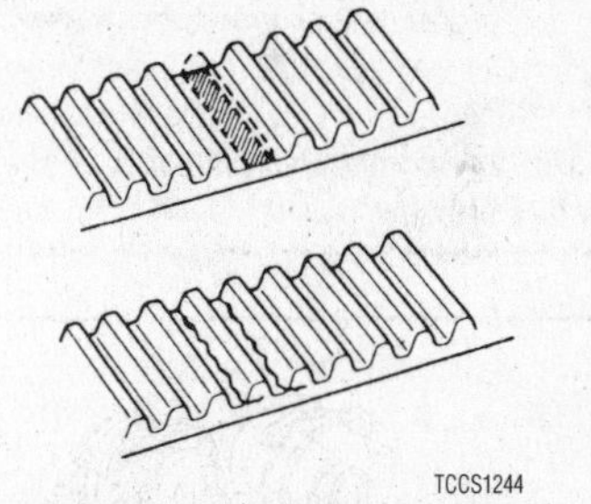

Fig. 81 Check if the teeth are cracked or damaged

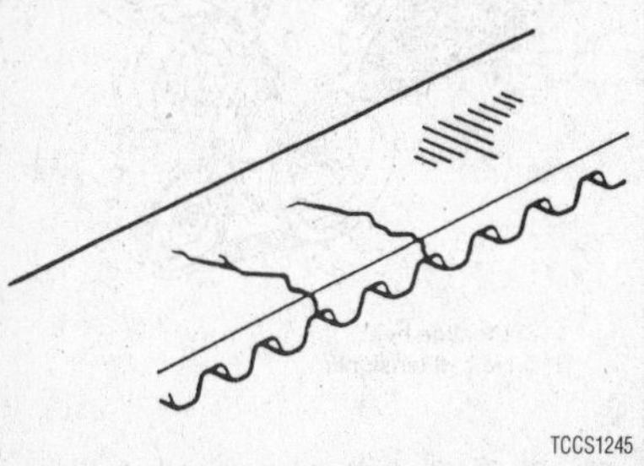

Fig. 82 Look for noticeable cracks or wear on the belt face

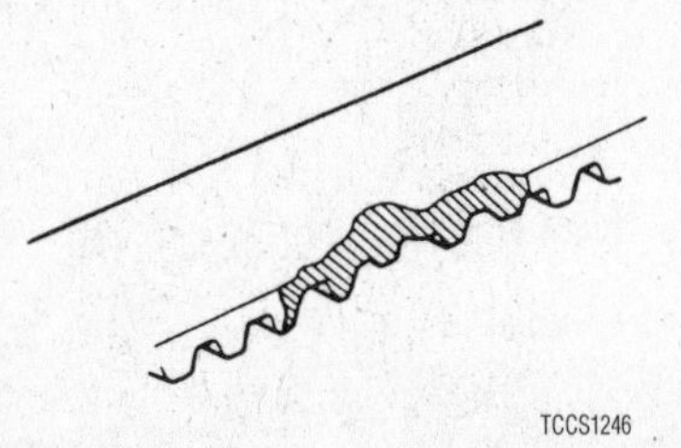

Fig. 83 You may only have damage on one side of the belt; if so, the guide could be the culprit

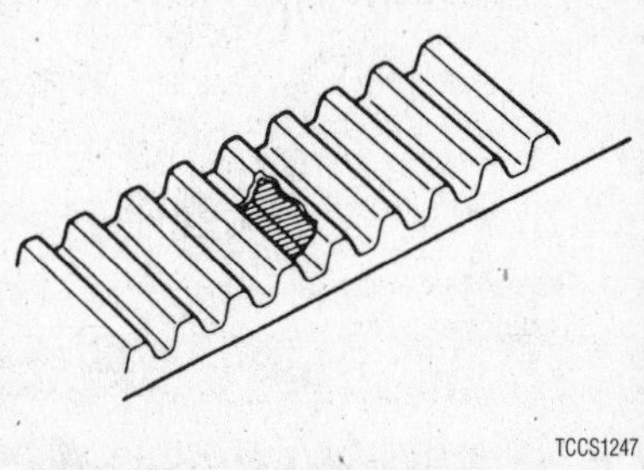

Fig. 84 Foreign materials can get in between the teeth and cause damage

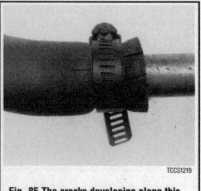

Fig. 85 The cracks developing along this hose are a result of age-related hardening

Fig. 86 A hose clamp that is too tight can cause older hoses to separate and tear on either side of the clamp

Fig. 87 A soft spongy hose (identifiable by the swollen section) will eventually burst and should be replaced

Fig. 88 Hoses are likely to deteriorate from the inside if the cooling system is not periodically flushed

the connection and/or hose may become damaged. Heater connections especially may be easily damaged by such a procedure. If the hose is to be replaced, use a single-edged razor blade to make a slice along the portion of the hose which is stuck on the connection, perpendicular to the end of the hose. Do not cut deep so as to prevent damaging the connection. The hose can then be peeled from the connection and discarded.

5. Clean both hose mounting connections. Inspect the condition of the hose clamps and replace them, if necessary.

To install:

6. Dip the ends of the new hose into clean engine coolant to ease installation.

7. Slide the clamps over the replacement hose, then slide the hose ends over the connections into position.

8. Position and secure the clamps at least ¼ in. (6.35mm) from the ends of the hose. Make sure they are located beyond the raised bead of the connector.

9. Close the radiator or engine drains and properly refill the cooling system with the clean drained engine coolant or a suitable mixture of ethylene glycol coolant and water.

10. If available, install a pressure tester and check for leaks. If a pressure tester is not available, run the engine until normal operating temperature is reached (allowing the system to naturally pressurize), then check for leaks.

✷✷ CAUTION

If you are checking for leaks with the system at normal operating temperature, BE EXTREMELY CAREFUL not to touch any moving or hot engine parts. Once temperature has been reached, shut the engine OFF, and check for leaks around the hose fittings and connections which were removed earlier.

CV-Boots

INSPECTION

▶ **See Figures 89 and 90**

The CV (Constant Velocity) boots should be checked for damage each time the oil is changed and any other time the vehicle is raised for service. These

Fig. 89 CV-Boots must be inspected periodically for damage

Fig. 90 A torn boot should be replaced immediately

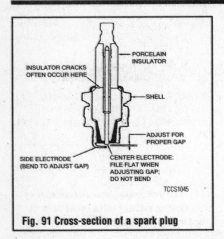

Fig. 91 Cross-section of a spark plug

Fig. 92 A variety of tools and gauges are needed for spark plug service

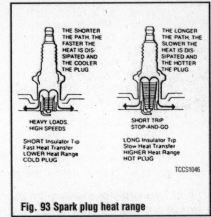

Fig. 93 Spark plug heat range

boots keep water, grime, dirt and other damaging matter from entering the CV-joints. Any of these could cause early CV-joint failure which can be expensive to repair. Heavy grease thrown around the inside of the front wheel(s) and on the brake caliper can be an indication of a torn boot. Thoroughly check the boots for missing clamps and tears. If the boot is damaged, it should be replaced immediately. Please refer to Section 7 for procedures.

Spark Plugs

▶ See Figures 91 and 92

A typical spark plug consists of a metal shell surrounding a ceramic insulator. A metal electrode extends downward through the center of the insulator and protrudes a small distance. Located at the end of the plug and attached to the side of the outer metal shell is the side electrode. The side electrode bends in at a 90° angle so that its tip is just past and parallel to the tip of the center electrode. The distance between these two electrodes (measured in thousandths of an inch or hundredths of a millimeter) is called the spark plug gap.

The spark plug does not produce a spark but instead provides a gap across which the current can arc. The coil produces anywhere from 20,000 to 50,000 volts (depending on the type and application) which travels through the wires to the spark plugs. The current passes along the center electrode and jumps the gap to the side electrode, and in doing so, ignites the air/fuel mixture in the combustion chamber.

SPARK PLUG HEAT RANGE

▶ See Figure 93

Spark plug heat range is the ability of the plug to dissipate heat. The longer the insulator (or the farther it extends into the engine), the hotter the plug will operate; the shorter the insulator (the closer the electrode is to the block's cooling passages) the cooler it will operate. A plug that absorbs little heat and remains too cool will quickly accumulate deposits of oil and carbon since it is not hot enough to burn them off. This leads to plug fouling and consequently to misfiring. A plug that absorbs too much heat will have no deposits but, due to the excessive heat, the electrodes will burn away quickly and might possibly lead to preignition or other ignition problems. Preignition takes place when plug tips get so hot that they glow sufficiently to ignite the air/fuel mixture before the actual spark occurs. This early ignition will usually cause a pinging during low speeds and heavy loads.

The general rule of thumb for choosing the correct heat range when picking a spark plug is: if most of your driving is long distance, high speed travel, use a colder plug; if most of your driving is stop and go, use a hotter plug. Original equipment plugs are generally a good compromise between the 2 styles and most people never have the need to change their plugs from the factory-recommended heat range.

REMOVAL & INSTALLATION

➡Remove the spark plugs and wires one at a time to avoid confusion and miswiring during installation.

※ WARNING

To avoid engine damage, do NOT remove spark plugs when the engine is warm; the spark plug threads may be stripped if removed on a hot engine.

2.2L Engine

1. Disconnect the negative battery cable. If the vehicle has been run recently, allow the engine to thoroughly cool.
2. Carefully twist the spark plug wire boot to loosen it, then pull upward and remove the boot from the plug. Be sure to pull on the boot and not on the wire, otherwise the connector located inside the boot may become separated.
3. Using compressed air, blow any water or debris from the spark plug well to assure that no harmful contaminants are allowed to enter the combustion chamber when the spark plug is removed. If compressed air is not available, use a rag or a brush to clean the area.

➡Remove the spark plugs when the engine is cold, if possible, to prevent damage to the threads. If removal of the plugs is difficult, apply a few drops of penetrating oil or silicone spray to the area around the base of the plug, and allow it a few minutes to work.

4. Using a spark plug socket that is equipped with a rubber insert to properly hold the plug, turn the spark plug counterclockwise to loosen and remove the spark plug from the bore.

※ WARNING

Be sure not to use a flexible extension on the socket. Use of a flexible extension may allow a shear force to be applied to the plug. A shear force could break the plug off in the cylinder head, leading to costly and frustrating repairs.

To install:
5. Inspect the spark plug boot for tears or damage. If a damaged boot is found, the spark plug wire must be replaced.
6. Using a wire feeler gauge, check and adjust the spark plug gap. When using a gauge, the proper size should pass between the electrodes with a slight drag. The next larger size should not be able to pass while the next smaller size should pass freely.
7. Carefully thread the plug into the bore by hand. If resistance is felt before the plug is almost completely threaded, back the plug out and begin threading again. In small to reach areas, an old spark plug wire and boot could be used as a threading tool. The boot will hold the plug while you twist the end of the wire and the wire is supple enough to twist before it would allow the plug to crossthread.

※ WARNING

Do not use the spark plug socket to thread the plugs. Always carefully thread the plug by hand or using an old plug wire to prevent the possibility of cross-threading and damaging the cylinder head bore.

8. Carefully tighten the spark plug. If the plug you are installing is equipped with a crush washer, seat the plug, then tighten about ¼ turn to crush the washer. If you are installing a tapered seat plug, tighten the plug to specifications provided by the vehicle or plug manufacturer.

9. Apply a small amount of silicone dielectric compound to the end of the spark plug lead or inside the spark plug boot to prevent sticking, then install the boot to the spark plug and push until it clicks into place. The click may be felt or heard, then gently pull back on the boot to assure proper contact.

2.3L Engine

The spark plugs on this engine are located under the ignition coil and module assembly. To gain access to the spark plugs, the coil and module assembly must be removed. For more details, refer to Section 2 of this manual.

1. Remove the air cleaner assembly.

2. Disconnect the negative battery cable. If the vehicle has been run recently, allow the engine to thoroughly cool.

3. Detach the ignition coil cover electrical connector.

4. Unfasten the four ignition cover-to-cylinder head bolts.

5. If any of the boots stick to the spark plug, use a spark plug connector removing tool J-36011 or equivalent to remove the boot using a twisting motion.

6. Remove the ignition cover and set aside.

7. Clean any dirt away from the spark plug recess area, then remove the spark plugs using a suitable spark plug socket.

To install:

8. Using a wire feeler gauge, check and adjust the spark plug gap. When using a gauge, the proper size should pass between the electrodes with a slight drag. The next larger size should not be able to pass while the next smaller size should pass freely.

9. Carefully thread the plug into the bore by hand. If resistance is felt before the plug is almost completely threaded, back the plug out and begin threading again. In small to reach areas, an old spark plug wire and boot could be used as a threading tool. The boot will hold the plug while you twist the end of the wire and the wire is supple enough to twist before it would allow the plug to crossthread.

※※ WARNING

Do not use the spark plug socket to thread the plugs. Always carefully thread the plug by hand or using an old plug wire to prevent the possibility of cross-threading and damaging the cylinder head bore.

10. Tighten the plugs to 17 ft. lbs. (23 Nm).

11. If removed, install the plug boots and retainers-to-ignition cover.

12. Apply a suitable silicone dielectric compound to the plug boot.

13. Install the ignition cover-to-engine while carefully aligning the boots with the spark plug terminals.

14. Apply thread locking compound Loctite® or equivalent to the ignition cover bolts. Install the bolts and tighten to 15 ft. lbs. (20 Nm).

15. Attach the ignition cover electrical connectors.

16. Connect the negative battery cable, then install the air cleaner.

2.5L Engine

1. Disconnect the negative battery cable. If the vehicle has been run recently, allow the engine to thoroughly cool.

2. Remove air cleaner components in order to gain access to the spark plugs.

3. Carefully twist the spark plug wire boot to loosen it, then pull upward and remove the boot from the plug. Be sure to pull on the boot and not on the wire, otherwise the connector located inside the boot may become separated.

4. Using compressed air, blow any water or debris from the spark plug well to assure that no harmful contaminants are allowed to enter the combustion chamber when the spark plug is removed. If compressed air is not available, use a rag or a brush to clean the area.

➡**Remove the spark plugs when the engine is cold, if possible, to prevent damage to the threads. If removal of the plugs is difficult, apply a few drops of penetrating oil or silicone spray to the area around the base of the plug, and allow it a few minutes to work.**

5. Using a spark plug socket that is equipped with a rubber insert to properly hold the plug, turn the spark plug counterclockwise to loosen and remove the spark plug from the bore.

※※ WARNING

Be sure not to use a flexible extension on the socket. Use of a flexible extension may allow a shear force to be applied to the plug. A shear force could break the plug off in the cylinder head, leading to costly and frustrating repairs.

To install:

6. Using a wire feeler gauge, check and adjust the spark plug gap. When using a gauge, the proper size should pass between the electrodes with a slight drag. The next larger size should not be able to pass while the next smaller size should pass freely.

7. Carefully thread the plug into the bore by hand. If resistance is felt before the plug is almost completely threaded, back the plug out and begin threading again. In small to reach areas, an old spark plug wire and boot could be used as a threading tool. The boot will hold the plug while you twist the end of the wire and the wire is supple enough to twist before it would allow the plug to crossthread.

※※ WARNING

Do not use the spark plug socket to thread the plugs. Always carefully thread the plug by hand or using an old plug wire to prevent the possibility of cross-threading and damaging the cylinder head bore.

8. Tighten the spark plug to 20 ft. lbs. (27 Nm).

9. Fasten the cable on the plug, making sure it snaps into place. Repeat for the remaining spark plugs.

10. Install the air cleaner components.

11. Connect the negative battery cable.

2.8L and 3.1L Engines

▶ **See Figures 94, 95 and 96**

➡**In order to gain access to the spark plugs, the engine must first be rotated.**

1. Disconnect the negative battery cable. If the vehicle has been run recently, allow the engine to thoroughly cool.

2. For vehicles through 1994, rotate the engine as follows:

a. Place the transaxle in Neutral.

b. Remove the air cleaner assembly and coolant recovery bottle.

c. Unfasten the torque strut-to-engine bracket bolts and swing the torque struts aside.

d. Replace the passenger side torque strut-to-engine bracket bolt in the engine bracket.

e. Position a prybar in the bracket so that it contacts the bracket and the bolt.

f. Rotate the engine by pulling forward on the prybar.

g. Align the slave hole in the driver side torque strut to the engine bracket hole.

h. Retain the engine in this position using the torque strut-to-engine bracket bolt.

3. For 1995–96 vehicles, rotate the engine as follows:

a. Place the transaxle in Neutral.

b. Remove the air cleaner assembly and coolant recovery bottle.

c. Unfasten the torque strut-to-engine bracket bolts and swing the torque struts aside.

d. Install engine tilter J 41131 or equivalent, then rotate the engine forward.

4. Carefully twist the spark plug wire boot to loosen it, then pull upward and remove the boot from the plug. Be sure to pull on the boot and not on the wire, otherwise the connector located inside the boot may become separated.

5. Using compressed air, blow any water or debris from the spark plug well to assure that no harmful contaminants are allowed to enter the combustion chamber when the spark plug is removed. If compressed air is not available, use a rag or a brush to clean the area.

Fig. 94 When removing the spark plug wires, pull on the boot, NOT on the wire itself

Fig. 95 Use a socket and suitable extension . . .

Fig. 96 . . . then remove the spark plug from the cylinder head

➡Remove the spark plugs when the engine is cold, if possible, to prevent damage to the threads. If removal of the plugs is difficult, apply a few drops of penetrating oil or silicone spray to the area around the base of the plug, and allow it a few minutes to work.

6. Using a spark plug socket that is equipped with a rubber insert to properly hold the plug, turn the spark plug counterclockwise to loosen and remove the spark plug from the bore.

✳✳ WARNING

Be sure not to use a flexible extension on the socket. Use of a flexible extension may allow a shear force to be applied to the plug. A shear force could break the plug off in the cylinder head, leading to costly and frustrating repairs.

To install:

7. Using a wire feeler gauge, check and adjust the spark plug gap. When using a gauge, the proper size should pass between the electrodes with a slight drag. The next larger size should not be able to pass while the next smaller size should pass freely.

8. Carefully thread the plug into the bore by hand. If resistance is felt before the plug is almost completely threaded, back the plug out and begin threading again. In small to reach areas, an old spark plug wire and boot could be used as a threading tool. The boot will hold the plug while you twist the end of the wire and the wire is supple enough to twist before it would allow the plug to crossthread.

✳✳ WARNING

Do not use the spark plug socket to thread the plugs. Always carefully thread the plug by hand or using an old plug wire to prevent the possibility of cross-threading and damaging the cylinder head bore.

9. Tighten the spark plug to 18 ft. lbs. (24 Nm). Install the cable on the plug. Make sure it snaps in place.

10. Repeat for the remaining spark plugs.

11. For vehicles through 1994, proceed as follows to bring the engine back to its original position:

a. To bring the engine back into position, pull forward on the prybar to relieve the engine's weight. Then remove the driver side torque strut-to-engine bracket bolt from the torque strut slave hole and engine bracket.

b. Allow the engine to rotate back to its original position.

c. Remove the prybar.

d. Remove the passenger side torque strut-to-engine bracket bolt from the bracket.

e. Install the torque struts and strut-to-engine bracket bolts. Torque the bolts to 51 ft. lbs. (70 Nm).

f. Put the transaxle in Park.

12. For 1995–96 vehicles, proceed as follows to bring the engine back to its original position:

a. Rotate the engine backward, then remove J 41131.

b. Fasten the torque strut-to-engine bracket bolts.

c. Put the transaxle in Park.

13. Install the coolant recovery bottle and air cleaner assembly.

14. Connect the negative battery cable.

3.4L Engine

1. Disconnect the negative battery cable. If the vehicle has been run recently, allow the engine to thoroughly cool.

2. If necessary for access, remove the upper intake manifold, as outlined in Section 3 of this manual.

3. Carefully twist the spark plug wire boot to loosen it, then pull upward and remove the boot from the plug. Be sure to pull on the boot and not on the wire, otherwise the connector located inside the boot may become separated.

4. Using compressed air, blow any water or debris from the spark plug well to assure that no harmful contaminants are allowed to enter the combustion chamber when the spark plug is removed. If compressed air is not available, use a rag or a brush to clean the area.

➡Remove the spark plugs when the engine is cold, if possible, to prevent damage to the threads. If removal of the plugs is difficult, apply a few drops of penetrating oil or silicone spray to the area around the base of the plug, and allow it a few minutes to work.

5. Using a spark plug socket that is equipped with a rubber insert to properly hold the plug, turn the spark plug counterclockwise to loosen and remove the spark plug from the bore.

✳✳ WARNING

Be sure not to use a flexible extension on the socket. Use of a flexible extension may allow a shear force to be applied to the plug. A shear force could break the plug off in the cylinder head, leading to costly and frustrating repairs.

6. Tag the spark plug wires to avoid confusion during installation.

7. Disconnect the spark plug wire by pulling and twisting the boot; then remove the spark plug.

To install:

8. Using a wire feeler gauge, check and adjust the spark plug gap. When using a gauge, the proper size should pass between the electrodes with a slight drag. The next larger size should not be able to pass while the next smaller size should pass freely.

9. Carefully thread the plug into the bore by hand. If resistance is felt before the plug is almost completely threaded, back the plug out and begin threading again. In small to reach areas, an old spark plug wire and boot could be used as a threading tool. The boot will hold the plug while you twist the end of the wire and the wire is supple enough to twist before it would allow the plug to crossthread.

✳✳ WARNING

Do not use the spark plug socket to thread the plugs. Always carefully thread the plug by hand or using an old plug wire to prevent the possibility of cross-threading and damaging the cylinder head bore.

10. Tighten the spark plugs to 18 ft. lbs. (24 Nm).

11. Fasten the spark plug wire on the plug, as tagged during removal. Make sure it snaps in place.

12. Repeat for the remaining spark plugs.

13. Connect the negative battery cable.

3.8L Engine

▶ See Figure 97

1. Disconnect the negative battery cable. If the vehicle has been run recently, allow the engine to thoroughly cool.

2. Tag the spark plug wires to avoid confusion during installation.

3. Carefully twist the spark plug wire boot ½ a turn to loosen it, then pull upward and remove the boot from the plug. Be sure to pull on the boot and not on the wire, otherwise the connector located inside the boot may become separated.

4. On the right rear cylinders only, use tool J 38491, or equivalent small pry tool, to carefully pry the heat shields up from the spark plugs.

5. Using compressed air, blow any water or debris from the spark plug well to assure that no harmful contaminants are allowed to enter the combustion chamber when the spark plug is removed. If compressed air is not available, use a rag or a brush to clean the area.

➡Remove the spark plugs when the engine is cold, if possible, to prevent damage to the threads. If removal of the plugs is difficult, apply a few drops of penetrating oil or silicone spray to the area around the base of the plug, and allow it a few minutes to work.

6. Using a spark plug socket that is equipped with a rubber insert to properly hold the plug, turn the spark plug counterclockwise to loosen and remove the spark plug from the bore.

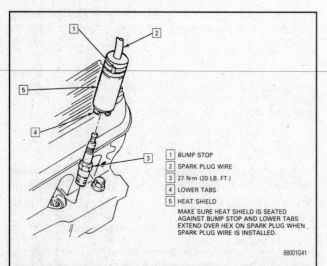

1	BUMP STOP
2	SPARK PLUG WIRE
3	27 N·m (20 LB. FT.)
4	LOWER TABS
5	HEAT SHIELD

MAKE SURE HEAT SHIELD IS SEATED AGAINST BUMP STOP AND LOWER TABS EXTEND OVER HEX ON SPARK PLUG WHEN SPARK PLUG WIRE IS INSTALLED.

88001G41

Fig. 97 When installing the heat shields, make sure they are seated against the bump stop and the lower tabs extend over the plug's hex

✳✳ WARNING

Be sure not to use a flexible extension on the socket. Use of a flexible extension may allow a shear force to be applied to the plug. A shear force could break the plug off in the cylinder head, leading to costly and frustrating repairs.

To install:

7. Using a wire feeler gauge, check and adjust the spark plug gap. When using a gauge, the proper size should pass between the electrodes with a slight drag. The next larger size should not be able to pass while the next smaller size should pass freely.

8. Carefully thread the plug into the bore by hand. If resistance is felt before the plug is almost completely threaded, back the plug out and begin threading again. In small to reach areas, an old spark plug wire and boot could be used as a,threading tool. The boot will hold the plug while you twist the end of the wire and the wire is supple enough to twist before it would allow the plug to crossthread.

✳✳ WARNING

Do not use the spark plug socket to thread the plugs. Always carefully thread the plug by hand or using an old plug wire to prevent the possibility of cross-threading and damaging the cylinder head bore.

9. Tighten the spark plugs to 20 ft. lbs. (27 Nm) for vehicles through 1991 and to 11 ft. lbs. (15 Nm) for 1992–96 vehicles.

10. Install the heat shields. When installing the heat shields, make sure they are seated against the bump stop and the lower tabs extend over the spark plug's hex.

11. Connect the negative battery cable.

INSPECTION & GAPPING

▶ See Figures 98, 99, 100 and 101

Check the plugs for deposits and wear. If they are not going to be replaced, clean the plugs thoroughly. Remember that any kind of deposit will decrease the efficiency of the plug. Plugs can be cleaned on a spark plug cleaning machine, which can sometimes be found in service stations, or you can do an acceptable job of cleaning with a stiff brush. If the plugs are cleaned, the electrodes must be filed flat. Use an ignition points file, not an emery board or the like, which will leave deposits. The electrodes must be filed perfectly flat with sharp edges; rounded edges reduce the spark plug voltage by as much as 50%.

Check spark plug gap before installation. The ground electrode (the L-shaped one connected to the body of the plug) must be parallel to the center electrode and the specified size wire gauge (please refer to the Tune-Up Specifications chart for details) must pass between the electrodes with a slight drag.

➡NEVER adjust the gap on a used platinum type spark plug.

Always check the gap on new plugs as they are not always set correctly at the factory. Do not use a flat feeler gauge when measuring the gap on a used

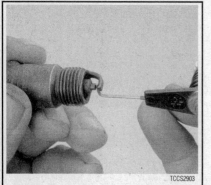

TCCS2903

Fig. 98 Checking the spark plug gap with a feeler gauge

TCCS2904

Fig. 99 Adjusting the spark plug gap

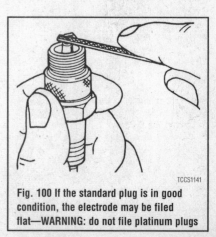

TCCS1141

Fig. 100 If the standard plug is in good condition, the electrode may be filed flat—WARNING: do not file platinum plugs

plug, because the reading may be inaccurate. A round-wire type gapping tool is the best way to check the gap. The correct gauge should pass through the electrode gap with a slight drag. If you're in doubt, try one size smaller and one larger. The smaller gauge should go through easily, while the larger one shouldn't go through at all. Wire gapping tools usually have a bending tool attached. Use that to adjust the side electrode until the proper distance is obtained. Absolutely never attempt to bend the center electrode. Also, be careful not to bend the side electrode too far or too often as it may weaken and break off within the engine, requiring removal of the cylinder head to retrieve it.

Spark Plug Wires

TESTING

▶ See Figures 102 and 103

At every tune-up/inspection, visually check the spark plug cables for burns cuts, or breaks in the insulation. Check the boots and the nipples on the coil. Replace any damaged wiring.

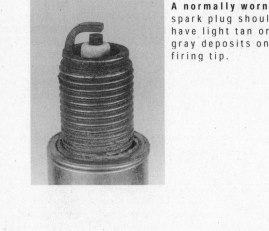
A normally worn spark plug should have light tan or gray deposits on the firing tip.

A carbon fouled plug, identified by soft, sooty, black deposits, may indicate an improperly tuned vehicle. Check the air cleaner, ignition components and engine control system.

This spark plug has been **left in the engine too long,** as evidenced by the extreme gap- Plugs with such an extreme gap can cause misfiring and stumbling accompanied by a noticeable lack of power.

An oil fouled spark plug indicates an engine with worn poston rings and/or bad valve seals allowing excessive oil to enter the chamber.

A physically damaged spark plug may be evidence of severe detonation in that cylinder. Watch that cylinder carefully between services, as a continued detonation will not only damage the plug, but could also damage the engine.

A bridged or almost bridged spark plug, identified by a build-up between the electrodes caused by excessive carbon or oil build-up on the plug.

TCCA1P40

Fig. 101 Inspect the spark plug to determine engine running conditions

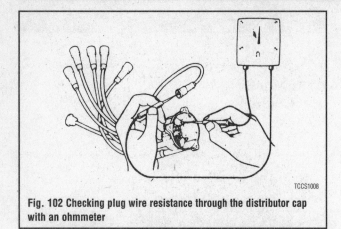

Fig. 102 Checking plug wire resistance through the distributor cap with an ohmmeter

Fig. 103 Checking individual plug wire resistance with an digital ohmmeter

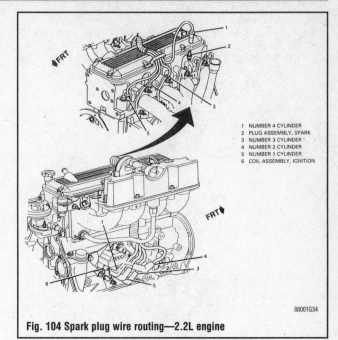

1 NUMBER 4 CYLINDER
2 PLUG ASSEMBLY, SPARK
3 NUMBER 3 CYLINDER
4 NUMBER 2 CYLINDER
5 NUMBER 1 CYLINDER
6 COIL ASSEMBLY, IGNITION

Fig. 104 Spark plug wire routing—2.2L engine

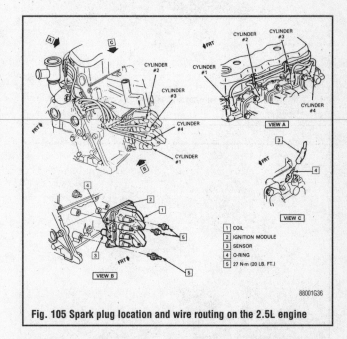

1 COIL
2 IGNITION MODULE
3 SENSOR
4 O-RING
5 27 N·m (20 LB. FT.)

Fig. 105 Spark plug location and wire routing on the 2.5L engine

Every 50,000 miles (80,000 Km) or 60 months, the resistance of the wires should be checked with an ohmmeter. Wires with excessive resistance will cause misfiring, and may make the engine difficult to start in damp weather.

To check resistance, connect one lead of an ohmmeter to an electrode on the ignition coil; connect the other lead to the corresponding spark plug terminal (remove it from the spark plug for this test). Replace any wire which shows a resistance over 30,000 ohms. Generally speaking, it is preferable that resistance be below 25,000 ohms, but 30,000 ohms must be considered the outer limit of acceptability. It should be remembered that resistance is also a function of length; the longer the wire, the greater the resistance. Thus, if the wires on your car are longer than the factory originals, resistance will be higher, quite possible outside these limits.

Wire length can therefore be used to determine appropriate resistance values:
- 0–15 in. (0–38cm)—3,000–10,000 ohms
- 15–25 in. (38–64cm)—4,000–15,000 ohms
- 25–35 in. (64–89cm)—6,000–20,000 ohms
- Wire over 35 in. (89cm)—25,000 ohms

REMOVAL & INSTALLATION

▶ See Figures 104 thru 109

➡ If all of the wires must be disconnected from the spark plugs or from the ignition coil pack at the same time, be sure to tag the wires to assure proper reconnection.

When installing a new set of spark plug wires, replace the wires one at a time so there will be no mix-up. Start by replacing the longest cable first. Twist the

boot of the spark plug wire ½ turn in each direction before pulling if off. Install the boot firmly over the spark plug. Route the wire exactly the same as the original. Insert the nipple firmly onto the tower on the ignition coil. Be sure to apply silicone dielectric compound to the spark plug wire boots and tower connectors prior to installation. On some vehicles, the engine must be rotated to allow for access to the rear spark plug wires. For details regarding rotating the engine, please refer to Section 3 of this manual.

Ignition Timing

GENERAL INFORMATION

All of the vehicles covered by this manual are equipped with distributorless ignition systems. Accordingly, ignition timing is controlled by the Engine/Powertrain Control Module (ECM/PCM) and is not adjustable.

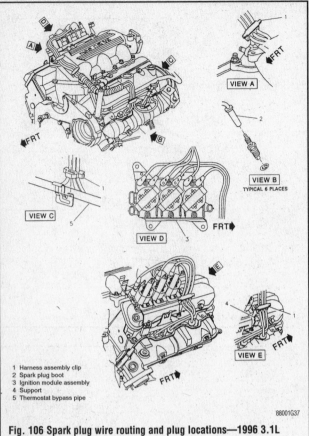

1 Harness assembly clip
2 Spark plug boot
3 Ignition module assembly
4 Support
5 Thermostat bypass pipe

88001G37

Fig. 106 Spark plug wire routing and plug locations—1996 3.1L engine shown

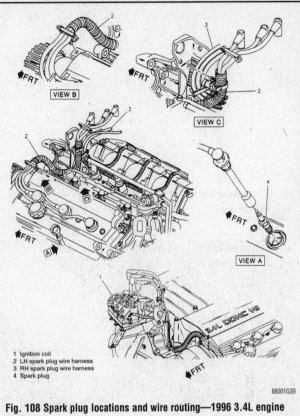

1 Ignition coil
2 LH spark plug wire harness
3 RH spark plug wire harness
4 Spark plug

88001G39

Fig. 108 Spark plug locations and wire routing—1996 3.4L engine shown

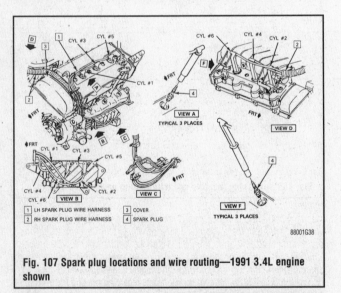

1 LH SPARK PLUG WIRE HARNESS   3 COVER
2 RH SPARK PLUG WIRE HARNESS   4 SPARK PLUG

88001G38

Fig. 107 Spark plug locations and wire routing—1991 3.4L engine shown

Valve Lash

All engines in the vehicles covered by this manual are equipped with hydraulic valve lifters that do not require periodic valve lash adjustment. Adjustment to zero is maintained automatically by hydraulic pressure in the valves.

Idle Speed and Mixture Adjustments

Idle speed and mixture for all engines covered by this manual are electronically controlled by computerized fuel injection system. Adjustments are neither necessary nor possible.

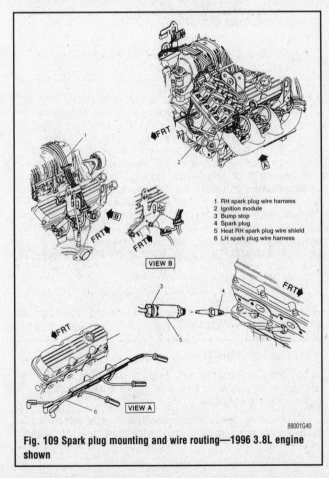

1 RH spark plug wire harness
2 Ignition module
3 Bump stop
4 Spark plug
5 Heat RH spark plug wire shield
6 LH spark plug wire harness

88001G40

Fig. 109 Spark plug mounting and wire routing—1996 3.8L engine shown

GASOLINE ENGINE TUNE-UP SPECIFICATIONS

Year	Engine ID/VIN	Engine Displacement Liters (cc)	Spark Plugs Gap (in.)	Ignition Timing (deg.) MT	Ignition Timing (deg.) AT	Fuel Pump (psi)	Idle Speed (rpm) MT	Idle Speed (rpm) AT	Valve Clearance In.	Valve Clearance Ex.
1988	W	2.8 (2837)	0.045	①	①	41-47	②	②	HYD	HYD
1989	T	3.1 (3135)	0.045	①	①	41-47	②	②	HYD	HYD
	W	2.8 (2837)	0.045	①	①	41-47	②	②	HYD	HYD
	V	3.1 (3135)	0.045	-	①	41-47	-	②	HYD	HYD
1990	A	2.3 (2260)	0.035	①	①	41-47	②	②	HYD	HYD
	D	2.3 (2260)	0.035	-	①	41-47	-	②	HYD	HYD
	R	2.5 (2471)	0.060	-	①	26-32	-	②	HYD	HYD
	T	3.1 (3135)	0.045	-	①	41-47	②	②	HYD	HYD
	V	3.1 (3135)	0.045	-	①	41-47	-	②	HYD	HYD
1991	D	2.3 (2260)	0.035	-	①	41-47	-	②	HYD	HYD
	L	3.8 (3791)	0.060	-	①	41-47	-	②	HYD	HYD
	R	2.5 (2471)	0.060	-	①	26-32	-	②	HYD	HYD
	T	3.1 (3135)	0.045	-	①	41-47	-	②	HYD	HYD
	X	3.4 (3350)	0.045	①	①	41-47	②	②	HYD	HYD
1992	L	3.8 (3791)	0.060	-	①	41-47	-	②	HYD	HYD
	R	2.5 (2471)	0.060	-	①	26-32	-	②	HYD	HYD
	T	3.1 (3135)	0.045	-	①	41-47	-	②	HYD	HYD
	X	3.4 (3350)	0.045	①	①	41-47	②	②	HYD	HYD
1993	4	2.2 (2190)	0.045	-	①	41-47	-	②	HYD	HYD
	L	3.8 (3791)	0.060	-	①	41-47	-	②	HYD	HYD
	M	3.1 (3135)	③	-	①	41-47	-	②	HYD	HYD
	T	3.1 (3135)	0.045	-	①	41-47	-	②	HYD	HYD
	X	3.4 (3350)	0.045	①	①	41-47	②	②	HYD	HYD
1994	L	3.8 (3791)	0.060	-	①	41-47	-	②	HYD	HYD
	M	3.1 (3135)	0.060	-	①	41-47	-	②	HYD	HYD
	T	3.1 (3135)	0.045	-	①	41-47	-	②	HYD	HYD
	X	3.4 (3350)	0.045	-	①	41-47	-	②	HYD	HYD
1995	L	3.8 (3791)	0.060	-	①	41-47	-	②	HYD	HYD
	M	3.1 (3135)	0.060	-	①	41-47	-	②	HYD	HYD
	X	3.4 (3350)	0.045	-	①	41-47	-	②	HYD	HYD
1996	K	3.8 (3791)	0.060	-	①	41-47	-	②	HYD	HYD
	M	3.1 (3135)	0.060	-	①	41-47	-	②	HYD	HYD
	X	3.4 (3350)	0.045	-	①	41-47	-	②	HYD	HYD

NOTE: The Vehicle Emission Control Information label often reflects specification changes made during production. The label figures must be used if they differ from those in this chart.

HYD - Hydraulic

① Distributorless ignition system, no adjustment is possible.

② Idle speed is computer controlled, no adjustment is possible.

③ Refer to Vehicle Emission Control Information label.

88001C06

Air Conditioning System

SYSTEM SERVICE & REPAIR

➡ It is recommended that the A/C system be serviced by an EPA Section 609 certified automotive technician utilizing a refrigerant recovery/recycling machine.

The do-it-yourselfer should not service his/her own vehicle's A/C system for many reasons, including legal concerns, personal injury, environmental damage and cost.

According to the U.S. Clean Air Act, it is a federal crime to service or repair (involving the refrigerant) a Motor Vehicle Air Conditioning (MVAC) system for money without being EPA certified. It is also illegal to vent R-12 and R-134a refrigerants into the atmosphere. State and/or local laws may be more strict than the federal regulations, so be sure to check with your state and/or local authorities for further information.

➡ Federal law dictates that a fine of up to $25,000 may be levied on people convicted of venting refrigerant into the atmosphere.

When servicing an A/C system you run the risk of handling or coming in contact with refrigerant, which may result in skin or eye irritation or frostbite. Although low in toxicity (due to chemical stability), inhalation of concentrated refrigerant fumes is dangerous and can result in death; cases of fatal cardiac arrhythmia have been reported in people accidentally subjected to high levels of refrigerant. Some early symptoms include loss of concentration and drowsiness.

➡ Generally, the limit for exposure is lower for R-134a than it is for R-12. Exceptional care must be practiced when handling R-134a.

Also, some refrigerants can decompose at high temperatures (near gas heaters or open flame), which may result in hydrofluoric acid, hydrochloric acid and phosgene (a fatal nerve gas).

It is usually more economically feasible to have a certified MVAC automotive technician perform A/C system service on your vehicle.

R-12 Refrigerant Conversion

If your vehicle still uses R-12 refrigerant, one way to save A/C system costs down the road is to investigate the possibility of having your system converted to R-134a. The older R-12 systems can be easily converted to R-134a refrigerant by a certified automotive technician by installing a few new components and changing the system oil.

The cost of R-12 is steadily rising and will continue to increase, because it is no longer imported or manufactured in the United States. Therefore, it is often possible to have an R-12 system converted to R-134a and recharged for less than it would cost to just charge the system with R-12.

If you are interested in having your system converted, contact local automotive service stations for more details and information.

PREVENTIVE MAINTENANCE

Although the A/C system should not be serviced by the do-it-yourselfer, preventive maintenance should be practiced to help maintain the efficiency of the vehicle's A/C system. Be sure to perform the following:

• The easiest and most important preventive maintenance for your A/C system is to be sure that it is used on a regular basis. Running the system for five minutes each month (no matter what the season) will help ensure that the seals and all internal components remain lubricated.

➡ **Some vehicles automatically operate the A/C system compressor whenever the windshield defroster is activated. Therefore, the A/C system would not need to be operated each month if the defroster was used.**

• In order to prevent heater core freeze-up during A/C operation, it is necessary to maintain proper antifreeze protection. Be sure to properly maintain the engine cooling system.

• Any obstruction of or damage to the condenser configuration will restrict air flow which is essential to its efficient operation. Keep this unit clean and in proper physical shape.

➡ **Bug screens which are mounted in front of the condenser (unless they are original equipment) are regarded as obstructions.**

• The condensation drain tube expels any water which accumulates on the bottom of the evaporator housing into the engine compartment. If this tube is obstructed, the air conditioning performance can be restricted and condensation buildup can spill over onto the vehicle's floor.

SYSTEM INSPECTION

Although the A/C system should not be serviced by the do-it-yourselfer, system inspections should be performed to help maintain the efficiency of the vehicle's A/C system. Be sure to perform the following:

The easiest and often most important check for the air conditioning system consists of a visual inspection of the system components. Visually inspect the system for refrigerant leaks, damaged compressor clutch, abnormal compressor drive belt tension and/or condition, plugged evaporator drain tube, blocked condenser fins, disconnected or broken wires, blown fuses, corroded connections and poor insulation.

A refrigerant leak will usually appear as an oily residue at the leakage point in the system. The oily residue soon picks up dust or dirt particles from the surrounding air and appears greasy. Through time, this will build up and appear to be a heavy dirt impregnated grease.

For a thorough visual and operational inspection, check the following:

• Check the surface of the radiator and condenser for dirt, leaves or other material which might block air flow.

• Check for kinks in hoses and lines. Check the system for leaks.

• Make sure the drive belt is properly tensioned. During operation, make sure the belt is free of noise or slippage.

• Make sure the blower motor operates at all appropriate positions, then check for distribution of the air from all outlets.

➡ **Remember that in high humidity, air discharged from the vents may not feel as cold as expected, even if the system is working properly. This is because moisture in humid air retains heat more effectively than dry air, thereby making humid air more difficult to cool.**

Windshield Wipers

ELEMENT (REFILL) CARE & REPLACEMENT

▶ **See Figures 110, 111 and 112**

For maximum effectiveness and longest element life, the windshield and wiper blades should be kept clean. Dirt, tree sap, road tar and so on will cause streaking, smearing and blade deterioration if left on the glass. It is advisable to wash the windshield carefully with a commercial glass cleaner at least once a month. Wipe off the rubber blades with the wet rag afterwards. Do not attempt to move wipers across the windshield by hand; damage to the motor and drive mechanism will result.

To inspect and/or replace the wiper blade elements, place the wiper switch in the **LOW** speed position and the ignition switch in the **ACC** position. When the wiper blades are approximately vertical on the windshield, turn the ignition switch to **OFF**.

Examine the wiper blade elements. If they are found to be cracked, broken or torn, they should be replaced immediately. Replacement intervals will vary with usage, although ozone deterioration usually limits element life to about one year. If the wiper pattern is smeared or streaked, or if the blade chatters across the glass, the elements should be replaced. It is easiest and most sensible to replace the elements in pairs.

If your vehicle is equipped with aftermarket blades, there are several different types of refills and your vehicle might have any kind. Aftermarket blades and arms rarely use the exact same type blade or refill as the original equipment.

Regardless of the type of refill used, be sure to follow the part manufacturer's instructions closely. Make sure that all of the frame jaws are engaged as the refill is pushed into place and locked. If the metal blade holder and frame are allowed to touch the glass during wiper operation, the glass will be scratched.

Fig. 110 Most aftermarket blades are available with multiple adapters to fit different vehicles

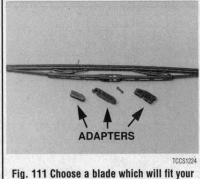

Fig. 111 Choose a blade which will fit your vehicle, and that will be readily available next time you need blades

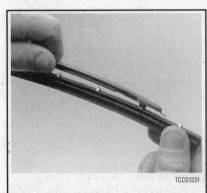

Fig. 112 When installed, be certain the blade is fully inserted into the backing

Tires and Wheels

Common sense and good driving habits will afford maximum tire life. Make sure that you don't overload the vehicle or run with incorrect pressure in the tires. Either of these will increase tread wear. Fast starts, sudden stops and sharp cornering are hard on tires and will shorten their useful life span.

➡ **For optimum tire life, keep the tires properly inflated, rotate them often and have the wheel alignment checked periodically.**

Inspect your tires frequently. Be especially careful to watch for bubbles in the tread or sidewall, deep cuts or underinflation. Replace any tires with bubbles in the sidewall. If cuts are so deep that they penetrate to the cords, discard the tire. Any cut in the sidewall of a radial tire renders it unsafe. Also look for uneven tread wear patterns that may indicate the front end is out of alignment or that the tires are out of balance.

TIRE ROTATION

▶ **See Figure 113**

Tires must be rotated periodically to equalize wear patterns that vary with a tire's position on the vehicle. Tires will also wear in an uneven way as the front steering/suspension system wears to the point where the alignment should be reset.

Rotating the tires will ensure maximum life for the tires as a set, so you will not have to discard a tire early due to wear on only part of the tread. Regular rotation is required to equalize wear.

When rotating "unidirectional tires," make sure that they always roll in the same direction. This means that a tire used on the left side of the vehicle must not be switched to the right side and vice-versa. Such tires should only be rotated front-to-rear or rear-to-front, while always remaining on the same side of the vehicle. These tires are marked on the sidewall as to the direction of rotation; observe the marks when reinstalling the tire(s).

Some styled or "mag" wheels may have different offsets front to rear. In these cases, the rear wheels must not be used up front and vice-versa. Furthermore, if these wheels are equipped with unidirectional tires, they cannot be rotated unless the tire is remounted for the proper direction of rotation.

➡ **The compact or space-saver spare is strictly for emergency use. It must never be included in the tire rotation or placed on the vehicle for everyday use.**

TIRE DESIGN

▶ **See Figure 114**

For maximum satisfaction, tires should be used in sets of four. Mixing of different brands or types (radial, bias-belted, fiberglass belted) should be avoided. In most cases, the vehicle manufacturer has designated a type of tire on which the vehicle will perform best. Your first choice when replacing tires should be to use the same type of tire that the manufacturer recommends.

When radial tires are used, tire sizes and wheel diameters should be selected to maintain ground clearance and tire load capacity equivalent to the original specified tire. Radial tires should always be used in sets of four.

✳✳ CAUTION

Radial tires should never be used on only the front axle.

When selecting tires, pay attention to the original size as marked on the tire. Most tires are described using an industry size code sometimes referred to as P-Metric. This allows the exact identification of the tire specifications, regardless of the manufacturer. If selecting a different tire size or brand, remember to check the installed tire for any sign of interference with the body or suspension while the vehicle is stopping, turning sharply or heavily loaded.

Snow Tires

Good radial tires can produce a big advantage in slippery weather, but in snow, a street radial tire does not have sufficient tread to provide traction and control. The small grooves of a street tire quickly pack with snow and the tire behaves like a billiard ball on a marble floor. The more open, chunky tread of a snow tire will self-clean as the tire turns, providing much better grip on snowy surfaces.

To satisfy municipalities requiring snow tires during weather emergencies, most snow tires carry either an M + S designation after the tire size stamped on the sidewall, or the designation "all-season." In general, no change in tire size is necessary when buying snow tires.

Most manufacturers strongly recommend the use of 4 snow tires on their vehicles for reasons of stability. If snow tires are fitted only to the drive wheels, the opposite end of the vehicle may become very unstable when braking or turning on slippery surfaces. This instability can lead to unpleasant endings if the driver can't counteract the slide in time.

Note that snow tires, whether 2 or 4, will affect vehicle handling in all non-snow situations. The stiffer, heavier snow tires will noticeably change the turning and braking characteristics of the vehicle. Once the snow tires are installed, you must re-learn the behavior of the vehicle and drive accordingly.

➡ **Consider buying extra wheels on which to mount the snow tires. Once done, the "snow wheels" can be installed and removed as needed. This eliminates the potential damage to tires or wheels from seasonal removal and installation. Even if your vehicle has styled wheels, see if inexpensive steel wheels are available. Although the look of the vehicle will change, the expensive wheels will be protected from salt, curb hits and pothole damage.**

TIRE STORAGE

If they are mounted on wheels, store the tires at proper inflation pressure. All tires should be kept in a cool, dry place. If they are stored in the garage or basement, do not let them stand on a concrete floor; set them on strips of wood, a mat or a large stack of newspaper. Keeping them away from direct moisture is of paramount importance. Tires should not be stored upright, but in a flat position.

INFLATION & INSPECTION

▶ **See Figures 115 thru 120**

The importance of proper tire inflation cannot be overemphasized. A tire employs air as part of its structure. It is designed around the supporting

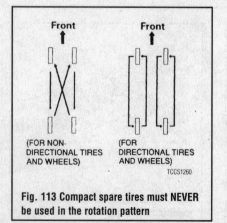

(FOR NON-DIRECTIONAL TIRES AND WHEELS)

(FOR DIRECTIONAL TIRES AND WHEELS)

TCCS1260

Fig. 113 Compact spare tires must NEVER be used in the rotation pattern

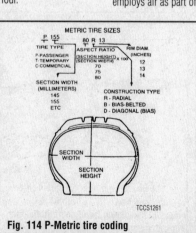

METRIC TIRE SIZES

TCCS1261

Fig. 114 P-Metric tire coding

TCCS1095

Fig. 115 Tires with deep cuts, or cuts which bulge, should be replaced immediately

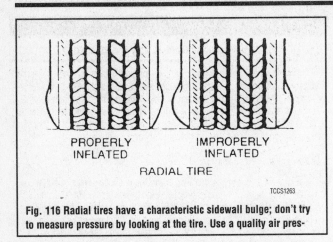

Fig. 116 Radial tires have a characteristic sidewall bulge; don't try to measure pressure by looking at the tire. Use a quality air pres-

A plate or sticker is normally provided somewhere in the vehicle (door post, hood, tailgate or trunk lid) which shows the proper pressure for the tires. Never counteract excessive pressure build-up by bleeding off air pressure (letting some air out). This will cause the tire to run hotter and wear quicker.

✳ CAUTION

Never exceed the maximum tire pressure embossed on the tire! This is the pressure to be used when the tire is at maximum loading, but it is rarely the correct pressure for everyday driving. Consult the owner's manual or the tire pressure sticker for the correct tire pressure.

strength of the air at a specified pressure. For this reason, improper inflation drastically reduces the tire's ability to perform as intended. A tire will lose some air in day-to-day use; having to add a few pounds of air periodically is not necessarily a sign of a leaking tire.

Two items should be a permanent fixture in every glove compartment: an accurate tire pressure gauge and a tread depth gauge. Check the tire pressure (including the spare) regularly with a pocket type gauge. Too often, the gauge on the end of the air hose at your corner garage is not accurate because it suffers too much abuse. Always check tire pressure when the tires are cold, as pressure increases with temperature. If you must move the vehicle to check the tire inflation, do not drive more than a mile before checking. A cold tire is generally one that has not been driven for more than three hours.

Once you've maintained the correct tire pressures for several weeks, you'll be familiar with the vehicle's braking and handling personality. Slight adjustments in tire pressures can fine-tune these characteristics, but never change the cold pressure specification by more than 2 psi. A slightly softer tire pressure will give a softer ride but also yield lower fuel mileage. A slightly harder tire will give crisper dry road handling but can cause skidding on wet surfaces. Unless you're fully attuned to the vehicle, stick to the recommended inflation pressures.

All automotive tires have built-in tread wear indicator bars that show up as 1/2 in. (13mm) wide smooth bands across the tire when 1/16 in. (1.5mm) of tread remains. The appearance of tread wear indicators means that the tires should be replaced. In fact, many states have laws prohibiting the use of tires with less than this amount of tread.

You can check your own tread depth with an inexpensive gauge or by using a Lincoln head penny. Slip the Lincoln penny (with Lincoln's head upside-down) into several tread grooves. If you can see the top of Lincoln's head in 2 adjacent grooves, the tire has less than 1/16 in. (1.5mm) tread left and should be replaced. You can measure snow tires in the same manner by using the "tails" side of the Lincoln penny. If you can see the top of the Lincoln memorial, it's time to replace the snow tire(s).

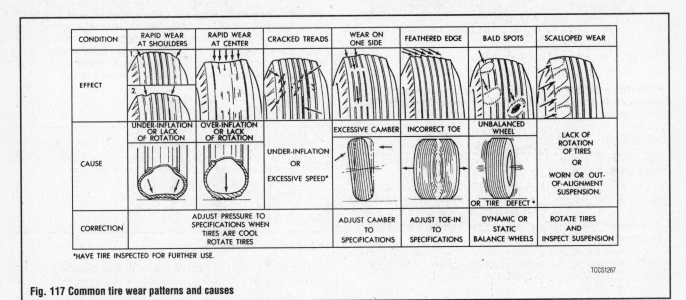

Fig. 117 Common tire wear patterns and causes

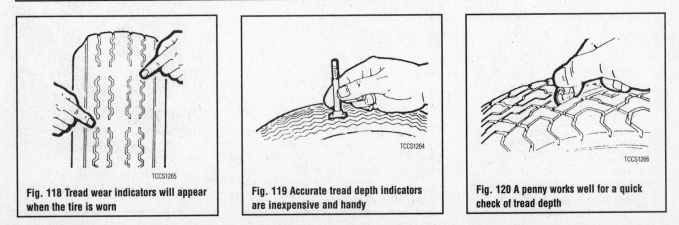

Fig. 118 Tread wear indicators will appear when the tire is worn

Fig. 119 Accurate tread depth indicators are inexpensive and handy

Fig. 120 A penny works well for a quick check of tread depth

FLUIDS AND LUBRICANTS

Fluid Disposal

Used fluids such as engine oil, transmission fluid, antifreeze and brake fluid are hazardous wastes and must be disposed of properly. Before draining any fluids, consult with your local authorities; in many areas waste oil, etc. is being accepted as a part of recycling programs. A number of service stations and auto parts stores are also accepting waste fluids for recycling.

Be sure of the recycling center's policies before draining any fluids, as many will not accept different fluids that have been mixed together.

Fuel and Engine Oil Recommendations

FUEL

➡ Some fuel additives contain chemicals that can damage the catalytic converter and/or oxygen sensor. Read all of the labels carefully before using any additive in the engine or fuel system.

All of the vehicles covered by this manual are designed to run on unleaded fuel. The use of a leaded fuel in a car requiring unleaded fuel will plug the catalytic converter and render it inoperative. It will also increase exhaust backpressure to the point where engine output will be severely reduced. The minimum octane rating of the unleaded fuel being used must be at least 87, which usually means regular unleaded, but some high performance engines may require higher ratings. Fuel should be selected for the brand and octane which performs best with your engine. Judge a gasoline by its ability to prevent pinging, its engine starting capabilities (cold and hot) and general all weather performance.

As far as the octane rating is concerned, refer to the general engine specifications chart in Section 3 of this manual to find your engine and its compression ratio. If the compression ratio is 9.0:1 or lower, in most cases a regular unleaded grade of gasoline can be used. If the compression ratio is higher than 9.0:1 use a premium grade of unleaded fuel.

The use of a fuel too low in octane (a measure of anti-knock quality) will result in spark knock. Since many factors such as altitude, terrain, air temperature and humidity affect operating efficiency, knocking may result even though the recommended fuel is being used. If persistent knocking occurs, it may be necessary to switch to a higher grade of fuel. Continuous or heavy knocking may result in engine damage.

➡ Your engine's fuel requirement can change with time, mainly due to carbon build-up, which will in turn change the compression ratio. If you engine pings, knocks or diesels (runs with the ignition OFF) switch to a higher grade of fuel. Sometimes, just changing brands will cure the problem. If it becomes necessary to retard the timing from the specifications, don't change it more than a few degrees. Retarded timing will reduce power output and fuel mileage, in addition to making the engine run hotter.

ENGINE OIL

▶ See Figures 121 and 122

The Society Of Automotive Engineer (SAE) grade number indicates the viscosity of the engine oil and thus its ability to lubricate at a given temperature. The lower the SAE grade number, the lighter the oil; the lower the viscosity, the easier it is to crank the engine in cold weather. Oil viscosities should be chosen from those oils recommended for the lowest anticipated temperatures during the oil change interval. With the proper viscosity, you will be assured of easy cold starting and sufficient engine protection.

Multi-viscosity oils (5W-30, 10W-30 etc.) offer the important advantage of being adaptable to temperature extremes. They allow easy starting at low temperatures, yet they give good protection at high speeds and engine temperatures. This is a decided advantage in changeable climates or in long distance driving.

The American Petroleum Institute (API) designation indicates the classification of engine oil used under certain given operating conditions. Only oil designated for Service SH, or latest superseding oil grade, should be used. Oils of the SH type perform a variety of functions inside the engine in addition to their

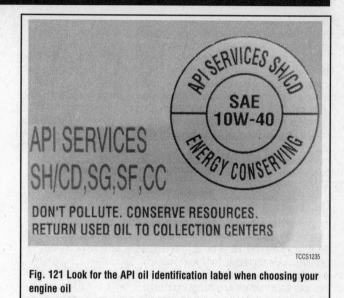

Fig. 121 Look for the API oil identification label when choosing your engine oil

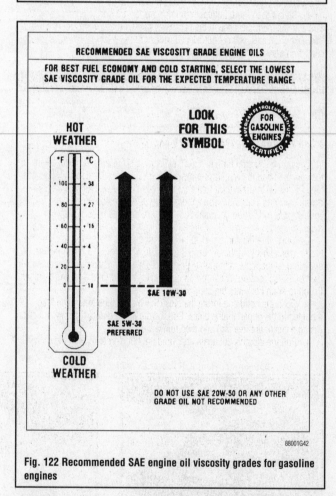

Fig. 122 Recommended SAE engine oil viscosity grades for gasoline engines

basic function as a lubricant. Through a balanced system of metallic detergents and polymeric dispersants, the oil prevents the formation of high and low temperature deposits and also keeps sludge and particles of dirt in suspension. Acids, particularly sulfuric acid, as well as other byproducts of combustion, are neutralized. Both the SAE grade number and the API designation can be found on the side of the oil bottle.

Synthetic Oils

There are excellent synthetic and fuel-efficient oils available that, under the right circumstances, can help provide better fuel mileage and better engine protection. However, these advantages come at a price, which can be significantly more than the price per quart of conventional motor oils.

Before pouring any synthetic oils into your car's engine, you should consider the condition of the engine and the type of driving you do. It is also wise to check the vehicle manufacturer's position on synthetic oils.

Generally, it is best to avoid the use of synthetic oil in both brand new and older, high mileage engines. New engines require a proper break-in, and the synthetics are so slippery that they can impede this; most manufacturers recommend that you wait at least 5,000 miles (8,000 km) before switching to a synthetic oil. Conversely, older engines are looser and tend to lose more oil; synthetics will slip past worn parts more readily than regular oil. If your car already leaks oil, (due to worn parts or bad seals/gaskets), it may leak more with a synthetic inside.

Consider your type of driving. If most of your accumulated mileage is on the highway at higher, steadier speed, a synthetic oil will reduce friction and probably help deliver better fuel mileage. Under such ideal highway conditions, the oil change interval can be extended, as long as the oil filter can operated effectively for the extended life of the oil. If the filter can't do its job for this extended period, dirt and sludge will build up in your engine's crankcase, sump, oil pump and lines, no matter what type of oil is used. If using synthetic oil in this manner, your should continue to change the oil filter at the recommended intervals.

Cars used under harder, stop-and-go, short hop circumstances should always be serviced more frequently, and for these cars synthetic oil may not be a wise investment. Because of the necessary shorter change interval needed for this type of driving, you cannot take advantage of the long recommended change interval of most synthetic oils.

Engine

OIL LEVEL CHECK

▶ See Figures 123, 124, 125, 126 and 127

Every time you stop for fuel, check the engine oil making sure the engine has fully warmed and the vehicle is parked on a level surface. Because it takes some time for the oil to drain back to the oil pan, you should wait a few minutes before checking your oil. If you are doing this at a fuel stop, first fill the fuel tank, then open the hood and check the oil, but don't get so carried away as to forget to pay for the fuel. Most station attendants won't believe that you forgot.

1. Make sure the car is parked on level ground.
2. When checking the oil level, it is best for the engine to be at normal operating temperature, although checking the oil immediately after stopping will lead to a false reading. Wait a few minutes after turning off the engine to allow the oil to drain back in the crankcase.
3. Open the hood and locate the dipstick which will be in a guide tube mounted in the upper engine block. Pull the dipstick from its tube, wipe it clean (using a clean, lint free rag) and then reinsert it.
4. Pull the dipstick out again and, holding it horizontally, read the oil level.

The oil should be between the FULL and ADD marks on the dipstick. The oil is below the ADD mark, add oil of the proper viscosity through the capped opening in the top of the valve cover. See the oil and fuel recommendations listed earlier in this section for the proper viscosity and rating of oil to use.

5. Insert the dipstick and check the oil level again after adding any oil. Approximately one quart of oil will raise the level from the ADD mark to the FULL mark. Be sure not to overfill the crankcase and waste the oil. Excess oil will generally be consumed at an accelerated rate.

✳✳ WARNING

DO NOT overfill the crankcase. It may result in oil-fouled spark plugs, oil leaks cause by oil seal failure or engine damage due to oil foaming.

6. Close the hood.

OIL AND FILTER CHANGE

▶ See Figures 128 thru 134

The manufacturer's recommended oil change interval is 7500 miles (12,000 km) under normal operating conditions. We recommend an oil change interval of 3000–3500 miles (4800–5600 km) under normal conditions; more frequently under severe conditions such as when the average trip is less than 4 miles (6 km), the engine is operated for extended periods at idle or low-speed, when towing a trailer or operating is dusty areas.

In addition, we recommend that the filter be replaced EVERY time the oil is changed.

➡**Please be considerate of the environment. Dispose of waste oil properly by taking it to a service station, municipal facility or recycling center.**

1. Run the engine until it reaches normal operating temperature. The turn the engine **OFF**.
2. Raise and safely support the front of the vehicle using jackstands.
3. Slide a drain pan of at least 5 quarts capacity under the oil pan. Wipe the drain plug and surrounding area clean using an old rag.
4. Loosen the drain plug using a ratchet, short extension and socket, or a box-wrench. Turn the plug out by hand, using a rag to shield your fingers from the hot oil. By keeping an inward pressure on the plug as you unscrew it, oil won't escape past the threads and you can remove it without being burned by hot oil.
5. Quickly withdraw the plug and move your hands out of the way, but be careful not to drop the plug into the drain pan, as fishing it out can be an unpleasant mess. Allow the oil to drain completely, then reinstall the drain plug (except on 2.5L engines). Do not overtighten the plug.
6. Move the drain pan under the oil filter. Use a strap-type or cap-type wrench to loosen the oil filter. Cover your hand with a rag, and spin the filter off by hand; turn it slowly. Keep in mind that it's holding about one quart of dirty, hot oil.
7. On some vehicles such as the 2.5L Lumina engine, the oil filter is mounted inside the engine. The filter on these engines is serviced through the oil pan drain plug. To remove the oil filter on the 2.5L engines:

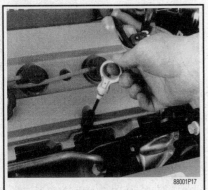

Fig. 123 Open the hood and locate the dip-stick

Fig. 124 Wipe the dipstick with a clean, lint free rag, then reinsert it in the tube

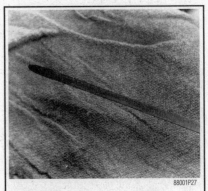

Fig. 125 The oil should be within the crosshatched area of the dipstick

Fig. 126 If the oil level is low, remove the fill cap . . .

Fig. 127 . . . then add the correct amount of oil through the opening in the valve cover

Fig. 128 Loosen the drain plug using a proper sized wrench

Fig. 129 Quickly withdraw the plug and move your hands out of the way

Fig. 130 Allow the oil to completely drain from the pan, then reinstall the drain plug

Fig. 131 Use a strap-type or cap-type wrench to loosen the oil filter

Fig. 132 Before installing a new oil filter, lightly coat the rubber gasket with clean oil

Fig. 133 Remove the oil fill cap on the valve cover to refill the crankcase with oil

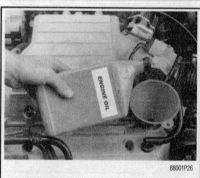

Fig. 134 Using a funnel will help prevent unnecessary mess while refilling the crankcase with fresh oil

a. After removing the drain plug and completely draining the oil, slowly turn the filter to begin removal, then pull it downward.

b. Remove the filter, using pliers at the tab, then remove and discard the O-ring if it is stuck to the housing.

➡ **Be careful when removing the oil filter, because the filler contains about 1 quart of hot, dirty oil.**

8. Empty the old oil filter into the drain pan, then properly dispose of the filter.

9. Using a clean shop towel, wipe off the filter adapter on the engine block. Be sure the towel does not leave any lint which could clog an oil passage.

10. For all vehicles except the 2.5L, coat the rubber gasket on the new filter with fresh oil. Spin the filter onto the adapter by hand until it contacts the mounting surface. Tighten the filter ¾ to 1 full turn.

11. For the 2.5L engine, coat the O-ring and grommet with clean engine oil, then press the oil filter into the housing by hand. Clean the oil pan drain plug,

then coat the drain plug gasket with clean engine oil and install the plug. Tighten the plug ¼ turn after gasket contact.

12. If raised, carefully lower the vehicle.

13. Refill the crankcase with the correct amount of fresh engine oil. Please refer to the Capacities chart in this section.

14. Check the oil level on the dipstick. It is normal or the level to be a bit above the full mark until the engine is run and the new filter is filled with oil. Start the engine and allow it to idle for a few minutes.

✳✳ CAUTION

Do not run the engine above idle speed until it has built up oil pressure, as indicated when the oil light goes out.

15. Shut off the engine and allow the oil to flow back to the crankcase for a minute, then recheck the oil level. Check around the filter and drain plug for any leaks, and correct as necessary.

When you have finished this job, you will notice that you now possess four or five quarts of dirty oil. The best thing to do is to pour it into plastic jugs, such as milk or old antifreeze containers. Then, locate a service station or automotive parts store where you can pour it into their used oil tank for recycling.

➡ **Improperly disposing of used motor oil not only pollutes the environment, it violates Federal law. Dispose of waste oil properly.**

Manual Transaxle

FLUID RECOMMENDATIONS

According to General Motors, manual transaxle fluid should be checked every 15,000 miles (24,000km) to make sure the level is full. The manufacturer does not recommends an interval for a manual transaxle fluid change, but after 100,000 miles (160,000km) the fluid should probably be changed.

The proper fluid for all manual transaxles is manual transaxle oil No. 12345349 or equivalent. DO NOT use any other fluid as damage may occur.

FLUID LEVEL CHECK

▶ **See Figures 135 and 136**

To check for proper fluid level on the HM-282 or 5TM40, remove the fluid level dipstick located on the driver's side (left) in the transaxle case. The dipstick is located on the top of the differential housing on the Getrag 284 transaxle. With the engine warm, add enough fluid to bring the level to the proper level.

DRAIN AND REFILL

1. Raise the vehicle and support with jackstands.
2. Position a drain pan under the transaxle drain plug. Remove the drain plug/magnet and allow the fluid to drain completely.
3. Clean and install the drain plug, then tighten to 18 ft. lbs. (24 Nm).
4. Using a long thin funnel, refill with the proper amount of 2 qts. of manual transaxle oil No. 12345349 or equivalent.
5. Check the fluid level and add oil as required.
6. Install the fluid level dipstick. Drive the vehicle for a short distance, then stop and inspect for leaks.

Automatic Transaxle

FLUID RECOMMENDATIONS

When adding fluid or refilling the transaxle, use Dexron®IIE or Dexron® III automatic transmission fluid.

LEVEL CHECK

▶ **See Figures 137, 138 and 139**

1. Start the engine and drive the vehicle for a minimum of 15 miles (24 km).

➡ **The automatic transmission fluid level must be checked with the vehicle at normal operating temperature; 180–200°F (82–93°C). Temperature will greatly affect transaxle fluid level.**

2. Park the vehicle on a level surface.
3. Place the transaxle gear selector in **P**.
4. Apply the parking brake and block the drive wheels.
5. With the brakes applied, move the shift lever through all the gear ranges, ending in **P**.

➡ **The fluid level must be checked with the engine running at slow idle, with the car level, and the fluid at least at room temperature. The correct fluid level cannot be read if you have just driven the car for a long time at high speed, city traffic in hot weather or if the car has been pulling a trailer. In these cases, wait at least 30 minutes for the fluid to cool down.**

6. Pull the dipstick, located at the rear end of the engine, out and wipe with a clean, lint-free rag.
7. Push the dipstick completely into the filler tube, then wait 3 seconds and pull the dipstick out again.
8. Check both sides of the dipstick and read the lower level. The fluid level should be in the crosshatch area.

➡ **The fluid level is acceptable if it is anywhere within the crosshatch area. The fluid level does not have to be at the top of the crosshatch area. DO NOT add fluid unless the level is below the crosshatch area.**

9. Inaccurate fluid level readings may result if the fluid is checked immediately after the vehicle has been operated under any or all of the following conditions:
   a. In high ambient temperatures above 90°F (32°C).
   b. At sustained high speeds.
   c. In heavy city traffic during hot weather.
   d. As a towing vehicle.
   e. In commercial service (taxi or police use).
10. If the vehicle has been operated under these conditions, shut the engine **OFF** and allow the vehicle to cool for 30 minutes. After the cooldown period, restart the vehicle and continue from Step 2.
11. If it is determined that the fluid level is low, add only enough fluid to bring the level into the crosshatch area. It generally takes less than a pint. DO NOT overfill the transaxle! If the fluid level is within specifications, simply push the dipstick back into the filler tube completely.

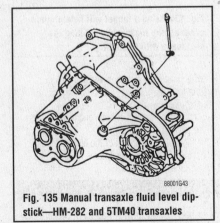

Fig. 135 Manual transaxle fluid level dipstick—HM-282 and 5TM40 transaxles

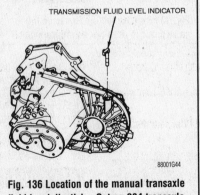

TRANSMISSION FLUID LEVEL INDICATOR

Fig. 136 Location of the manual transaxle fluid level dipstick—Getrag 284 transaxle

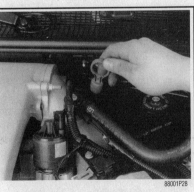

Fig. 137 Pull out the dipstick, wipe clean, then reinsert it in the filler tube

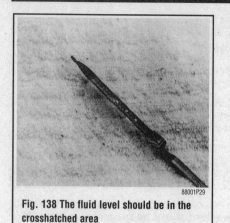

Fig. 138 The fluid level should be in the crosshatched area

Fig. 139 Use a funnel to aid in filling the transaxle

Fig. 140 Remove the bolts from the front and sides on the fluid pan only

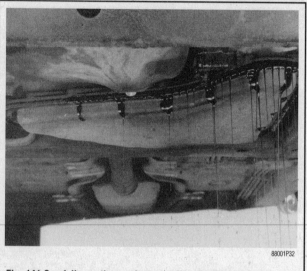

Fig. 141 Carefully pry the pan loose to allow the fluid to drain

12. After adding fluid, if necessary, recheck the level, making sure it is within the crosshatch area. Turn the engine **OFF**, then unblock the drive wheels.

DRAIN AND REFILL

▶ **See Figures 140 thru 145**

The car should be driven approximately 15 miles (24 km) to warm the transaxle fluid before the pan is removed.

➡ **The fluid should be drained while the transaxle is warm.**

❊❊ WARNING

Use only fluid labeled Dexron®II. Use of other fluids could cause erratic shifting and transaxle damage.

1. Raise and safely support the vehicle with jackstands.
2. Place a suitable drain pan under the transaxle fluid pan.
3. Remove the fluid pan bolts/screws from the front and sides of the pan.
4. Loosen the rear bolts/screws about four turns.

❊❊ WARNING

Be careful not to damage the mating surfaces of the oil pan and case. Any damage could result in fluid leaks.

5. Lightly tap the pan with a rubber mallet or carefully pry the fluid pan loose and allow the fluid to drain.

➡ If the transaxle fluid is dark or has a burnt smell, transaxle damage is indicated. Have the transaxle checked professionally.

6. Remove the remaining bolts, the pan, and the gasket or RTV sealant. Discard the old gasket. Use a suitable gasket scraper to clean the gasket mating surfaces.
7. Clean the pan with solvent and dry it thoroughly.
8. Remove the filter and O-ring seal.

To install:

9. Install a new transaxle filter and O-ring seal, locating the filter against the dipstick stop. Always replace the filter with a new one. Do not attempt to clean the old one!

➡ For the 3T40 transaxle, it is necessary to use GM Thread Locker part no. 12345382 or equivalent sealant on the specified bolt in the accompanying figure to prevent leaks.

10. Install a new gasket or RTV sealant. Thoroughly clean and dry all bolts and bolt holes. Install the pan and tighten the bolts in a crisscross manner, starting from the middle and working outward. Tighten the bolts/screws to the following specifications:
   a. 440-T4 automatic transaxle: 10 ft. lbs. (13 Nm)
   b. THM-125C and 3T40 automatic transaxles: 97 inch lbs. (11 Nm)

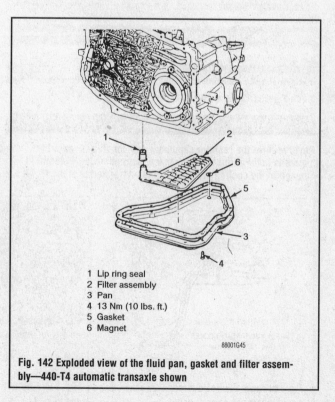

1 Lip ring seal
2 Filter assembly
3 Pan
4 13 Nm (10 lbs. ft.)
5 Gasket
6 Magnet

Fig. 142 Exploded view of the fluid pan, gasket and filter assembly—440-T4 automatic transaxle shown

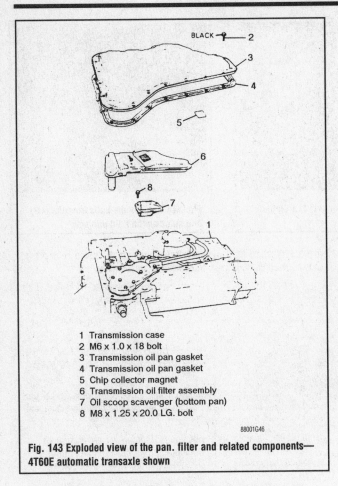

1 Transmission case
2 M6 x 1.0 x 18 bolt
3 Transmission oil pan gasket
4 Transmission oil pan gasket
5 Chip collector magnet
6 Transmission oil filter assembly
7 Oil scoop scavenger (bottom pan)
8 M8 x 1.25 x 20.0 LG. bolt

88001G46

Fig. 143 Exploded view of the pan. filter and related components— 4T60E automatic transaxle shown

c. 4T60 and 4T60E automatic transaxles: 13 ft. lbs. (17 Nm)

11. Carefully lower the vehicle, then add the correct amount of Dexron®III, IIE, or equivalent, transmission fluid. Refer to the Capacities chart for fluid specifications.

12. Follow the fluid check procedure earlier in this section.

13. Check the pan for leaks.

Cooling System

▶ See Figures 146 and 147

✷✷ CAUTION

Never remove the radiator cap under any conditions while the engine is hot! Failure to follow these instructions could result in damage to the cooling system, engine and/or personal injury. To

avoid having scalding hot coolant or steam blow out of the radiator, use extreme care whenever you are removing the radiator cap. Wait until the engine has cooled, then wrap a thick cloth around radiator cap and turn it slowly to the first stop. Step back while the pressure is released from the cooling system. When you are sure the pressure has been released, press down on the radiator cap (still have the cloth in position), turn and remove the cap.

FLUID RECOMMENDATIONS

▶ See Figure 148

✷✷ WARNING

For 1996 vehicles, when adding coolant, it is important that you use DEX-COOL®, an orange colored, silicate free coolant meeting GM specifications 6277M. If silicated coolant is added to the system, premature engine, heater core or radiator corrosion may result.

The cooling system should be inspected, flushed and refilled with fresh coolant at least every 30,000 miles (48,000 km) or 24 months. If the coolant is left in the system too long, it loses its ability to prevent rust and corrosion.

When the coolant is being replaced, use a good quality antifreeze that is safe to be used with aluminum cooling system components. The ratio of antifreeze to water should always be a 50/50 mixture. This ratio will ensure the proper balance of cooling ability, corrosion protection and antifreeze protection. At this ratio, the antifreeze protection should be good to −34°F (−37°C). If greater antifreeze protection is needed, the ratio should not exceed 70% antifreeze to 30% water.

LEVEL CHECK

▶ See Figures 149 and 150

➡ **When checking the coolant level, the radiator cap need not be removed. Simply check the coolant level in the recovery bottle or surge tank.**

Check the coolant level in the recovery bottle or surge tank, usually mounted on the inner fender. With the engine cold, the coolant level should be at the FULL COLD level. With the engine at normal operating temperature, the coolant level should be at the FULL HOT mark. Only add coolant to the recovery bottle or surge tank as necessary to bring the system up to a proper level.

✷✷ CAUTION

Should it be necessary to remove the radiator cap, make sure the system has had time to cool, reducing the internal pressure.

On any vehicle that is not equipped with a coolant recovery bottle or surge tank, the level must be checked by removing the radiator cap. This should only be done when the cooling system has had time to sufficiently cool after the engine has been run. The coolant level should be within 2 in. (51mm) of the

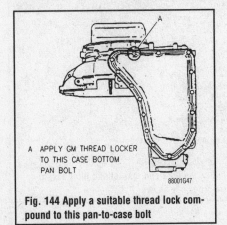

A APPLY GM THREAD LOCKER TO THIS CASE BOTTOM PAN BOLT

88001G47

Fig. 144 Apply a suitable thread lock compound to this pan-to-case bolt

88001P33

Fig. 145 After filling the transaxle, check the fluid level

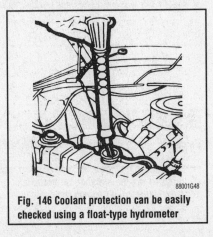

88001G48

Fig. 146 Coolant protection can be easily checked using a float-type hydrometer

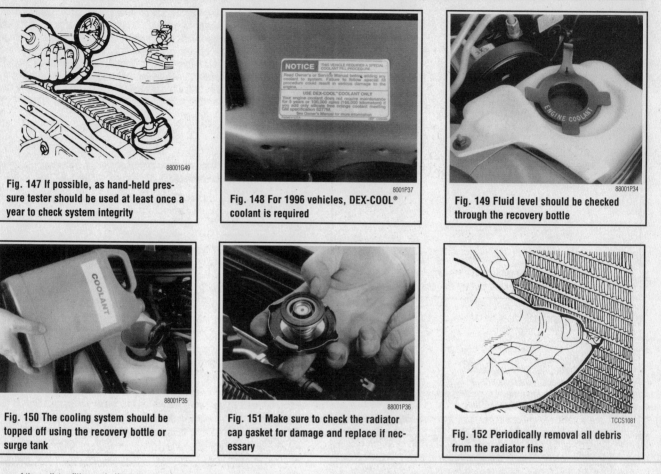

Fig. 147 If possible, as hand-held pressure tester should be used at least once a year to check system integrity

Fig. 148 For 1996 vehicles, DEX-COOL® coolant is required

Fig. 149 Fluid level should be checked through the recovery bottle

Fig. 150 The cooling system should be topped off using the recovery bottle or surge tank

Fig. 151 Make sure to check the radiator cap gasket for damage and replace if necessary

Fig. 152 Periodically removal all debris from the radiator fins

base of the radiator filler neck. If necessary, coolant can then be added directly to the radiator.

COOLING SYSTEM INSPECTION

Checking the Radiator Cap Seal

▶ See Figure 151

While you are checking the coolant level, check the radiator cap for a worn or cracked gasket. If the cap doesn't seal properly, fluid will be lost and the engine will overheat.

Worn caps should be replaced with a new one.

Checking the Radiator for Debris

▶ See Figure 152

Periodically clean any debris; leaves, paper, insects, etc. from the radiator fins. Pick the large pieces off by hand. The smaller pieces can be washed away with water pressure from a hose.

Carefully straighten any bent radiator fins with a pair of needle nose pliers. Be careful, the fins are very soft. Don't wiggle the fins back and forth too much. Straighten them once and try not move them again.

DRAIN AND REFILL

▶ See Figures 153 and 154

✱✱ CAUTION

When draining the coolant, keep in mind that cats and dogs are attracted by ethylene glycol antifreeze and are quite likely to drink any that is left in an uncovered container or in puddles on the ground. This will prove fatal in sufficient quantity. Always drain the coolant into a sealable container. Coolant should be reused until it

is contaminated or several years old. To avoid injuries from scalding fluid and steam, DO NOT remove the radiator cap while the engine and radiator are still hot.

1. Make sure the engine is cool and the vehicle is parked on a level surface, remove the radiator cap by performing the following:
    a. Slowly rotate the cap counterclockwise to the detent.
    b. If any residual pressure is present, WAIT until the hissing stops.
    c. After the hissing noise has ceased, press down on the cap and continue rotating it counterclockwise to remove it.
2. Remove the recovery bottle or surge tank cap.

Fig. 153 When the engine is cool, carefully remove the radiator cap, then remove the recovery bottle cap

88001P39

Fig. 154 When draining the cooling system, placing a piece of tubing over the drain valve may help control spillage

3. Place a fluid catch pan under the radiator. Open the radiator drain valve, which is located at the bottom of the radiator tank.

4. Remove the thermostat housing cap and thermostat or open the air bleed vent(s), if applicable.

5. Remove the engine block drain plug.

6. Allow the coolant to drain completely from the vehicle.

7. Close the radiator drain valve, then reinstall any block drains which were removed.

8. Using a 50/50 mixture of antifreeze and clean water, fill the radiator to the bottom of the filler neck and the coolant tank to the FULL mark.

9. Install the radiator cap, making sure the arrows line up over the overflow tube leading the reservoir or surge tank. Place the cap back on the recovery bottle or surge tank.

10. Start the engine. Select heat on the climate control panel and turn the temperature valve to full warm. Run the engine until it reaches normal operating temperature. Check to make sure there is hot air flowing from the floor ducts.

11. Check the fluid level in the reservoir or surge tank and add as necessary.

FLUSHING AND CLEANING

1. Refer to the drain and refill procedure in this section, then drain the cooling system.

2. Close the drain valve.

➡A flushing solution may be used. Ensure it is safe for use with aluminum cooling system components. Follow the directions on the container.

3. If using a flushing solution, remove the thermostat. Reinstall the thermostat housing.

4. Add sufficient water to fill the system.

5. Start the engine and run for a few minutes. Drain the system.

6. If using a flushing solution, disconnect the heater hose that connects the cylinder head to the heater core (that end of the hose will clamp to a fitting on the firewall. Connect a water hose to the end of the heater hose that runs to the cylinder head and run water into the system until it begins to flow out of the top of the radiator.

7. Allow the water to flow out of the radiator until it is clear.

8. Reconnect the heater hose.

9. Drain the cooling system.

10. Reinstall the thermostat.

11. Empty the coolant reservoir or surge tank and flush it.

12. Fill the cooling system, using the correct ratio of antifreeze and water, to the bottom of the filler neck. Fill the reservoir or surge tank to the FULL mark.

13. Install the radiator cap, making sure that the arrows align with the overflow tube.

Brake Master Cylinder

FLUID RECOMMENDATION

Use only heavy duty brake fluid meeting DOT 3 specifications from a clean, sealed container. Using any other type of fluid may result in severe brake system damage.

❊❊❊ WARNING

Brake fluid damages paint. It also absorbs moisture from the air; never leave a container or the master cylinder uncovered longer than necessary. All parts in contact with the brake fluid (master cylinder, hoses, plunger assemblies and etc.) must be kept clean, since any contamination of the brake fluid will adversely affect braking performance.

LEVEL CHECK

◆ See Figures 155, 156 and 157

It should be obvious how important the brake system is to safe operation of your vehicle. The brake fluid is key to the proper operation of your vehicle. Low levels of fluid indicate a need for service (there may be a leak in the system or the brake pads may just be worn and in need of replacement). In any case, the brake fluid level should be inspected at least during every oil change, but more often is desirable. Every time you open the hood is a good time to glance at the master cylinder reservoir.

To check the fluid level on most vehicles covered by this manual, remove the master cylinder reservoir cap and diaphragm (if applicable) and check the level against the markings on the inside of the reservoir.

88001P41

Fig. 155 Remove the brake master cylinder reservoir cap . . .

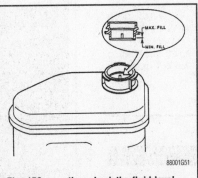

88001G51

Fig. 156 . . . then check the fluid level against the marks on the neck of the reservoir

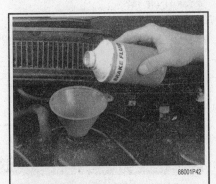

88001P42

Fig. 157 When adding brake fluid to the master cylinder, use only clean, fresh fluid from a sealed container

Fig. 158 The power steering reservoir cap/dipstick is marked for proper fluid levels

Fig. 159 Make sure the cap is clean before removing it; this will prevent dirt from contaminating the system

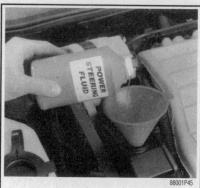

Fig. 160 Add power steering fluid through the opening while the cap is removed

When making additions of brake fluid, use only fresh, uncontaminated brake fluid which meets or exceeds DOT-3 standards. Be careful not to spill any brake fluid on painted surfaces, as it will quickly eat the paint. Do not allow the brake fluid container or the master cylinder to remain open any longer than necessary; brake fluid absorbs moisture from the air, reducing the fluid's effectiveness and causing corrosion in the lines.

Clutch Master Cylinder

FLUID RECOMMENDATION

Use only heavy duty brake fluid meeting DOT 3 specifications. DO NOT use any other fluid because severe clutch system damage will result.

LEVEL CHECK

The clutch system fluid in the master cylinder should be checked every 6 months or 6000 miles (9600km).

The clutch master cylinder reservoir is located on top of the left (driver) strut tower. Check the fluid level on the side of the reservoir. If fluid is required, remove the screw on filler cap and gasket from the master cylinder. Fill the reservoir to the full line in the reservoir with heavy duty brake fluid meeting DOT 3 specifications ONLY. Install the filler cap, making sure the gasket is properly seated in the cap. Make sure no dirt enters the system when adding fluid.

If fluid has to be added frequently, the system should be checked for a leak. Check for leaks at the master cylinder, slave cylinder and hose. If a leak is found, replace the component and bleed the system as outlined in Section 7.

Power Steering

FLUID RECOMMENDATIONS

When adding fluid or making a complete fluid change, always use GM P/N 1050017, 1052884, power steering fluid or equivalent. DO NOT use automatic transmission fluid. Failure to use the proper fluid may cause hose and seal damage and fluid leaks.

LEVEL CHECK

▶ See Figures 158, 159 and 160

The power steering fluid reservoir is directly above the steering pump. The pump is located on top of the engine on the right (passenger's) side.

Power steering fluid level is indicated either by marks on a see through reservoir or by marks on a fluid level indicator in the reservoir cap.

If the fluid is warmed up (about 150°F/66°C), the level should be between the HOT and COLD marks.

If the fluid is cooler than 150°F (66°C), the level should be between the ADD and COLD marks.

Chassis Greasing

Lubricate the chassis lubrication points every 7500 miles (12,000km) or 12 months. If your vehicle is equipped with grease fittings, lubricate the suspension and steering linkage with heavy duty chassis grease. Lubricate the transaxle shift linkage, parking cable guides, under body contact points and linkage with white lithium grease.

Body Lubrication and Maintenance

LOCK CYLINDERS

Apply graphite lubricant sparingly though the key slot. Insert the key and operate the lock several times to be sure that the lubricant is worked completely into the lock cylinder.

DOOR HINGES AND HINGE CHECKS

Spray a silicone lubricant on the hinge pivot points to eliminate any binding conditions. Open and close the door several times to be sure that the lubricant is evenly and thoroughly distributed.

TRUNK LID OR TAILGATE

Spray a silicone lubricant on all of the pivot and friction surfaces to eliminate any squeaks or binds. Work the tailgate to distribute the lubricant

BODY DRAIN HOLES

Be sure that the drain holes in the doors and rocker panels are cleared of obstruction. A small screwdriver can be used to clear them of any debris.

Wheel Bearings

The W-body models are equipped with sealed hub and bearing assemblies for the front and rear wheels. The hub and bearing assemblies are non-serviceable. If the assembly is damaged, the complete unit must be replaced. Refer to Section 8 for the hub and bearing removal and installation procedure.

JUMP STARTING A DEAD BATTERY

▶ See Figure 161

Whenever a vehicle is jump started, precautions must be followed in order to prevent the possibility of personal injury. Remember that batteries contain a small amount of explosive hydrogen gas which is a by-product of battery charging. Sparks should always be avoided when working around batteries, especially when attaching jumper cables. To minimize the possibility of accidental sparks, follow the procedure carefully.

✳✳ CAUTION

NEVER hook the batteries up in a series circuit or the entire electrical system will go up in smoke, including the starter!

Vehicles equipped with a diesel engine may utilize two 12 volt batteries. If so, the batteries are connected in a parallel circuit (positive terminal to positive terminal, negative terminal to negative terminal). Hooking the batteries up in parallel circuit increases battery cranking power without increasing total battery voltage output. Output remains at 12 volts. On the other hand, hooking two 12 volt batteries up in a series circuit (positive terminal to negative terminal, positive terminal to negative terminal) increases total battery output to 24 volts (12 volts plus 12 volts).

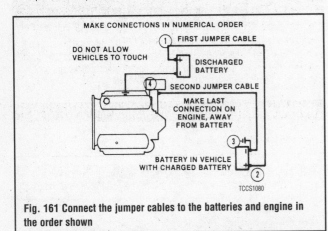

Fig. 161 Connect the jumper cables to the batteries and engine in the order shown

Jump Starting Precautions

- Be sure that both batteries are of the same polarity (have the same terminal, in most cases NEGATIVE grounded).
- Be sure that the vehicles are not touching or a short could occur.
- On non-sealed batteries, be sure the vent cap holes are not obstructed.
- Do not smoke or allow sparks anywhere near the batteries.
- In cold weather, make sure the battery electrolyte is not frozen. This can occur more readily in a battery that has been in a state of discharge.
- Do not allow electrolyte to contact your skin or clothing.

JACKING

▶ See Figures 162 and 163

Your vehicle was supplied with a jack for emergency road repairs. This jack is fine for changing a flat tire or other short term procedures not requiring you to go beneath the vehicle. If it is used in an emergency situation, carefully follow the instructions provided either with the jack or in your owner's manual. Do not attempt to use the jack on any portions of the vehicle other than specified by the vehicle manufacturer. Always block the diagonally opposite wheel when using a jack.

A more convenient way of jacking is the use of a garage or floor jack. You may use the floor jack to lift the front of the vehicle by positioning the jack in

Jump Starting Procedure

1. Make sure that the voltages of the 2 batteries are the same. Most batteries and charging systems are of the 12 volt variety.
2. Pull the jumping vehicle (with the good battery) into a position so the jumper cables can reach the dead battery and that vehicle's engine. Make sure that the vehicles do NOT touch.
3. Place the transmissions/transaxles of both vehicles in **Neutral** (MT) or **P** (AT), as applicable, then firmly set their parking brakes.

➡ If necessary for safety reasons, the hazard lights on both vehicles may be operated throughout the entire procedure without significantly increasing the difficulty of jumping the dead battery.

4. Turn all lights and accessories OFF on both vehicles. Make sure the ignition switches on both vehicles are turned to the **OFF** position.
5. Cover the battery cell caps with a rag, but do not cover the terminals.
6. Make sure the terminals on both batteries are clean and free of corrosion for good electrical contact.
7. Identify the positive (+) and negative (−) terminals on both batteries.
8. Connect the first jumper cable to the positive (+) terminal of the dead battery, then connect the other end of that cable to the positive (+) terminal of the booster (good) battery.
9. Connect one end of the other jumper cable to the negative (−) terminal on the booster battery and the final cable clamp to an engine bolt head, alternator bracket or other solid, metallic point on the engine with the dead battery. Try to pick a ground on the engine that is positioned away from the battery in order to minimize the possibility of the 2 clamps touching should one loosen during the procedure. DO NOT connect this clamp to the negative (−) terminal of the bad battery.

✳✳ CAUTION

Be very careful to keep the jumper cables away from moving parts (cooling fan, belts, etc.) on both engines.

10. Check to make sure that the cables are routed away from any moving parts, then start the donor vehicle's engine. Run the engine at moderate speed for several minutes to allow the dead battery a chance to receive some initial charge.
11. With the donor vehicle's engine still running slightly above idle, try to start the vehicle with the dead battery. Crank the engine for no more than 10 seconds at a time and let the starter cool for at least 20 seconds between tries. If the vehicle does not start in 3 tries, it is likely that something else is also wrong or that the battery needs additional time to charge.
12. Once the vehicle is started, allow it to run at idle for a few seconds to make sure that it is operating properly.
13. Turn ON the headlights, heater blower and, if equipped, the rear defroster of both vehicles in order to reduce the severity of voltage spikes and subsequent risk of damage to the vehicles' electrical systems when the cables are disconnected. This step is especially important to any vehicle equipped with computer control modules.
14. Carefully disconnect the cables in the reverse order of connection. Start with the negative cable that is attached to the engine ground, then the negative cable on the donor battery. Disconnect the positive cable from the donor battery and finally, disconnect the positive cable from the formerly dead battery. Be careful when disconnecting the cables from the positive terminals not to allow the alligator clips to touch any metal on either vehicle or a short and sparks will occur.

the center of the front crossmember. When raising the rear of the vehicle, position the jack on the rear jack pad.

Never place the jack under the radiator, engine or transmission components. Severe and expensive damage will result when the jack is raised. Additionally, never jack under the floorpan or bodywork; the metal will deform.

Whenever you plan to work under the vehicle, you must support it on jackstands or ramps. Never use cinder blocks or stacks of wood to support the vehicle, even if you're only going to be under it for a few minutes. Never crawl under the vehicle when it is supported only by the tire-changing jack or other floor jack.

Fig. 162 When raising the front of your vehicle, position the jack in the center of the front crossmember

Fig. 163 Position the floor jack on the rear jack pad to raise the rear of the car

➨Always position a block of wood or small rubber pad on top of the jack or jackstand to protect the lifting point's finish when lifting or supporting the vehicle.

Small hydraulic, screw, or scissors jacks are satisfactory for raising the vehicle. Drive-on trestles or ramps are also a handy and safe way to both raise and support the vehicle. Be careful though, some ramps may be too steep to drive your vehicle onto without scraping the front bottom panels. Never support the vehicle on any suspension member (unless specifically instructed to do so by a repair manual) or by an underbody panel.

Jacking Precautions

The following safety points cannot be overemphasized:
• Always block the opposite wheel or wheels to keep the vehicle from rolling off the jack.
• When raising the front of the vehicle, firmly apply the parking brake.
• When the drive wheels are to remain on the ground, leave the vehicle in gear to help prevent it from rolling.
• Always use jackstands to support the vehicle when you are working underneath. Place the stands beneath the vehicle's jacking brackets. Before climbing underneath, rock the vehicle a bit to make sure it is firmly supported.

MAINTENANCE INTERVAL CHARTS

FOLLOW SCHEDULE I IF THE CAR IS MAINLY OPERATED UNDER ONE OR MORE OF THE FOLLOWING CONDITIONS:
• When most trips are less than 4 miles (6 kilometers).
• When most trips are less than 10 miles (16 kilometers) and outside temperature remains below freezing.
• When most trips include extended idling and/or frequent low-speed operation as in stop-and-go traffic.
• When vehicle is used for delivery service, police, taxi or other commercial applications.
• Towing a trailer.**
• Operating in dusty areas.

Schedule I should also be followed if the car is used for delivery service, police, taxi, or other commercial application.

TO BE SERVICED	WHEN TO PERFORM Miles (Kilometers) or Months Whichever Occurs First	The service shown in this schedule up to 60,000 miles (100 000 km) are to be performed after 60,000 miles (100 000 km) at the same intervals.																			
	MILES (000)	5	10	15	20	25	30	35	40	45	50	55	60	65	70	75	80	85	90	95	100
	KILOMETERS (000)	3	6	9	12	15	18	21	24	27	30	33	36	39	42	45	48	51	54	57	60
Engine Oil & Oil Filter change*	Every 3,000 (5 000 km) or 3 mos.	●	●	●	●	●	●	●	●	●	●	●	●	●	●	●	●	●	●	●	●
Chassis Lubrication	Every other oil change.		●		●		●		●		●		●		●		●		●		●
Service To Be Performed at Least Twice a Year (See Explanation)																					
Service To Be Performed at Least Once a Year (See Explanation)																					
Throttle Body Mount Bolt Torque (Some Models)*	At 6,000 mi. (10 000 km) only.	●																			
Tire & Wheel Insp. and Rotation	At 6,000 mi. (10 000 km) and then every 15,000 mi. (25 000 km).	●					●					●					●				
Engine Accessory Drive Belt(s) Insp.*	Every 30,000 mi. (50 000 km) or 24 mos.						●														●
Cooling System Service*							●														●
Transmission/Transaxle Service							●														●
Spark Plug Replacement*	Every 30,000 mi. (50 000 km).						●														●
Spark Plug Wire Insp. (Some Models)							●														●
EGR System Insp.* ‡							●														●
Air Cleaner & PVC Inlet Filter Element Replacement	Every 30,000 mi. (50 000 km) or 36 mos.						●														●
Fuel Tank, Cup & Lines Inspection* ‡	Every 30,000 mi. (50 000 km).						●														●

* An Emission Control Service.

• Trailer is not recommended for some models, see the owners manual for complete details

‡ The U.S. Enviromental Protection Agency or the California Air Resources Board has determined that the failure to perform this maintenance item will not nullify the emission warranty or limit recall liability prior to the completion of vehicle useful life. General Motors, however, urges that all recommended maintenance services be performed at the indicated intervals and the maintenance be recorded in section E of the owner's maintenance schedule.

Fig. 164 Maintenance Interval Chart—Schedule I (severe usage)

FOLLOW SCHEDULE II ONLY IF NONE OF THE DRIVING CONDITIONS SPECIFIED IN SCHEDULE I APPLY:

The service shown in this schedule up to 60,000 miles (100 000 km) are to be performed after 60,000 miles (100 000 km) at the same intervals.

TO BE SERVICED	WHEN TO PERFORM — Miles (Kilometers) or Months Whichever Occurs First	MILES (000) 7.5 / KILOMETERS (000) 12.5	15 / 25	22.5 / 37.5	30 / 50	37.5 / 62.5	45 / 75	52.5 / 87.5	60 / 100
Engine Oil change* Plus Other Required Services (See explanation)	Every 7,500 mi. (12 500 km) or 12 months.	●	●	●	●	●	●	●	●
Oil Filter Change*	At first and every other oil change or 12 mos.	●		●		●		●	
Chassis Lubrication	Every 7,500 mi. (12 000 km) or 12 mos.	●	●	●	●	●	●	●	●
Service To Be Performed at Least Twice a Year (See Explanation)									
Service To Be Performed at Least Once a Year (See Explanation)									
Throttle Body Mount Bolt Torque (Some Models)*	At 7,500 mi. (12 000 km) only.	●							
Tire & Wheel Insp. and Rotation	At 7,500 mi. (12 500 km) and then every 15,000 mi. (25 000 km).	●		●		●		●	
Engine Accessory Drive Belt(s) Insp.*	Every 30,000 mi. (50 000 km) or 24 mos.				●				●
Cooling System Service*					●				●
Transmission/Transaxle Service									
Spark Plug Replacement*	Every 30,000 mi. (50 000 km).				●				●
Spark Plug Wire Insp. (Some Models)					●				●
EGR System Insp.* ‡					●				●
Air Cleaner & PVC Inlet Filter Element Replacement	Every 30,000 mi. (50 000 km) or 36 mos.				●				●
Fuel Tank, Cap & Lines Inspection* ‡	Every 30,000 mi. (50 000 km).				●				●

* An Emission Control Service.

‡ The U.S. Environmental Protection Agency or the California Air Resources Board has determined that the failure to perform this maintenance item will not nullify the emission warranty or limit recall liability prior to the completion of vehicle useful life. General Motors, however, urges that all recommended maintenance services be performed at the indicated intervals and the maintenance be recorded in section E of the owner's maintenance schedule.

Fig. 165 Maintenance Interval Chart—Schedule II (normal usage)

CAPACITIES

Year	Model	Engine ID/VIN	Engine Displacement Liters (cc)	Engine Oil with Filter (qts.)	Transaxle (pts.) 4-Spd	5-Spd	Auto.	Transfer Case (pts.)	Drive Axle Front (pts.)	Rear (pts.)	Fuel Tank (gal.)	Cooling System (qts.)
1993	Cutlass Supreme	M	3.1 (3135)	4.0 [3]			12.0 [2]				16.0	12.5
	Cutlass Supreme	T	3.1 (3135)	4.0 [3]			12.0 [2]				16.0	12.7 [19]
	Cutlass Supreme	X	3.4 (3350)	5.0 [3]			12.0 [2]				16.0	12.7
	Grand Prix	T	3.1 (3135)	4.0 [3]			12.0 [9]				16.0	12.7 [19]
	Grand Prix	X	3.4 (3350)	5.0 [3]		4.5	12.0 [2]				16.0	12.7
	Lumina	4	2.2 (2190)	4.0 [3]			8.0 [2]				17.1	11.7
	Lumina	T	3.1 (3135)	4.0 [3]			12.0 [2]				16.0	12.7
	Lumina	X	3.4 (3350)	5.0 [3]		4.5	12.0 [2]				16.0	12.7
	Regal	T	3.1 (3135)	4.0 [3]			12.0 [2]				16.0	12.6
	Regal	L	3.8 (3791)	4.0 [3]			12.0 [2]				16.0	11.1
1994	Cutlass Supreme	M	3.1 (3135)	4.0 [3]			12.0 [2]				16.0	12.5
	Cutlass Supreme	X	3.4 (3350)	5.0 [3]			12.0 [2]				16.0	12.7
	Grand Prix	M	3.1 (3135)	4.0 [3]			12.0 [9]				16.0	12.7 [19]
	Grand Prix	X	3.4 (3350)	5.0 [3]			12.0 [2]				16.0	12.7
	Lumina	M	3.1 (3135)	4.0 [3]			12.0 [2]				16.0	12.5
	Lumina	X	3.4 (3350)	5.0 [3]			12.0 [2]				16.0	12.7
	Regal	M	3.1 (3135)	4.0 [3]			12.0 [2]				16.0	11.8
	Regal	L	3.8 (3791)	4.0 [3]			12.0 [2]				16.0	11.1
1995	Cutlass Supreme	M	3.1 (3135)	4.0 [3]			12.0 [2]				17.1	12.5
	Cutlass Supreme	X	3.4 (3350)	5.0 [3]			12.0 [2]				17.1	12.7
	Grand Prix	M	3.1 (3135)	4.0 [3]			12.0 [9]				17.1	12.7 [19]
	Grand Prix	X	3.4 (3350)	5.0 [3]			12.0 [2]				17.1	12.7
	Lumina	M	3.1 (3135)	4.0 [3]			12.0 [2]				17.1	12.7
	Monte Carlo	M	3.1 (3135)	4.0 [3]			12.0 [2]				17.1	12.7
	Monte Carlo	X	3.4 (3350)	5.0 [3]			12.0 [2]				17.1	12.5
	Regal	M	3.1 (3135)	4.0 [3]			12.0 [2]				17.1	11.1
	Regal	L	3.8 (3791)	4.0 [3]			12.0 [2]				17.1	12.7
1996	Cutlass Supreme	M	3.1 (3135)	4.0 [3]			12.0 [2]				17.1	12.7
	Cutlass Supreme	X	3.4 (3350)	5.0 [3]			12.0 [2]				17.1	12.5
	Grand Prix	M	3.1 (3135)	4.0 [3]			12.0 [2]				17.1	12.7
	Grand Prix	X	3.4 (3350)	5.0 [3]			12.0 [2]				16.1	12.7
	Lumina	M	3.1 (3135)	4.0 [3]			12.0 [2]				17.1	12.7
	Monte Carlo	M	3.1 (3135)	4.0 [3]			12.0 [2]				16.1	12.5
	Monte Carlo	X	3.4 (3350)	5.0 [3]			12.0 [2]				17.1	12.5
	Regal	M	3.1 (3135)	4.0 [3]			12.0 [2]				17.1	12.5
	Regal	K	3.8 (3791)	4.0 [3]			12.0 [2]				17.1	11.1

[5] With std. cooling: 11.75 qts. With A/C: 12.60 qts. With heavy duty cooling: 12.75 qts.

[6] Figure shown is for pan removal - for overhaul use 20 pts.

[7] Exc. A/C with heavy duty cooling: 9.20 qts. Exc. A/C with heavy duty cooling: 9.40 qts.

[8] 3T40 transaxle: use 8 pts. for pan removal.

[9] Figure shown is for pan removal - for overhaul use 14 pts.

[13] With A/C and 3 speed automatic transaxle: 12.7 qts.

[14] With manual transaxle: 12.6 qts.

[15] With 4T60E transaxle: 12.5 qts.

[10] With manual transaxle use 12.9 qts.

[11] Figure shown is for pan removal - for overhaul use 20 pts.

[12] Figure shown is for pan removal - for overhaul use 14 pts.

3140 transaxle: use 8 pts. for pan removal, 14 pts. for overhaul. 4T60 & 4T60E transaxle: use 12 pts. for pan removal, 16 pts. for overhaul.

88001C08

CAPACITIES

Year	Model	Engine ID/VIN	Engine Displacement Liters (cc)	Engine Oil with Filter (qts.)	Transaxle (pts.) 4-Spd	5-Spd	Auto.	Transfer Case (pts.)	Drive Axle Front (pts.)	Rear (pts.)	Fuel Tank (gal.)	Cooling System (qts.)
1988	Cutlass Supreme	W	2.8 (2837)	4.0 [3]		5.0	12.0 [2]				16.0	12.6 [4]
	Grand Prix	W	2.8 (2837)	4.0 [3]		5.0	12.0 [2]				16.0	12.6 [4]
	Regal	W	2.8 (2837)	4.0 [3]			12.0 [2]				16.0	12.6 [4]
1989	Cutlass Supreme	W	2.8 (2837)	4.0 [3]		5.0	12.0 [2]				16.0	[5]
	Cutlass-Supreme	T	3.1 (3135)	4.0 [3]		5.0	12.0 [2]				16.0	[5]
	Grand Prix	W	2.8 (2837)	4.0 [3]		5.0	12.0 [2]				16.0	12.6 [4]
	Grand Prix	T	3.1 (3135)	4.0 [3]			12.0 [2]				16.0	12.6 [4]
	Grand Prix	V	3.1 (3135)	4.0 [3]			12.0 [2]				16.0	12.7
	Regal	W	2.8 (2837)	4.0 [3]			12.0 [2]				16.0	13.2
	Regal	T	3.1 (3135)	4.0 [3]			12.0 [2]				16.0	12.6
1990	Cutlass Supreme	A	2.3 (2260)	4.0 [3]		4.4					16.0	8.9 [7]
	Cutlass Supreme	D	2.3 (2260)	4.0 [3]			14.0 [6]				16.0	9.2 [7]
	Cutlass Supreme	T	3.1 (3135)	4.0 [3]			12.0 [2]				16.0	12.5
	Grand Prix	D	2.3 (2260)	5.0 [3]			14.0 [6]				16.0	9.2
	Grand Prix	T	3.1 (3135)	4.0 [3]		4.4					16.0	12.6
	Grand Prix	V	3.1 (3135)	4.0 [3]			12.0 [2]				16.0	13.2
	Lumina	R	2.5 (2471)	4.0 [3]			14.0 [6]				16.0	9.4
	Lumina	T	3.1 (3135)	4.0 [3]			12.0 [1]				16.0	12.6
	Regal	T	3.1 (3135)	4.0 [3]			12.0 [2]				16.0	12.5
1991	Cutlass Supreme	D	2.3 (2260)	4.0 [3]			14.0 [6]				16.0	8.9 [7]
	Cutlass Supreme	T	3.1 (3135)	4.0 [3]			12.0 [2]				16.0	12.5 [12]
	Cutlass Supreme	X	3.4 (3350)	5.0 [3]		4.2					16.0	12.8
	Grand Prix	D	2.3 (2260)	4.0 [3]			14.0 [6]				16.0	9.2
	Grand Prix	T	3.1 (3135)	4.0 [3]		4.2					16.0	12.5 [12]
	Lumina	X	3.4 (3350)	5.0 [3]			12.0 [2]				16.0	12.8
	Lumina	R	2.5 (2471)	4.0 [3]			14.0 [6]				16.0	9.4
	Lumina	T	3.1 (3135)	4.0 [3]		4.2					16.0	12.6
	Regal	T	3.1 (3135)	4.0 [3]			12.0 [2]				16.0	12.8
	Regal	L	3.8 (3791)	4.0 [3]			12.0 [2]				16.0	11.1
1992	Cutlass Supreme	D	2.3 (2260)	4.0 [3]			14.0 [11]				16.0	12.0
	Cutlass Supreme	X	3.4 (3350)	5.0 [3]		4.2					16.0	12.4 [13]
	Grand Prix	X	3.4 (3350)	5.0 [3]			12.0 [2]				16.0	12.0
	Grand Prix	T	3.1 (3135)	4.0 [3]		4.2					16.0	12.4 [13]
	Lumina	R	2.5 (2471)	5.0 [3]		4.5	14.8 [11]				16.0	9.1
	Lumina	4	2.2 (2190)	4.0 [3]			8.0 [8]				16.0	12.0
	Lumina	T	3.1 (3135)	4.0 [3]			14.8 [11]				17.1	12.4 [13]
	Lumina	X	3.4 (3350)	5.0 [3]		4.5	12.0 [2]				16.0	12.7
	Regal	T	3.1 (3135)	4.0 [3]			12.0 [2]				16.0	12.6
	Regal	L	3.8 (3791)	4.0 [3]			12.0 [2]				16.0	11.1
1993	Cutlass Supreme	M	3.1 (3135)	4.0 [3]			12.0 [2]				16.0	12.5
	Cutlass Supreme	T	3.1 (3135)	4.0 [3]			12.0 [9]				16.0	12.7 [19]
	Cutlass Supreme	X	3.4 (3350)	5.0 [3]			12.0 [2]				16.0	12.7
	Grand Prix	T	3.1 (3135)	4.0 [3]			12.0 [2]				16.0	12.7 [19]
	Grand Prix	X	3.4 (3350)	5.0 [3]		4.5	12.0 [2]				16.0	11.7
	Lumina	4	2.2 (2190)	4.0 [3]			8.0 [2]				17.1	11.7
	Lumina	T	3.1 (3135)	4.0 [3]			12.0 [2]				16.0	12.7
	Lumina	X	3.4 (3350)	5.0 [3]		4.5	12.0 [2]				16.0	12.7
	Regal	T	3.1 (3135)	4.0 [3]			12.0 [2]				16.0	12.6
	Regal	L	3.8 (3791)	4.0 [3]			12.0 [2]				16.0	11.1

[1] Hydra-matic 3T40: drain and refill only-14 pts., complete overhaul-18 pts.

[2] Hydra-matic 4T60: drain and refill only: 12.0 pts., complete overhaul-16 pts.

[3] Figure shown is for pan removal - for overhaul use 18.0 qts.

[4] Capacity is without filter replacement. Additional oil may be required.

[5] With A/C shown. Without A/C: 12.3 qts.

88001C07

ENGLISH TO METRIC CONVERSION: MASS (WEIGHT)

Current mass measurement is expressed in pounds and ounces (lbs. & ozs.). The metric unit of mass (or weight) is the kilogram (kg). Even although this table does not show conversion of masses (weights) larger than 15 lbs, it is easy to calculate larger units by following the data immediately below.

To convert ounces (oz.) to grams (g): multiply th number of ozs. by 28
To convert grams (g) to ounces (oz.): multiply the number of grams by .035

To convert pounds (lbs.) to kilograms (kg): multiply the number of lbs. by .45
To convert kilograms (kg) to pounds (lbs.): multiply the number of kilograms by 2.2

lbs	kg	lbs	kg	oz	kg	oz	kg
0.1	0.04	0.9	0.41	0.1	0.003	0.9	0.024
0.2	0.09	1	0.4	0.2	0.005	1	0.03
0.3	0.14	2	0.9	0.3	0.008	2	0.06
0.4	0.18	3	1.4	0.4	0.011	3	0.08
0.5	0.23	4	1.8	0.5	0.014	4	0.11
0.6	0.27	5	2.3	0.6	0.017	5	0.14
0.7	0.32	10	4.5	0.7	0.020	10	0.28
0.8	0.36	15	6.8	0.8	0.023	15	0.42

ENGLISH TO METRIC CONVERSION: TEMPERATURE

To convert Fahrenheit (°F) to Celsius (°C): take number of °F and subtract 32; multiply result by 5; divide result by 9

To convert Celsius (°C) to Fahrenheit (°F): take number of °C and multiply by 9; divide result by 5; add 32 to total

Fahrenheit (F)	Celsius (C)			Fahrenheit (F)	Celsius (C)			Fahrenheit (F)	Celsius (C)		
°F	°C	°C	°F	°F	°C	°C	°F	°F	°C	°C	°F
−40	−40	−38	−36.4	80	26.7	18	64.4	215	101.7	80	176
−35	−37.2	−36	−32.8	85	29.4	20	68	220	104.4	85	185
−30	−34.4	−34	−29.2	90	32.2	22	71.6	225	107.2	90	194
−25	−31.7	−32	−25.6	95	35.0	24	75.2	230	110.0	95	202
−20	−28.9	−30	−22	100	37.8	26	78.8	235	112.8	100	212
−15	−26.1	−28	−18.4	105	40.6	28	82.4	240	115.6	105	221
−10	−23.3	−26	−14.8	110	43.3	30	86	245	118.3	110	230
−5	−20.6	−24	−11.2	115	46.1	32	89.6	250	121.1	115	239
0	−17.8	−22	−7.6	120	48.9	34	93.2	255	123.9	120	248
1	−17.2	−20	−4	125	51.7	36	96.8	260	126.6	125	257
2	−16.7	−18	−0.4	130	54.4	38	100.4	265	129.4	130	266
3	−16.1	−16	3.2	135	57.2	40	104	270	132.2	135	275
4	−15.6	−14	6.8	140	60.0	42	107.6	275	135.0	140	284
5	−15.0	−12	10.4	145	62.8	44	112.2	280	137.8	145	293
10	−12.2	−10	14	150	65.6	46	114.8	285	140.6	150	302
15	−9.4	−8	17.6	155	68.3	48	118.4	290	143.3	155	311
20	−6.7	−6	21.2	160	71.1	50	122	295	146.1	160	320
25	−3.9	−4	24.8	165	73.9	52	125.6	300	148.9	165	329
30	−1.1	−2	28.4	170	76.7	54	129.2	305	151.7	170	338
35	1.7	0	32	175	79.4	56	132.8	310	154.4	175	347
40	4.4	2	35.6	180	82.2	58	136.4	315	157.2	180	356
45	7.2	4	39.2	185	85.0	60	140	320	160.0	185	365
50	10.0	6	42.8	190	87.8	62	143.6	325	162.8	190	374
55	12.8	8	46.4	195	90.6	64	147.2	330	165.6	195	383
60	15.6	10	50	200	93.3	66	150.8	335	168.3	200	392
65	18.3	12	53.6	205	96.1	68	154.4	340	171.1	205	401
70	21.1	14	57.2	210	98.9	70	158	345	173.9	210	410
75	23.9	16	60.8	212	100.0	75	167	350	176.7	215	414

TCCS1C01

ENGLISH TO METRIC CONVERSION: LENGTH

To convert inches (ins.) to millimeters (mm): multiply number of inches by 25.4

To convert millimeters (mm) to inches (ins.): multiply number of millimeters by .04

Inches		Decimals	Milli-meters	Inches to millimeters		Inches		Decimals	Milli-meters	Inches to millimeters	
				inches	mm					inches	mm
	1/64	0.051625	0.3969	0.0001	0.00254		33/64	0.515625	13.0969	0.6	15.24
1/32		0.03125	0.7937	0.0002	0.00508	17/32		0.53125	13.4937	0.7	17.78
	3/64	0.046875	1.1906	0.0003	0.00762		35/64	0.546875	13.8906	0.8	20.32
1/16		0.0625	1.5875	0.0004	0.01016	9/16		0.5625	14.2875	0.9	22.86
	5/64	0.078125	1.9844	0.0005	0.01270		37/64	0.578125	14.6844	1	25.4
3/32		0.09375	2.3812	0.0006	0.01524	19/32		0.59375	15.0812	2	50.8
	7/64	0.109375	2.7781	0.0007	0.01778		39/64	0.609375	15.4781	3	76.2
1/8		0.125	3.1750	0.0008	0.02032	5/8		0.625	15.8750	4	101.6
	9/64	0.140625	3.5719	0.0009	0.02286		41/64	0.640625	16.2719	5	127.0
5/32		0.15625	3.9687	0.001	0.0254	21/32		0.65625	16.6687	6	152.4
	11/64	0.171875	4.3656	0.002	0.0508		43/64	0.671875	17.0656	7	177.8
3/16		0.1875	4.7625	0.003	0.0762	11/16		0.6875	17.4625	8	203.2
	13/64	0.203125	5.1594	0.004	0.1016		45/64	0.703125	17.8594	9	228.6
7/32		0.21875	5.5562	0.005	0.1270	23/32		0.71875	18.2562	10	254.0
	15/64	0.234375	5.9531	0.006	0.1524		47/64	0.734375	18.6531	11	279.4
1/4		0.25	6.3500	0.007	0.1778	3/4		0.75	19.0500	12	304.8
	17/64	0.265625	6.7469	0.008	0.2032		49/64	0.765625	19.4469	13	330.2
9/32		0.28125	7.1437	0.009	0.2286	25/32		0.78125	19.8437	14	355.6
	19/64	0.296875	7.5406	0.01	0.254		51/64	0.796875	20.2406	15	381.0
5/16		0.3125	7.9375	0.02	0.508	13/16		0.8125	20.6375	16	406.4
	21/64	0.328125	8.3344	0.03	0.762		53/64	0.828125	21.0344	17	431.8
11/32		0.34375	8.7312	0.04	1.016	27/32		0.84375	21.4312	18	457.2
	23/64	0.359375	9.1281	0.05	1.270		55/64	0.859375	21.8281	19	482.6
3/8		0.375	9.5250	0.06	1.524	7/8		0.875	22.2250	20	508.0
	25/64	0.390625	9.9219	0.07	1.778		57/64	0.890625	22.6219	21	533.4
13/32		0.40625	10.3187	0.08	2.032	29/32		0.90625	23.0187	22	558.8
	27/64	0.421875	10.7156	0.09	2.286		59/64	0.921875	23.4156	23	584.2
7/16		0.4375	11.1125	0.1	2.54	15/16		0.9375	23.8125	24	609.6
	29/64	0.453125	11.5094	0.2	5.08		61/64	0.953125	24.2094	25	635.0
15/32		0.46875	11.9062	0.3	7.62	31/32		0.96875	24.6062	26	660.4
	31/64	0.484375	12.3031	0.4	10.16		63/64	0.984375	25.0031	27	690.6
1/2		0.5	12.7000	0.5	12.70						

ENGLISH TO METRIC CONVERSION: TORQUE

To convert foot-pounds (ft. lbs.) to Newton-meters: multiply the number of ft. lbs. by 1.3

To convert inch-pounds (in. lbs.) to Newton-meters: multiply the number of in. lbs. by .11

in lbs	N-m	in lbs	N-m	in lbs	N-m	in lbs	N-m	in lbs	N-m
0.1	0.01	1	0.11	10	1.13	19	2.15	28	3.16
0.2	0.02	2	0.23	11	1.24	20	2.26	29	3.28
0.3	0.03	3	0.34	12	1.36	21	2.37	30	3.39
0.4	0.04	4	0.45	13	1.47	22	2.49	31	3.50
0.5	0.06	5	0.56	14	1.58	23	2.60	32	3.62
0.6	0.07	6	0.68	15	1.70	24	2.71	33	3.73
0.7	0.08	7	0.78	16	1.81	25	2.82	34	3.84
0.8	0.09	8	0.90	17	1.92	26	2.94	35	3.95
0.9	0.10	9	1.02	18	2.03	27	3.05	36	4.0

TCCS1C02

ENGLISH TO METRIC CONVERSION: TORQUE

Torque is now expressed as either foot-pounds (ft./lbs.) or inch-pounds (in./lbs.). The metric measurement unit for torque is the Newton-meter (Nm). This unit—the Nm—will be used for all SI metric torque references, both the present ft./lbs. and in./lbs.

ft lbs	N-m	ft lbs	N-m	ft lbs	N-m	ft lbs	N-m
0.1	0.1	33	44.7	74	100.3	115	155.9
0.2	0.3	34	46.1	75	101.7	116	157.3
0.3	0.4	35	47.4	76	103.0	117	158.6
0.4	0.5	36	48.8	77	104.4	118	160.0
0.5	0.7	37	50.7	78	105.8	119	161.3
0.6	0.8	38	51.5	79	107.1	120	162.7
0.7	1.0	39	52.9	80	108.5	121	164.0
0.8	1.1	40	54.2	81	109.8	122	165.4
0.9	1.2	41	55.6	82	111.2	123	166.8
1	1.3	42	56.9	83	112.5	124	168.1
2	2.7	43	58.3	84	113.9	125	169.5
3	4.1	44	59.7	85	115.2	126	170.8
4	5.4	45	61.0	86	116.6	127	172.2
5	6.8	46	62.4	87	118.0	128	173.5
6	8.1	47	63.7	88	119.3	129	174.9
7	9.5	48	65.1	89	120.7	130	176.2
8	10.8	49	66.4	90	122.0	131	177.6
9	12.2	50	67.8	91	123.4	132	179.0
10	13.6	51	69.2	92	124.7	133	180.3
11	14.9	52	70.5	93	126.1	134	181.7
12	16.3	53	71.9	94	127.4	135	183.0
13	17.6	54	73.2	95	128.8	136	184.4
14	18.9	55	74.6	96	130.2	137	185.7
15	20.3	56	75.9	97	131.5	138	187.1
16	21.7	57	77.3	98	132.9	139	188.5
17	23.0	58	78.6	99	134.2	140	189.8
18	24.4	59	80.0	100	135.6	141	191.2
19	25.8	60	81.4	101	136.9	142	192.5
20	27.1	61	82.7	102	138.3	143	193.9
21	28.5	62	84.1	103	139.6	144	195.2
22	29.8	63	85.4	104	141.0	145	196.6
23	31.2	64	86.8	105	142.4	146	198.0
24	32.5	65	88.1	106	143.7	147	199.3
25	33.9	66	89.5	107	145.1	148	200.7
26	35.2	67	90.8	108	146.4	149	202.0
27	36.6	68	92.2	109	147.8	150	203.4
28	38.0	69	93.6	110	149.1	151	204.7
29	39.3	70	94.9	111	150.5	152	206.1
30	40.7	71	96.3	112	151.8	153	207.4
31	42.0	72	97.6	113	153.2	154	208.8
32	43.4	73	99.0	114	154.6	155	210.2

TCCS1C03

ENGLISH TO METRIC CONVERSION: FORCE

Force is presently measured in pounds (lbs.). This type of measurement is used to measure spring pressure, specifically how many pounds it takes to compress a spring. Our present force unit (the pound) will be replaced in SI metric measurements by the Newton (N). This term will eventually see use in specifications for electric motor brush spring pressures, valve spring pressures, etc.

To convert pounds (lbs.) to Newton (N): multiply the number of lbs. by 4.45

lbs	N	lbs	N	lbs	N	oz	N
0.01	0.04	21	93.4	59	262.4	1	0.3
0.02	0.09	22	97.9	60	266.9	2	0.6
0.03	0.13	23	102.3	61	271.3	3	0.8
0.04	0.18	24	106.8	62	275.8	4	1.1
0.05	0.22	25	111.2	63	280.2	5	1.4
0.06	0.27	26	115.6	64	284.6	6	1.7
0.07	0.31	27	120.1	65	289.1	7	2.0
0.08	0.36	28	124.6	66	293.6	8	2.2
0.09	0.40	29	129.0	67	298.0	9	2.5
0.1	0.4	30	133.4	68	302.5	10	2.8
0.2	0.9	31	137.9	69	306.9	11	3.1
0.3	1.3	32	142.3	70	311.4	12	3.3
0.4	1.8	33	146.8	71	315.8	13	3.6
0.5	2.2	34	151.2	72	320.3	14	3.9
0.6	2.7	35	155.7	73	324.7	15	4.2
0.7	3.1	36	160.1	74	329.2	16	4.4
0.8	3.6	37	164.6	75	333.6	17	4.7
0.9	4.0	38	169.0	76	338.1	18	5.0
1	4.4	39	173.5	77	342.5	19	5.3
2	8.9	40	177.9	78	347.0	20	5.6
3	13.4	41	182.4	79	351.4	21	5.8
4	17.8	42	186.8	80	355.9	22	6.1
5	22.2	43	191.3	81	360.3	23	6.4
6	26.7	44	195.7	82	364.8	24	6.7
7	31.1	45	200.2	83	369.2	25	7.0
8	35.6	46	204.6	84	373.6	26	7.2
9	40.0	47	209.1	85	378.1	27	7.5
10	44.5	48	213.5	86	382.6	28	7.8
11	48.9	49	218.0	87	387.0	29	8.1
12	53.4	50	224.4	88	391.4	30	8.3
13	57.8	51	226.9	89	395.9	31	8.6
14	62.3	52	231.3	90	400.3	32	8.9
15	66.7	53	235.8	91	404.8	33	9.2
16	71.2	54	240.2	92	409.2	34	9.4
17	75.6	55	244.6	93	413.7	35	9.7
18	80.1	56	249.1	94	418.1	36	10.0
19	84.5	57	253.6	95	422.6	37	10.3
20	89.0	58	258.0	96	427.0	38	10.6

TCCS1C04

2

ENGINE ELECTRICAL

INTEGRATED DIRECT IGNITION (IDI) SYSTEM

➥For information on understanding electricity and troubleshooting electrical circuits, please refer to Section 6 of this manual.

General Description

▶ See Figure 1

Vehicles with the 2.3L engine are equipped with the Integrated Direct Ignition (IDI) system. This system features a distributorless ignition. The IDI system consists of two separate ignition coils, an ignition module and a secondary conductor housing mounted to an aluminum cover plate. The system also consists of a crankshaft sensor, connecting wires and the Electronic Spark Timing (EST) portion of the Electronic Control Module (ECM).

➥When the term Electronic Control Module (ECM) is used in this manual, it refers to the engine control computer; regardless, if the term Powertrain Control Module (PCM) or Electronic Control Module (ECM) is used.

The IDI ignition system uses a magnetic crankshaft sensor, mounted remotely from the ignition module, and a reluctor to determine crankshaft position and engine speed. The reluctor is a special wheel cast into the crankshaft, with 7 slots machined into it. Six of the slots are equally spaced 60 degrees apart and the seventh slot is spaced 10 degrees from 1 of the other slots. This seventh slot is used to generate a sync-pulse.

The ECM uses the EST circuit to control spark advance and ignition dwell, when the ignition system is operating in the EST mode.

To control spark knock and to use maximum spark advance to improve driveability and fuel economy, an Electronic Spark Control (ESC) system is used. This system consists of a knock sensor and an ESC module. The ECM monitors the ESC signal to determine when engine detonation occurs.

SYSTEM COMPONENTS

Crankshaft Sensor

The crankshaft sensor, mounted remotely from the ignition module on an aluminum cover plate, is used to determine crankshaft position and engine speed.

Ignition Coil

The ignition coil assemblies are mounted inside the ignition module housing. Each coil distributes the spark for two plugs simultaneously.

Electronic Spark Timing (EST)

The EST system is basically the same EST to ECM circuit use on the distributor type ignition systems with EST. This system includes the following circuits:

• Reference circuit (CKT 430)— provides the ECM with rpm and crankshaft position information from the IDI module. The IDI module receives this signal from the crank sensor.
• Bypass signal (CKT 424)— above 700 rpm, the ECM applies 5 volts to this circuit to switch spark timing control from the IDI module to the ECM.
• EST signal (CKT 42)—reference signal is sent to the ECM via the DIS module during cranking. Under 700 rpm, the IDI module controls the ignition timing. Above 700 rpm, the ECM applies 5 volts to the bypass line to switch the timing to the ECM control.
• Reference ground circuit (CKT 453)—this wire is grounded through the module and insures that the ground circuit has no voltage drop between the ignition module and the ECM which could affect performance.

ESC Sensor

The ESC sensor, mounted in the engine block near the cylinders, detects abnormal vibration (spark knock) in the engine.

Diagnosis and Testing

SERVICE PRECAUTIONS

✳✳ CAUTION

The ignition coil's secondary voltage output capabilities can exceed 40,000 volts. Avoid body contact with the IDI high voltage secondary components when the engine is running, or personal injury may result.

➥To avoid damage to the ECM or other ignition system components, do not use electrical test equipment such as battery or AC powered voltmeter, ohmmeter, etc. or any type of tester other than specified.

• When performing electrical tests on the system, use a high impedance multimeter, digital voltmeter (DVM) J-34029-A or equivalent. Use of a 12 volt test light is not recommended.
• To prevent Electrostatic Discharge damage, when working with the ECM, do not touch the connector pins or soldered components on the circuit board.
• When handling a PROM, CAL-PAK or MEM-CAL, do not touch the component leads. Also, do not remove the integrated circuit from the carrier.
• Never pierce a high tension lead or boot for any testing purpose; otherwise, future problems are guaranteed.
• Leave new components and modules in the shipping package until ready to install them.
• Never detach any electrical connection with the ignition switch ON unless instructed to do so in a test.

SYMPTOM DIAGNOSIS

▶ See Figures 2 and 3

The ECM uses information from the MAP and coolant sensors, in addition to rpm to calculate spark advance as follows:
1. Low MAP output voltage—more spark advance
2. Cold engine—more spark advance
3. High MAP output voltage—less spark advance
4. Hot engine—less spark advance

Therefore, detonation could be caused by low MAP output or high resistance in the coolant sensor circuit. And poor performance could be caused by high MAP output or low resistance in the coolant sensor circuit.

To diagnose what may be an ignition-related problem, first check for codes, as described in Section 4. If codes, exist, refer to the corresponding diagnostic information in Section 4. Otherwise, the accompanying charts may be helpful.

Ignition Coil and Module Assembly

REMOVAL & INSTALLATION

▶ See Figure 4

1. Make sure the ignition switch is OFF.
2. Disconnect the negative battery cable.
3. Detach the 11-pin IDI ignition harness connector.
4. Unfasten the ignition system assembly-to-camshaft housing bolts.
5. Remove the ignition coil and module assembly from the engine.

➥If the boots are difficult to remove from the spark plugs, use tool J36011 or equivalent, to remove them. First twist and then pull upward on the retainers. Reinstall the boots and retainers on the ignition coil and module housing secondary terminals. The boots and retainers must be in place on the housing secondary terminals before to ignition system assembly installation or ignition system damage may result.

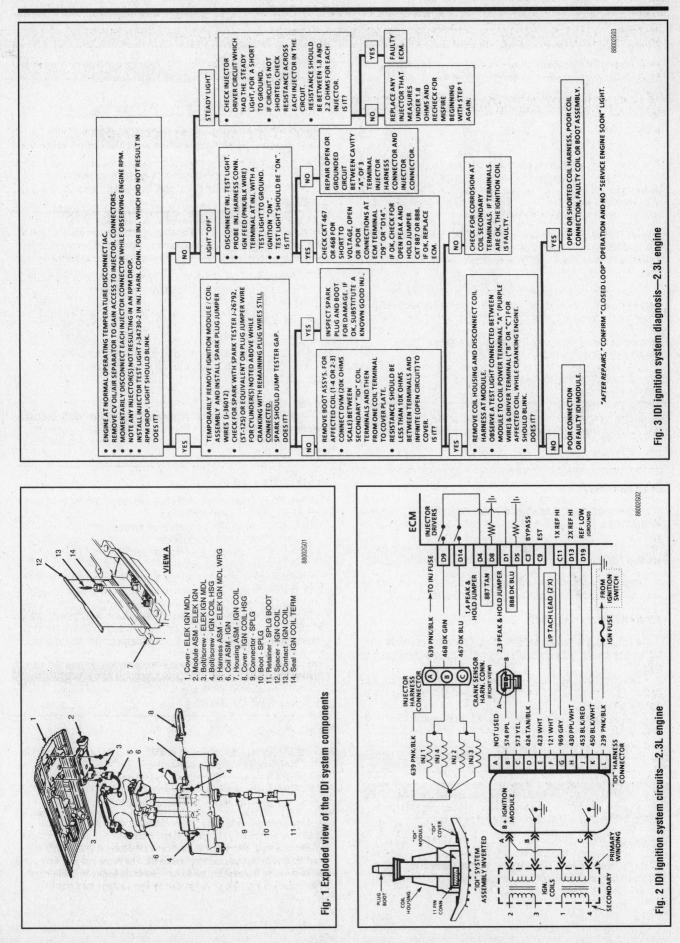

Fig. 3 IDI ignition system diagnosis—2.3L engine

Fig. 1 Exploded view of the IDI system components

1. Cover - ELEK IGN MDL
2. Module ASM - ELEK IGN
3. Bolt/screw - ELEK IGN MDL
4. Bolt/screw - IGN COIL HSG
5. Harness ASM - ELEK IGN MDL WRG
6. Coil ASM - IGN
7. Housing ASM - IGN COIL
8. Cover - IGN COIL HSG
9. Connector - SPLG
10. Boot - SPLG
11. Retainer - SPLG BOOT
12. Spacer - IGN COIL
13. Contact - IGN COIL
14. Seal - IGN COIL TERM

VIEW A

Fig. 2 IDI ignition system circuits—2.3L engine

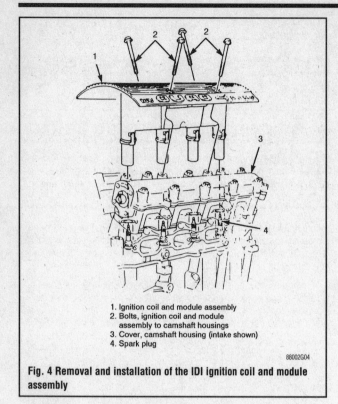

1. Ignition coil and module assembly
2. Bolts, ignition coil and module assembly to camshaft housings
3. Cover, camshaft housing (intake shown)
4. Spark plug

88002G04

Fig. 4 Removal and installation of the IDI ignition coil and module assembly

To install:

6. Install the spark plug boots and retainers to the housing.

7. Carefully align the boots to the spark plug terminals, while installing the ignition system assembly to the engine.

8. Coat the threads of the retaining bolts with 1052080 or equivalent, then install them. Tighten the bolts to 19 ft. lbs. (26 Nm).

9. Attach the 11-pin harness connector.

10. Make sure the ignition switch is **OFF**, then connect the negative battery cable.

Ignition Coil

REMOVAL & INSTALLATION

♦ See Figure 1

1. Disconnect the negative battery cable.
2. Detach the 11-pin IDI ignition harness connector.
3. Remove the ignition coil and module assembly from the engine, as outlined earlier in this section.
4. Unfasten the four housing-to-cover screws, then remove the housing from the cover.
5. Disengage the coil harness connector(s).
6. Remove the coil(s), contact(s) and seal(s) from the cover.

DIRECT IGNITION SYSTEM (DIS)

General Description

Vehicles which are equipped with the 2.2L, 2.5L, 2.8L, 3.1L and 3.4L engines utilize the Direct Ignition System (DIS). This system is called the Electronic Ignition (EI) in later model years. This system features a distributorless ignition. The DIS/EI system consists of two separate ignition coils on 4 cylinder engines or 3 separate coils on V6 engines, an Ignition Control Module (ICM), and a secondary conductor housing which is mounted to an aluminum cover plate. The system also consist of one or two Crankshaft Position (CKP) sensors,

To install:

7. Install the coil(s) to the cover.
8. Attach the coil harness connector(s).
9. Install new seals to the housing.
10. Using petroleum jelly to retain the contact, install the contacts to the housing.
11. Install the housing cover and secure using the retaining screws. Tighten the screws to 35 inch lbs. (4 Nm).
12. Fit the spark plug boots and retainers to the housing.
13. Install the IDI assembly to the engine, as outlined earlier in this section.
14. Attach the 11-pin harness connector.
15. Connect the negative battery cable.

Ignition Module

REMOVAL & INSTALLATION

♦ See Figure 1

1. Disconnect the negative battery cable.
2. Remove the ignition coil and module assembly from the engine, as outlined earlier in this section.
3. Unfasten the housing-to-cover retaining screws, then remove the housing from the cover.
4. Detach the coil harness connector from the module.
5. Unfasten the module-to-cover retaining screws, then remove the module from the cover.

➡Do not wipe the grease from the module or coil, if the same module is to be replaced. If a new module is to be installed, spread the grease (included in package) on the metal face of the new module and on the cover where the module seats. This grease is necessary from module cooling.

To install:

6. Position the module to the cover and secure using the retaining screws. Tighten the screws to 35 inch lbs. (4 Nm).
7. Attach the coil harness connector to the module.
8. Install the housing cover, then secure using the retaining screws. Tighten the screws to 35 inch lbs. (4 Nm).
9. Fit the spark plug boots and retainers to the housing.
10. Install the ignition coil and module assembly to the engine, as outlined earlier in this section.
11. Connect the negative battery cable.

Crankshaft Sensor

For testing and removal and installation procedures for the crankshaft position sensor, please refer to Section 4 of this manual.

Camshaft Position Sensor

For removal and installation of the camshaft position sensor, please refer to the procedure located in Section 4 of this manual.

crankshaft reluctor ring, related connecting wires and the Electronic Spark Timing (EST) or Ignition Control (IC) portion of the Electronic Control Module (ECM). A Camshaft Position (CMP) sensor may also be incorporated on some engines.

➡When the term Electronic Control Module (ECM) is used in this manual, it refers to the engine control computer; regardless, if the term Powertrain Control Module (PCM) or Electronic Control Module (ECM) is used.

The DIS/EI ignition system uses a magnetic crankshaft sensor (mounted remotely from the ignition module) and a reluctor to determine crankshaft position and engine speed. The reluctor is a special wheel cast into the crankshaft with several machined slots. A specific slot on the reluctor wheel is used to generate a sync-pulse.

The camshaft sensor, used on some engines, provides a cam signal to identify correct firing sequence. The crankshaft sensor signal triggers each coil at the proper time.

The ECM uses the EST circuit to control spark advance and ignition dwell, when the ignition system is operating in the EST/IC mode.

The Electronic Spark Control (ESC) system is used to control spark knock and enable maximum spark advance to improve driveability and fuel economy. This system is consists of a knock sensor and an ESC module. The computer control module (ECM/PCM) monitors the ESC signal to determine when engine detonation occurs.

SYSTEM COMPONENTS

Crankshaft Position (CKP) Sensor

The Crankshaft Position (CKP) sensor is mounted on the bottom of the DIS module on the 2.2L and 2.5L engines. The sensor is located toward the bottom of the rear (right side) of the engine block on V6 engines. It is used to determine crankshaft position and engine speed.

Ignition Coils

The ignition coil assemblies are mounted inside the module assembly housing. Each coil distributes the spark for two plugs simultaneously.

Electronic Spark Timing (EST)

The EST system, used on 1988–92 models, includes the following circuits:

The EST system is basically the same EST to ECM circuit used on the distributor type ignition systems with EST. This system includes the following circuits:
- Reference circuit (CKT 430)—provides the ECM with rpm and crankshaft position information from the IDI module. The IDI module receives this signal from the crank sensor.
- Bypass signal (CKT 424)—above 700 rpm, the ECM applies 5 volts to this circuit to switch spark timing control from the IDI module to the ECM.
- EST signal (CKT 42)—reference signal is sent to the ECM via the DIS module during cranking. Under 700 rpm, the IDI module controls the ignition timing. Above 700 rpm, the ECM applies 5 volts to the bypass line to switch the timing to the ECM control.
- Reference ground circuit (CKT 45)—this wire is grounded through the module and insures that the ground circuit has no voltage drop between the ignition module and the ECM which could affect performance.

Ignition Control (IC)

The IC system, used on 1993–96 models, includes the following circuits:
- 3X Reference high (CKT 430)—The CKP sensor generates a signal to the ICM, resulting in a reference pulse which is sent to the PCM. The PCM uses this signal to determine crankshaft position, engine speed and injector pulse width. The engine will not start or run if this circuit is open or grounded.
- 3X Reference low (CKT 453)—This wire is grounded through the module and insures that the ground circuit has no voltage drop between the ICM and the PCM which may affect engine performance.
- Ignition control (CKT 423)—The PCM uses this circuit to trigger the electronic ignition control module. The PCM uses the crankshaft reference signal to base its calculation of the amount of spark advance needed under present engine conditions.
- 24X reference signal—Additional to the electronic ignition system is the

24X crankshaft position sensor. Its function is to smooth idle quality and provide improved low speed driveability.

Diagnosis and Testing

SERVICE PRECAUTIONS

✱✱ CAUTION

The ignition coil's secondary voltage output capabilities can exceed 40,000 volts. Avoid body contact with the DIS high voltage secondary components when the engine is running, or personal injury may result.

➡To avoid damage to the computer control module or other ignition system components, do not use electrical test equipment such as battery or AC powered voltmeter, ohmmeter, etc. or any type of tester other than specified.

- When performing electrical tests on the system, use a high impedance multimeter or quality digital voltmeter (DVM). Use of a 12 volt test light is not recommended.
- To prevent electrostatic discharge damage, when working with the ECM, do not touch the connector pins or soldered components on the circuit board.
- When handling a PROM, CAL-PAK or MEM-CAL, do not touch the component leads. Also, do not remove the integrated circuit from the carrier.
- When performing electrical tests on the system, use a high impedance multimeter, digital voltmeter (DVM) J-34029-A or equivalent.
- Never pierce a high tension lead or boot for any testing purpose; otherwise, future problems are guaranteed.
- Leave new components and modules in the shipping package until ready to install them.
- Never disconnect any electrical connection with the ignition switch **ON** unless instructed to do so in a test.

SYMPTOM DIAGNOSIS

▶ **See Figures 5 thru 14**

The ECM uses information from the MAP and coolant sensors, in addition to rpm to calculate spark advance as follows:
1. Low MAP output voltage—more spark advance
2. Cold engine—more spark advance
3. High MAP output voltage—less spark advance
4. Hot engine—less spark advance

Therefore, briefly, detonation could be caused by low MAP output or high resistance in the coolant sensor circuit. And poor performance could be caused by high MAP output or low resistance in the coolant sensor circuit.

To diagnose what may be an ignition-related problem, first check for codes, as described in Section 4. If codes, exist, refer to the corresponding diagnostic charts in Section 4. Otherwise, the following charts may be helpful.

Ignition Coil

TESTING

1. Remove the ignition coil(s).
2. Using an ohmmeter, check the resistance between the primary terminals on the underside of the coil. The resistance should be 0.50–0.90 ohms.
3. Check the resistance between the secondary terminals. It should be 5000–10,000 ohms.
4. If the coil failed either test, replace the coil.

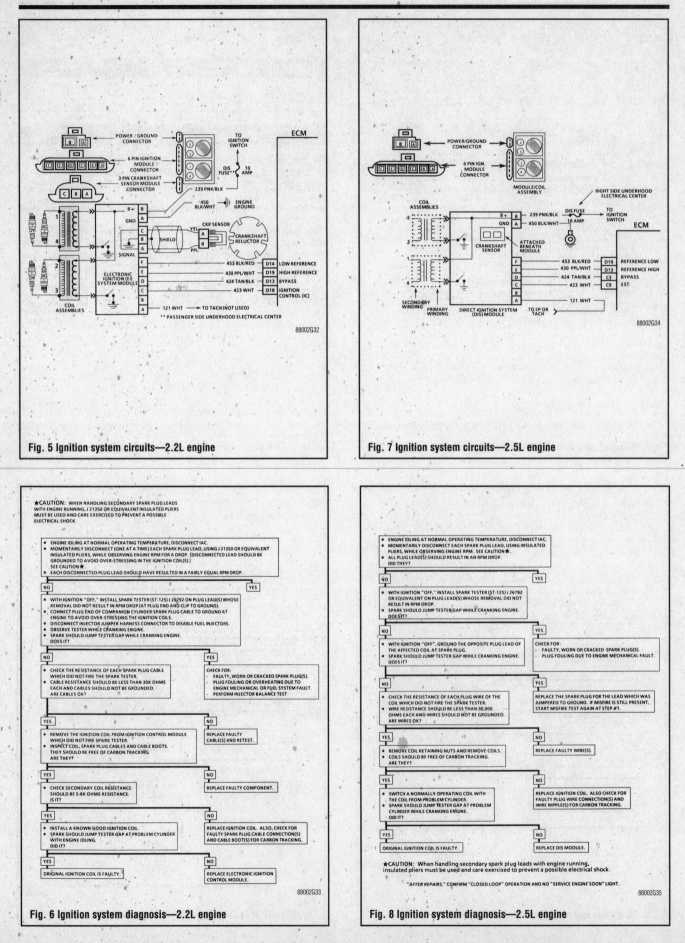

Fig. 5 Ignition system circuits—2.2L engine

Fig. 7 Ignition system circuits—2.5L engine

Fig. 6 Ignition system diagnosis—2.2L engine

Fig. 8 Ignition system diagnosis—2.5L engine

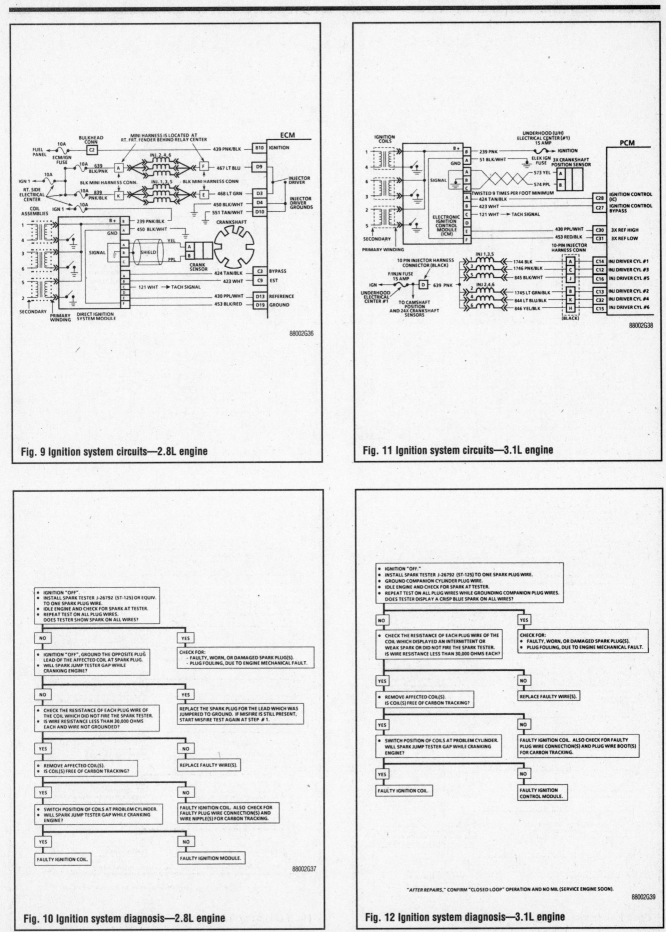

Fig. 9 Ignition system circuits—2.8L engine

Fig. 11 Ignition system circuits—3.1L engine

Fig. 10 Ignition system diagnosis—2.8L engine

Fig. 12 Ignition system diagnosis—3.1L engine

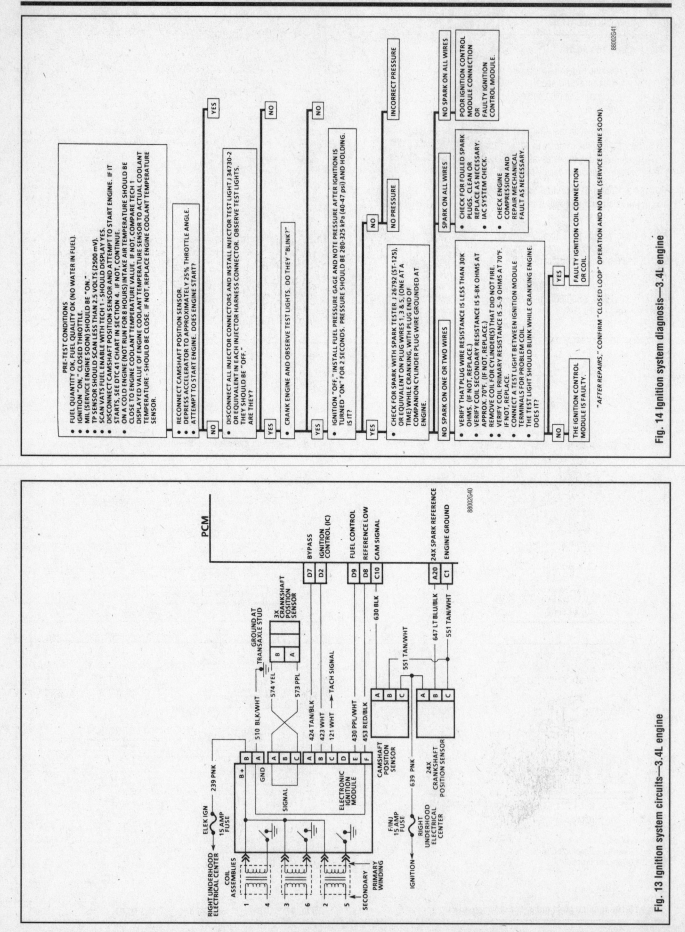

Fig. 13 Ignition system circuits—3.4L engine

Fig. 14 Ignition system diagnosis—3.4L engine

REMOVAL & INSTALLATION

♦ **See Figures 15 and 16**

1. Disconnect the negative battery cable.
2. Tag and disconnect the spark plug wires.
3. Unfasten the coil retaining nuts/screws, then separate and remove the coils from the module.

To install:

4. Position the coils to the module, then secure using the retaining nuts/screws. Tighten the retainers to 40 inch lbs. (4.5 Nm).
5. Attach the spark plug wires, as tagged during removal.
6. Connect the negative battery cable.

➡ **On the 3.1L or 3.4L engines, this procedure must be performed before the engine is started and requires the use of a Tech 1®, or equivalent, scan tool.**

7. If equipped with the 3.1L or 3.4L engine, perform the idle learn procedure to allow the ECM/PCM memory to be updated with the correct IAC valve pintle position and provide for a stable idle speed.
   a. Install a Tech 1®, or equivalent scan tool.
   b. Turn the ignition to the **ON** position, engine not running.
   c. Select **IAC SYSTEM**, then **IDLE LEARN** in the **MISC TEST** mode.

d. Place the transaxle in **P** or **N**, as applicable.
e. Proceed with idle learn as directed by the scan tool.

Ignition Coil and Module Assembly

REMOVAL & INSTALLATION

♦ **See Figure 17**

1. Make sure the ignition switch is **OFF**.
2. Disconnect the negative battery cable.
3. Tag and detach the electrical connectors and the spark plug wires from the coil assembly.
4. Unfasten the ignition coil and module assembly retaining bolts, then remove the unit from the engine.

To install:

➡ **On 2.2L and 2.5L engines, before installing the DIS assembly, check the crankshaft sensor O-ring for damage or leakage. Replace if necessary. Lubricate the O-ring with engine oil before installing.**

5. Position the coil and module assembly to the engine and install the retaining bolts. Tighten the bolts to 20 ft. lbs. (27 Nm).
6. Connect the spark plug wires to the coils, as tagged during removal.

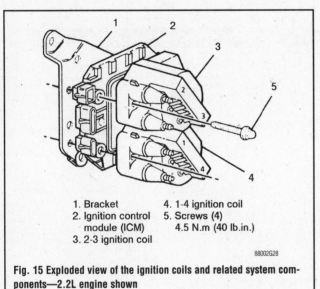

1. Bracket
2. Ignition control module (ICM)
3. 2-3 ignition coil
4. 1-4 ignition coil
5. Screws (4) 4.5 N.m (40 lb.in.)

88002G28

Fig. 15 Exploded view of the ignition coils and related system components—2.2L engine shown

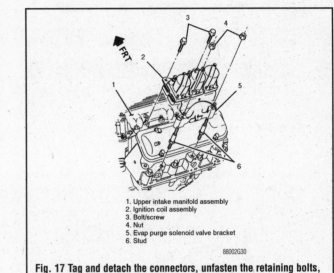

1. Upper intake manifold assembly
2. Ignition coil assembly
3. Bolt/screw
4. Nut
5. Evap purge solenoid valve bracket
6. Stud

88002G30

Fig. 17 Tag and detach the connectors, unfasten the retaining bolts, then remove the coil and module assembly from the engine

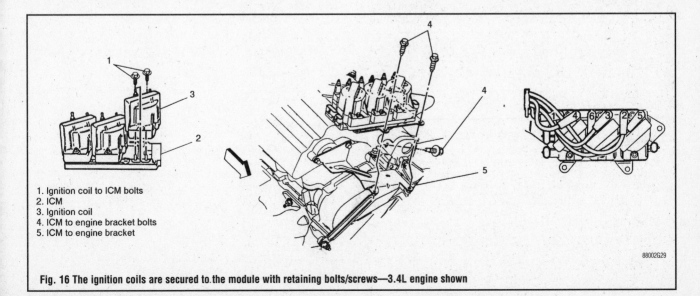

1. Ignition coil to ICM bolts
2. ICM
3. Ignition coil
4. ICM to engine bracket bolts
5. ICM to engine bracket

88002G29

Fig. 16 The ignition coils are secured to the module with retaining bolts/screws—3.4L engine shown

7. Attach the coil and module assembly electrical connectors, as tagged during removal.

8. Connect the negative battery cable.

➡On the 3.1L or 3.4L engines, this procedure must be performed before the engine is started and requires the use of a Tech 1®, or equivalent, scan tool.

9. If equipped with the 3.1L or 3.4L engine, perform the idle learn procedure, as outlined under the Ignition Coil removal & installation procedure.

Ignition Module

REMOVAL & INSTALLATION

▶ See Figure 18

1. Disconnect the negative battery cable.
2. Remove the ignition coil and module assembly from the engine, as outlined earlier in this section.
3. Remove the ignition coils from the module, as previously outlined.
4. Remove the module from the assembly plate.

To install:

5. Position the module to the assembly plate. Carefully engage the sensor to the module terminals.
6. Install the ignition coils.

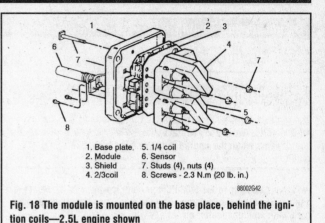

1. Base plate   5. 1/4 coil
2. Module   6. Sensor
3. Shield   7. Studs (4), nuts (4)
4. 2/3 coil   8. Screws - 2.3 N.m (20 lb. in.)

88002G42

Fig. 18 The module is mounted on the base place, behind the ignition coils—2.5L engine shown

7. Install the ignition coil and module assembly to the engine.

➡On the 3.1L or 3.4L engines, this procedure must be performed before the engine is started and requires the use of a Tech 1®, or equivalent, scan tool.

8. If equipped with the 3.1L or 3.4L engine, perform the idle learn procedure, as outlined under the Ignition Coil removal & installation procedure.

COMPUTER CONTROLLED COIL IGNITION (C³I) SYSTEM

General Description

Vehicles with the 3.8L engine are equipped with the Computer Controlled Coil (C³I). This system may also be called the Electronic Ignition (EI) system on later models. This system features a distributorless ignition engine. The C³I/EI system consists of 3 ignition coils, an Ignition Control Module (ICM), a dual crank sensor also, camshaft sensor, connecting wires, and the Electronic Spark Timing (EST) portion of the Electronic Control Module (ECM).

➡When the term Electronic Control Module (ECM) is used in this manual, it refers to the engine control computer; regardless, if the term Powertrain Control Module (PCM) or Electronic Control Module (ECM) is used.

The ECM uses the EST circuit to control spark advance and ignition dwell, when the ignition system is operating in the EST mode. There are 2 modes of ignition system operation. These modes are as follows:

• Module mode—the ignition system operates independently of the ECM/PCM, with module mode spark advance always at 10 degrees BTDC. The ECM has no control of the ignition system when in this mode.

• EST mode—the ignition spark timing and ignition dwell time is fully controlled by the ECM. EST spark advance and ignition dwell is calculated by the ECM.

To control spark knock, and to use maximum spark advance to improve driveability and fuel economy, an Electronic Spark Control (ESC) system is used. This system consists of a knock sensor and an ESC module. The ECM monitors the ESC signal to determine when engine detonation occurs.

SYSTEM COMPONENTS

C³I Module

The C³I module monitors the sync-pulse and the crank signal. During cranking the C³I module monitors the sync-pulse to begin the ignition firing sequence. During this time, each of the 3 coils are fired at a pre-determined interval based on engine speed only. Above 400 rpm, the C³I module is only use as a reference signal.

Ignition Coil

The ignition coil assemblies are mounted on the C³I module. Each coil distributes the spark for 2 plugs simultaneously.

Electronic Spark Control (ESC)

The ESC system incorporates a knock sensor and the ECM. The knock sensor detects engine detonation. When engine detonation occurs, the ECM receives the ESC signal and retards EST to reduce detonation.

Electronic Spark Timing (EST)

The EST system includes the following circuits:

• Reference circuit—provides the ECM with rpm and crankshaft position information from the C³I module. The C³I module receives this signal from the crank sensor hall-effect switch.

• Bypass signal—above 400 rpm, the ECM applies 5 volts to this circuit to switch spark timing control from the C³I module to the ECM.

• EST signal—reference signal is sent to the ECM via the C³I module during cranking. Under 400 rpm, the C³I module controls the ignition timing. Above 400 rpm, the ECM applies 5 volts to the bypass line to switch the timing to the ECM control.

Electronic Control Module (ECM) or Powertrain Control Module (PCM)

The ECM/PCM is responsible for maintaining proper spark and fuel injection timing for all driving conditions.

Dual Crank Sensor

The dual crank sensor is mounted in a pedestal on the front of the engine near the harmonic balancer. The sensor consists of 2 hall-effect switches, which depend on 2 metal interrupter rings mounted on the balancer to activate them. Windows in the interrupters activate the hall-effect switches as they provide a path for the magnetic field between the switches transducers and magnets.

Diagnosis and Testing

SERVICE PRECAUTIONS

✳✳ CAUTION

The ignition coil's secondary voltage output capabilities can exceed 40,000 volts. Avoid body contact with the C³I high voltage secondary components when the engine is running, or personal injury may result.

➡To avoid damage to the ECM/PCM or other ignition system components, do not use electrical test equipment such as battery or AC-powered voltmeter, ohmmeter, etc. or any type of tester other than specified.

- Check for codes, as described in Section 4. If any are found, refer to the appropriate diagnostic procedure in Section 4.
- When performing electrical tests on the system, use a high impedance multimeter or quality digital voltmeter (DVM). Use of a 12 volt test light is not recommended.
- To prevent electrostatic discharge damage, when working with the ECM, do not touch the connector pins or soldered components on the circuit board.
- When handling a PROM, CAL-PAK or MEM-CAL, do not touch the component leads. Also, do not remove the integrated circuit from the carrier.
- Never pierce a high tension lead or boot for any testing purpose; otherwise, future problems are guaranteed.
- Do not allow extension cords for power tools or droplights to lie on, near or across any vehicle electrical wiring.
- Leave new components and modules in the shipping package until ready to install them.

Ignition Coil

TESTING

1. Remove the ignition coil(s).
2. Using an ohmmeter, check the resistance between the primary terminals on the underside of the coil. The resistance should be 0.50–0.90 ohms.
3. Check the resistance between the secondary terminals. It should be 5000–10,000 ohms.
4. If the coil failed either test, replace the coil.

REMOVAL & INSTALLATION

▶ See Figure 19

1. Disconnect the negative battery cable.
2. Tag and disconnect the spark plug wires.
3. Unfasten the 2 retaining screws securing the coil to the ignition module, then remove the remove the coil assembly.
4. Installation is the reverse of the removal procedure. Tighten the retaining screws to 40 inch lbs. (4–5 Nm).
5. Connect the negative battery cable.

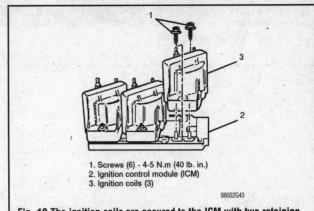

1. Screws (6) - 4-5 N.m (40 lb. in.)
2. Ignition control module (ICM)
3. Ignition coils (3)

88002G43

Fig. 19 The ignition coils are secured to the ICM with two retaining screws

Ignition Control Module (ICM)

REMOVAL & INSTALLATION

▶ See Figure 20

1. Disconnect the negative battery cable.
2. Detach the 14-way connector at the ignition module.
3. Tag and disconnect the spark plug wires at the coil assembly.
4. Remove the 6 screws securing the coil assemblies to the ignition control module, then disconnect the coils from the module.
5. Unfasten the nuts and washers that retain the module to the bracket, then remove the ignition module from the vehicle.

To install:

6. Position the coils to the ignition control module, then secure with the retaining screws. Tighten the screws to 40 inch lbs. (4.5 Nm).
7. Fit the module assembly to the bracket and install the retaining nuts and washers. Tighten to 70 inch lbs. (8 Nm).
8. Connect the spark plug wires, as tagged during removal.
9. Attach the 14-way connector to the module.
10. Connect the negative battery cable.

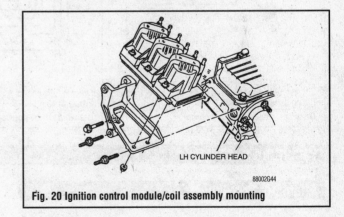

LH CYLINDER HEAD

88002G44

Fig. 20 Ignition control module/coil assembly mounting

FIRING ORDERS

♦ See Figures 21, 22, 23, 24 and 25

➡To avoid confusion, removal and tag the wires one at a time, for replacement.

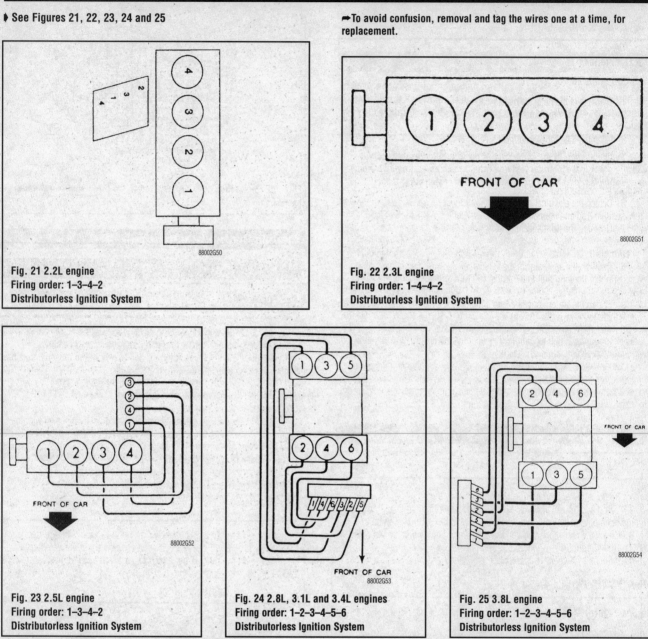

Fig. 21 2.2L engine
Firing order: 1–3–4–2
Distributorless Ignition System

Fig. 22 2.3L engine
Firing order: 1–4–4–2
Distributorless Ignition System

Fig. 23 2.5L engine
Firing order: 1–3–4–2
Distributorless Ignition System

Fig. 24 2.8L, 3.1L and 3.4L engines
Firing order: 1–2–3–4–5–6
Distributorless Ignition System

Fig. 25 3.8L engine
Firing order: 1–2–3–4–5–6
Distributorless Ignition System

CHARGING SYSTEM

Alternator Precautions

To prevent damage to the on-board computer, alternator, and regulator, the following precautions must be taken when working with the electrical system.

• If the battery is removed for any reason, make sure it is reconnected with the correct polarity. Reversing the battery connections may result in damage to the one-way rectifiers. Always check the battery polarity visually. This is to be done before any connections are made to be sure that all of the connections correspond to the battery ground polarity.

• When utilizing a booster battery as a starting aid, always connect the positive-to-positive terminals and the negative terminals from the booster battery to a good engine ground on the vehicle being started.

• Never use a fast charger as a booster to start vehicles.

• Disconnect the battery cables when charging the battery with a fast charger; the charger has a tendency to force current through the diodes in the opposite direction for which they were designed. This burns out the diodes.

• Make sure the ignition switch if **OFF** when connecting or disconnecting any electrical component, especially on cars with any on-board computer system.

• Never attempt to polarize the alternator.

• Do not use test lights of more than 12 volts when checking diode continuity.

• Do not short across or ground any of the alternator terminals.

• The polarity of the battery, alternator and regulator must be matched and considered before making any electrical connections within the system.

• Never separate the alternator on an open circuit. Make sure all connections within the circuit are clean and tight.

• Disconnect the battery ground terminal when performing any service on electrical components.

• Disconnect the battery if arc welding is to be done on the vehicle.

Alternator

REMOVAL & INSTALLATION

2.2L Engine

▶ **See Figure 26**

1. Disconnect the negative battery cable.
2. Remove the serpentine drive belt, as outlined in Section 1 of this manual.
3. Unfasten the rear bracket/heat shield nuts from the exhaust manifold.
4. Remove the rear bracket/heat shield bolts from the block, near the water pump.
5. Unfasten the rear bracket/heat shield retaining nuts at the alternator, then remove the bracket/heat shield.
6. Detach the electrical connections from the alternator, including the battery positive lead and the nuts from the alternator output (BAT) terminal.
7. Unfasten the front attaching bolts, then remove the alternator from the vehicle.

To install:

8. Position the alternator in the vehicle, then secure using the retaining bolts. Tighten the long bolt to 37 ft. lbs. (50 Nm) and the short bolt to 18 ft. lbs. (25 Nm).
9. Fasten the battery positive lead and nut to the alternator output terminal and tighten to 70 inch lbs. (8 Nm).
10. Attach the electrical connector to the alternator.
11. Position the rear bracket/heat shield, then install the retaining bolt at the alternator. Tighten the bolt to 18 ft. lbs. (25 Nm).
12. Fasten the rear bracket/heat shield bolts to the block, near the water pump. Tighten to 63 ft. lbs. (85 Nm). Install the bracket/shield-to-exhaust manifold nuts and tighten to 37 ft. lbs. (50 Nm).
13. Install the serpentine drive belt, as outlined in Section 1 of this manual.
14. Connect the negative battery cable.

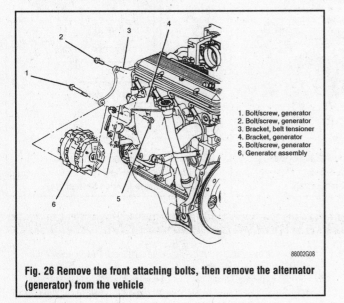

1. Bolt/screw, generator
2. Bolt/screw, generator
3. Bracket, belt tensioner
4. Bracket, generator
5. Bolt/screw, generator
6. Generator assembly

88002G08

Fig. 26 Remove the front attaching bolts, then remove the alternator (generator) from the vehicle

2.3L Engine

▶ **See Figure 27**

1. Disconnect the negative battery cable.
2. Remove the electrical center fuse block shield.
3. Remove the serpentine belt, as outlined in Section 1 of this manual.
4. Label and detach the alternator electrical connector(s). Unfasten the nut and the battery positive connector from the alternator.
5. Unfasten the alternator brace bolt and the rear and front retaining bolts.

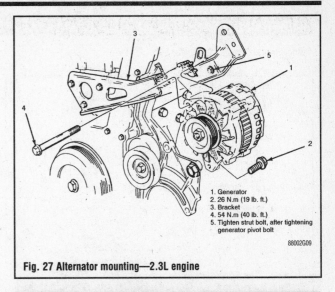

1. Generator
2. 26 N.m (19 lb. ft.)
3. Bracket
4. 54 N.m (40 lb. ft.)
5. Tighten strut bolt, after tightening generator pivot bolt

88002G09

Fig. 27 Alternator mounting—2.3L engine

✳✳ WARNING

Be very careful not to damage the A/C compressor and condenser hose when removing the alternator.

6. Lift the alternator out between the engine lifting eyelet and the A/C compressor and condenser hose, to the passenger side, then up and out.

To install:

7. Position the alternator in the vehicle, then install the front attaching bolt, but do not tighten at this time. Install rear and brace retaining bolts.
8. Tighten the long bolt to 40 ft. lbs. (54 Nm), the short bolt to 19 ft. lbs. (26 Nm) and the brace bolt to 18 ft. lbs. (25 Nm).
9. Fasten the battery positive connector and nut to the alternator.
10. Attach the alternator electrical connector, then install the serpentine belt and fuse block shield.
11. Connect the negative battery cable and check for proper operation.

2.5L Engine

▶ **See Figure 28**

1. Disconnect the negative battery cable.
2. Remove the serpentine belt, as outlined in Section 1 of this manual.
3. Detach the electrical connector(s) from the back of the alternator.
4. Unfasten the nut and the battery positive lead from the alternator output (BAT) terminal.

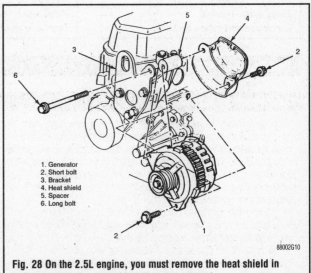

1. Generator
2. Short bolt
3. Bracket
4. Heat shield
5. Spacer
6. Long bolt

88002G10

Fig. 28 On the 2.5L engine, you must remove the heat shield in order to remove the alternator from the vehicle

5. Remove the rear then the front attaching bolts and remove the heat shield.

6. Carefully remove the alternator assembly, making sure all wires are disconnected.

To install:

7. Position the alternator into the mounting bracket and install the front mounting bolts but do not tighten at this time.

8. Install the heat shield and the rear the rear mounting bolt.

9. Tighten the long bolts to 37 ft. lbs. (50 Nm) and the short bolt and heat shield bolt to 20 ft. lbs. (27 Nm).

10. Attach the electrical connector(s).

11. Install the serpentine belt, as outlined in Section 1 of this manual.

12. Connect the negative battery cable.

2.8L and 3.1L Engines

1988–93 VEHICLES

▶ See Figures 29, 30, 31 and 32

1. Disconnect the negative battery cable.

2. If necessary for access to the alternator, remove the air cleaner assembly.

3. Remove the serpentine belt, as outlined in Section 1 of this manual.

4. Label and detach the electrical connector(s) from the back of the alternator.

5. Remove the rear and front attaching bolts, and unfasten the brace-to-alternator bolt.

6. Carefully remove the alternator assembly, making sure all wires are disconnected.

➡If the alternator brace is removed, the studs must be retightened before installation or damage to the brace may result.

To install:

7. Position the alternator into the mounting bracket.

8. If necessary, attach the battery positive lead and nut to the alternator output terminal. Tighten to 71 inch lbs. (8 Nm).

9. Install the brace-to-alternator bolt, but do not tighten at this time.

10. Install the front and rear mounting bolts. Tighten the bolts as follows:
   a. Long bolt to 35 ft. lbs. (47 Nm)
   b. Short bolt to 18 ft. lbs. (25 Nm)
   c. Bracket bolt to 18 ft. lbs. (25 Nm)

11. Check that tightening of the brace bolts did not bind the alternator.

12. Attach the electrical connector(s).

13. Install the serpentine belt, as outlined in Section 1 of this manual.

14. If removed, install the air cleaner.

15. Connect the negative battery cable.

1994–96 VEHICLES

▶ See Figure 33

1. Disconnect the negative battery cable.

2. Remove the serpentine belt at the alternator, as outlined in Section 1 of this manual.

3. Unfasten the bolt/screw from the alternator.

4. Remove the power steering gear pipe clip and nut.

5. Remove the stud from the alternator.

6. Detach the electrical connector from the alternator.

7. Loosen the alternator front and rear braces from the upper intake manifold.

8. Unfasten the nut and battery positive lead from the alternator output (BAT) terminal.

9. Remove the alternator from the vehicle.

Fig. 29 After removing the serpentine belt, detach the electrical connector from the rear of the alternator

Fig. 30 Unfasten the front and rear mounting bolts . . .

Fig. 31 . . . then remove the brace-to-alternator bolt

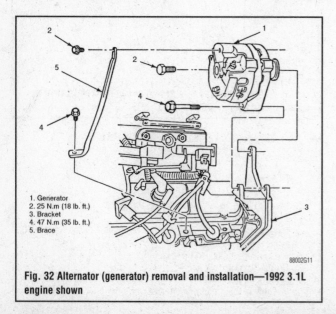

1. Generator
2. 25 N.m (18 lb. ft.)
3. Bracket
4. 47 N.m (35 lb. ft.)
5. Brace

Fig. 32 Alternator (generator) removal and installation—1992 3.1L engine shown

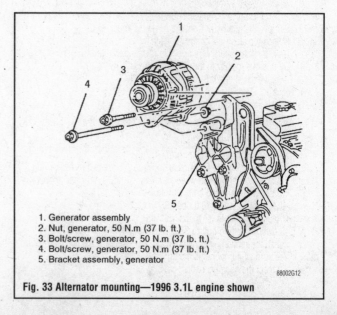

1. Generator assembly
2. Nut, generator, 50 N.m (37 lb. ft.)
3. Bolt/screw, generator, 50 N.m (37 lb. ft.)
4. Bolt/screw, generator, 50 N.m (37 lb. ft.)
5. Bracket assembly, generator

Fig. 33 Alternator mounting—1996 3.1L engine shown

To install:

10. Position the alternator in the mounting bracket.

11. Attach the battery positive lead and the nut to the alternator output terminal. Tighten the nut to 15 ft. lbs. (20 Nm).

12. Hand start the alternator front and rear braces to the intake manifold.

13. Attach the electrical connector to the alternator. The connector will snap into place when it is correctly installed.

14. Install the retaining bolts/screws to the alternator. Tighten to 37 ft. lbs. (50 Nm).

15. Fasten the alternator front and rear brace nuts to the intake manifold, then tighten the nuts to 18 ft. lbs. (25 Nm). Make sure the alternator does not bind when tightening the brace nuts.

16. Install the stud on the alternator, then tighten to 18 ft. lbs. (25 Nm).

17. Fasten the power steering gear pipe clip and nut.

18. Install the drive belt on the alternator as outlined in Section 1 of this manual.

19. Connect the negative battery cable.

3.4L Engine

→Vehicles with the 3.4L engine will also be equipped with an alternator cooling fan behind the right side headlight, used to cool the unit through a duct hose.

AUTOMATIC TRANSAXLE VEHICLES THROUGH 1994

♦ See Figures 34 and 35

1. Remove the air cleaner assembly.
2. Disconnect the negative battery cable.
3. Remove the serpentine belt, as outlined in Section 1 of this section.
4. Remove the coolant recovery reservoir and set it aside.
5. Unfasten the upper alternator stud nut and remove the power steering pipe retaining clip from the stud.
6. Loosen the upper alternator stud.
7. Raise and safely support the vehicle.
8. Remove the front tire and wheel assemblies.
9. Unfasten the right engine splash shield upper retaining clips, then pull down the shield.
10. Remove the upper alternator stud.
11. Remove the cotter pin and lower ball joint castle nut from the right lower ball joint, then separate the lower ball joint from the lower control arm.
12. Remove the metal halfshaft shield retaining screws, then remove the shield.
13. If equipped, detach the knock sensor electrical connector.
14. Disconnect the right halfshaft from the transaxle.
15. Remove the front exhaust pipe and converter assembly.
16. Unfasten the lower alternator mounting bolt.
17. Remove the alternator rear brace-to-alternator bolt. The bolt can best be accessed using a 4 ft. (1.2m) extension through the left side wheel well opening.
18. Remove the alternator rear brace nut from the engine. The nut can be best accessed through the right wheel well behind the alternator.
19. Remove the alternator from the mounting bracket.
20. Detach the electrical connector from the alternator.
21. Unfasten the battery wire nut from the alternator stud, then disconnect the battery positive lead from the alternator output terminal.
22. Remove the alternator from the vehicle.

To install:

23. Attach the alternator electrical connector and battery wire to the alternator. Tighten the mounting nut on the battery wire to 71 inch lbs. (8 Nm).

24. Position the alternator and loosely install the mounting bolts. If the replacement alternator does not fit into the bracket, remove the adhesive-backed shim from the rear of the alternator bracket.

25. Install the alternator rear brace, cooling duct bracket and mounting. Access the bolt through the left wheel opening using a 4 ft. (1.2m) extension.

26. Tighten the mounting bolts as follows:
  a. Rear brace bolt to 18 ft. lbs. (25 Nm)
  b. Rear brace nut to 37 ft. lbs. (50 Nm)
  c. Lower mounting bolt to 37 ft. lbs. (50 Nm)

27. Install the remaining components in the reverse of the removal procedure. Make sure all components are tightly secured.

28. Connect the negative battery cable.

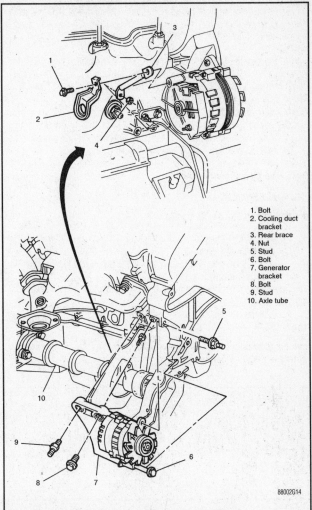

1. Bolt
2. Cooling duct bracket
3. Rear brace
4. Nut
5. Stud
6. Bolt
7. Generator bracket
8. Bolt
9. Stud
10. Axle tube

88002G14

Fig. 34 Alternator mounting—1993 3.4L engine shown

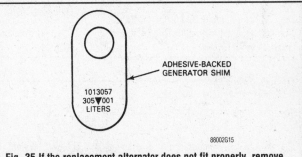

ADHESIVE-BACKED GENERATOR SHIM

1013057
305▼001
LITERS

88002G15

Fig. 35 If the replacement alternator does not fit properly, remove the shim from the rear of the bracket

MANUAL TRANSAXLE VEHICLES THROUGH 1994

♦ See Figures 34, 35 and 36

1. Remove the air cleaner assembly.
2. Disconnect the negative battery cable.
3. Remove the serpentine belt, as outlined in Section 1 of this manual.
4. Remove the coolant recovery reservoir.
5. Unfasten the upper alternator stud nut, and remove the power steering pipe retaining clip from the stud.
6. Raise and safely support the vehicle.
7. Remove the right front wheel and tire assembly.

8. Unfasten the right engine splash shield upper retaining clips and pull down the shield.

9. Remove the plastic outboard halfshaft shield retaining screws and the shield.

10. Unfasten the alternator rear brace-to-alternator bolt and nut.

11. Detach the electrical connector from the alternator.

12. Unfasten the battery wire nut from the alternator stud and disconnect the battery positive lead form the alternator output terminal.

13. Remove the cotter pin and lower ball joint castle nut from the right lower ball joint and separate the lower ball joint from the lower control arm.

14. Disconnect the right halfshaft from the transaxle.

15. Remove the metal outer drive axle shield.

16. Remove the rear engine mount bracket brace mounting bolts with the metal inner halfshaft shield attached.

17. Unfasten the alternator mounting stud and lower mounting bolt, then remove the alternator.

To install:

18. Position the alternator, then loosely install the mounting bolts. If the replacement alternator does not fit into the bracket, remove the adhesive-backed shim from the rear of the alternator bracket.

19. Tighten the lower mounting bolt to 37 ft. lbs. (50 Nm) and the mounting stud to 18 ft. lbs. (25 Nm).

20. Install the rear engine mount bracket brace retaining bolts and the inboard halfshaft shield.

21. Install the metal drive axle shield and retaining screws.

22. Attach the right halfshaft to the transaxle.

23. Connect the lower ball joint to the lower control arm and tighten the castle nut to 63 ft. lbs. (85 Nm).

24. Attach the alternator electrical connector and battery wire to the alternator. Tighten the mounting nut on the battery wire to 71 inch lbs. (8 Nm).

25. Install the alternator rear brace, cooling duct bracket and mounting nut and bolt. Tighten the rear brace bolt to 18 ft. lbs. (25 Nm) and the rear brace nut to 37 ft. lbs. (50 Nm).

26. Install the plastic outboard halfshaft shield.

27. Position the right engine splash shield and secure with the retaining clips.

28. Install the tire and wheel assembly, then carefully lower the vehicle.

29. Fasten the power steering pipe retaining clip and mounting nut.

30. Install the coolant recovery reservoir.

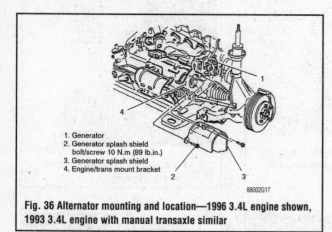

1. Generator
2. Generator splash shield bolt/screw 10 N.m (89 lb.in.)
3. Generator splash shield
4. Engine/trans mount bracket

88002G17

Fig. 36 Alternator mounting and location—1996 3.4L engine shown, 1993 3.4L engine with manual transaxle similar

31. Install the serpentine belt, as outlined in Section 1 this manual.

32. Connect the negative battery cable, then install the air cleaner assembly.

1995–96 VEHICLES

♦ **See Figure 36**

1. Remove the air cleaner and duct.

2. Disconnect the negative battery cable.

3. Remove the cross brace.

4. Remove the coolant recovery reservoir.

5. Remove the serpentine belt, as outlined in Section 1 of this manual.

6. Disconnect the power steering gear pipe from the clip mounting to the alternator upper stud.

7. Unfasten and remove the alternator upper stud and nut.

8. Raise and safely support the vehicle.

9. Remove the right tire and wheel.

10. Unfasten the right engine splash shield upper retaining clips, then pull down the shield.

11. Remove the front exhaust pipe and converter.

12. Detach the alternator splash shield fastened to the cowl.

13. Install a suitable jacking fixture to support the engine.

14. Unfasten the rear two cradle bolts.

15. Remove the intermediate shaft lower pinch bolt at the steering gear.

16. Unfasten the right front cradle bolt, then remove the right side tie rod.

17. Remove the alternator splash shield at the drive axle.

18. Detach the alternator electrical connectors.

19. Remove the alternator cooling duct and rear brace.

20. Unfasten the alternator rear brace nut at the engine, then remove the alternator from the vehicle.

To install:

21. Position the alternator in the vehicle, then install the lower bolt. Tighten the bolt to 37 ft. lbs. (50 Nm).

➥**The part should fit together easily. Tightening the bolts and nuts must NOT bind the alternator.**

22. Install the alternator rear brace, bolt and nut. Tighten the rear brace nut to 37 ft. lbs. (50 Nm) and the bolt to 18 ft. lbs. (25 Nm).

23. Connect the cooling duct.

24. Attach the electrical connectors to the alternator.

25. Attach the alternator splash shield at the drive axle.

26. Install the remaining components in the reverse of the removal procedure. Tighten the alternator upper stud and nut to 18 ft. lbs. (25 Nm).

27. Connect the negative battery cable, then install the air cleaner and duct assembly.

28. Bleed the power steering system, as outlined in Section 8 of this manual.

3.8L Engine

♦ **See Figures 37 and 38**

1. Disconnect the negative battery cable.

2. Remove the serpentine belt, as outlined in Section 1 of this manual.

3. Unfasten the alternator retaining bolts.

4. Detach the electrical connector from the alternator.

5. Unfasten the nut and the positive battery lead from the alternator output (BAT) terminal.

6. Remove the alternator from the vehicle.

7. If removing, unfasten the brace-to-engine bolt.

To install:

8. If removed, fasten the brace-to-engine bolt.

9. Position the alternator in the vehicle.

10. Attach the battery positive lead and nut to the alternator output terminal. Tighten the nut to 71 inch lbs. (8 Nm).

11. Attach the electrical connector to the alternator.

➥**Make sure that tightening the bolts does not bind the alternator.**

12. Install the alternator mounting bolts and tighten them to 20 ft. lbs. (27 Nm).

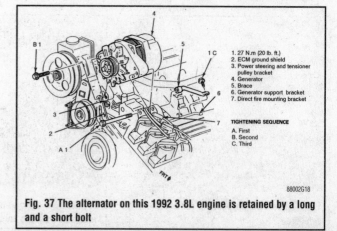

1. 27 N.m (20 lb. ft.)
2. ECM ground shield
3. Power steering and tensioner pulley bracket
4. Generator
5. Brace
6. Generator support bracket
7. Direct fire mounting bracket

TIGHTENING SEQUENCE

A. First
B. Second
C. Third

88002G18

Fig. 37 The alternator on this 1992 3.8L engine is retained by a long and a short bolt

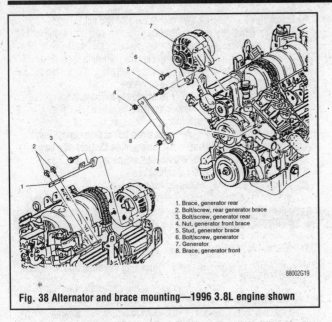

1. Brace, generator rear
2. Bolt/screw, rear generator brace
3. Bolt/screw, generator rear
4. Nut, generator front brace
5. Stud, generator brace
6. Bolt/screw, generator
7. Generator
8. Brace, generator front

88002G19

Fig. 38 Alternator and brace mounting—1996 3.8L engine shown

13. Install the serpentine belt, as outlined in Section 1 of this manual.
14. Connect the negative battery cable.

Regulator

REMOVAL & INSTALLATION

The alternators used in these vehicles have an internal regulator. The alternator is serviced as a complete unit and cannot be overhauled.

Battery

REMOVAL & INSTALLATION

♦ See Figures 39 thru 45

❊❊ CAUTION

Always make sure that the ignition is OFF when disconnecting or connecting the battery cables. Failure to do so may cause dam-

88002P04

Fig. 39 Unfasten the retaining bolts . . .

88002P05

Fig. 40 . . . then remove the cross brace

88002P06

Fig. 41 On vehicles with ABS, remove the relay center and bracket, then position them aside

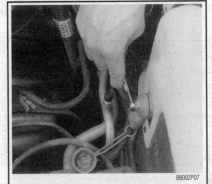

88002P07

Fig. 42 Unfasten the windshield washer reservoir retaining nuts

88002P08

Fig. 43 Use a suitable tool to remove the retainers . . .

88002P09

Fig. 44 . . . then remove the washer reservoir from the vehicle

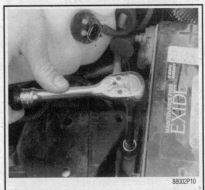

88002P10

Fig. 45 Unfasten any remaining retainers, then remove the battery from the vehicle

age to the computer control module or other electronic components.

1. Make sure the ignition is **OFF**. Remove the air cleaner assembly if necessary, and disconnect the negative battery cable, then the positive cable.
2. Unfasten the retaining bolts, then remove the cross brace.
3. If equipped with Anti-Lock Brakes (ABS), remove the relay center and bracket, then position aside.
4. If necessary, detach the electrical connector and hose from the windshield washer pump, then unfasten the reservoir retaining nut and remove the reservoir.
5. Remove the air cleaner bracket upper attachment bolt.
6. Unfasten the battery heat shield, hold-down bolt, and retainer.
7. Remove the battery from the battery tray.

To install:

8. Place the heat shield on the battery, then position the battery in the vehicle.
9. Install the retainer, air cleaner bracket and hold-down bolt. Tighten the hold-down bolt to 13 ft. lbs. (18 Nm).
10. Install the air cleaner bracket upper attachment bolt. Tighten the bolt to 35 inch lbs. (4 Nm).
11. Position the windshield washer reservoir and secure with the retainers. Attach the hose and electrical connector to the windshield washer pump.
12. If equipped with ABS, install the relay center bracket and relay center.
13. Position the cross brace, then secure with the retaining bolts. Tighten the front bolt to 18 ft. lbs. (25 Nm) and the rear bolt to 35 ft. lbs. (47 Nm).
14. Connect the positive battery cable, then the negative battery cable. Tighten the cable bolts to 11 ft. lbs. (15 Nm).
15. If removed, install the air cleaner assembly.

STARTING SYSTEM

Starter

TESTING

♦ **See Figure 46**

1. Make the connections as shown in the accompanying figure.
2. Close the switch and compare the RPM, current and voltage readings with the following values.
- 2.2L engine: No load test @ 10 volts—45–75 amps, RPM at drive pinion—6,000–11,000 rpm
- 2.3L engine: No load test @ 10 volts—52–76 amps, RPM at drive pinion—6,000–12,000 rpm
- 2.5L engine: No load test @ 10 volts—50–75 amps, RPM at drive pinion—6,000–11,900 rpm
- 2.8L engine: No load test @ 10 volts—50–75 amps, RPM at drive pinion—6,000–11,900 rpm
- 3.1L engine: No load test @ 10 volts—45–75 amps, RPM at drive pinion—6,000–11,000 rpm
- 1991–92 3.4L engine: No load test @ 10 volts—50–75 amps, RPM at drive pinion—7,000–11,000 rpm
- 1992–95 3.4L engine: No load test @ 10 volts—45–70 amps, RPM at drive pinion—6,500–11,000 rpm
- 1996 3.4L engine: No load test @ 10 volts—64–95 amps, RPM at drive pinion—2,825–3,275 rpm
- 3.8L engine: No load test @ 10 volts—45–75 amps, RPM at drive pinion—8,600–13,000 rpm

3. Rated current draw and no load speed indicates normal condition of the starter motor.
4. Low free speed and high current draw indicates:
- Too much friction. Tight, dirty, or worn bushings, bent armature shaft allowing armature to drag.
- Shorted armature. This can be further checked on a growler after disassembly.
- Grounded armature or fields. Check further after assembly.
5. Failure to operate with high current draw indicates:
- A direct ground in the terminal or fields.
- "Frozen" bearings.
6. Failure to operate with low or no current draw indicates:
- Open solenoid windings.
- Open field circuit. This can be checked after disassembly by inspecting internal connections and tracing the circuit with a test lamp.
- Open armature coils. Inspect the commutator for badly burned bar after disassembly.
- Broken brush springs, worn brushes, high insulation between the commutator bars of other causes which would prevent good contact between the brushes and commutator.
7. Low no-load speed and low current draw indicates:
- High internal resistance due to poor connections, defective leads, dirty commutator and causes listed under Step 6.
8. High free speed and high current drain usually indicate shorted fields. If shorted fields are suspected, replace the field and frame assembly. Also check for shorted armature using a growler.

REMOVAL & INSTALLATION

2.2L Engine

♦ **See Figure 47**

1. Disconnect the negative battery cable.
2. Raise and safely support the vehicle.
3. Unfasten the bolts from the flywheel inspection cover, then remove the cover.
4. Detach the starter electrical connector.
5. Remove the stud from the bracket.
6. Unfasten the starter motor retaining bolts, then remove the starter motor from the engine.
7. Remove the bracket from the starter.

To install:

8. Install the bracket on the starter and tighten the retaining nuts to 80 inch lbs. (9 Nm).

❊❊❊ WARNING

Before installing the starter in the vehicle, make sure the electrical terminals are secure by tightening the nut next to the cap on the solenoid battery terminal. If this terminal is not tight, starter damage may occur.

9. Secure the electrical terminal on the solenoid. Tighten the solenoid battery terminal inside nut to 84 inch lbs. (9.5 Nm).

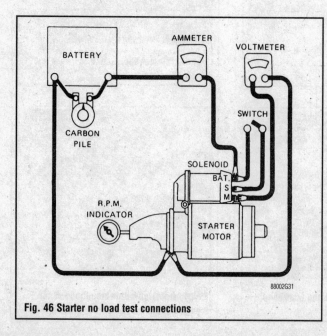

Fig. 46 Starter no load test connections

88002G31

10. Attach the electrical connections to the starter. Tighten the solenoid battery outside nut to 84 inch lbs. (9.5 Nm) and the solenoid "S" terminal outside nut to 22 inch lbs. (2.5 Nm).

11. Position the starter in the engine and install the retaining bolts. Tighten the bolts to 32 ft. lbs. (43 Nm).

12. Install the bracket to the engine. Tighten the retaining bolt to 26 ft. lbs. (32 Nm).

13. Install the flywheel inspection cover and tighten the retaining bolts to 89 inch lbs. (10 Nm).

14. Carefully lower the vehicle, then connect the negative battery cable.

2.3L Engine

▶ See Figure 48

1. Loosen the air inlet hose clamp at the throttle body.
2. Disconnect the negative battery cable.
3. Remove the air cleaner assembly.
4. Detach and plug the coolant reservoir hose at the radiator filler neck.
5. Remove the coolant recovery reservoir.
6. Unfasten the intake manifold brace bolts.
7. Place a suitable drain pan under the oil filter, then remove the filter.
8. Unfasten the starter retaining bolts, lower the starter onto the frame member, detach the starter electrical connectors, then remove the starter from the vehicle.

To install:

9. Position the starter into the vehicle, attach the electrical connectors, then tighten the retaining bolts to 32 ft. lbs. (43 Nm).
10. Install a new oil filter and add engine oil, as needed.
11. Install the intake manifold brace, coolant reservoir and hoses.
12. Add coolant, if needed.
13. Install the air cleaner assembly and connect the air inlet hose at the throttle body.
14. Connect the negative battery cable, then check the oil level and add if necessary.

2.5L Engine

▶ See Figure 49

1. Disconnect the negative battery cable.
2. Raise and safely support the vehicle.
3. Unfasten the flywheel inspection cover bolts, then remove the cover.
4. Remove the stud from the starter support bracket.
5. Unfasten the starter mounting bolts and shim(s), if used.
6. Remove the starter motor. Be careful not to damage the starter wires by letting the starter hang.

7. While holding the starter motor, detach the electrical connectors from the starter solenoid.
8. Remove the bracket from the starter.

To install:

9. Install the bracket to the starter.
10. Attach the starter electrical connectors.
11. Install the starter adjustment shims, if used.
12. Position the starter to the engine mounting flange, then tighten the retaining bolts to 32 ft. lbs. (43 Nm).
13. Install the bracket to the engine, then tighten the stud to 18 ft. lbs. (25 Nm).
14. Install the inspection cover and secure with the retaining bolts. Tighten the bolts to 89 inch lbs. (10 Nm).
15. Carefully lower the vehicle, then connect the negative battery cable.

2.8L and 3.1L Engines

1988–94 VEHICLES

▶ See Figures 50, 51, 52 and 53

1. Remove the air cleaner and duct assembly.
2. Disconnect the negative battery cable.
3. Raise and safely support the vehicle.
4. If equipped with an engine oil cooler, drain the engine oil, remove the oil filter and position the hose next to the starter motor to the side.
5. Remove the nut from the brace at the air conditioning compressor, nut from the brace at the engine and the brace.
6. Unfasten the retaining bolts, then remove the flywheel inspection cover.
7. Remove the starter bolts and shims, if equipped. Do not let the starter hang from the starter wires.
8. Detach the starter wires from the solenoid, then remove the starter from the vehicle.

To install:

9. While supporting the starter, connect the starter wires at the solenoid.
10. Install the starter motor-to-engine mount with the shims, if equipped, and the mounting bolts. Tighten the bolts to 32 ft. lbs. (43 Nm).
11. If equipped with an engine oil cooler, reposition the hose next to the starter motor, install the oil filter and refill the engine with the proper amount of engine oil.
12. Install the flywheel inspection cover and tighten the bolts.
13. Install the starter support brace to the air conditioning compressor and tighten the nut to 23 ft. lbs. (31 Nm).
14. Carefully lower the vehicle, then connect the negative battery cable.
15. Install the air cleaner and duct assembly.

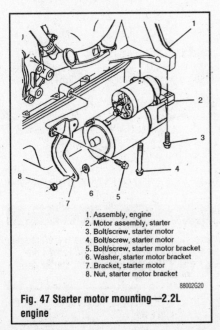

1. Assembly, engine
2. Motor assembly, starter
3. Bolt/screw, starter motor
4. Bolt/screw, starter motor
5. Bolt/screw, starter motor bracket
6. Washer, starter motor bracket
7. Bracket, starter motor
8. Nut, starter motor bracket

88002G20

Fig. 47 Starter motor mounting—2.2L engine

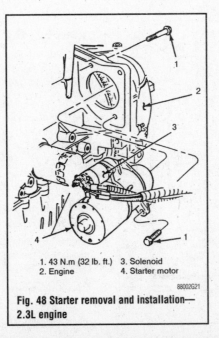

1. 43 N.m (32 lb. ft.)   3. Solenoid
2. Engine   4. Starter motor

88002G21

Fig. 48 Starter removal and installation—2.3L engine

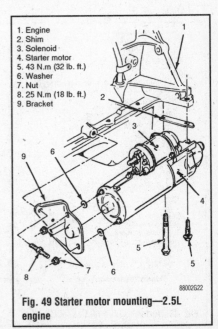

1. Engine
2. Shim
3. Solenoid
4. Starter motor
5. 43 N.m (32 lb. ft.)
6. Washer
7. Nut
8. 25 N.m (18 lb. ft.)
9. Bracket

88002G22

Fig. 49 Starter motor mounting—2.5L engine

Fig. 50 Unfasten the retaining bolts . . .

Fig. 51 . . . then remove the flywheel cover

Fig. 52 An extension may be needed to access the starter mounting bolts

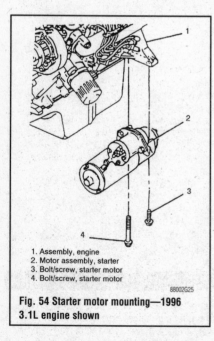

Fig. 53 Remove the starter motor and any shims that may have been used

1995–96 VEHICLES

▶ See Figure 54

1. Remove the air cleaner and duct assembly.
2. Disconnect the negative battery cable.
3. Raise and safely support the vehicle.
4. Remove the oil filter splash shield.
5. Detach the starter electrical connector(s).
6. Unfasten the starter mounting bolts, remove any shims, then remove the starter from the vehicle.

To install:

7. Position the starter to the engine. Install the mounting bolts and shims (if equipped). Tighten the bolts to 32 ft. lbs. (43 Nm).
8. Attach the electrical connector(s) to the starter. Tighten the starter solenoid switch BAT terminal outer nut to 84 inch lbs. (9.5 Nm) and the starter solenoid switch "S" terminal nut to 22 inch lbs. (2.5 Nm).
9. Install the oil filter splash shield.
10. Carefully lower the vehicle, then connect the negative battery cable.
11. Install the air cleaner and duct assembly.

3.4L Engine

▶ See Figures 55 and 56

1. Disconnect the negative battery cable.
2. Remove the engine oil cooler assembly. For details, please refer to the procedure located in Section 3 of this manual.

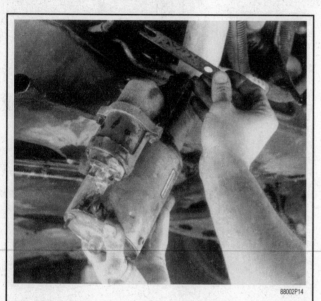

1. Assembly, engine
2. Motor assembly, starter
3. Bolt/screw, starter motor
4. Bolt/screw, starter motor

Fig. 54 Starter motor mounting—1996 3.1L engine shown

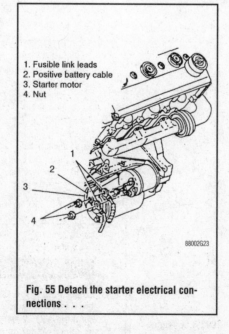

1. Fusible link leads
2. Positive battery cable
3. Starter motor
4. Nut

Fig. 55 Detach the starter electrical connections . . .

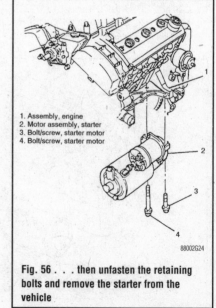

1. Assembly, engine
2. Motor assembly, starter
3. Bolt/screw, starter motor
4. Bolt/screw, starter motor

Fig. 56 . . . then unfasten the retaining bolts and remove the starter from the vehicle

3. If equipped with an automatic transaxle, unfasten the flywheel inspection cover bolts, then remove the cover.

4. Detach the electrical connections from the starter.

5. Unfasten the starter motor retaining bolts, then remove the starter.

To install:

✳✳ WARNING

Before installing the starter to the engine, make sure the electrical terminals are secure by tightening the nut next to the cap on the solenoid battery terminal. If this terminal is not tight, starter damage may occur.

6. Secure the electrical terminal on the solenoid. Tighten the solenoid battery terminal inside nut to 84 inch lbs. (9.5 Nm).

7. Attach the electrical connectors to the starter. Tighten the solenoid battery terminal outside nut to 9.5–12 ft. lbs. (13–16 Nm). Tighten the "S" terminal nut to 22–27 inch lbs. (22–27 Nm).

8. Position the starter motor, then install the retaining bolts. Tighten the bolts to 32 ft. lbs. (43 Nm).

9. If equipped, install the flywheel inspection cover and tighten the retaining bolts to 89 inch lbs. (10 Nm).

10. Install the engine oil cooler assembly, as outlined in Section 3 of this manual.

11. Connect the negative battery cable.

3.8L Engine

1991–92 VEHICLES

▶ See Figure 57

1. Disconnect the negative battery cable.

2. Remove the right side cooling fan.

3. Remove the serpentine drive belt, as outlined in Section 1 of this manual.

4. Disconnect the A/C compressor upper support brace, then lay the compressor in the fan opening.

5. Raise and safely support the vehicle.

6. Detach the engine oil cooler lines at the flex connector.

7. Unfasten the retaining bolts, then remove the flywheel inspection cover.

8. Remove the starter motor retaining bolts, carefully lower the starter and remove the shims, if used.

9. Detach the starter motor wiring, then remove the starter from the vehicle.

To install:

10. Attach the electrical connectors to the starter terminals. Tighten the battery terminal nut to 80 inch lbs. (9 Nm) for 1991 vehicles and to 12 ft. lbs. (16 Nm) for 1992 vehicles. Tighten the "S" terminal nut to 27–35 inch lbs. (3–4 Nm).

11. Position the starter motor and shims, if used, to the engine and tighten the mounting bolts to 32 ft. lbs. (43 Nm).

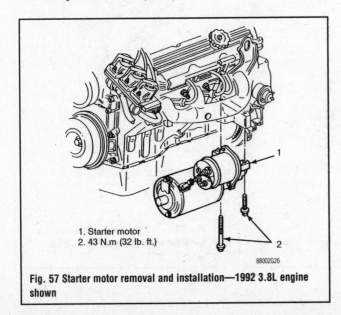

1. Starter motor
2. 43 N.m (32 lb. ft.)

88002G26

Fig. 57 Starter motor removal and installation—1992 3.8L engine shown

12. Install the flywheel inspection cover. Tighten the retaining bolts to 89 inch lbs. (10 Nm).

13. Attach the engine oil cooler lines at the flex connector.

14. Carefully lower the vehicle and position the A/C compressor.

15. Install the A/C compressor upper support brace.

16. Install the serpentine drive belt, as outlined in Section 1 of this manual.

17. Install the right side cooling fan.

18. Connect the negative battery cable.

1993 VEHICLES

1. Disconnect the negative battery cable.

2. Remove the left side cooling fan.

3. Raise and safely support the vehicle.

4. Detach the engine oil level sensor and knock sensor electrical connectors.

5. Disconnect the engine oil cooler pipe from the pipe clip.

6. Unfasten the retaining bolts, then remove the flywheel inspection cover.

7. Remove the starter mounting bolts, then detach the electrical connections from the starter.

8. Carefully lower the vehicle, then remove the starter motor from the engine.

To install:

9. Position the starter motor to the engine, then raise and safely support the vehicle.

✳✳ WARNING

Before bolting the starter to the engine, make sure the electrical terminals are secure by tightening the nut next to the cap on the solenoid battery terminal. If this terminal is not tight, the cap may be damaged during installation and starter failure may result.

10. Secure the electrical terminals on the solenoid. Tighten the battery terminal inside nut to 12 ft. lbs. (16 Nm) and the "S" terminal inside nut to 22 inch lbs. (2.5 Nm).

11. Attach the starter electrical connections. Tighten the battery terminal outside nut to 12 ft. lbs. and the "S" terminal nut to 22 inch lbs. (2.5 Nm).

12. Install the starter mounting bolts and tighten to 32 ft. lbs. (43 Nm).

13. Install the flywheel inspection cover and secure with the retaining bolts. Tighten the bolts to 89 inch lbs. (10 Nm).

14. Connect the engine oil cooler pipe to the pipe clip.

15. Attach the engine oil level sensor and knock sensor electrical connectors.

16. Carefully lower the vehicle.

17. Install the left side cooling fan.

18. Connect the negative battery cable, then check the engine oil level and add if necessary.

1994 VEHICLES

1. Disconnect the negative battery cable.

2. Remove the coolant recovery reservoir.

3. Remove the ECM cover.

4. Remove the serpentine belt, as outlined in Section 1 of this manual.

5. Remove the right side cooling fan.

6. Unfasten the A/C compressor heat shield and screw. Detach the compressor electrical connectors. Remove the A/C compressor bracket brace, nut and bolt.

7. Remove the A/C compressor bolts and move the compressor aside.

8. Raise and safely support the vehicle.

9. Disconnect the engine wiring harness clamps at the lower front of the frame.

10. Unfasten the flywheel inspection cover screws, then remove the cover.

11. Detach the oil level sensor electrical connector.

12. Unfasten the starter motor bolts, pull the starter down, detach the electrical connections, then remove the starter from the vehicle.

To install:

✳✳ WARNING

Before bolting the starter to the engine, make sure the electrical terminals are secure by tightening the nut next to the cap on the solenoid battery terminal. If this terminal is not tight, the cap may be damaged during installation and starter failure may result.

13. Secure the electrical terminals on the solenoid. Tighten the battery terminal inside nut to 12 ft. lbs. (16 Nm) and the "S" terminal inside nut to 22 inch lbs. (2.5 Nm).

14. Attach the starter electrical connections. Tighten the battery terminal outside nut to 12 ft. lbs. and the "S" terminal nut to 22 inch lbs. (2.5 Nm).

15. Install the starter motor, then secure using the retaining bolts. Tighten the bolts to 32 ft. lbs. (43 Nm).

16. Attach the oil level sensor electrical connector.

17. Install the flywheel cover and secure with the retaining screws. Tighten the screws to 89 inch lbs. (10 Nm).

18. Connect the engine wiring harness clamps to the lower front of the frame.

19. Carefully lower the vehicle.

20. Install the A/C compressor and secure with the retaining bolts. Tighten the front bolts to 39 ft. lbs. (53 Nm) and the rear bolts to 23 ft. lbs. (31 Nm).

21. Install the A/C compressor bracket brace, bolt and nut. Tighten the bolt to 19 ft. lbs. (26 Nm) and the nut to 24 ft. lbs. (33 Nm). Attach the A/C compressor electrical connectors, then install the compressor heat shield and screw.

22. Install the right side engine cooling fan.

23. Install the serpentine drive belt.

24. Fasten the ECM cover.

25. Install the coolant recovery reservoir.

26. Connect the negative battery cable, then check the engine oil level and adjust as necessary.

1995–96 VEHICLES

▶ **See Figure 58**

1. Disconnect the negative battery cable.
2. Remove the upper mounting bracket above the radiator.
3. Detach the electrical connections at the coolant fan, then remove the fan.
4. Disconnect the upper and lower oil cooler pipes from the radiator.
5. Raise and safely support the vehicle.
6. Unfasten the retainers from the engine harness and position them away from the starter.
7. Disconnect both lower oil cooler hoses from the radiator.
8. Detach the starter electrical connections.
9. Remove the upper flywheel inspection cover.
10. Unfasten the mounting bolts/screws, then remove the starter and shims (if used) from the engine.

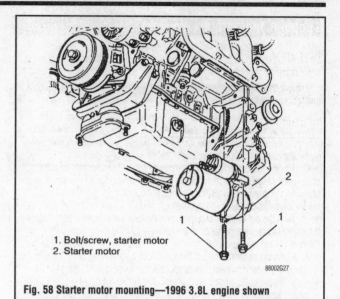

1. Bolt/screw, starter motor
2. Starter motor

88002G27

Fig. 58 Starter motor mounting—1996 3.8L engine shown

To install:

11. Position the starter and shims (if used) to the engine, then secure with the mounting bolts/screws. Tighten to 32 ft. lbs. (43 Nm).

12. Attach the electrical connections to the starter. Tighten the solenoid battery terminal outside nut to 12 ft. lbs. (16 Nm). and the solenoid "S" terminal inside nut to 22 inch lbs. (2.5 Nm).

13. Position the upper inspection cover, then secure with the retainers to 89 inch lbs. (10 Nm).

14. Attach both lower oil cooler hoses to the radiator.

15. Fasten the engine wire harness and retainers.

16. Carefully lower the vehicle.

17. Attach the oil cooler pipes to the radiator.

18. Install the coolant fan and attach the electrical connectors.

19. Install the upper engine mounting bracket and tighten the bolt/screws to 32 ft. lbs. (43 Nm).

20. Connect the negative battery cable, then check the engine oil level and add as necessary.

SENDING UNITS AND SENSORS

The sensors covered in this section are not related to engine control. They are for gauges and warning lights only. For sensors related to engine control refer to Electronic Engine Controls in Section 4.

Low Coolant Sensor

OPERATION

The low coolant sensor activates a light in the instrument cluster when the coolant in the radiator goes below a certain level. The sensor is mounted on the radiator's right side tank.

REMOVAL & INSTALLATION

▶ **See Figure 59**

1. Disconnect the negative battery cable.
2. Partially drain the radiator, into a suitable container, to a level below the sensor.
3. Detach the electrical connector from the sensor.
4. Remove the sensor. To unlock the sensor, lift one leg of the snap clip from its locked position and pull outward with a slight twisting motion. Remove and discard the O-ring.

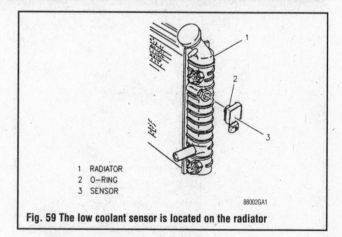

1 RADIATOR
2 O–RING
3 SENSOR

88002GA1

Fig. 59 The low coolant sensor is located on the radiator

To install:

5. Lubricate a new O-ring seal with clean coolant.
6. Place the snap clip leg in the place.
7. Install the sensor. Attach the electrical connector to the sensor.
8. Fill the radiator to the proper level with coolant.
9. Connect the negative battery cable.

Coolant Temperature Sensor

OPERATION

The coolant temperature sensor changes resistance as the coolant temperature increases and decreases.

TESTING

1. Remove the temperature sender from the engine.
2. Position the water temperature sending unit in such a way that the metal shaft (opposite end from the electrical connectors) is situated in a pot of water. Make sure that the electrical connector is not submerged and that only the tip of the sending unit's body is in the water.
3. Heat the pot of water at a medium rate. While the water is warming, continue to measure the resistance of the terminal and the metal body of the sending unit:

   a. As the water warms up, the resistance exhibited by the ohmmeter goes down in a steady manner: the sending unit is good.

   b. As the water warms up, the resistance does not change or changes in erratic jumps: the sender is bad, replace it with a new one.
4. Install the good or new sending unit into the engine, then connect the negative battery cable.

REMOVAL & INSTALLATION

▶ **See Figure 60**

1. Disconnect the negative battery cable.
2. Properly drain the engine coolant into a suitable container.
3. Disconnect the sensor electrical lead and unscrew the sensor. The coolant sensor can be found on the front, left side of the engine block, visible through, or below, the manifold, or threaded into the thermostat housing or water outlet.

To install:

4. Install the sensor and tighten it to 17 ft. lbs. (23 Nm).
5. Connect the sensor electrical lead.
6. Connect the battery cable and fill the engine with the proper type and amount of coolant.

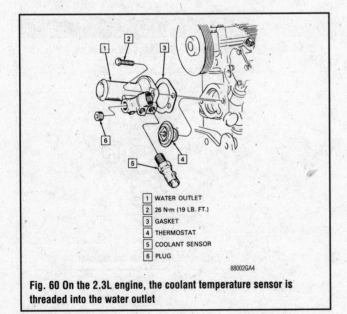

1	WATER OUTLET
2	26 N·m (19 LB. FT.)
3	GASKET
4	THERMOSTAT
5	COOLANT SENSOR
6	PLUG

88002GA4

Fig. 60 On the 2.3L engine, the coolant temperature sensor is threaded into the water outlet

Oil Level Sensor

OPERATION

The low oil level sensor activates a light in the instrument cluster when the oil level in the pan goes below a certain level. The sensor is mounted on the oil pan.

REMOVAL & INSTALLATION

▶ **See Figures 61 and 62**

1. Disconnect the negative battery cable.
2. Raise and safely support the vehicle.
3. Detach the sensor connector harness.
4. Drain the engine oil into a suitable container.
5. Remove the oil level sensor.

To install:

6. Install the oil level sensor and tighten it to 89 inch lbs. (10 Nm).
7. Attach the sensor harness connector, then carefully lower the vehicle.
8. Add the correct type and amount of engine oil to the crankcase, then connect the negative battery cable.

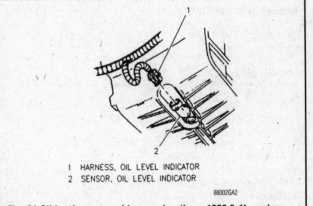

1 HARNESS, OIL LEVEL INDICATOR
2 SENSOR, OIL LEVEL INDICATOR

88002GA2

Fig. 61 Oil level sensor and harness location—1996 3.1L engine shown

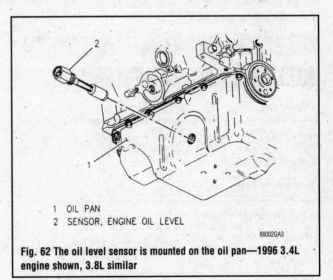

1 OIL PAN
2 SENSOR, ENGINE OIL LEVEL

88002GA3

Fig. 62 The oil level sensor is mounted on the oil pan—1996 3.4L engine shown, 3.8L similar

Oil Pressure Sender

OPERATION

The oil pressure sender relays to the dash gauge the oil pressure in the engine.

TESTING

1. To test the normally closed oil lamp circuit, disengage the locking connector and measure the resistance between the switch terminal (terminal for the wire to the warning lamp) and the metal housing. The ohmmeter should read 0 ohms.
2. To test the sending unit, measure the resistance between the sending unit terminal and the metal housing. The ohmmeter should read an open circuit (infinite resistance).
3. Start the engine.
4. Once again, test each terminal against the metal housing:
   a. The oil switch terminal-to-housing circuit should read an open circuit if there is oil pressure present.
   b. The sending unit-to-housing circuit should read between 15–80 ohms, depending on the engine speed, oil temperature and oil viscosity.
5. To test the oil pressure sender only, rev the engine and watch the ohms reading, which should fluctuate slightly (within the range of 15–80 ohms) as rpm increases.
6. If the above results were not obtained, replace the sending unit/switch with a new one.

REMOVAL & INSTALLATION

▶ **See Figures 63, 64 and 65**

1. Remove the air cleaner assembly.
2. Disconnect the negative battery cable.
3. Raise and safely support the vehicle.
4. If the vehicle is equipped with a gauge package (large sensor assembly) and does not have and oil cooler, drain the engine oil, then remove the oil filter.
5. Detach the sensor electrical connector.
6. Remove the sensor.
To install:
7. Coat the first two or three threads with sealer. Install the sensor and tighten until snug. Engage the electrical lead.
8. If removed, install the oil filter, then carefully lower the vehicle.
9. Connect the negative battery cable and fill the engine with oil.

Fan Switch

OPERATION

The fan circuit contains the auxiliary fan, coolant temperature sensor and a relay. When the sensor reaches a predetermined temperature, it closes the circuit to the relay. This energizes the relay sending 12 volts to the fan. When the temperature decreases below the set point of the sensor, the circuit opens and the voltage is no longer applied to the fan.

REMOVAL & INSTALLATION

1. Disconnect the negative battery cable.
2. Disconnect the sensor electrical lead and unscrew the sensor.
To install:
3. Install the sensor or relay and connect the electrical lead.
4. Connect the battery cable.

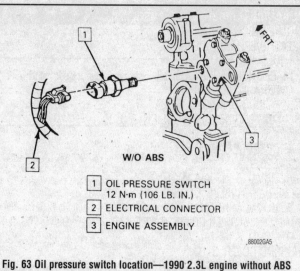

W/O ABS

1	OIL PRESSURE SWITCH 12 N·m (106 LB. IN.)
2	ELECTRICAL CONNECTOR
3	ENGINE ASSEMBLY

88002GA5

Fig. 63 Oil pressure switch location—1990 2.3L engine without ABS shown

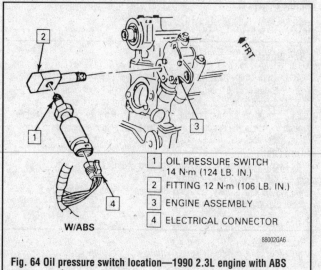

1	OIL PRESSURE SWITCH 14 N·m (124 LB. IN.)
2	FITTING 12 N·m (106 LB. IN.)
3	ENGINE ASSEMBLY
4	ELECTRICAL CONNECTOR

W/ABS

88002GA6

Fig. 64 Oil pressure switch location—1990 2.3L engine with ABS shown

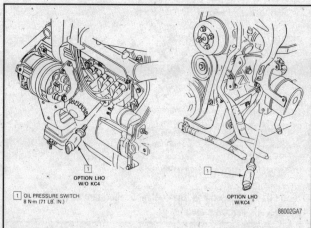

OPTION LHO W/O KC4

| 1 | OIL PRESSURE SWITCH 8 N·m (71 LB. IN.) |

OPTION LHO W/KC4

88002GA7

Fig. 65 Oil pressure switch location—1990 3.1L engine shown

3

ENGINE AND ENGINE OVERHAUL

ENGINE MECHANICAL

Engine Overhaul Tips

Most engine overhaul procedures are fairly standard. In addition to specific parts replacement procedures and specifications for your individual engine, this section is also a guide to acceptable rebuilding procedures. Examples of standard rebuilding practice are given and should be used along with specific details concerning your particular engine.

Competent and accurate machine shop services will ensure maximum performance, reliability and engine life. In most instances it is more profitable for the do-it-yourself mechanic to remove, clean and inspect the component, buy the necessary parts and deliver these to a shop for actual machine work.

On the other hand, much of the rebuilding work (crankshaft, block, bearings, piston rods, and other components) is well within the scope of the do-it-yourself mechanic's tools and abilities. You will have to decide for yourself the depth of involvement you desire in an engine repair or rebuild.

TOOLS

The tools required for an engine overhaul or parts replacement will depend on the depth of your involvement. With a few exceptions, they will be the tools found in a mechanic's tool kit (see Section 1 of this manual). More in-depth work will require some or all of the following:

- A dial indicator (reading in thousandths) mounted on a universal base
- Micrometers and telescope gauges
- Jaw and screw-type pullers
- Scraper
- Valve spring compressor
- Ring groove cleaner
- Piston ring expander and compressor
- Ridge reamer
- Cylinder hone or glaze breaker
- Plastigage®
- Engine stand

The use of most of these tools is illustrated in this chapter. Many can be rented for a one-time use from a local parts jobber or tool supply house specializing in automotive work.

Occasionally, the use of special tools is called for. See the information on Special Tools and the Safety Notice in the front of this book before substituting another tool.

INSPECTION TECHNIQUES

Procedures and specifications are given in this chapter for inspecting, cleaning and assessing the wear limits of most major components. Other procedures such as Magnaflux® and Zyglo® can be used to locate material flaws and stress cracks. Magnaflux® is a magnetic process applicable only to ferrous materials. The Zyglo® process coats the material with a fluorescent dye penetrant and can be used on any material.

Checking for suspected surface cracks can be more readily made using spot check dye. The dye is sprayed onto the suspected area, wiped off and the area sprayed with a developer. Cracks will show up brightly.

OVERHAUL TIPS

Aluminum has become extremely popular for use in engines, due to its low weight. Observe the following precautions when handling aluminum parts:

- Never hot tank aluminum parts (the caustic hot tank solution will eat the aluminum.
- Remove all aluminum parts (identification tag, etc.) from engine parts prior to the tanking.
- Always coat threads lightly with engine oil or anti-seize compounds before installation, to prevent seizure.
- Never overtorque bolts or spark plugs especially in aluminum threads.

Stripped threads in any component can be repaired using any of several commercial repair kits (Heli-Coil®, Microdot®, Keenserts®, etc.).

When assembling the engine, any parts that will be exposed to frictional contact must be prelubed to provide lubrication at initial start-up. Any product specifically formulated for this purpose can be used, but engine oil is not recommended as a prelube in most cases.

When semi-permanent (locked, but removable) installation of bolts or nuts is desired, threads should be cleaned and coated with Loctite® or another similar, commercial non-hardening sealant.

REPAIRING DAMAGED THREADS

▶ **See Figures 1, 2, 3, 4 and 5**

Several methods of repairing damaged threads are available. Heli-Coil® (shown here), Keenserts® and Microdot® are among the most widely used. All involve basically the same principle—drilling out stripped threads, tapping the hole and installing a prewound insert—making welding, plugging and oversize fasteners unnecessary.

Two types of thread repair inserts are usually supplied: a standard type for most inch coarse, inch fine, metric course and metric fine thread sizes and a spark lug type to fit most spark plug port sizes. Consult the individual tool manufacturer's catalog to determine exact applications. Typical thread repair kits will contain a selection of prewound threaded inserts, a tap (corresponding to the outside diameter threads of the insert) and an installation tool. Spark plug inserts usually differ because they require a tap equipped with pilot threads and a combined reamer/tap section. Most manufacturers also supply blister-packed thread repair inserts separately in addition to a master kit containing a variety of taps and inserts plus installation tools.

Before attempting to repair a threaded hole, remove any snapped, broken or damaged bolts or studs. Penetrating oil can be used to free frozen threads. The offending item can usually be removed with locking pliers or using a screw/stud

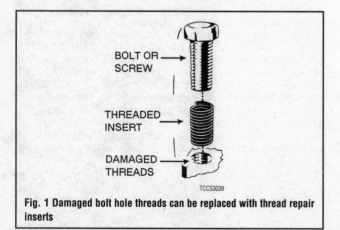

Fig. 1 Damaged bolt hole threads can be replaced with thread repair inserts

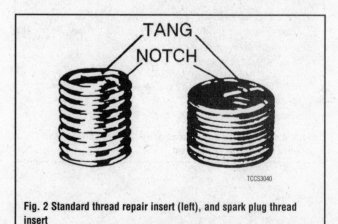

Fig. 2 Standard thread repair insert (left), and spark plug thread insert

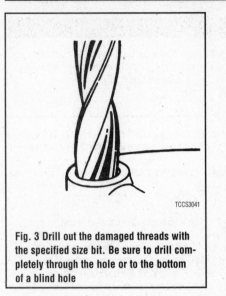

TCCS3041

Fig. 3 Drill out the damaged threads with the specified size bit. Be sure to drill completely through the hole or to the bottom of a blind hole

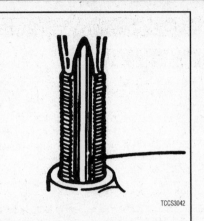

TCCS3042

Fig. 4 Using the kit, tap the hole in order to receive the thread insert. Keep the tap well oiled and back it out frequently to avoid clogging the threads.

TCCS3043

Fig. 5 Screw the insert onto the installer tool until the tang engages the slot. Thread the insert into the hole until it is ¼–½ turn below the top surface, then remove the tool and break off the tang using a punch.

extractor. After the hole is clear, the thread can be repaired, as shown in the series of accompanying illustrations and in the kit manufacturer's instructions.

Checking Engine Compression

▶ See Figure 6

A noticeable lack of engine power, excessive oil consumption and/or poor fuel mileage measured over an extended period are all indicators of internal engine wear. Worn piston rings, scored or worn cylinder bores, blown head gaskets, sticking or burnt valves and worn valve seats are all possible culprits here. A check of each cylinder's compression will help you locate the problems.

As mentioned in the Tools and Equipment section of Section 1, a screw-in type compression gauge is more accurate that the type you simply hold against the spark plug hole, although it takes slightly longer to use. It's worth it to obtain a more accurate reading. Follow the procedures given:

1. Warm up the engine to normal operating temperature.
2. Tag the spark plug wires and remove all the spark plugs.
3. Disable the fuel and ignition systems.
4. Remove the air cleaner assembly and fully open the throttle plates by operating the throttle linkage by hand or by having an assistant floor the accelerator pedal.

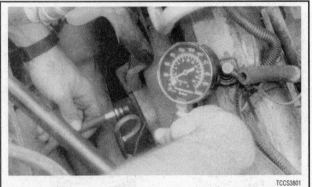

TCCS3801

Fig. 6 A screw-in type compression gauge is more accurate and easier to use without an assistant

5. Coat the gauge threads with oil and screw the compression gauge into the no. 1 spark plug hole until the fitting is snug.

❋❋ WARNING

Be careful not to crossthread the plug hole. On aluminum cylinder heads use extra care, as the threads in these heads are easily ruined.

6. Ask an assistant to depress the accelerator pedal fully. Then, while you read the compression gauge, ask the assistant to crank the engine two or three times in short bursts using the ignition switch. There should be four puffs per cylinder.
7. Read the compression gauge at the end of each series of cranks, and record the highest of these readings. Repeat this procedure for each of the engine's cylinders. Compare the highest reading of each cylinder to the compression pressure specification. The lowest cylinder reading should not be less than 70% of the highest reading. Examples follow:

   a. NORMAL: Compression builds up quickly and evenly to the specified compression on each cylinder.

   b. PISTON RINGS: Compression low on the first stroke, tends to build up on the following strokes, but does not reach normal. This reading should be tested with the addition of a few shots of engine oil into the cylinder. If the compression increases considerably, the rings are leaking compression.

   c. VALVES: Low on the first stroke, does not tend to build up on following strokes. This reading will stay around the same with a few shots of engine oil.

   d. HEAD GASKET: The compression reading is low between two adjacent cylinders. the head gasket between the two cylinders may be blown. If there is the sign of white smoke coming from the exhaust while the engine is running may indicate water leaking into the cylinder.

8. If a cylinder is unusually low, shoot about a tablespoon of clean engine oil into the cylinder through the spark plug hole and repeat the compression test. If the compression comes up after adding the oil, it appears that the cylinder's piston rings or bore are damaged or worn. If the pressure remains low, the valves may not be seating properly (a valve job is needed), or the head gasket may be blown near that cylinder. If compression in any two adjacent cylinders is low, and if the addition of oil does not help the compression, there is leakage past the head gasket. Oil and coolant water in the combustion chamber can result from this problem. There may be evidence of water droplets on the engine dipstick when a head gasket has blown.

VALVE SPECIFICATIONS

Year	Engine ID/VIN	Engine Displacement Liters (cc)	Seat Angle (deg.)	Face Angle (deg.)	Spring Test Pressure (lbs. @ In.)	Spring Installed Height (in.)	Stem-to-Guide Clearance (in.) Intake	Stem-to-Guide Clearance (in.) Exhaust	Stem Diameter (in.) Intake	Stem Diameter (in.) Exhaust
1988	W	2.8 (2837)	46	45	90@1.701	1.5748	0.0010-0.0027	0.0010-0.0027	0.3410-0.3416	0.3410-0.3416
1989	T	3.1 (3135)	46	45	215@1.291	1.5748	0.0010-0.0027	0.0010-0.0027	0.3416	0.3416
	V	3.1 (3135)	46	45	90@1.701	1.5748	0.0010-0.0027	0.0010-0.0027	NA	NA
	W	2.8 (2837)	46	45	90@1.701	1.5748	0.0010-0.0027	0.0010-0.0027	0.3410-0.3416	0.3410-0.3416
1990	A	2.3 (2260)	45	①	193-207@1.043	NA	0.0010-0.0027	0.0015-0.0032	0.2751-0.2745	0.2740-0.2747
	D	2.3 (2260)	45	①	193-207@1.043	NA	0.0010-0.0027	0.0015-0.0032	0.2751-0.2745	0.2740-0.2747
	R	2.5 (2471)	46	45	75@1.68	1.68	0.0010-0.0027	0.0010-0.0027	0.3418-0.3425	0.3418-0.3425
	T	3.1 (3135)	46	45	90@1.701	1.5748	0.0010-0.0027	0.0010-0.0027	NA	NA
	V	3.1 (3135)	46	45	90@1.701	1.5748	0.0010-0.0027	0.0010-0.0027	NA	NA
1991	D	2.3 (2260)	45	①	193-207@1.043	NA	0.0010-0.0027	0.0015-0.0032	0.2751-0.2745	0.2740-0.2747
	L	3.8 (3791)	45	45	210@1.315	1.69-1.72	0.0015-0.0035	0.0015-0.0032	NA	NA
	R	2.5 (2471)	46	45	75@1.68	1.68	0.0010-0.0028	0.0010-0.0041	NA	NA
	T	3.1 (3135)	46	45	90@1.701	1.5748	0.0010-0.0027	0.0010-0.0027	NA	NA
	X	3.4 (3350)	46	45	75@1.40	NA	0.0011-0.0026	0.0014-0.0031	NA	NA
1992	L	3.8 (3791)	45	45	210@1.315	1.690-1.720	0.0015-0.0035	0.0015-0.0032	NA	NA
	R	2.5 (2471)	46	45	75@1.68	1.68	0.0010-0.0028	0.0010-0.0041	NA	NA
	T	3.1 (3135)	46	45	90@1.701	1.5748	0.0010-0.0027	0.0010-0.0027	NA	NA
	X	3.4 (3350)	46	45	75@1.40	NA	0.0011-0.0026	0.0014-0.0031	NA	NA

⑥ High Output (H.O.)

88003C02

GENERAL ENGINE SPECIFICATIONS

Year	Engine ID/VIN	Engine Displacement Liters (cc)	Fuel System Type	Net Horsepower @ rpm	Net Torque @ rpm (ft. lbs.)	Bore x Stroke (in.)	Compression Ratio	Oil Pressure @ rpm
1988	W	2.8 (2837)	MFI	125@4500	160@3600	3.50x2.99	8.9:1	15@1100
1989	T	3.1 (3135)	MFI ①	140@4500	185@3200	3.50x3.31	8.8:1	15@1100
	V	3.1 (3135)	MFI	205@4800	220@3200	3.50x2.99	8.75:1	15@1100
	W	2.8 (2837)	MFI ①	130@4500	170@3600	3.50x2.99	8.9:1	15@1100
1990	A ③	2.3 (2260)	MFI	180@6200	160@5200	3.62x3.35	10.0:1	30@2000
	D	2.3 (2260)	MFI	160@6200	155@5200	3.62x3.35	9.5:1	30@2000
	R	2.5 (2471)	TFI	105@4800	135@3200	3.50x3.31	8.3:1	26@800
	T	3.1 (3135)	MFI	140@4500	185@3600	3.50x3.31	8.8:1	15@1100
	V ③	3.1 (3135)	MFI ①	205@4800	220@3200	3.50x2.99	8.75:1	15@1100
1991	D	2.3 (2260)	MFI	160@6200	155@5200	3.62x3.35	9.5:1	30@2000
	L	3.8 (3791)	MFI	170@4800	220@3200	3.80x3.40	8.5:1	60@1850
	R	2.5 (2471)	TFI	105@4800	135@3200	3.50x3.31	8.3:1	26@800
	X	3.4 (3350)	MFI	140@4400	185@3200	3.62x3.31	8.8:1	15@1100
1992	L	3.8 (3791)	MFI	170@4800	220@3200	3.80x3.40	8.5:1	60@1850
	R	2.5 (2471)	TFI	105@4800	135@3200	4.00x3.00	8.3:1	26@800
	T	3.1 (3135)	MFI	140@4400	185@3200	3.50x3.31	8.8:1	15@1100
	X ②	3.4 (3350)	MFI	140@4400	215@4000	3.62x3.31	9.25:1	15@1100
1993	4	2.2 (2190)	MFI	110@5200	130@3200	3.50x3.46	9.0:1	56@3000
	L	3.8 (3791)	SFI	160@4800	225@3200	3.80x3.40	9.0:1	60@1850
	M	3.1 (3135)	SFI	160@5200	185@4000	3.50x3.31	9.6:1	15@1100
	T	3.1 (3135)	MFI	140@4400	185@3200	3.50x3.31	8.8:1	15@1100
	X ②	3.4 (3350)	MFI	210@5200	215@4000	3.62x3.31	9.25:1	15@1100
1994	L	3.8 (3791)	SFI	170@4800	225@3200	3.80x3.40	9.0:1	60@1850
	M	3.1 (3135)	SFI	160@5200	185@4000	3.50x3.31	9.6:1	15@1100
	T	3.1 (3135)	MFI	140@4400	185@3200	3.50x3.31	8.8:1	15@1100
	X	3.4 (3350)	SFI	210@5200	215@4000	3.62x3.31	9.25:1	15@1100
1995	L	3.8 (3791)	SFI	170@4800	225@3200	3.80x3.40	9.0:1	60@1850
	M	3.1 (3135)	SFI	160@5200	185@4000	3.50x3.31	9.6:1	15@1100
	X	3.4 (3350)	SFI	210@5200	215@4000	3.62x3.31	9.25:1	15@1100
1996	K	3.8 (3791)	SFI	205@5200	230@4000	3.80x3.40	9.4:1	60@1850
	M	3.1 (3135)	SFI	160@5200	185@4000	3.50x3.31	9.6:1	15@1100
	X	3.4 (3350)	SFI	215@5200	220@4000	3.62x3.31	9.7:1	15@1100

MFI - Multi-port Fuel Injection
SFI - Sequential Fuel Injection
TFI - Throttle body Fuel Injection

① Turbocharged
② Manual - 210@5200 Automatic - 200@5000
③ High Output (H.O.)

88003C01

CAMSHAFT SPECIFICATIONS
All measurements given in inches.

Year	Engine ID/VIN	Engine Displacement Liters (cc)	Journal Diameter 1	2	3	4	5	Elevation In.	Ex.	Bearing Clearance	Camshaft End Play
1988	W	2.8 (2837)	1.8678-1.8815	1.8678-1.8815	1.8678-1.8815	1.8678-1.8815	NA	0.2626	0.2732	0.0010-0.0040	NA
1989	T	3.1 (3135)	1.8678-1.8815	1.8678-1.8815	1.8678-1.8815	1.8678-1.8815	NA	0.2626	0.2732	0.0010-0.0040	NA
	V	3.1 (3135)	1.8678-1.8815	1.8678-1.8815	1.8678-1.8815	1.8678-1.8815	NA	0.2626	0.2732	0.0010-0.0040	NA
	W	2.8 (2837)	1.8678-1.8815	1.8678-1.8815	1.8678-1.8815	1.8678-1.8815	NA	0.2626	0.2732	0.0010-0.0040	NA
1990	A	2.3 (2260)	1.5720-1.5728	1.3751-1.3760	1.3751-1.3760	1.3751-1.3760	1.3751-1.3760	0.4100	0.4100	0.0019-0.0043	0.0009-0.0088
	D	2.3 (2260)	1.5720-1.5728	1.3751-1.3760	1.3751-1.3760	1.3751-1.3760	1.3751-1.3760	0.3750	0.3750	0.0019-0.0043	0.0009-0.0088
	R	2.5 (2471)	1.8690	1.8690	1.8690	NA	NA	0.2480	0.2480	0.0007-0.0027	0.0015-0.0050
1991	T	3.1 (3135)	1.8677-1.8815	1.8677-1.8815	1.8677-1.8815	1.8677-1.8815	NA	0.2626	0.2732	0.0010-0.0040	NA
	V	3.1 (3135)	1.8678-1.8815	1.8678-1.8815	1.8678-1.8815	1.8678-1.8815	NA	0.2626	0.2732	0.0010-0.0040	NA
	D	2.3 (2260)	1.5720-1.5728	1.3751-1.3760	1.3751-1.3760	1.3751-1.3760	1.3751-1.3760	0.3750	0.3750	0.0019-0.0043	0.0009-0.0088
	L	3.8 (3791)	1.7850-1.7860	1.7850-1.7860	1.7850-1.7860	1.7850-1.7860	NA	0.2500	0.2550	0.0005-0.0035	NA
	R	2.5 (2471)	1.8690	1.8690	1.8690	NA	NA	0.2480	0.2480	0.0007-0.0027	0.0015-0.0050
1992	T	3.1 (3135)	1.8677-1.8815	1.8677-1.8815	1.8677-1.8815	1.8677-1.8815	NA	0.2626	0.2732	0.0010-0.0040	NA
	X	3.4 (3350)	2.1643-2.1657	2.1643-2.1657	2.1660-2.1660	2.1650-2.1660	NA	0.3700	0.3700	0.0019-0.0040	NA
	L	3.8 (3791)	1.7850-1.7860	1.7850-1.7860	1.7850-1.7860	1.7850-1.7860	NA	0.2500	0.2550	0.0005-0.0035	NA
	R	2.5 (2471)	1.8690	1.8690	1.8690	NA	NA	0.2480	0.2480	0.0007-0.0027	0.0015-0.0050

88003C04

VALVE SPECIFICATIONS

Year	Engine ID/VIN	Engine Displacement Liters (cc)	Seat Angle (deg.)	Face Angle (deg.)	Spring Test Pressure (lbs. @ in.)	Spring Installed Height (in.)	Stem-to-Guide Clearance (in.) Intake	Exhaust	Stem Diameter (in.) Intake	Exhaust
1993	4	2.2 (2190)	46	45	225-233@1.247	1.637	0.0011-0.0026	0.0014-0.0031	NA	NA
	L	3.8 (3791)	45	45	210@1.315	1.690-1.720	0.0015-0.0035	0.0015-0.0032	NA	NA
	M	3.1 (3135)	45	45	80@1.710	1.710	0.0010-0.0027	0.0010-0.0032	NA	NA
	T	3.1 (3135)	46	45	90@1.693	1.693	0.0008-0.0021	0.0014-0.0030	NA	NA
	X	3.4 (3350)	46	45	65@1.40	NA	0.0011-0.0026	0.0018-0.0033	NA	NA
1994	L	3.8 (3791)	45	45	210@1.315	1.690-1.720	0.0015-0.0035	0.0015-0.0032	NA	NA
	M	3.1 (3135)	45	45	80@1.710	1.710	0.0010-0.0027	0.0010-0.0027	NA	NA
	T	3.1 (3135)	46	45	90@1.693	1.693	0.0008-0.0021	0.0014-0.0030	NA	NA
	X	3.4 (3350)	46	45	65@1.40	NA	0.0011-0.0026	0.0018-0.0033	NA	NA
1995	L	3.8 (3791)	45	45	210@1.315	1.690-1.720	0.0015-0.0035	0.0015-0.0032	NA	NA
	M	3.1 (3135)	45	45	80@1.710	1.710	0.0010-0.0027	0.0010-0.0027	NA	NA
	X	3.4 (3350)	46	45	65@1.40	NA	0.0011-0.0026	0.0018-0.0033	NA	NA
1996	K	3.8 (3791)	45	45	210@1.315	1.690-1.720	0.0015-0.0035	0.0015-0.0035	NA	NA
	M	3.1 (3135)	45	45	75@1.710	1.710	0.0010-0.0027	0.0010-0.0027	NA	NA
	X	3.4 (3350)	46	45	65@1.40	NA	0.0011-0.0026	0.0018-0.0033	NA	NA

NA - Not Available
① Intake face angle: 44 degrees
② Exhaust face angle: 44.5 degrees

88003C03

CRANKSHAFT AND CONNECTING ROD SPECIFICATIONS
All measurements are given in inches.

Year	Engine ID/VIN	Engine Displacement Liters (cc)	Crankshaft Main Brg. Journal Dia.	Main Brg. Oil Clearance	Shaft End-play	Thrust on No.	Connecting Rod Journal Diameter	Oil Clearance	Side Clearance
1988	W	2.8 (2837)	2.6473-2.6483	0.0016-0.0032	0.0024-0.0083	3	1.9983-1.9994	0.0013-0.0026	0.0060-0.0170
1989	T	3.1 (3135)	2.6473-2.6483	0.0012-0.0027	0.0024-0.0083	3	1.9983-1.9994	0.0014-0.0036	0.0140-0.0270
	V	3.1 (3135)	2.6473-2.6483	0.0012-0.0027	0.0024-0.0083	3	1.9983-1.9994	0.0014-0.0036	0.0140-0.0270
	W	2.8 (2837)	2.6473-2.6483	0.0012-0.0027	0.0024-0.0083	3	1.9983-1.9994	0.0014-0.0036	0.0060-0.0170
1990	A	2.3 (2260)	2.0470-2.0480	0.0005-0.0023	0.0034-0.0095	3	1.8887-1.8897	0.0005-0.0020	0.0059-0.0177
	D	2.3 (2260)	2.0470-2.0480	0.0005-0.0023	0.0034-0.0095	3	1.8887-1.8897	0.0005-0.0020	0.0059-0.0177
	R	2.5 (2471)	2.2991-2.3000	0.0005-0.0022	0.0051-0.0102	5	1.9964-2.0002	0.0011-0.0034	0.0060-0.0236
	T	3.1 (3135)	2.6473-2.6483	0.0012-0.0030	0.0024-0.0083	3	1.9983-1.9994	0.0011-0.0034	0.0140-0.0270
	V	3.1 (3135)	2.6473-2.6483	0.0012-0.0030	0.0024-0.0083	3	1.9983-1.9994	0.0011-0.0034	0.0140-0.0270
1991	D	2.3 (2260)	2.0470-2.0480	0.0005-0.0023	0.0034-0.0095	3	1.8887-1.8897	0.0005-0.0020	0.0059-0.0177
	L	3.8 (3791)	2.4988-2.4998	0.0003-0.0018	0.0110	2	2.2487-2.2499	0.0003-0.0026	0.0030-0.0150
	R	2.5 (2471)	2.2991-2.3000	0.0005-0.0022	0.0051-0.0102	5	1.9964-2.0002	0.0011-0.0027	0.0060-0.0236
	T	3.1 (3135)	2.6473-2.6483	0.0012-0.0030	0.0024-0.0083	3	1.9983-1.9994	0.0011-0.0034	0.0140-0.0270
	X	3.4 (3350)	2.6473-2.6479	0.0013-0.0030	0.0024-0.0083	3	1.9987-1.9994	0.0011-0.0032	0.0140-0.0250
1992	L	3.8 (3791)	2.4988-2.4998	0.0008-0.0022	0.0030-0.0110	2	2.2487-2.2499	0.0008-0.0022	0.0030-0.0150
	R	2.5 (2471)	2.2991-2.3000	0.0005-0.0022	0.0102	5	1.9964-2.0002	0.0005-0.0027	0.0060-0.0236
	T	3.1 (3135)	2.6473-2.6483	0.0012-0.0030	0.0024-0.0083	3	1.9983-1.9994	0.0011-0.0034	0.0140-0.0270
	X	3.4 (3350)	2.6473-2.6479	0.0013-0.0030	0.0024-0.0083	3	1.9987-1.9994	0.0011-0.0032	0.0140-0.0250

88003C06

CAMSHAFT SPECIFICATIONS
All measurements given in inches.

Year	Engine ID/VIN	Engine Displacement Liters (cc)	Journal Diameter 1	2	3	4	5	Elevation In.	Ex.	Bearing Clearance	Camshaft End Play
1993	4	2.2 (2190)	1.8670-1.8690	1.8670-1.8690	1.8670-1.8690	1.8670-1.8690	1.8670-1.8690	0.2590	0.2500	0.0010-0.0039	NA
	L	3.8 (3791)	1.7850-1.7860	1.7850-1.7860	1.7850-1.7860	1.7850-1.7860	NA	0.2500	0.2550	0.0005-0.0035	NA
	M	3.1 (3135)	1.8680-1.8690	1.8680-1.8690	1.8680-1.8690	1.8680-1.8690	NA	0.2727	0.2727	0.0010-0.0040	NA
	T	3.1 (3135)	1.8677-1.8815	1.8677-1.8815	1.8677-1.8815	1.8677-1.8815	NA	0.2626	0.2732	0.0010-0.0040	NA
	X	3.4 (3350)	2.1643-2.1654	2.1643-2.1654	2.1643-2.1654	2.1643-2.1654	NA	0.3700	0.3700	0.0019-0.0040	NA
1994	L	3.8 (3791)	1.7850-1.7860	1.7850-1.7860	1.7850-1.7860	1.7850-1.7860	NA	0.2500	0.2550	0.0005-0.0035	NA
	M	3.1 (3135)	1.8680-1.8690	1.8680-1.8690	1.8680-1.8690	1.8680-1.8690	NA	0.2727	0.2727	0.0010-0.0040	NA
	T	3.1 (3135)	1.8677-1.8815	1.8677-1.8815	1.8677-1.8815	1.8677-1.8815	NA	0.2626	0.2732	0.0010-0.0040	NA
	X	3.4 (3350)	2.1643-2.1654	2.1643-2.1654	2.1643-2.1654	2.1643-2.1654	NA	0.3700	0.3700	0.0019-0.0040	NA
1995	L	3.8 (3791)	1.7850-1.7860	1.7850-1.7860	1.7850-1.7860	1.7850-1.7860	NA	0.2500	0.2550	0.0005-0.0035	NA
	M	3.1 (3135)	1.8680-1.8690	1.8680-1.8690	1.8680-1.8690	1.8680-1.8690	NA	0.2727	0.2727	0.0010-0.0040	NA
	X	3.4 (3350)	2.1643-2.1654	2.1643-2.1654	2.1643-2.1654	2.1643-2.1654	NA	0.3700	0.3700	0.0019-0.0040	NA
1996	K	3.8 (3791)	1.7850-1.7860	1.7850-1.7860	1.7850-1.7860	1.7850-1.7860	NA	0.2500	0.2550	0.0005-0.0035	NA
	M	3.1 (3135)	1.8680-1.8690	1.8680-1.8690	1.8680-1.8690	1.8680-1.8690	NA	0.2727	0.2727	0.0010-0.0040	NA
	X	3.4 (3350)	2.1643-2.1654	2.1643-2.1654	2.1643-2.1654	2.1643-2.1654	NA	0.3700	0.3700	0.0019-0.0040	NA

NA - Not Available

88003C05

PISTON AND RING SPECIFICATIONS
All measurements are given in inches.

Year	Engine ID/VIN	Engine Displacement Liters (cc)	Piston Clearance	Ring Gap			Ring Side Clearance		
				Top Compression	Bottom Compression	Oil Control	Top Compression	Bottom Compression	Oil Control
1988	W	2.8 (2837)	0.0020-0.0028	0.010-0.020	0.010-0.020	0.020-0.055	0.0010-0.0030	0.0010-0.0030	0.0080 (MAX)
1989	T	3.1 (3135)	0.0009-0.0022	0.0100-0.0200	0.0100-0.0200	0.0100-0.0500	0.0020-0.0035	0.0020-0.0035	0.0080 (MAX)
	V	3.1 (3135)	0.0009-0.0022	0.0100-0.0200	0.0100-0.0200	0.0100-0.0500	0.0020-0.0035	0.0020-0.0035	0.0060 (MAX)
	W	2.8 (2837)	0.0009-0.0022	0.010-0.020	0.010-0.020	0.020-0.055	0.0010-0.0030	0.0010-0.0030	0.0080 (MAX)
1990	A	2.3 (2260)	0.0007-0.0020	0.0138-0.0236	0.0157-0.0256	0.0157-0.0551	0.0027-0.0047	0.0016-0.0032	NA
	D	2.3 (2260)	0.0007-0.0020	0.0138-0.0236	0.0157-0.0256	0.0157-0.0551	0.0020-0.0039	0.0016-0.0032	NA
	R	2.5 (2471)	0.0014-① 0.0022	0.020-0.020	0.010-0.020	0.020-0.060	0.0020-0.0030	0.0010-0.0030	0.0150-0.0550
	T	3.1 (3135)	0.0009-0.0022	0.020-0.020	0.020-0.028	0.020-0.030	0.0020-0.0035	0.0020-0.0035	0.0080 (MAX)
	V	3.1 (3135)	0.0009-0.0022	0.010-0.020	0.010-0.020	0.010-0.030	0.0020-0.0035	0.0020-0.0035	0.0080 (MAX)
1991	D	2.3 (2260)	0.0007-0.0020	0.0138-0.0236	0.0157-0.0256	0.0157-0.0551	0.0020-0.0039	0.0013-0.0032	NA
	L	3.8 (3791)	0.0004-② 0.0022	0.010-0.025	0.010-0.025	0.015-0.055	0.0013-0.0031	0.0013-0.0031	0.0011-0.0081
	R	2.5 (2471)	0.0014-① 0.0022	0.010-0.020	0.010-0.020	0.020-0.060	0.0010-0.0030	0.0010-0.0030	0.0150-0.0550
	T	3.1 (3135)	0.0009-0.0022	0.010-0.020	0.020-0.028	0.010-0.030	0.0020-0.0035	0.0020-0.0035	0.0080 (MAX)
	X	3.4 (3350)	0.0009-0.0022	0.012-0.019	0.019-0.028	0.010-0.030	0.0016-0.0035	0.0016-0.0035	0.0020-0.0080
1992	L	3.8 (3791)	0.0004-② 0.0022	0.010-0.025	0.010-0.025	0.015-0.055	0.0013-0.0031	0.0013-0.0031	0.0011-0.0081
	R	2.5 (2471)	0.0014-① 0.0022	0.010-0.020	0.010-0.020	0.020-0.060	0.0020-0.0030	0.0010-0.0030	0.0150-0.0550
	T	3.1 (3135)	0.0009-0.0022	0.010-0.020	0.010-0.020	0.010-0.030	0.0020-0.0035	0.0020-0.0035	0.0080 (MAX)
	X	3.4 (3350)	0.0009-0.0023	0.012-0.022	0.019-0.029	0.010-0.030	0.0016-0.0035	0.0016-0.0035	0.0020-0.0080

88003C08

CRANKSHAFT AND CONNECTING ROD SPECIFICATIONS
All measurements are given in inches.

Year	Engine ID/VIN	Engine Displacement Liters (cc)	Main Brg. Journal Dia.	Crankshaft			Connecting Rod		
				Main Brg. Oil Clearance	Shaft End-play	Thrust on No.	Journal Diameter	Oil Clearance	Side Clearance
1993	4	2.2 (2190)	2.4945-2.4954	0.0006-0.0019	0.0020-0.0070	4	1.9983-1.9994	0.0010-0.0031	0.0039-0.0149
	L	3.8 (3791)	2.4988-2.4998	0.0008-0.0022	0.0030-0.0110	2	2.2487-2.2499	0.0008-0.0022	0.0030-0.0150
	M	3.1 (3135)	2.6473-2.6483	0.0012-0.0030	0.0024-0.0083	3	1.9987-1.9994	0.0011-0.0030	0.0071-0.0173
	T	3.1 (3135)	2.6473-2.6479	0.0013-0.0030	0.0024-0.0083	3	1.9987-1.9994	0.0011-0.0032	0.0071-0.0173
	X	3.4 (3350)	2.6472-2.6479	0.0013-0.0030	0.0024-0.0083	3	1.9987-1.9994	0.0011-0.0032	0.0071-0.0173
1994	L	3.8 (3791)	2.4988-2.4998	0.0008-0.0022	0.0030-0.0110	2	2.2487-2.2499	0.0008-0.0022	0.0030-0.0150
	M	3.1 (3135)	2.6473-2.6483	0.0012-0.0030	0.0024-0.0083	3	1.9987-1.9994	0.0011-0.0030	0.0071-0.0173
	T	3.1 (3135)	2.6472-2.6479	0.0013-0.0030	0.0024-0.0083	3	1.9987-1.9994	0.0011-0.0032	0.0071-0.0173
	X	3.4 (3350)	2.6472-2.6479	0.0013-0.0030	0.0024-0.0083	3	1.9987-1.9994	0.0011-0.0032	0.0071-0.0173
1995	L	3.8 (3791)	2.4988-2.4998	0.0008-0.0022	0.0030-0.0110	2	2.2487-2.2499	0.0008-0.0022	0.0030-0.0150
	M	3.1 (3135)	2.6473-2.6483	0.0012-0.0030	0.0024-0.0083	3	1.9987-1.9994	0.0011-0.0030	0.0071-0.0173
	X	3.4 (3350)	2.6472-2.6479	0.0013-0.0030	0.0024-0.0083	3	1.9987-1.9994	0.0011-0.0032	0.0071-0.0173
1996	K	3.8 (3791)	2.4988-2.4998	0.0008-0.0022	0.0030-0.0110	2	NA	NA	0.0030-0.0150
	M	3.1 (3135)	2.6473-2.6483	0.0008-0.0025	0.0024-0.0083	3	1.9987-1.9994	0.0007-0.0024	0.0071-0.0173
	X	3.4 (3350)	2.6472-2.6479	0.0008-0.0025	0.0024-0.0083	3	1.9987-1.9994	0.0007-0.0024	0.0071-0.0173

88003C07

TORQUE SPECIFICATIONS
All readings in ft. lbs.

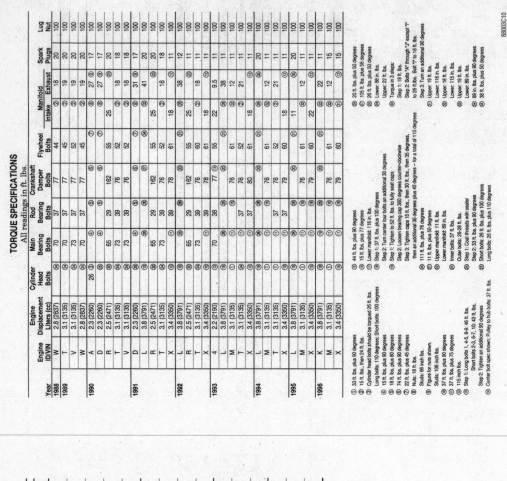

Year	Engine ID/VIN	Engine Displacement Liters (cc)	Cylinder Head Bolts	Main Bearing Bolts	Rod Bearing Bolts	Crankshaft Damper Bolts	Flywheel Bolts	Manifold Intake	Manifold Exhaust	Spark Plugs	Lug Nut
1988	W	2.8 (2837)		70	37	77	44		18	20	100
1989	T	3.1 (3135)		70	37	77	45		19	20	100
	V	3.1 (3135)		73	37	77	52		19	20	100
	W	2.8 (2837)		70	37	77	45		19	20	100
1990	A	2.3 (2260)							27	17	100
	D	2.3 (2260)	26					25	27	17	100
	R	2.5 (2471)		65	29	162	55	25	18	20	100
	T	3.1 (3135)		73	39	76	52		18	18	100
	V	3.1 (3135)		73	39	76	52		18	18	100
1991	D	2.3 (2260)							31	17	100
	L	3.8 (3791)							41	20	100
	R	2.5 (2471)		65	29	162	55	25	18	20	100
	T	3.1 (3135)		73	39	76	52	18	18	11	100
	X	3.4 (3350)		73	39	78	61	18	11	11	100
1992	L	3.8 (3791)							38	12	100
	R	2.5 (2471)		65	29	162	55	25	18	11	100
	T	3.1 (3135)		73	39	76	60	18	18	11	100
	X	3.4 (3350)		73	39	78	61	18	11	11	100
1993	4	2.2 (2190)		70	38	77	55	22	9.5	11	100
	L	3.8 (3791)				76	61		38	11	100
	M	3.1 (3135)			37	76	52		12	11	100
	T	3.1 (3135)			37	80	61	18	21	11	100
	X	3.4 (3350)			37						100
1994	L	3.8 (3791)				76	61		12	20	100
	M	3.1 (3135)				76	52		12	11	100
	T	3.1 (3135)			37	79	60	18	21	11	100
	X	3.4 (3350)								11	100
1995	M	3.1 (3135)				76	61	11	12	20	100
	T	3.1 (3135)			37	79	60			11	100
	X	3.4 (3350)						22		11	100
1996	M	3.1 (3135)				76	61		22	11	100
	X	3.4 (3350)				79	60		12	15	100

① 33 ft. lbs. plus 90 degrees
② 15 ft. lbs. then 24 ft. lbs.
③ Cylinder head bolts should be torqued 26 ft. lbs. Long bolts: 110 degrees; Short bolts: 100 degrees
④ 15 ft. lbs. plus 90 degrees
⑤ 18 ft. lbs. plus 80 degrees
⑥ 74 ft. lbs. plus 90 degrees
⑦ 22 ft. lbs. plus 45 degrees
⑧ Nuts: 18 ft. lbs.
⑨ Studs: 96 inch lbs.
⑩ Figure for nuts shown.
Studs: 106 inch lbs.
⑪ 37 ft. lbs. plus 90 degrees
⑫ 37 ft. lbs. plus 75 degrees
⑬ 115 inch lbs.

⑭ 44 ft. lbs. plus 90 degrees
⑮ 15 ft. lbs. plus 77 degrees
⑯ Lower manifold: 116 in. lbs.
⑰ Step 1: 37 ft. lbs. plus 130 degrees
Step 2: Turn center four bolts an additional 30 degrees
⑱ Step 1: Tighten to 52 ft. lbs. to fully seat caps
Step 2: Loosen bearing cap 360 degrees counter-clockwise
Step 3: Tighten caps 15 ft. lbs., then 30 ft. lbs., then 35 degrees.
⑲ 111 ft. lbs. plus 76 degrees
then an additional 35 degrees plus 40 degrees — for a total of 110 degrees
⑳ 11 ft. lbs. plus 50 degrees
㉑ Upper manifold: 11 ft. lbs.
㉒ Lower manifold: 89 in. lbs.
㉓ Inner bolts: 37 ft. lbs.
Outer bolts: 26-28 ft. lbs.
㉔ Step 1: Coat threads with sealer
Step 2: 33 ft. lbs. plus 90 degrees
Short bolts: 26 ft. lbs. plus 100 degrees
Long bolts: 26 ft. lbs. plus 110 degrees

㉕ 20 ft. lbs. plus 50 degrees
㉖ 105 ft. lbs. plus 50 degrees
㉗ 26 ft. lbs. plus 50 degrees
㉘ Lower: 86 in. lbs.
Upper: 22 ft. lbs.
㉙ Torque in 3 steps:
Step 1: 18 ft. lbs.
Step 2: Bolts "A" through "J" except "I"
to 26 ft. lbs. Bolt "I" to 18 ft. lbs.
Step 3: Turn an additional 30 degrees
㉚ Upper: 19 ft. lbs.
Lower: 116 in. lbs.
㉛ Upper: 18 in. lbs.
Lower: 115 in. lbs.
㉜ Upper: 19 ft. lbs.
Lower: 89 in. lbs.
㉝ 89 in. lbs. plus 90 degrees
㉞ 38 ft. lbs. plus 50 degrees

88003C10

PISTON AND RING SPECIFICATIONS
All measurements are given in inches.

Year	Engine ID/VIN	Engine Displacement Liters (cc)	Piston Clearance	Ring Gap Top Compression	Ring Gap Bottom Compression	Ring Gap Oil Control	Ring Side Clearance Top Compression	Ring Side Clearance Bottom Compression	Ring Side Clearance Oil Control
1993	4	2.2 (2190)	0.0007- 0.0017	0.010- 0.020	0.010- 0.020	0.010- 0.050	0.0019- 0.0027	0.0019- 0.0027	0.0019- 0.0082
	L	3.8 (3791)	0.0004- ② 0.0022	0.010- 0.025	0.010- 0.025	0.015- 0.055	0.0013- 0.0031	0.0013- 0.0031	0.0011- 0.0081
	M	3.1 (3135)	0.0013- 0.0027	0.007- 0.016	0.0197- 0.0280	0.0098- 0.0295	0.0020- 0.0035	0.0020- 0.0035	0.0080 (MAX)
	T	3.1 (3135)	0.0009- 0.0023	0.0071- 0.0161	0.0197- 0.0280	0.0098- 0.0295	0.0016- 0.0035	0.0016- 0.0035	0.0080 (MAX)
	X	3.4 (3350)	0.0013- 0.0027	0.0098- 0.0197	0.0189- 0.0291	0.0098- 0.0299	0.0016- 0.0035	0.0016- 0.0035	0.0019- 0.0080
1994	L	3.8 (3791)	0.0004- ② 0.0022	0.010- 0.022	0.030- 0.040	0.010- 0.030	0.0013- 0.0031	0.0013- 0.0031	0.0011- 0.0081
	M	3.1 (3135)	0.0013- 0.0027	0.007- 0.016	0.0197- 0.0280	0.0098- 0.0295	0.0020- 0.0035	0.0020- 0.0035	0.0080 (MAX)
	X	3.4 (3350)	0.0013- 0.0027	0.0098- 0.0197	0.0189- 0.0291	0.0098- 0.0299	0.0016- 0.0035	0.0016- 0.0035	0.0019- 0.0080
1995	K	3.8 (3791)	0.0004- ③ 0.0020	0.012- 0.022	0.030- 0.040	0.010- 0.030	0.0013- 0.0031	0.0013- 0.0031	0.0009- 0.0079
	M	3.1 (3135)	0.0013- 0.0027	0.006- 0.014	0.0197- 0.0280	0.0500 (MAX)	0.0020- 0.0033	0.0020- 0.0035	0.0080 (MAX)
	X	3.4 (3350)	0.0008- 0.0020	0.008- 0.018	0.022- 0.032	0.0098- 0.0299	0.0013- 0.0031	0.0013- 0.0031	0.0011- 0.0081

NA - Not Available
① Measured 1/8 inch down from piston top
② Measured 44mm from top of piston
③ Measured 39mm from top of piston

88003C09

Rotating the Engine

PROCEDURE

1988–94 Vehicles

1. For vehicles through 1994, rotate the engine, as follows:
   a. Place the transaxle in Neutral.
   b. Remove the air cleaner assembly and coolant recovery bottle.
   c. Unfasten the torque strut-to-engine bracket bolts and swing the torque struts aside.
   d. Replace the passenger side torque strut-to-engine bracket bolt in the engine bracket.
   e. Position a prybar in the bracket so that it contacts the bracket and the bolt.
   f. Rotate the engine by pulling forward on the prybar.
   g. Align the slave hole in the driver side torque strut to the engine bracket hole.
   h. Retain the engine in this position using the torque strut-to-engine bracket bolt.
2. For vehicles through 1994, proceed as follows to rotate the engine back to its original position:
   a. To bring the engine back into position, pull forward on the prybar to relieve the engine's weight. Then remove the driver side torque strut-to-engine bracket bolt from the torque strut slave hole and engine bracket.
   b. Allow the engine to rotate back to its original position.
   c. Remove the prybar.
   d. Remove the passenger side torque strut-to-engine bracket bolt from the bracket.
   e. Install the torque struts and strut-to-engine bracket bolts. Tighten the bolts to 51 ft. lbs. (70 Nm).
   f. Put the transaxle in Park.

1995–96 Vehicles

1. For 1995–96 vehicles, rotate the engine, as follows:
   a. Place the transaxle in Neutral.
   b. Remove the air cleaner assembly and coolant recovery bottle.
   c. Unfasten the torque strut-to-engine bracket bolts and swing the torque struts aside.
   d. Install engine tilter J 41131 or equivalent, then rotate the engine forward.
2. For 1995–96 vehicles, proceed as follows to rotate the engine back to its original position:
   a. Rotate the engine backward, then remove J 41131.
   b. Fasten the torque strut-to-engine bracket bolts.
   c. Put the transaxle in Park.

Engine

REMOVAL & INSTALLATION

✳✳ CAUTION

The EPA warns that prolonged contact with used engine oil may cause a number of skin disorders, including cancer! You should make every effort to minimize your exposure to used engine oil. Protective gloves should be worn when changing the oil. Wash your hands and any other exposed skin areas as soon as possible after exposure to used engine oil. Soap and water, or waterless hand cleaner should be used.

In the process of removing the engine, you will come across a number of steps which call for the removal of a separate component or system, i.e. "disconnect the exhaust system" or "remove the radiator." In most instances, a detailed removal procedure can be found elsewhere in this manual.

It is virtually impossible to list each individual wire and hose which must be disconnected, simply because so many different model and engine combinations have been manufactured. Careful observation and common sense are the best possible additions to any repair procedure. Be absolutely sure to tag and wire or hose before it is disconnected, so that you can be assured of proper reconnection during installation.

2.2L Engine

1. Disconnect the negative battery cable.
2. With the help of an assistant, matchmark the hood hinges, then remove the hood.
3. Properly relieve the fuel system pressure.
4. Remove the air cleaner and duct assembly.
5. Properly drain the cooling system into an approved container.
6. Remove the engine torque strut, as follows:
   a. Unfasten the torque strut-to-engine bracket bolt and nut.
   b. Remove the torque strut-to-upper tie bar bracket bolt and nut, then remove the torque strut.
7. Remove the air intake silencer assembly.
8. Remove the coolant recovery reservoir.
9. Disconnect the upper radiator hose at the engine, then disconnect the lower radiator/heater hose at the water pump, at the rear of the engine.
10. Detach the brake booster vacuum hose at the intake manifold.
11. Disconnect the throttle control cables at the throttle body.
12. Remove the serpentine drive belt, as outlined in Section 1 of this manual.
13. Detach the electrical connection, unfasten retaining screws at the right side engine cooling fan, then remove the fan.
14. Remove the power steering pump. Refer to Section 8 for details regarding this procedure.
15. Disconnect the fuel lines.
16. Unfasten the retaining screws, then remove the alternator heat shield.
17. Detach the electrical connections at the alternator.
18. Disengage the electrical connector at the exhaust oxygen sensor.
19. Unfasten the nuts retaining the engine torque strut mount bracket, battery cable/ground wires, bracket at the bellhousing and the bolt retaining the torque strut bracket at the engine lift bracket.
20. Raise and safely support the vehicle.
21. Unfasten the retaining screws, then remove the flywheel cover. Remove the flywheel-to-torque converter retaining bolts.
22. Disconnect the front exhaust pipe from the exhaust manifold.
23. Carefully lower the vehicle.
24. Rotate the engine and install the strut to the bolt hole in the engine lift bracket and torque strut mount bracket. This holds the engine forward and gives access to the rear of the engine.
25. Detach the electrical connections at the starter motor and the ground wires at the engine block in front of the starter.
26. Unfasten the bolts retaining the A/C compressor to the mount bracket, then position the compressor aside.
27. Remove the bolts retaining the engine to the transaxle bracket at the transaxle.
28. Disconnect the vacuum hose at the intake manifold.
29. Detach the electrical connections at the Vehicle Speed Sensor (VSS), knock sensor, engine block ground wires and the wire harness clamp nut under the intake manifold.
30. Disengage the electrical connectors at the throttle body and injector harness. Leave the harness on the injectors and pull the harness from the manifold.
31. Remove the bellhousing-to-engine bolts/nuts, ground wires and battery ground cable.
32. Remove the engine torque struts.
33. Install a suitable engine lifting device.
34. With the help of an assistant, pull the engine assembly halfway out.
35. Detach the electrical connections at the ignition module, then carefully remove the engine from the vehicle.

To install:

36. Partially install the engine to the vehicle, then attach the electrical connectors at the ignition module.
37. Carefully lower the engine into the vehicle, with the help of an assistant, then remove the engine lifting device.
38. Install the engine torque struts and tighten the retainers to 39 ft. lbs. (53 Nm). If removed, tighten the engine mount-to-chassis nuts and the engine mount-to-bracket nuts to 39 ft. lbs. (53 Nm).

39. Install the remaining components in the reverse of the removal procedure. Make sure all components are tightened securely

40. Properly fill the engine cooling system.

41. Install the air cleaner and duct assembly.

42. With the help of an assistant, install the hood.

43. Connect the negative battery cable, inspect the fluid levels, then start the engine and check for proper operations and/or leaks.

2.3L Engine

▶ **See Figures 7 and 8**

1. If equipped with A/C, have a certified repair shop recover the refrigerant using the proper equipment.

2. Disconnect the negative battery cable.

3. Relieve the fuel system pressure, as outlined in Section 5 of this manual.

4. Properly drain the engine cooling system into an approved container.

5. Scribe a mark around the hood hinges, then remove the hood with the help of an assistant.

6. Remove the heater hoses at the heater core and thermostat housing.

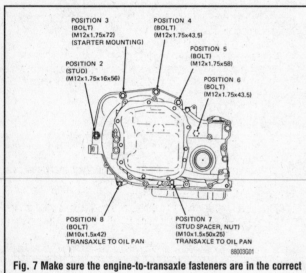

Fig. 7 Make sure the engine-to-transaxle fasteners are in the correct positions

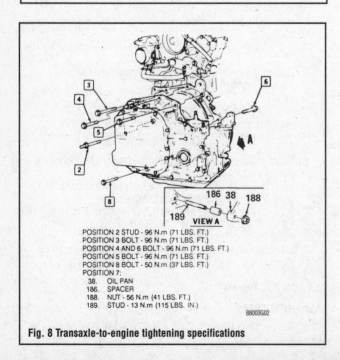

POSITION 2 STUD - 96 N.m (71 LBS. FT.)
POSITION 3 BOLT - 96 N.m (71 LBS. FT.)
POSITION 4 AND 6 BOLT - 96 N.m (71 LBS. FT.)
POSITION 5 BOLT - 96 N.m (71 LBS. FT.)
POSITION 8 BOLT - 50 N.m (37 LBS. FT.)
POSITION 7:
38. OIL PAN
186. SPACER
188. NUT - 56 N.m (41 LBS. FT.)
189. STUD - 13 N.m (115 LBS. IN.)

Fig. 8 Transaxle-to-engine tightening specifications

7. Disconnect the radiator upper (inlet) hose.

8. Remove the air cleaner-to-throttle body duct..

9. If equipped with A/C, remove the compressor and condenser hose at the compressor.

10. Tag and disconnect the two vacuum hoses from the front of the engine.

11. Label and detach the following electrical connectors:

• Alternator

• A/C compressor (if equipped)

• Fuel injector harness (position the harness aside)

12. Detach the electrical connectors from the starter solenoid

13. Disengage the ground connections at the front of the engine, and the negative battery cable from the transaxle.

14. Tag and detach the following electrical connectors:

• Ignition coil and module assembly

• Coolant sensors (there are 2)

• Oil pressure sensor/switch

• Knock sensor

• Oxygen sensor

• Idle Air Control (IAC) valve and Throttle Position Sensor (TPS) at the throttle body and position the harness aside

15. Disconnect the power brake vacuum hose from the throttle body, then remove the throttle cable and bracket.

16. Remove the power steering pump, hydraulic lines and the front/rear brackets.

17. Remove the power steering pivot bolt and drive belt.

18. If not done already, relieve the fuel system pressure and disconnect the fuel lines.

19. Remove the engine torque strut mounts.

20. For vehicles equipped with an automatic transaxle, remove the transaxle fill tube.

21. Remove the exhaust heat shield.

22. As outlined in Section 1 of this manual, remove the serpentine belt.

23. Remove the upper transaxle-to-engine bolts.

24. Raise and safely support the vehicle.

25. Unfasten the exhaust pipe-to-manifold bolts.

26. Remove the remaining transaxle-to-cylinder block retaining bolts.

27. Remove the exhaust-to-transaxle brace.

28. Disconnect the lower radiator (outlet) hose.

29. Remove the flywheel or converter cover.

30. Scribe a mark on the torque converter and flywheel. Unfasten the retaining nuts and remove the torque converter.

31. Remove the transaxle-to-engine bracket.

32. Remove the lower engine mount.

33. Carefully lower the vehicle.

34. Properly support the transaxle.

35. Install a suitable engine lifting fixture and remove the engine. Disconnect the vacuum lines and pull the vacuum harness back through the front lift bracket.

To install:

➡**Make sure all the engine mounting bolts are in their correct location to prevent transaxle and engine damage.**

36. Install the engine to a lifting fixture and position the engine in the vehicle. With the help of an assistant, align the engine to transaxle. Make sure the bolts are in the proper locations, as shown in the accompanying figure. If not engine damage may occur. Tighten to the specifications shown.

37. Raise and safely support the vehicle.

38. Install the transaxle-to-engine brace.

39. Apply a suitable thread locking compound, then install the torque converter-to-flywheel bolts. Tighten the bolts to 46 ft. lbs. (63 Nm). Install the flywheel cover.

40. At the right side of the vehicle, install the engine mount bolt.

41. Connect the lower (outlet) radiator hose.

42. Attach the ground connections at the front of the engine and the negative battery cable to the transaxle.

43. Fasten the A/C compressor (if equipped) and alternator electrical harnesses.

44. If equipped with A/C, connect the compressor and condenser hose at the compressor.

45. Connect the lower heater hose.

46. Install the exhaust-to-transaxle brace.

47. Fasten the exhaust pipe-to-manifold bolts.
48. Carefully lower the vehicle.
49. Install the remaining components in the reverse of the removal procedure. Make sure all components are tightened securely and all connectors proper attached.
50. Connect the upper radiator hose. Fill the radiator with coolant until the coolant reaches the heater hose water outlet, then install the hose. This assists with the complete cylinder block fill. Finish filling the cooling system.
51. Check the engine oil level, and add as necessary.
52. Fill and bleed the power steering system.
53. Install the hood assembly with the help of an assistant.
54. Recheck all procedures for completion of repair.
55. Recheck all fluid levels.
56. Connect the negative battery cable. Start the engine and check for fluid leaks.
57. If equipped, have a certified repair shop evacuate and recharge the A/C system.

2.5L Engine

1990–91 VEHICLES

1. Properly relieve the fuel system pressure as outlined in Section 5 of this manual.
2. Disconnect the negative, then the positive battery cables.
3. Place a suitable drain pan under the radiator drain valve and drain the engine coolant into a suitable container.
4. Remove the air cleaner assembly.
5. Mark the hood hinges with a scribe mark, then remove the hood assembly.
6. Mark and remove all engine wiring. Place all the wire assemblies out of the way.
7. Tag and disconnect the vacuum, heater and radiator hoses.
8. If equipped, remove the A/C from the engine and position it aside with the lines attached. Do NOT disconnect the hoses from the compressor.
9. Remove the alternator and bracket.
10. Remove the engine torque strut.
11. Unfasten the throttle and transaxle linkage.
12. Remove the transaxle-to-engine bolts except the 2 upper bolts.
13. Raise and safely support the vehicle.
14. Unfasten the engine mount-to-frame nuts.
15. Remove the exhaust pipe from the manifold.
16. Remove the flywheel cover.
17. Unfasten the torque converter-to-flywheel bolts.
18. Remove the starter motor. For details, please refer to the procedure in Section 2 of this manual.
19. Unfasten the power steering pump and position it aside with the lines attached.
20. Disconnect the fuel lines at the throttle body assembly.
21. Unfasten the retaining bolts, then remove the rear engine support bracket.
22. Support the transaxle assembly with a suitable holding fixture or jack.
23. Separate the transaxle from the engine.
24. Attach an suitable engine lifting device, then remove the engine from the vehicle.
25. Place the engine on a suitable workstand.
To install:
26. Place the engine assembly onto a lifting device.
27. With an assistant, install the engine into the vehicle. Remove the lifting device.
28. Position the engine into the engine mounts and engage the transaxle with the engine.
29. Remove the transaxle support fixture.
30. Install the rear support bracket bolts.
31. Install the engine mount nuts. Tighten to 35 ft. lbs. (47 Nm).
32. Install the rear transaxle bracket bolts. Tighten all bolts except the right bolt to 35 ft. lbs. (48 Nm). Tighten the right bolt to 61 ft. lbs. (83 Nm).
33. Install the remaining components in the reverse of the removal procedure. Make sure all components are tightened securely and all connectors proper attached.
34. Fill the cooling system with the proper type and quantity of engine coolant.

35. Connect the positive, then the negative battery cables.
36. Install the air cleaner assembly.
37. Check for proper fluid levels, then start the vehicle and inspect for any fluid leaks.

1992 VEHICLES

1. Matchmark the hood hinges for installation reference and remove the hood.

➡ **For the procedure to relieve the fuel system pressure, please refer to Section 5 of this manual.**

2. Properly relieve the fuel system pressure and disconnect the negative, then the positive battery cables.
3. Properly drain the cooling system into an approved container.
4. Remove the coolant recovery reservoir.
5. Remove the air cleaner assembly.
6. Detach the plastic ECM cover.
7. Remove the serpentine drive belt, as outlined in Section 1 of this manual.
8. Unfasten the radiator and heater hose clamps, then disconnect the hoses at the engine.
9. Disconnect the throttle control cables and position them aside.
10. Rotate the engine forward, as outlined earlier in this section.
11. Unfasten the power steering pump bolts, then position the pump aside. Do NOT disconnect the fluid lines.
12. Rotate the engine back to its original position.
13. Raise and safely support the vehicle.
14. Unfasten the front exhaust pipe bolts at the converter and manifold.
15. Remove the starter motor. For details, please refer to the procedure located in Section 2 of this manual.
16. Detach the right engine splash shield.
17. Unfasten the flywheel-to-torque converter bolts.
18. Remove the transaxle support bracket-to-transaxle bolts.
19. Unfasten the engine and transaxle mount nuts at the frame.
20. Carefully lower the vehicle.
21. Unfasten the front exhaust pipe bracket bolts and detach the exhaust pipe.
22. Tag and detach the engine electrical connectors.
23. Unfasten the engine wiring harness clips.
24. If equipped, unfasten the A/C compressor bolts and use a piece of wire or coat hanger to hang the compressor aside. Do NOT disconnect the refrigerant lines.
25. Detach the fuel line quick connect fittings. Unfasten the fuel line bracket screws and remove the bracket. Remove the fuel line bracket at the transaxle bolt.
26. Tag and disconnect all necessary vacuum lines.
27. Remove the exhaust pipe bracket at the transaxle bolt.
28. Unfasten the transaxle-to-engine bolts. Support the transaxle with a suitable fixture.
29. Attach a suitable engine lifting device. Carefully lift the engine from the vehicle.
30. Unfasten the flywheel bolts, remove the flywheel and spacer.
31. Place the engine on an engine stand.
To install:
32. Remove the engine from the engine stand.
33. Install the spacer, flywheel and secure with the retaining bolts.
34. Use the engine lifting device to position the engine into the vehicle.
35. Remove the lifting device.
36. Install the transaxle-to-engine bolts and tighten to 55 ft. lbs. (75 Nm).
37. Remove the transaxle support.
38. Install the remaining components in the reverse of the removal procedure. Tighten the following to the specifications given:
   • Engine and transaxle-to-frame mount nuts at the frame: 35 ft. lbs. (47 Nm)
   • Flywheel-to-converter bolts: 44 ft. lbs. (60 Nm)
39. Install the hood, using the marks made during removal.
40. Fill the cooling system with the proper type and quantity of coolant.
41. Check all fluid levels, then start the engine and check for leaks.

2.8L and 3.1L Engines

1988–93 VEHICLES

1. Remove the air cleaner and duct assembly, including the air flow tube from the throttle body.

2. Properly relieve the fuel system pressure.

3. Disconnect the negative, then the positive battery cables.

4. Scribe a mark around the hood hinges to ensure proper reinstallation. With the help of an assistant, remove the hood assembly.

5. Drain the coolant into a suitable container. Remove the coolant recovery reservoir.

6. For 1992–93 vehicles, rotate the engine forward. Disconnect the brake vacuum tube at the plenum and the booster.

7. Tag and detach all necessary engine wiring and place the harnesses out of the way.

8. Disconnect the throttle, TV and cruise control cables, if equipped, from the throttle body assembly.

9. For 1992–93 vehicles, rotate the engine back to its original position.

10. Unfasten the fuel lines at engine.

11. If equipped remove the AIR belt.

12. For 1991 vehicles, remove the crossover pipe.

13. Remove the serpentine belt.

14. Disconnect the upper and lower radiator hoses.

15. If equipped, remove the A/C compressor mounting bolts at the front mounting bracket.

16. Remove the power steering pump and position it aside. Do not disconnect the pump hoses.

17. Disconnect the heater hoses from the engine.

18. If not already done, detach the brake booster vacuum supply line.

19. Remove the EGR hose from the exhaust manifold. Remove pipe from EGR valve, if equipped.

20. Raise the vehicle and support it safely.

21. If equipped, remove the A/C conditioning compressor from the engine and position it aside, but DO NOT disconnect the refrigerant lines.

22. Remove the flywheel cover(s).

23. As outlined in Section 2, remove the starter motor.

24. Remove the right engine splash shield.

25. Unfasten the torque converter bolts.

26. For 1992–93 vehicles, drain the engine oil, then remove the oil filter.

27. Remove the transaxle bracket.

28. Unfasten the engine front mount nuts.

29. For vehicles through 1991, disconnect the exhaust pipe at the crossover.

30. For 1992–93 vehicles, unfasten the exhaust pipe bolts at the rear exhaust manifold.

31. Carefully lower the vehicle.

32. For vehicles through 1991, remove the engine torque struts.

33. For 1992–93 vehicles, remove the exhaust crossover pipe.

34. For vehicles through 1990, remove the left crossover pipe-to-manifold clamp.

35. For vehicle through 1990, pull the engine assembly forward and suitably support it.

36. Detach the bulkhead electrical connector.

37. For vehicles through 1990, remove the right crossover pipe-to-manifold clamp.

38. For vehicles through 1990, remove the engine support, and allow the engine to move to the normal position.

39. For 1992–93 vehicles, disconnect the vacuum modulator line at the modulator.

40. Support the transaxle with a suitable floor jack or equivalent.

41. Unfasten the transaxle-to-engine bolts.

42. Attach an engine lifting device and remove the engine from the vehicle. Check for connected wires and hoses as the engine is coming out of the body.

43. For 1992–93 vehicles, remove the flywheel bolts, flywheel and spacer.

44. Place the engine on a workstand.

To install:

45. For vehicles through 1991, with an assistant, install a lifting device onto the engine and position into the vehicle.

46. Remove the lifting device.

47. Install the transaxle-to-engine bolts.

48. Remove the transaxle support.

49. For 1992–93 vehicles, perform the following:

    a. Install the flywheel, spacer and retaining bolts. Tighten the bolts to 60 ft. lbs. (82 Nm).

    b. Use a lifting device to position the engine assembly into the vehicle, then install two engine-to-transaxle retaining bolts.

    c. Remove the lifting device and transaxle support.

    d. Install the retaining transaxle-to-engine bolts. Tighten to 55 ft. lbs. (75 Nm).

    e. Connect the vacuum modulator line to the modulator.

    f. Fasten the power steering lines to the pump. Tighten to 20 ft. lbs. (27 Nm).

    g. Install the crossover pipe.

50. The remainder of installation is the reverse of the removal procedure. Make sure all components are securely tightened, and all connectors properly attached.

51. Fill the engine with clean engine oil, coolant and transaxle fluid, if needed.

➡**On the 1991–93 3.1L engines, the following test, which requires the use of a Tech 1® or equivalent scan tool, must be done before the engine is started.**

52. If equipped with a 1991–93 3.1L, perform the idle learn procedure to allow the ECM/PCM memory to be updated with the correct IAC valve pintle position and provide for a stable idle speed.

    a. Install a Tech 1® or equivalent scan tool.

    b. Turn the ignition to the **ON** position, engine not running.

    c. Select **IAC SYSTEM**, then **IDLE LEARN** in the **MISC TEST** mode.

    d. Place the transaxle in Park or Neutral, as applicable.

    e. Proceed with idle learn as directed by the scan tool.

53. Turn ignition **ON** for 3 seconds and turn **OFF**. Check for fuel leaks. Repeat this procedure a second time and recheck for fuel leaks.

54. Inspect the vehicle for fluid leaks before and after starting the engine. Check the fluid levels, and add as necessary.

55. Road test the vehicle and recheck for fluid leaks.

1994–96 VEHICLES

1. Properly relieve the fuel system pressure as outlined in Section 5 of this manual.

2. Disconnect the negative battery cable.

3. Scribe a mark around the hood hinges to ensure proper reinstallation. With the help of an assistant, remove the hood assembly.

4. Properly drain the engine coolant into a suitable container.

5. Remove the air cleaner and duct assembly.

6. Remove the transaxle fluid filler tube.

7. Remove the engine mount strut brackets.

8. Raise and safely support the vehicle.

9. Position a drain pan under the oil pan, then drain the engine oil.

10. Remove the front exhaust manifold pipe. Remove the front exhaust pipe heat shield.

11. Unfasten the lower rear transaxle bolt/screw.

12. Detach the electrical connector from the Vehicle Speed Sensor (VSS).

13. Unfasten the engine mount frame side nuts.

14. Remove the flywheel inspection cover.

15. Remove the starter motor. For details, please refer to the procedure in Section 2 of this manual.

16. Unfasten the torque converter bolts/screws.

17. Remove the transaxle mount.

18. Carefully lower the vehicle.

19. Remove the coolant recovery reservoir.

20. Remove the serpentine drive belt, as outlined in Section 1 of this manual.

21. Disconnect the accelerator control and cruise control servo cable from the throttle body.

22. Remove the accelerator control cable bracket and position the cable aside.

23. Disconnect the power brake booster vacuum hose from the upper intake manifold.

24. Unfasten the plastic cover from the shock tower.

25. Remove the alternator front and rear braces, then remove the alternator from the vehicle.

26. Disconnect the fuel feed and return pipes.

27. Tie straps around the ignition wiring harness and the engine mount strut and A/C compressor bracket.

28. Remove the power steering pump pulley, then unfasten the pump retaining bolts/screws and position the pump aside. Leave the fluid lines attached.

29. Disconnect the heater inlet and outlet hoses.

30. Detach the upper radiator hose from the engine and lower radiator hose from the water pump.

31. Unfasten the engine mount strut and A/C compressor bracket bolts/screw and position the compressor aside. Do NOT disconnect the refrigerant lines.

32. Disconnect the automatic transaxle vacuum pipe.

33. Tag and detach the electrical connectors from the following components:
- Knock sensor
- Heated oxygen sensor
- Engine Coolant Temperature (ECT) sensor
- Camshaft Position (CMP) sensor
- Crankshaft Position (CKP) sensor
- Wheel speed sensors

34. Detach the electrical connectors from the ignition coil.

35. Tag and detach the Idle Air Control (IAC) valve and the Throttle Position (TP) sensor electrical connectors.

36. Disconnect the vacuum hoses from the upper intake manifold.

37. Unfasten the transaxle-to-engine bolts/screws.

38. Install a safely bolt between the alternator bracket and the engine lift bracket.

39. Suitable support the transaxle with a jack or floor stands.

40. Attach a suitable engine lifting device and remove the engine from the vehicle. Check for connected wires and hoses as the engine is coming out of the body.

41. Place the engine on a workstand.

To install:

42. With an assistant, install a lifting device onto the engine and position into the vehicle.

43. Remove the lifting device.

44. Remove the floor stands or jack from under the transaxle.

45. Remove the safely bolt from the alternator bracket and front engine lift bracket.

46. Install the transaxle-to-engine bolts. Tighten to 55 ft. lbs. (75 Nm).

47. Install the remaining components in the reverse of the removal procedure. Make sure all components are securely tightened, and all connectors properly attached.

48. With the help of an assistant, install the hood assembly, making sure to align the marks made during removal.

49. Connect the negative battery cable.

50. Refill the engine with the proper type and amount of coolant and engine oil.

51. Check the fluid levels and inspect vehicle for fluid leaks before and after starting the engine.

52. Road test the vehicle and recheck for fluid leaks.

3.4L Engine

1. Take the car to a certified repair shop to have the A/C system discharged.

2. Remove the air cleaner assembly.

3. Scribe a mark around the hood hinges, then remove the hood with the help of an assistant.

4. Properly drain the engine cooling system into a suitable container.

5. Relieve the fuel system pressure, as outlined in Section 5 of this manual.

6. Disconnect the negative battery cable.

7. Unfasten the heater hoses from the engine.

8. Remove the engine mount torque strut and mount.

9. Remove the coolant fan assemblies.

10. Disconnect the radiator hoses from the engine.

11. If equipped, disconnect the transaxle cooler lines.

12. Remove the radiator and hoses.

13. Detach the control cables from the bracket and throttle body.

14. Disengage the electrical bulkhead connector at the right side dash mat.

15. Disconnect the fuel lines.

16. Remove the exhaust crossover.

17. Unfasten the transaxle-to-engine retaining bolts, Remove the ground wires/straps from the bellhousing.

18. If equipped, remove the fuel injector cover.

19. Disconnect the power steering lines at the pump and front cover.

20. Remove the serpentine drive belt.

21. Unfasten the upper A/C compressor bolts. Detach the compressor electrical connector.

22. Detach the EGR pipe from the EGR valve.

23. Raise and safely support the vehicle.

24. Remove the right front wheel and tire assembly, then remove the right front splash shield.

25. For vehicles through 1993, remove the A/C manifold from the compressor.

26. For 1994–96 vehicles, unfasten the lower compressor bolts and position the compressor aside.

27. Unfasten the flywheel inspection cover(s).

28. Position a suitable drain pan under the oil pan, then drain the engine oil and remove the oil filter.

29. Remove the starter motor, as outlined in Section 2 of this manual.

30. Remove the front exhaust pipe and converter.

31. Remove the engine mount nuts from the frame.

32. Tag and detach the electrical connections from the rear of the engine.

33. Remove the steel torque converter inspection cover. Unfasten the torque converter bolts.

34. Tag and detach the electrical connections from the front of the engine.

35. Unfasten the right ball joint nut, then separate the ball joint from the control arm.

36. Remove the outer tie rod.

37. Remove the drive axle assembly.

38. If equipped, remove the transaxle shield.

39. Support the transaxle with a suitable jacking fixture.

40. Unfasten the motor mount bracket-to-transaxle bolts and nuts.

41. Detach the electrical connections from the alternator.

42. Carefully lower the vehicle.

43. Remove the plastic cover from the shock tower.

44. Detach the engine quick connects from the ECM/PCM.

45. Install an engine lifting device.

46. Unfasten the remaining engine-to-transaxle bolts, then lift the engine from the vehicle. Make sure to disconnect any remaining vacuum lines or electrical connectors from the rear of the engine while removing the engine.

To install:

47. Lower the engine into the vehicle, making sure to connect the vacuum lines to the rear of the engine. Attach any necessary electrical connectors.

48. Install the two transaxle-to-engine bolts.

49. Attach the electrical quick connects to the ECM/PCM.

50. Remove the engine lifting device and the transaxle support.

51. Raise and safely support the vehicle.

52. Attach the alternator electrical connections.

53. Fasten the motor mount bracket-to-transaxle nuts and bolts and tighten to 32 ft. lbs. (43 Nm).

54. Install the remaining components in the reverse of the removal procedure. Make sure all components are securely tightened, and all connectors properly attached.

55. Refill the engine cooling system with the proper type and amount of coolant.

56. Install the hood assembly with the help of an assistant.

57. Install the air cleaner assembly.

58. Connect the negative battery cable.

59. Perform the idle learn procedure to allow the ECM/PCM memory to be updated with the correct IAC valve pintle position and provide for a stable idle speed.
   a. Install a Tech 1® or equivalent scan tool.
   b. Turn the ignition to the **ON** position, engine not running.
   c. Select **IAC SYSTEM**, then **IDLE LEARN** in the **MISC TEST** mode.
   d. Place the transaxle in park or neutral, as applicable.
   e. Proceed with idle learn as directed by the scan tool.

60. Bleed the power steering system, as outlined in Section 8 of this manual.

61. Check the fluid levels and inspect the vehicle for fluid leaks before and after starting the engine.

62. Road test the vehicle and recheck for fluid leaks.

63. Take the vehicle to a certified repair shop to have the A/C system charged.

3.8L Engine

▶ **See Figure 9**

1. Scribe a mark around the hood hinges for installation reference, then remove the hood with the help of an assistant.

2. Properly relieve the fuel system pressure. For details, please refer to the procedure in Section 5 of this manual.

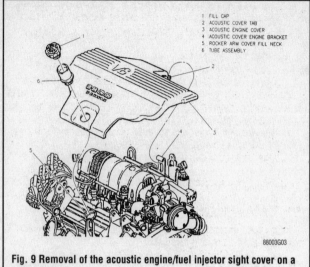

1 FILL CAP
2 ACOUSTIC COVER TAB
3 ACOUSTIC ENGINE COVER
4 ACOUSTIC COVER ENGINE BRACKET
5 ROCKER ARM COVER FILL NECK
6 TUBE ASSEMBLY

88003G03

Fig. 9 Removal of the acoustic engine/fuel injector sight cover on a 1996 vehicle

3. Disconnect the negative battery cable.

4. Remove the air cleaner assembly.

5. Disconnect the fuel lines from the fuel rail and mounting brackets and position aside.

6. Drain the engine coolant into a suitable container, then remove the coolant recovery reservoir.

7. Remove the inner fender electrical cover.

8. Remove the fuel injector sight/acoustic engine cover as follows:
   a. Twist to unlock tube/oil fill cap from the engine.
   b. Lift the cover up at the front and slid the tab out of the engine bracket.
   c. Replace the tube/oil fill cap in the rocker arm (valve) cover.

9. Disconnect the throttle cables from the throttle body and mounting bracket.

10. Remove the rear heat shield from the crossover pipe.

11. Remove the throttle cable mounting bracket and vacuum line as an assembly.

12. Disconnect the exhaust crossover from the manifolds.

13. Unfasten the engine mount/torque strut bolt, then remove the strut from the engine.

14. Remove the engine cooling fans.

15. Detach the oil cooler hoses at the radiator.

16. Disconnect the vacuum line from the transaxle module.

17. Remove the serpentine belt as outlined in Section 1 of this manual.

18. Remove the power steering pump. For details, please refer to the procedure in Section 8 of this manual.

19. Remove the alternator, as outlined in Section 2 of this manual.

20. Remove the alternator support brace and engine strut bracket with the coil pack.

21. Tag and detach all electrical connections from the engine.

22. Disconnect the upper and lower radiator and heater hoses from the engine.

23. Unfasten the transaxle-to-engine bolts and remove the ground wire harness by unfastening the retaining bolt.

24. Raise and support the vehicle safely.

25. Remove the right front wheel and tire assembly.

26. Remove the inner splash shield.

27. Remove the flywheel cover, scribe a mark on the torque converter and flywheel, for installation purposes, and unfasten the flywheel to torque converter bolts.

28. Unfasten the wire harness clamps from the frame near the radiator.

29. Remove the A/C compressor from the bracket position it aside. Do NOT disconnect the refrigerant lines.

30. Disconnect the wires and remove the starter motor assembly. For details, please refer to the procedure in Section 2 of this manual.

31. Safely support the transaxle, then use a long extension through the wheel well to unfasten the transaxle-to-engine bolt.

32. Attach a suitable engine lifting device and unfasten the engine mount-to-frame nuts.

33. Drain the engine oil into a suitable container, then remove the oil filter.

34. Disconnect the oil cooler pipes from the hose connections.

35. Detach the exhaust pipe from the manifold.

36. Carefully lower the vehicle, then remove the engine assembly from the vehicle.

To install:

37. With an assistant, install a lifting device onto the engine and position into the vehicle. Make sure to align the engine with the transaxle dowel pins.

38. With the transaxle supported, install the transaxle-to-engine bolts and ground wire harness. Tighten the bolts to 46 ft. lbs. (62 Nm).

39. Remove the engine lifting device and transaxle support fixture.

40. Install the remaining components in the reverse of the removal procedure. Tighten the following components to the specifications given:
   - Engine torque strut bolts: 41 ft. lbs. (56 Nm)
   - Engine mount-to-frame nuts: 32 ft. lbs. (43 Nm)
   - Transaxle-to-engine bolt (through wheel well): 46 ft. lbs. (62 Nm)
   - Torque converter-to-flywheel bolts: 46 ft. lbs. (62 Nm)
   - Flywheel cover bolts: 53 inch lbs. (6 Nm)

41. Refill the cooling system with the proper type and amount of coolant.

42. Bleed the power steering system, as outlined in Section 8 of this manual.

43. Connect the negative battery cable and install the hood, aligning the marks made during removal.

44. Check and add fluids as required. Test drive the vehicle and check for leaks and correct fluid levels.

Rocker Arm (Valve) Cover

REMOVAL & INSTALLATION

2.2L Engine

▶ See Figure 10

1. Disconnect the negative battery cable.

2. Remove the air cleaner and duct assembly.

3. Tag and disconnect the spark plug wires from the spark plugs, and disconnect the spark plug wire clips from the rocker arm cover and position aside.

4. Detach the PCV hose from the rocker arm cover.

5. Disconnect the throttle cables from the throttle body and remove the throttle cable bracket from the intake plenum and move aside.

6. Unfasten the rocker arm cover bolts, then remove the rocker arm cover from the vehicle. Remove and discard the gasket. Thoroughly clean all gasket mating surfaces.

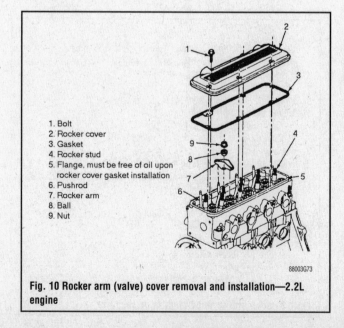

1. Bolt
2. Rocker cover
3. Gasket
4. Rocker stud
5. Flange, must be free of oil upon rocker cover gasket installation
6. Pushrod
7. Rocker arm
8. Ball
9. Nut

88003G73

Fig. 10 Rocker arm (valve) cover removal and installation—2.2L engine

To install:

7. Install a new gasket into the cut out in the rocker arm cover.

8. Position the rocker arm cover on the cylinder head, then tighten the retaining bolts to 89 inch lbs. (10 Nm).

9. Install the remaining components in the reverse of the removal procedure.

10. Connect the negative battery cable. Check the engine oil level, and add if necessary.

11. Start the engine and verify no leaks.

2.3L Engine

The camshaft housing covers and cylinder heads use the same retaining bolts. When the bolts are removed to service the camshaft cover, the cylinder head gasket MUST be replaced also. Refer to the Cylinder Head removal procedure for details.

2.5L Engine

▶ **See Figures 11 and 12**

1. Disconnect the negative battery cable.
2. Remove the air cleaner assembly.
3. Remove the spark plug wire guides from the rocket arm (valve) cover and lay wires to the side.
4. Remove the PCV valve and hose from the cover.
5. If necessary for access, remove the EGR valve bolts, valve and gasket.
6. Unfasten the valve cover retaining bolts.

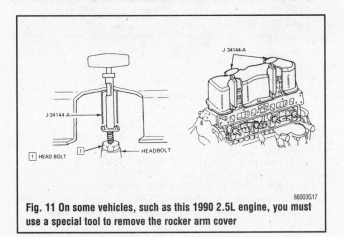

Fig. 11 On some vehicles, such as this 1990 2.5L engine, you must use a special tool to remove the rocker arm cover

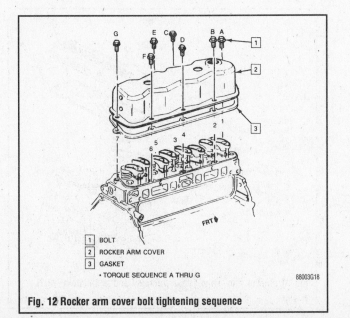

Fig. 12 Rocker arm cover bolt tightening sequence

7. Remove the valve cover, using the Rocker Arm Cover Removing tool No. J34144-A or equivalent if necessary, and lightly tap with a rubber hammer.

➡ **Prying on the cover could cause damage to the sealing surfaces.**

To install:

8. Clean the rocker arm cover with solvent and dry with a clean rag.

9. Apply a continuous 3/16 in. (5mm) diameter bead of RTV sealant or equivalent around the cylinder head sealing surfaces inboard at the bolt holes.

10. Install the rocker arm cover, then tighten the attaching bolts to 80 inch lbs. (9 Nm) using the proper sequence.

11. If removed, install the EGR gasket and valve and secure with the retaining bolts. Tighten the bolts to 16 ft. lbs. (22 Nm).

12. Fasten the spark plug wire guide and the PCV valve and hose to the cover.

13. Install the air cleaner assembly, then connect the negative battery cable.

2.8L and 3.1L (VIN T and V) Engines

➡ **On the 1991 and later 3.1L engines, a Tech 1® scan tool is needed to perform the "Idle Learn" procedure.**

LEFT (FRONT) COVER

▶ **See Figures 13 thru 19**

1. Remove the air cleaner assembly.
2. Disconnect the negative battery cable.
3. Properly drain the engine coolant into a suitable container.
4. Remove the ignition wire clamps and guide from the coolant tube.
5. Remove the coolant tube mount at the left cylinder head, the coolant tube at each end, coolant tube at the water pump, then remove the coolant tube.
6. Remove the crankcase vent tube.
7. Unfasten the torque strut-to-engine bracket bolts, then swing the torque strut up, out of the way.
8. If necessary for access, remove the ignition wire guide.
9. Unfasten the rocker arm (valve) cover retaining bolts, then remove the cover. If the cover is stuck to the cylinder head, remove it by bumping the end of the cover with the palm of your hand or a soft rubber mallet. Do not pry on the cover to remove it.

➡ **Prying on the cover could cause damage to the sealing surfaces.**

To install:

10. Clean all sealing surfaces on the cylinder head and rocker cover with degreaser and a gasket scraper.

11. Position a new gasket and install new bolt grommets. Make sure the gasket is properly seated in the rocker arm cover groove.

12. Apply a continuous 3/16 in. (5mm) diameter bead of RTV sealant surfaces inboard at the bolt holes.

13. Install the rocker cover and tighten the retaining bolts to 89 inch lbs. (10 Nm).

14. Fasten the torque strut-to-engine bracket bolt and tighten the nut to 41 ft. lbs. (56 Nm).

15. Install the remaining components in the reverse of the removal procedure.

Fig. 13 Remove the crankcase vent tube from the rocker arm cover

Fig. 14 Unfasten the torque strut-to-engine bracket bolts . . .

Fig. 15 . . . then swing the torque strut up out of the way

Fig. 16 Remove the spark plug wire guide, if necessary

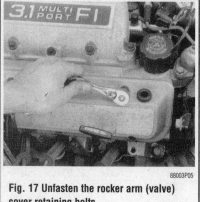

Fig. 17 Unfasten the rocker arm (valve) cover retaining bolts . . .

Fig. 18 . . . then remove the cover from the cylinder head. Do not pry on the cover during removal

Fig. 19 Remove and discard the rocker arm cover gasket

16. Properly fill the cooling system with the proper type and amount of coolant.

17. Connect the negative battery cable.

18. If equipped with a 1991 or later 3.1L engine perform the following "Idle Learn" procedure, as follows:
   a. Install a Tech 1® scan tool.
   b. Turn the ignition to the **ON** position, engine not running.
   c. Select **IAC SYSTEM**, then **IDLE LEARN** in the **MISC TEST** mode.
   d. Place the transaxle in park or neutral, as applicable.
   e. Proceed with idle learn as directed by the scan tool.

19. Start the engine and check for correct operation.

RIGHT (REAR) COVER

1. Remove the air cleaner assembly.
2. Disconnect the negative battery cable.
3. Properly drain the engine coolant into a suitable container.
4. Detach the vacuum hoses at the intake plenum.
5. Remove the EGR tube at the crossover pipe.
6. Remove the ignition wire guide and harness at the intake plenum and at spark plugs.
7. Detach the coolant hoses at the throttle base and electrical wiring from the intake plenum.
8. Remove the throttle, TV and cruise control cables from the throttle body assembly.
9. Remove the bracket from the right side of the intake plenum.
10. Disconnect the brake booster vacuum hose from the plenum.
11. Remove the serpentine belt.
12. Remove the coolant recovery bottle, exhaust pipe at the crossover and engine struts at the engine.
13. Rotate the engine as outlined earlier in this section.
14. Remove the alternator and set aside.
15. Remove the PCV valve from the rocker cover.
16. Unfasten the four rocker cover retaining bolts, then remove the cover.

➡Prying on the cover could cause damage to the sealing surfaces.

To install:

17. Clean all sealing surfaces on the cylinder head and rocker cover with degreaser and a gasket scraper.

18. Install a new gasket and bolt grommets. Make sure the gasket is properly seated in the rocker cover groove.

19. Apply a continuous ³⁄₁₆ in. (5mm) diameter bead of RTV sealant or equivalent around the cylinder head sealing surfaces inboard at the bolt holes.

20. Install the rocker cover and tighten the retaining bolts to 89 inch lbs. (10 Nm).

21. Installation of the remaining components is the reverse of the removal procedure.

22. Properly refill the cooling system with the specified type and amount of engine coolant.

23. Connect the negative battery cable.

24. Install the air cleaner assembly.

25. If equipped with a 1991 or later 3.1L engine perform the "Idle Learn" procedure, as outlined under the left (front) cover procedure.

26. Start the vehicle and check for oil, coolant, vacuum and exhaust leaks.

3.1L (VIN M) Engine

LEFT (FRONT) COVER

1. Properly drain the engine coolant into a suitable container.
2. Remove the air cleaner and duct assembly.
3. Disconnect the negative battery cable.
4. Remove the thermostat bypass pipe clip nut.
5. Remove the automatic transaxle vacuum modulator pipe assembly.
6. Remove the right engine mount strut assembly from the engine. For details, please refer to the procedure located earlier in this section.
7. Disconnect the upper radiator hose from the engine assembly.
8. Detach the PCV valve hose from the cover.
9. Remove the heater outlet hose and the thermostat bypass pipe assemblies.

10. Unfasten the rocker arm cover retaining bolts/screws, then remove the cover and gasket from the cylinder head. Discard the gasket.

11. Thoroughly clean the rocker arm cover and cylinder head mating surfaces.

To install:

12. Apply sealant No. 12345739 or equivalent at the cylinder head-to-lower manifold joint.

13. Position a new gasket, then install the rocker arm cover and hand-tighten all the retaining bolts. After all the bolts are installed, tighten them to 89 inch lbs. (10 Nm).

14. Install the remaining components in the reverse of the removal procedure.

15. Refill the engine cooling system with the proper type and amount of coolant, then add two engine coolant sealant pellets 3634621 or equivalent.

16. Connect the negative battery cable, then properly bleed the cooling system.

RIGHT (REAR) COVER

1. Disconnect the negative battery cable.
2. Remove the serpentine drive belt.
3. Remove the engine mount strut assemblies from the engine.
4. Rotate the engine, as outlined earlier in this section.
5. Detach the electrical connectors from the ignition coil, then remove the coil assembly from the vehicle.
6. Remove the plastic cover from the shock tower.
7. Remove the alternator front and rear braces, then remove the alternator from the vehicle.
8. Remove the EGR valve and position it aside.
9. Unfasten the retaining bolts/screws, then remove the cover and gasket from the vehicle. Discard the gasket.
10. Thoroughly clean the rocker arm cover and cylinder head mating surfaces.

To install:

11. Apply sealant No. 12345739 or equivalent at the cylinder head-to-lower manifold joint.

12. Position a new gasket, then install the rocker arm cover and hand-tighten all the retaining bolts. After all the bolts are installed, tighten them to 89 inch lbs. (10 Nm).

13. Install the remaining components in the reverse of the removal procedure.

14. Connect the negative battery cable, then start the engine and check for leaks and proper operation.

3.8L Engine

♦ See Figure 20

LEFT SIDE (FRONT COVER)

1. Disconnect the negative battery cable.
2. Remove the engine lift bracket from the exhaust manifold studs.
3. Remove the fuel injector sight shield.
4. For 1993–96 vehicles, remove the serpentine drive belt.

5. For 1993–96 vehicles, unfasten the alternator-to-brace bolt, then remove the alternator brace.

6. Tag and disconnect the spark plug cables from the plugs, then remove the wire cover from the valve cover.

7. Remove the valve cover retaining bolts and remove the cover with a light tap with a rubber mallet, if necessary.

To install:

8. Installation is the reverse of the removal procedure. Be sure to thoroughly clean and dry all parts prior to installing them.

9. Replace the gasket, apply thread-locking compound to the threads, and tighten the retaining bolts to 89 inch lbs. (10 Nm).

10. Connect the negative battery cable, then start the engine and check for leaks.

RIGHT SIDE (REAR COVER)

1. Disconnect the negative battery cable.
2. Remove the coolant recovery bottle.
3. Remove the serpentine drive belt.
4. Without disconnecting the hoses, remove the power steering pump and position aside.
5. Remove the fuel injector sight shield.
6. Remove the canister purge sensor valve from the bracket and remove the power steering pump support braces.
7. Tag and disconnect the spark plug wires from the spark plugs.
8. Remove the engine lift brackets from the exhaust manifold studs.
9. Unfasten the valve cover retaining bolts, then remove the cover. If necessary use a light tap with a rubber mallet on the cover to remove it.

To install:

10. Be sure to thoroughly clean and dry all parts prior to installing them.

11. Replace the gasket, apply thread-locking compound to the threads, and tighten the retaining bolts to 89 inch lbs. (10 Nm).

12. Install the engine lift brackets to the exhaust manifold studs. Tighten the nuts to 41 ft. lbs. (55 Nm).

13. Installation of the remaining components is the reverse of the removal procedure.

14. Connect the negative battery cable.
15. Run the engine and check for leaks.

Camshaft Carrier Cover

REMOVAL & INSTALLATION

3.4L Engine

♦ See Figure 21

LEFT (FRONT) COVER

1. Disconnect the negative battery cable.
2. Remove the oil/air breather hose from the cover.
3. Tag and disconnect the spark plug cables from the spark plugs.
4. Remove the rear spark plug wires cover.

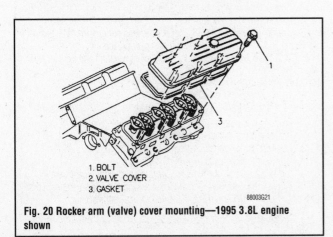

Fig. 20 Rocker arm (valve) cover mounting—1995 3.8L engine shown

1. BOLT
2. VALVE COVER
3. GASKET

88003G21

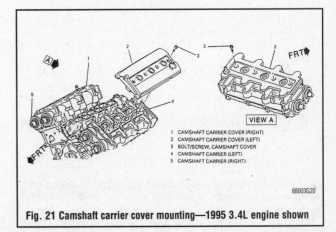

Fig. 21 Camshaft carrier cover mounting—1995 3.4L engine shown

1 CAMSHAFT CARRIER COVER (RIGHT)
2 CAMSHAFT CARRIER COVER (LEFT)
3 BOLT/SCREW, CAMSHAFT COVER
4 CAMSHAFT CARRIER (LEFT)
5 CAMSHAFT CARRIER (RIGHT)

VIEW A

88003G20

5. Unfasten the cam carrier cover retaining bolts, then remove the cover, with a light tap with a rubber mallet, if necessary. Remove and discard the gasket and O-rings.

To install:

6. Thoroughly clean and dry all parts prior to installing them.

7. Replace the gasket and O-rings on the cover, then position the cover and install the retaining bolts. Fully seat the isolators into the cover, then tighten the retaining bolts to 97 inch lbs. (11 Nm).

8. Fasten the rear spark plug wire cover.

9. Attach the spark plug wires to the plugs, as tagged during removal.

10. Fasten the oil/air breather hose to the cover.

11. Connect the negative battery cable, then start the engine and check for leaks.

RIGHT (REAR COVER)

1. Disconnect the negative battery cable.

2. Remove the upper intake manifold (plenum) assembly, as outlined later in this section.

3. Remove the right side timing belt cover.

4. Tag and disconnect the right side spark plug cables.

5. Detach the oil/air separator hose from the cover.

6. Unfasten the cam carrier cover retaining bolts and remove the cover, with a light tap with a rubber mallet, if necessary.

To install:

7. The installation is the reverse of the removal procedure. Be sure to thoroughly clean and dry all parts prior to installing them.

8. Replace all gasket and O-rings and tighten the cover retaining bolts to 89 inch lbs. (10 Nm).

9. Connect the negative battery cable.

10. Start the engine and check for leaks.

Pushrod Cover

REMOVAL & INSTALLATION

2.5L Engine

1. Disconnect the negative battery cable.

2. Remove the intake manifold as outlined later in this section.

3. Unfasten the four pushrod cover attaching nuts.

➡**Do not pry on the cover or damage to the sealing surface may result.**

4. To remove the pushrod cover, proceed as follows:

a. Unscrew the four nuts from the cover attaching studs, then reverse the two nuts so the washers face outward and screw them back onto the inner two studs. Assemble the remaining nuts to the same two inner studs with the washers facing inward.

b. Using a small wrench on the inner nut on each stud, jam the two nuts tightly together. Again, using the small wrench on the inner nut, unscrew the studs until the cover breaks loose.

c. After breaking the cover loose, remove the jammed nuts from each stud. Remove the cover from the studs. Examine the stud and rubber washer assembly and replace if either stud or washer is damaged.

To install:

5. Clean the sealing surfaces on the cover and cylinder block.

6. Apply a continuous ³⁄₁₆ in. (5mm) bead of RTV sealer or equivalent around the pushrod cover.

7. Install the cover, then tighten the retaining bolts to 90 inch lbs. (10 Nm).

8. Install the intake manifold as outlined later in this section.

9. Connect the negative battery cable.

Rocker Arms

REMOVAL & INSTALLATION

2.2L Engine

1. Disconnect the negative battery cable.

2. Remove the rocker arm (valve) cover, as outlined earlier in this section.

➡**When removing the valve train components, any components that are to be reused, must be kept in order for installation in the same locations from which they were removed.**

3. Remove the rocker arm nut(s), ball(s) and rocker arms from the vehicle.

4. Carefully remove the pushrods.

To install:

5. Clean the gasket surfaces completely.

6. Coat the bearing surfaces of the rocker arm(s) and the rocker arm ball(s) with Molykote® or equivalent engine assembly lube, engine oil supplement, etc.

7. Seat the pushrods in the lifters.

8. Install the rocker arm(s), ball(s) and nut(s). Components being reused must be installed in the same location from which they were removed. Tighten the rocker arm nut(s) to 22 ft. lbs. (30 Nm).

9. Install the rocker arm cover, using a new gasket, as outlined earlier in this section.

10. Connect the negative battery cable.

2.5L Engine

▶ **See Figure 22**

1. Disconnect the negative battery cable.

2. Remove the rocker arm (valve) cover, as outlined earlier in this section.

➡**Mark all valve components so they are reinstalled in their original locations.**

3. Remove the rocker arm bolt and ball.

4. Remove the rocker arm, guide, and pushrod.

To install:

5. If removed, install the pushrod through the cylinder head and into the lifter seat.

6. Install the guide, rocker arm, ball and bolt. Tighten the rocker arm bolts to 20–24 ft. lbs. (27–32 Nm)

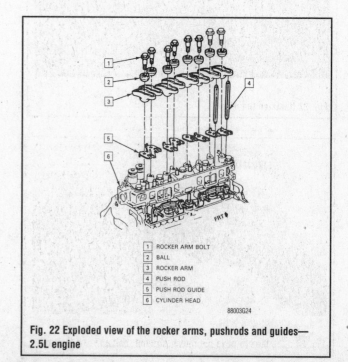

1	ROCKER ARM BOLT
2	BALL
3	ROCKER ARM
4	PUSH ROD
5	PUSH ROD GUIDE
6	CYLINDER HEAD

88003G24

Fig. 22 Exploded view of the rocker arms, pushrods and guides— 2.5L engine

7. Install the rocker arm cover, as outlined in this section.
8. Connect the negative battery cable.

2.8L and 3.1L Engines

▶ **See Figures 23, 24 and 25**

➡The intake pushrods and exhaust pushrods are different lengths. To distinguish the different pushrods, paint has been used, although this paint may be hard to identify after prolonged use. The intake pushrods are color-coded orange and are 6 in. (152mm) long. The exhaust pushrods are color-coded blue and are 6⅜ in. (162mm) long.

1. Disconnect the negative battery cable.
2. Remove the rocket arm cover, as outlined earlier in this section.
3. Remove the rocker arm nuts and balls and remove the rocker arms. Make sure to keep the components in order for installation purposes.

❋❋ WARNING

Be careful when removing the pushrods, so they do not fall into the lifter valley!

4. Remove the pushrod assemblies.

➡Place the rocker arms, balls and pushrod assemblies in a rack so they can be installed in their original positions.

5. Clean the gasket mounting surfaces.

To install:

➡When installing the rocker arms, balls and pushrod assemblies, coat their bearing surface with prelube 1052365 or equivalent. Make sure to install these components in the locations from which they were removed.

6. Install the pushrods in their original location, making sure they seat in the lifter sockets.

Fig. 23 Unfasten the nuts . . .

Fig. 24 . . . then remove the rocker arm nut, ball and rocker arm

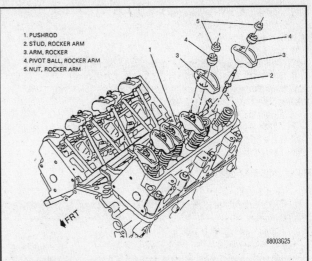

1. PUSHROD
2. STUD, ROCKER ARM
3. ARM, ROCKER
4. PIVOT BALL, ROCKER ARM
5. NUT, ROCKER ARM

FRT

88003G25

Fig. 25 Exploded view of the valve rocker arms and pushrod assemblies—1995 3.1L engine shown

7. Install the rocker arms and ball, then tighten the nuts to 14–20 ft. lbs. (19–27 Nm).
8. Install the rocker arm (valve) cover, as outlined earlier in this section.
9. Connect negative battery cable.
10. Start the vehicle and check for leaks.

3.8L Engine

▶ **See Figure 26**

1. Disconnect the negative battery cable.
2. Remove the valve cover(s), as outlined in this section.
3. Remove the rocker arm pedestal retaining bolts and remove the pedestal, bearing and rocker arm assembly.
4. Remove the pushrods.

➡Intake and exhaust pushrods are the same length. Store components in order so they can reassembled in the same location.

To install:

5. Install the pushrods and make sure they seat in the lifter.
6. Apply a thread lock compound to the bolt threads before reassembly.
7. Install the retainer, bearing, pedestal and rocker arm assemblies and tighten the retaining bolts to 18 ft. lbs. (27 Nm), plus an additional 70° using tool J 36660, or equivalent.

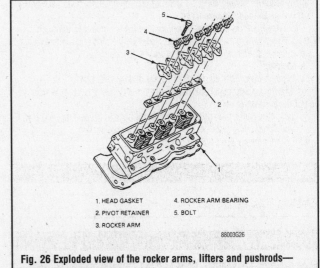

1. HEAD GASKET
2. PIVOT RETAINER
3. ROCKER ARM
4. ROCKER ARM BEARING
5. BOLT

88003G26

Fig. 26 Exploded view of the rocker arms, lifters and pushrods—1995 3.8L engine shown

8. Install the valve cover(s), as outlined earlier in this section.
9. Connect the negative battery cable.
10. Start engine and check for fluid leaks.

Thermostat

The thermostat is used to control the flow of engine coolant. When the engine is cold, the thermostat is closed to prevent coolant from circulating through the engine. As the engine begins to warm up, the thermostat opens to allow the coolant to flow through the radiator and cool the engine to its normal operating temperature. Fuel economy and engine durability is increased when operated at normal operating temperature.

REMOVAL & INSTALLATION

✳✳ CAUTION

Never open the radiator cap or the cooling system when the engine is hot. The system is under pressure and will release scalding hot coolant and steam which can cause severe burns and other bodily harm. When draining the coolant, keep in mind that cats and dogs are attracted by ethylene glycol antifreeze, and are quite likely to drink any that is left in an uncovered container or in puddles on the ground. This will prove fatal in sufficient quantity. Always drain the coolant into a sealable container. Coolant should be reused unless it is contaminated or several years old.

2.2L Engine

▶ See Figure 27

1. Disconnect the negative battery cable.
2. Partially drain the coolant, into a suitable container, to a level below the thermostat housing.
3. If replacing the coolant outlet, disconnect the upper coolant hose from the outlet.
4. Unfasten the three retaining nuts, then remove the outlet and thermostat.
5. If damaged remove and discard the studs from the housing.
6. Thoroughly clean the gasket mating surfaces.

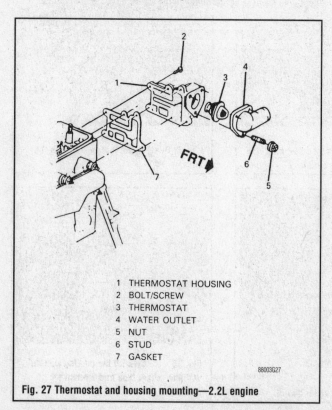

1	THERMOSTAT HOUSING
2	BOLT/SCREW
3	THERMOSTAT
4	WATER OUTLET
5	NUT
6	STUD
7	GASKET

88003G27

Fig. 27 Thermostat and housing mounting—2.2L engine

To install:

7. If removed, install new studs and tighten to 89 inch lbs. (10 Nm).
8. Apply a suitable sealer, then install the thermostat and the thermostat housing and secure with the three nuts. Tighten the nuts to 89 inch lbs. (10 Nm).
9. If removed, connect the upper coolant hose to the outlet.
10. Refill the cooling system to the proper level with the correct type of coolant.
11. Connect the negative battery cable.

2.3L Engine

▶ See Figure 28

1. Remove the air cleaner assembly.
2. Disconnect the negative battery cable.
3. Partially drain the engine coolant, into a suitable drain pan, to a level below the thermostat.
4. Disconnect the radiator and heater hoses from the coolant outlet.
5. Detach the electrical connectors from the coolant outlet.
6. Remove the pipe and retaining bolts from the coolant outlet.
7. Remove the outlet and thermostat.

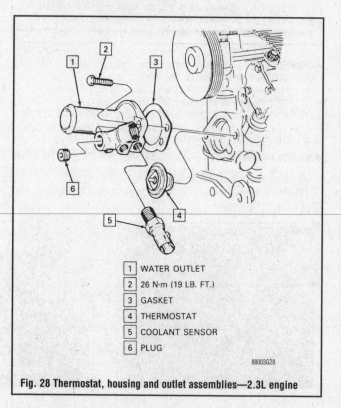

1	WATER OUTLET
2	26 N·m (19 LB. FT.)
3	GASKET
4	THERMOSTAT
5	COOLANT SENSOR
6	PLUG

88003G28

Fig. 28 Thermostat, housing and outlet assemblies—2.3L engine

To install:

8. Thoroughly clean the gasket mating surfaces.
9. Using a new gasket and RTV sealant, install the thermostat and outlet. Tighten the retaining bolts to 19 ft. lbs. (26 Nm).
10. Connect the pipe to the coolant outlet.
11. Attach the electrical connectors and the hoses to the coolant outlet.
12. Refill the radiator with the specified amount of engine coolant
13. Connect the negative battery cable, then install the air cleaner.
14. Start the engine and check for leaks.

2.5L Engine

▶ See Figure 29

1. Disconnect the negative battery cable.
2. Partially drain the engine coolant from the radiator to a level below the thermostat.
3. Remove the thermostat housing cap.
4. Remove the thermostat by using the wire handle to lift it out of the housing.

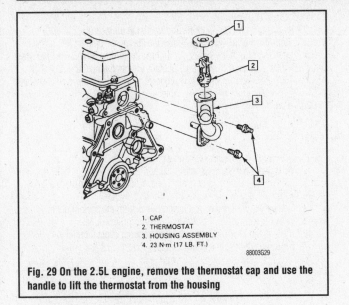

Fig. 29 On the 2.5L engine, remove the thermostat cap and use the handle to lift the thermostat from the housing

1. CAP
2. THERMOSTAT
3. HOUSING ASSEMBLY
4. 23 N·m (17 LB. FT.)

88003G29

To install:
5. Insert the thermostat and seal into the housing.
6. Install the thermostat housing cap
7. Refill the engine with the proper amount of engine coolant.
8. Connect the negative battery cable. Start the engine and check for leaks.

2.8L, 3.1L and 1991 3.4L Engines

▶ See Figures 30 thru 37

1. Disconnect the negative battery cable.
2. Partially drain the engine cooling system, into a suitable container, to a level below the thermostat.

3. If replacing the water outlet, detach the radiator hose from the outlet.
4. Unfasten the water outlet attaching bolts and remove the water outlet.
5. Remove the thermostat. Remove and discard the gasket.
6. Thoroughly clean the manifold water inlet and water outlet mating surfaces.
To install:
7. Position the thermostat into the inlet manifold.
8. Apply a 0.125 in. (3mm) bead of RTV sealer to the thermostat housing.
9. Install the water outlet to the inlet manifold, then tighten the attaching bolts to 18 ft. lbs. (23 Nm).
10. Attach the radiator hose to the water outlet housing.
11. Refill the engine with the specified type and amount of engine coolant. Connect the negative battery cable, start the engine and check for coolant leaks.

1992–96 3.4L Engines

▶ See Figure 38

1. Disconnect the negative battery cable.
2. Remove the air cleaner and duct assembly.
3. Partially drain the engine cooling system, into a suitable container, to a level below the thermostat.
4. Remove the engine torque strut bolt from the engine.
5. Disconnect the upper radiator hose from the housing.
6. Properly relieve the fuel system pressure. For details, please refer to Section 5 of this manual.
7. Disconnect the fuel lines from the fuel rail.
8. Remove the heater hose bracket at the thermostat housing stud.
9. Disconnect the heater hose from the throttle body.
10. Unfasten the thermostat housing retaining bolts, then remove the housing.
11. Remove the thermostat. Remove and discard the gasket.
To install:
12. Thoroughly clean the gasket mating surfaces.
13. Position the thermostat, then install a new gasket.

Fig. 30 View of the thermostat location—1992 3.1L engine

88003P09

Fig. 31 Unfasten the water outlet attaching bolts, then remove the outlet

88003P08

Fig. 32 Remove the thermostat from the housing . . .

88003P10

Fig. 33 . . . then remove and discard the gasket from the thermostat

88003P11

Fig. 34 Remove the radiator cap . . .

88003P12

Fig. 35 . . . then fill the cooling system with the proper type and amount of coolant

88003P13

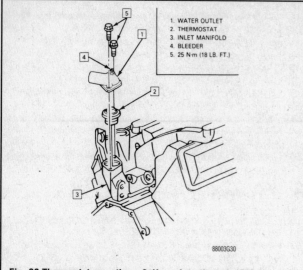

Fig. 36 Thermostat mounting—3.1L engines through 1993

1. WATER OUTLET
2. THERMOSTAT
3. INLET MANIFOLD
4. BLEEDER
5. 25 N·m (18 LB. FT.)

88003G30

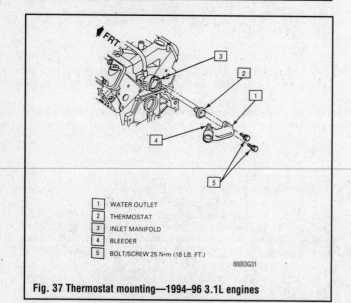

1. WATER OUTLET
2. THERMOSTAT
3. INLET MANIFOLD
4. BLEEDER
5. BOLT/SCREW 25 N·m (18 LB. FT.)

88003G31

Fig. 37 Thermostat mounting—1994–96 3.1L engines

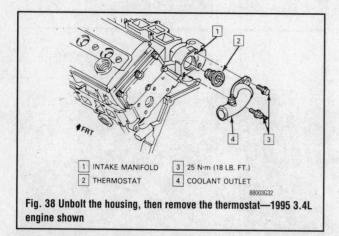

1. INTAKE MANIFOLD   3. 25 N·m (18 LB. FT.)
2. THERMOSTAT   4. COOLANT OUTLET

88003G32

Fig. 38 Unbolt the housing, then remove the thermostat—1995 3.4L engine shown

14. Attach the thermostat housing to the inlet manifold. Coat the retaining bolts with RTV sealer before installing them. Tighten the bolts to 18 ft. lbs. (25 Nm).
15. Connect the heater hose to the throttle body.
16. Install the heater hose bracket at the thermostat housing stud.

17. Connect the fuel lines to the fuel rails.
18. Attach the upper radiator hose to the thermostat housing.
19. Install the engine torque strut-to-engine bolt.
20. Install the air cleaner assembly, then connect the negative battery cable.
21. Refill the engine with the specified type and amount of engine coolant. Start the engine and check for coolant leaks.

3.8L Engine

▶ **See Figure 39**

1. Disconnect the negative battery cable.
2. Remove the air cleaner and duct assembly.
3. Partially drain the engine cooling system, into a suitable container, to a level below the thermostat.
4. Disconnect the radiator hose from the water outlet.
5. If necessary, detach the electrical connections from the throttle body assembly.
6. Unfasten the water outlet attaching bolts, then remove the water outlet.
7. Remove the thermostat. Remove and discard the gasket.
8. Thoroughly clean the manifold water inlet and water outlet mating surfaces.

To install:

9. Position the thermostat into the intake manifold with a new gasket.
10. Install the water outlet to the intake manifold with RTV sealer. Tighten the attaching bolts to 20 ft. lbs. (27 Nm).
11. Connect the radiator hose to the water outlet housing.
12. If necessary, attach the electrical connections to the throttle body assembly.
13. Install the air cleaner assembly, then connect the negative battery cable.
14. Refill the engine with the specified type and amount of engine coolant. Start the engine and check for coolant leaks.

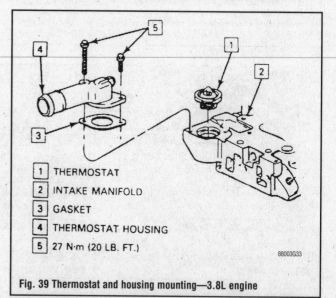

1. THERMOSTAT
2. INTAKE MANIFOLD
3. GASKET
4. THERMOSTAT HOUSING
5. 27 N·m (20 LB. FT.)

88003G33

Fig. 39 Thermostat and housing mounting—3.8L engine

Intake Manifold

REMOVAL & INSTALLATION

✳✳ CAUTION

When draining the coolant, keep in mind that cats and dogs are attracted by ethylene glycol antifreeze, and are quite likely to drink any that is left in an uncovered container or in puddles on the ground. This will prove fatal in sufficient quantity. Always drain the coolant into a sealable container. Coolant should be reused unless it is contaminated or several years old.

2.2L Engine

♦ **See Figures 40 and 41**

1. Disconnect the negative battery cable.
2. Properly relieve the fuel system pressure, as outlined in Section 5 of this manual.
3. Remove the air cleaner assembly.
4. Properly drain the coolant into a suitable container.
5. Remove the serpentine drive belt.

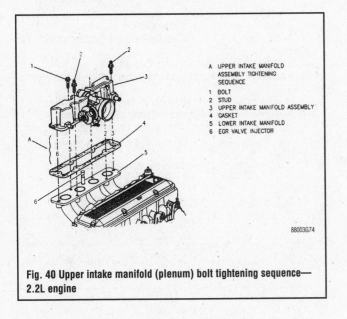

A   UPPER INTAKE MANIFOLD
     ASSEMBLY TIGHTENING
     SEQUENCE
1   BOLT
2   STUD
3   UPPER INTAKE MANIFOLD ASSEMBLY
4   GASKET
5   LOWER INTAKE MANIFOLD
6   EGR VALVE INJECTOR

88003G74

Fig. 40 Upper intake manifold (plenum) bolt tightening sequence—2.2L engine

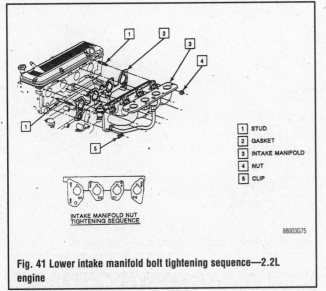

1   STUD
2   GASKET
3   INTAKE MANIFOLD
4   NUT
5   CLIP

INTAKE MANIFOLD NUT
TIGHTENING SEQUENCE

88003G75

Fig. 41 Lower intake manifold bolt tightening sequence—2.2L engine

6. Unbolt the power steering pump and set it aside. Do NOT disconnect the fluid lines.
7. Tag and detach any necessary vacuum lines or electrical connectors.
8. Remove the accelerator cable bracket.
9. Remove the MAP sensor and EGR solenoid valve.
10. Unfasten the retaining nuts, then remove the upper intake manifold.
11. Remove the EGR valve injector.
12. Remove the fuel injector retainer bracket, regulator and the injectors.
13. Unfasten the manifold retaining nuts, then remove the lower intake manifold. Remove and discard the gasket.
14. Thoroughly clean the gasket mating surfaces with a suitable gasket scraper.

To install:

15. Position a new gasket, then place the lower manifold over it. Install the retaining nuts and tighten to 22 ft. lbs. (30 Nm).
16. Install the fuel injector retainer bracket, regulator and the injectors. Tighten the bolt/screw to 31 inch lbs. (3.5 Nm).
17. Position the EGR valve injector so the port is facing directly towards the throttle body.
18. Install the upper intake manifold and secure with the retaining nuts. Tighten the nuts to 22 ft. lbs. (30 Nm).
19. Install the EGR solenoid valve and the MAP sensor and seal. Be sure the MAP sensor is installed properly. Tighten the sensor retaining bolt to 27 inch lbs. (3 Nm); do not overtighten.
20. Position the accelerator cable bracket and secure with the retaining bolts and nut. Tighten the bolts to 18 ft. lbs. (25 Nm) and the nut to 22 ft. lbs. (30 Nm).
21. Attach the vacuum lines and electrical connectors, as tagged during removal.
22. Position the power steering pump and secure with the retaining bolts.
23. Install the serpentine drive belt.
24. Install the air cleaner assembly, then connect the negative battery cable.
25. Refill the engine with the specified type and amount of engine coolant. Start the engine and check for coolant leaks.

2.3L Engine

♦ **See Figures 42 and 43**

1. Disconnect the negative battery cable. Properly drain the cooling system.
2. Properly relieve the fuel system pressure as outlined in Section 5 of this manual.
3. If necessary for access, remove the coolant recovery tank.
4. Disconnect the vacuum hose and the electrical connector from the MAP sensor.
5. Detach the electrical connectors from the MAP sensor, MAT sensor, Purge solenoid and the fuel injector harness and position the harness aside.
6. Tag and disconnect the vacuum hoses from the intake manifold and hose at the fuel regulator and purge solenoid to canister.
7. Disconnect the throttle body-to-air cleaner duct.
8. Remove the vent tube-to-air cleaner duct.
9. Remove the throttle cable bracket.
10. Remove the power brake vacuum hose, including the retaining bracket-to-power steering bracket, and position it aside.
11. Disconnect the coolant hoses from the throttle body, then remove the throttle body from the intake manifold.
12. Remove the oil/air separator (crankcase ventilation system). Leave the hoses attached to the separator, disconnect them from the oil fill, chain cover, intake duct and the intake manifold. Remove as an assembly.
13. Disconnect the oil/air separator from the oil fill tube.

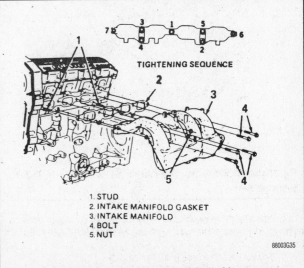

TIGHTENING SEQUENCE

1. STUD
2. INTAKE MANIFOLD GASKET
3. INTAKE MANIFOLD
4. BOLT
5. NUT

88003G35

Fig. 42 The intake manifold bolts must be tightened in sequence

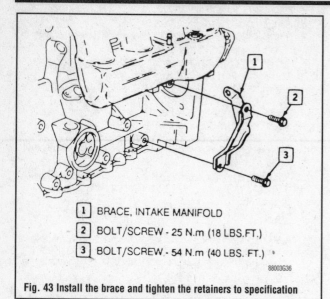

1 BRACE, INTAKE MANIFOLD

2 BOLT/SCREW - 25 N.m (18 LBS.FT.)

3 BOLT/SCREW - 54 N.m (40 LBS. FT.)

88003G36

Fig. 43 Install the brace and tighten the retainers to specification

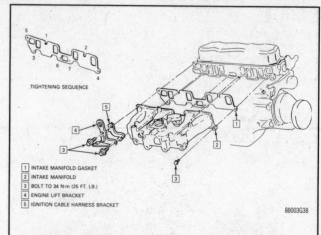

TIGHTENING SEQUENCE

1 INTAKE MANIFOLD GASKET
2 INTAKE MANIFOLD
3 BOLT TO 34 N·m (25 FT. LB.)
4 ENGINE LIFT BRACKET
5 IGNITION CABLE HARNESS BRACKET

88003G38

Fig. 44 Intake manifold bolt tightening sequence—2.5L engine

14. Remove the oil fill cap and oil level indicator dipstick.

15. Unfasten the retaining bolts, then pull the oil tube fill upward to unseat from block and remove.

16. Detach the injector harness connector.

17. Remove the fill tube out the top, rotating as necessary to gain clearance for the oil/air separator nipple between the intake tubes and fuel rail electrical harness.

18. Unfasten the intake manifold support brace bolts and nut, then remove the brace.

19. Remove the intake manifold retaining nuts and bolts, then remove the intake manifold. The hole closest to the chain housing is slotted for additional clearance. Remove and discard the gasket.

20. Thoroughly clean the gasket mating surfaces with a suitable gasket scraper.

To install:

21. Thoroughly clean and dry the mating surfaces. Install new gaskets and place the intake manifold in position.

22. Tighten the intake manifold bolts/nuts, in sequence, to 18 ft. lbs. (25 Nm). Tighten intake manifold brace and retainers hand-tight. Tighten, in sequence, as follows:

   a. Nut to stud bolt: 18 ft. lbs. (25 Nm)

   b. Bolt to intake manifold: 40 ft. lbs. (55 Nm)

   c. Bolt to cylinder block: 40 ft. lbs. (55 Nm)

23. Lubricate a new oil fill tube ring seal with engine oil and install tube between No. 1 and 2 intake tubes. Rotate as necessary to gain clearance for oil/air separator nipple on fill tube.

24. Locate the oil fill tube in its cylinder block opening. Align the fill tube so it is approximately in its installed position. Press straight down to seat fill tube and seal into cylinder block.

25. Lubricate the hoses and install the oil/air separator assembly.

26. Install the remaining components in the reverse of the removal procedure.

27. Fill all fluids to their proper levels.

28. Connect the negative battery cable, then start the engine and check for leaks.

2.5L Engine

▶ See Figure 44

1. Relieve the fuel system pressure as outlined in Section 5.

2. Disconnect the negative battery cable.

3. Remove the air cleaner assembly.

4. Detach the MAP sensor connector.

5. Properly drain the cooling system into a suitable container.

6. Rotate the engine forward, as outlined earlier in this section.

7. Remove the PCV valve and hose from the throttle body assembly and valve cover.

8. Remove the fuel lines from the throttle body and position them aside.

9. Tag and disconnect the vacuum lines and brake booster hose from the throttle body.

10. Detach all electrical connectors and control cables from the TBI assembly.

11. Unfasten the control cable bracket bolts, then position the bracket aside.

12. Unfasten the heater hose clamps, then detach the hose from the intake manifold.

13. Remove the power steering pump bolts then position it aside. Do NOT disconnect the pump fluid lines.

14. Unfasten the intake manifold retaining bolts, then remove the manifold. Remove and discard the gasket.

To install:

15. Clean all gasket surfaces on the cylinder head and intake manifold.

16. Position the intake manifold with a new gasket on the engine.

17. Install all the retaining bolts and washers hand-tight. Tighten the bolts, in proper sequence, to 25 ft. lbs. (34 Nm).

18. Install the remaining components in the reverse of the removal procedure.

19. Refill the engine cooling system to the proper level with the correct type of coolant.

20. Install the air cleaner assembly and MAP sensor connector.

21. Connect the negative battery cable, then start the engine and check for fluid leaks.

2.8L and 3.1L Engines

1988–90 VEHICLES

▶ See Figure 45

1. Disconnect the negative battery cable.

2. Drain the cooling system into a suitable container.

3. Properly relieve the fuel system pressure as outlined in Section 5.

4. Disconnect the TV and accelerator cables from the plenum.

5. Unfasten the throttle body-to-plenum bolts, then remove the throttle body. Remove the EGR valve.

6. Remove the plenum-to-intake manifold bolts, then remove the plenum.

7. Disconnect and plug the fuel lines and return pipes from the fuel rail.

8. Remove the serpentine drive belt cover and belt.

9. Unfasten the power steering pump-to-bracket bolts and support the pump out of the way. Do NOT disconnect the pressure hoses.

10. Remove the alternator-to-bracket bolts and support the alternator out of the way. Remove the alternator bracket.

11. From the throttle body, disconnect the idle air vacuum hose.

12. Label and detach the electrical connectors from the fuel injectors. Remove the fuel rail.

13. Remove the breather tube. Disconnect the runners.

14. Unfasten the rocker arm cover-to-cylinder head bolts and remove both covers.

15. Disconnect the radiator hose from the thermostat housing.

16. Tag and detach the electrical connectors from the coolant temperature sensor and oil pressure sending unit. Remove the coolant sensor.

17. Disconnect the heater inlet pipe from the manifold.

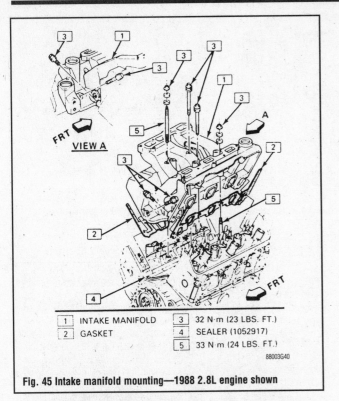

	INTAKE MANIFOLD		3	32 N·m (23 LBS. FT.)
	GASKET		4	SEALER (1052917)
			5	33 N·m (24 LBS. FT.)

88003G40

Fig. 45 Intake manifold mounting—1988 2.8L engine shown

18. Unfasten the intake manifold-to-cylinder head bolts, then remove the manifold. Remove and discard the gasket.

19. Loosen the rocker arm nuts, turn them 90° and remove the pushrods; be sure to keep the components in order for installation purposes.

20. Thoroughly clean all of the gasket mounting surfaces.

To install:

21. Place a bead of RTV sealer or equivalent on each ridge where the intake manifold and block meet. Install the intake manifold gasket in place on the block.

22. Install the pushrods and reposition the rocker arms. Make sure the pushrods seat properly in the lifter. Tighten the rocker arm nuts to 18 ft. lbs. (25 Nm).

23. Mount the intake manifold on the engine, using a new gasket, then tighten the bolts to 23 ft. lbs. 32 (Nm).

24. Connect the heater inlet pipe to the manifold.

25. Install and connect the coolant sensor. Attach the wire at the oil sending switch.

26. Connect the radiator hose at the thermostat outlet.

27. Install the rocker arm (valve) covers and tighten the retaining bolts to 90 inch lbs. (10 Nm)

28. Install the runners, breather tube, fuel rail and connect the wires at the fuel injectors.

29. Attach the idle air vacuum hose to the throttle body.

30. Install the alternator bracket and the alternator. Install the power steering pump.

31. Install the serpentine belt and belt cover.

32. Connect the fuel lines to the fuel rail.

33. Install the plenum,

34. Attach the EGR valve to the plenum.

35. Mount the throttle body to the plenum.

36. Connect the accelerator cable and the TV cable to the plenum.

37. Fill the cooling system. Connect the negative battery cable.

38. Run the engine until it reaches normal operating temperature and check for coolant and oil leaks.

1991–93 VEHICLES

▶ See Figures 46 thru 54

1. Remove the air cleaner assembly.

2. Disconnect the negative battery cable.

3. Properly relieve the fuel system pressure as outlined in Section 5.

4. If equipped, unfasten the engine strut mounts at the engine strut mount bracket, then pull the strut up and out of the way.

5. Drain the cooling system into a suitable container.

6. Remove the throttle body from the plenum. For details, please refer to Section 5 of this manual.

7. Remove the EGR valve from the plenum.

8. If equipped, disconnect the brake booster pipe at the plenum.

9. Remove the plenum-to-intake manifold bolts and the plenum. Remove the plenum gaskets.

10. Unfasten the fuel line bracket bolt, then remove the bracket.

11. Disconnect the fuel lines from the fuel rail.

12. Rotate the engine forward, as outlined earlier in this section.

13. Remove the alternator bolts and support the alternator out of the way.

14. Remove the power steering line clamp nut at the alternator bracket.

15. Unfasten the alternator mounting bracket bolts, then remove the bracket.

16. Remove the front engine lift bracket studs, then remove the lift bracket.

17. Unfasten the power steering pump mounting bolts and support the pump out of the way. Do NOT disconnect the pressure hoses.

18. Disconnect the power brake booster pipe bracket at the rear cylinder head.

19. Unfasten the rear alternator pencil brace bolt, then remove the brace.

20. Tag and disconnect the spark plug wires from the rear cylinder head. Remove the rear valve cover, as outlined earlier in this section.

21. Rotate the engine back to its original position.

22. Unfasten the upper radiator hose clamp, then disconnect the hose from the engine.

23. Remove the coolant bypass pipe retaining bolts and the bracket nut. Remove the bypass pipe and gasket.

24. Remove the front valve cover, as outlined earlier in this section.

25. Detach the electrical connections from the intake manifold and fuel injectors.

26. Remove the coolant sensor.

27. Remove the heater inlet pipe assembly from the cylinder head and intake manifold.

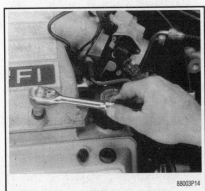

88003P14

Fig. 46 Use the correct size socket to unfasten the intake plenum retaining bolts

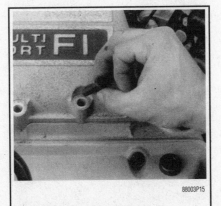

88003P15

Fig. 47 Remove the retaining bolts . . .

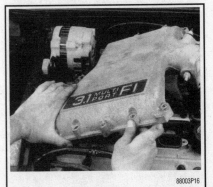

88003P16

Fig. 48 . . . then remove the intake plenum from the vehicle

Fig. 49 Remove the plenum gaskets and thoroughly clean the mating surfaces

Fig. 50 Disconnect the fuel feed and return lines from the fuel rail

Fig. 51 Unfasten the bolts, then remove the power steering pump and position aside. DO NOT disconnect the fluid lines

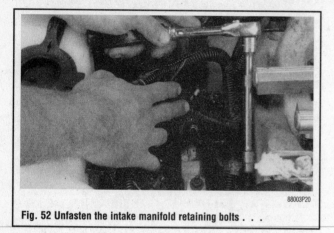

Fig. 52 Unfasten the intake manifold retaining bolts . . .

Fig. 53 . . . then remove the intake manifold from the vehicle

28. Remove the bypass hose from the filler neck and cylinder head. Remove top radiator hose.

29. Unfasten the intake manifold-to-cylinder head bolts, then remove the manifold. If necessary, tag and detach any necessary vacuum lines. Remove and discard the gasket.

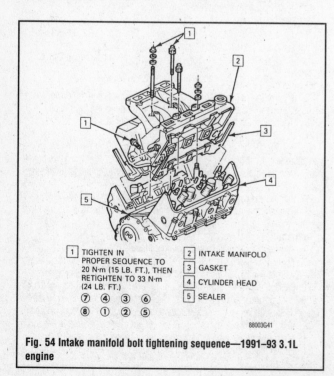

Fig. 54 Intake manifold bolt tightening sequence—1991–93 3.1L engine

Legend for Fig. 54:

1	TIGHTEN IN PROPER SEQUENCE TO 20 N·m (15 LB. FT.), THEN RETIGHTEN TO 33 N·m (24 LB. FT.)
2	INTAKE MANIFOLD
3	GASKET
4	CYLINDER HEAD
5	SEALER

⑦ ④ ③ ⑥
⑧ ① ② ⑤

30. Loosen the rocker arm nuts, turn them 90° and remove the pushrods; be sure to keep the components in order for installation purposes.

31. Clean all of the gasket mounting surfaces.

To install:

32. Place a bead of RTV sealer or equivalent on each ridge where the intake manifold and block meet. Install the intake manifold gasket in place on the block.

33. Install the pushrods and reposition the rocker arms. Tighten the rocker arm nuts to 18 ft. lbs. (25 Nm).

34. Mount the intake manifold on the engine, using a new gasket, then tighten the bolts, in two steps, as follows:

 a. 1st step: tighten in sequence to 15 ft. lbs. (20 Nm).
 b. 2nd step: tighten in sequence to 23 ft. lbs. (29 Nm).

35. Connect any necessary vacuum lines, as tagged during removal.

36. Connect the heater inlet pipe to the cylinder head and intake manifold. Install and connect the coolant sensor.

37. Attach the electrical connectors at the intake manifold and fuel injectors.

38. Install the front valve cover, using a new gasket and bolts grommets. Tighten the bolts to 89 inch lbs. (10 Nm).

39. Install the coolant bypass pipe and gasket. Secure the coolant bypass pipe retaining bolts and bracket nut.

40. Connect the upper radiator hose to the engine and secure with the retaining clamp.

41. Rotate the engine assembly forward, as outlined earlier in this section.

42. Install the rear valve cover, using a new gasket and bolts grommets. Tighten the bolts to 89 inch lbs. (10 Nm).

43. Connect the spark plug wires to the rear plugs, as tagged during removal.

44. Install the rear alternator pencil brace and secure with the retaining bolt.

45. Attach the power brake booster pipe bracket at the rear of the cylinder head.

46. Place the power steering pump in its original position and install the retaining bolts.

47. Install the front engine lift bracket and studs. Tighten the studs to 40 ft. lbs. (55 Nm).

48. Install the alternator bracket and secure with the retaining bolts. Tighten the bolts to 37 ft. lbs. (50 Nm).

49. Fasten the power steering line clamp nut at the alternator bracket.

50. Install the alternator and secure with the retaining bolts.

51. Rotate the engine back to its original position.

52. Connect the fuel lines to the fuel rail. Install the fuel line bracket and retaining bolt.

53. Install the intake plenum. Tighten the retaining bolts to 88 inch lbs. (10 Nm). If equipped, connect the brake booster pipe at the plenum.

54. Attach the EGR valve to the plenum.

55. Install the throttle body, as outlined in Section 5 of this manual.

56. Install the engine strut mounts at the engine strut mount bracket. Tighten the nuts to 41 ft. lbs. (56 Nm).

57. Fill the cooling system. Connect the negative battery cable.

58. Run the engine until it reaches normal operating temperature and check for coolant and oil leaks.

1994–96 VEHICLES

▶ See Figures 55 and 56

1. Disconnect the negative battery cable.
2. Remove the air cleaner and duct assembly.
3. Properly relieve the fuel system pressure as outlined in Section 5.
4. Drain the cooling system into a suitable container.
5. Remove the coolant recovery reservoir.
6. Remove the serpentine drive belt.
7. Disconnect the accelerator control and cruise control servo cables from the throttle body.
8. Remove the accelerator control cable bracket and move the cable assemblies aside.
9. Unfasten the thermostat bypass pipe clip nut from the upper intake manifold.
10. Remove the automatic transaxle vacuum modulator pipe assembly.
11. Disconnect the power brake booster vacuum hose from the manifold.
12. Unfasten the engine mount strut assemblies from the engine.
13. Rotate the engine assembly, as outlined earlier in this section.

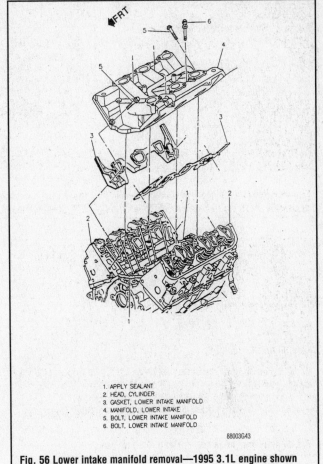

1. APPLY SEALANT
2. HEAD, CYLINDER
3. GASKET, LOWER INTAKE MANIFOLD
4. MANIFOLD, LOWER INTAKE
5. BOLT, LOWER INTAKE MANIFOLD
6. BOLT, LOWER INTAKE MANIFOLD

88003G43

Fig. 56 Lower intake manifold removal—1995 3.1L engine shown

14. Detach the electrical connectors from the ignition coil assembly, then remove the ignition coil.

15. Remove the alternator front and rear braces.

16. Tag and detach the electrical connectors from the manifold assembly.

17. Disconnect any necessary vacuum hoses.

18. Remove the MAP sensor and the EGR valve assembly.

19. Unfasten the retaining bolts and screws, then remove the upper intake manifold (plenum) assembly. Remove and discard the gaskets.

20. Disconnect the fuel feed and return lines from the lower manifold assembly.

21. Remove the fuel rail.

22. Remove the power steering pump pulley, then unfasten the power steering bolts. Position the pump aside but do NOT disconnect the fluid lines.

23. Disconnect the heater inlet pipe from the manifold.

24. Detach the upper radiator hose from the engine.

25. Remove the tie straps from the heater outlet pipe and the ignition wiring harness assembly.

26. Disconnect the heater pipe from the heater core-to-water pump assembly.

27. Remove the rocker arm (valve) covers. Remove and discard the gaskets.

28. Unfasten the lower manifold retaining screws, then remove the manifold from the vehicle.

To install:

29. Thoroughly clean all gasket mating surfaces.

30. Apply a 0.08–0.11 in. (8–12mm) bead of RTV sealer on the each ridge where the front and rear of the manifold assembly contact the engine block.

31. Position the manifold on the block using a new gasket. Hand-tighten the vertical, then the diagonal retaining bolts/screws after applying suitable sealer to the threads. Tighten the vertical, then the diagonal bolts/screws to 115 inch lbs. (5 Nm).

32. Install the rocker arm (valve) covers, as outlined earlier in this section.

33. Attach the heater pipe to the heater core-to-water pump assembly.

34. Fasten the tie straps around the heater outlet pipe and ignition wiring harness assembly.

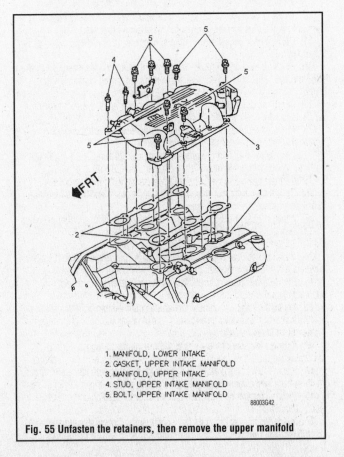

1. MANIFOLD, LOWER INTAKE
2. GASKET, UPPER INTAKE MANIFOLD
3. MANIFOLD, UPPER INTAKE
4. STUD, UPPER INTAKE MANIFOLD
5. BOLT, UPPER INTAKE MANIFOLD

88003G42

Fig. 55 Unfasten the retainers, then remove the upper manifold

35. Connect the upper radiator hose to the engine.
36. Position the power steering pump and secure with the retainers.
37. Install the power steering pump pulley.
38. Install the fuel rail assembly. Connect the fuel feed and return pipes to the fuel rail.
39. Position the upper manifold assembly, using new gaskets. Secure with the studs and bolts/screws. Tighten the bolts/screws to 18 ft. lbs. (25 Nm).
40. Install the EGR valve and the MAP sensor.
41. Connect any necessary vacuum hoses and electrical connectors to the manifold assembly.
42. Install the alternator front and rear braces.
43. Install the ignition coil and attach the electrical connector.
44. Rotate the engine assembly back to its original position.
45. Install the engine mount strut assemblies to the engine.
46. Connect the power brake booster vacuum hose to the manifold.
47. Install the automatic transaxle vacuum module pipe assembly.
48. Fasten the thermostat bypass clip nut to the upper intake manifold assembly.
49. Install the accelerator control cable bracket and the accelerator control and cruise control cable servo assemblies to the throttle body.
50. Install the serpentine drive belt and the coolant recovery reservoir.
51. Install the air cleaner assembly.
52. Fill the cooling system. Connect the negative battery cable.
53. Run the engine until it reaches normal operating temperature and check for coolant and oil leaks.

3.4L Engine

♦ See Figures 57 and 58

➡Much of this procedure involves servicing the intake plenum. Do not confuse it with the intake manifold. They are separate entities and are separately serviceable, although the intake plenum must first be removed to gain access to the fuel rail and intake manifold.

1. Properly relieve the fuel system pressure as outlined in Section 5.
2. Disconnect the negative battery cable and remove the air cleaner assembly.
3. Detach the control cables from the connections from the throttle body portion of the plenum.
4. Unfasten the retaining bolts, then remove the fuel rail cover.
5. If necessary, disconnect the vacuum module line at the intake manifold.
6. Disconnect the fuel feed line and return line from the fuel rail assembly; be sure to use a backup wrench on the inlet fitting to prevent turning.
7. Disconnect the heater hose from the lower intake manifold.
8. Disconnect the PCV valve and vacuum line from the throttle body portion of the plenum (upper intake manifold).
9. Tag and detach the AIR solenoid, EGR valve, and TPS connectors.
10. Unfasten the retaining bolts, then remove the EGR valve.

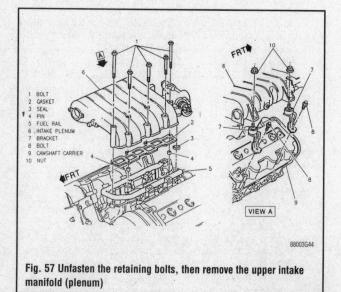

1 BOLT
2 GASKET
3 SEAL
4 PIN
5 FUEL RAIL
6 INTAKE PLENUM
7 BRACKET
8 BOLT
9 CAMSHAFT CARRIER
10 NUT

VIEW A

88003G44

Fig. 57 Unfasten the retaining bolts, then remove the upper intake manifold (plenum)

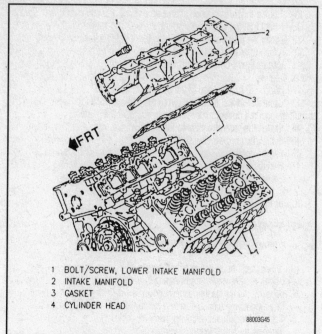

1 BOLT/SCREW, LOWER INTAKE MANIFOLD
2 INTAKE MANIFOLD
3 GASKET
4 CYLINDER HEAD

88003G45

Fig. 58 Lower intake manifold removal—1995 3.1L engine shown

11. Remove the fuel line bracket from the throttle body portion of the plenum.
12. Loosen the throttle body heater hose clamp from the upper intake manifold (plenum).
13. Disconnect the canister purge solenoid and MAP sensor connectors.
14. Carefully disconnect the vacuum hoses from the vacuum tee on the plenum.
15. Remove the wiring loom bracket for the rear spark plug cables.
16. Unfasten the plenum (upper manifold) support bracket nuts.
17. Remove the plenum mounting bolts and remove the intake plenum. Remove and discard the gaskets.
18. Remove the vacuum line at the pressure regulator. Remove the fuel rail assembly retaining bolts.
19. Push in the wire connector clip, while pulling the connector away from the injector.
20. Remove the fuel rail assembly and cover all openings with masking tape to prevent dirt from entering.
21. Detach the electrical connector, then remove the temperature sensor.
22. Remove the heater hose pipe bracket at the thermostat housing.
23. Disconnect the radiator hose from thermostat housing.
24. Unfasten the mounting bolts, then remove the lower intake manifold. Remove and discard the gaskets.
To install:
25. Thoroughly clean and dry all mating surfaces and install new intake manifold gaskets.

➡Tighten the manifold bolts evenly. DO NOT tighten one side or end of the manifold fully.

26. Position the intake manifold. Insert new rubber isolators into manifold flange and tighten the mounting evenly bolts to 18–22 ft. lbs. (25–30 Nm). Start with center bolts and work outwards in a circular pattern.
27. Install the heater hose pipe bracket to the thermostat housing.
28. Install the temperature sensor and attach the connector.
29. Connect the radiator hose to thermostat housing.
30. Install the fuel rail assembly and secure with the retaining bolts.
31. Connect the vacuum line to the pressure regulator.
32. Install the intake plenum, using new gaskets and install the retaining bolts. Tighten the bolts 18–22 ft. lbs. (25–30 Nm), starting in the center and working outwards in a circular pattern.
33. Install the plenum support bracket nuts.
34. Install the wiring loom bracket for the rear spark plug cables.
35. Carefully connect the vacuum hoses to the vacuum tee on the plenum.
36. Connect the canister purge solenoid and MAP sensor connectors.

37. Tighten the throttle body hose clamp.
38. Install the fuel line bracket to the throttle body portion of the plenum.
39. Install the EGR valve.
40. Attach the AIR solenoid, EGR valve, and TPS connectors.
41. Connect the PCV valve and vacuum line to the throttle body portion of the plenum.
42. Attach the heater hose to the intake manifold.
43. Connect the fuel feed line and return line to the fuel rail assembly and install the fuel rail cover.
44. Fasten the control cables to the throttle body portion of the plenum.
45. Install the air cleaner assembly.
46. Fill the cooling system. Connect the negative battery cable.
47. Run the engine until it reaches normal operating temperature and check for coolant and oil leaks.

3.8L Engine

♦ See Figures 59 and 60

1. Properly relieve the fuel system pressure as outlined in Section 5 of this manual.
2. Disconnect the negative battery cable. Place a clean drain pan under the radiator, open the drain cock and drain the cooling system.
3. Remove the air cleaner assembly and the fuel injector sight shield.
4. Disconnect the cables from the throttle body and mount bracket.
5. Remove the coolant recovery reservoir.
6. Remove the inner fender electrical cover on the right side.
7. Remove the right rear crossover pipe heat shield.
8. Disconnect the fuel lines from the fuel rail and from the cable bracket.
9. Remove the alternator and brace.
10. Remove the throttle body cable mounting bracket with the vacuum lines and disconnect the vacuum lines.
11. Tag and detach the electrical connections at the throttle body and both banks of fuel injectors.
12. Disconnect the vacuum hoses from the canister purge solenoid valve and transaxle module and intake connection.

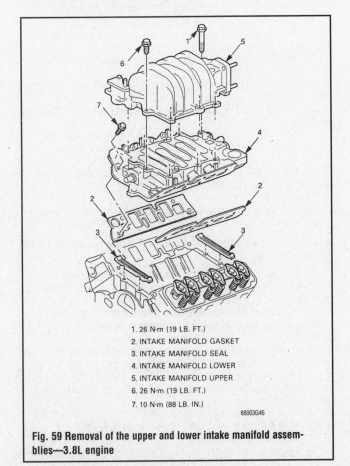

1. 26 N·m (19 LB. FT.)
2. INTAKE MANIFOLD GASKET
3. INTAKE MANIFOLD SEAL
4. INTAKE MANIFOLD LOWER
5. INTAKE MANIFOLD UPPER
6. 26 N·m (19 LB. FT.)
7. 10 N·m (88 LB. IN.)

88003G46

Fig. 59 Removal of the upper and lower intake manifold assemblies—3.8L engine

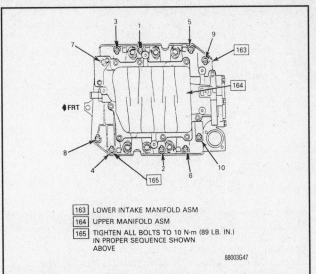

163 LOWER INTAKE MANIFOLD ASM
164 UPPER MANIFOLD ASM
165 TIGHTEN ALL BOLTS TO 10 N·m (89 LB. IN.)
     IN PROPER SEQUENCE SHOWN
     ABOVE

88003G47

Fig. 60 Lower intake manifold tightening sequence—3.8L engine

13. Unbolt the power steering pump and move forward. DO NOT disconnect the fluid lines.
14. Tag and disconnect the spark plug wires position lay aside.
15. Disconnect the coolant bypass hose from the intake manifold.
16. Remove the solenoid valve mounting bracket and power steering support brace from the intake manifold.
17. Disconnect the heater pipes from the intake and front cover.
18. Remove the alternator support brace from the intake.
19. Disconnect the upper radiator hose from the housing.
20. Remove the thermostat housing and thermostat from the intake.
21. Detach the electrical connector from the temperature sensor and sensor switch.
22. Unfasten the intake manifold bolts, then remove the manifold as an assembly. Remove and discard the gaskets.
23. If separating the upper manifold from the lower, proceed as follows:
   a. Remove the fuel rail and fuel injectors.
   b. Detach the coolant sensor switch.
   c. Remove the manifold end cap cover.
   d. Remove the upper intake manifold and throttle body assembly from the lower manifold. Remove and discard the gaskets.

To install:
24. Thoroughly clean all gasket mating surfaces.
25. If replacing the upper manifold, proceed as follows:
   a. Apply a 1/16 in. bead of Loctite® Instant Gasket Eliminator 51845 or equivalent to the lower manifold mating surface. Make sure to circle all bolt holes.
   b. Carefully lower the upper manifold and throttle body assembly onto the lower manifold.
   c. Tighten the upper manifold retaining bolts to 19 ft. lbs. (26 Nm).
   d. Install the manifold end cap cover and the coolant sensor switch.
   e. Install the fuel injectors and rail to the manifold assembly.
26. Clean the mating surfaces and install the intake manifold gaskets and seals. Apply sealer to the ends of the of the intake manifold seals.
27. Position the intake manifold and apply a suitable thread lock compound to the bolt threads. Tighten the retaining bolts to 88 inch lbs. (10 Nm), twice, in the sequence shown in the accompanying figure.
28. Attach the electrical connector to the temperature sensor and sensor switch.
29. Install the thermostat housing and thermostat with a new gasket.
30. Connect the alternator support brace to the intake.
31. Install the solenoid valve mounting bracket and power steering support brace to the intake manifold.
32. Connect the heater pipes to the intake and front cover.
33. Attach the coolant bypass hose to the intake manifold.
34. Install the power steering pump support bracket and tighten to 37 ft. lbs. (50 Nm).
35. Install the spark plug wires on both sides.
36. Install the belt tensioner pulley and tighten to 33 ft. lbs. (45 Nm).

37. Install the power steering pump.
38. Connect the vacuum hoses to the canister purge solenoid valve and transaxle module and intake connection.
39. Attach the electrical connections at the throttle body and both banks of fuel injectors.
40. Install the alternator and brace.
41. Connect the throttle body cable mounting bracket with the vacuum lines.
42. Install the right rear crossover pipe heat shield.
43. Install the cables to the throttle body.
44. Connect the fuel lines to the fuel rail and mount bracket.
45. Install the inner fender electrical cover on the right side.
46. Install the coolant recovery reservoir and upper radiator hose. Fill the cooling system.
47. Install the air cleaner assembly and the fuel injector sight shield.
48. Connect the negative battery cable.

Exhaust Manifold

REMOVAL & INSTALLATION

2.2L Engine

▶ See Figure 61

1. Disconnect the negative battery cable.
2. Detach the wiring harness from the oxygen sensor.
3. Remove the serpentine drive belt.
4. Remove the alternator.
5. Raise and safely support the vehicle.
6. Unfasten the retaining and separate the exhaust pipe from the manifold.
7. Carefully lower the vehicle.
8. Remove the bolt securing the oil fill tube to the engine block, then pull the tube from the engine.
9. If the coolant inlet pipe interferes with removal, disconnect the mounting bracket from the transaxle stud.
10. Unfasten the manifold retaining nuts, then remove the manifold from the cylinder head. Remove and discard the gasket from the mating surfaces.

To install:
11. Install the manifold to the cylinder head, using a new gasket. Tighten the retaining nuts to 115 inch lbs. (13 Nm).
12. Raise and safely support the vehicle, then attach the exhaust pipe to the manifold. Tighten the retaining nuts to 18 ft. lbs. (25 Nm), then carefully lower the vehicle.
13. Install the alternator and serpentine drive belt.
14. If disconnected, attach the coolant inlet pipe.
15. Lubricate the oil fill tube seal, then install the tube.
16. Attach the wiring harness to the oxygen sensor.
17. Connect the negative battery cable.
18. Start the engine and check for exhaust leaks.

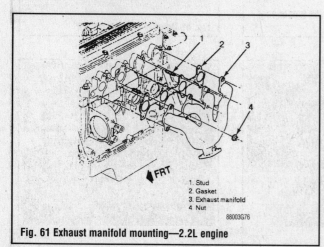

1. Stud
2. Gasket
3. Exhaust manifold
4. Nut

88003G76

Fig. 61 Exhaust manifold mounting—2.2L engine

2.3L Engine

▶ See Figures 62 and 63

1. Disconnect the negative battery cable.
2. Detach the oxygen sensor connector.
3. Remove the upper and lower exhaust manifold heat shields.
4. Unfasten the bolt that attaches the exhaust manifold brace to the manifold.
5. Break loose the manifold to exhaust pipe spring loaded bolts using a 13mm box wrench.
6. Raise the vehicle and support safely.

➡It is necessary to relieve the spring pressure from 1 bolt prior to removing the second bolt. If the spring pressure is not relieved it will cause the exhaust pipe to twist and bind up the bolt as it is removed.

7. Remove the manifold to exhaust pipe bolts from the exhaust pipe flange as follows:

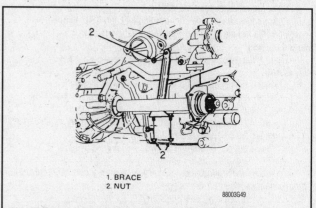

1. BRACE
2. NUT

88003G49

Fig. 62 Remove the exhaust manifold brace-to-manifold bolt

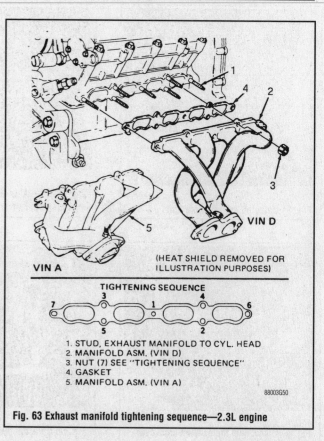

VIN D

VIN A

(HEAT SHIELD REMOVED FOR ILLUSTRATION PURPOSES)

TIGHTENING SEQUENCE

1. STUD, EXHAUST MANIFOLD TO CYL. HEAD
2. MANIFOLD ASM. (VIN D)
3. NUT (7) SEE "TIGHTENING SEQUENCE"
4. GASKET
5. MANIFOLD ASM. (VIN A)

88003G50

Fig. 63 Exhaust manifold tightening sequence—2.3L engine

a. Unscrew either bolt clockwise 4 turns.

b. Remove the other bolt.

c. Remove the first bolt.

8. Pull down and back on the exhaust pipe to disengage it from the exhaust manifold bolts.

9. Lower the vehicle.

10. Remove the exhaust manifold mounting bolts and remove the manifold.

To install:

11. The installation is the reverse of the removal procedure.

12. Tighten the mounting bolts in sequence to 27 ft. lbs. (37 Nm). Install the exhaust pipe flange bolts evenly and gradually to avoid binding.

13. Connect the negative battery cable and check for leaks.

2.5L Engine

1. Disconnect the negative battery cable.

2. Remove the torque strut bolts at the radiator panel and cylinder head.

3. Disconnect the oxygen sensor and remove the oil level indicator tube.

4. Raise and safely support the vehicle.

5. Remove the exhaust pipe from the manifold and lower the vehicle.

6. Bend the locking tabs away from the bolts and remove the retaining bolts and washers.

7. Remove the exhaust manifold and gasket. Discard the gasket.

To install:

8. Clean the sealing surfaces of the cylinder head and manifold.

9. Lubricate the bolt threads with anti-seize compound and install the exhaust manifold with a new gasket.

10. Tighten the bolts to the specifications shown in the accompanying figure.

11. Bend the locking tabs against the bolts.

12. Raise and support the vehicle safely.

13. Attach the exhaust pipe to the manifold, then carefully lower the vehicle.

14. Install the oil level indicator tube, oxygen sensor and torque rod bracket at the cylinder head and radiator support.

15. Connect the negative battery cable.

2.8L and 1989–93 3.1L Engines

▶ See Figures 64 thru 70

LEFT SIDE

1. Disconnect the negative battery cable.

2. Remove the coolant recovery bottle.

3. Relieve the accessory drive belt tension, then remove the belt.

4. If equipped, remove the A/C compressor mounting bolts and support the compressor aside. DO NOT disconnect the refrigerant lines.

5. Remove the right side engine torque strut. Unfasten the bolts retaining the A/C compressor (if equipped) and torque strut mounting bracket, then remove the bracket.

6. Remove the heat shield and crossover pipe at the manifold.

7. Unfasten the exhaust manifold mounting bolts and remove the manifold. Remove and discard the gasket.

To install:

8. Clean the gasket mounting surfaces.

9. Install the exhaust manifold to the engine, loosely install the mounting bolts.

10. Install the exhaust crossover pipe. Tighten the exhaust manifold bolts to 18 ft. lbs. (25 Nm)

11. Attach the heat shield. Install the A/C compressor and torque strut mounting bracket.

12. Install the torque strut. Mount the A/C compressor.

13. Install the accessory drive belt.

14. Install the coolant recovery bottle.

15. Connect the negative battery cable.

RIGHT SIDE

1. Disconnect the negative battery cable.

2. Raise and safely support the vehicle.

3. Remove the exhaust pipe at the crossover. Carefully lower the vehicle.

4. Remove the coolant recovery bottle and remove the engine torque struts.

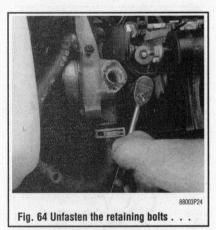

Fig. 64 Unfasten the retaining bolts . . .

Fig. 65 . . . then remove the torque strut mounting bracket

Fig. 66 Remove the heat shield

Fig. 67 Disconnect the exhaust crossover pipe

Fig. 68 Unfasten the exhaust manifold retaining bolts . . .

Fig. 69 . . . then remove the front manifold from the vehicle

Fig. 70 Remove the exhaust manifold gasket and replace with a new one during installation

5. Pull the engine forward and securely support it.
6. Remove the air cleaner, breather, mass air flow sensor and heat shield.
7. Remove the crossover at the manifold. Disconnect the accelerator and TV cables.
8. Unfasten the manifold mounting bolts, then remove the manifold. Remove and discard the gasket. Clean the manifold mounting surfaces.

To install:
9. Install the exhaust manifold, loosely install the mounting bolts.
10. Attach the crossover at the manifold. Tighten the manifold mounting bolts to 18 ft. lbs. (25 Nm).
11. Connect the accelerator and TV cables.
12. Attach the air cleaner, breather and mass air flow sensor.
13. Remove the engine support and allow the engine to roll back into position.
14. Install the coolant recovery bottle and the engine torque struts.
15. Raise and safely support the vehicle. Install the exhaust pipe to the crossover.
16. Carefully lower the vehicle.
17. Connect the negative battery cable.

1994–96 3.1L Engines

LEFT SIDE (FRONT)

1. Disconnect the negative battery cable.
2. Remove the air cleaner and duct assembly.
3. Properly drain the engine cooling system into a suitable container.
4. Remove the engine mount strut assemblies from the engine.
5. Rotate the engine forward, as outlined earlier in this section.
6. Remove the coolant recovery reservoir.
7. Remove the serpentine drive belt.
8. Disconnect the upper and lower radiator hoses from the engine.
9. Detach the tie straps from the heater outlet pipe and the ignition wiring harness.
10. Disconnect the automatic transaxle vacuum module pipe assembly.
11. Remove the heater pipe from the heater core-to-water pump assembly.
12. Remove the exhaust crossover shield and pipe assemblies.
13. Remove the engine mount strut and the A/C compressor bracket, if equipped.
14. Remove the heat shield retaining bolts/screws, then remove the shield.
15. Unfasten the retaining nuts, then remove the front exhaust manifold assembly. Remove and discard the gasket.
16. Thoroughly clean all the gasket mating surfaces.

To install:
17. Position a new gasket, then install the exhaust manifold and secure with the retaining nuts. Tighten the nuts to 11 ft. lbs. (15 Nm).
18. Install the heat shield and the retaining bolts/screws. Tighten to 89 inch lbs. (10 Nm).
19. Install the engine mount strut and the A/C mounting bracket, if equipped.
20. Install the exhaust crossover pipe and shield assemblies.
21. Fasten the heater pip to the heater core-to-water pump assembly.
22. Connect the automatic transaxle vacuum module pipe assembly.
23. Secure the tie straps around the heater outlet pipe and ignition wiring harness assembly.

24. Attach the upper and lower radiator hoses.
25. Install the serpentine drive belt.
26. Install the coolant recovery reservoir.
27. Rotate the engine assembly, as outlined earlier in this section.
28. Attach the engine mount strut assemblies at the engine assembly.
29. Refill the engine cooling system with the proper type and amount of coolant, then add two engine coolant sealant pellets, 3634621 or equivalent.
30. Install the air cleaner and duct assembly.
31. Connect the negative battery cable, then bleed the cooling system. Start the engine and check for proper operation.

RIGHT SIDE (REAR)

1. Properly drain the engine coolant into a suitable container.
2. Remove the air cleaner and duct assembly.
3. Disconnect the negative battery cable.
4. Remove the engine mount strut assemblies at the engine assembly.
5. Disconnect the upper radiator hose from the engine.
6. Detach the tie straps from the heater outlet pipe and the ignition wiring harness.
7. Disconnect the automatic transaxle vacuum modulator pipe.
8. Remove the heater pipe from the heater core-to-water pump assembly.
9. Remove the exhaust crossover heat shield and pipe assemblies.
10. Detach the oxygen sensor connector.
11. Rotate the engine assembly, as outlined earlier in this section.
12. Raise and safely support the vehicle.
13. Unfasten the rear drivetrain the front suspension frame bolts/screws. Carefully lower the drivetrain and front suspension frame assembly.
14. Disconnect the exhaust pipe assembly.
15. Detach the EGR tube from the rear exhaust manifold assembly.
16. Remove the oxygen sensor.
17. Remove the automatic transaxle fluid filler tube and position aside.
18. Remove the retaining bolts/screws, then remove the upper and lower heat shields.
19. Unfasten the retaining nuts, then remove the manifold assembly and gasket. Discard the gasket.
20. Thoroughly clean the gasket mating surfaces.

To install:
21. Install a new gasket, then position the exhaust manifold and secure with the retaining nuts. Tighten the nuts to 12 ft. lbs. (16 Nm).
22. Position the upper and lower heat shields, then install the retaining bolts/screws. Tighten to 89 inch lbs. (10 Nm).
23. Install the automatic transaxle fluid filler tube.
24. Install the oxygen sensor.
25. Attach the EGR tube assembly to the rear exhaust manifold.
26. Connect the exhaust pipe assembly.
27. Carefully raise the drivetrain and front suspension frame assembly, then secure with the retaining bolts/screws.
28. Carefully lower the vehicle.
29. Rotate the engine assembly, as outlined earlier in this section.
30. Attach the oxygen sensor electrical connector.
31. Install the exhaust crossover pipe and heat shield assemblies.
32. Attach the heater pipe to the heater core-to-water pump assembly.
33. Install the automatic transaxle vacuum modulator pipe.
34. Secure the tie straps around the heater outlet pipe and ignition wiring harness assembly.
35. Connect the upper radiator hose at the engine assembly.
36. Rotate the engine back to its original position.
37. Fasten the engine mount strut assemblies to the engine.
38. Refill the engine cooling system with the proper type and amount of coolant, then add two engine coolant sealant pellets, 3634621 or equivalent.
39. Install the air cleaner and duct assembly.
40. Connect the negative battery cable, then bleed the cooling system. Start the engine and check for proper operation.

1991–93 3.4L Engine

LEFT SIDE (FRONT)

▶ See Figure 71

1. Remove air cleaner assembly. Disconnect the negative battery cable.
2. Remove exhaust crossover.

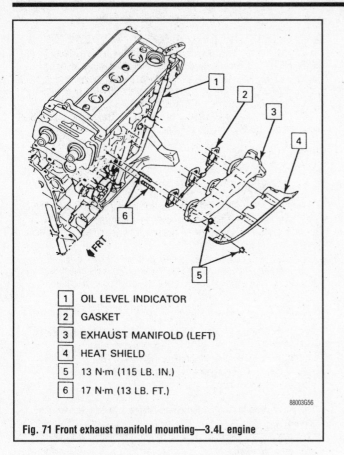

1 OIL LEVEL INDICATOR
2 GASKET
3 EXHAUST MANIFOLD (LEFT)
4 HEAT SHIELD
5 13 N·m (115 LB. IN.)
6 17 N·m (13 LB. FT.)

88003G56

Fig. 71 Front exhaust manifold mounting—3.4L engine

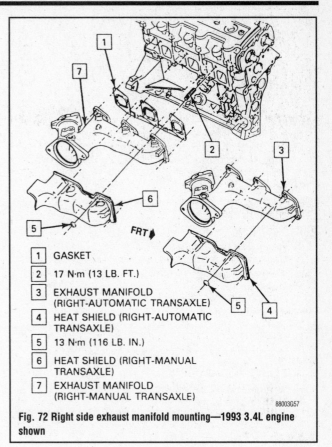

1 GASKET
2 17 N·m (13 LB. FT.)
3 EXHAUST MANIFOLD (RIGHT-AUTOMATIC TRANSAXLE)
4 HEAT SHIELD (RIGHT-AUTOMATIC TRANSAXLE)
5 13 N·m (116 LB. IN.)
6 HEAT SHIELD (RIGHT-MANUAL TRANSAXLE)
7 EXHAUST MANIFOLD (RIGHT-MANUAL TRANSAXLE)

88003G57

Fig. 72 Right side exhaust manifold mounting—1993 3.4L engine shown

3. Remove the engine torque strut bracket at frame and position out of the way.
4. Remove the upper radiator shroud.
5. Remove the cooling fans.
6. For vehicles equipped with a manual transaxle, detach the front hose from air pipe.
7. Unfasten the front exhaust manifold retaining nuts, then remove the manifold. Remove the old gasket and discard.

To install:
8. Position a new gasket, then install the manifold and heat shields. Install the manifold retaining nuts and tighten to 115 inch lbs. (14 Nm).
9. Install the cooling fans and the radiator shroud.
10. Move the torque strut into position and secure.
11. Install the exhaust crossover.
12. Install the air cleaner assembly.
13. Connect the negative battery cable, then start the engine and check for leaks.

RIGHT SIDE (REAR)—WITH AUTOMATIC TRANSAXLE

▶ See Figure 72

1. Disconnect the negative battery cable.
2. Remove right side cam carrier as follows:
   a. Remove intake plenum and right timing belt cover, as outlined in this section.
   b. Tag and disconnect the right side spark plug wires.
   c. Detach air/oil separator hose at cam carrier cover.
   d. Remove cam carrier cover bolts and lift of cover. Remove gasket and O-rings from cover.
   e. Remove secondary timing belt by removing secondary timing belt actuator and tensioner assembly and sliding belt from pulleys.
   f. Install 6 sections of fuel line hoses under the camshaft and between the lifters. This will hold the lifters in the carrier. For this procedure use 5/16 in. (8mm) fuel line hose for exhaust valves and 7/32 in. (5.5mm) fuel line hose for the intake valves.
   g. Remove exhaust crossover pipe and torque strut.
   h. Remove torque strut bracket at engine. Remove front engine lift hook.

   i. Unfasten the cam carrier mounting bolts and nuts and remove cam carrier.
   j. Remove cam carrier gasket from cylinder head.
3. Remove exhaust manifold to crossover pipe nuts.
4. Raise and safely support vehicle.
5. Disconnect the front exhaust pipe from the manifold. Carefully lower vehicle.
6. Detach electrical connector from oxygen sensor.
7. Unfasten the exhaust manifold nuts then remove the heat shield and manifold. Remove and discard the gasket.

To install:
8. Clean all mating surfaces, then install manifold gasket and heat shields.
9. Install exhaust manifold. Tighten the retaining nuts to 116 inch lbs. (14 Nm).
10. Attach electrical connector to the oxygen sensor.
11. Raise and safely support vehicle.
12. Connect the exhaust pipe to the manifold. Carefully lower the vehicle.
13. Install exhaust crossover pipe.
14. Install right cam carrier as follows:
   a. Install new gasket on cam carrier to cylinder mounting surface.
   b. Install cam hold-down tool J–38613 or equivalent, to carrier assembly.
   c. Install cam carrier to cylinder head. Install mounting bolts and nuts. Torque bolts and nuts to 18 ft. lbs.
   d. Remove lifter hold-down hoses and cam hold-down tool.
   e. Install torque strut bracket to engine and install torque strut.
   f. Install engine crossover pipe and engine lift hook.
   g. Install secondary timing belt and cam carrier cover and gasket.
   h. Attach the spark plug wires, as tagged during removal, then install the cover.
15. Connect negative battery cable.

RIGHT SIDE (REAR)—WITH MANUAL TRANSAXLE

▶ See Figure 72

1. Disconnect the negative battery cable.
2. Remove the exhaust crossover pipe.
3. Raise and safely support vehicle.

4. Remove the exhaust pipe and converter assembly.
5. Detach oxygen sensor connector.
6. Remove EGR pipe at manifold and manifold heat shields.
7. Unfasten the exhaust manifold retaining nuts, then remove the manifold and gasket.
To install:
8. Clean all gasket mating surfaces.
9. Position a new gasket, then install the manifold. Tighten retaining nuts to 116 inch lbs. (14 Nm).
10. Install EGR pipe and heat shields to exhaust manifold.
11. Attach the electrical connector to the oxygen sensor.
12. Connect exhaust pipe to manifold, then carefully lower the vehicle.
13. Install exhaust crossover
14. Connect the negative battery cable.

1994–96 3.4L Engine

LEFT SIDE (FRONT)

1. Disconnect the negative battery cable.
2. Remove the air cleaner assembly.
3. Disconnect the exhaust crossover.
4. Remove the cooling fans.
5. Unfasten the exhaust manifold retaining nuts, then remove the exhaust manifold and heat shields.
6. Remove and discard the gasket. Thoroughly clean all gasket mating surfaces.
To install:
7. Position a new gasket, then position the exhaust manifold and heat shield. Tighten the retaining nuts to 18 ft. lbs. (25 Nm).
8. Install the cooling fans.
9. Attach the exhaust crossover.
10. Install the air cleaner assembly.
11. Connect the negative battery cable, then start the engine and check for leaks.

RIGHT SIDE (REAR)

▶ See Figure 73

1. Disconnect the negative battery cable.
2. Remove the air cleaner assembly.
3. Disconnect the exhaust crossover.
4. Detach the EGR tube from the exhaust manifold.
5. Raise and safely support the vehicle.
6. Remove the front exhaust pipe and converter assembly.
7. Remove the oxygen sensor.
8. Disconnect the exhaust pipe from the heat shield.
9. Remove the rear alternator brace.
10. Remove the transaxle dipstick tube.
11. Detach the intermediate shaft from the steering gear.
12. Remove the exhaust manifold nuts.
13. Install a suitable jacking fixture to support the rear cradle. Unfasten the rear cradle bolts, then carefully lower the cradle.
14. Remove the steering gear heat shield.
15. Remove the exhaust manifold and heat shield. Remove and discard the gasket.
16. Thoroughly clean all gasket mating surfaces.
To install:
17. Position a new gasket, then install the exhaust manifold and heat shield. Install the exhaust manifold retaining nuts and tighten to 115 inch lbs. (13 Nm).
18. Install the steering gear heat shield.
19. Carefully raise the cradle, then install the rear cradle retaining bolts. Carefully remove the jacking fixture.
20. Attach the intermediate shaft to the steering gear.
21. Install the transaxle dipstick tube.
22. Fasten the rear alternator brace.
23. Install the exhaust pipe front heat shield.
24. Install the oxygen sensor.
25. Attach the front exhaust pipe and converter assembly.
26. Carefully lower the vehicle.
27. Attach the EGR tube to exhaust manifold.
28. Install the front exhaust crossover pipe.
29. Install the air cleaner and duct assembly.
30. Connect the negative battery cable.

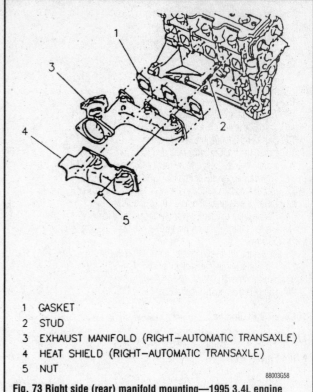

1	GASKET
2	STUD
3	EXHAUST MANIFOLD (RIGHT–AUTOMATIC TRANSAXLE)
4	HEAT SHIELD (RIGHT–AUTOMATIC TRANSAXLE)
5	NUT

88003G58

Fig. 73 Right side (rear) manifold mounting—1995 3.4L engine shown

1991–92 3.8L Engine

LEFT SIDE (FRONT)

▶ See Figure 74

1. Disconnect the negative battery cable.
2. Remove the air cleaner assembly and disconnect the spark plug wires.
3. Disconnect the exhaust crossover pipe.
4. Remove the oil level indicator and tube from the manifold.
5. Disconnect the engine lift bracket and the air conditioner compressor support brace.
6. Remove the exhaust manifold.
To install:
7. Clean the mating surfaces and loosely install the exhaust manifold and retaining bolts.
8. Install the crossover pipe to the manifold and support bracket.
9. Tighten the manifold retaining bolts to 41 ft. lbs. (55 Nm).
10. Install the engine lift bracket and the air conditioner compressor support brace.
11. Install the oil level indicator and tube to the manifold.
12. Install the air cleaner assembly and connect the spark plug wires.
13. Connect the negative battery cable.

RIGHT SIDE (REAR)

▶ See Figure 75

1. Disconnect the negative battery cable.
2. Remove the air cleaner assembly and tag and disconnect the spark plug wires.
3. Disconnect the exhaust crossover pipe.
4. Remove the oil level indicator and tube from the manifold.
5. Detach the oxygen sensor electrical connector.
6. Disconnect the engine torque strut and bolt from the engine.
7. Remove the engine lift bracket from the engine.
8. Tag and disconnect the spark plugs from the right side rear bank.
9. Raise and support the vehicle safely.
10. Remove the front exhaust pipe and the converter from the vehicle.

11. Remove the right rear engine mount to frame nuts and lower the engine.

12. Use a floor jack to carefully raise and support safely the right rear corner of the engine for access.

13. Remove the exhaust manifold retaining bolts and remove the exhaust manifold.

To install:

14. Clean the mating surfaces and loosely install the exhaust manifold and retaining bolts.

15. Install the crossover pipe to the manifold and support bracket.

16. Tighten the manifold retaining bolts to 41 ft. lbs. (55 Nm).

17. Carefully lower the engine and remove the floor jack.

18. Raise and support the vehicle safely.

19. Install the front exhaust pipe and the converter.

20. Install the right rear engine mount to frame nuts and lower the engine.

21. Tighten the crossover bolts.

22. Install the spark plugs to the right side rear bank.

23. Install the engine lift bracket to the engine.

24. Connect the oxygen sensor electrical connector.

25. Connect the engine torque strut and bolt to the engine and tighten to 41 ft. lbs. (55 Nm).

26. Install the oil level indicator and tube to the manifold.

27. Install the air cleaner assembly and connect the spark plug wires, as tagged during removal.

28. Connect the negative battery cable.

1993–96 3.8L Engine

LEFT SIDE (FRONT)

▶ **See Figure 74**

1. Disconnect the negative battery cable.

2. Remove the exhaust manifold.

3. Remove the engine torque strut.

4. Remove the right side engine cooling fan.

5. Detach the front-to-rear exhaust manifold connection and heat shield.

6. Properly drain the cooling system into a suitable container.

7. Detach the upper radiator hose from the intake manifold.

8. Remove the fuel rail cover.

9. Detach the EGR adapter from the upper intake manifold pipe. Include the EGR cover and pipe retaining bolt.

10. Remove the EGR valve and adapter assembly, including the pipe at the manifold.

11. Remove the left engine lift hook.

12. Remove the engine torque strut bracket from the cylinder head.

13. Remove the oil level indicator tube from the exhaust manifold.

14. Tag and disconnect the spark plug wires from the plugs and rocker arm cover.

15. If equipped, remove the A/C compressor support brace from the exhaust manifold stud.

16. Remove the spark plugs.

17. Unfasten the exhaust manifold bolts, then remove the manifold. Remove and discard the gasket.

18. Thoroughly clean all gasket mating surfaces.

To install:

19. Position a new gasket, then install the exhaust manifold. Tighten the retaining bolts/studs to 38 ft. lbs. (52 Nm).

20. Install the spark plugs.

21. If equipped, attach the A/C compressor bracket to the exhaust manifold stud.

22. Attach the spark plug wires to the rocker arm cover and plugs.

23. Install the oil level indicator tube assembly.

24. Fasten the engine torque strut bracket to the cylinder head.

25. Install the engine lift hook.

26. Install the EGR valve and adapter assembly.

27. Connect the EGR adapter to the upper intake manifold pipe.

28. Install the fuel rail cover.

29. Connect the upper radiator hose to the intake manifold.

30. Properly refill the cooling system.

31. Fasten the front-to-rear exhaust manifold connection and heat shield.

32. Install the right engine cooling fan.

33. Install the engine torque strut.

34. Connect the negative battery cable. Start the engine and check for leaks.

RIGHT SIDE (REAR)

▶ **See Figure 75**

1. Remove the air cleaner and the fuel injector sight shield.

2. Disconnect the negative battery cable.

3. Remove the coolant recovery reservoir.

4. Detach the exhaust crossover pipe.

5. Remove the transaxle oil level indicator tube support brace bolt and tube for access.

6. Tag and disconnect the spark plug wires.

7. Detach the oxygen sensor electrical connector.

8. Remove the engine torque strut and bolt from the engine.

9. Remove the engine lift bracket from the manifold.

10. Remove the spark plugs from the rear bank.

11. Raise and safely support the vehicle.

12. Remove the front exhaust pipe and converter from the vehicle.

13. Remove the right rear engine mount-to-frame nuts.

14. Carefully lower the vehicle.

15. Use a suitable floor jack at the right rear corner of the engine with a suitable support. Carefully raise the engine slightly for access.

16. Unfasten the manifold retaining bolts, then remove the manifold. Remove and discard the gasket. Thoroughly clean the gasket mating surfaces.

To install:

17. Install a new gasket, then position the exhaust manifold and install the retaining bolts loosely. Install the exhaust crossover at the manifold, then loosely install the nuts.

18. Tighten the manifold bolts/studs to 38 ft. lbs. (52 Nm).

19. Carefully lower the engine and remove the floor jack.

20. Raise and safely support the vehicle.

21. Install the front exhaust pipe and converter to the vehicle.

22. Fasten the engine mount-to-frame nuts.

23. Carefully lower the vehicle.

24. Tighten the exhaust crossover nuts.

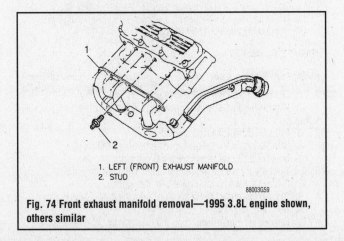

1. LEFT (FRONT) EXHAUST MANIFOLD
2. STUD

88003G59

Fig. 74 Front exhaust manifold removal—1995 3.8L engine shown, others similar

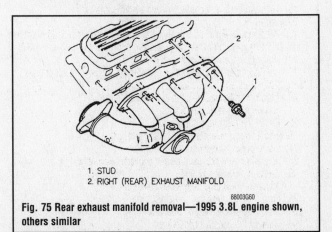

1. STUD
2. RIGHT (REAR) EXHAUST MANIFOLD

88003G60

Fig. 75 Rear exhaust manifold removal—1995 3.8L engine shown, others similar

25. Install the engine lift brackets.
26. Install the spark plugs, then attach the oxygen sensor connector.
27. Install the transaxle oil level indicator tube and bolt.
28. Connect the spark plug wires, as tagged during removal.
29. Position the engine torque strut, then secure with the bolt and nut. Tighten the nut to 32 ft. lbs. (43 Nm).
30. Install the coolant recovery reservoir.
31. Connect the negative battery cable.
32. Install the fuel injector sight shield and air cleaner assembly.
33. Start the engine and check for leaks.

Turbocharger

REMOVAL & INSTALLATION

3.1L (VIN V) Engine

▶ See Figures 76 and 77

➡ For this procedure, a Tech 1® scan tool must be used for the idle relearn procedure.

1. Disconnect the negative battery cable.
2. Properly drain the coolant from the radiator into a suitable container.
3. Unfasten the intercooler-to-intake manifold duct attaching bolt at the thermostat housing, then remove the intercooler to intake manifold duct.
4. Disconnect the air cleaner-to-turbocharger duct from the turbocharger.
5. Detach the air cleaner inlet duct.
6. Remove the air cleaner and duct assembly.
7. Disconnect the turbocharger-to-intercooler duct from the turbocharger.
8. Remove the turbocharger heat covers.
9. Detach the oxygen sensor electrical connector and remove the oxygen sensor.
10. Disconnect the turbo water and oil lines at the turbocharger.
11. Tag and disconnect the vacuum lines at the turbocharger compressor outlet and actuator assembly.
12. Disconnect the actuator arm from the wastegate.
13. Detach the wastegate actuator from the turbocharger.
14. Remove the cruise control servo and set aside.
15. Disconnect the turbocharger downpipe at the turbocharger.
16. Unfasten the water supply clamp and rubber hose.
17. Disconnect the turbocharger drain hose at the drain pipe.
18. Remove the turbocharger to exhaust crossover attaching bolts and remove the turbocharger from the engine.
   To install:
19. Install the turbocharger to the engine compartment, then tighten the turbocharger-to-exhaust crossover bolts to 17 ft. lbs. (23 Nm)

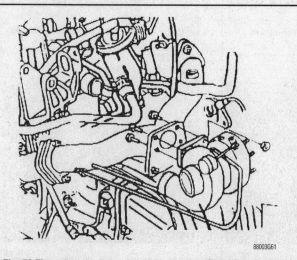

Fig. 76 The only turbocharged vehicles are the 1989-90 3.1L (VIN V) Grand Prix

88003G61

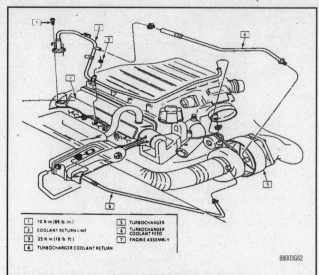

```
1  10 N·m (89 lb. in.)        5  TURBOCHARGER
2  COOLANT RETURN LINE        6  TURBOCHARGER
3  25 N·m (18 lb ft)             COOLANT FEED
4  TURBOCHARGER COOLANT RETURN  7  ENGINE ASSEMBLY
```

88003G62

Fig. 77 Turbocharger mounting and coolant line routing

20. Connect the turbocharger drain hose at the drain pipe.
21. Attach the water supply clamp and rubber hose.
22. Connect the turbocharger downpipe at the turbocharger, then tighten to 17 ft. lbs. (23 Nm)
23. Install the cruise control servo.
24. Connect the wastegate actuator to the turbocharger.
25. Attach the actuator arm to the wastegate.
26. Connect the vacuum lines at the turbocharger compressor outlet and actuator assembly.
27. Attach the turbo water line and tighten to 21 ft. lbs. (28 Nm).
28. Connect the oil line at the turbocharger and tighten to 15 ft. lbs. (20 Nm).
29. Install the oxygen sensor and tighten to 31 ft. lbs. (42 Nm). Attach the electrical connector.
30. Install the turbocharger heat covers.
31. Connect the turbocharger to intercooler duct at the turbocharger.
32. Install the air cleaner and duct assembly.
33. Install the air cleaner to turbocharger duct at the turbo.
34. Install the intercooler to intake manifold duct attaching bolt at the thermostat housing and tighten to 17 ft. lbs. (23 Nm).
35. Fill the engine cooling system with the proper type and amount of coolant.
36. Connect the negative battery cable.

➡ Prime the turbocharger with oil before running the engine. Crank the engine with the fuel pump fuse removed until normal operating oil pressure is achieved.

37. Perform the idle learn procedure to allow the ECM memory to be updated with the correct IAC valve pintle position and provide for a stable idle speed.
   a. Install a Tech 1® scan tool.
   b. Turn the ignition to the **ON** position, engine not running.
   c. Select **IAC SYSTEM**, then **IDLE LEARN** in the **MISC TEST** mode.
   d. Proceed with idle learn as directed by the scan tool.

Intercooler

REMOVAL & INSTALLATION

3.1L (VIN V) Engine

▶ See Figure 78

1. Disconnect the negative battery cable.
2. Detach the air cleaner-to-turbocharger duct at the turbocharger.
3. Remove the air cleaner assembly along with all adjoining duct work.
4. Remove the intercooler-to-intake manifold duct assembly.

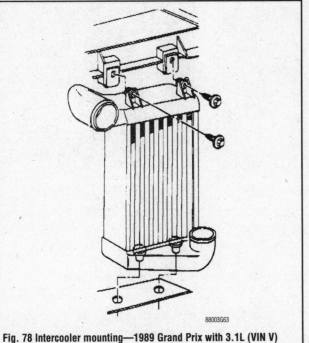

Fig. 78 Intercooler mounting—1989 Grand Prix with 3.1L (VIN V) engine

5. Remove the turbocharger-to-intercooler duct.
6. Unfasten the upper intercooler attaching bolts, then remove the intercooler.
7. The installation is the reverse of the removal procedure.
8. Make sure that no duct work is leaking when reassembling.

Radiator

REMOVAL & INSTALLATION

▶ **See Figures 79 thru 88**

1. Disconnect the negative battery cable.
2. Remove the air cleaner, mounting stud and duct.

✷ CAUTION

When draining the coolant, keep in mind that cats and dogs are attracted by ethylene glycol antifreeze, and are quite likely to drink any that is left in an uncovered container or in puddles on the ground. This will prove fatal in sufficient quantity. Always drain the coolant into a sealable container. Coolant should be reused unless it is contaminated or several years old. To avoid being burned, do NOT remove the thermostat housing cap while the engine is at normal operating temperature. The cooling system will release scalding fluid and steam under pressure if the cap is removed while the engine is still hot.

3. Properly drain the engine cooling system into a suitable container.
4. Remove the coolant recovery reservoir.
5. Remove the engine strut brace bolts from the upper tie bar and rotate the struts and brace rearward.

➡ To prevent shearing of the rubber bushing, loosen the bolts on the engine strut before swinging the struts.

6. Remove the air intake resonator mounting nut, upper radiator mounting panel bolts and clamps. Tighten to 89 inch lbs. (10 Nm).
7. Detach the cooling fan electrical connectors.
8. Remove the upper radiator mounting panel with the fans attached or the fan assembly, as applicable.

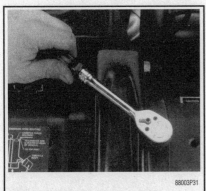

Fig. 79 Unfasten the engine strut brace bolts . . .

Fig. 80 . . . then swing the struts and brace rearward

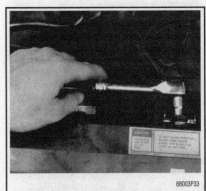

Fig. 81 Remove the upper panel mounting bolts and other retainers

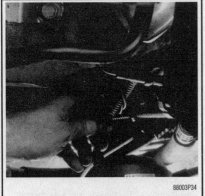

Fig. 82 Detach the fan electrical connector

Fig. 83 Remove the electric cooling fan assemblies

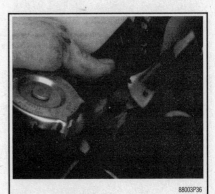

Fig. 84 Disconnect the upper, then the lower radiator hoses

Fig. 85 If equipped with an automatic transaxle, disconnect the transaxle cooler lines from the radiator

88003P37

Fig. 86 Unfasten the radiator mounting bolts

88003P38

Fig. 87 If necessary remove the radiator shroud . . .

88003P39

Fig. 88 . . . then remove the radiator from the vehicle

88003P40

9. Disconnect the upper and lower radiator hoses.

10. Detach the low coolant sensor electrical connector, then remove the sensor, if used.

11. If equipped, remove the automatic transaxle cooler lines from the radiator.

12. Unfasten any necessary retainers, then remove the radiator.

To install:

➡If a new radiator is being used, transfer all necessary fittings from the old radiator to the new one.

13. Position the radiator into the lower insulator pads

14. If equipped, attach the automatic transaxle cooler lines to radiator.

15. Install the low coolant sensor and attach the electrical connector.

16. Connect the upper and lower radiator hoses and secure with the clamps.

17. Install the upper radiator mounting panel with the fans attached or install the fan assemblies. Tighten the fan mounting bolts to 53 inch lbs. (6 Nm). Connect the fan wires

18. Install the mounting panel bolts and clamps. Tighten the bolts to 89 inch lbs. (10 Nm).

19. Install the coolant recovery bottle.

20. Swing the engine strut to the proper position and tighten the bolts.

21. Refill the engine with the specified amount and type of engine coolant.

22. Install the air cleaner, then connect the negative battery cable.

23. Start the engine and check for coolant leaks.

Engine Oil Cooler

REMOVAL & INSTALLATION

1. Disconnect the negative battery cable.
2. Remove the air cleaner assembly.
3. Properly drain the cooling system into a suitable container.
4. Raise and safely support the vehicle.

5. Place a drain pan under the oil filter and remove the filter.
6. Disconnect the oil cooler outlet hose, then position it aside.
7. Detach the inlet hose and position it aside.
8. Remove the connector piece.
9. Remove the oil cooler and adapter.

To install:

10. Clean the mating surfaces of the block and cooler.
11. Coat the gasket with oil and install the adapter.
12. The remainder of installation is the reverse of the removal procedure. Coat a new connector O-ring with oil before installation.
13. Properly fill the cooling system, then check the oil level. Add oil to the crankcase, if necessary.
14. Connect the negative battery cable, then start the engine and check for leaks.

Electric Cooling Fan

REMOVAL & INSTALLATION

▶ See Figure 89

1. Disconnect the negative battery cable.
2. Remove the coolant reservoir and/or the air cleaner assembly, as applicable.
3. Remove engine strut brace bolts from upper tie bar and rotate strut and brace rearward.

➡To prevent shearing of the rubber bushing, loosen the bolts on the engine strut before swinging the struts.

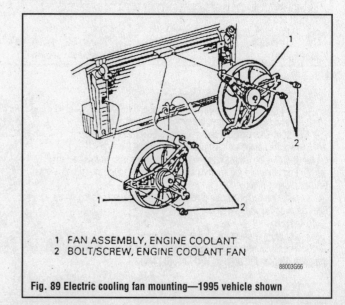

1 FAN ASSEMBLY, ENGINE COOLANT
2 BOLT/SCREW, ENGINE COOLANT FAN

88003G66

Fig. 89 Electric cooling fan mounting—1995 vehicle shown

4.. Disconnect the electrical wiring harness from the cooling fan frame.

5. Remove the fan assembly from the radiator support.

To install:

6. Install the fan assembly to the radiator support. Tighten the fan assembly-to-radiator support bolts to 7 ft. lbs. (9.5 Nm). Attach electrical connector.

7. Place the engine strut in its proper position, then secure with the retaining bolt.

8. Install the coolant recovery reservoir and/or the air cleaner assembly, as applicable.

9. Attach the fan wiring harness.

10. Connect the negative battery cable, start the engine, let it warm up and check for proper fan operation.

Water Pump

REMOVAL & INSTALLATION

❊❊ CAUTION

When draining the coolant, keep in mind that cats and dogs are attracted by ethylene glycol antifreeze, and are quite likely to drink any that is left in an uncovered container or in puddles on the ground. This will prove fatal in sufficient quantity. Always drain the coolant into a sealable container. Coolant should be reused unless it is contaminated or several years old.

2.2L Engine

1. Disconnect the negative battery cable.

2. Properly drain the engine coolant into a suitable container.

3. Remove the serpentine drive belt, as outlined in Section 1 of this manual.

4. Unfasten the water pump pulley bolts, then remove the pulley.

5. Remove the alternator and side bracket.

6. Disconnect the water pump hoses.

7. Unfasten the water pump retaining bolts, then remove the water pump from the vehicle. Remove and discard the gasket. Thoroughly clean all gasket mating surfaces.

To install:

8. Position a new water pump gasket, then install the water pump. Tighten the attaching bolts to 18 ft. lbs. (25 Nm).

9. Install the water pump pulley and secure with the retaining bolts. Tighten the bolts to 22 ft. lbs. (30 Nm).

10. Attach the water pump hoses.

11. Install the alternator bracket and the alternator.

12. Install the serpentine drive belt.

13. Properly refill the engine cooling system using the correct type and amount of coolant.

14. Connect the negative battery cable.

2.3L Engine

▶ **See Figure 90**

1. Disconnect the negative battery cable.

2. Unfasten the upper engine torque strut and rotate the engine rearward.

3. Disconnect and remove the oxygen sensor, if needed.

4. Remove the exhaust heat shield and EGR valve, if equipped.

5. Disconnect the exhaust pipe from manifold.

6. Remove the exhaust manifold, as outlined earlier in this section.

7. Partially drain the engine coolant, into a suitable container, to a level below the water pump.

8. Unfasten the water pump retaining bolts, then remove the pump. Remove and discard the gasket.

To install

9. Thoroughly clean the gasket mating surfaces.

10. Position a new gasket, then install the pump and secure with the retaining bolts. Tighten the bolts to 19 ft. lbs. (26 Nm).

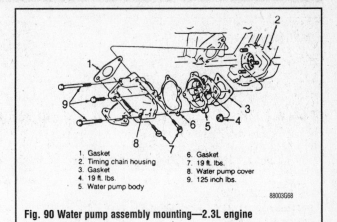

1. Gasket
2. Timing chain housing
3. Gasket
4. 19 ft. lbs.
5. Water pump body
6. Gasket
7. 19 ft. lbs.
8. Water pump cover
9. 125 inch lbs.

88003G68

Fig. 90 Water pump assembly mounting—2.3L engine

11. Attach the lower coolant pipe and tighten to 124 inch lbs. (14 Nm).

12. Connect the coolant return hose.

13. Install the exhaust manifold and pipe, oxygen sensor, EGR valve and heat shield.

14. Return the engine to its proper position and install the torque strut.

15. Refill the engine with the proper type and amount of coolant.

16. Connect the negative battery cable then start the engine and check for coolant leaks.

2.5L Engine

▶ **See Figure 91**

1. Disconnect the negative battery cable.

2. Remove the alternator. For details, please refer to the procedure in Section 2 of this manual.

3. Remove the convenience center heat shield.

4. Partially drain the coolant, into a suitable container, to a level below the water pump.

5. Unfasten the 4 water pump-to-engine attaching bolts, then remove the water pump and gasket.

6. Thoroughly clean all gasket mating surfaces.

7. If a new pump is being installed, remove the pulley from the old pump and install on the new pump.

To install:

8. Position a new gasket, then install the pump and pulley assembly.

9. Install the water pump attaching bolts and tighten to 24 ft. lbs. (33 Nm).

10. Install the remaining components in the reverse of the removal procedure.

11. Refill the cooling system with the specified amount of engine coolant, then start the engine and check for coolant leaks.

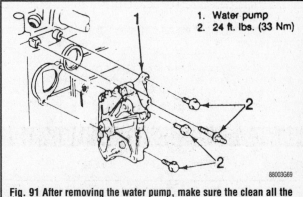

1. Water pump
2. 24 ft. lbs. (33 Nm)

88003G69

Fig. 91 After removing the water pump, make sure the clean all the old gasket material from the mating surfaces

2.8L, 3.1L and 3.4L Engines

▶ See Figures 92 thru 97

1. Disconnect the negative battery cable.
2. Remove the air cleaner assembly.
3. If necessary for access, remove the coolant recovery reservoir.
4. Partially drain the coolant, into a suitable container, to a level below the water pump.
5. If equipped, remove the serpentine belt guard/cover.
6. Remove the serpentine belt.
7. Remove the retaining bolts, then remove the water pump pulley.
8. Unfasten the 5 water pump attaching bolts, then remove the water pump and gasket. Discard the gasket.

To install:

9. Thoroughly clean the water pump mounting surfaces.
10. Position a new gasket, then install the water pump.

11. Install the attaching bolts and tighten them to 89 inch lbs. (10 Nm).
12. Install the water pump pulley.
13. Install the serpentine belt and belt cover/guard (if equipped).
14. Refill the cooling system with the specified type and amount of engine coolant.
15. Install the air cleaner assembly.
16. Connect the negative battery cable, then start the engine and check for coolant leaks.

3.8L Engine

▶ See Figure 98

1. Disconnect the negative battery cable.
2. Properly drain the engine coolant from the radiator into a suitable container.
3. Remove the coolant recovery reservoir.

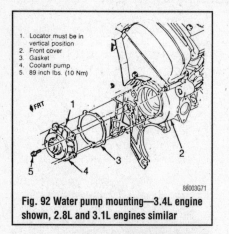

1. Locator must be in vertical position
2. Front cover
3. Gasket
4. Coolant pump
5. 89 inch lbs. (10 Nm)

◆FRT

88003G71

Fig. 92 Water pump mounting—3.4L engine shown, 2.8L and 3.1L engines similar

88003P41

Fig. 93 Unfasten the water pump pulley retaining bolts . . .

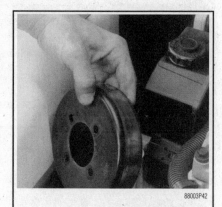

88003P42

Fig. 94 . . . then remove the pulley

88003P43

Fig. 95 Use the correct size socket to remove the water pump retaining bolts . . .

88003P44

Fig. 96 . . . then remove the water pump from the vehicle

88003P45

Fig. 97 Use a suitable gasket scraper to carefully remove old gasket material from the mating surfaces

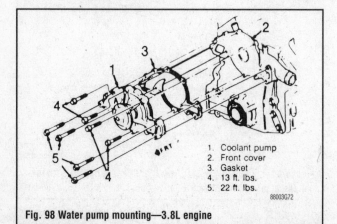

1. Coolant pump
2. Front cover
3. Gasket
4. 13 ft. lbs.
5. 22 ft. lbs.

◆FRT

88003G72

Fig. 98 Water pump mounting—3.8L engine

4. Remove the serpentine belt.
5. If more access is needed, remove the inner fender electrical cover.
6. For 1992–96 vehicles, remove the alternator and position it aside.
7. Remove the serpentine belt tensioner pulley and/or the water pump pulley.
8. Unfasten the water pump attaching bolts, then remove the water pump and gasket. Discard the gasket.

To install:

9. Thoroughly clean the water pump mounting surfaces.
10. Position a new gasket, then install the water pump.
11. Install the attaching bolts, then tighten the long bolts to 22 ft. lbs. (30 Nm) and the short bolts to 13 ft. lbs. (18 Nm).
12. Install the pulley(s) and the serpentine belt. Tighten the pulley bolts to 115 inch lbs. (13 Nm).
13. If removed, install the alternator.
14. Attach the inner fender electrical cover, if removed.
15. Install the coolant recovery reservoir.

16. Refill the cooling system with the specified amount of engine coolant.
17. Connect the negative battery cable.
18. Start the engine and check for coolant leaks.

Cylinder Head

REMOVAL & INSTALLATION

2.2L Engine

▶ **See Figure 99**

1. Properly relieve the fuel system pressure, as outlined in Section 5 of this manual.
2. Disconnect the negative battery cable.
3. Remove the air cleaner assembly.
4. Properly drain the engine cooling system into a suitable container.
5. Tag and disconnect the vacuum lines and electrical connectors from the intake manifold and cylinder head.
6. Detach the control cables from the throttle body and remove the cable bracket at the throttle body and rocker arm cover.
7. Remove the serpentine belt and belt tensioner.
8. Tag and disconnect the spark plug wires, then lay them out of the way.
9. Disconnect the canister purge lines under the manifold.
10. Detach the upper radiator hose from the engine.
11. Disconnect the upper and lower heater hoses from the intake manifold.
12. Detach the coolant inlet hose from the cylinder head.
13. Remove the intake manifold brace from the power steering pump bracket.
14. Disconnect and cap the fuel lines at the quick connects.

➡ **When removing valve train components, they must be kept in order for installation in the same locations they were removed from.**

15. Remove the rocker arm cover, rocker arm nuts, rocker arms and pushrods.
16. Remove the engine oil fill tube.

➡ **Removal of the intake and exhaust manifolds from the vehicle should not be necessary. However, if additional room is needed, remove them.**

17. Remove the engine lift brackets.
18. Unfasten the cylinder head retaining bolts, then remove the cylinder head from the vehicle. Remove and discard the gasket and thoroughly clean all mating surfaces. Clean the threads on the cylinder head bolts and the block threads.
   To install:
19. Place a new cylinder head gasket in position over the dowel pins on the block. Carefully guide the cylinder head into position.

20. Install all the cylinder head bolts finger-tight. New replacement bolts are recommended. The long bolts go into bolt positions 1, 4, 5, 8 and 9. The short bolts are in positions 2, 3, 6 and 7. The stud is in position 10.
21. Tighten the bolts in the sequence shown in the accompanying figure. Tighten the long bolts to 23 ft. lbs. (32 Nm) and the short bolts and stud to 22 ft. lbs. (29 Nm). Make a final pass over all bolts, tightening each an additional 90 degrees (¼-turn) using a torque angle meter.
22. Install the engine lift brackets. Tighten the front bracket bolt to 41 ft. lbs. (55 Nm) and the rear bracket bolt to 32 ft. lbs. (43 Nm).
23. If applicable, install the intake and exhaust manifolds to the cylinder head.
24. Install the oil fill tube.
25. Install the pushrods, rocker arms, rocker arm ball and tighten the rocker arm nuts to 22 ft. lbs. (30 Nm).
26. Position the rocker arm cover and secure with the retaining bolts. Tighten the bolts to 89 inch lbs. (10 Nm).
27. Uncap and connect the fuel lines to the fuel rail.
28. Install the intake manifold brace.
29. Attach the coolant hose to the cylinder head.
30. Connect the upper and lower heater hoses to the intake manifold.
31. Attach the upper radiator hose.
32. Connect the canister purge hose under the intake manifold.
33. Attach the spark plug wires, as tagged during removal.
34. Install serpentine belt tensioner and tighten the mounting bolt to 37 ft. lbs. (50 Nm). Install the serpentine belt.
35. Connect the control cables to the intake manifold bracket and throttle body lever.
36. Attach the vacuum lines and electrical connectors to the intake manifold and cylinder head.
37. Install the air cleaner assembly.
38. An oil and filter change is recommended since coolant can get into the oil system during cylinder head service.
39. Connect the negative battery cable.
40. Refill and bleed the cooling system. Start the engine and verify proper engine operation.

2.3L Engine

▶ **See Figures 100 and 101**

1. Disconnect the negative battery cable. Properly relieve the fuel system pressure as outlined in Section 5 of this manual.
2. Properly drain the cooling system into a suitable container.
3. Disconnect the heater inlet and throttle body heater hoses from the water inlet.
4. Remove the exhaust manifold, as outlined earlier in this section.
5. Remove the intake and exhaust camshaft housing.
6. Remove the oil fill cap, tube and retainer. Pull the tube up and out of the block.
7. Disconnect and move the fuel injector harness.
8. Release the fuel system pressure.
9. Remove the throttle body and air inlet tube with the hoses and cables still connected. Position the assembly out of the way.
10. Remove the power brake booster hose and throttle cable bracket.

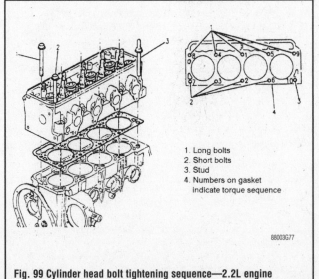

1. Long bolts
2. Short bolts
3. Stud
4. Numbers on gasket indicate torque sequence

88003G77

Fig. 99 Cylinder head bolt tightening sequence—2.2L engine

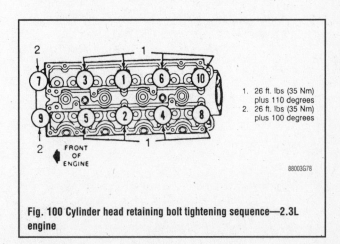

1. 26 ft. lbs (35 Nm) plus 110 degrees
2. 26 ft. lbs (35 Nm) plus 100 degrees

FRONT OF ENGINE

88003G78

Fig. 100 Cylinder head retaining bolt tightening sequence—2.3L engine

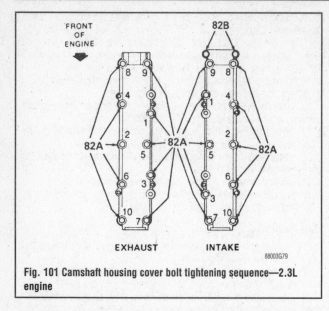

Fig. 101 Camshaft housing cover bolt tightening sequence—2.3L engine

11. Remove the MAP sensor vacuum hose and all electrical connectors from the intake manifold and cylinder head.

12. Remove the radiator inlet hose and coolant sensor connectors.

13. In the reverse order of installation, remove the cylinder head-to-block retaining bolts.

14. Gently tap the outer edges of the cylinder head with a rubber hammer to dislodge the head gasket. Do not pry a screwdriver between the 2 surfaces.

15. Remove the cylinder head and intake manifold as an assembly.

To install:

16. Clean all gasket mating surfaces with a plastic scraper and solvent. Remove all dirt from the bolts with a wire brush.

17. Clean and inspect the oil flow check valve but do not remove the valve.

18. Check the cylinder head mating surface for flatness using a straight-edge and a feeler gauge. Resurface the head, if the warpage exceeds 0.010 in. (0.25mm).

19. Check to see if the dowel pins are installed properly, and replace if necessary.

➡**To avoid damage, install new spark plugs after the cylinder head has been installed on the engine. In the mean time, plug the holes to prevent dirt from entering the combustion chamber during reinstallation.**

20. Do not use any sealing compounds on the new cylinder head gasket. Match the new gasket with the old one to ensure a perfect match.

21. Install the cylinder head and camshaft housing covers.

22. Tighten all bolts to 26 ft. lbs. (35 Nm) plus an additional 100° for bolts No. 7 and 9. Tighten an additional 110° for all bolts except No. 7 and 9.

23. Install the throttle body heater hoses, upper radiator hose and intake manifold bracket.

24. Attach the cylinder head and intake manifold electrical connectors and vacuum hoses.

25. Install the throttle body-to-intake manifold with a new gasket. Install the throttle cable, MAP sensor vacuum hose and air cleaner duct.

26. Lubricate the new oil fill tube O-ring and install the fill tube. Make sure the tube is fully seated in the block.

27. Install the exhaust manifold, as outlined earlier in this section.

28. Fill the radiator with the specified amount of engine coolant.

29. Recheck all procedures to ensure completion of repair.

30. Connect the negative battery cable, start the engine and check for fluid leaks.

2.5L Engine

♦ **See Figure 102**

1. Properly relieve the fuel system pressure as outlined in Section 5.
2. Disconnect the negative battery cable.
3. Drain the cooling system into a suitable container.
4. Raise and safely support the vehicle.

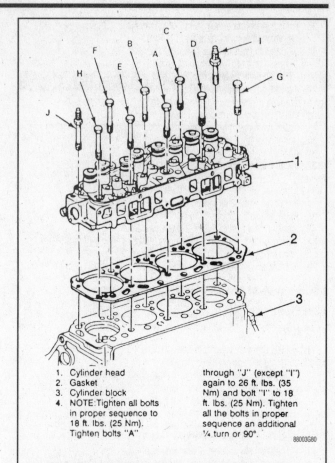

1. Cylinder head
2. Gasket
3. Cylinder block
4. NOTE: Tighten all bolts in proper sequence to 18 ft. lbs. (25 Nm). Tighten bolts "A" through "J" (except "I") again to 26 ft. lbs. (35 Nm) and bolt "I" to 18 ft. lbs. (25 Nm). Tighten all the bolts in proper sequence an additional ¼ turn or 90°.

Fig. 102 Cylinder head bolt tightening sequence—2.5L engine

5. Remove the exhaust pipe and oxygen sensor.

6. Carefully lower the vehicle.

7. Remove the oil level indicator tube and auxiliary ground cable.

8. Remove the air cleaner assembly.

9. Label and disconnect the vacuum hoses.

10. Detach the fuel injection wiring connectors, throttle linkage and fuel lines.

11. Disconnect the heater hose from the intake manifold.

12. Tag and detach the wiring connectors from the manifold and cylinder head.

13. Remove the vacuum hoses, serpentine belt and alternator bracket.

14. Disconnect the radiator hoses.

15. Remove the rocker arm cover, as outlined earlier in this section.

16. Loosen the rocker arm nuts and move the rocker arms to the side enough to remove the pushrods.

17. Mark each pushrod and remove from the engine.

➡**Mark each valve component to ensure that they are replaced in the same location as removed.**

18. Unfasten the cylinder head bolts.

19. Tap the sides of the cylinder head with a plastic hammer to dislodge the gasket. Remove the cylinder head with the intake and exhaust manifold still attached.

20. If the cylinder head has to be serviced or replaced, remove the intake manifold, exhaust manifold and remaining hardware.

To install:

21. Before installing, clean the gasket surfaces of the head and block.

22. Check the cylinder head for warpage using a straight-edge.

23. Match up the old head gasket with the new one to ensure the holes are exact. Install a new gasket over the dowel pins in the cylinder block.

24. Install the cylinder head in place over the dowel pins.

25. Coat the cylinder head bolt threads with sealing compound and install finger-tight.

26. Tighten the cylinder head bolts, in sequence, as follows:
   a. Tighten all bolts to 18 ft. lbs. (24 Nm).
   b. Tighten bolts A through J, except I, to 26 ft. lbs. (35 Nm).
   c. Tighten bolt I to 18 ft. lbs. (24 Nm).
   d. Turn all bolts an additional 90° (¼ turn).

27. Install the pushrods, rocker arms and nuts (or bolts) in the same location as removed. Tighten the nuts (or bolts) to 24 ft. lbs. (32 Nm).

28. Install the rocker arm cover, as outlined earlier in this section.

29. Install the radiator hoses, alternator bracket and serpentine belt.

30. Connect all intake manifold and cylinder head wiring.

31. Attach the vacuum hoses and heater hose at manifold.

32. Install the wiring, throttle linkage and fuel lines to the throttle body assembly.

33. Install the oil level indicator tube-to-exhaust manifold.

34. Install the air cleaner assembly and refill the cooling system.

35. Raise and safely support the vehicle.

36. Install the exhaust pipe and oxygen sensor.

37. Carefully lower the vehicle. Properly fill the cooling system with the correct type and amount of coolant.

38. Connect the negative battery cable. Start the engine and check for leaks.

2.8L and 1989–91 3.1L Engines

▶ See Figure 103

LEFT SIDE

1. Relieve the fuel system pressure, as outlined in Section 5 of this manual. Disconnect the negative battery cable.

2. Properly drain the cooling system into a suitable container.

3. Remove the rocker arm (valve) cover, as outlined earlier in this section.

4. Remove the intake manifold from the vehicle, as outlined earlier in this section.

5. Remove the exhaust crossover pipe.

6. Remove the left side exhaust manifold, as outlined earlier in this section.

7. Disconnect the oil level indicator tube bracket.

8. Loosen the rocker arms nuts, turn the rocker arms and remove the pushrods. Intake and exhaust pushrods are different lengths and are color coded for identification; intake pushrods are marked orange and exhaust pushrods are marked blue in color.

➡ **Be sure to keep the parts in order for installation purposes.**

9. Tag and disconnect the spark plug wires from the spark plugs.

10. Unfasten the cylinder head-to-engine bolts; start with the outer bolts and work toward the center. Remove the cylinder head with the exhaust manifold as an assembly.

To install:

11. Clean the gasket mounting surfaces. Inspect the surfaces of the cylinder head, block and intake manifold for damage and/or warpage. Clean the threaded holes in the block and the cylinder head bolt threads.

12. Use new gaskets, align the new cylinder head gasket over the dowels on the block with the note **THIS SIDE UP** facing the cylinder head.

13. Install the cylinder head and exhaust manifold crossover assembly on the engine.

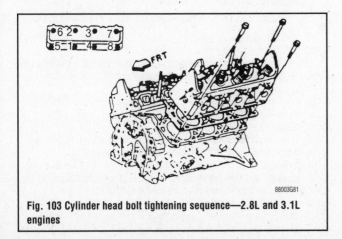

88003G81

Fig. 103 Cylinder head bolt tightening sequence—2.8L and 3.1L engines

14. Using GM sealant 1052080 or equivalent, coat the cylinder head bolts and install the bolts hand-tight.

15. Using the correct sequence, tighten the bolts to 33 ft. lbs. (45 Nm). After all bolts are tightened to 33 ft. lbs. (45 Nm), rotate the torque wrench another 90° or ¼ turn. This will apply the correct torque to the bolts.

16. Install the left exhaust manifold.

17. Connect the plug wires to the spark plugs.

18. Install the pushrods in the same order that they were removed. Tighten the rocker arm nuts to 14–20 ft. lbs. (19–27 Nm).

19. Install the intake manifold using a new gasket and following the correct sequence, tighten the bolts to the correct specification.

20. Install the oil level indicator tube and install the rocker cover. Install the air inlet tube and spark plug wires.

21. Reinstall engine strut bracket and exhaust manifold.

22. Connect the negative battery cable. Refill the cooling system. Start the engine and check for leaks.

RIGHT SIDE

1. Disconnect the negative battery cable. Properly drain the cooling system into a suitable container.

2. Relieve the fuel system pressure, as outlined in Section 5 of this manual.

3. Remove the air cleaner assembly. Remove the torque strut from the engine.

4. Raise and safely support the vehicle. Remove the exhaust manifold-to-exhaust pipe bolts and separate the pipe from the manifold.

5. Carefully lower the vehicle. Remove the coolant recovery tank.

6. Remove the exhaust manifold-to-cylinder head bolts and the manifold.

7. Remove exhaust crossover heat shield and crossover pipe at right exhaust manifold.

8. Tag and disconnect right side spark plug wires at cylinder head.

9. Remove the rocker arm cover. Remove the intake manifold-to-cylinder head bolts and the intake manifold.

10. Loosen the rocker arms nuts, turn the rocker arms and remove the pushrods. Intake and exhaust pushrods are different lengths and are color coded for identification; intake pushrods are marked orange and exhaust pushrods are marked blue in color.

➡ **Be sure to keep the components in order for reassembly purposes.**

11. Remove the cylinder head-to-engine bolts, starting with the outer bolts and working toward the center of the cylinder head.

To install:

12. Clean the gasket mounting surfaces. Inspect the parts for damage and/or warpage. Clean the engine block threaded holes and the cylinder head bolt threads.

13. Place a new cylinder head gasket on the engine block dowels with the note **THIS SIDE UP** facing the cylinder head.

14. Using GM sealant 1052080 or equivalent, coat the cylinder head bolts and install the bolts hand-tight.

15. Using the tightening sequence, tighten the bolts to 33 ft. lbs. (45 Nm). After all bolts are torqued to 33 ft. lbs. (45 Nm), rotate the torque wrench another 90° or ¼ turn. This will apply the correct torque to the bolts.

16. Install the pushrods in the same order as they were removed. Tighten the rocker arm nuts to 14–20 ft. lbs. (19–27 Nm).

17. Follow the tightening sequence, use a new gasket and install the intake manifold.

18. Connect the spark plug wires to cylinder head.

19. Install the right side exhaust crossover pipe, heat shield and manifold.

20. Connect the exhaust pipe to the manifold.

21. Install the oil level indicator tube and install the rocker cover. Install the air inlet tube.

22. Install the coolant recovery tank. Refill the cooling system.

23. Connect the negative battery cable. Start the engine, allow it to reach normal operating temperatures and check for leaks.

1992–93 3.1L Engine

▶ See Figures 103, 104, 105 and 106

LEFT SIDE

1. Relieve the fuel system pressure, as outlined in Section 5 of this manual. Disconnect the negative battery cable.

2. Properly drain the cooling system into a suitable container.

3. Remove the intake manifold from the vehicle, as outlined earlier in this section.

Fig. 104 Unfasten the cylinder head bolts, then remove the head

Fig. 105 Remove and discard the cylinder head gasket

Fig. 106 Use a suitable scraper to thoroughly clean the gasket mating surfaces

4. Remove the exhaust crossover pipe.

5. Raise and safely support the vehicle.

6. Remove the oil filter and adapter.

7. If equipped, position the oil cooler aside.

8. Carefully lower the vehicle.

9. Unbolt the A/C compressor, if equipped, and position it aside.

10. Remove the radiator hose clamp at the water pump, then disconnect the hose.

11. Remove the A/C (if equipped) and torque strut mounting bracket.

12. Tag and disconnect the plug wires from the spark plugs.

13. Remove the left side exhaust manifold, as outlined earlier in this section.

14. Remove the vacuum pipe nut.

15. Unfasten the cylinder head-to-engine bolts; start with the outer bolts and work toward the center. Remove the cylinder head and gasket. Discard the gasket.

To install:

16. Clean the gasket mounting surfaces. Inspect the surfaces of the cylinder head, block and intake manifold for damage and/or warpage. Clean the threaded holes in the block and the cylinder head bolt threads.

17. Use new gaskets, align the new cylinder head gasket over the dowels on the block with the note **THIS SIDE UP** facing the cylinder head.

18. Install the cylinder head and exhaust manifold crossover assembly on the engine.

19. Using GM sealant 1052080 or equivalent, coat the cylinder head bolts and install the bolts hand-tight.

20. Using the correct sequence, tighten the bolts to 33 ft. lbs. (45 Nm). After all bolts are tightened to 33 ft. lbs. (45 Nm), use tool J36660, or equivalent torque wrench to rotate the bolts another 90° or ¼ turn. This will apply the correct torque to the bolts.

21. Install the vacuum pipe nut.

22. Install the left exhaust manifold.

23. Connect the plug wires to the spark plugs.

24. Install the A/C and torque strut mounting bracket.

25. Attach the radiator hose to the water pump and secure with the clamp.

26. If equipped, position the A/C compressor and install the retaining bolts.

27. Raise and safely support the vehicle.

28. Install the exhaust crossover pipe.

29. Install the intake manifold, using a new gasket, as outlined earlier in this section.

30. Connect the negative battery cable. Refill the cooling system. Start the engine and check for leaks.

RIGHT SIDE

1. Relieve the fuel system pressure, as outlined in Section 5 of this manual.

2. Disconnect the negative battery cable.

3. Properly drain the cooling system into a suitable container.

4. Remove the intake manifold and gasket, as outlined earlier in this section.

5. Raise and safely support the vehicle. Remove the exhaust manifold-to-exhaust pipe bolts and separate the pipe from the manifold.

6. Carefully lower the vehicle.

7. Remove the exhaust crossover pipe nuts to the right exhaust manifold.

8. Rotate the engine forward, as outlined earlier in this section.

9. If equipped, remove the secondary air injection pipe.

10. Detach the oxygen sensor electrical connector.

11. Unfasten the cylinder head retaining bolts, then remove the cylinder head and gasket. Discard the gasket.

To install:

12. Clean the gasket mounting surfaces. Inspect the parts for damage and/or warpage. Clean the engine block threaded holes and the cylinder head bolt threads.

13. Place a new cylinder head gasket on the engine block dowels with the note **THIS SIDE UP** facing the cylinder head.

14. Using GM sealant 1052080 or equivalent, coat the cylinder head bolts and install the bolts hand-tight.

15. Using the correct sequence, tighten the bolts to 33 ft. lbs. (45 Nm). After all bolts are tightened to 33 ft. lbs. (45 Nm), use tool J36660, or equivalent torque wrench to rotate the bolts another 90° or ¼ turn. This will apply the correct torque to the bolts.

16. Attach the oxygen sensor electrical connector.

17. If equipped, install the secondary air injection pipe.

18. Rotate the engine back to its original location.

19. Fasten the exhaust crossover pipe nuts to the right exhaust manifold.

20. Raise and safely support the vehicle.

21. Connect the exhaust pipe at the rear exhaust manifold.

22. Carefully lower the vehicle.

23. Install the intake manifold, as outlined earlier in this section.

24. Refill the cooling system.

25. Connect the negative battery cable. Start the engine, allow it to reach normal operating temperatures and check for leaks.

1994–96 3.1L Engine

♦ See Figure 103

1. Disconnect the negative battery cable.

2. Properly drain the engine cooling system into a suitable container.

3. Raise and safely support the vehicle.

4. Drain the engine oil into a suitable container, then carefully lower the vehicle.

5. Remove the upper and lower intake manifolds, as outlined earlier in this section.

6. Remove the valve rocker arm and pushrod assemblies. Make sure to keep all components in order for installation purposes.

7. Remove the exhaust crossover pipe assembly.

8. Remove the engine mount strut and A/C compressor bracket.

9. Oil level indicator tube assembly.

10. Tag and disconnect the spark plug wires, then remove the spark plugs.

11. Unfasten the cylinder head retaining bolts and screws, then remove the cylinder head and gasket from the vehicle. Discard the gasket.

To install:

12. Clean the gasket mounting surfaces. Inspect the parts for damage and/or warpage. Clean the engine block threaded holes and the cylinder head bolt threads.

13. Place a new cylinder head gasket on the engine block dowels with the note **THIS SIDE UP** facing the cylinder head.

14. Using GM sealant 1052080 or equivalent, coat the cylinder head bolts and install the bolts hand-tight.

15. Using the correct sequence, tighten the bolts to 33 ft. lbs. (45 Nm). After all bolts are tightened to 33 ft. lbs. (45 Nm), use tool J36660, or equivalent torque wrench to rotate the bolts another 90° or ¼ turn. This will apply the correct torque to the bolts.

16. Install the spark plugs and connect the plug wires.
17. Install the oil level indicator tube assembly.
18. Install the engine mount strut and A/C compressor bracket.
19. Install the exhaust crossover pipe assembly.
20. Install the valve rocker arm and pushrod assemblies.
21. Install the lower and upper intake manifold assemblies.
22. Refill the crankcase with engine oil. Refill the cooling system.
23. Connect the negative battery cable, then start the engine and check for proper operation.

3.4L Engine

LEFT SIDE (FRONT)

▶ See Figures 107 and 108

1. Properly relieve the fuel system pressure as outlined in Section 5.
2. Disconnect the negative battery cable.
3. Drain cooling system into a suitable container.
4. Remove the intake manifold, as outlined earlier in this section.
5. Remove left side cam carrier as follows:
   a. Disconnect oil/air breather hose from cam carrier cover. Tag and detach the spark plug wires from plugs and remove rear spark plug wire cover.

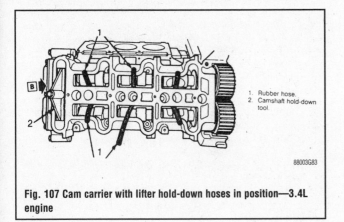

1. Rubber hose.
2. Camshaft hold-down tool.

88003G83

Fig. 107 Cam carrier with lifter hold-down hoses in position—3.4L engine

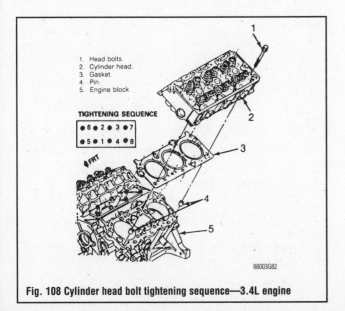

1. Head bolts.
2. Cylinder head.
3. Gasket.
4. Pin.
5. Engine block

TIGHTENING SEQUENCE

6 2 3 7
5 1 4 8

FRT

88003G82

Fig. 108 Cylinder head bolt tightening sequence—3.4L engine

   b. Remove cam carrier cover bolts and lift the cover off. Remove gasket and O-rings from cover.
   c. Remove secondary timing belt by removing secondary timing belt actuator and tensioner assembly and sliding belt from pulleys.
   d. Install 6 sections of fuel line hoses under the camshaft and between the lifters. This will hold the lifters in the carrier. For this procedure use ⁵⁄₁₆ in. fuel line hose for the exhaust valves and ⁷⁄₃₂ in. (5.5mm) fuel line hose for the intake valves.
   e. Remove exhaust crossover pipe and torque strut.
   f. Remove torque strut bracket at engine.
   g. Unfasten the cam carrier mounting bolts and nuts and remove the cam carrier.
   h. Remove cam carrier gasket from cylinder head.
6. On vehicles equipped with a manual transaxle, remove the front air hose.
7. Remove the right side cooling fan.
8. Remove exhaust manifold mounting bolts, then remove the manifold.
9. Remove oil level indicator tube bolt and tube.
10. Detach the electrical connector from temperature sending unit.
11. Unfasten the cylinder head bolts, then remove the cylinder head. Remove and discard the gasket.

To install:

12. Clean the gasket mounting surfaces. Inspect the parts for damage and/or warpage.
13. Clean the engine block threaded holes and the cylinder head bolt threads. Remove oil from threaded holes in block.
14. Install new cylinder head gasket to block with tabs between cylinders facing up.
15. Install cylinder head and bolts and tighten in proper sequence. Tighten the bolts to 33 ft. lbs. (45 Nm) plus an additional 90 degree (¼) turn using tool J 36660 or equivalent torque angle meter.
16. Attach electrical connector to coolant temperature sending unit.
17. Install oil level tube and bolt. Tighten to 89 inch lbs. (10 Nm).
18. Install exhaust manifold and nuts. Tighten to 116 inch lbs. (13 Nm).
19. Install the front air pipe, if equipped with a manual transaxle.
20. Install the right side cooling fan.
21. Install cam carrier following these steps:
   a. Install new gasket on cam carrier to cylinder mounting surface.
   b. Install cam hold-down tool J–38613 or equivalent, to carrier assembly.
   c. Install cam carrier to cylinder head. Install mounting bolts and nuts. Torque bolts and nuts to 18 ft. lbs. (25 Nm).
   d. Remove lifter hold-down hoses and cam hold-down tool.
   e. Install torque strut bracket to engine and install torque strut.
   f. Install engine crossover pipe.
   g. Install secondary timing belt and cam carrier cover.
22. Install the intake manifold.
23. Refill fluid levels as required. Connect the negative battery cable.
24. Start the engine and check for fluid leaks.

RIGHT SIDE (REAR)

1. Relieve the fuel system pressure as outlined in Section 5 of this manual.
2. Disconnect the negative battery cable.
3. Drain cooling system into a suitable container.
4. Remove intake manifold, as outlined earlier in this section.
5. Remove right side cam carrier as follows:
   a. Remove intake plenum and right timing belt cover.
   b. Tag and disconnect the right spark plug wires.
   c. Remove air/oil separator hose at cam carrier cover.
   d. Remove cam carrier cover bolts and lift of cover. Remove gasket and O-rings from cover.
   e. Remove secondary timing belt by removing secondary timing belt actuator and tensioner assembly and sliding belt from pulleys.
   f. Install 6 sections of fuel line hoses under the camshaft and between the lifters. This will hold the lifters in the carrier. For this procedure use ⁵⁄₁₆ in. (8mm) fuel line hose for the exhaust valves and ⁷⁄₃₂ in. (5.5mm) fuel line hose for the intake valves.
   g. Remove exhaust crossover pipe and torque strut.
   h. Remove torque strut bracket at engine. Remove front engine lift hook.
   i. Unfasten the cam carrier mounting bolts and nuts and remove the cam carrier.
   j. Remove cam carrier gasket from cylinder head.

6. Raise and support vehicle safely.

7. Remove front exhaust pipe at manifold.

8. If equipped with a manual transaxle, remove the rear air hose from air pipe.

9. Carefully lower the vehicle and detach the electrical connector from the oxygen sensor.

10. Remove rear timing belt tensioner bracket.

11. Unfasten the cylinder head bolts, then remove the cylinder head. Remove and discard the gasket.

To install:

12. Clean the gasket mounting surfaces. Inspect the parts for damage and/or warpage.

13. Clean the engine block threaded holes and the cylinder head bolt threads. Remove oil from threaded holes in block.

14. Install new cylinder head gasket to block with tabs between cylinders facing up.

15. Install cylinder head and bolts and tighten in the proper sequence. Tighten the bolts to 33 ft. lbs. (45 Nm) plus an additional ¼ turn using tool J 36660 or equivalent torque angle meter.

16. Install rear timing belt tensioner bracket.

17. Attach the electrical connector to oxygen sensor.

18. Raise the vehicle and support safely.

19. Connect rear air hose to air pipe for vehicles with a manual transaxle.

20. Install front exhaust pipe to the manifold. Carefully lower the vehicle.

21. Install the cam carrier following these steps:

  a. Install a new gasket on cam carrier to cylinder mounting surface.

  b. Install cam hold-down tool J–38613 or equivalent, to carrier assembly.

  c. Install the cam carrier to the cylinder head. Install mounting bolts and nuts. Tighten the bolts and nuts to 18 ft. lbs. (26 Nm).

  d. Remove the lifter hold-down hoses and cam hold-down tool.

  e. Install the torque strut bracket to engine and install torque strut.

  f. Install the engine crossover pipe and engine lift hook.

  g. Install the secondary timing belt and cam carrier cover.

  h. Connect the spark plug wires and install the cover.

22. Install the intake manifold, as outlined earlier in this section.

23. Refill fluid levels as required. Connect the negative battery cable.

24. Start vehicle and check for fluid leaks.

3.8L Engine

▶ See Figure 109

LEFT SIDE (FRONT)

1. Properly relieve the fuel system pressure.

2. Disconnect the negative battery cable and remove the air cleaner assembly.

3. Drain the cooling system into a suitable container.

4. Remove the intake manifold, as outlined earlier in this section.

5. Remove the valve covers, then remove the rocker arm assemblies.

6. Detach the torque strut from the bracket at cylinder head.

7. Disconnect the vacuum line from the transaxle.

8. Remove the left exhaust manifold, as outlined earlier in this section.

9. Tag and disconnect the spark plug wires and remove the spark plugs.

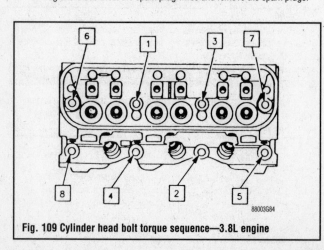

Fig. 109 Cylinder head bolt torque sequence—3.8L engine

10. Remove the alternator front mount bracket and ignition module with the bracket.

11. Unfasten the cylinder head bolts and remove the cylinder head. Remove and discard the gasket.

12. Clean all gasket mating surfaces and the cylinder head bolt holes in the block.

To install:

13. Place the cylinder head gasket on the engine block dowels with the note **THIS SIDE UP** facing the cylinder head and the arrow facing the front of the engine.

14. Install the cylinder head bolts and tighten as follows:

  a. Tighten the cylinder head bolts, in sequence, to 35 ft. lbs. (47 Nm).

  b. Rotate each bolt 130°, in sequence.

  c. Rotate the center 4 bolts an additional 30°, in sequence.

15. Install the rocker arm assemblies and valve covers.

16. Install the intake and exhaust manifolds.

17. Install the alternator front mount bracket and ignition module with bracket.

18. Install the spark plugs and connect the wires, as tagged during removal.

19. Install the torque strut to the bracket, at the head and tighten to 41 ft. lbs. (55 Nm).

20. Fill the cooling system with the proper type and amount of coolant.

21. Connect the negative battery cable and install the air cleaner assembly.

22. Start the engine and check for proper operation.

RIGHT SIDE (REAR)

1. Properly relieve the fuel system pressure.

2. Disconnect the negative battery cable and remove the air cleaner assembly.

3. Drain the cooling system into a suitable container.

4. Disconnect the exhaust crossover pipe.

5. Remove the intake manifold, as outlined earlier in this section.

6. Raise and support the vehicle safely.

7. Disconnect the front exhaust pipe from the manifold.

8. Remove the valve covers, as outlined earlier in this section.

9. Remove the belt tensioner pulley.

10. Disconnect the heater hose from the engine.

11. Remove the power steering pump mounting bracket and lay the pump to aside. DO NOT disconnect the fluid lines.

12. Tag and disconnect the spark plug wires and remove the spark plugs.

13. Disconnect the exhaust manifold and leave in place.

14. Detach the electrical connection from the oxygen sensor.

15. Remove the rocker arm assemblies.

16. Unfasten the cylinder head bolts and remove the cylinder head. Remove and discard the gasket.

17. Clean all gasket mating surfaces and the cylinder head bolt holes in the block.

To install:

18. Place the cylinder head gasket on the engine block dowels with the note **THIS SIDE UP** facing the cylinder head and the arrow facing the front of the engine.

19. Install the cylinder head bolts and tighten as follows:

  a. Tighten the cylinder head bolts, in sequence, to 35 ft. lbs. (47 Nm).

  b. Rotate each bolt 130°, in sequence.

  c. Rotate the center 4 bolts an additional 30°, in sequence.

20. Attach the electrical connection to the oxygen sensor.

21. Install the exhaust manifold and intake manifold, as outlined earlier in this section.

22. Install the rocker arm assemblies and the valve cover(s).

23. Install the spark plugs and connect the wires, as tagged during removal.

24. Install the power steering pump bracket and tighten the bolts to 37 ft. lbs. (50 Nm).

25. Install the belt tensioner pulley.

26. Fasten the heater hose to the engine.

27. Connect the exhaust crossover pipe.

28. Raise and support the vehicle safely.

29. Attach the front exhaust pipe to the manifold, then carefully lower the vehicle.

30. Fill the cooling system with the proper type and amount of coolant.

31. Connect the negative battery cable and install the air cleaner assembly.

32. Start the engine and check for proper operation.

CLEANING AND INSPECTION

▶ See Figure 110

※※ CAUTION

To avoid personal injury ALWAYS wear safety glasses when using a power drill and wire brush.

1. With the valves installed to protect the valve seats, remove carbon deposits from the combustion chambers and valve heads with a drill-mounted wire brush. Be careful not to damage the cylinder head gasket surface. If the head is to be disassembled, proceed to Step 3. If the head is not to be disassembled, proceed to Step 2.

2. Remove all dirt, oil and old gasket material from the cylinder head with solvent. Clean the bolt holes and the oil passage. Be careful not to get solvent on the valve seals as the solvent may damage them. If available, dry the cylinder head with compressed air. Check the head for cracks or other damage, and check the gasket surface for burrs, nicks and flatness. If you are in doubt about the head's serviceability, consult a reputable automotive machine shop.

3. Remove the valves, springs and retainers, then clean the valve guide bores with a valve guide cleaning tool. Remove all dirt, oil and old gasket material from the cylinder head with solvent. Clean the bolt holes and the oil passage.

4. Remove all deposits from the valves with a wire brush or buffing wheel. Inspect the valves as described later in this section.

5. Check the head for cracks using a dye penetrant in the valve seat area and ports, head surface and top. Check the gasket surface for burrs, nicks and flatness. If you are in doubt about the head's serviceability, consult a reputable automotive machine shop.

➡ **If the cylinder head was removed due to an overheating condition and a crack is suspected, do not assume that the head is not cracked because a crack is not visually found. A crack can be so small that it cannot be seen by eye, but can pass coolant when the engine is at oper-** ating temperature. Consult an automotive machine shop that has testing equipment to make sure the head is not cracked.

RESURFACING

▶ See Figure 111

Whenever the cylinder head is removed, check the flatness of the cylinder head gasket surface as follows:

1. Make sure all dirt and old gasket material has been cleaned from the cylinder head. Any foreign material left on the head gasket surface can cause a false measurement.

2. Place a straightedge straight across and diagonally across the gasket surface of the cylinder head (in the positions shown in the figures). Using feeler gauges, determine the clearance at the center of the straightedge.

3. If the surfaces are "out of flat" by more than 0.005 in. (0.127mm) the surface should be milled.

4. If warpage exceeds 0.010 in. (0.25mm) then the cylinder head should likely be replaced. Contact a reputable machine shop for machining service and recommendations.

➡ **When resurfacing the cylinder head(s) on V-type engines, the intake manifold mounting position is altered and must be corrected by machining a proportionate amount from the intake manifold flange.**

Valves

REMOVAL & INSTALLATION

▶ See Figures 112 and 113

1. Disconnect the negative battery cable.
2. Remove the cylinder head(s) from the vehicle, as outlined earlier in this section, as place on a clean surface.

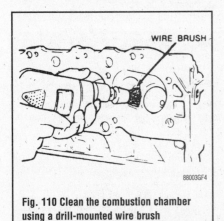

Fig. 110 Clean the combustion chamber using a drill-mounted wire brush

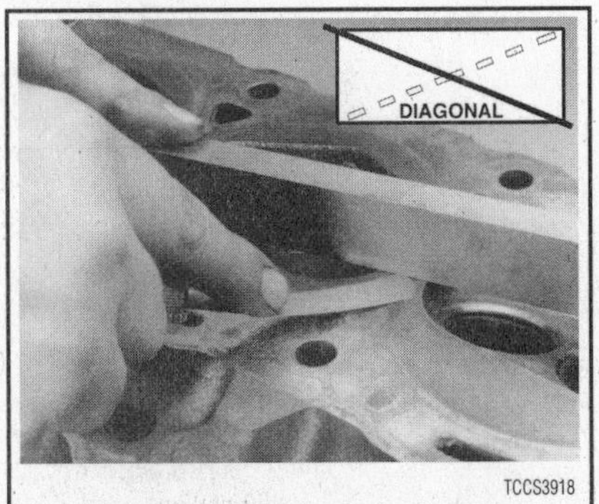

Fig. 111 Checking the cylinder head for flatness diagonally (shown) and straight across the head surface

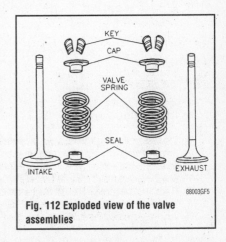

Fig. 112 Exploded view of the valve assemblies

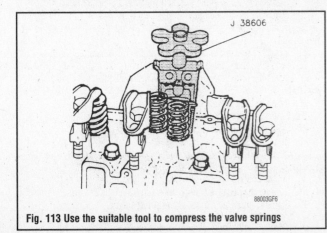

Fig. 113 Use the suitable tool to compress the valve springs

3. Remove the rocker arms or camshafts, as applicable. Using a suitable valve spring compressor, compress the valve spring and remove the valve keys using a magnetic retrieval tool.

※※ CAUTION

The valve springs are under high spring load, always wear safety glasses when removing valve springs. Decompressing a valve spring quickly may cause personal injury.

4. Slowly release the compressor and remove the valve spring caps (or rotors) and the valve springs.

5. Fabricate a valve arrangement board (piece of cardboard with holes punched through) to use when you remove the valves, which will indicate the port in which each valve was originally installed (and which cylinder head on V6 models). Also note that the valve keys, rotators, caps, etc. should be arranged in a manner which will allow you to install them on the valve on which they were originally removed.

6. Remove the discard the valve seals. On models using the umbrella type seals, note the location of the large and small seals for assembly purposes.

7. Thoroughly clean the valves on the wire wheel of a bench grinder, then clean the cylinder head mating surface with a soft wire wheel, a soft wire brush, or a wooden scraper. Avoid using a metallic scraper, since this can cause damage to the cylinder head mating surface, especially on models with aluminum heads.

8. Using a valve guide cleaner chucked into a drill, clean all of the valve guides.

To install:

➡Be sure that all traces of lapping compound have been cleaned off before the valves are installed.

9. Lubricate all of the valve stems with a light coating of engine oil, then install the valves into the proper ports/guides.

10. If the umbrella-type valve seals are used, install them at this time. Be sure to use a seal protector to prevent damage to the seals as they are pushed over the valve keeper grooves. If O-ring seals are used, don't install them yet.

11. Install the valve springs and the spring retainers (or rotators), and using the valve compressing tool, compress the springs.

12. If umbrella-type seals are used, just install the valve keepers (white grease may be used to hold them in place) and release the pressure on the compressing tool. If O-ring type seals are used, carefully work the seals into the second groove of the valve (closest to the head), install the valve keepers and release the pressure on the tool.

➡If the O-ring seals are installed BEFORE the springs and retainers are compressed, the seal will be destroyed.

13. After all of the valves are installed and retained, tap each valve spring retainer with a rubber mallet to seat the keepers in the retainer.

REFACING

Valve refacing should only be handled by a reputable machine shop, as the experience and equipment needed to do the job are beyond that of the average owner/mechanic. During the course of a normal valve job, refacing is necessary when simply lapping the valves into their seats will not correct the seat and face wear. When the valves are reground (resurfaced), the valve seats must also be recut, again requiring special equipment and experience.

VALVE LAPPING

▶ **See Figures 114 and 115**

After machine work has been performed on the valves, it may be necessary to lap the valve to assure proper contact. For this, you should first contact your machine shop to determine if lapping is necessary. Some machine shops will perform this for you as part of the service, but the precision machining which is available today often makes lapping unnecessary. Additionally, the hardened valves/seats used in modern automobiles may make lapping difficult or impossible. If your machine shop recommends that you lap the valves, proceed as follows:

1. Set the cylinder head on the workbench, combustion chamber side up. Rest the head on wooden blocks on either end, so there are two or three inches between the tops of the valve guides and the bench.

2. Lightly lube the valve stem with clean engine oil. Coat the valve seat completely with valve grinding compound. Use just enough compound that the full width and circumference of the seat are covered.

3. Install the valve in its proper location in the head. Attach the suction cup end of the valve lapping tool to the valve head. It usually helps to put a small amount of saliva into the suction cup to aid it sticking to the valve.

4. Rotate the tool between the palms, changing position and lifting the tool often to prevent grooving. Lap the valve in until a smooth, evenly polished seat and valve face are evident.

5. Remove the valve from the head. Wipe away all traces of grinding compound from the valve face and seat. Wipe out the port with a solvent soaked rag, and swab out the valve guide with a piece of solvent soaked rag to make sure there are no traces of compound grit inside the guide. This cleaning is important.

6. Proceed through the remaining valves, one at a time. Make sure the valve faces, seats, cylinder ports and valve guides are clean before reassembling the valve train.

Fig. 114 Lapping the valves by hand

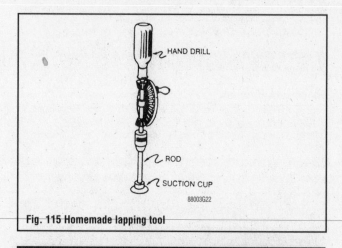

Fig. 115 Homemade lapping tool

Valve Stem Seals

REPLACEMENT

➡This procedure is for removing the seals with the head installed on the vehicle. If the head is removed, refer to the valve removal and installation procedure.

1. Disconnect the negative battery cable.
2. Remove the rocker arm cover as previously outlined in this section.
3. Remove the rocker arm assembly at the valve being serviced.
4. Remove the spark plug at the cylinder being serviced.
5. On DOHC engines, remove the camshaft over the valve being serviced.
6. Install a spark plug port adapter tool No. J–23590 onto the spark plug hole. Apply compressed air to the cylinder to keep the valve in the closed position.
7. Using a valve compressor tool J–5892–B or equivalent, remove the valve keepers, cap, keepers and seal.

To install:

8. Position the valve seal over the end of the valve.
9. Install the spring, cap and keepers using the spring compressor. Carefully release the spring compressor and make sure the keepers are in the proper position.
10. Release the air pressure from the cylinder and remove the spark plug port adapter.
11. Install the spark plug and wire.
12. Install the rocker arm assembly as previously outlined in this section. Reconnect the negative battery cable. Start the engine and check for oil leaks.

Valve Springs

REMOVAL & INSTALLATION

Please refer to the procedure for valve removal and installation.

INSPECTION

▶ **See Figures 116, 117 and 118**

Valve spring squareness, length and tension should be checked while the valve train is disassembled. Place each valve spring on a flat surface next to a steel square. Measure the length of the spring, and rotate it against the edge of the square to measure distortion. If spring length varies (by comparison) by more than 0.06 in. (1.6mm) or if distortion exceeds 0.06 in. (1.6mm), replace the spring.

Spring tension must be checked on a spring tester. Springs used on most engines should be within one pound of each other when tested at their specified installed heights.

Valve Seats

REMOVAL & INSTALLATION

The valve seats in these engines are not removable. Refer all servicing of the valve seats to a qualified machine shop.

Valve Guides

REMOVAL & INSTALLATION

The engines covered in this guide use integral valve guides. That is, they are a part of the cylinder head and cannot be replaced. The guides can, however, be reamed oversize if they are found to be worn past an acceptable limit. Occasionally, a valve guide bore will be oversize as manufactured. These are marked on the inboard side of the cylinder heads on the machined surface just above the intake manifold.

If the guides must be reamed (this service is available at most machine shops), then valves with oversize stems must be fitted. Valves are usually available in 0.001 in. (0.025mm), 0.003 in. (0.076mm), and 0.005 in. (0.12mm) stem oversizes. Valve guides which are not excessively worn or distorted may, in some cases, be knurled rather than reamed. Knurling is a process in which the metal on the valve guide bore is displaced and raised, thereby reducing clearance. Knurling also provides excellent oil control. The option of knurling rather than reaming valve guides should be discussed with a reputable machinist or engine specialist.

INSPECTION

1. Install each valve into its respective port (guide) of the cylinder head.
2. Mount a dial indicator so that the stem is at 90° to the valve stem, as close to the valve guide as possible.
3. Move the valve off its seat, and measure the valve guide-to-stem clearance by rocking the stem back and forth to actuate the dial indicator.

4. Measure the valve stems using a micrometer, and compare to specifications to determine whether stem or guide wear is responsible for excessive clearance. Consult the machine shop for valve guide reconditioning.

Valve Lifters

REMOVAL & INSTALLATION

2.2L Engine

1. Disconnect the negative battery cable.
2. Remove the valve (rocker arm) cover, as outlined in this section.
3. Loosen the rocker arm nut and swing the rocker arm aside. Remove the pushrod.
4. Remove the engine lift bracket, located at the rear of the engine.

➡When removing the cylinder head to service the lifters, camshaft, camshaft bearing or pistons and connecting rods, it is NOT necessary to remove the oil fill tube or intake and exhaust manifolds.

5. Route the spark plug wires down below the lower intake manifold.
6. With the help of an assistant, carefully remove the cylinder head with the exhaust and intake manifolds attached.
7. Remove and discard the cylinder head gasket.
8. Remove the valve lifter(s).
9. Inspect the lifter. The lifter foot is slightly convex. This can be detected by holding a good straight edge to the surface while looking into a light source. If the lifter foot is flat or grooved, it MUST be replaced.

To install:

➡Whenever new valve lifters are being installed, coat the foot of the lifters with Camshaft Assembly Lube 1052365 or equivalent.

10. Install the valve lifter(s).
11. Position a new cylinder head gasket, then install the cylinder head assembly with the help of an assistant. Tighten the retaining bolts to the specifications in the "Cylinder Head" procedure located in this section.
12. Install the lift bracket and tighten the nuts to 32 ft. lbs. (43 Nm).
13. Route the spark plug wires up through the lower intake manifold.
14. Install the pushrod(s), making sure they seat in the lifter(s).
15. Install the rocker and nut.
16. Install the valve (rocker arm) cover, as outlined earlier in this section.
17. Connect the negative battery cable.

Fig. 116 Use a caliper gauge to check the valve spring free-length

Fig. 117 Check the valve spring for squareness on a flat service; a carpenter's square can be used

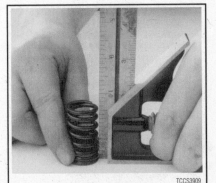

Fig. 118 The valve spring should be straight up and down when placed like this

2.3L Engine

INTAKE LIFTERS

1. Disconnect the negative battery cable.
2. Remove the ignition coil and module assembly electrical connections.
3. Remove the ignition coil and module from engine.
4. Remove idle speed power steering pressure switch connector.
5. Remove power steering drive belt and remove power steering pump as required.
6. Remove oil/air separator hose, fuel harness connector, vacuum hose to fuel regulator and fuel rail as required. Position fuel rail out of the way leaving fuel rail attached to fuel lines.
7. Disconnect timing chain housing but do not remove from vehicle. Install 2 bolts in timing chain housing to hold into place.
8. Remove intake cam housing cover to housing bolts.
9. Remove intake cam housing to cylinder head retaining bolts using the reverse of the tightening procedure.
10. Remove the cover off of the housing by threading 4 of the housing to head bolts into the tapped holes in the camshaft cover. Tighten bolts in evenly so not to bind the cover on the dowel pins.
11. Remove 2 loosely installed bolts in cover and remove cover. Discard gasket from cover.
12. Note position of chain sprocket dowel pin for reassembly. Remove camshaft.
13. Remove valve lifters keeping in order of removal.

To install:

14. Install lifters into bores. Used lifters must be returned to their original position. Replace all lifters if new camshaft is being installed.
15. Prelube camshaft lobes and journals and install into same position as when removed.
16. Install new camshaft housing to camshaft housing cover seals into cover. Remove bolts holding housing into place and install cover and retaining bolts. Coat housing and cover retaining bolts with pipe sealer prior to installing. Torque bolts 82A, in proper sequence, to 11 ft. lbs. plus an additional 75°; on 82B bolts, tighten to 11 ft. lbs. plus an additional 25°.
17. Install timing chain and housing.
18. Install new O-rings on injectors and install fuel rail into cylinder head. Install fuel rail to camshaft housing bolts and tighten to 19 ft. lbs.
19. Install injector wiring harness, vacuum hose to fuel pressure regulator and oil/air separator assembly.
20. Lube inner sealing surface of intake camshaft seal with clean engine oil and install seal into housing using tool J–36009 or equivalent.
21. Install drive pulley onto intake camshaft using tool J–36015 or equivalent.
22. Install power steering pump and drive belt.
23. Install idle speed power steering switch connector.
24. Install ignition module and coil assembly with retainer bolts and reconnect electrical connector.
25. Connect negative battery cable, start engine and check for oil leaks.

EXHAUST LIFTERS

1. Disconnect the negative battery cable.
2. Disconnect electrical connection from ignition coil and module assembly.
3. Remove ignition coil and module assembly from camshaft housing.
4. Disconnect electrical connector from oil pressure switch.
5. Remove transaxle fluid level indicator tube from exhaust camshaft cover and set aside for automatic transaxle only.
6. Remove exhaust camshaft cover and gasket.
7. Disconnect timing chain housing but do not remove from vehicle.
8. Remove exhaust housing to cylinder head bolts reversing the order of tightening. Leave 2 bolts loosely in place while removing cover from housing.
9. Remove the cover off of the housing by threading 4 of the housing to head retaining bolts into the tapped holes in the camshaft cover. Tighten bolts in evenly so not to bind the cover on the dowel pins.
10. Remove 2 loosely installed bolts in cover and remove cover.
11. Note position of chain sprocket dowel pin for reassembly. Remove camshaft.
12. Remove valve lifters keeping in order of removal.
13. Remove camshaft housing.

To install:

14. Install camshaft housing to cylinder head with a new gasket. Loosely install one bolt to hold into place.

15. Install lifters into bores. Used lifters must be returned to their original position. Replace all lifters if new camshaft is being installed.
16. Prelube camshaft lobes and journals and install into same position as when removed.
17. Install new camshaft housing to camshaft housing cover seals into cover. Remove bolt holding housing into place and install cover and retaining bolts. Coat housing and cover retaining bolts with pipe sealer prior to installing. Torque bolts, in proper sequence, to 11 ft. lbs. plus an additional 75°.
18. Install timing chain and housing.
19. Install exhaust camshaft housing cover with new gasket in place.
20. Install transaxle level indicator tube to exhaust camshaft cover.
21. Install electrical connection to oil pressure switch.
22. Install ignition coil and module assembly and connect electrical connector.
23. Install negative battery cable and start vehicle. Inspect for leaks.

2.5L Engine

1. Disconnect the negative battery cable.
2. Remove the rocker arm cover.
3. Remove the intake manifold.
4. Remove the pushrod cover.
5. Loosen the rocker arms and move to the side.
6. Mark and remove the pushrods, retainer and lifter guides.
7. Mark and remove the lifters.

➡**Mark each valve component location for reassembly.**

8. Lubricate all bearing surfaces and lifters with engine oil and install the lifters.
9. Install the lifter guides, retainers and pushrods.
10. Position the rocker arms over the pushrods and tighten the rocker arm nuts to 24 ft. lbs. (32 Nm) with the lifter at the base circle of the camshaft.
11. Install the pushrod cover, intake manifold and rocker arm cover.
12. Connect the negative battery cable.

2.8L and 3.1L Engines

1. Disconnect the negative terminal from the battery.
2. Drain the cooling system.
3. Remove the rocker arm covers and intake manifold.
4. Loosen the rocker arms nuts enough to move the rocker arms to 1 side and remove the pushrods.
5. Remove the lifters from the engine.
6. Using Molykote® or equivalent, coat the base of the new lifters and install them into the engine.
7. Position the pushrods and the rocker arms correctly into their original positions. Tighten the rocker arm nuts to 18 ft. lbs. (25 Nm)
8. Install the intake manifold and tighten the intake manifold-to-cylinder head bolts to specification.
9. Install the rocker cover. Connect the negative battery cable.
10. Fill the cooling system.

3.4L Engine

LEFT SIDE (FRONT)

1. Disconnect the negative battery cable.
2. Remove left side cam carrier as follows:
   a. Disconnect oil/air breather hose from cam carrier cover. Remove spark plug wires from plugs and remove rear spark plug wire cover.
   b. Remove cam carrier cover bolts and lift off cover. Remove gasket and O-rings from cover.
   c. Remove secondary timing belt by removing secondary timing belt actuator and tensioner assembly and sliding belt from pulleys.
   d. Install 6 sections of fuel line hoses under camshaft and between lifters. This will hold lifters in the carrier. For this procedure use 5/16 in. (8mm) fuel line hose for exhaust valves and 7/32 in. (5.5mm) fuel line hose for the intake valves.
   e. Remove exhaust crossover pipe and torque strut.
   f. Remove torque strut bracket at engine.
   g. Remove cam carrier mounting bolts and nuts and remove cam carrier.
   h. Remove cam carrier gasket from cylinder head.
3. Remove the 6 lifter hold-down hoses. Remove the lifters.

To install

4. Lubricate lifters with clean engine oil and install lifters into original position.

5. Install lifter hold-down hoses to cam carrier.

6. Install cam carrier following these steps:
   a. Install new gasket on cam carrier to cylinder mounting surface.
   b. Install cam hold-down tool J–38613 or equivalent, to carrier assembly.
   c. Install cam carrier to cylinder head. Install mounting bolts and nuts. Torque bolts and nuts to 18 ft. lbs.
   d. Remove lifter hold-down hoses and cam hold-down tool.
   e. Install torque strut bracket to engine and install torque strut.
   f. Install engine crossover pipe.
   g. Install secondary timing belt and cam carrier cover.
   h. Reconnect spark plug cover and wires.
   i. Connect breather hose to cam carrier cover.

7. Add fluids as required, reconnect negative battery cable. Start engine and recheck for leaks.

RIGHT SIDE (REAR)

1. Disconnect the negative battery cable. Drain cooling system.
2. Remove right side cam carrier as follows:
   a. Remove intake plenum and right timing belt cover.
   b. Remove right spark plug wires.
   c. Remove air/oil separator hose at cam carrier cover.
   d. Remove cam carrier cover bolts and lift of cover. Remove gasket and O-rings from cover.
   e. Remove secondary timing belt by removing secondary timing belt actuator and tensioner assembly and sliding belt from pulleys.
   f. Install 6 sections of fuel line hoses under camshaft and between lifters. This will hold lifters in carrier. For this procedure use 5⁄16 in. (8mm) fuel line hose for exhaust valves and 7⁄32 in. (5.5mm) fuel line hose for the intake valves.
   g. Remove exhaust crossover pipe and torque strut.
   h. Remove torque strut bracket at engine. Remove front engine lift hook.
   i. Remove cam carrier mounting bolts and nuts and remove cam carrier.
   j. Remove cam carrier gasket from cylinder head.
3. Remove 6 lifter hold-down hoses.
4. Remove lifters.

To install

5. Lubricate lifters with clean engine oil and install lifters into original position.

6. Install lifter hold-down hoses to cam carrier.

7. Install cam carrier following these steps:
   a. Install new gasket on cam carrier to cylinder mounting surface.
   b. Install cam hold-down tool J–38613 or equivalent, to carrier assembly.
   c. Install cam carrier to cylinder head. Install mounting bolts and nuts. Torque bolts and nuts to 18 ft. lbs.
   d. Remove lifter hold-down hoses and cam hold-down tool.
   e. Install torque strut bracket to engine and install torque strut.
   f. Install engine crossover pipe and engine lift hook.
   g. Install secondary timing belt and cam carrier cover.
   h. Install spark plug wires and cover.

8. Add fluids as required. Connect negative battery cable. Start engine and check for fluid leaks.

3.8L Engine

1. Disconnect the negative terminal from the battery.
2. Drain the cooling system.
3. Remove the rocker arm covers and intake manifold.
4. Remove the rocker arm assemblies.
5. Remove the guide retainer bolts and retainer.
6. Remove the valve lifter guides and valve lifters.

To install:

7. Prelube (dip) the valve lifters with oil before installation.
8. Install the lifter guides, guide retainer and bolts and tighten to 27 ft. lbs.
9. Install the rocker arm assemblies, intake manifold and valve covers.
10. Fill the cooling system and connect the negative battery cable.

Oil Pan

REMOVAL & INSTALLATION

✲✲ CAUTION

The EPA warns that prolonged contact with used engine oil may cause a number of skin disorders, including cancer! You should make every effort to minimize your exposure to used engine oil. Protective gloves should be worn when changing the oil. Wash your hands and any other exposed skin areas as soon as possible after exposure to used engine oil. Soap and water, or waterless hand cleaner should be used.

2.2L Engine

▶ See Figure 119

1. Disconnect the negative battery cable.
2. Raise and safely support the vehicle.
3. Properly drain the engine oil into a suitable container.
4. Detach the starter bracket from the block, then remove the starter and position it aside.
5. Remove the flywheel cover.
6. Remove the oil filter. Make sure the gasket is removed with the filter.
7. Unfasten the oil pan bolts and nuts, then remove the oil pan from the vehicle. Remove and discard the oil pan gasket and seal(s).
8. Thoroughly clean the gasket mating surfaces.

To install:

9. Place a 0.079 in. (2mm) diameter bead of a suitable RTV sealer on the oil pan-to-block side sealing flanges. Apply a suitable bead of RTV sealant to the oil pan surface which fits to the engine front cover.

10. Using a new oil pan rear seal, apply a thin coat of RTV sealant on the ends down to the ears, then install the pan against the cylinder case and install the retaining bolts and nuts. Tighten the bolts and nuts to 124 inch lbs. (14 Nm).

11. Lubricate a new oil filter gasket with clean engine oil. Install the filter and tighten to 13 ft. lbs. (17 Nm).

12. Install the starter, as outlined in Section 2 of this manual.
13. Carefully lower the vehicle.
14. Fill the crankcase with the proper type and amount of engine oil.
15. Connect the negative battery cable, then start the engine and check for leaks.

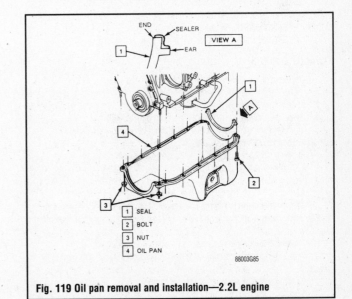

Fig. 119 Oil pan removal and installation—2.2L engine

2.3L Engine

♦ **See Figure 120**

1. Disconnect the negative battery cable.
2. Raise and support the vehicle safely.
3. Remove the flywheel inspection cover.
4. Unfasten the splash shield-to-suspension support bolt. If equipped, Remove the exhaust manifold brace.
5. Remove the radiator outlet pipe-to-oil pan bolt.
6. Unfasten the transaxle-to-oil pan nut and stud using a 7mm socket.
7. Gently pry the spacer out from between oil pan and transaxle.
8. Unfasten the oil pan retaining bolts. Rotate the crankshaft if necessary and remove the oil pan and gasket from the engine.
9. Inspect the silicone strips across the top of the aluminum carrier at the oil pan-cylinder block-seal housing 3-way joint. If damaged, these strips must be repaired with silicone sealer. Use only enough sealer to restore the strips to their original dimension; too much sealer could cause leakage.

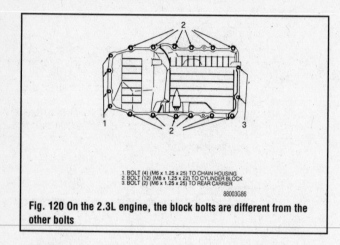

1. BOLT (4) (M6 x 1.25 x 25) TO CHAIN HOUSING
2. BOLT (12) (M8 x 1.25 x 22) TO CYLINDER BLOCK
3. BOLT (2) (M6 x 1.25 x 25) TO REAR CARRIER

88003G86

Fig. 120 On the 2.3L engine, the block bolts are different from the other bolts

To install:
10. Thoroughly clean and dry the mating surfaces, bolts and bolt holes. Install the oil pan with a new gasket; do not use sealer on the gasket. Loosely install the pan bolts.
11. Place the spacer in its approximate installed position but allow clearance to tighten the pan bolt above it.
12. Tighten the pan-to-block bolts to 17 ft. lbs. (24 Nm) and the remaining bolts to 106 inch lbs. (12 Nm)
13. Install the spacer and stud.
14. Install the oil pan transaxle nut and bolt.
15. Install the splash shield to suspension support.
16. Fasten the radiator outlet pipe bolt.
17. Install the exhaust manifold brace, if removed.
18. Install the flywheel inspection cover.
19. Carefully lower the vehicle.
20. Fill the crankcase with the proper type and amount oil.
21. Connect the negative battery cable, then start the engine and check for leaks.

2.5L Engine

♦ **See Figure 121**

1. Disconnect the negative battery cable.
2. Remove the coolant recovery bottle, engine torque strut, air cleaner and the air inlet.
3. Remove the serpentine belt.
4. If equipped, loosen and move the A/C compressor from the bracket. Position the compressor aside, but do not disconnect the refrigerant lines.
5. Remove the oil level indicator and fill tube.
6. Support the engine using an engine support tool J–28467–A and J–36462, or equivalent.
7. Raise and safely support the vehicle, drain the engine oil and remove the oil filter.

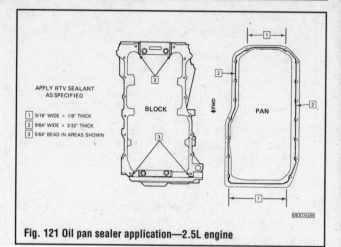

APPLY RTV SEALANT AS SPECIFIED

BLOCK ⬦FWD PAN

1 5/16" WIDE x 1/8" THICK
2 9/64" WIDE x 3/32" THICK
3 5/64" BEAD IN AREAS SHOWN

88003G88

Fig. 121 Oil pan sealer application—2.5L engine

8. Remove the starter motor, flywheel cover and turn the front wheels to full right.
9. Remove the engine wiring harness retainers under the oil pan on the right and left sides.
10. Remove the right engine splash shield, front engine mount bracket bolts and nuts.
11. Remove the transaxle mount nuts.
12. Using the engine support fixture tool J–28467–A and J–36462, raise the engine about 2 in. (51mm).
13. Remove the front engine mount, bracket and loosen the frame bolts.
14. Remove the oil pan retaining bolts and oil pan.
To install:
15. Clean all gasket surfaces and apply RTV sealer to the oil pan and engine surfaces.
16. Install the oil pan and retaining bolts and tighten to 89 inch lbs. (10 Nm)
17. Install the frame bolts and tighten to 103 ft. lbs. (140 Nm)
18. Install the engine mount, bracket, lower the engine into position and install the transaxle mount nuts.
19. Install the engine mount nuts and bracket bolts.
20. Install the engine splash shield, wiring harness to the oil pan, flywheel cover and the starter motor.
21. Lower the vehicle and remove the engine support fixtures.
22. Install the oil level indicator and tube assembly.
23. If equipped, reinstall the A/C compressor to its original location.
24. Install the serpentine belt.
25. Install the air inlet, air cleaner, torque strut and coolant recovery bottle.
26. Connect the negative battery cable and fill the engine with the correct type and amount of oil.
27. Start the engine and check for leaks.

2.8L and 3.1L Engines

1988–93 VEHICLES

♦ **See Figure 122**

1. Disconnect the negative battery cable.
2. Remove the serpentine belt and the tensioner.
3. Support the engine with tool J–28467 or equivalent.
4. Raise and safely support the vehicle. Drain the engine oil.
5. Remove the right tire and wheel assembly. Remove the right inner fender splash shield.
6. Remove the steering gear pinch bolt. Remove the transaxle mount retaining bolts. Failure to disconnect intermediate shaft from rack and pinion stub shaft can result in damage to the steering gear and/or intermediate shaft. This could cause a loss of steering control which could result in personal injury.
7. Remove the engine-to-cradle mounting nuts. Remove the front engine collar bracket from the block.
8. Remove the starter shield and the flywheel cover. Remove the starter.
9. Loosen, but do not remove the rear engine cradle bolts. Remove electrical connector at DIS sensor.

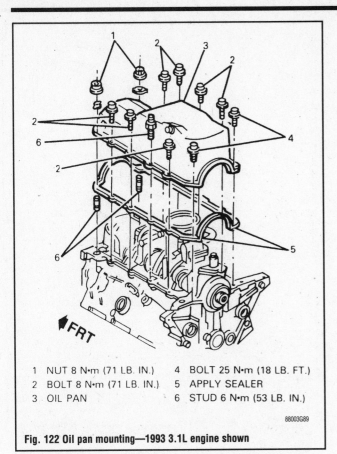

1 NUT 8 N•m (71 LB. IN.)   4 BOLT 25 N•m (18 LB. FT.)
2 BOLT 8 N•m (71 LB. IN.)   5 APPLY SEALER
3 OIL PAN   6 STUD 6 N•m (53 LB. IN.)

88003G89

Fig. 122 Oil pan mounting—1993 3.1L engine shown

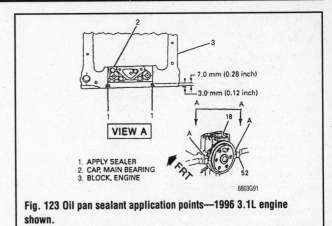

1. APPLY SEALER
2. CAP, MAIN BEARING
3. BLOCK, ENGINE

8803G91

Fig. 123 Oil pan sealant application points—1996 3.1L engine shown.

10. Unfasten the front cradle bolts and lower the front of the frame.

11. If equipped, remove secondary air injection pipe retaining nuts from the oil pan stud.

12. Unfasten the oil pan retaining bolts and nuts, then remove the oil pan. Remove and discard the gasket.

To install:

13. Clean the gasket mating surfaces.

14. Install a new gasket on the oil pan. Apply silicon sealer to the portion of the pan that contacts the rear of the block.

15. Install the oil pan, nuts and retaining bolts. Tighten the rear bolts to 18 ft. lbs. (25 Nm), and the remaining nuts and bolts to 89 inch lbs. (10 Nm).

16. If equipped, install the secondary air injection pipe retaining nut to the oil pan stud.

17. Install the front cradle bolts and tighten the rear cradle bolts. Install DIS connector. Install the starter and splash shield. Install the flywheel shield.

18. Attach the collar bracket to the block, install the engine-to-cradle nuts. Install the transaxle mount nuts.

19. Install the steering pinch bolt. Install the right inner fender splash shield and tire assembly. Lower the vehicle.

20. Remove the engine support tool. Install the serpentine belt and tensioner.

21. Fill the crankcase to the correct level. Connect the negative battery cable. Run the engine to normal operating temperature and check for leaks.

1994–96 VEHICLES

▶ See Figure 123

1. Disconnect the negative battery cable.

➡It may be necessary to remove the hood, with the help of an assistant, for access.

2. Remove the engine mount strut and A/C compressor (if equipped) and the engine mount strut bracket assemblies.

3. Remove the electric cooling fan assemblies.

4. Support the engine with tools J—28467 and J 26462, or equivalent.

5. Raise and safely support the vehicle. Drain the engine oil.

6. Remove the front exhaust manifold pipe.

7. Remove the intermediate shaft bolt/screw.

8. Remove the oil level sensor.

9. Remove the engine splash shield.

10. Suitable support the drivetrain and front suspension with jack stands.

11. Remove the transaxle mount side frame retaining nuts from the drivetrain and suspension frame assembly.

12. Remove the engine mount side frame nuts from the drivetrain and suspension frame assembly.

13. Unfasten the rear drivetrain and front suspension frame bolts/screws.

14. If equipped, remove the lower drivetrain and front suspension frame bolts/screws.

15. Remove the engine mount assembly.

16. Remove the flywheel inspection cover.

17. Remove the starter, as outlined in Section 2 of this manual.

18. Disconnect the transaxle mount assembly from the oil pan.

19. Unfasten the side bolts and screws and the retaining bolts and screws, then remove the oil pan. Remove and discard the oil pan gasket.

To install:

13. Clean the gasket mating surfaces.

14. Apply a small amount of sealer on either side of the rear main bearing cap, where the seal surface on the cap meets the cylinder block. Install a new gasket on the oil pan.

15. Position the oil pan and secure with the retaining bolts and screws. Tighten the retaining bolts and screws to 18 ft. lbs. (25 Nm) and the side bolts/screws using tool J 39505 or equivalent.

16. Fasten the transaxle mount assembly to the oil pan.

17. Install the starter motor, as outlined in Section 2 of this manual.

18. Install the flywheel inspection cover.

19. Install the engine mount assembly.

20. Carefully raise the drivetrain and front suspension assembly. Install the rear drivetrain and front suspension frame bolts/screws.

21. Fasten the engine mount frame side nuts to the drivetrain and front suspension frame assembly. Install the transaxle mount frame side nuts to the drivetrain and suspension frame assembly.

22. Remove the jackstands from the drivetrain and front suspension frame assembly.

23. Install the engine splash shield and the oil level sensor.

24. Install the intermediate steering shaft bolt/screw. Connect the front exhaust manifold pipe.

25. Carefully lower the vehicle.

26. Remove the engine support tools.

27. Install the electric cooling fan assemblies.

28. Install the engine mount strut and A/C compressor, bracket and the engine mount strut bracket.

29. If removed, install the hood assembly.

30. Fill the crankcase to the correct level. Connect the negative battery cable. Run the engine to normal operating temperature and check for leaks.

3.4L Engine

▶ See Figure 124

1. Disconnect the negative battery cable.

2. Raise and safely support vehicle. Drain the engine oil into a suitable container.

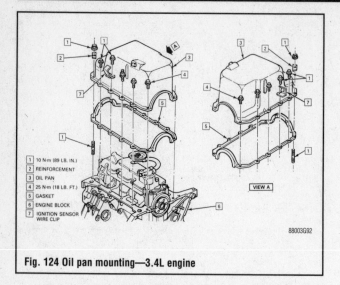

[1] 10 N·m (89 LB. IN.)
[2] REINFORCEMENT
[3] OIL PAN
[4] 25 N·m (18 LB. FT.)
[5] GASKET
[6] ENGINE BLOCK
[7] IGNITION SENSOR WIRE CLIP

88003G92

Fig. 124 Oil pan mounting—3.4L engine

3. Remove right front wheel and tire assemblies and the steering gear heat shield.

4. Unfasten the steering gear retaining bolts and support steering gear to body.

5. Separate right and left lower ball joints, using a suitable puller.

6. Disconnect power steering cooler line clamps at frame.

7. Safely support frame and remove engine mount nuts at frame.

8. Unfasten the frame retaining bolts and remove frame assembly.

9. Remove starter assembly and the flywheel cover.

10. Unfasten the oil pan retaining nuts and bolts, then remove the oil pan.

11. Remove and discard the old pan gasket. Clean all mating surfaces.

To install:

12. Install a new gasket, adding sealer to gasket next to rear main bearing cap. Position the oil pan and secure using the retaining bolts. Tighten the rear bolts to 18 ft. lbs. (24 Nm) and all other bolts and nuts to 89 inch lbs. (10 Nm).

13. Install the flywheel cover and starter motor.

14. Install the frame assembly and secure all bolts.

15. Install the engine mount nuts at frame. Remove frame support.

16. Connect the power steering cooler lines at frame.

17. Install the lower ball joints. Install steering gear to steering gear mounts.

18. Install steering gear retainer bolts and the heat shield.

19. Install the front tire and wheel assemblies and carefully lower the vehicle.

20. Connect the negative battery cable, then add the correct type and quantity of engine oil.

21. Start vehicle and check for leaks.

3.8L Engine

♦ **See Figure 125**

1. Disconnect the negative battery cable.

2. Remove the engine torque strut from the engine.

3. Raise and support the vehicle safely.

4. Disconnect the front exhaust pipe from the manifold.

5. Remove the right front wheel and tire assembly, then remove the inner fender splash shield.

6. Drain the engine oil into a suitable container, then remove the oil filter.

7. Disconnect the oil cooler pipes and allow to hang loose for access.

8. Remove both front engine mounts from the frame.

9. Remove the flywheel cover.

10. Raise the engine assembly safely, using a suitable jack.

11. If necessary, detach the oil level sensor electrical connector, then remove the sensor.

12. Unfasten the oil pan retaining bolts, then lower the oil pan and disconnect the oil pump screen assembly. Remove and discard the oil pan gasket.

13. Remove the oil pan and pump screen assembly.

To install:

14. Clean the gasket mating surfaces.

15. Use a new oil pan gasket and install the oil pan and screen assembly to the engine.

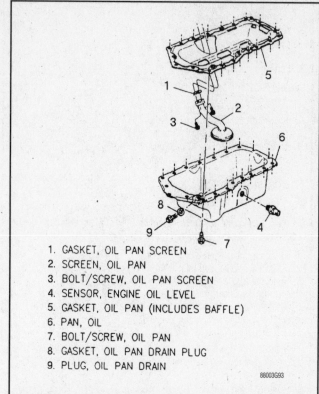

1. GASKET, OIL PAN SCREEN
2. SCREEN, OIL PAN
3. BOLT/SCREW, OIL PAN SCREEN
4. SENSOR, ENGINE OIL LEVEL
5. GASKET, OIL PAN (INCLUDES BAFFLE)
6. PAN, OIL
7. BOLT/SCREW, OIL PAN
8. GASKET, OIL PAN DRAIN PLUG
9. PLUG, OIL PAN DRAIN

88003G93

Fig. 125 Oil pan removal and installation—1996 3.8L engine shown

➡ **If the rear main bearing cap is being installed, then RTV sealant must be placed on the oil pan gasket tabs that insert into the gasket groove of the outer surface on the rear main bearing cap.**

16. Tighten the screen assembly bolts to 115 inch lbs. (13 Nm) and the oil pan retaining bolts to 124 inch lbs. (14 Nm). Do not overtighten.

17. If removed, install the oil level sensor and attach the connector.

18. Lower the engine and install the transaxle converter cover.

19. Install the engine mount nuts to the frame and tighten to 32 ft. lbs. (43 Nm).

20. Attach the oil cooler pipes and install the oil filter.

21. Install the inner fender splash shield and wheel assembly.

22. Connect the front exhaust pipe to the manifold.

23. Lower the vehicle, then install the engine torque strut to the engine.

24. Fill the crankcase with the proper amount and type of engine oil. Connect the negative battery cable, then start the engine and check for leaks.

Oil Pump

REMOVAL

※ CAUTION

The EPA warns that prolonged contact with used engine oil may cause a number of skin disorders, including cancer! You should make every effort to minimize your exposure to used engine oil. Protective gloves should be worn when changing the oil. Wash your hands and any other exposed skin areas as soon as possible after exposure to used engine oil. Soap and water, or waterless hand cleaner should be used.

2.2L Engine

1. Disconnect the negative battery cable.

2. Raise and safely support the vehicle, then drain the engine oil.

3. Remove the oil pan, as outlined earlier in this section.

4. Unfasten the pump retaining bolt from the rear main bearing cap, then remove the pump and extension shaft.

5. Remove the extension shaft and retainer, but be very careful NOT to crack the retainer.

2.3L Engine

▶ See Figure 126

1. Disconnect the negative battery cable.
2. Raise and support the vehicle safely.
3. Drain the engine oil and remove the oil pan.
4. Unfasten the oil pump retaining bolts and nut.
5. Remove the oil pump assembly, shims, if equipped, and screen.

2.5L, 2.8L, 3.1L and 3.4L Engines

▶ See Figures 127, 128 and 129

➡On the 2.5L engine, the force balancer assembly does not have to be removed to service the oil pump or pressure regulator assemblies.

1. Disconnect the negative battery cable.
2. Raise and safely support the vehicle.
3. Drain the engine oil into a suitable container.
4. Remove the oil pan, as outlined earlier in this section.
5. On 3.4L engine, it will be necessary to remove the oil pan baffle by extracting the nuts and rotating the oil pick up tube out of the way.
6. Unfasten the oil pump retaining bolts and remove the oil pump and pump driveshaft.

3.8L Engine

▶ See Figure 130

1. Disconnect the negative battery cable.
2. Raise and safely support the vehicle.
3. Drain the engine oil.
4. Remove the front cover assembly.
5. Remove the oil filter adapter, pressure regulator valve and spring.
6. Remove the oil pump cover attaching screws and remove the cover.
7. Remove the oil pump gears.

INSPECTION

2.2L Engine

1. Inspect all components carefully for physical damage of any type and replace worn parts.
2. Check the gear pocket depth. The specification is 1.195–1.198 in. (30.36–30.44mm).

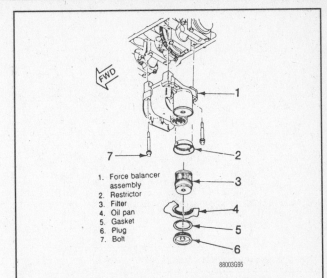

1. Force balancer assembly
2. Restrictor
3. Filter
4. Oil pan
5. Gasket
6. Plug
7. Bolt

88003G95

Fig. 127 Exploded view of the oil pump assembly—2.5L engine

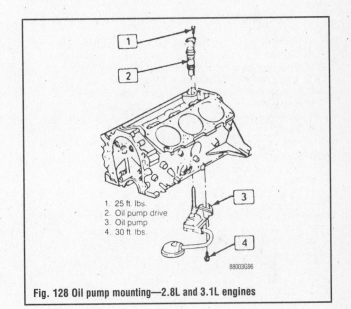

1. 25 ft. lbs.
2. Oil pump drive
3. Oil pump
4. 30 ft. lbs.

88003G96

Fig. 128 Oil pump mounting—2.8L and 3.1L engines

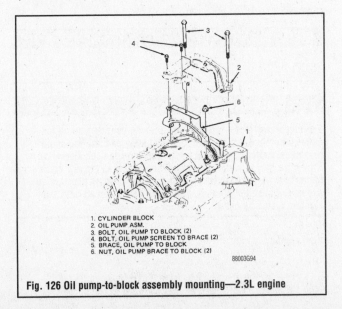

1. CYLINDER BLOCK
2. OIL PUMP ASM.
3. BOLT, OIL PUMP TO BLOCK (2)
4. BOLT, OIL PUMP SCREEN TO BRACE (2)
5. BRACE, OIL PUMP TO BLOCK
6. NUT, OIL PUMP BRACE TO BLOCK (2)

88003G94

Fig. 126 Oil pump-to-block assembly mounting—2.3L engine

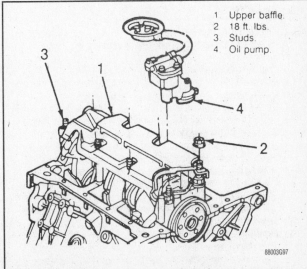

1. Upper baffle.
2. 18 ft. lbs.
3. Studs.
4. Oil pump.

88003G97

Fig. 129 View of the oil pump assembly mounting—3.4L engine

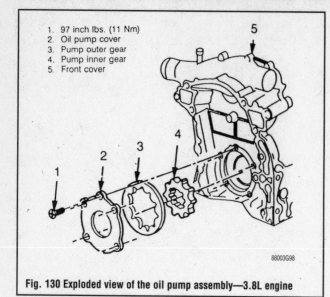

1. 97 inch lbs. (11 Nm)
2. Oil pump cover
3. Pump outer gear
4. Pump inner gear
5. Front cover

88003G98

Fig. 130 Exploded view of the oil pump assembly—3.8L engine

3. Check the gear pocket diameter. The specification is 1.503–1.506 in. (38.18–38.25mm).
4. Check the gear length. The measurement is 1.199–1.200 in. (30.45–30.48mm).
5. Check the outer gear diameter clearance. The specification is 1.498–1.500 in. (38.05–38.10mm).
6. Replace the oil pump assembly if any specification is out of range.

2.3L Engine

1. Inspect all components carefully for physical damage of any type and replace worn parts.
2. Check the gerotor cavity depth. The specification is 0.674–0.676 in. (17.11–17.16mm).
3. Check the gerotor cavity diameter. The specification is 2.127–2.129 in. (53.95–54.00mm).
4. Check the inner gerotor tip clearance. The maximum clearance is 0.006 in. (0.15mm).
5. Check the outer gerotor diameter clearance. The specification is 0.010–0.014 in. (0.254–0.354mm).
6. Replace the oil pump assembly if any specification is out of range.

2.5L Engine

1. Inspect all components carefully for physical damage of any type and replace worn parts.
2. Check the gerotor cavity depth. The specification for 1988 is 0.995–0.998 in. (25.27–25.35mm). The specification for 1989–92 is 0.514–0.516 in. (13.05–13.10mm).
3. Check the gear lash. The specification is 0.009–0.015 in. (0.23–0.38mm).
4. Check the clearance of both gears. The maximum clearance is 0.004 in. (0.10mm).
5. Replace the oil pump assembly if any specification is out of range. (0.10mm).

2.8L, 3.1L and 3.4L Engines

1. Inspect all components carefully for physical damage of any type and replace worn parts.
2. Check the gear pocket depth. The specification is 1.195–1.198 in. (30.36–30.44mm).
3. Check the gear pocket diameter. The specification is 1.503–1.506 in. (38.18–38.25mm).
4. Check the gear length. The measurement is 1.199–1.200 in. (30.45–30.48mm).
5. Check the outer gear diameter clearance. The specification is 1.498–1.500 in. (38.05–38.10mm).

6. The pressure regulator valve-to-bore clearance should be 0.0015–0.0035 in. (0.038mm–0.089mm).
7. Replace the oil pump assembly if any specification is out of range.

3.8L Engine

1. Inspect all components carefully for physical damage of any type and replace worn parts.
2. The inner tip clearance should be 0.006 in. (0.15mm).
3. The outer gear diameter clearance should be 0.008–0.015 in. (0.20–0.38mm).
4. The gear end clearance or the drop in the housing should be 0.001–0.0035 in. (0.025–0.089mm).
5. The pressure regulator valve-to-bore clearance should be 0.0015–0.003 in. (0.038–0.076mm).
6. Replace the oil pump assembly if any specification is out of range.

INSTALLATION

2.2L Engine

1. Remove oil pump from block, fill the cavity with petroleum jelly and reinstall driven gear cover assembly to pump. Tighten the bolts to 89 inch lbs. (10 Nm).
2. Heat the extension shaft in hot water before assembling the extension shaft.
3. Attach the extension to the oil pump. Make sure the retainer does not crack during installation.
4. Install the pump-to-rear bearing cap, then install the retaining bolt. Tighten the bolt to 32 ft. lbs. (43 Nm).
5. Install the oil pan, as outlined earlier in this section.
6. Carefully lower the vehicle, then fill the crankcase with the proper type and amount of engine oil.
7. Connect the negative battery cable, then start the engine and check for proper operation.

2.3L Engine

1. With oil pump assembly off engine, remove 3 retaining bolts and separate the driven gear cover and screen assembly from the oil pump.
2. Install the oil pump on the block using the original shims, if equipped. Tighten the bolts to 33 ft. lbs. (45 Nm).
3. Mount a dial indicator assembly to measure backlash between oil pump to drive gear.
4. Record oil pump drive to driven gear backlash. Proper backlash is 0.010–0.018 in. (0.25–0.45mm). When measuring, do not allow the crankshaft to move.
5. If equipped with shims, remove shims to decrease clearance and add shims to increase clearance. If no shims were present, replace the assembly if proper backlash cannot be obtained.
6. When the proper clearance is reached, rotate crankshaft ½ turn and recheck clearance.
7. Remove oil pump from block, fill the cavity with petroleum jelly and reinstall driven gear cover and screen assembly to pump. Tighten the bolts to 106 inch lbs. (13 Nm).
8. Reinstall the pump assembly to the block. Torque oil pump-to-block bolts 33 ft. lbs. (45 Nm).
9. Install the oil pan.
10. Fill the crankcase with the proper oil.
11. Start the engine, check the oil pressure and check for leaks. Do not run the engine without measurable oil pressure.

2.5L, 2.8L, 3.1L and 3.4L Engines

1. Pack the pump with petroleum jelly.
2. Install the oil pump and pump driveshaft. Tighten the oil pump mounting bolts to 30 ft. lbs. (41 Nm) for the 2.8L and 3.1L engines, 40 ft. lbs. (54 Nm) for 3.4L engine or to 89 inch lbs. (10 Nm) for 2.5L engine.
3. Install oil pan baffle, if equipped, and tighten nuts to 18 ft. lbs. (25 Nm).
4. Install the oil pan, then carefully lower the vehicle.
5. Fill the crankcase to the correct level with oil.
6. Connect the negative battery cable, then start the engine, check the oil

pressure and check for leaks. Do not run the engine without measurable oil pressure.

3.8L Engine

1. Lubricate the gears with petroleum jelly and install the gears into the housing.
2. Pack the gear cavity with petroleum jelly after the gears have been installed in the housing.
3. Install the oil pump cover and screws and tighten to 97 inch lbs.
4. Install the oil filter adapter with new gasket, pressure regulator valve and spring.
5. Install the front cover assembly.
6. Fill with clean engine oil. Start the engine, check the oil pressure and check for leaks. Do not run the engine without measurable oil pressure.

Timing Chain Front Cover

REMOVAL & INSTALLATION

2.2L Engine

▶ See Figures 131 and 132

1. Disconnect the negative battery cable.
2. Remove the serpentine drive belt.
3. Raise and safely support the vehicle.
4. Remove the right side tire and wheel assembly. Mark a relationship between the wheel and the wheel stud for reinstallation purposes.
5. Unfasten the crankshaft pulley bolts, then remove the pulley.
6. Install puller J 24420-B or equivalent and remove the hub.
7. Remove the electrical center cover.
8. Remove the serpentine belt tensioner and bracket.
9. Remove the oil pan, as outlined earlier in this section.
10. Unfasten the timing chain cover bolts, then remove the cover. If the cover is difficult to removed, use a rubber mallet to carefully loosen the cover. Remove and discard the timing chain cover gasket.
11. Thoroughly clean all gasket mating surfaces.

To install:

12. Position the timing chain cover to the engine, using a new gasket, guiding the cover over the dowel pins.
13. Install the timing chain cover retaining bolts, then tighten to 97 inch lbs. (11 Nm).
14. Install the crankshaft pulley hub using tool J 29113 or equivalent, and using RTV sealant at the keyway in the crankshaft.
15. Install the oil pan, as outlined earlier in this section.
16. Install the crankshaft belt pulley, then tighten the retaining bolts to 37 ft. lbs. (50 Nm).

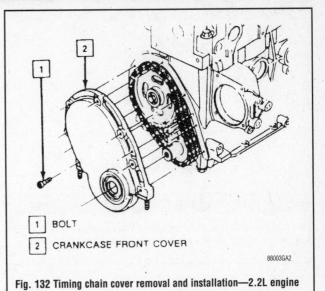

1	BOLT
2	CRANKCASE FRONT COVER

88003GA2

Fig. 132 Timing chain cover removal and installation—2.2L engine

17. Install the crankshaft hub bolt, then tighten to 77 ft. lbs. (105 Nm).
18. Install the serpentine belt and the electrical cover.
19. Install the right side inner wheel well splash shield.
20. Install the wheel and tire assembly, then carefully lower the vehicle.
21. Tighten the lug nuts to specification, then connect the negative battery cable.
22. Fill the crankcase to the correct level with the proper type of oil.
23. Start the engine and check for proper operation and/or leakage.

2.3L Engine

▶ See Figure 133

1. Disconnect the negative battery cable. Remove the coolant recovery reservoir.
2. Remove the serpentine drive belt using a 13mm wrench that is at least 24 in. (61cm) long.
3. Remove upper cover fasteners.
4. Disconnect the cover vent hose.
5. Remove the engine lift bracket.
6. Raise and safely support the vehicle.
7. Remove the right front wheel assembly and lower splash shield.
8. Remove the crankshaft balancer assembly.
9. Detach the lower cover fasteners.
10. Carefully lower the vehicle.

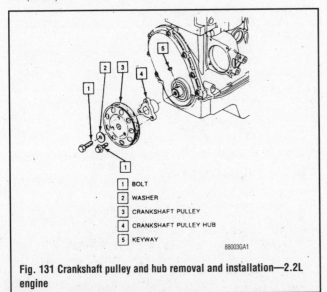

1	BOLT
2	WASHER
3	CRANKSHAFT PULLEY
4	CRANKSHAFT PULLEY HUB
5	KEYWAY

88003GA1

Fig. 131 Crankshaft pulley and hub removal and installation—2.2L engine

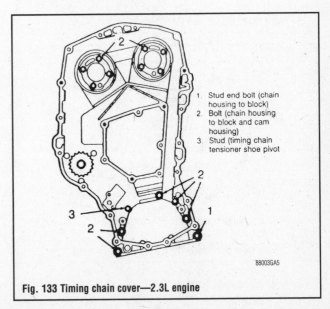

1. Stud end bolt (chain housing to block)
2. Bolt (chain housing to block and cam housing)
3. Stud (timing chain tensioner shoe pivot

88003GA5

Fig. 133 Timing chain cover—2.3L engine

11. Remove the timing chain front cover and gaskets. Discard the gaskets.
To install:
12. Install the cover and new gaskets. Place the nuts on the studs to retain the cover, then install the bolts and tighten to 106 inch lbs. (12 Nm).
13. Install the engine lift bracket.
14. Raise and safely support the vehicle.
15. Install the remaining cover fasteners and tighten to 106 inch lbs. (12 Nm).
16. Lubricate the front oil seal and the sealing surface of the crankshaft balancer with a suitable chassis grease.
17. Install the crankshaft balancer and tighten the balancer retaining bolt to 74 ft. lbs. (100 Nm) plus an additional 90° turn.
18. Install the right front wheel and tire assembly.
19. Carefully lower the vehicle.

⁂ CAUTION

To avoid personal injury when rotating the serpentine belt tensioner, use a tight fitting 13mm wrench that is at least 24 inches (61cm) long.

20. Install the serpentine drive belt.
21. Attach the cover vent hose.
22. Install the coolant recovery tank.
23. Connect the negative battery cable, then start the engine and check for leaks.

2.5L Engine

▶ **See Figure 134**

1. Disconnect the negative battery cable.
2. Remove the torque strut bolt at the cylinder head bracket and move the strut out of the way.
3. Remove the serpentine belt.
4. Install the engine support fixture tool J–28467–A and J–36462.
5. Raise and safely support the vehicle.
6. Remove the right front tire assembly.
7. Disconnect the right lower ball joint from the knuckle.
8. Remove the 2 right frame attaching bolts.
9. Loosen the 2 left frame attaching bolts but do not remove.
10. Carefully lower the vehicle.
11. Lower the engine on the right side. Raise and safely support the vehicle.
12. Remove the engine vibration dampener using a suitable dampener puller.
13. Unfasten the timing cover retaining bolts, then remove the cover. Remove and discard the gasket.
To install:
14. Clean all gasket mating surfaces with solvent and a gasket scraper.
15. Apply a ³⁄₈ in. (10mm) wide by ¹⁄₁₆ in. (1.6mm) thick bead of RTV sealer to the joint at the oil pan and timing cover.

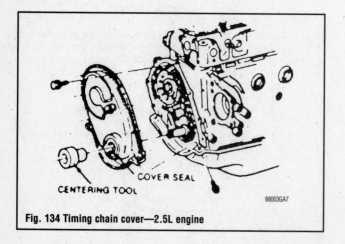

Fig. 134 Timing chain cover—2.5L engine

16. Apply a ¼ in. (6mm) wide by ⅛ in. (3mm) thick bead of RTV sealer to the timing cover at the block mating surface.
17. Install a new timing cover oil seal using a timing cover seal installer tool J–34995 or equivalent.
18. Position the cover onto the block and install the retaining bolts loosely.
19. Install the timing cover seal installer tool J–34995 to align the timing cover.
20. Tighten the opposing bolts to hold the cover in place.
21. Tighten the bolts, in sequence, to 89 inch lbs. (10 Nm). Remove the timing cover oil seal installer tool.
22. Install the crankshaft vibration dampener and tighten the bolt to 162 ft. lbs. (220 Nm).
23. Carefully lower the vehicle.
24. Raise the engine to its proper position using the support fixture.
25. Raise and safely support the vehicle.
26. Raise the frame and install the removed frame bolts. Tighten the bolts to 103 ft. lbs. (140 Nm).
27. Install the right ball joint, then tighten the nut.
28. Install the right front tire, tighten the lug nuts to 100 ft. lbs. (136 Nm) and lower the vehicle.
29. Remove the engine support fixture.
30. Install the torque strut and bolt to the cylinder head bracket.
31. Install the serpentine belt, connect the negative battery cable and check for oil leaks.

2.8L and 3.1L Engines

VEHICLES THROUGH 1993

▶ **See Figure 135**

1. Remove the air cleaner assembly.
2. Disconnect the negative battery cable. Drain the cooling system into a suitable container.
3. Remove the serpentine belt and the belt tensioner.
4. Remove the alternator-to-bracket bolts and remove the alternator, with the wires attached, then support it out of the way.
5. Unfasten the power steering pump-to-bracket bolts and support it out of the way. Do not disconnect the pressure hoses.
6. Raise and safely support the vehicle.
7. Remove the right side inner fender splash shield. Remove the flywheel dust cover.
8. Using a suitable crankshaft pulley puller tool, remove the crankshaft damper.
9. Label and disconnect the starter wires, then remove the starter.
10. Drain the engine oil into a suitable container, then remove the oil pan.
11. Remove the lower front cover bolts.
12. Carefully lower the vehicle.
13. Disconnect the radiator hose from the water pump.
14. Detach the heater coolant hose from the cooling system filler pipe.
15. Remove the bypass and overflow hoses.
16. Remove the water pump pulley. Disconnect the canister purge hose.
17. Remove the spark plug wire shield from the water pump.
18. Unfasten the upper front cover-to-engine bolts, then remove the front cover.
19. Remove and discard the gasket. Clean front cover mounting surfaces.
To install:
20. Apply a thin bead of silicone sealant on the front cover mating surface and using a new gasket, install the front cover on the engine with the top bolts to hold it in place.
21. Raise and safely support the vehicle.
22. Install the oil pan. Install the lower front cover bolts, tighten all of the front cover bolts to 26–35 ft. lbs. (35–48 Nm).
23. Install the serpentine belt and idler pulley. Install the damper on the engine using tool J–29113 or equivalent. Install the starter.
24. Install the inner fender splash shield. Lower the vehicle.
25. Attach the radiator hose to the water pump and attach the heater hoses.
26. Install the power steering pump and the alternator.
27. Attach the spark plug wire shield. Fill the cooling system.
28. Connect the negative battery cable. Check for coolant and oil leaks.

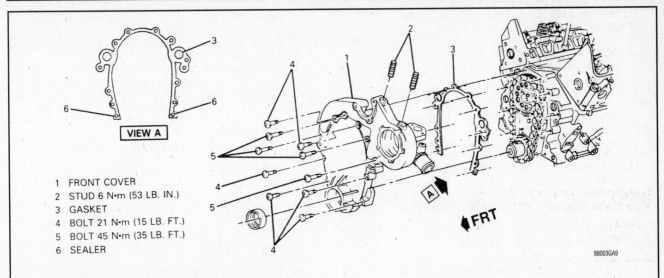

1 FRONT COVER
2 STUD 6 N•m (53 LB. IN.)
3 GASKET
4 BOLT 21 N•m (15 LB. FT.)
5 BOLT 45 N•m (35 LB. FT.)
6 SEALER

88003GA9

Fig. 135 Timing chain front cover removal—1993 3.1L engine shown

1994–96 VEHICLES

▶ See Figure 136

1. Disconnect the negative battery cable.
2. Drain the engine cooling system into a suitable container.
3. Remove the serpentine drive belt.
4. With the help of an assistant, remove the hood.
5. Remove the engine mount strut and A/C compressor bracket and the engine mount strut bracket.
6. Remove the electric cooling fan.
7. Install engine support tools J 28467-A and J 36462, or equivalent.
8. Raise and safely support the vehicle.
9. Remove the front exhaust manifold pipe.
10. Unfasten the intermediate steering shaft bolt/screw, then position the cover aside.
11. Drain the engine oil into a suitable container.
12. Remove the engine splash shield.
13. Remove the crankshaft balancer bolt/screw and washer, then remove the balancer using tool J 24420-B or equivalent.
14. Support the drivetrain and front suspension frame with suitable jackstands.
15. Remove the transaxle mount side frame retaining nuts from the drivetrain and suspension frame assembly.
16. Remove the engine mount side frame nuts from the drivetrain and suspension frame assembly.

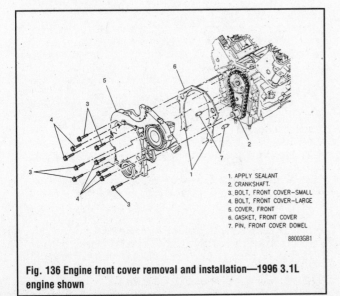

1. APPLY SEALANT
2. CRANKSHAFT
3. BOLT, FRONT COVER–SMALL
4. BOLT, FRONT COVER–LARGE
5. COVER, FRONT
6. GASKET, FRONT COVER
7. PIN, FRONT COVER DOWEL

88003GB1

Fig. 136 Engine front cover removal and installation—1996 3.1L engine shown

17. Unfasten the rear drivetrain and front suspension frame bolts/screws.
18. If equipped, remove the lower drivetrain and front suspension frame bolts/screws.
19. Remove the engine mount assembly.
20. Remove the flywheel inspection cover.
21. Remove the starter, as outlined in Section 2 of this manual.
22. Disconnect the transaxle mount assembly from the oil pan.
23. Unfasten the side bolts and screws and the retaining bolts and screws, then remove the oil pan.
24. Raise the drivetrain and front suspension frame, then install the retaining bolts/screws.
25. Carefully lower the vehicle.
26. Remove the coolant recovery reservoir.
27. Remove the serpentine drive belt shield.
28. Remove the power steering pump pulley.
29. Unfasten the power steering pump bolts, then position the pump aside. Do NOT disconnect the fluid lines.
30. Remove the thermostat bypass pipe clip nut from the upper intake manifold, then disconnect the pipe from the water pump.
31. Remove the water pump pulley.
32. Disconnect the lower radiator outlet hose from the water pump.
33. Remove the serpentine drive belt tensioner.
34. Remove the Crankshaft Position (CKP) sensor from the front cover.
35. Unfasten the front cover retaining bolts, and screws, then remove the front cover and gasket. Discard the gasket.
36. Remove the water pump from the front cover.

To install:

37. Thoroughly clean all the gasket mating surfaces.
38. Install the water pump to the front cover.
39. Coat both sides of the lower tabs of a new cover gasket with sealer 1052080 or equivalent. Position the gasket in the front cover, then install the cover and secure with the bolts and screws. Tighten the large bolts and screws to 35 ft. lbs. (47 Nm). and the small bolts/screws to 15 ft. lbs. (20 Nm).
40. Attach the crankshaft position sensor to the front cover.
41. Install the serpentine drive belt tensioner.
42. Connect the lower radiator outlet hose to the water pump.
43. Install the water pump pulley.
44. Attach the thermostat bypass pipe to the water pump and secure with the nut to the upper intake manifold.
45. Position the power steering pump and secure with the retaining bolts. Install the power steering pump pulley.
46. Install the serpentine belt shield.
47. Install the coolant recovery reservoir.
48. Raise and safely support the vehicle.
49. Safely support the drivetrain and front suspension frame with jackstands.
50. Remove the rear drivetrain and front suspension bolts/screws.

51. Carefully lower the drivetrain and front suspension frame.
52. Install the oil pan, as outlined earlier in this section.
53. Fasten the transaxle mount to the oil pan.
54. Install the starter and the flywheel cover.
55. Install the engine mount.
56. Raise the drivetrain and front suspension frame.
57. Install the rear drivetrain and front suspension frame retaining bolts/screws.
58. Fasten the engine mount frame side nuts to the drivetrain and front suspension frame.
59. Remove the jackstands from the drivetrain and front suspension frame.
60. Install the crankshaft balancer. Tighten the retaining washer and bolt/screw to 76 ft. lbs. (103 Nm).
61. Fasten the engine splash shield.
62. Install the intermediate steering shaft bolt/screw and cover.
63. Connect the front exhaust pipe.
64. Carefully lower the vehicle.
65. Remove the engine support fixtures.
66. Install the electric cooling fan.
67. Install the engine mount strut and A/C compressor bracket and the engine mount strut bracket.
68. With the help of an assistant, install the hood.
69. Install the serpentine drive belt.
70. Refill all necessary fluids.
71. Connect the negative battery cable.

3.4L Engines

▶ See Figures 137 and 138

1. Disconnect the negative battery cable.
2. Remove secondary timing belt tensioner mounting bracket and gasket by removing tensioner pulley and mounting bracket bolts.
3. For 1992–96 vehicles, remove the secondary timing belt, as outlined later in this section. Remove secondary timing belt idler pulleys.
4. Remove the front engine lift hook/bracket.
5. Remove engine torque strut mount bracket to frame bolts and position strut out of the way.
6. Unfasten the cooling fan bolts, then remove the upper radiator support. For 1991 vehicles, remove the right side cooling fan and for 1992–96 vehicles remove both cooling fans.
7. Properly drain the cooling system into a suitable container, then disconnect the lower radiator hose from coolant pump inlet pipe.
8. For vehicles equipped with a manual transaxle, disconnect the front air hose at the air pipe.
9. Detach the heater hose from the front cover and remove the heater pipe bracket retainer bolts at frame.

10. Raise and safely support vehicle. Drain the engine oil into a suitable container.
11. Remove right front tire and wheel assembly. Remove right splash shield.
12. Remove crankshaft pulley and damper.
13. Remove the oil filter.
14. For 1992–96 vehicles, remove the engine oil cooler assembly.
15. For 1992–96 vehicles, remove the front oil pan retaining nuts (2) and bolts (4). Loosen, but do not remove the remaining pan bolts.
16. If equipped, remove the A/C compressor mounting bracket bolts.
17. Remove the lower front cover bolts.
18. On vehicles equipped with an automatic transaxle vehicles, remove the halfshaft.
19. Remove the rear alternator bracket, then remove the starter motor. Carefully lower the vehicle.
20. Remove the camshaft drive belt sprocket retaining bolt, then extract the camshaft drive belt sprocket using tool J–38616 or equivalent.
21. Remove upper alternator retaining bolts. Unfasten the forward light relay center screws, then position the relay center aside.
22. Disconnect the oil cooler hose from the front cover, then remove the water pump pulley.
23. If equipped with a manual transaxle, remove the secondary air injection pipe check valve.
24. Unfasten the upper front cover bolts, then remove the front cover. Remove and discard the old gasket, then clean the mating surfaces of front cover and block.

To install:
25. Apply GM sealer 1052080 or equivalent, to lower edges of the sealing surface of the front cover and place the cover in position. Apply thread sealant to the large retaining bolts and secure the cover in place. Do not tighten the cover bolts at this time.
26. If equipped, install the secondary air injection pipe check valve.
27. Install the water pump pulley. Connect the oil cooler coolant hose to front cover.
28. Install the forward light relay center and upper alternator retaining bolts.
29. Install the camshaft drive belt sprocket secure the retaining bolt using tool J 31096, or equivalent.
30. Raise and safely support vehicle.
31. Install the starter motor, as outlined in Section 2 of this manual.
32. For vehicles equipped with an automatic transaxle, install the halfshaft.
33. Install the rear alternator bracket.
34. Install the lower front cover bolts and tighten to 18 ft. lbs. (25 Nm).
35. Install the A/C compressor mounting bolts.
36. If removed, install the oil pan retaining nuts and bolts. Tighten the rear bolts to 18 ft. lbs. (25 Nm) and the remaining bolts and nuts to 89 inch lbs. (10 Nm).
37. Install the oil filter and the crankshaft damper and pulley.
38. If equipped with a manual transaxle, remove the front-to-rear engine mount bracket brace.

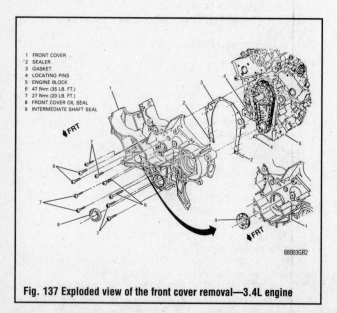

Fig. 137 Exploded view of the front cover removal—3.4L engine

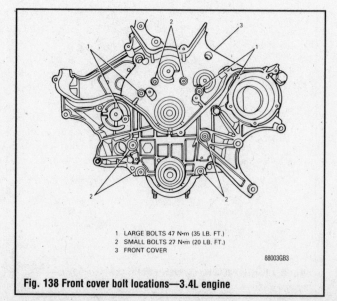

Fig. 138 Front cover bolt locations—3.4L engine

39. For 1992–96 vehicles, install the engine oil cooler and hoses.
40. Fasten the right side splash shield and the wheel and tire assembly. Carefully lower the vehicle.
41. Install and tighten the upper front cover small bolts to 18 ft. lbs. (25 Nm), and the front cover large bolts to 35 ft. lbs. (47 Nm).
42. Connect the heater hoses to the front cover and attach the lower radiator hose to the water pump.
43. If equipped connect the secondary air injection hose to the front exhaust manifold air injection pipe.
44. Install the coolant fans. Add coolant to the correct level.
45. Install the retainer screws into heater pipe bracket.
46. Install the upper radiator support and the torque strut-to-frame bolts.
47. Install front engine lift hook and secondary timing belt idler pulley.
48. For 1992–96 vehicles, install the secondary timing belt, as outlined later in this section. Install the secondary timing belt tensioner mounting bracket. Tighten the bolts to 37 ft. lbs. (50 Nm).
49. Connect the negative battery cable.

3.8L Engine

♦ See Figure 139

1. Disconnect the negative battery cable.
2. Remove the crankshaft balancer.
3. Remove the crankshaft sensor cover.
4. Tag and detach the electrical connections from the camshaft, crankshaft and oil pressure sensors.
5. Raise and support the vehicle safely.
6. Drain the engine oil into a suitable container, then remove the oil pan-to-front cover bolts.
7. Remove the oil filter, then disconnect the oil cooler pipes from the oil filter adapter housing.
8. Carefully lower the vehicle and drain the cooling system into a suitable container.
9. Remove the alternator and brace.
10. Disconnect the heater hoses, the pipe, and the bypass hose from the cover.

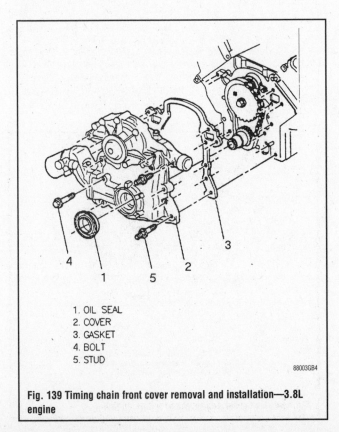

1. OIL SEAL
2. COVER
3. GASKET
4. BOLT
5. STUD

88003GB4

Fig. 139 Timing chain front cover removal and installation—3.8L engine

11. Detach the lower radiator hose.
12. Remove the water pump pulley.
13. Unfasten the front cover attaching bolts, then remove the cover with the oil filter adapter as an assembly.
14. Remove the oil filter adapter housing.
15. Remove the oil pressure valve, spring and oil pump from the front cover.
16. Remove the water pump from the front cover.
17. Carefully pry the oil seal out of the cover using a suitable tool.

To install:

➡The oil pan bolts can be loosened and the pan dropped slightly for front cover clearance. If the oil pan gasket is excessively swollen, the oil pan must be removed and the gasket replaced.

18. Clean the mating surfaces of the front cover and cylinder block with a degreaser.
19. Install the oil filter and adapter housing with the oil pressure valve and spring to the cover. Tighten the bolts to 24 ft. lbs. (32 Nm).
20. Install the oil pump assembly to the cover.
21. Use a new gasket, apply sealer to the bolt threads and install the coolant pump to the front cover.
22. Lubricate a new front cover oil seal with clean engine oil and install it to the front cover, using tool J–35354 or equivalent. Use the crankshaft balancer bolt with the tool and tighten the bolt until the seal is seated in the cover. Remove the tool.
23. Install the front cover to the engine and install the upper cover bolts. Tighten the upper cover bolts to 124 inch lbs. (14 Nm)
24. Install the crankshaft sensor and adjust, using tool J–37089 or equivalent.
25. Fasten the sensor cover and attach the electrical connections, as tagged during removal.
26. Install the crankshaft balancer.
27. Connect the oil cooler lines, then install the oil filter.
28. Carefully lower the vehicle, then install the water pump pulley.
29. Connect the lower radiator hose, bypass hose and heater hoses.
30. Install the alternator and brace.
31. Add the proper types and amount of coolant and engine oil.
32. Connect the negative battery cable.

Front Cover Oil Seal

REPLACEMENT

1. Disconnect the negative terminal from the battery. Remove the serpentine belt.
2. Raise and safely support the vehicle. Remove the right side inner fender splash shield.
3. Remove the damper retaining bolt.
4. Using a crankshaft pulley puller tool, press the damper pulley from the crankshaft.
5. Using a small prybar, carefully pry out the seal in the front cover.

➡Use care not to damage the seal seat or the crankshaft while removing or installing the seal. Inspect the crankshaft seal surface for signs of wear.

To install:

6. Coat the new seal with oil. Using a seal installer tool, drive the new seal in the cover with the lip facing towards the engine.
7. Using a crankshaft pulley installer tool, press the crankshaft pulley onto the crankshaft. Tighten the damper bolt to the following specifications:
   • 2.2L engine: 70 ft. lbs. (95 Nm)
   • 2.3L engine: 74 ft. lbs. plus an additional 90° turn
   • 2.5L engine: 162 ft. lbs. (220 Nm)
   • 2.8L and 3.1L engines: 67–85 ft. lbs. (90–115 Nm)
   • 3.4L engine: 95 ft. lbs. (130 Nm)
   • 3.8L engine: 105 ft. lbs. plus an additional 56° turn
8. Install the inner fender splash shield. Lower the vehicle.
9. Install the serpentine belt. Connect the negative battery cable. Run the engine to normal operating temperature and check for leaks.

Timing Chain

REMOVAL & INSTALLATION

2.2L Engine

▶ **See Figures 140 and 141**

1. Disconnect the negative battery cable.
2. Remove the timing chain cover, as outlined earlier in this section.
3. Align the marks on the timing gears before removing the timing chain and gears.
4. Remove the upper camshaft gear retaining bolt.
5. Loosen the timing chain tensioner bolt. DO NOT REMOVE THE BOLT.
6. Remove the camshaft sprocket and the timing chain.
7. If replacing the lower crankshaft gear, install puller J 22888-20 or equivalent and remove the gear.

To install:

8. Clean all the sealing surfaces where the gaskets are installed.
9. Install the lower crankshaft sprocket using J 5590 or the equivalent.
10. Compress the timing chain tensioner spring and install a cotter pin into the retaining hole.

11. Align the crankshaft and timing gears to the marks on the tensioner assembly.
12. Snug up on the tensioner bolt.
13. Align the dowel in the camshaft with the dowel in the camshaft sprocket and install the chain to the gear assemblies.
14. Tighten the timing chain tensioner retaining bolts to 18 ft. lbs. (24 Nm).
15. Tighten the camshaft sprocket retaining bolt to 77 ft. lbs. (105 Nm).
16. Remove the timing chain tensioner cotter pin.
17. Position the timing chain cover to the engine with a new gasket guiding the cover over the dowel pins.
18. Install the timing chain cover, as outlined earlier in this section.
19. Fill all fluid to their proper levels. Connect the negative battery cable, then start the engine and verify proper operation.

2.3L Engine

▶ **See Figure 142**

➡ **It is recommended that the entire procedure be reviewed before attempting to service this timing chain.**

1. Disconnect the negative battery cable.
2. Remove the front timing chain cover and crankshaft oil slinger.
3. Rotate the crankshaft clockwise, as viewed from front of engine (normal rotation) until the camshaft sprockets timing dowel pin holes line up with the holes in the timing chain housing. The mark on the crankshaft sprocket should line up with the mark on the cylinder block. The crankshaft sprocket keyway should point upwards and line up with the centerline of the cylinder bores. This is the normal "timed" position.
4. Remove the 3 timing chain guides.
5. Raise the vehicle and support safely.
6. Gently pry off timing chain tensioner spring retainer and remove spring.

➡ **Two styles of tensioner are used. Early production engines will have a spring post and late production ones will not. Both styles are identical in operation and are interchangeable.**

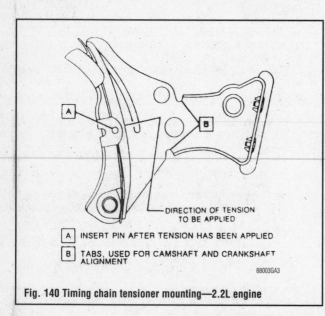

DIRECTION OF TENSION
TO BE APPLIED

A | INSERT PIN AFTER TENSION HAS BEEN APPLIED

B | TABS, USED FOR CAMSHAFT AND CRANKSHAFT ALIGNMENT

88003GA3

Fig. 140 Timing chain tensioner mounting—2.2L engine

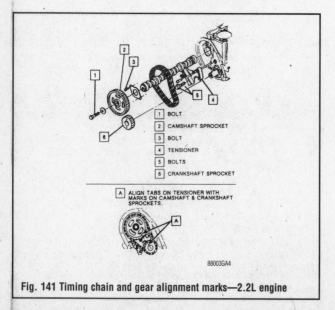

1 BOLT
2 CAMSHAFT SPROCKET
3 BOLT
4 TENSIONER
5 BOLTS
6 CRANKSHAFT SPROCKET

A | ALIGN TABS ON TENSIONER WITH MARKS ON CAMSHAFT & CRANKSHAFT SPROCKETS.

88003GA4

Fig. 141 Timing chain and gear alignment marks—2.2L engine

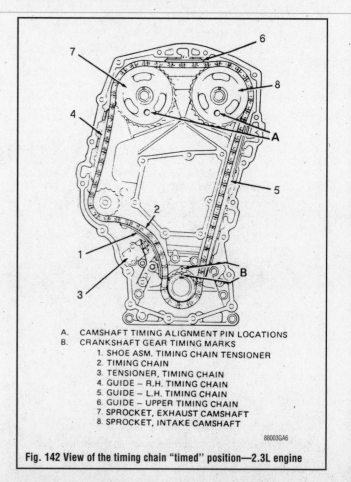

A. CAMSHAFT TIMING ALIGNMENT PIN LOCATIONS
B. CRANKSHAFT GEAR TIMING MARKS
1. SHOE ASM. TIMING CHAIN TENSIONER
2. TIMING CHAIN
3. TENSIONER, TIMING CHAIN
4. GUIDE – R.H. TIMING CHAIN
5. GUIDE – L.H. TIMING CHAIN
6. GUIDE – UPPER TIMING CHAIN
7. SPROCKET, EXHAUST CAMSHAFT
8. SPROCKET, INTAKE CAMSHAFT

88003GA6

Fig. 142 View of the timing chain "timed" position—2.3L engine

7. Remove the timing chain tensioner shoe retainer.

8. Make sure all the slack in the timing chain is above the tensioner assembly; remove the chain tensioner shoe. The timing chain must be disengaged from the wear grooves in the tensioner shoe in order to remove the shoe. Slide a prybar under the timing chain while pulling shoe outward.

9. If difficulty is encountered removing chain tensioner shoe, proceed as follows:

   a. Lower the vehicle.

   b. Hold the intake camshaft sprocket with a holding tool and remove the sprocket bolt and washer.

   c. Remove the washer from the bolt and rethread the bolt back into the camshaft by hand, the bolt provides a surface to push against.

   d. Remove intake camshaft sprocket using a 3-jaw puller in the 3 relief holes in the sprocket. Do not attempt to pry the sprocket off the camshaft or damage to the sprocket or chain housing could occur.

10. Remove the tensioner assembly retaining bolts and the tensioner.

⁂ CAUTION

The tensioner piston is spring loaded and could fly out causing personal injury.

11. Remove the chain housing to block stud (timing chain tensioner shoe pivot).

12. Remove the timing chain.

To install:

13. Tighten intake camshaft sprocket retaining bolt and washer, while holding the sprocket with tool J–36013 if removed.

14. Install the special tool through holes in camshaft sprockets into holes in timing chain housing. This positions the camshafts for correct timing.

15. If the camshafts are out of position and must be rotated more than ⅛ turn in order to install the alignment dowel pins:

   a. The crankshaft must be rotated 90° clockwise off of TDC in order to give the valves adequate clearance to open.

   b. Once the camshafts are in position and the dowels installed, rotate the crankshaft counterclockwise back to top dead center. Do not rotate the crankshaft clockwise to TDC, or valve or piston damage could occur.

16. Install the timing chain over the exhaust camshaft sprocket, around the idler sprocket and around the crankshaft sprocket.

17. Remove the alignment dowel pin from the intake camshaft. Using a dowel pin remover tool, rotate the intake camshaft sprocket counterclockwise enough to slide the timing chain over the intake camshaft sprocket. Release the camshaft sprocket wrench. The length of chain between the 2 camshaft sprockets will tighten. If properly timed, the intake camshaft alignment dowel pin should slide in easily. If the dowel pin does not fully index, the camshafts are not timed correctly and the procedure must be repeated.

18. Leave the alignment dowel pins installed.

19. With slack removed from chain between intake camshaft sprocket and crankshaft sprocket, the timing marks on the crankshaft and the cylinder block should be aligned. If marks are not aligned, move the chain 1 tooth forward or rearward, remove slack and recheck marks.

20. Tighten the chain housing to block stud (timing chain tensioner shoe pivot). the stud is installed under the timing chain. Tighten to 19 ft. lbs. (26 Nm).

21. Reload the timing chain tensioner assembly to its **0** position as follows:

   a. Assemble restraint cylinder, spring and nylon plug into plunger. Index slot in restraint cylinder with peg in plunger. While rotating the restraint cylinder clockwise, push the restraint cylinder into the plunger until it bottoms. Keep rotating the restraint cylinder clockwise but allow the spring to push it out of the plunger. The pin in the plunger will lock the restraint in the loaded position.

   b. Install tool J–36589 or equivalent, onto plunger assembly.

   c. Install plunger assembly into tensioner body with the long end toward the crankshaft when installed.

22. Install the tensioner assembly to the chain housing. Recheck plunger assembly installation. It is correctly installed when the long end is toward the crankshaft.

23. Install and tighten timing chain tensioner bolts and tighten to 10 ft. lbs. (14 Nm).

24. Install the tensioner shoe and tensioner shoe retainer.

25. Remove special tool J–36589 and squeeze plunger assembly into the tensioner body to unload the plunger assembly.

26. Lower vehicle and remove the alignment dowel pins. Rotate crankshaft clockwise 2 full rotations. Align crankshaft timing mark with mark on cylinder block and reinstall alignment dowel pins. Alignment dowel pins will slide in easily if engine is timed correctly.

➡**If the engine is not correctly timed, severe engine damage could occur.**

27. Install the 3 timing chain guides and crankshaft oil slinger.

28. Install the timing chain front cover.

29. Connect the negative battery cable and check for leaks.

2.5L, 2.8L and 3.1L Engines

▶ **See Figures 143, 144 and 145**

1. Disconnect the negative battery cable.

2. Remove the timing chain front cover assembly, as outlined earlier in this section.

3. Rotate the crankshaft until the timing marks on the crankshaft sprocket and camshaft sprocket locator hole are aligned to the marks on the engine block or timing chain dampener. This is the No. 1 piston at TDC (No. 4 firing position).

4. Unfasten the camshaft sprocket retaining bolt/screw, then remove the camshaft sprocket and the timing chain.

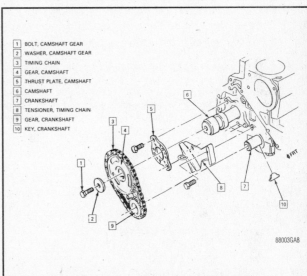

1	BOLT, CAMSHAFT GEAR
2	WASHER, CAMSHAFT GEAR
3	TIMING CHAIN
4	GEAR, CAMSHAFT
5	THRUST PLATE, CAMSHAFT
6	CAMSHAFT
7	CRANKSHAFT
8	TENSIONER, TIMING CHAIN
9	GEAR, CRANKSHAFT
10	KEY, CRANKSHAFT

88003GA8

Fig. 143 Timing chain and sprocket removal—2.5L engine

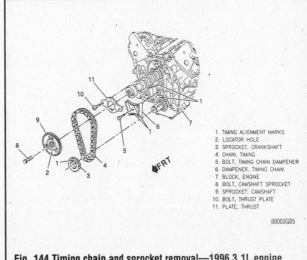

1. TIMING ALIGNMENT MARKS
2. LOCATOR HOLE
3. SPROCKET, CRANKSHAFT
4. CHAIN, TIMING
5. BOLT, TIMING CHAIN DAMPENER
6. DAMPENER, TIMING CHAIN
7. BLOCK, ENGINE
8. BOLT, CAMSHAFT SPROCKET
9. SPROCKET, CAMSHAFT
10. BOLT, THRUST PLATE
11. PLATE, THRUST

88003GB5

Fig. 144 Timing chain and sprocket removal—1996 3.1L engine shown

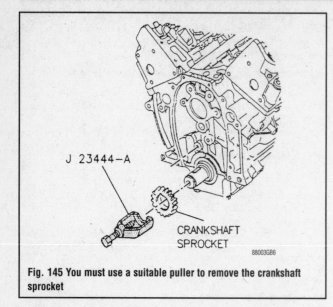

Fig. 145 You must use a suitable puller to remove the crankshaft sprocket

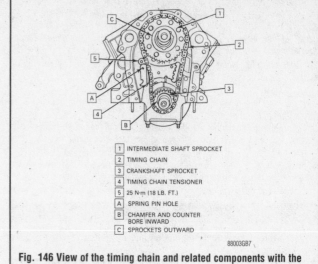

Fig. 146 View of the timing chain and related components with the front cover removed—3.4L engine

➡ If the camshaft sprocket does not come off easily, a light blow on the lower edge of the sprocket with a rubber mallet should loosen the sprocket.

5. Remove the crankshaft sprocket using tool J 23444-A or equivalent puller.

6. If necessary, remove the timing chain dampener retaining bolts, then remove the dampener.

To install:

7. Install the crankshaft sprocket using tool J 38612 until it the sprocket is fully seated on the flange of the crankshaft nose. Apply a coat of Molykote® or equivalent, to the sprocket thrust surface.

8. Hold the camshaft sprocket with the chain hanging down, and align the marks on the camshaft and crankshaft sprockets.

9. If removed, install the timing chain damper to the engine block.

10. Align the dowel in the camshaft with the dowel hole in the camshaft sprocket. Install the camshaft sprocket and chain, use the camshaft sprocket bolts to draw the sprocket on to the camshaft. Tighten the sprocket bolts to 18 ft. lbs. (25 Nm).

11. Lubricate the timing chain with engine oil.

12. Install the front cover assembly, as outlined earlier in this section.

13. Connect the negative battery cable.

3.4L Engine

▶ See Figures 146 thru 151

1. Disconnect the negative battery cable.

2. Raise and safely support the vehicle.

3. For 1991 vehicles, perform the following:

a. Remove the starter motor and flywheel cover.

b. Remove oil pan retaining nuts and bolts. Remove lower frame and powertrain onto transmission table.

4. Remove the front cover, as outlined earlier this section.

5. Matchmark the intermediate sprocket, chain link, front face of cylinder and crank sprocket for reference.

6. Retract the timing chain tensioner shoe by using J-33875 or equivalent, on both sides of the tensioner and pulling on the thru pin in the tensioner arm to retract the spring. While spring is retracted, insert a holding tool to hold it.

7. Remove the timing chain tensioner retaining bolts.

8. Raise and safely support the vehicle.

9. Remove the timing chain, crankshaft sprocket and intermediate sprocket using tools J 8433 and J 28611, as shown in the accompanying figure. If the intermediate gear does not slide off easily with the timing chain assembly, rotate the crankshaft back and forth to loosen the tight fit.

10. If necessary, remove the timing chain tensioner.

To install:

11. Check to ensure that crankshaft key is installed and fully seated and the chain tensioner is fully installed and blade retracted.

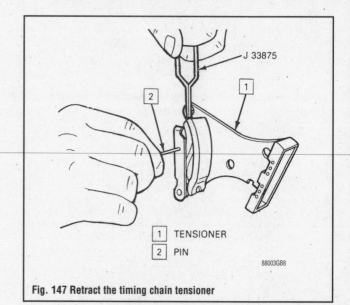

Fig. 147 Retract the timing chain tensioner

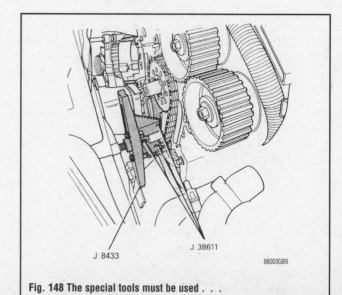

Fig. 148 The special tools must be used . . .

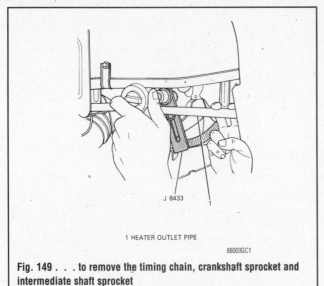

Fig. 149 . . . to remove the timing chain, crankshaft sprocket and intermediate shaft sprocket

1 HEATER OUTLET PIPE
J 8433
88003GC1

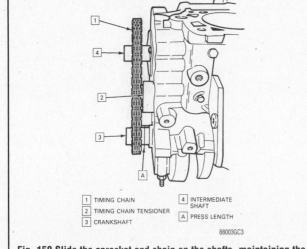

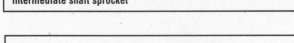

1 TIMING CHAIN	4 INTERMEDIATE SHAFT
2 TIMING CHAIN TENSIONER	A PRESS LENGTH
3 CRANKSHAFT	

88003GC3

Fig. 150 Slide the sprocket and chain on the shafts, maintaining the proper alignment

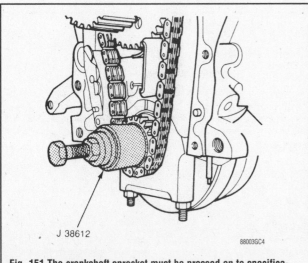

J 38612
88003GC4

Fig. 151 The crankshaft sprocket must be pressed on to specifications using a special tool

12. Slip both sprockets and chain over the proper shaft and engage the slot in the key. The intermediate shaft may move against the rear cover. Slide the sprocket and chain on the shafts, maintaining the proper alignment shown in the accompanying figure. While installing note the following:

a. Make sure the rubber and tension blade of the tensioner does not become caught, misaligned, or dislodged.

b. The large chamfer and counterbore of the crankshaft sprocket are installed towards the crankshaft. The intermediate sprocket spline sockets are installed away from the case.

c. The crankshaft sprocket must be pressed on for the final 0.31 in. (8mm) to the seated position using tool J38612 or equivalent, as shown in the accompanying figure.

d. Check to make sure timing was maintained. Remove the retaining pin from tensioner.

13. For 1991 vehicles, install the oil pan retaining nuts and bolts, and the flywheel cover and starter.

14. Install the front cover, as outlined earlier in this section.

15. Connect the negative battery cable. Start the engine and check for leaks.

3.8L Engine

▶ See Figures 152 and 153

1. Disconnect the negative battery cable.
2. Remove the timing chain front cover assembly, as outlined earlier in this section.
3. Align the timing marks on the sprockets, as shown in the accompanying figure.
4. Remove the timing chain damper.

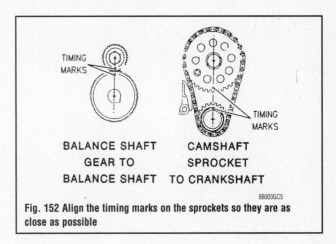

Fig. 152 Align the timing marks on the sprockets so they are as close as possible

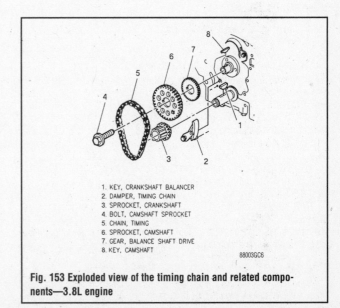

1. KEY, CRANKSHAFT BALANCER
2. DAMPER, TIMING CHAIN
3. SPROCKET, CRANKSHAFT
4. BOLT, CAMSHAFT SPROCKET
5. CHAIN, TIMING
6. SPROCKET, CAMSHAFT
7. GEAR, BALANCE SHAFT DRIVE
8. KEY, CAMSHAFT

88003GC6

Fig. 153 Exploded view of the timing chain and related components—3.8L engine

5. Unfasten the camshaft sprocket bolts, then remove the camshaft sprocket and chain.

6. Remove the crankshaft sprocket. If the sprocket does not come off easily, apply a light blow on the lower edge of the sprocket with a plastic mallet.

To install:

7. If the pistons have been moved in the engine, perform the following:

a. Turn the crankshaft so the No. 1 piston is at Top Dead Center (TDC).

b. Turn the camshaft so, with the sprocket temporarily installed, the timing mark is straight down.

8. Assemble the timing chain on the sprockets with the timing marks facing each other.

9. Install the timing chain and sprockets, then tighten the camshaft sprocket bolts to 52 ft. lbs. (70 Nm) plus an additional 110° turn.

10. Install the timing chain damper and tighten the bolt to 14 ft. lbs. (19 Nm).

11. Rotate the engine 2 revolutions and make sure the timing marks are aligned correctly.

12. Install the front cover assembly, as outlined earlier in this section.

13. Connect the negative battery cable.

Timing Belt Covers

REMOVAL & INSTALLATION

3.4L Engine

UPPER RIGHT SIDE COVER

▶ See Figure 154

1. Disconnect the negative battery cable.
2. Remove retaining bolts, then remove the cover.

To install:

3. Position cover and install retaining bolts. Tighten the bolts to 89 inch lbs. (10 Nm).

4. Connect the negative battery cable.

UPPER LEFT SIDE COVER

▶ See Figure 154

1. Disconnect the negative battery cable.
2. Remove spark plug wire cover or the coil pack and harness, bracket and bracket, as applicable.
3. Remove the retaining bolts, then remove the cover.

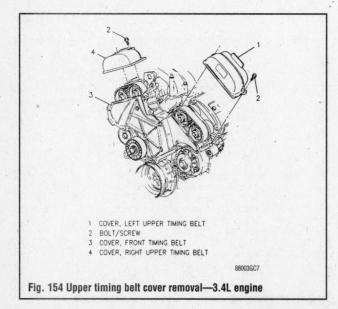

1 COVER, LEFT UPPER TIMING BELT
2 BOLT/SCREW
3 COVER, FRONT TIMING BELT
4 COVER, RIGHT UPPER TIMING BELT

88003GC7

Fig. 154 Upper timing belt cover removal—3.4L engine

To install:

4. Position the cover, then secure with the retaining bolts. Tighten the bolts to 89 inch lbs. (10 Nm).

5. Install spark plug wire cover or coil pack bracket, coil pack and harness, as applicable.

6. Connect the negative battery cable.

CENTER COVER

▶ See Figure 155

1. Disconnect the negative battery cable.
2. Remove the Electronic Control Module (ECM) harness cover.
3. Remove serpentine belt tensioner.
4. Remove the right and left side timing belt covers, as outlined earlier in this section.
5. Remove power steering pipe retaining clip nut at alternator stud.
6. Unfasten the center timing belt cover bolts, then remove the cover.

To install:

7. Position the cover on engine and secure with retainer bolts. Tighten bolts to 89 inch lbs.

8. Install power steering pipe retaining clip nut to alternator stud.

9. Fasten the right and left side covers. Install the serpentine belt tensioner.

10. Install Electronic Control Module (ECM) harness cover.

11. Connect negative battery cable.

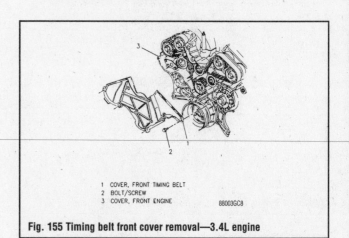

1 COVER, FRONT TIMING BELT
2 BOLT/SCREW
3 COVER, FRONT ENGINE

88003GC8

Fig. 155 Timing belt front cover removal—3.4L engine

Timing Belt and Tensioner

REMOVAL & INSTALLATION

▶ See Figures 156, 157, 158 and 159

1991–95 3.4L Engines

1. Disconnect the negative battery cable.

➡ **Siphon the power steering fluid from the reservoir before disconnecting the lines to avoid spilling fluid on the timing belt cover. Use shop rags when disconnecting the lines to insure any remaining fluid does NOT contact the timing belt cover. Power steering fluid can damage the timing belt.**

2. Remove secondary timing belt actuator/tensioner, as follows:

a. Remove the power steering pump, as outlined in Section 8.

b. Remove the camshaft timing belt covers, as outlined earlier in this section.

c. Rotate the engine clockwise to align the timing marks on the camshaft sprockets and crankshaft balancer to the front cover, if the marks are visible. If no timing marks are present, rotate the crankshaft to align the crankshaft balancer mark to the cast front cover timing arrow. Mark the camshaft

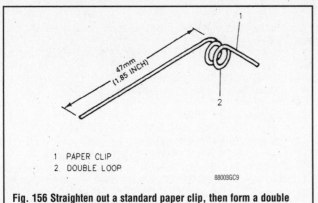

1 PAPER CLIP
2 DOUBLE LOOP

88003GC9

Fig. 156 Straighten out a standard paper clip, then form a double loop as shown

sprocket teeth facing each other with a permanent marker, for installation reference.

d. Loosely clamp the two camshaft sprockets on each side of the engine together using clamping pliers or equivalent. No deflection of the cam sprockets should be noted, if deflection is noted, loosen the clamping device.

e. Remove the bolts and side plate from the tensioner.

f. Rotate the tensioner assembly from the tensioner pulley socket and out of the mounting base. Removal of the tensioner from the tensioner pulley allows it to extend to its maximum travel.

➡**Do not install a rod tip or tensioner boot in the jaws of a vise or damage to the assembly may occur.**

g. Position the tensioner in a vertical position in a vise (rod tip down), then tensioner body in the vise lightly. Allow the oil to drain to the boot end, for at least 5 minutes before refilling.

h. Straighten out a paper clip (0.032 in. diameter, no serrations) to a minimum straight length of 1.85 in. (47mm). Form a double loop in the remaining end of the paper clip.

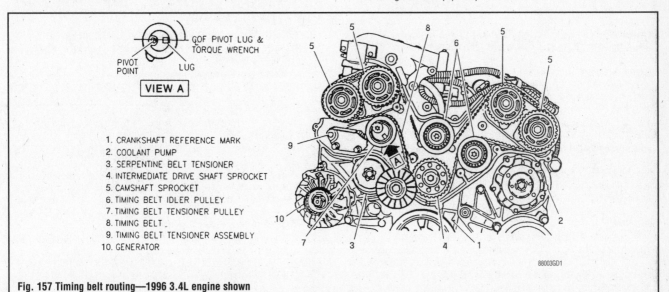

VIEW A

1. CRANKSHAFT REFERENCE MARK
2. COOLANT PUMP
3. SERPENTINE BELT TENSIONER
4. INTERMEDIATE DRIVE SHAFT SPROCKET
5. CAMSHAFT SPROCKET
6. TIMING BELT IDLER PULLEY
7. TIMING BELT TENSIONER PULLEY
8. TIMING BELT
9. TIMING BELT TENSIONER ASSEMBLY
10. GENERATOR

88003GD1

Fig. 157 Timing belt routing—1996 3.4L engine shown

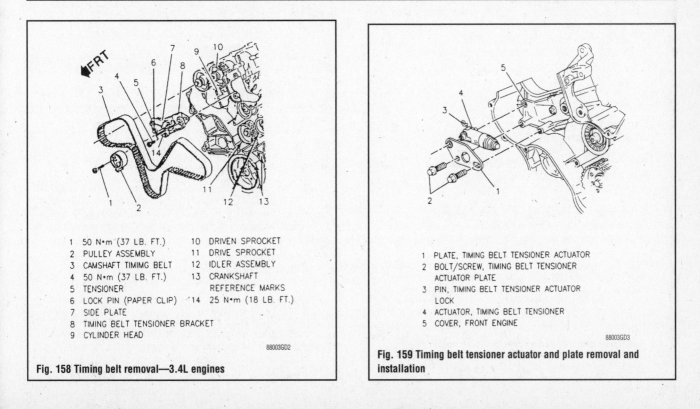

1	50 N•m (37 LB. FT.)	10	DRIVEN SPROCKET
2	PULLEY ASSEMBLY	11	DRIVE SPROCKET
3	CAMSHAFT TIMING BELT	12	IDLER ASSEMBLY
4	50 N•m (37 LB. FT.)	13	CRANKSHAFT
5	TENSIONER		REFERENCE MARKS
6	LOCK PIN (PAPER CLIP)	14	25 N•m (18 LB. FT.)
7	SIDE PLATE		
8	TIMING BELT TENSIONER BRACKET		
9	CYLINDER HEAD		

88003GD2

Fig. 158 Timing belt removal—3.4L engines

1 PLATE, TIMING BELT TENSIONER ACTUATOR
2 BOLT/SCREW, TIMING BELT TENSIONER ACTUATOR PLATE
3 PIN, TIMING BELT TENSIONER ACTUATOR LOCK
4 ACTUATOR, TIMING BELT TENSIONER
5 COVER, FRONT ENGINE

88003GD3

Fig. 159 Timing belt tensioner actuator and plate removal and installation

i. Remove the rubber end plug from the rear of the tensioner assembly. The assembly is filled with oil and removal of the plug may allow oil to escape. Do NOT remove the vent plug.

j. Push the paper clip through the center hole in the vent plug and into the pilot hole.

k. Insert a small screwdriver into the screw slot inside the tensioner, behind the rubber end plug.

l. Retract the tensioner plunger by rotating the screw in a clockwise direction, until it is fully retracted. Push on the paper clip and slowly rotate the screw counterclockwise until the paper clip engages.

m. If tensioner oil has been lost, fill the tensioner with synthetic engine oil through the end hole. Fill to the bottom of the plug hole ONLY when the tensioner is fully retracted and the pin is installed.

3. If the belt is to be reused, mark direction of rotation for installation purposes.

4. Remove tensioner and pulley arm assembly by removing the tensioner pulley bolt and remove the arm. The pivot bushing can fall out. Hold in the pulley with a flat magnet, tape or cup plug.

5. Remove timing belt by sliding off of pulleys. Do not bend, twist, or kink belt or damage to the belt may occur.

To install:

6. Install new belt or old belt taking note of direction of rotation.

7. Install the tensioner pulley to the mounting base. Tighten the bolt to 37 ft. lbs. (50 Nm).

8. Rotate the tensioner pulley counterclockwise into the belt using the cast square lug on body and engage ball end of the actuator into socket on pulley arm.

9. Remove the tensioner lockpin, allowing tensioner shaft to extend and the pulley to move into the belt.

10. Rotate the tensioner pulley counterclockwise applying 12–15 ft. lbs. (16–20 Nm) of torque.

11. Rotate the engine clockwise 3 times to seat belt. Align the crankshaft reference marks during final rotation to TDC. Do NOT allow crankshaft to spring back or reverse direction of rotation.

12. Seat the lockring on the right exhaust and right intake camshaft into the bore by threading in the attaching bolts.

13. Hold the sprocket from turning, using tool J–38614 or equivalent. Tighten the attaching bolt to 81 ft. lbs. (110 Nm), taking note of running torque; torque required to turn bolt before seating. Running torque of bolt should be 44–66 ft. lbs. (60–89 Nm). If less torque is required, replace the shim and lockrings and inspect the nose of the camshaft for brinelling. If more torque is required than replace the shim and lockrings and check the attaching bolt threads for burrs or foreign material.

14. Rotate engine clockwise 1 revolution and realign the balancer marks at TDC. Make sure timing mark on damper lines up with front cover timing mark.

15. Repeat steps, starting with left intake then left exhaust camshaft.

16. Install secondary timing belt covers and retaining bolts.

17. Connect negative battery cable.

1996 3.4L Engines

1. Disconnect the negative battery cable.

2. Remove the air cleaner assembly. Properly drain the engine coolant into a suitable container.

3. Disconnect the control cables from the throttle body.

4. Remove the fuel injector sight shield.

5. Relieve the fuel system pressure, as outlined in Section 5 of this manual.

6. Disconnect and cap the fuel lines from the fuel rail.

7. Remove the fuel mounting bracket.

8. Detach the heater hose and remove the bracket from the lower intake manifold.

9. Disconnect the PCV valve and the vacuum line from the throttle body.

10. Detach the EGR valve electrical connector, unfasten the retaining bolts, then remove the EGR valve from the upper intake and position it aside.

11. Disconnect the electrical connectors from the canister purge solenoid and MAP sensor.

12. Tag and disconnect the vacuum lines from the upper intake manifold tee.

13. Remove the wiring loom bracket from the rear band spark plug wires.

14. Detach the power brake vacuum hose.

15. Unfasten the nuts at the upper intake manifold support bracket.

16. Remove the upper intake manifold, as outlined earlier in this section.

17. Remove the coolant recovery tank.

18. Remove the serpentine drive belt and belt tensioner.

19. Remove the power steering pump, as outlined in Section 8 of this manual.

20. Detach the PCM electrical connectors.

21. Tag and disconnect the spark plug wires from the plugs.

22. Remove the wiring harness cover from the right strut tower.

23. Remove the fuel line bracket.

24. Remove the timing belt covers, as outlined earlier in this section.

25. Disconnect the breather hose from the rear camshaft cover and crankcase vent from the breather manifold.

26. Remove the camshaft carrier covers.

27. Remove the bolts and the side plate from the tensioner actuator.

28. Rotate the tensioner actuator from the tensioner actuator pulley socket and out of the mounting base. The removal of the tensioner actuator from the tensioner actuator pulley allow it to extend to its maximum travel.

➥Do not install a rod tip or tensioner boot in the jaws of a vise or damage to the assembly may occur.

29. Position the tensioner in a vertical position in a vise (rod tip down), then tensioner body in the vise lightly. Allow the oil to drain to the boot end, for at least 5 minutes before refilling.

30. Straighten out a paper clip (0.032 in. diameter, no serrations) to a minimum straight length of 1.85 in. (47mm). Form a double loop in the remaining end of the paper clip.

31. Remove the rubber end plug from the rear of the tensioner assembly. The assembly is filled with oil and removal of the plug may allow oil to escape. Do NOT remove the vent plug.

32. Push the paper clip through the center hole in the vent plug and into the pilot hole.

33. Insert a small screwdriver into the screw slot inside the tensioner, behind the rubber end plug.

34. Retract the tensioner plunger by rotating the screw in a clockwise direction, until it is fully retracted. Push on the paper clip and slowly rotate the screw counterclockwise until the paper clip engages.

35. Remove the timing belt from the vehicle. Remove the timing marks from the camshaft and intermediate shaft sprockets.

36. Rotate the crankshaft to the No. 1 cylinder is at TDC. Mark the timing indicator with white paint or equivalent on the crankshaft balancer and front cover.

37. Position the camshaft so the flat spots are up for installation of tool J 38613-A.

➥Make sure the bolt hole is free of any debris before installing J 38613-A or the camshaft carrier may be damaged.

38. Install tool J 38613-A on both camshaft carriers.

39. Remove the camshaft sprockets. Remove the bolts, taper lockrings and sprockets by lightly tapping on it with a soft faced hammer.

To install:

40. Install the camshaft sprockets finger-tight.

41. Route the timing belt in a counterclockwise direction around the sprockets. Make sure all of the timing belt teeth are fully engaged with all sprockets.

42. Install the timing belt tensioner actuator pulley. Tighten the retaining bolt/screw to 37 ft. lbs. (50 Nm).

43. If tensioner oil has been lost, fill the tensioner with synthetic engine oil through the end hole. Fill to the bottom of the plug hole ONLY when the tensioner is fully retracted and the pin is installed.

44. Install the rubber end plug to the rear of the tensioner actuator. Push until flush and snapped into place. Make sure the end plug has sealed against the case.

45. Install the tensioner actuator bushing into the side plate.

46. Install the tensioner actuator and side plate. Make sure the tapered fulcrum of the tensioner actuator is properly seated in the tensioner actuator bracket bushing. Tighten the retaining bolts to 18 ft. lbs. (25 Nm).

➥Rotate the pulley into the belt a maximum of 11 ft. lbs. (15 Nm) to allow engagement of the actuator shaft into the pulley arm socket.

47. Pull the lockpin and discard. Retighten the pulley to 15 Nm counterclockwise to seat the pulley into the belt.

48. Install both right hand (rear bank) camshaft sprockets. Tighten the bolts to 96 ft. lbs. (130 Nm).

49. Remove tool J 38613-A from the right hand (rear bank) camshaft carrier.
50. Rotate the crankshaft 360° clockwise while looking at the front of the engine and align the crankshaft reference marks.
51. Make sure both right hand camshaft flats are down, then tighten both left hand (front bank) camshaft sprockets to 96 ft. lbs. (130 Nm).
52. Remove tool J 38613-A from the left hand (front bank) camshaft carrier.
53. Rotate the crankshaft 720° clockwise while looking at the front of the engine to seat the timing belt and verify correct timing. Make sure both camshaft flat spots are up on one band and down on the opposing bank.
54. Install the camshaft carrier covers.
55. Connect the breather hose to the rear camshaft cover and crankcase vent to the breather manifold.
56. Install the camshaft timing belt covers, as outlined earlier in this section.
57. Install the fuel line bracket and bolt.
58. Install the wiring harness cover at the right strut tower.
59. Connect the spark plug wires, as tagged during removal.
60. Attach the PCM electrical connectors.
61. Connect the power steering lines to the pump.
62. Install the serpentine drive belt and tensioner.
63. Install the coolant recovery tank.
64. Install the upper intake manifold, using a new gasket. Tighten the retaining bolts to 19 ft. lbs. (26 Nm).
65. Fasten the nuts at the upper intake manifold support bracket. Tighten the nuts to 18 ft. lbs. (25 Nm).
66. Connect the power brake vacuum hose.
67. Install the wiring loom bracket for the rear spark plug wires.
68. Connect the vacuum lines to the upper intake manifold tee.
69. Attach the electrical connectors to the canister purge solenoid and MAP sensor.
70. Install the EGR valve, secure with the retaining bolts, then attach the connector.
71. Connect the PCV valve and vacuum line to the throttle body.
72. Install the heater hose and bracket to the lower intake manifold.
73. Install the fuel line bracket and bolt. Uncap and connect the fuel pipes to the fuel rail.
74. Install the fuel injector sight shield.
75. Connect the control cables to the throttle body.
76. Install the air cleaner assembly. Refill the cooling system and refill and bleed the power steering system. Connect the negative battery cable.

Camshaft

REMOVAL & INSTALLATION

2.2L Engine

1. Disconnect the negative battery cable.
2. Remove the engine from the vehicle, as outlined earlier in this section, then mount it on a suitable stand.
3. Remove the rocker arms and pushrods, as outlined earlier in this section.
4. Remove the valve lifters.
5. Remove the crankcase front cover.
6. Remove the camshaft sprocket, timing chain and tensioner.
7. Remove the oil pump drive.
8. Remove the camshaft thrust plate.

✳✳ WARNING

Care must be taken to avoid damaging the camshaft bearings with the cam when withdrawing the camshaft.

9. Carefully remove the camshaft.
To install:
10. Coat the camshaft lobes and bearings with a suitable lubricant. Insert the camshaft with extreme care to avoid personal injury and gouging of the camshaft bearings.
11. Install the thrust plate, then tighten the retaining bolts to 106 inch lbs. (12 Nm).
12. Install the timing chain and sprockets.

13. Install the remaining components in the reverse order of removal.
14. Install the engine in the vehicle, as outlined earlier in this section.

2.3L Engine

♦ See Figures 160, 161 and 162

INTAKE CAMSHAFT

➡ Any time the camshaft housing to cylinder head bolts are loosened or removed, the camshaft housing to cylinder head gasket must be replaced.

1. Relieve the fuel system pressure, as outlined in Section 5. Disconnect the negative battery cable.
2. Label and detach the ignition coil and module assembly electrical connections.
3. Remove the ignition coil and module assembly-to-camshaft housing bolts and remove the assembly by pulling it straight up. Use tool J 36011, or equivalent spark plug boot wire remover tool, to remove the connector assemblies if they have stuck to the spark plugs.
4. Remove the idle speed power steering pressure switch connector.
5. Loosen the 3 power steering pump pivot bolts and remove drive belt.
6. Disconnect the 2 rear power steering pump bracket-to-transaxle bolts.
7. Remove the front power steering pump bracket-to-cylinder block bolt.
8. Unbolt the power steering pump assembly and position to the side. Do NOT disconnect the fluid lines.
9. Using the special tool, remove the power steering pump drive pulley from the intake camshaft.
10. Remove oil/air separator bolts and hoses. Leave the hoses attached to the separator, disconnect from the oil fill, chain housing and intake manifold. Remove as an assembly.
11. Detach the vacuum line from the fuel pressure regulator and disconnect the fuel injector harness connector.
12. Disconnect the fuel line retaining clamp from bracket on top of intake camshaft housing.
13. Remove the fuel rail-to-camshaft housing retaining bolts.

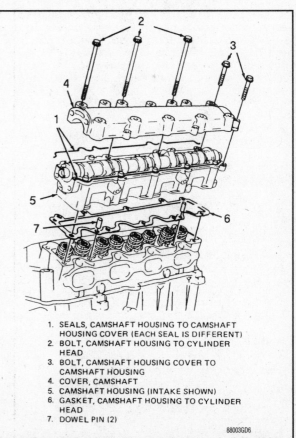

1. SEALS, CAMSHAFT HOUSING TO CAMSHAFT HOUSING COVER (EACH SEAL IS DIFFERENT)
2. BOLT, CAMSHAFT HOUSING TO CYLINDER HEAD
3. BOLT, CAMSHAFT HOUSING COVER TO CAMSHAFT HOUSING
4. COVER, CAMSHAFT
5. CAMSHAFT HOUSING (INTAKE SHOWN)
6. GASKET, CAMSHAFT HOUSING TO CYLINDER HEAD
7. DOWEL PIN (2)

88003GD6

Fig. 160 Camshaft housing, cover and gasket removal—2.3L engine

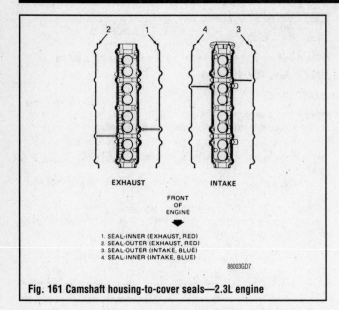

Fig. 161 Camshaft housing-to-cover seals—2.3L engine

1. SEAL-INNER (EXHAUST, RED)
2. SEAL-OUTER (EXHAUST, RED)
3. SEAL-OUTER (INTAKE, BLUE)
4. SEAL-INNER (INTAKE, BLUE)

88003GD7

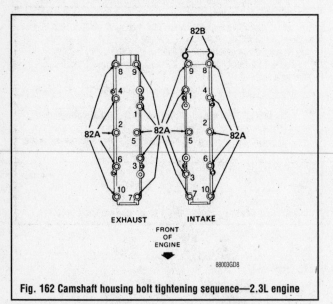

Fig. 162 Camshaft housing bolt tightening sequence—2.3L engine

88003GD8

14. Remove the fuel rail from the cylinder head. Cover injector openings in cylinder head and cover injector nozzles. Leave the fuel lines attached and position fuel rail aside.

15. Disconnect the timing chain and housing but do not remove from the engine.

16. Remove intake camshaft housing cover-to-camshaft housing retaining bolts.

17. Remove the intake camshaft housing-to-cylinder head retaining bolts, using the reverse of the tightening sequence. Leave 2 bolts loosely in place to hold the camshaft housing while separating camshaft cover from housing.

18. Push the cover off the housing by threading 4 of the housing to head retaining bolts into the tapped holes in the cam housing cover. Tighten the bolts in evenly so the cover does not bind on the dowel pins.

19. Remove the 2 loosely installed camshaft housing to head bolts and remove the cover. Discard the gaskets.

20. Note the position of the chain sprocket dowel pin for reassembly. Carefully remove the camshaft; do not damage the camshaft oil seal.

21. Remove intake camshaft oil seal from camshaft and discard seal. This seal must be replaced any time the housing and cover are separated.

22. Remove the camshaft carrier from the cylinder head and remove the gasket. Discard the gasket.

To install:

23. Thoroughly clean the mating surfaces of the camshaft carrier and the cylinder head, bolts and bolt holes. Install a new gasket and place the housing on the head. Install 1 bolt loosely to hold in place.

24. Install the lifters into their bores. If the camshaft is being replaced, the lifters must also be replaced. Lubricate camshaft lobes, journals and lifters with camshaft and lifter prelube. The camshaft lobes and journals must be adequately lubricated or engine damage could occur upon start up.

25. Install the camshaft in the same position as when removed. The timing chain sprocket dowel pin should be straight up and line up with the centerline of the lifter bores.

26. Install new camshaft housing to camshaft housing cover seals into cover; do not use sealer. Make sure the correct color seal is placed in each groove. Install the cover to the housing.

27. Apply a suitable thread locking compound to the camshaft housing and cover retaining bolt threads.

28. Install the bolts and tighten to 11 ft. lbs. (15 Nm). Rotate the bolts (except the 2 rear bolts that hold fuel pipe to camshaft housing) an additional 75° in sequence. Rotate the 2 rear bolts an additional 25°.

29. Install the timing chain housing and timing chain.

30. Uncover fuel injectors, then install new fuel injector ring seals lubricated with oil. Install the fuel rail.

31. Install the fuel line retaining clamp and retainer to bracket on top of the intake camshaft housing.

32. Connect the vacuum line to the fuel pressure regulator.

33. Attach the fuel injector harness connectors.

34. Install the oil/air separator assembly.

35. Lubricate the inner sealing surface of the intake camshaft seal with oil and install the seal to the housing.

36. Install the power steering pump pulley onto the intake camshaft.

37. Install the power steering pump assembly and drive belt.

38. Attach the idle speed power steering pressure switch connector.

39. Clean any loose lubricant that is present on the ignition coil and module assembly to camshaft housing bolts. Apply Loctite® 592 or equivalent, onto the ignition coil and module assembly to camshaft housing bolts. Install the bolts and tighten to 13 ft. lbs. (18 Nm).

40. Attach the electrical connectors to ignition coil and module assembly.

41. Connect the negative battery cable and road test the vehicle. Check for leaks.

EXHAUST CAMSHAFT

➡**Any time the camshaft housing to cylinder head bolts are loosened or removed the camshaft housing to cylinder head gasket must be replaced.**

1. Relieve the fuel system pressure, as outlined in Section 5. Disconnect the negative battery cable.

2. Label and detach the ignition coil and module assembly electrical connections.

3. Remove the ignition coil and module assembly-to-camshaft housing bolts and remove the assembly by pulling it straight up. Use tool J 36011, or equivalent spark plug boot wire remover tool, to remove connector assemblies if they have stuck to the spark plugs.

4. Remove the idle speed power steering pressure switch connector.

5. Remove the transaxle fluid level indicator tube assembly from exhaust camshaft cover and position aside.

6. Remove the exhaust camshaft cover and gasket.

7. Disconnect the timing chain and housing but do not remove from the engine.

8. Remove the exhaust camshaft housing-to-cylinder head bolts using the reverse of the tightening sequence.

9. Push the cover off the housing by threading 4 of the housing to head retaining bolts into the tapped holes in the camshaft cover. Tighten the bolts evenly so the cover does not bind on the dowel pins.

10. Remove the 2 loosely installed camshaft housing to cylinder head bolts and remove cover, discard gaskets.

11. Loosely install 1 camshaft housing to cylinder head bolt to retain the housing during camshaft and lifter removal.

12. Note the position of the chain sprocket dowel pin for reassembly. Remove camshaft being careful not to damage the camshaft or journals.

13. Remove the camshaft carrier from the cylinder head and remove and discard the gasket.

To install:

14. Thoroughly clean the mating surfaces of the camshaft carrier and the cylinder head, bolts and bolt holes. Install a new gasket and place the housing on the head. Install 1 bolt loosely to hold the assembly in place.

15. Install the lifters into their bores. If the camshaft is being replaced, the lifters must also be replaced. Lubricate camshaft lobes, journals and lifters with camshaft and lifter prelube. The camshaft lobes and journals must be adequately lubricated or engine damage could occur upon start up.

16. Install camshaft in same position as when removed. The timing chain sprocket dowel pin should be straight up and align with the centerline of the lifter bores.

17. Install new camshaft housing-to-camshaft housing cover seals into the cover; do not use sealer. Make sure the correct color seal is placed in each groove. Install the cover to the housing.

18. Apply a suitable thread locking compound to the camshaft housing and cover retaining bolt threads.

19. Install the retaining bolts and tighten in sequence to 11 ft. lbs. (15 Nm). Rotate the bolts an additional 75°, in sequence.

20. Install the timing chain housing and timing chain.

21. Install the transaxle fluid level indicator tube assembly to exhaust camshaft cover.

22. Attach the idle speed power steering pressure switch connector.

23. Clean any loose lubricant that is present on the ignition coil and module assembly to camshaft housing bolts. Apply Loctite® 592 or equivalent, onto the ignition coil and module assembly to camshaft housing bolts. Install the bolts and tighten to 13 ft. lbs. (18 Nm)

24. Attach the electrical connectors to ignition coil and module assembly.

25. Connect the negative battery cable and road test the vehicle. Check for leaks.

2.5L Engine

➡**For the removal of the camshaft, the engine assembly must be removed from the vehicle.**

1. Disconnect the negative battery cable.
2. Remove the engine assembly from the vehicle, as outlined earlier in this section.
3. Remove the rocker arm cover and pushrods.
4. Remove the pushrod cover and valve lifters.
5. Remove the serpentine belt, crankshaft pulleys and vibration dampener.
6. Remove the front cover.
7. Unfasten the camshaft thrust plate screws.

➡**The camshaft journals are the same diameter. Care must be taken when removing the camshaft to avoid damage to the cam bearings.**

8. Carefully slide the camshaft and gear through the front of the block.
9. To remove the camshaft gear, use a arbor press and adapter.
10. Old and new camshafts should be cleaned with solvent and compressed air before being installed.

To install:

11. Install the camshaft gear onto the camshaft with an arbor press.

12. Measure the end clearance with a feeler gauge between the cam journal and thrust plate. The measurement should be between 0.0015–0.0050 in. (0.038–0.127mm). If the measurement is less than 0.0015 in. (0.127mm), replace the spacer ring. If the measurement is more than 0.0050 in. (0.038mm), replace the thrust plate.

➡**Always apply assembly lube, GM Engine Oil Supplement (E.O.S) or equivalent, to the cam journals and lobes. If this procedures is not done, cam damage may result.**

13. Carefully install the camshaft into the engine block by rotating and pushing forward until seated.

14. Install the thrust plate screws and tighten to 89 inch lbs, (10 Nm).

15. Install the front cover, vibration dampener and serpentine belt.

16. Install the valve lifter and pushrod cover.

17. Install the pushrods and rocker arm cover.

18. Install the engine into the vehicle, as outlined earlier in this section.

19. Refill all necessary fluids, then connect the negative battery cable.

20. Start the engine and check for leaks.

2.8L, 3.1L and 3.8L Engines

♦ **See Figure 163**

➡**For the removal of the camshaft, the engine assembly must be removed from the vehicle.**

1. Disconnect the negative battery cable.
2. Remove the engine assembly from the vehicle, as outlined earlier in this section.
3. Remove the rocker covers and remove the valve lifters.
4. Remove the front cover assembly, timing chain and sprockets.
5. Carefully remove the camshaft by sliding it from the block.

To install:

6. Coat the camshaft journals with engine oil. Coat the camshaft lobes with GM Engine Oil Supplement (E.O.S) or equivalent.
7. Slide the camshaft into the block.
8. Install the timing chain and sprockets, making sure to align the timing marks.
9. Install the front cover assembly. Install the valve lifters.
10. Install the engine assembly into the vehicle, as outlined earlier in this section.
11. Connect the negative battery cable, then start the engine and check for leaks.

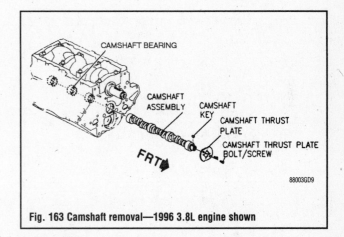

Fig. 163 Camshaft removal—1996 3.8L engine shown

3.4L Engine

♦ **See Figure 164**

LEFT SIDE (FRONT)

1. Disconnect the negative battery cable.
2. Properly drain the cooling system into a suitable container.
3. Remove the left side cam carrier as follows:

a. Disconnect oil/air breather hose from cam carrier cover. Tag and disconnect the spark plug wires from plugs, then remove the rear spark plug wire cover.

b. Remove the cam carrier cover bolts and lift off cover. Remove gasket and O-rings from cover.

c. Remove the secondary timing belt by removing secondary timing belt actuator and tensioner assembly and sliding belt from pulleys.

d. Install 6 sections of fuel line hoses under the camshaft and between the lifters. This will hold the lifters in the carrier. For this procedure use 5/16 in. (8mm) fuel line hose for exhaust valves and 7/32 in. (5.5mm) fuel line hose for the intake valves.

e. Remove the exhaust crossover pipe and torque strut.

f. Remove the torque strut bracket from the engine.

g. Unfasten the cam carrier mounting bolts and nuts, then remove the cam carrier.

h. Remove cam carrier gasket from cylinder head.

4. Remove the 6 lifter hold-down hoses. Remove the lifters.

5. Install the cam hold-down tool J–38613 or equivalent, in place and remove the cam sprockets.

6. Remove the cam carrier end caps and retainer plate bolts and plate.

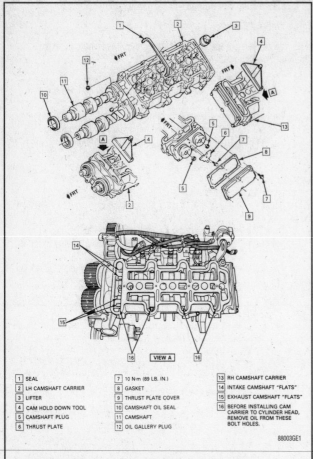

1	SEAL	7	10 N·m (89 LB. IN.)	13	RH CAMSHAFT CARRIER
2	LH CAMSHAFT CARRIER	8	GASKET	14	INTAKE CAMSHAFT "FLATS"
3	LIFTER	9	THRUST PLATE COVER	15	EXHAUST CAMSHAFT "FLATS"
4	CAM HOLD DOWN TOOL	10	CAMSHAFT OIL SEAL	16	BEFORE INSTALLING CAM CARRIER TO CYLINDER HEAD, REMOVE OIL FROM THESE BOLT HOLES.
5	CAMSHAFT PLUG	11	CAMSHAFT		
6	THRUST PLATE	12	OIL GALLERY PLUG		

88003GE1

Fig. 164 Camshaft and related components—3.4L engine

7. Remove camshaft hold hold-down tool, then carefully remove camshaft out the back of the carrier.

To install:

8. Coat the camshaft lobes and journals with clean engine oil and install the camshaft into carrier. Install retaining plate and bolts and tighten to 89 inch lbs. (10 Nm). Install the cam carrier end caps.

9. Install the cam sprocket(s).

10. Adjust cam timing and install cam hold-down tool.

11. Lubricate the lifters with clean engine oil, then install them into their original positions.

12. Install the lifter hold-down hoses to cam carrier.

13. Install the left side cam carrier as follows:

a. Install a new gasket on cam carrier to cylinder mounting surface.

b. Install cam hold-down tool J–38613 or equivalent, to the carrier assembly.

c. Install the cam carrier to the cylinder head. Install mounting bolts and nuts and tighten to 18 ft. lbs. (25 Nm).

d. Remove the lifter hold-down hoses and cam hold-down tool.

e. Install the torque strut bracket to the engine and install torque strut.

f. Install the engine crossover pipe.

g. Install the secondary timing belt and cam carrier cover.

h. Install the spark plug cover and connect the wires.

i. Connect the breather hose to cam carrier cover.

14. Add fluids as required, then connect the negative battery cable. Start engine and check for leaks.

RIGHT SIDE (REAR)

1. Disconnect the negative battery cable. Properly drain the cooling system into a suitable container.

2. Remove the right side cam carrier as follows:

a. Remove the intake plenum and right timing belt cover.

b. Tag and disconnect the right spark plug wires.

c. Disconnect the air/oil separator hose from the cam carrier cover.

d. Unfasten the cam carrier cover bolts, then lift the cover off. Remove the gasket and O-rings from cover.

e. Remove the secondary timing belt by removing secondary timing belt actuator and tensioner assembly and sliding belt from pulleys.

f. Install 6 sections of fuel line hoses under the camshaft and between the lifters. This will hold the lifters in the carrier. For this procedure use 5/16 in. (8mm) fuel line hose for exhaust valves and 7/32 in. (5.5mm) fuel line hose for the intake valves.

g. Remove the exhaust crossover pipe and torque strut.

h. Remove the torque strut bracket from the engine. Remove the front engine lift hook.

i. Unfasten the cam carrier mounting bolts, then remove the cam carrier.

j. Remove the cam carrier gasket from cylinder head.

3. Remove 6 lifter hold-down hoses, then remove the lifters.

4. Install cam hold-down tool J–38613 or equivalent, and remove the cam sprocket.

5. Remove the cam carrier end caps and retainer plate. Remove cam hold-down tool, then carefully slide the camshaft out the rear of the carrier.

To install

6. Lubricate the camshaft lobes and journals with clean engine oil and carefully slide into the cam carrier. Install the retainer plate and bolts and tighten bolts to 89 inch lbs. (10 Nm).

7. Install the cam carrier end caps and cam sprockets.

8. Install the camshaft carrier hold-down tool and adjust cam timing.

9. Lubricate the lifters with clean engine oil, then install them into their original positions.

10. Attach the lifter hold-down hoses to cam carrier.

11. Install the right side cam carrier, as follows:

a. Install new gasket on cam carrier to cylinder mounting surface.

b. Install cam hold-down tool J–38613 or equivalent, to the carrier assembly.

c. Install the cam carrier to the cylinder head. Install the mounting bolts and nuts and tighten to 18 ft. lbs. (25 Nm).

d. Remove the lifter hold-down hoses and cam hold-down tool.

e. Install the torque strut bracket to engine, then install the torque strut.

f. Install the engine crossover pipe and engine lift hook.

g. Install the secondary timing belt and cam carrier cover.

h. Connect the spark plug wires, then install the cover.

12. Add fluids as required. Connect the negative battery cable, then start engine and check for fluid leaks.

INSPECTION

1. Check the camshaft sprocket, keyway and threads, bearing journals and lobes for wear, galling, gouges or overheating. If any of these conditions exist, replace the camshaft.

➡Do NOT attempt to repair the camshaft. Always replace the camshaft and lifters as an assembly. Old valve lifters will destroy a new camshaft in less time than it took you to replace the camshaft.

2. Camshaft Lift Measurement:

a. Lubricate the camshaft bearings with Assembly Lube 1051396 or equivalent.

b. Carefully install the camshaft into the block. If the cam bearings are damaged badly, set the camshaft on "V" blocks instead.

c. Install a dial indicator J–8520 and measure the camshaft lift.

d. Measure the bearing journals with a micrometer. Take measurements for run-out and diameter. If not within specification in the "Camshaft" chart in the beginning of this section, replace the camshaft.

Camshaft Bearings

REMOVAL & INSTALLATION

♦ **See Figure 165**

2.2L and 2.5L Engines

➡Camshaft bearing removal and installation should be done by a qualified machine shop since the tools needed are expensive and would not be economical to purchase for a one time usage.

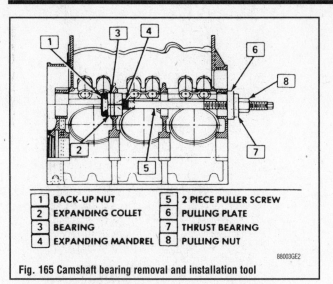

1	BACK-UP NUT	5	2 PIECE PULLER SCREW
2	EXPANDING COLLET	6	PULLING PLATE
3	BEARING	7	THRUST BEARING
4	EXPANDING MANDREL	8	PULLING NUT

88003GE2

Fig. 165 Camshaft bearing removal and installation tool

1. Remove the engine from the vehicle as outlined earlier in this section.
2. Remove the camshaft from the engine, as previously outlined.
3. Unbolt and remove the engine flywheel.
4. Using a long prybar, carefully drive the rear camshaft expansion plug out of the engine block from the inside.
5. Using camshaft bearing service tool No. J33049 or equivalent, drive the front camshaft bearing towards the rear and the rear bearing towards the front.
6. Install the appropriate extension on the service tool and drive the center bearing out towards the rear.
7. Drive all of the new bearings into place in the opposite direction of which they were removed, making sure to align the oil holes in the engine block bores.

To install:

✳ WARNING

Never reuse camshaft bearings. Always use new bearings.

➡The front camshaft bearing must be driven approximately ⅛ in. (3mm) behind the front of the cylinder block to uncover the oil hole to the timing gear oiling nozzle.

8. Install the camshaft and timing gear as outlined earlier in this section.
9. Install the timing gear cover, vibration dampener, all accessories and install the engine into the vehicle as outlined earlier in this section.

2.8L and 3.1L Engines

➡Camshaft bearing removal should be done by a qualified machine shop since the tools needed are expensive and would not be economical to purchase for a one time usage.

Camshaft bearings can be replaced with engine completely or partially disassembled. To replace bearings without complete disassembly remove the camshaft and crankshaft leaving cylinder heads attached and pistons in place. Before removing crankshaft, install 2 in. (51mm) pieces of rubber hose to the threads of connecting rod bolts to prevent damage to crankshaft. Fasten connecting rods against sides of engine so they will not be in the way while replacing camshaft bearings.

1. Remove the timing chain front cover and camshaft rear cover as outlined earlier in this section.
2. Using camshaft bearing Tool J-33049 or its equivalent, with the nut and thrust washer installed to the end of the threads, index the pilot in the camshaft front bearing and install the puller screw through the pilot.
3. Install the remover and installer tool with the shoulder toward the bearing, making sure a sufficient number of threads are engaged.
4. Using two wrenches, hold the puller screw while turning the nut. When the bearing has been pulled from the bore, remove the remover and installer tool and bearing from the puller screw.
5. Remove the remaining bearings (except front and rear) in the same manner. It will be necessary to index the pilot in the camshaft rear bearing to remove the rear intermediate bearing.

6. Assemble the remover and installer tool on the driver handle and remove the camshaft front and rear bearings by driving towards the center of the cylinder block. The camshaft front and rear bearings should be installed first. These bearings will act as guides for the pilot, and center the remaining bearings being pulled into place.

To install:

7. Assemble the remover and installer tool on the driver handle and install the camshaft front and rear bearings by driving them towards the center of the cylinder block. Make sure the oil holes in the bearing line up with the holes in the block.
8. Using Tool Set J-6098, or its equivalent with the nut and thrust washer installed to end of the threads, index the pilot into the camshaft front bearing and install the puller screw through the pilot.
9. Index the camshaft bearing into the bore, then install the remover and installer tool on the puller screw with the shoulder toward the bearing.
10. Using two wrenches, hold the puller screw while turning the nut. After the bearing has been pulled into the bore, remove the remover and installer tool from the puller screw and check the alignment of the oil holes in the camshaft bearings.
11. Install the remaining bearings in the same manner. It will be necessary to index the pilot in the camshaft rear bearing to install the rear intermediate bearing.
12. Clean the rear cover mating surfaces and apply a ⅛ in. (3mm) bead of RTV to the cover. Install the rear cover using the appropriate size core plug installer.
13. Install the camshaft as outlined earlier in this section. Install the timing gear cover, all accessories and install the engine into the vehicle.

Intermediate Shaft

REMOVAL & INSTALLATION

3.4L Engine

1. Disconnect the negative battery cable.
2. Remove the engine from the vehicle, as outlined earlier in this section.
3. Remove the right side cylinder head and oil pump drive assembly.
4. Remove the timing chain assembly.
5. Unfasten the thrust plate screws, then remove the plate.
6. Remove the intermediate shaft, using care not to damage journals or bearings.

To install:

7. Lubricate the intermediate shaft journals and gear with engine oil. Install the intermediate shaft, thrust plate and retainer screws. Tighten the screws to 89 inch lbs. (10 Nm).
8. Replace the O-ring after the sprocket is installed, then install timing chain and gear assembly.
9. Install oil pump drive assembly and cylinder head.
10. Install engine assembly, as outlined earlier in this section.

Balance Shaft

REMOVAL & INSTALLATION

2.5L Engine

▶ See Figure 166

The 2.5L engine uses a force balancer assembly that is driven directly from the crankshaft. Two eccentrically weighted shafts and gears are counter rotated by a concentric gear on the crankshaft at twice the crankshaft speed. The balancer helps dampen engine vibration and includes a sump pickup screen, a gerotor-type oil pump and an oil filter. The filter is serviced through an opening in the bottom of the oil pan.

1. Disconnect the negative battery cable.
2. Raise and safely support the vehicle.
3. Drain the engine oil into a suitable container, then remove the oil filter assembly.
4. Remove the oil pan assembly, as outlined earlier in this section.

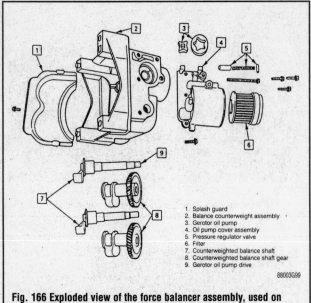

1. Splash guard
2. Balance counterweight assembly
3. Gerotor oil pump
4. Oil pump cover assembly
5. Pressure regulator valve
6. Filter
7. Counterweighted balance shaft
8. Counterweighted balance shaft gear
9. Gerotor oil pump drive

88003G99

Fig. 166 Exploded view of the force balancer assembly, used on 2.5L engines

➡ **When installing the balancer, the end of the housing without the dowel pins MUST remain in contact with the block surface. If it loses contact, gear engagement may be lost and permanent damage to either the crank or balancer gears may result.**

5. Unfasten the four force balancer attaching bolts and remove the balancer assembly. Refer to the accompanying force balancer illustration in this section.

To install:

6. Rotate the engine to Top Dead Center (TDC) on the No. 1 and No. 4 cylinders.

7. Position the balancer assembly onto the crankshaft with the balancer weights at BDC (bottom dead center), plus or minus one half of a gear tooth.

8. Tighten the bolts in the following sequence in two steps, 3–1–2–4.

9. The first torque step to 107 inch lbs. (12 Nm). The second torque step to 11 ft. lbs. (15 Nm) plus 75° (1 flat) for the short bolts and 11 ft. lbs. (15 Nm) plus 90° (1½ flats) for the long bolts.

10. Install the oil pan assembly as outlined earlier in this section.

11. Carefully lower the vehicle.

12. Refill the crankcase with the specified amount and type of engine oil. Start the engine and check for oil leaks.

3.8L Engine

1. Disconnect the negative battery cable.

2. Remove the engine from the vehicle, as outlined earlier, then secure it to a suitable workstand.

3. Remove the flywheel-to-crankshaft bolts and the flywheel.

4. Unfasten the timing chain cover-to-engine bolts, then remove the cover.

5. Remove the camshaft sprocket-to-camshaft gear bolts, the sprocket, the timing chain and the gear.

6. To remove the balance shaft, perform the following:

a. Remove the balance shaft gear-to-shaft bolt and the gear.

b. Remove the balance shaft retainer-to-engine bolts and the retainer.

c. Using the slide hammer tool, pull the balance shaft from the front of the engine.

7. If replacing the rear balance shaft bearing, perform the following procedures:

a. Drive the rear plug from the engine.

b. Using the camshaft remover/installer tool, press the rear bearing from the rear of the engine.

c. Dip the new bearing in clean engine oil.

d. Using the balance shaft rear bearing installer tool, press the new rear bearing into the rear of the engine.

e. Install the rear cup plug.

To install:

8. Using the balance shaft installer tool, screw it into the balance shaft and install the shaft into the engine; remove the installer tool.

9. Clean the gasket mounting surfaces. Inspect the parts for wear and/or damage; replace the parts, if necessary.

10. Install the balance shaft retainer. Tighten the balance shaft retainer-to-engine bolts to 27 ft. lbs. (37 Nm).

11. Align the balance shaft gear with the camshaft gear timing marks. Install the balance shaft gear onto the balance shaft. Tighten the balance gear-to-balance shaft bolt to 15 ft. lbs. (20 Nm), then using a torque angle meter tool, rotate another 35°.

12. Align the marks on the balance shaft gear and the camshaft gear by turning the balance shaft.

13. Turn the crankshaft so the No. 1 piston is at TDC.

14. Install the timing chain and sprocket.

15. Replace the balance shaft front bearing retainer and bolts. Tighten the bolts to 26 ft. lbs. (35 Nm).

16. Install the front timing cover and the lifter guide retainer.

17. Install the intake manifold and flywheel assembly. Tighten the flywheel bolts to 89 inch lbs. (10 Nm), plus an additional 90° turn.

18. Install the engine assembly and connect the negative battery cable. Start the engine and check for leaks.

Pistons and Connecting Rods

❊❊ CAUTION

The EPA warns that prolonged contact with used engine oil may cause a number of skin disorders, including cancer! You should make every effort to minimize your exposure to used engine oil. Protective gloves should be worn when changing the oil. Wash your hands and any other exposed skin areas as soon as possible after exposure to used engine oil. Soap and water, or waterless hand cleaner should be used.

REMOVAL

◆ **See Figures 167 thru 172**

❊❊ CAUTION

Fuel injection systems remain under pressure, even after the engine has been turned OFF. The fuel system pressure must be relieved before disconnecting any fuel lines. Failure to do so may result in fire and/or personal injury.

1. Disconnect the negative battery cable.

➡ **While it may be possible to remove the oil pan and cylinder heads to access the pistons and connecting rods for removal, it is recommended that the engine be removed from the vehicle and secured to a suitable engine stand. This is especially true if a defective connecting rod bearing is suspected, since the crankshaft will have to be removed as part of the service.**

2. Remove the engine assembly from the vehicle, as outlined earlier in this section.

3. On 6 cylinder engines: remove the intake manifold and the cylinder head located over the piston assembly being removed. On 4 cylinder engines: remove the cylinder head and manifolds as an assembly.

4. Drain the oil and remove the oil pan.

5. Remove the oil pump and sump assembly. Remove the force balancer assembly on 2.5L engines.

6. Stamp the cylinder number on the machined surfaces of the bolt bosses of the connecting rod and cap for identification when reinstalling. If the pistons are to be removed from the connecting rod, mark the cylinder number on the

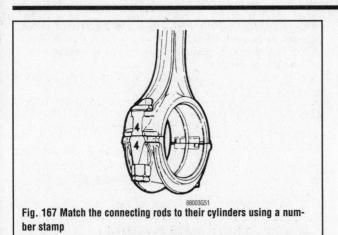

Fig. 167 Match the connecting rods to their cylinders using a number stamp

Fig. 168 Place lengths of rubber hose over the connecting rod studs

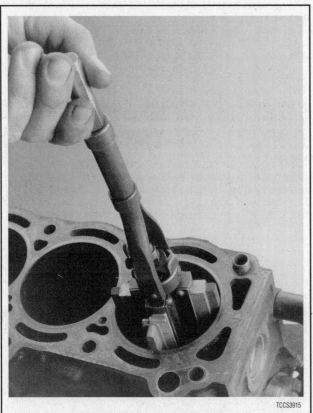

Fig. 169 Remove the ridge from the cylinder bore using a ridge cutter

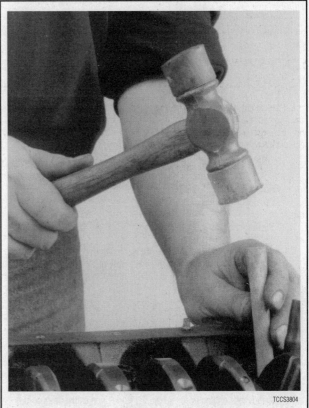

Fig. 170 Carefully tap the piston out of the bore using a wooden dowel

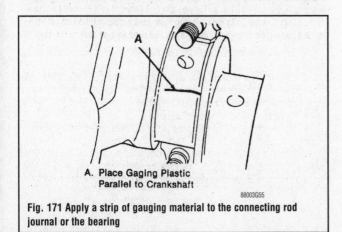

Fig. 171 Apply a strip of gauging material to the connecting rod journal or the bearing

Fig. 172 Remove the bearing cap and compare the gauging material to the scale provided with the package

piston with a silver pencil or quick drying paint for proper cylinder identification and cap-to-rod location. On 4-cylinder engines, the cylinders are numbered 1–4 from front to back; for 6-cylinder engines, the cylinders are numbered 1–3–5 on the right bank, 2–4–6 on the left bank.

➡**If the pistons or connecting rods are not marked from the factory, mark each assembly with paint before removal.**

7. Rotate the crankshaft until the piston to be removed is at the bottom of the cylinder. Examine the cylinder bore above the ring travel. If the bore is worn so that a shoulder or ridge exists at the top of the cylinder, remove the ridge with a ridge reamer to avoid damaging the rings or cracking the ring lands in the piston during removal. Before operating the ridge reamer, place a shop towel on top of the piston to catch the metal shavings.

✳✳ WARNING

Be very careful when using a ridge reamer. Only remove the cylinder bore material that is necessary to remove the ridge. If too much cylinder bore material is removed, cylinder overboring and piston replacement may be necessary.

8. Examine the cylinder bore above the ring travel. If a ridge exists, remove the ridge with a ridge reamer before attempting to remove the piston and rod assembly. This tool can be purchased at your local parts distributor or rented at a tool rental.
9. Remove the rod bearing cap and bearing. Tap on the lower cap to dislodge it from the connecting rod.
10. Install a guide hose over threads of rod bolts. This is to prevent damage to bearing journal and rod bolt threads. Use two pieces of ⅜ in. (10mm) fuel hose.
11. Remove the rod and piston assembly through the top of the cylinder bore by lightly tapping the connecting rod with a wooden hammer handle. Do NOT use any metal tools to remove the piston and connecting rod assembly.

➡**If the piston rings will not clear the top of the cylinder, check to see if the ridge is completely removed.**

12. Loosen the connecting rod bolt nuts until the nuts are flush with the ends of the bolts. Using a hammer and a brass drift or piece of wood, lightly tap on the nuts/bolts until the connecting rod cap is loosened from the connecting rod. Remove the nuts, rod cap and lower bearing shell.
13. Slip a piece of snug fitting rubber hose over each rod bolt, to prevent the bolt threads from damaging the crankshaft during removal. Using a hammer handle or piece of wood or plastic, push the rod and piston upward in the bore until the connecting rod is clear of the crankshaft journal.
14. Inspect the rod bearings for scoring, chipping or other wear.
15. Inspect the crankshaft rod bearing journal for wear. Measure the journal diameter in several locations around the journal and compare to specification. If the crankshaft journal is scored or has deep ridges, or its diameter is below specification, the crankshaft must be removed from the engine and reground.
16. If the crankshaft journal appears usable, clean it and the rod bearing shells until they are completely free of oil. Blow any oil from the oil hole in the crankshaft.

➡**The journal surfaces and bearing shells must be completely free of oil to get an accurate reading with Plastigage®.**

17. Pull the connecting rod back onto the crankshaft rod journal and remove the rubber hoses.
18. Place a strip of Plastigage® lengthwise along the bottom center of the lower bearing shell, then install the cap with the shell and torque the connecting rod nuts to specification. Do not turn the crankshaft with the Plastigage® installed in the bearing.
19. Remove the bearing cap with the shell. The flattened Plastigage® will either be sticking to the bearing shell or the crankshaft journal.
20. Using the printed scale on the Plastigage® package, measure the flattened Plastigage® at its widest point. The number on the scale that most closely corresponds to the width of the Plastigage® indicates the bearing clearance in thousandths of an inch or hundredths of a millimeter.
21. Compare the actual bearing clearance with the bearing clearance specification. If the bearing clearance is excessive, the bearing must be replaced or the crankshaft must be ground and the bearing replaced.

➡**If the crankshaft is still at standard size (has not been ground undersize), bearing shell sets of 0.001, (0.0254mm) 0.002 (0.050mm) and 0.003 in. (0.0762mm) over standard size may be available to correct excessive bearing clearance.**

22. After clearance measuring is completed, be sure to remove the Plastigage® from the crankshaft and/or bearing shell.
23. Again remove the connecting rod cap and install the rubber hose on the rod bolts. Push the rod and piston upward in the bore until the piston rings clear the cylinder block. Remove the piston and connecting rod assembly from the top of the cylinder bore.

CLEANING AND INSPECTION

▶ **See Figures 173 thru 178**

1. Remove the piston rings from the piston. The compression rings must be removed using a piston ring expander, to prevent breakage.
2. Clean the ring grooves with a ring groove cleaner, being careful not to cut into the piston metal. Heavy carbon deposits can be cleaned from the top of the piston with a scraper or wire brush, however, do not use a wire wheel on the ring grooves or lands. Clean the oil drain holes in the ring grooves. Clean all remaining dirt, carbon and varnish from the piston with a suitable solvent and a brush; do not use a caustic solution.
3. After cleaning, inspect the piston for scuffing, scoring, cracks, pitting or excessive ring groove wear. Replace any piston that is obviously worn.
4. If the piston appears okay, measure the piston diameter using a micrometer. Measure the piston diameter in the thrust direction, 90° to the piston pin axis, 3/4 in. (19mm) below the center line of the piston pin bore.
5. Measure the cylinder bore diameter using a bore gauge, or with a telescope gauge and micrometer. The measurement should be made in the piston thrust direction at the top, middle and bottom of the bore.

➡**Piston diameter and cylinder bore measurements should be made with the parts at room temperature, 70°F (21°C).**

6. Subtract the piston diameter measurement made in Step 4 from the cylinder bore measurement made in Step 5. This is the piston-to-bore clearance. If the clearance is within specification, light finish honing is all that is necessary. If the clearance is excessive, the cylinder must be bored and the piston replaced. If the pistons are replaced, the piston rings must also be replaced.
7. If the piston-to-bore clearance is okay, check the ring groove clearance. Roll the piston ring around the ring groove in which it is to be installed and check the clearance with a feeler gauge. Compare the measurement with specification. High points in the ring groove that may cause the ring to bind may be cleaned up carefully with a points file. Replace the piston if the ring groove clearance is not within specification.
8. Check the connecting rod for damage or obvious wear. Check for signs of fractures and check the bearing bore for out-of-round and taper.
9. A shiny surface on the pin boss side of the piston usually indicates that the connecting rod is bent or the wrist pin hole is not in proper relation to the piston skirt and ring grooves.
10. Abnormal connecting rod bearing wear can be caused by either a bent connecting rod, an improperly machined journal, or a tapered connecting rod bore.
11. Twisted connecting rods will not create an easily identifiable wear pattern, but badly twisted rods will disturb the action of the entire piston, rings, and connecting rod assembly and may be the cause of excessive oil consumption.
12. If the piston must be removed from the connecting rod, mark the side of the connecting rod that corresponds with the side of the piston that faces the front of the engine, so the new piston will be installed facing the same direction. Most pistons have an arrow or notch on the top of the piston, indicating that this side should face the front of the engine. If the original piston is to be reinstalled, use paint or a marker to indicate the cylinder number on the piston, so it can be reinstalled on the same connecting rod.
13. The piston pin is a press fit in the connecting rod. If the piston and/or connecting rod must be replaced, the pin must be pressed into the connecting rod using a fixture that will not damage or distort the piston and/or connecting rod. The piston must move freely on the pin after installation.

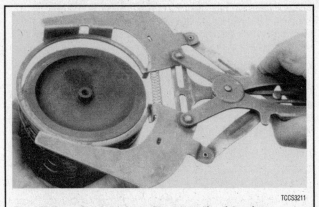

Fig. 173 Use a ring expander tool to remove the piston rings

Fig. 174 Clean the piston grooves using a ring groove cleaner

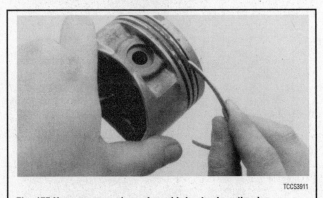

Fig. 175 You can use a piece of an old ring to clean the ring grooves, BUT be careful the ring is sharp

Fig. 176 Measure the piston's outer diameter using a micrometer

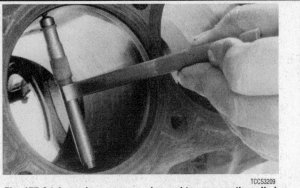

Fig. 177 A telescoping gauge may be used to measure the cylinder bore diameter

Fig. 178 Checking the ring-to-ring groove clearance

HONING

▶ **See Figures 179 and 180**

1. After the piston and connecting rod assembly have been removed, check the clearances as explained in the cleaning and inspection procedure, to determine whether boring and honing or just light honing are required.

2. Honing is best done with the crankshaft removed. This prevents damage to the crankshaft and makes post-honing cleaning easier, as the honing process will scatter metal particles. However, if the crankshaft is in the cylinder block, position the connecting rod journal for the cylinder being honed as far away from the bottom of the cylinder bore as possible, and wrap a shop cloth around the journal.

3. Honing can be done either with a flexible glaze breaker type hone or with a rigid hone that has honing stones and guide shoes. The flexible hone removes the least amount of metal, and is especially recommended if the piston-to-cylinder bore clearance is on the loose side. The flexible hone is useful to provide a

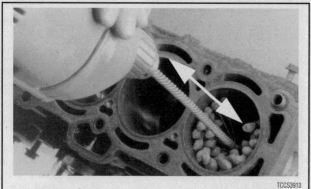

Fig. 179 Using a ball type cylinder hone is an easy way to hone the cylinder bore

Fig. 180 A properly cross-hatched cylinder bore

finish on which the new piston rings will seat. A rigid hone will remove more material than the flexible hone and requires more operator skill.

4. Regardless of the type of hone used, carefully follow the manufacturers instructions for operation.

5. The hone should be moved up and down the bore at sufficient speed to obtain a uniform finish. A rigid hone will provide a more definite cross-hatch finish; operate the rigid hone at a speed to obtain a 45° included angle in the cross-hatch. The finish marks should be clean but not sharp, free from embedded particles and torn or folded metal.

6. Periodically during the honing procedure, thoroughly clean the cylinder bore and check the piston-to-bore clearance with the piston for that cylinder.

7. After honing is completed, thoroughly wash the cylinder bores and the rest of the engine with hot water and detergent. Scrub the bores well with a stiff bristle brush and rinse thoroughly with hot water. Thorough cleaning is essential, for if any abrasive material is left in the cylinder bore, it will rapidly wear the new rings and the cylinder bore. If any abrasive material is left in the rest of the engine, it will be picked up by the oil and carried throughout the engine, damaging bearings and other parts.

8. After the bores are cleaned, wipe them down with a clean cloth coated with light engine oil, to keep them from rusting.

PISTON PIN REPLACEMENT

Use care at all times when handling and servicing connecting rods and pistons. To prevent possible damage to these units, do not clamp the rod or piston in a vise since they may become distorted. Do not allow the pistons to strike against one another, against hard objects or bench surfaces, since distortion of the piston contour or nicks in the soft aluminum material may result.

Removing the piston from the connecting rod requires the use of expensive tools that would not be practical to purchase for a one time basis (except 2.3L QUAD 4). This procedure should be performed by a qualified engine machine shop.

2.3L Engine

The piston pin is held in by retaining clips on either side of the pin, requiring no special tools to remove. Remove the retaining clips and push out the piston pin. Reuse the old retainers if not damaged. Make sure the clips are fully seated before installing into cylinder block.

All Other Engines

▶ See Figures 181 and 182

1. Remove the piston rings using a suitable piston ring removal tool.
2. Remove the piston pin lockring, if used.
3. Install the guide bushing of the piston pin removal and installation tool.
4. Install the piston and rod assembly on a support and place the assembly in an arbor press. Press the pin out of the connecting rod using the proper piston pin tool.
5. Assembly is the reverse of the removal procedure.

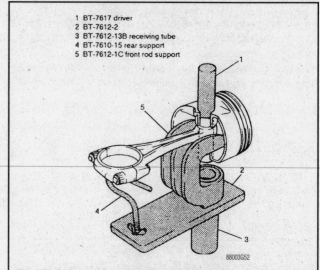

```
1 BT-7617 driver
2 BT-7612-2
3 BT-7612-13B receiving tube
4 BT-7610-15 rear support
5 BT-7612-1C front rod support
```

Fig. 181 Removing the piston pin using a suitable tool—3.1L engine shown

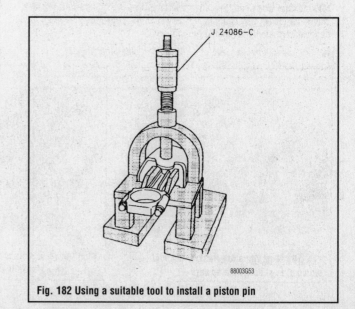

Fig. 182 Using a suitable tool to install a piston pin

PISTON RING REPLACEMENT

▶ **See Figure 183**

1. After the cylinder bores have been finish honed and cleaned, check the piston ring end-gap. Compress the piston rings to be used in the cylinder, one at a time, into that cylinder. Using an inverted piston, push the ring down into the cylinder bore area where normal ring wear is not encountered.

2. Measure the ring end-gap with a feeler gauge and compare to specification. A gap that is too tight is more harmful than one that is too loose (If ring end-gap is excessively loose, the cylinder bore is probably worn beyond specification).

3. If the ring end-gap is too tight, carefully remove the ring and file the ends squarely with a fine file to obtain the proper clearance.

4. Install the rings on the piston, lowest ring first. The lowest (oil) ring is installed by hand; the top 2 (compression) rings must be installed using a piston ring expander tool. There is a high risk of breaking or distorting the compression rings if they are installed by hand.

5. Install the oil ring expander in the bottom ring groove. Make sure the ends butt together and do not overlap. The expander end-gap should be parallel to the piston pin, facing the right cylinder bank.

6. Start the end of an oil ring rail ring into the oil ring groove above the expander. The rail end-gap should be positioned 135° from the expander end-gap. Finish installing the rail ring by spiraling it the remainder of the way on. Repeat the rail installation with the other rail ring. Its gap position must be 135° from the other side of the expander end-gap, 90° from the other rail ring end-gap.

➡ **If the instructions on the ring packaging differ from this information regarding ring gap positioning, follow the ring manufacturers instructions.**

7. Install the lower compression ring in the piston ring expander tool with the proper side up (usually the manufacturer's mark faces UP). The piston ring packaging should contain instructions as to the directions the ring sides should face. Spread the ring with the expander tool and install it on the piston. Position the end-gap 180° from the oil ring expander end-gap.

8. Repeat Step 7 to install the top compression ring. Position the end-gap in line with the oil ring expander end-gap. The compression ring end-gaps must not be aligned.

INSTALLATION

▶ **See Figures 184 and 185**

1. Make sure the connecting rod and rod cap bearing saddles are clean and free of nicks or burrs. Install the bearing shells in the connecting rod, making sure the bearing shell tangs are seated in the notches.

➡ **Be careful when handling any plain bearings. Hands and working area should be clean. Dirt is easily embedded in the bearing surface and the bearings are easily scratched or damaged.**

2. Make sure the cylinder bore and crankshaft journal are clean.
3. Position the crankshaft journal at its furthest position away from the bottom of the cylinder bore.
4. Coat the cylinder bore with light engine oil.
5. Install the rubber hoses over the connecting rod bolts to protect the crankshaft during installation.
6. Make sure the piston rings are properly installed and the ring end-gaps are correctly positioned. Install a piston ring compressor over the piston and rings and compress the piston rings into their grooves. Follow the ring compressor manufacturers instructions.
7. Place the piston and connecting rod assembly into the cylinder bore. Make sure the assembly is the correct one for that bore and that the piston and connecting rod are facing in the proper direction. Most pistons have an arrow or notch on the top of the piston, indicating that this side should face the front of the engine.
8. Make sure the ring compressor is seated squarely on the block deck surface. If the compressor is not seated squarely, a ring could pop out from beneath the compressor and hang up on the deck surface, as the piston is tapped into the bore, possibly breaking the ring.
9. Make sure that the connecting rod is not hung up on the crankshaft counterweights and is in position to come straight on to the crankshaft.
10. Tap the piston slowly into the bore, making sure the compressor remains squarely against the block deck. When the piston is completely in the bore, remove the ring compressor.

➡ **If the connecting rod bearings were replaced, recheck the bearing clearance as described during the removal procedure, before proceeding further.**

11. Coat the crankshaft journal and the bearing shells with engine assembly lube or clean engine oil. Pull the connecting rod onto the crankshaft journal. After the rod is seated, remove the rubber hoses.
12. Install the rod bearing cap, making sure it is the correct one for the connecting rod. Lightly oil the connecting rod bolt threads and install the rod nuts. Tighten the nuts to 15 ft. lbs. (20 Nm) plus 75° additional rotation.
13. After each piston and connecting rod assembly is installed, turn the crankshaft over several times and check for binding. If there is a problem and the crankshaft will not turn, or turns with great difficulty, it will be easier to find the problem (rod cap on backwards, broken ring, etc.) than if all the assemblies are installed.
14. Check the clearance between the sides of the connecting rods and the crankshaft using a feeler gauge. Spread the rods slightly with a screwdriver to insert the gauge. If the clearance is below the minimum specification, the connecting rod will have to be removed and machined to provide adequate clearance. If the clearance is excessive, substitute an unworn rod and recheck. If the clearance is still excessive, the crankshaft must be welded and reground, or replaced.
15. Install the oil pump and oil pan.
16. Install the cylinder heads and intake manifold.
17. Install the engine in the vehicle.
18. Start and run the engine, then check for leaks and proper engine operation.

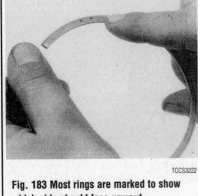

TCCS3222

Fig. 183 Most rings are marked to show which side should face upward

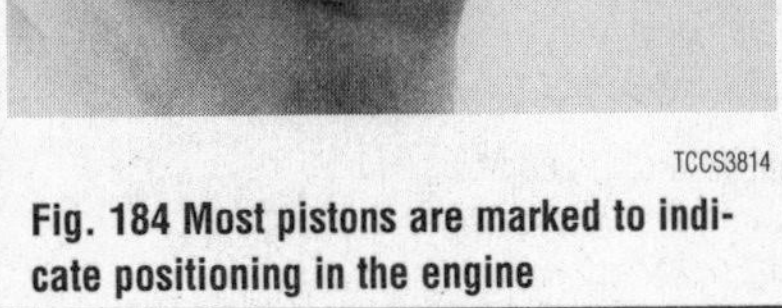

TCCS3814

Fig. 184 Most pistons are marked to indicate positioning in the engine

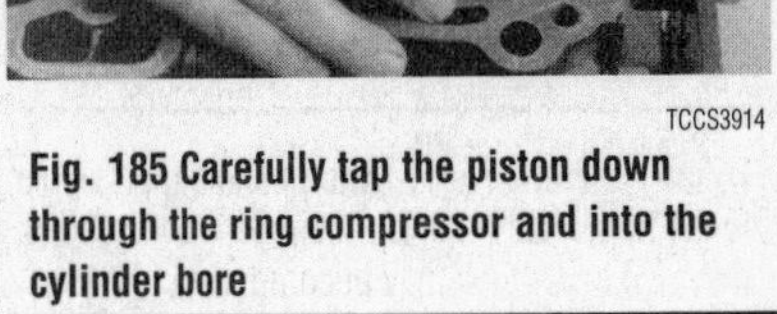

TCCS3914

Fig. 185 Carefully tap the piston down through the ring compressor and into the cylinder bore

Rear Main Bearing Oil Seal

REMOVAL & INSTALLATION

2.2L Engine

▶ **See Figures 186 and 187**

1. Disconnect the negative battery cable.
2. Remove the transaxle.
3. Use a suitable tool to prevent crankshaft rotation, then unfasten the flywheel-to-crankshaft bolts and remove the flywheel. Inspect for a rear main seal leak.

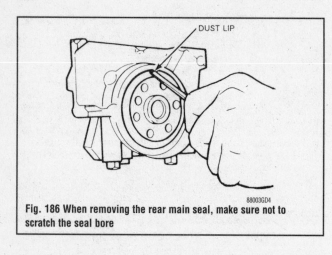

Fig. 186 When removing the rear main seal, make sure not to scratch the seal bore

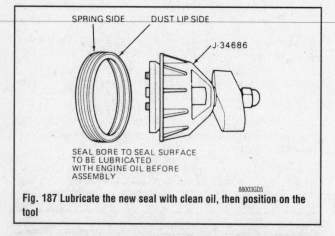

Fig. 187 Lubricate the new seal with clean oil, then position on the tool

✳✳ WARNING

Be very careful not to damage the crankshaft seal surfaces with the prytool.

4. Remove the seal by carefully inserting a suitable prytool in through the dust lip. Pry out the seal, moving the tool around the seal as required until the seal is removed.

To install:

5. Lubricate the seal bore-to-seal surface with clean engine oil.
6. Install a new seal using tool J 34686 or equivalent, as follows:

a. Slide the new seal over the mandrel until the dust lip bottoms squarely against the tool collar.

b. Align the dowel pin of the tool with the dowel pin hole in the crankshaft and attach the tool to the crankshaft. Tighten the attaching screws to 44 inch lbs. (5 Nm).

c. Tighten the "T" handle of the tool to push the seal into the bore. Continue until the tool collar is flush against the block.

d. Loosen the "T" handle completely. Remove the attaching screws and the tool. Check to make sure the seal is properly seated in the bore.

7. Install the flywheel and the transaxle.
8. Connect the negative battery cable. Check the oil level and add, if necessary. Start the engine and check for leaks.

2.3L Engine

▶ **See Figure 188**

1. Disconnect the negative battery cable.
2. Remove the transaxle, as outlined in Section 7.
3. If equipped with a manual transaxle, remove the clutch and clutch cover. Mark the relationship of the pressure plate to the flywheel for reassembly in the same position for proper balance.
4. Unfasten the flywheel-to-crankshaft bolts, then remove the flywheel.
5. Remove the 2 the oil pan-to-seal housing bolts.
6. Unfasten the 6 seal housing-to-block bolts, then remove the seal housing and gasket.
7. Support the seal housing for seal removal using two wood blocks of equal thickness. With the wood blocks on a flat surface, position the seal housing and block so the transaxle side of the seal housing is supported across the dowel pin and center bolt holes on both sides of the seal opening.

➡ **The seal housing could be damaged if it is not properly supported during seal removal.**

8. Drive the crankshaft/rear main seal evenly out of the transaxle side of the seal housing using a small chisel in the relief grooves on the crankshaft side of the seal housing.

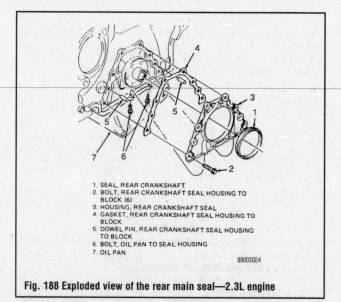

1. SEAL, REAR CRANKSHAFT
2. BOLT, REAR CRANKSHAFT SEAL HOUSING TO BLOCK (6)
3. HOUSING, REAR CRANKSHAFT SEAL
4. GASKET, REAR CRANKSHAFT SEAL HOUSING TO BLOCK
5. DOWEL PIN, REAR CRANKSHAFT SEAL HOUSING TO BLOCK
6. BOLT, OIL PAN TO SEAL HOUSING
7. OIL PAN

Fig. 188 Exploded view of the rear main seal—2.3L engine

✳✳ WARNING

Use care to avoid damage to the seal housing sealing surface. Damage to the sealing surfaces will result in an oil leak.

To install:

9. Press a new seal into the housing using tool J 36005 or equivalent seal installer.
10. Inspect the oil pan gasket inner silicone bead for any damage and replace if necessary. Also inspect the silicone across the top of the aluminum carrier at the oil pan, to cylinder block, to the seal housing three way joint. If these strips are damaged, they may be repaired using a suitable silicone sealant. Use only enough sealant to restore the silicone strips to their original dimension.

➡ **Excessive application of the sealant may cause part misalignment and oil leaks.**

11. Position the seal housing to the block gasket over the alignment dowel pins. The gasket is reversible. No sealant is necessary unless a gasket repair was necessary.

12. Lubricate the lip of the rear main seal with clean engine oil.

13. Position the seal housing assembly and secure with the housing-to-cylinder block bolts. Tighten to 106 inch lbs. (12 Nm).

14. Install the oil pan-to-seal housing bolts and tighten to 106 inch lbs. (12 Nm).

15. Install the flywheel and tighten the bolts evenly to the specifications listed in this section. Use tools J 36660 and J 37086 to prevent crankshaft rotation.

16. If equipped with a manual transaxle, install the clutch and clutch cover.

17. Install the transaxle, as outlined in Section 7 of this manual.

18. Connect the negative battery cable, then start the engine and check for leaks.

2.5L Engine

1. Disconnect the negative battery cable.
2. Remove the transaxle assembly, as outlined in Section 7.
3. Remove the flywheel.
4. Carefully pry out the seal, using a suitable tool.

To install:

5. Clean the block and crankshaft to seal mating surfaces.
6. Apply clean engine oil to the inside and outside diameter of the new seal.
7. Press the new seal evenly into place, using tool J-34924-A or equivalent seal installer.
8. Install the flywheel and transaxle.
9. Connect the negative battery cable, then start the engine and check for leaks.

2.8L, 3.1L, 3.4L and 3.8L Engines

▶ **See Figures 186, 187 and 189**

➡ **These engines use a round rear oil seal that requires removal of the transaxle and flywheel.**

1. Support the engine with tool J-28467 or equivalent. Raise and safely support the vehicle.
2. Remove the transaxle assembly, as outlined in Section 7.
3. Remove the flywheel, as outlined later in this section.
4. Using a small prybar or equivalent, insert it through the dust lip at an angle shown in the accompanying figure. Pry the seal out by moving the handle of the tool toward the end of the crankshaft pilot. Repeat as required around the seal until it is removed.

To install:

5. Inspect the seal bore and the crankshaft end for any damage.
6. Coat the inside lip of the seal with clean engine oil.
7. Install a new seal using tool J 34686 or equivalent, as follows:

   a. Slide the new seal over the mandrel until the dust lip bottoms squarely against the tool collar.

   b. Align the dowel pin of the tool with the dowel pin hole in the crankshaft and attach the tool to the crankshaft. Tighten the attaching screws to 44 inch lbs. (5 Nm).

c. Tighten the "T" handle of the tool to push the seal into the bore. Continue until the tool collar is flush against the block.

   d. Loosen the "T" handle completely. Remove the attaching screws and the tool. Check to make sure the seal is properly seated in the bore.

8. Install the flywheel and the transaxle.
9. Connect the negative battery cable. Check the oil level and add, if necessary. Start the engine and check for leaks.

Crankshaft and Main Bearings

REMOVAL & INSTALLATION

▶ **See Figure 190**

1. Disconnect the negative battery cable.
2. Remove the engine assembly as outlined earlier in this section.
3. Remove the engine front timing cover, then remove the timing chain and sprockets.
4. Remove the oil pan as outlined earlier in this section.
5. Remove the oil pump. On the 2.5L engine, remove the force balancer assembly.
6. Stamp the cylinder number on the machined surfaces of the bolt bosses of the connecting rods and caps, if not done by the factory, for identification when installing. If the pistons are to be removed from the connecting rod, mark the cylinder number on each piston with an indelible marker, silver pencil or quick drying paint for proper cylinder identification and cap to rod location.
7. Remove the connecting rod caps and store them so that they can be installed in their original positions. Put pieces of rubber fuel hose on the rod bolts before removal to protect the connecting rod journals.
8. Mark and remove all the main bearing caps.
9. Note the position of the keyway in the crankshaft so it can be installed in the same position.
10. With an assistant, lift the crankshaft out of the block. The rods will pivot to the center of the engine when the crankshaft is removed.
11. Remove the rear main oil seal.

To install:

12. Measure the crankshaft journals with Plastigage® to determine the correct size rod and main bearings to be used. Whenever a new or reconditioned crankshaft is installed, new connecting rod bearings and main bearings must be installed. The bearing undersize are usually 0.010 in. (0.254mm), 0.020 in. (0.501mm) and 0.030 in. (0.762mm). Do not go any further undersize than 0.030 in. (0.762mm).
13. Clean all oil passages in the block (and crankshaft if it is being reused).

➡ **A new rear main seal should be installed any time the crankshaft is removed or replaced.**

14. Install sufficient oil pan bolts in the block to align with the connecting rod bolts. Use rubber bands between the bolts to position the connecting rods

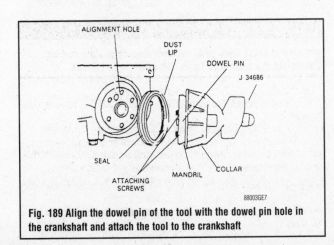

Fig. 189 Align the dowel pin of the tool with the dowel pin hole in the crankshaft and attach the tool to the crankshaft

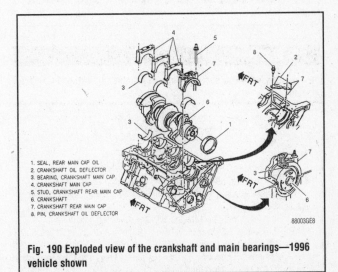

1. SEAL, REAR MAIN CAP OIL
2. CRANKSHAFT OIL DEFLECTOR
3. BEARING, CRANKSHAFT MAIN CAP
4. CRANKSHAFT MAIN CAP
5. STUD, CRANKSHAFT REAR MAIN CAP
6. CRANKSHAFT
7. CRANKSHAFT REAR MAIN CAP
8. PIN, CRANKSHAFT OIL DEFLECTOR

Fig. 190 Exploded view of the crankshaft and main bearings—1996 vehicle shown

as required. Connecting rod position can be adjusted by increasing the tension on the rubber bands with additional turns around the pan bolts or thread protectors. Install, if not already done, pieces of rubber hose on the connecting rod bolts to protect the crankshaft journals during installation.

15. Position the upper half of main bearings in the block and lubricate them with assembly lube. Position crankshaft keyway in the same position as removed. With an assistant, lower the crankshaft into the block. The connecting rods will follow the crank pins into the correct position as the crankshaft is lowered.

16. Lubricate the thrust flanges with Assembly Lube 10501609 or equivalent. Install rod caps with the lower half of the bearings lubricated with assembly lube. Lubricate the cap bolts with assembly lube and install, but do not tighten.

17. With a block of wood, bump the crankshaft in each direction to align the thrust flanges of the main bearing. After bumping the shaft in each direction, wedge the shaft to the front and hold it while tightening the thrust bearing cap bolts.

➡️In order to prevent the possibility of cylinder block and/or main bearing cap damage, the main bearing caps are to be tapped into their cylinder block cavity using a wood or rubber mallet before the bolts are installed. Do not use attaching bolts to pull the main bearing caps into their seats. Failure to observe this information may damage the cylinder block or a bearing cap.

18. Tighten all main bearing caps to the figures listed in the torque specifications chart in this section.

19. Remove the connecting rod bolt thread protectors and lubricate the connecting rod bearings with suitable assembly lube.

20. Install the connecting rod bearing caps in their original position. Tighten the nuts to the figures listed in the torque specifications chart in this section.

21. Install the oil pump, oil pan, timing cover, accessories and install the engine assembly into the vehicle as outlined earlier in this section.

22. Connect the negative battery cable.

CLEANING AND INSPECTION

♦ **See Figures 191, 192 and 193**

1. Clean the crankshaft with solvent and brush. Clean the oil passages with a suitable brush, then blow them out using compressed air.

2. Inspect the crankshaft for obvious damage or wear. Check the main and connecting rod journals for cracks, scratches, grooves or scores. Inspect the crankshaft oil seal surface for nicks, sharp edges or burrs that could damage the oil seal or cause premature wear.

3. If the crankshaft passes a visual inspection, check journal runout using a dial indicator. Support the crankshaft in V-blocks as shown in the figure and check the runout as shown. Compare to specifications.

4. Measure the main and connecting rod journals for wear, out-of-roundness or taper, using a micrometer. Measure in at least four places around each journal and compare your findings with the journal diameter specifications.

5. If the crankshaft fails any inspection for wear or damage, it must be reground or replaced.

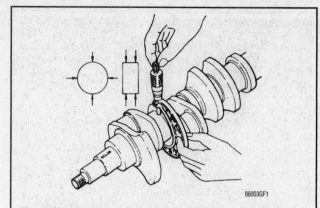

Fig. 192 Checking the main bearing journal using a micrometer

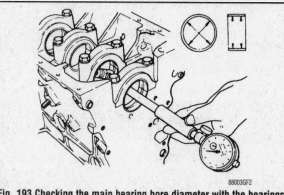

Fig. 193 Checking the main bearing bore diameter with the bearings installed

MAIN BEARING REPLACEMENT

♦ **See Figures 194 and 195**

➡️The following procedure requires the use of Plastigage® or a micrometer set consisting of inside and outside micrometers, and a dial indicator.

1. Inspect the bearings for scoring, chipping or other wear.

2. Inspect the crankshaft journals as details in the Cleaning and Inspection procedure

3. If the crankshaft journals appear usable, clean them and the bearing shells until they are completely free of oil. Blow any oil from the oil hole in the crankshaft.

4. To check the crankshaft/rod bearing clearances using a micrometer, use the perform the following procedures:

   a. Set the crankshaft on V-blocks Using a dial indicator set on the center bearing journal, check the crankshaft runout. Repair or replace the crankshaft if out of specification.

   b. Using an outside micrometer, measure the crankshaft bearing journals for diameter and out-of-round conditions; if necessary, regrind the bearing journals.

   c. Install the bearings and caps, then tightening the nuts/bolts to specifications. Using an inside micrometer, check the bearing bores in the engine block. If out of specification, regrind the bearing bores to the next largest oversize.

   d. The difference between the two readings is the bearing clearance. If out of specification, inspect for the cause and repair as necessary.

5. To inspect the main bearing surfaces using the Plastigage® method, perform the following procedures:

➡️The journal surfaces and bearing shells must be completely free of oil to get an accurate reading with Plastigage®

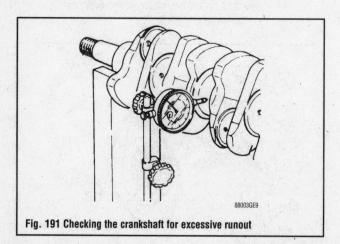

Fig. 191 Checking the crankshaft for excessive runout

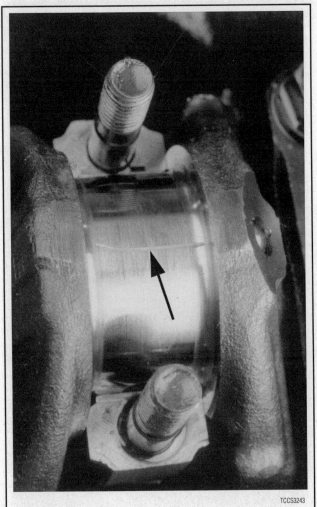

Fig. 194 Apply a strip of gauging material to the bearing, then install the cap

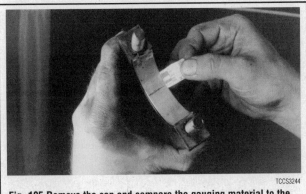

Fig. 195 Remove the cap and compare the gauging material to the provided scale

a. Place a strip of Plastigage® or equivalent gauging material, lengthwise along the bottom center of the lower bearing shell, then install the cap with the shell and tightening the connecting rod nuts or main cap bolt to specification.

➡ When the Plastigage® material is installed on the bearing surfaces, DO NOT rotate the crankshaft.

b. Remove the bearing cap with the shell. The flattened Plastigage® will either be sticking to the bearing shell or the crankshaft journal.

c. Using the printed scale on the Plastigage® package, measure the flattened material at its widest point. the number on the scale that most closely corresponds to the width of the Plastigage® indicates the bearing clearance in thousandths of an inch or hundredths of a millimeter.

d. Compare your findings with the bearing clearance specification. If the bearing clearance is excessive. the bearing must be replaced or the crankshaft must be ground and the bearing replaced.

➡ Bearing shell sets over the standard size are available to correct excessive bearing clearance.

e. After clearance measurement is completed, be sure to remove the Plastigage® from the crankshaft and/or bearing shell.

f. For final bearing shell installation, make sure the connecting rod and rod cap and/or cylinder block and main cap bearing saddles are clean and free of nicks or burrs. Install the bearing shells in the bearing saddles, making sure the shell tangs are seated in the notches.

➡ Be careful when handling any plain bearings. Your hands and the working area should be clean. Dirt is easily embedded in the bearing surface and the bearings are easily scratched or damaged.

Flywheel

REMOVAL & INSTALLATION

▸ See Figure 196

➡ On some vehicles, it may be necessary to remove the chamfer (bevel) from the edge of the socket to get full socket engagement on the thin headed flywheel bolts.

1. Disconnect the negative battery cable.
2. Remove the transaxle assembly as outlined in Section 7 of this manual.
3. If necessary for access, remove the right side splash shield.

➡ To assure proper balance during reassembly, matchmark the relationship of the pressure plate assembly to the flywheel.

4. If equipped with a manual transaxle, remove the clutch and pressure plate.
5. Using special tool J38122, J37096, or equivalent, secure the crankshaft, then unfasten the flywheel mounting bolts. Remove the flywheel and spacer (if equipped). For the 3.8L engine, discard the retaining bolts.

To install:
6. Remove all thread adhesive from the bolts and from the holes before installation.
7. Apply locking type adhesive to all of the flywheel-to-crankshaft mounting bolts.
8. The remaining installation steps are the reverse of the removal procedure. Tighten the flywheel bolts in stages to the following specifications:
   a. 2.2L and 2.5L engines: 55 ft. lbs. (75 Nm).
   b. 2.3L engine: 22 ft. lbs. (30 Nm) plus an additional 45° turn.
   c. 2.8L and 3.1L engines: 61 ft. lbs. (83 Nm).
   d. 3.4L engine: 60 ft. lbs. (82 Nm).
   e. 3.8L engine: 11 ft. lbs. (15 Nm) plus an additional 50° turn.
9. Connect the negative battery cable.

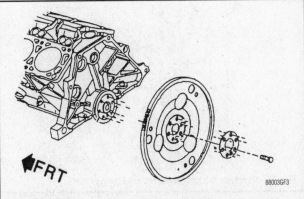

Fig. 196 Exploded view of the flywheel—1996 3.1L engine shown

EXHAUST SYSTEM

Inspection

▶ See Figures 197 thru 203

➡Safety glasses should be worn at all times when working on or near the exhaust system. Older exhaust systems will almost always be covered with loose rust particles which are more than a nuisance and could injure your eye.

✳✳ CAUTION

DO NOT perform exhaust repairs or inspection with the engine or exhaust hot. Allow the system to cool completely. Exhaust systems are noted for sharp edges, flaking metal and rusted bolts. Gloves and eye protection are required. A healthy supply of penetrating oil and rags is highly recommended.

Your vehicle must be raised and supported safely at four points to inspect the exhaust system properly. Start the inspection at the exhaust manifold where the header pipe is attached and work your way to the back of the vehicle. On dual exhaust systems, remember to inspect both sides of the vehicle. Check the complete exhaust system for open seams, holes, loose connections, or other deterioration which could permit exhaust fumes to seep into the passenger compartment. Inspect all mounting brackets and hangers for deterioration, some may have rubber O-rings that can become overstretched and non-supportive (and should be replaced if worn). Many technicians use a pointed tool to poke

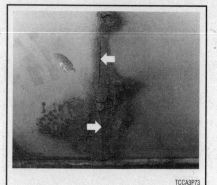

Fig. 197 Cracks in the muffler are a guaranteed leak

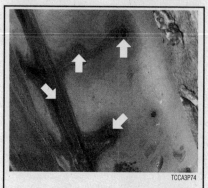

Fig. 198 Check the muffler for rotted spot welds and seams

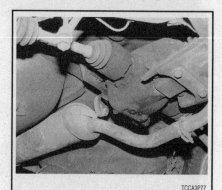

Fig. 199 Make sure the exhaust does contact the body or suspension

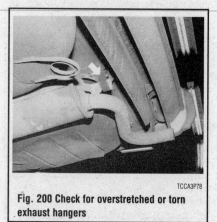

Fig. 200 Check for overstretched or torn exhaust hangers

Fig. 201 Example of a badly deteriorated exhaust pipe

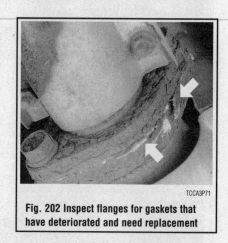

Fig. 202 Inspect flanges for gaskets that have deteriorated and need replacement

up into the exhaust system at rust spots to see whether or not they crumble. Most models have heat shield(s) covering certain parts of the exhaust system, it is often necessary to remove these shields to visually inspect those components.

REPLACEMENT

▶ See Figures 204, 205, 206, 207 and 208

There are basically two types of exhaust systems. One is the flange type where the component ends are attached with bolts and a gasket in-between. The other exhaust system is the slip joint type. These components slip into one another using clamps to retain them together.

✳✳ CAUTION

Allow the exhaust system to cool sufficiently before spraying a solvent exhaust fasteners. Some solvents are highly flammable and could ignite when sprayed on hot exhaust components.

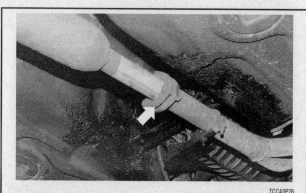

Fig. 203 Some systems, like this one, use large O-rings (donuts) in between the flanges

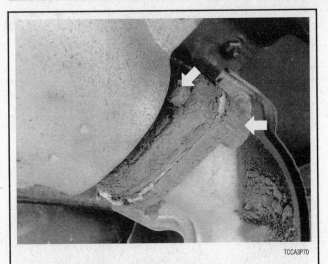

Fig. 204 Nuts and bolts will be extremely difficult to remove when deteriorated with rust

Before removing any component of the exhaust system, ALWAYS squirt a liquid rust dissolving agent onto the fasteners for ease of removal. A lot of knuckle skin will be saved by following this rule. It may even be wise to spray the fasteners and allow them to sit overnight.

❈❈ CAUTION

Do NOT perform exhaust repairs or inspection with the engine or exhaust hot. Allow the system to cool. Exhaust systems are noted for sharp edges, flaking metal and rusted bolts. Gloves and eye protection are required.

1. Raise and support the vehicle safely, as necessary for access. Remember that some longer exhaust pipes may be difficult to wrestle out from under the vehicle if it is not supported high enough.

2. If you haven't already, apply a generous amount of penetrating oil or solvent to any rusted fasteners.

3. On flange joints, carefully loosen and remove the retainers at the flange. If bolts or nuts are difficult to break loose, apply more penetrating liquid and give it some additional time to set. If the fasteners still will not come loose an impact driver may be necessary to jar it loose (and keep the fastener from breaking).

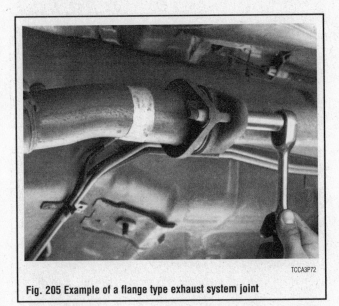

Fig. 205 Example of a flange type exhaust system joint

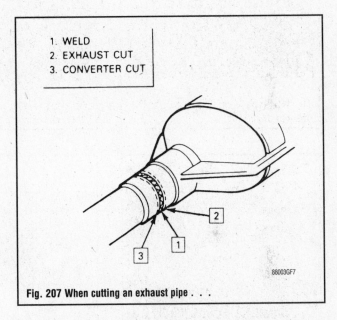

1. WELD
2. EXHAUST CUT
3. CONVERTER CUT

Fig. 207 When cutting an exhaust pipe . . .

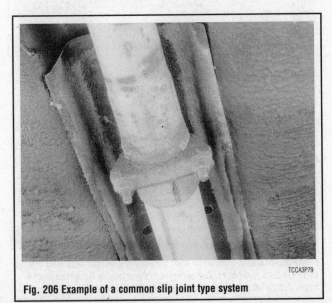

Fig. 206 Example of a common slip joint type system

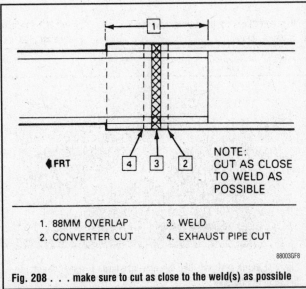

1. 88MM OVERLAP
2. CONVERTER CUT
3. WELD
4. EXHAUST PIPE CUT

NOTE: CUT AS CLOSE TO WELD AS POSSIBLE

◀ FRT

Fig. 208 . . . make sure to cut as close to the weld(s) as possible

➡**When unbolting the headpipe from the manifold, make sure that the bolts are free before trying to remove them. If you snap a stud in the exhaust manifold, the stud will have to be removed with a bolt extractor, which often means removal of the manifold itself.**

4. On slip joint components, remove the mounting U-bolts from around the exhaust pipe you are extracting from the vehicle. Don't be surprised if the U-bolts break while removing the nuts.

5. Loosen the exhaust pipe from any mounting brackets retaining it to the floor pan and separate the components. Slight twisting and turning may be required to remove the component completely from the vehicle. You may need to tap on the component with a rubber mallet to loosen it. If all else fails, use a hacksaw to separate the parts. An oxy-acetylene cutting torch may be faster but the sparks are DANGEROUS near the fuel tank, and at the very least, accidents could happen, resulting in damage to the under-vehicle parts, not to mention yourself.

6. When installing exhaust components, you should loosely position all components before tightening any of the joints. Once you are certain that the system is run correctly, begin tightening the fasteners at the front of the vehicle and work your way back.

4

DRIVEABILITY AND EMISSION CONTROLS

EMISSION CONTROLS

Crankcase Ventilation System

OPERATION

▶ **See Figures 1, 2 and 3**

The Positive Crankcase Ventilation (PCV) or Crankcase Ventilation (CV) system is used on all vehicles to evacuate the crankcase vapors. Fresh air from the air cleaner or intake duct is supplied to the crankcase, mixed with blow-by gases and then passed through a Positive Crankcase Ventilation (PCV) valve into the intake manifold or the air plenum.

When manifold vacuum is high, such as at idle, the orifice or valve restricts the flow of blow-by gases allowed into the manifold. If abnormal operating conditions occur, the system will allow excessive blow-by gases to back flow through the hose into the air cleaner. These blow-by gases will then be mixed with the intake air in the air cleaner instead of in the manifold. The air cleaner has a small filter attached to the inside wall that connects to the breather hose to trap impurities flowing in either direction.

A plugged PCV valve, orifice or hose may cause rough idle, stalling or slow idle speed, oil leaks, oil in the air cleaner or sludge in the engine. A leak could cause rough idle, stalling or high idle speed. The condition of the grommets in the valve cover will also affect system and engine performance.

Other than checking and replacing the PCV valve and associated hoses, there is no service required. Engine operating conditions that would direct suspicion to the PCV system are rough idle, oil present in the air cleaner, oil leaks and excessive oil sludging or dilution. If any of the above conditions exist, remove the PCV valve and shake it. A clicking sound indicates that the valve is free. If no clicking sound is heard, replace the valve. Inspect the PCV breather in the air cleaner. Replace the breather if it is so dirty that it will not allow gases to pass through. Check all the PCV hoses for condition and tight connections. Replace any hoses that have deteriorated.

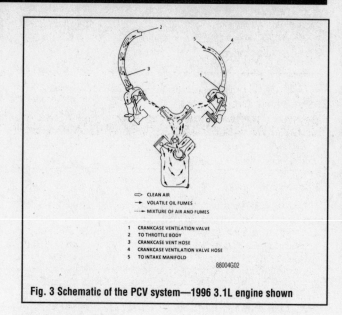

⇨ CLEAN AIR
→ VOLATILE OIL FUMES
----- MIXTURE OF AIR AND FUMES

1 CRANKCASE VENTILATION VALVE
2 TO THROTTLE BODY
3 CRANKCASE VENT HOSE
4 CRANKCASE VENTILATION VALVE HOSE
5 TO INTAKE MANIFOLD

88004G02

Fig. 3 Schematic of the PCV system—1996 3.1L engine shown

COMPONENT TESTING

▶ **See Figure 4**

PCV Valve

1. Start the engine.
2. With the engine at normal operating temperature, run at idle.
3. Remove the PCV valve or orifice from the grommet in the valve cover and place thumb over the end to check if vacuum is present. If vacuum is not present, check for plugged hoses or manifold port. Repair or replace as necessary.
4. Stop the engine and remove the valve. Shake the valve and listen for the rattle of the check valve needle. If there is no rattle heard when the valve is shaken, replace the valve.

PCV System

1. Check to make sure the engine has the correct PCV valve or bleed orifice.
2. Start the engine and bring to normal operating temperature.
3. Block off the PCV system fresh air intake passage.
4. Remove the engine oil dipstick and install a vacuum gauge on the dipstick tube.
5. Run the engine at 1500 rpm for 30 seconds then read the vacuum gauge with the engine at 1500 rpm.
   • If vacuum is present, the PCV system is functioning properly.

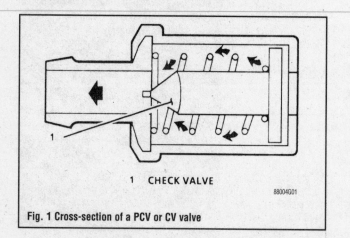

1 CHECK VALVE

88004G01

Fig. 1 Cross-section of a PCV or CV valve

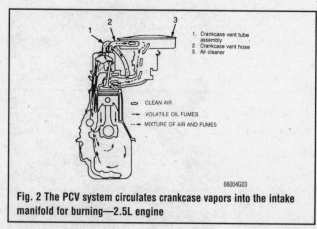

1. Crankcase vent tube assembly
2. Crankcase vent hose
3. Air cleaner

⇨ CLEAN AIR
→ VOLATILE OIL FUMES
----- MIXTURE OF AIR AND FUMES

88004G03

Fig. 2 The PCV system circulates crankcase vapors into the intake manifold for burning—2.5L engine

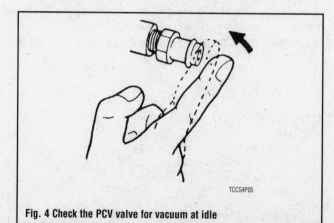

TCCS4P05

Fig. 4 Check the PCV valve for vacuum at idle

• If there is no vacuum, the engine may not be sealed and/or is drawing in outside air. Check the grommets and valve cover or oil pan gasket for leaks.

• If the vacuum gauge registers a pressure or the vacuum gauge is pushed out of the dipstick tube, check for the correct PCV valve or bleed orifice, a plugged hose or excessive engine blow-by.

REMOVAL & INSTALLATION

Removal and installation procedures of the PCV or CV valve is located in Section 1 of this manual.

Evaporative Emission Controls

OPERATION

▶ See Figures 5 and 6

The Evaporative Emission Control System (EECS) is designed to prevent fuel tank vapors from being emitted into the atmosphere. When the engine is not running, gasoline vapors from the tank are stored in a charcoal canister, mounted inside the left rear wheel well. The charcoal canister absorbs the gasoline vapors and stores them until certain engine conditions are met and the vapors can be purged and burned by the engine. In some vehicles, any liquid fuel entering the canister goes into a reservoir in the bottom of the canister to protect the integrity of the carbon element in the canister above. Three different methods are used to control the purge cycle of the charcoal canister.

First, the charcoal canister purge cycle is controlled by throttle position without the use of a valve on the canister. A vacuum line connects the canister to a ported vacuum source on the throttle body. When the throttle is at any position above idle, fresh air is drawn into the bottom of the canister and the fuel vapors are carried into the throttle body at that port. The air/vapor flow volume is only what can be drawn through the vacuum port and is fairly constant.

Second, the flow volume is modulated with throttle position through a vacuum valve. The ported vacuum from the throttle body is used to open a diaphragm valve on top of the canister. When the valve is open, air and vapors are drawn into the intake manifold, usually through the same manifold port as the PCV system. With this method, the purge valve cycle is slaved to the throttle opening; more throttle opening, more purge air flow.

And third, the charcoal canister purge valve cycle is controlled by the ECM through a solenoid valve on the canister. When the solenoid is activated, full manifold vacuum is applied to the top of the purge valve diaphragm to open the valve all the way. A high volume of fresh air is drawn into the canister and the gasoline vapors are purged quickly. The ECM activates the solenoid valve when the following conditions are met:

• The engine is at normal operating temperature.
• After the engine has been running a specified period of time.
• Vehicle speed is above a predetermined speed.
• Throttle opening is above a predetermined value.

A vent pipe allows fuel vapors to flow to the charcoal canister. On some vehicles, the tank is isolated from the charcoal canister by a tank pressure control valve, located either in the tank or in the vapor line near the canister. It is a com-

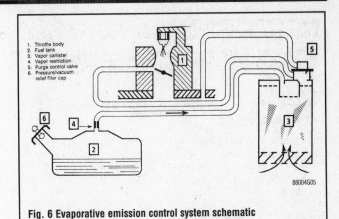

Fig. 6 Evaporative emission control system schematic

bination roll-over, integral pressure and vacuum relief valve. When the vapor pressure in the tank exceeds 0.72 psi (5 kPa), the valve opens to allow vapors to vent to the canister. The valve also provides vacuum relief to protect against vacuum build-up in the fuel tank and roll-over spill protection.

Poor engine idle, stalling and poor driveability can be caused by an inoperative canister purge solenoid, a damaged canister or split, damaged or improperly connected hoses.

The most common symptom of problems in this system is fuel odors coming from under the hood. If there is no liquid fuel leak, check for a cracked or damaged vapor canister, inoperative or always open canister control valve, disconnected, misrouted, kinked or damaged vapor pipe or canister hoses; or a damaged air cleaner or improperly seated air cleaner gasket.

TESTING

Tank Pressure Control Valve

1. Using a hand-held vacuum pump, apply a vacuum of 15 in. Hg (51 kPa) through the control vacuum signal tube to the purge valve diaphragm. If the diaphragm does not hold vacuum for at least 20 seconds, the diaphragm is leaking. Replace the control valve.

2. With the vacuum still applied to the control vacuum tube, attach a short piece of hose to the valve's tank tube side and blow into the hose. Air should pass through the valve. If it does not, replace the control valve.

Canister Purge Control Valve

1. Connect a clean length of hose to the fuel tank vapor line connection on the canister and attempt to blow through the purge control valve. It should be difficult or impossible to blow through the valve. If air passes easily, the valve is stuck open and should be replaced.

2. Connect a hand-held vacuum pump to the top vacuum line fitting of the purge control valve. Apply a vacuum of 15 in. Hg (51kPa) to the purge valve diaphragm. If the diaphragm does not hold vacuum for at least 20 seconds the diaphragm is leaking. Replace the control valve. If it is impossible to blow through the valve, it is stuck closed and must be replaced.

3. On vehicles with a solenoid activated purge control valve, unplug the connector and use jumper wires to supply 12 volts to the solenoid connections on the valve. With the vacuum still applied to the control vacuum tube, the purge control valve should open and it should be easy to blow through. If not, replace the valve.

REMOVAL & INSTALLATION

Evaporative Canister

▶ See Figure 7

1. Disconnect the negative battery cable.
2. If necessary for access, raise and safely support the vehicle, then remove the left (driver) side rear wheel and tire assembly.
3. Remove the left (driver) side rear wheel well liner.
4. Tag and disconnect the vacuum hoses from the canister.
5. Unfasten the retainers, then remove the canister from the vehicles.

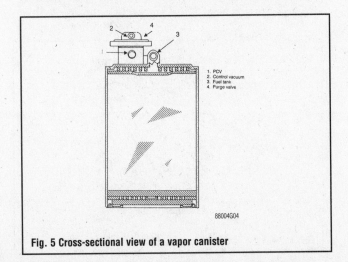

1. PCV
2. Control vacuum
3. Fuel tank
4. Purge valve

Fig. 5 Cross-sectional view of a vapor canister

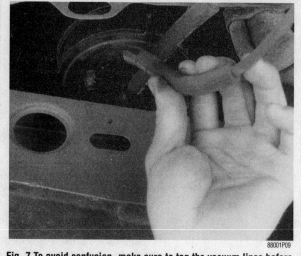

Fig. 7 To avoid confusion, make sure to tag the vacuum lines before disconnecting them

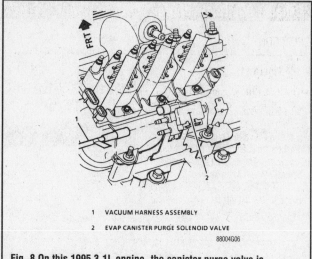

1   VACUUM HARNESS ASSEMBLY

2   EVAP CANISTER PURGE SOLENOID VALVE

Fig. 8 On this 1995 3.1L engine, the canister purge valve is mounted near the ignition coil

To install:

6. Position the canister into the vehicle, then secure with the retainers.
7. Attach the vacuum lines as tagged during removal.
8. Fasten the left (driver) side rear wheel well liner.
9. If removed, install the left rear wheel and tire assembly, then carefully lower the vehicle.
10. Connect the negative battery cable.

Tank Pressure Control Valve

1. Disconnect the negative battery cable.
2. Tag and disconnect the hoses from the control valve.
3. Remove the mounting hardware.
4. Remove the control valve from the vehicle.

To install:

5. Position the control valve in the vehicle, then secure using the mounting hardware.
6. Attach the hoses to the control valve, as tagged during removal.
7. Connect the negative battery cable.

Canister Purge Solenoid Valve

▶ See Figures 8, 9 and 10

1. Disconnect the negative battery cable.
2. Tag and detach the electrical connector and vacuum hose(s) from the valve.
3. Either unfasten the mounting nut or release the locktab on the solenoid bracket.
4. Remove the canister purge solenoid valve from the vehicle.

To install:

5. Position the purge solenoid valve to the bracket. Either snap the valve over the locktabs of the bracket or fasten the retaining nut to secure the valve.
6. Attach the vacuum hose(s) and electrical connector to the valve, as tagged during removal.
7. Connect the negative battery cable.

EVAP Vacuum Switch

1. Disconnect the negative battery cable.
2. Label and detach the switch electrical connector(s) and vacuum hoses.
3. Bend the retaining tab on the bracket to remove the switch, then remove the switch from the vehicle.

To install:

4. Connect the vacuum hoses to the switch.
5. Position the vacuum switch on the bracket.
6. Bend the retaining tab to secure the switch to the bracket.
7. Attach the switch electrical connector.
8. Connect the negative battery cable.

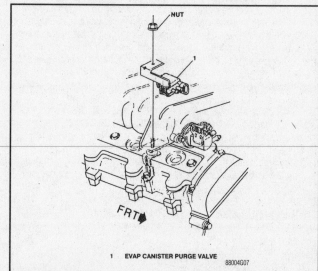

1   EVAP CANISTER PURGE VALVE

Fig. 9 Evaporative canister purge solenoid valve mounting—1995 3.4L engine shown

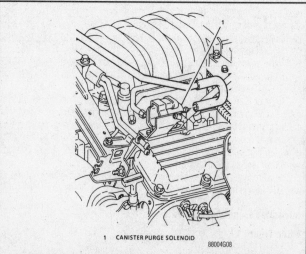

1   CANISTER PURGE SOLENOID

Fig. 10 The canister purge solenoid is located near the intake plenum—1995 3.8L engine shown

Exhaust Gas Recirculation (EGR) System

OPERATION

▶ See Figure 11

➡ **The 2.3L (VIN A) and 1991–92 3.8L engines do not use an EGR valve.**

The EGR system is used to reduce oxides of nitrogen (NOx) emission levels caused by high combustion chamber temperatures. This is accomplished by the use of an EGR valve which opens, under specific engine operating conditions, to admit a small amount of exhaust gas into the intake manifold, below the throttle plate. The exhaust gas mixes with the incoming air charge and displaces a portion of the oxygen in the air/fuel mixture entering the combustion chamber. The exhaust gas does not support combustion of the air/fuel mixture but it takes up volume, the net effect of which is to lower the temperature of the combustion process. This lower temperature also helps control detonation.

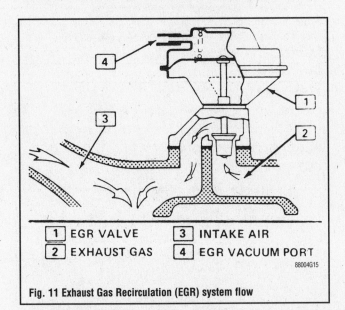

| 1 | EGR VALVE | 3 | INTAKE AIR |
| 2 | EXHAUST GAS | 4 | EGR VACUUM PORT |

88004G15

Fig. 11 Exhaust Gas Recirculation (EGR) system flow

The EGR valve is a mounted on the intake manifold and has an opening into the exhaust manifold. Except for the digital and linear versions, the EGR valve is opened by manifold vacuum to permit exhaust gas to flow into the intake manifold. With the digital and linear versions, the EGR valve is purely electrical and uses solenoid valves to open the flow passage. If too much exhaust gas enters, combustion will not occur. Because of this, very little exhaust gas is allowed to pass through the valve. The EGR system will be activated once the engine reaches normal operating temperature and the EGR valve will open when engine operating conditions are above idle speed and below Wide Open Throttle (WOT). On California vehicles equipped with a Vehicle Speed Sensor (VSS), the EGR valve opens when the VSS signal is greater than 2 mph (3.2 kph). The EGR system is deactivated on vehicles equipped with a Transmission Converter Clutch (TCC) when the TCC is engaged.

Too much EGR flow at idle, cruise, or during cold operation may result in the engine stalling after cold start, the engine stalling at idle after deceleration, vehicle surge during cruise and rough idle. If the EGR valve is always open, the vehicle may not idle. Too little or no EGR flow allows combustion temperatures to get too high which could result in spark knock (detonation), engine overheating and/or emission test failure.

There are four basic types of systems as described below, differing in the way EGR flow is modulated.

Integrated Electronic EGR Valve

▶ See Figure 12

The integrated electronic EGR valve, used on 1988–89 engines, functions like a port valve with a remote vacuum regulator, except the regulator and a pintle position sensor are sealed in the black plastic cover. The regulator and posi-

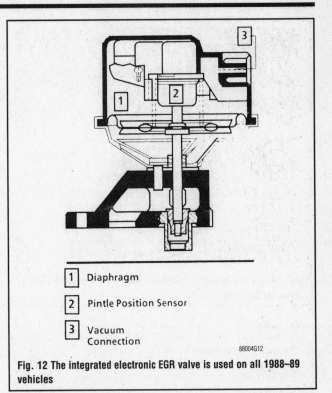

1	Diaphragm
2	Pintle Position Sensor
3	Vacuum Connection

88004G12

Fig. 12 The integrated electronic EGR valve is used on all 1988–89 vehicles

tion sensor are not serviceable items; there is a serviceable filter that provides fresh air to the regulator, along side the vacuum tube.

This valve has a vacuum regulator, to which the ECM provides variable current. This current produces the desired EGR flow using inputs from the manifold air temperature sensor, coolant temperature sensor and engine rpm.

Negative Backpressure EGR Valve

▶ See Figure 13

The negative backpressure EGR valve, used on the 2.5L engine, varies the amount of exhaust gas flow into the intake manifold depending on manifold vacuum and variations in exhaust backpressure. An air bleed valve, located inside the EGR valve assembly acts as a vacuum regulator. The bleed valve controls the amount of vacuum in the vacuum chamber by bleeding vacuum to outside air during the open phase of the cycle. The diaphragm on the valve has an internal air bleed hole which is held closed by a small spring when there is no exhaust backpressure. Engine vacuum opens the EGR valve against the pressure

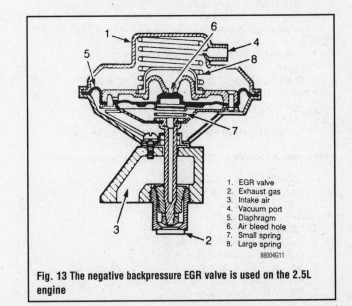

1. EGR valve
2. Exhaust gas
3. Intake air
4. Vacuum port
5. Diaphragm
6. Air bleed hole
7. Small spring
8. Large spring

88004G11

Fig. 13 The negative backpressure EGR valve is used on the 2.5L engine

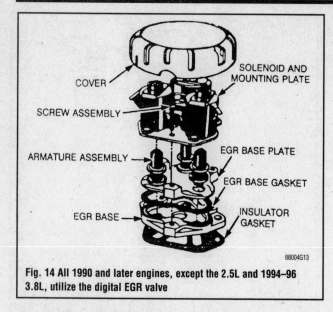

COVER

SOLENOID AND MOUNTING PLATE

SCREW ASSEMBLY

ARMATURE ASSEMBLY

EGR BASE PLATE

EGR BASE GASKET

EGR BASE

INSULATOR GASKET

88004G13

Fig. 14 All 1990 and later engines, except the 2.5L and 1994–96 3.8L, utilize the digital EGR valve

of a spring. When manifold vacuum combines with negative exhaust backpressure, the vacuum bleed hole opens and the EGR valve closes. This valve will open if vacuum is applied with the engine not running.

Digital EGR Valve

▶ See Figure 14

The digital EGR valve, used on all 1990 and later EGR-equipped engines (except the 2.5L and 1994–96 3.8L engine) is designed to control the flow of EGR independent of intake manifold vacuum. The valve controls EGR flow through 3 solenoid-opened orifices, which increase in size, to produce 7 possible combinations. When a solenoid is energized, the armature with attached shaft and swivel pintle, is lifted, opening the orifice.

The digital EGR valve is opened by the ECM, grounding each solenoid circuit individually. The flow of EGR is regulated by the ECM which uses information from the Coolant Temperature Sensor (CTS), Throttle Position Sensor (TPS) and Manifold Absolute Pressure (MAP) sensor to determine the appropriate rate of flow for a particular engine operating condition.

Linear EGR Valve

The linear EGR valve, used on the 1994–96 3.8L engine, is designed to accurately supply EGR to an engine, independent of intake manifold vacuum. The valve controls EGR flow from the exhaust to the intake manifold through an orifice with a PCM controlled pintle. During operation, the PCM controls pintle position by monitoring the pintle position feedback signal. The PCM uses information from the Engine Coolant Temperature (ECT) sensor, Throttle Position (TP) sensor and the Mass Air Flow (MAF) sensor to determine the appropriate rate of flow for a particular engine operating condition.

COMPONENT TESTING

Negative Backpressure EGR Valve

1. Inspect all passages and moving parts for plugging, sticking and deposits.
2. Inspect the entire system (hoses, tubes, connections, etc.) for leakage. Replace any part that is leaking, hardened, cracked, or melted.
3. Run the engine to normal operating temperature, and allow the engine to idle for 2 minutes. Quickly accelerate the engine to 2,500 rpm. Visible movement of the EGR stem should occur indicating proper system function. If no movement occurs, check the vacuum source and hose.
4. To determine if gas is flowing through the system, connect a vacuum pump to the valve.
5. With the engine idling, slowly apply vacuum. Engine speed should start to decrease when applied vacuum reaches 3 in. Hg. (10 kPa) The engine speed may drop quickly and could even stall; this indicates proper function.

6. If engine speed does not drop off, remove the EGR valve and check for plugged passages. If everything checks out, replace the valve.

Digital EGR Valve

➡ **This system must be checked using a Tech 1® or equivalent scan tool. Steps 4, 5 and 6 must be done very quickly, as the ECM will adjust the idle air control valve to compensate for idle speed.**

1. Using a Tech 1® or equivalent scan tool, check for any diagnostic trouble codes and solve those problems first. Refer to the Diagnostic Trouble Code (DTC) lists later in this section.
2. Select "EGR CONTROL" on the scan tool.
3. Start and run the engine, until it reaches normal operating temperature, then allow the engine to idle for 2 minutes.
4. Energize EGR SOL #1; engine rpm should drop slightly.
5. Energize EGR SOL #2; the engine should have a rough idle.
6. Energize EGR SOL #3; the engine should idle rough or stall.
7. If all tests were as specified, the system is functioning properly.
8. If not, check the EGR valve, pipe, adapter, gaskets, fittings, and all passages for damage, leakage or plugging. If all is OK, replace the EGR valve assembly.

Linear EGR Valve

▶ See Figure 15

To check this system, refer to the accompanying diagnostic chart for 1994–96 3.8L engines.

Integrated Electronic EGR Valve

▶ See Figure 16

To check this system, refer to the accompanying diagnostic chart.

REMOVAL & INSTALLATION

Except Digital EGR Valve

▶ See Figure 17

1. Disconnect the negative battery cable.
2. If necessary for access, remove the air cleaner assembly.
3. Tag and disconnect the necessary hoses and wiring to gain access to the EGR valve.
4. Unfasten the EGR valve retaining bolts.
5. Remove the EGR valve and gasket. Discard the gasket.
6. Buff the exhaust deposits from the mounting surface and around the valve using a wire wheel.
7. Remove deposits from the valve outlet.
8. Clean the mounting surfaces of the intake manifold and valve assembly.
To install:
9. Install a new EGR gasket.
10. Position the EGR valve to the manifold.
11. Install the retaining bolts and tighten to 16 ft. lbs. (22 Nm).
12. Connect the wiring and hoses.
13. Install the air cleaner assembly, if removed.
14. Connect the negative battery cable.

Digital EGR Valve

▶ See Figures 18, 19, 20, 21 and 22

1. Disconnect the negative battery cable.
2. Detach the electrical connector from the solenoid.
3. Unfasten the 2 base-to-flange bolts, then remove the digital EGR valve.
4. Remove and discard the gasket. Thoroughly clean the gasket mating surfaces.

To install:
5. Position a new gasket, then install the digital EGR valve.
6. Install the 2 base-to-flange bolts. Tighten to 22 ft. lbs. (30 Nm).
7. Attach the electrical connector to the solenoid.
8. Connect the negative battery cable.

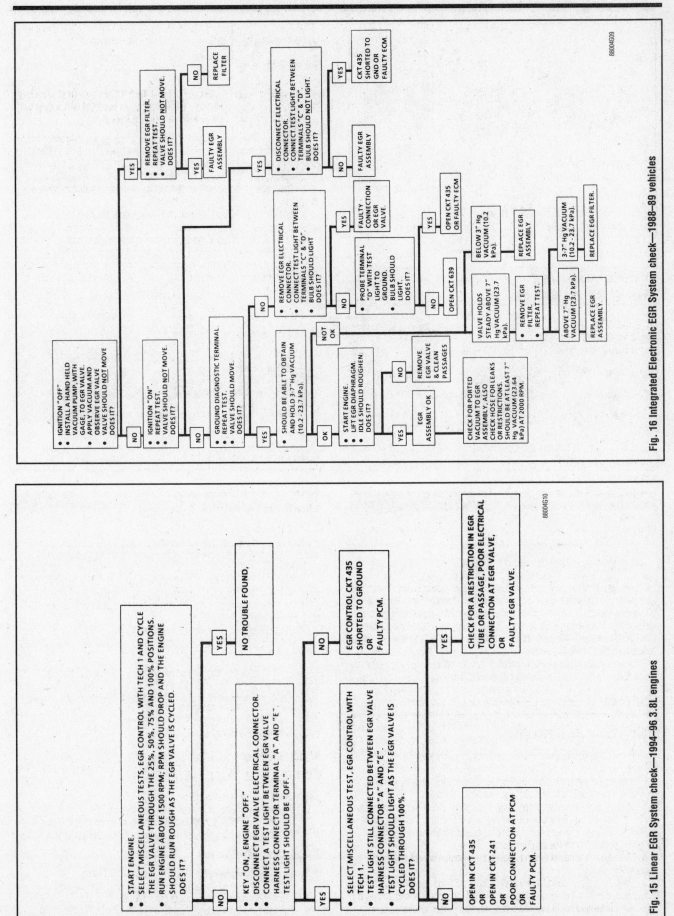

Fig. 16 Integrated Electronic EGR System check—1988-89 vehicles

Fig. 15 Linear EGR System check—1994-96 3.8L engines

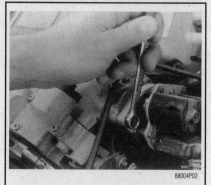

Fig. 17 Negative backpressure EGR valve mounting—2.5L engine

Fig. 18 Detach the electrical connector

Fig. 19 Unfasten the base-to-flange bolts . . .

Fig. 20 . . . then remove the digital EGR valve from the vehicle

Fig. 21 Remove and discard the EGR valve gasket

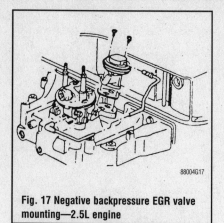

Fig. 22 Use a suitable scraper to thoroughly clean the gasket mating surfaces

Catalytic Converter

OPERATION

The catalytic converter is mounted in the engine exhaust stream ahead of the muffler. Its function is to combine carbon monoxide (CO) and hydrocarbons (HC) with oxygen and break down nitrogen oxide (NOx) compounds. These gasses are converted to mostly CO_2 and water. It heats to operating temperature within about 1–2 minutes, depending on ambient and driving conditions and will operate at temperatures up to about 1500 °F (816 °C). Inside the converter housing is a single or dual bed ceramic monolith, coated with various combinations of platinum, palladium and rhodium.

The catalytic converter is not serviceable. If tests and visual inspection show the converter to be damaged, it must be replaced. There are 2 types of failures: melting or fracturing. The most common failure is melting, resulting from unburned gasoline contacting the monolith, such as when a cylinder does not fire. Usually when the monolith melts, high backpressure results. When it cracks, it begins to break up into small particles that get blown out the tail pipe.

Poor fuel mileage and/or a lack of power can often be traced to a melted or plugged catalytic converter. The damage may be the result of engine malfunction or the use of leaded gasoline in the vehicle. Proper diagnosis for a restricted exhaust system is essential before any components are replaced. The following procedure that can be used to determine if the exhaust system is restricted.

INSPECTION

1. Raise and safely support the vehicle.
2. Inspect the catalytic converter protector for any damage.

➡ If any part of the protector is dented to the extent that is contacts the converter, replace it.

3. Check the heat insulator for adequate clearance between the converter and the heat insulator. Repair or replace any damaged components.

Air Injection Reaction (AIR) System

OPERATION

The Air Injection Reaction (AIR) system is used to reduce carbon monoxide (CO), hydrocarbon (HC) and oxides of nitrogen (NOx) emissions. The system also heats up the catalytic converter on engine start-up so the exhaust gases will be converted more quickly. This system is only utilized on 6-cylinder engines with manual transaxles.

The system consists of the following components.

Air Pump

An air pump may be either belt driven off the crankshaft (2.8L and 3.1L engines) or electric and accessed from under the vehicle, after the right front inner fender splash shield is removed (3.4L engine). The air pump supplies air to the AIR system.

Control Valve

Air flows through the pump through an ECM controlled valve (called a control valve) through a check valve to the exhaust ports or to the atmosphere.

Check Valve

The check valve prevents back flow of exhaust into the pump in the event of an exhaust backfire.

AIR System Control Valve

2.8L AND 3.1L ENGINES

The Electric Air Control (EAC) valve combines electronic control with the normal diverter valve function. This valve can be electronically controlled to provide divert air under any driving mode.

When the solenoid is de-energized, the pressurized air from the air pump is allowed to enter the decel timing chamber. This places sufficient pressure on the metering valve diaphragm to overcome spring tension, closing the valve, causing air to divert to the atmosphere (silencer).

At higher engine speeds, excess air is exhausted to the atmosphere (silencer) through the pressure relief valve.

Pulsair Shut-off Valve

3.4L ENGINES

▶ **See Figure 23**

A pulsair air management system makes the use of the vacuum peaks naturally occurring at the exhaust ports. This vacuum draws air through the shut-off valve through a one-way valve, and into the exhaust ports.

A pulsair shut-off valve shuts off air to the pulsair system when the ECM decides air is not desirable, such as during deceleration. When the solenoid is energized, intake manifold vacuum is applied to the bottom of the diaphragm and pulls the valve open against spring tension, allowing air to flow from the clean side of the air cleaner to the exhaust ports.

When the ECM de-energizes the solenoid, no vacuum can be applied to the diaphragm, and spring tension forces the valve closed.

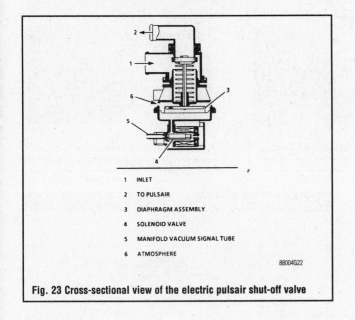

1	INLET
2	TO PULSAIR
3	DIAPHRAGM ASSEMBLY
4	SOLENOID VALVE
5	MANIFOLD VACUUM SIGNAL TUBE
6	ATMOSPHERE

88004G22

Fig. 23 Cross-sectional view of the electric pulsair shut-off valve

INSPECTION

Air Pump

1. Check the pump for a seized condition.
2. Check hoses, tubes, and connections for leaks and proper routing.
3. Check for air flow from the control/divert valve.
4. Check the pump for proper mounting.
5. If no irregularities exist and the pump is noisy, replace the pump assembly.

➡**Do not attempt to lubricate the pump.**

Hoses and Pipes

1. Check the hoses or pipes for deterioration or holes.
2. Inspect all hoses for pipe connections, and clamp tightness.
3. Check hose and pipe routing. Interference may cause wear.
4. If a leak is suspected on the pressure side of the system, or if a hose or pipe has been disconnected on the pressure side, the connections should be checked for leaks with a soapy water solution. With the air pump running, bubbles will form if a leak exists.

Check Valve

1. A check valve should be inspected whenever the hose is disconnected from a check valve or whenever check valve failure is suspected.
2. Blow through the check valve (toward the exhaust manifold) then, attempt to suck back through the check valve. Flow should only be in one direction (toward the manifold). Replace a valve which does not operate properly

COMPONENT TESTING

▶ **See Figures 24, 25 and 26**

Please refer to the accompanying charts for AIR system testing.

REMOVAL & INSTALLATION

Air Pump

2.8L AND 3.1L ENGINES

▶ **See Figure 27**

1. Disconnect the negative battery cable.
2. Hold the pump pulley from turning by compressing the drive belt, then loosen the pump pulley bolts.
3. Loosen the pump mounting bracket bolts and release the tension from the belt.
4. Move the belt out of the way.
5. Remove the hoses, vacuum and electrical connections from the pump.
6. Remove the pulley from the pump.
7. If required, insert needle nose pliers and pull the filter fan from the hub.
To install:
8. Install the air pump to the mounting brackets, then tighten the bolts to the specifications shown in the accompanying illustration.
9. Attach the hoses, vacuum and electrical connections to the pump.
10. Install the control valve.
11. Install a new filter fan onto the pump hub.
12. Install the spacer and pump pulley against the centrifugal filter fan.
13. Tighten the pulley bolts to 10 ft. lbs. (13 Nm).

➡**The preceding procedure will compress the centrifugal filter fan onto the pump hole. Do NOT drive the filter fan on with a hammer. There**

- CHECK FOR AT LEAST 34 KPA (10") OF VACUUM AT VALVE WITH ENGINE IDLING.
- RUN ENGINE AT PART THROTTLE (UNDER 2000 RPM).
- AIR SHOULD GO TO EXHAUST PORTS UNTIL SYSTEM GOES "CLOSED LOOP", THEN DIVERT.

NOT OK →
- IGN "ON", ENGINE STOPPED.
- REMOVE CONNECTOR FROM DIVERT VALVE AND CONNECT A TEST LIGHT BETWEEN CONNECTOR TERMINALS.

OK → NO TROUBLE FOUND

LIGHT "OFF" →
- GROUND DIAGNOSTIC TERM.
- NOTE LIGHT.

LIGHT "ON" → CKT 429 SHORTED TO GROUND OR FAULTY ECM.

LIGHT "OFF" → PROBE EACH TERMINAL WITH A TEST LIGHT TO GROUND.

LIGHT "ON" → FAULTY DIVERT VALVE CONNECTIONS OR VALVE.

LIGHT "ON" ONE → OPEN CKT 429 OR FAULTY ECM.

LIGHT "ON" BOTH → REPAIR SHORT TO VOLTAGE IN CKT 429.

NO LIGHT → OPEN CKT 250

88004G23

Fig. 24 AIR system testing—2.8L and 3.1L engines

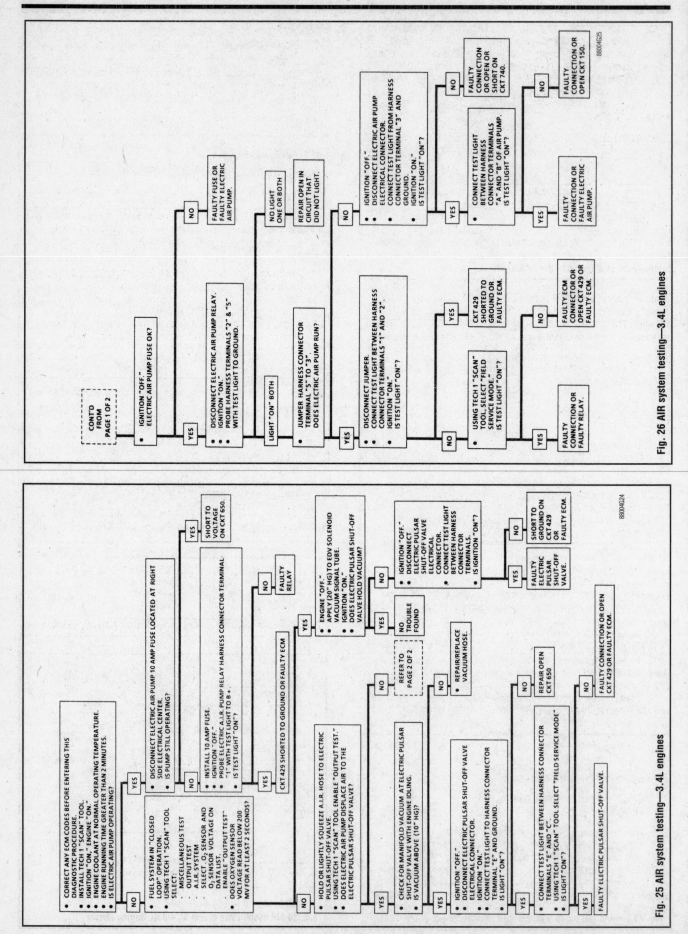

Fig. 26 AIR system testing—3.4L engines

Fig. 25 AIR system testing—3.4L engines

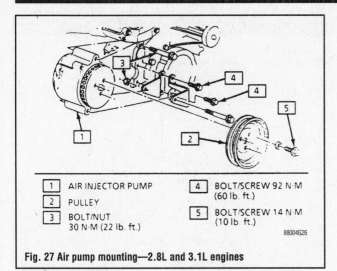

Fig. 27 Air pump mounting—2.8L and 3.1L engines

1	AIR INJECTOR PUMP	4	BOLT/SCREW 92 N·M (60 lb. ft.)
2	PULLEY	5	BOLT/SCREW 14 N·M (10 lb. ft.)
3	BOLT/NUT 30 N·M (22 lb. ft.)		

88004G26

might be a slight amount of interference with the housing bore, this is normal. After the new filter has been installed, it may squeal upon initial operation until the outside diameter sealing lip has worn in. This may require a short period of pump operation at various engine speeds.

14. Install the pump drive belt and adjust.
15. Connect the negative battery cable, then start the engine and check for air injection system operation.

3.4L ENGINE

▶ See Figure 28

1. Disconnect the negative battery cable.
2. Raise and safely support the vehicle. Remove the right front wheel and tire assembly.
3. Unfasten the 3 right side inner fender splash shield retaining bolts/screws. Remove the 2 inner fender support bracket bolts/screws.
4. Disconnect the air outlet hose from the electric air pump.
5. Detach the vacuum hose from the electric pulsair shut-off valve.
6. Remove the 3 air pump retaining bolts/screws.
7. Carefully lower the air pump assembly, then detach the 4-pin harness connector and the wiring harness clip.
8. Remove the electric air pump assembly.
9. Unfasten the electric pulsair shut-off valve bolt/screw from the pump bracket.
10. Detach the inlet hose and the 2-pin wire harness connector from the pulsair shut-off valve.
11. Remove the electric pulsair shut-off valve from the bracket.
To install:
12. Fasten the pulsair shut-off valve bolt/screw to the air pump bracket.
13. Attach the inlet hose and 2-pin wire harness connector to the pulsair shut-off valve.
14. Position the electric air pump assembly in the upper right front fender well while attaching the 4-pin harness connector.

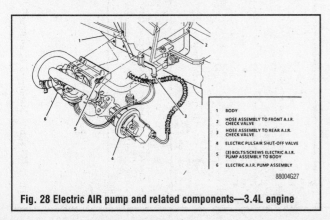

1	BODY
2	HOSE ASSEMBLY TO FRONT A.I.R. CHECK VALVE
3	HOSE ASSEMBLY TO REAR A.I.R. CHECK VALVE
4	ELECTRIC PULSAIR SHUT-OFF VALVE
5	(3) BOLTS/SCREWS ELECTRIC A.I.R. PUMP ASSEMBLY TO BODY
6	ELECTRIC A.I.R. PUMP ASSEMBLY

88004G27

Fig. 28 Electric AIR pump and related components—3.4L engine

15. Install the 3 air pump retaining bolts/screws.
16. Fasten the 4-pin harness connector body clip.
17. Attach the air outlet hose and vacuum hose.
18. Install the 2 inner fender support bracket bolts/screws and the 3 right side inner fender splash shield bolts/screws.
19. Install the right front wheel and tire assembly, then carefully lower the vehicle.
20. Connect the negative battery cable, then start the engine and check for proper system operation.

AIR System Check Valve

▶ See Figures 29 and 30

1. Disconnect the negative battery cable.

➡The 2.8L and 3.1L engines use one check valve. The 3.4L engine may utilize two check valves; one on the right side and one on the left.

2. Remove any engine components necessary for access to the right or left side check valve, as applicable.
3. Unfasten the clamp, then disconnect the air hose from the check valve(s).
4. Unscrew the check valve from the air injection pipe.
To install:
5. Screw the check valve onto the air injection pipe.
6. Connect the air hose to the check valve(s) and secure with the clamp.
7. Install any components removed for access to the check valve(s).
8. Connect the negative battery cable.

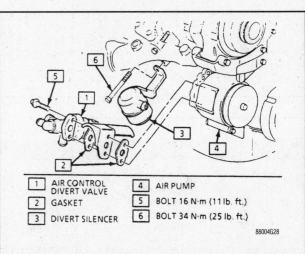

1	AIR CONTROL DIVERT VALVE	4	AIR PUMP
2	GASKET	5	BOLT 16 N·m (11 lb. ft.)
3	DIVERT SILENCER	6	BOLT 34 N·m (25 lb. ft.)

88004G28

Fig. 29 Control valve and related components—3.1L engine shown

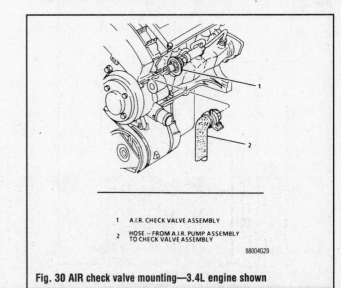

1	A.I.R. CHECK VALVE ASSEMBLY
2	HOSE — FROM A.I.R. PUMP ASSEMBLY TO CHECK VALVE ASSEMBLY

88004G29

Fig. 30 AIR check valve mounting—3.4L engine shown

ELECTRONIC ENGINE CONTROLS

Electronic Control Module (ECM)

OPERATION

➡When the term Electronic Control Module (ECM) is used in this manual it will refer to the engine control computer regardless that it may be a Powertrain Control Module (PCM) or Electronic Control Module (ECM).

The heart of the electronic control system, which is found on the vehicles covered by this manual, is a computer control module. The module gathers information from various sensors, then controls fuel supply and engine emission systems. Most early model vehicles are equipped with an Engine Control Module (ECM) which, as its name implies, controls the engine and related emissions systems. Some ECMs may also control the Torque Converter Clutch (TCC) on automatic transaxle vehicles or the manual upshift light on manual transmission vehicles. Later model vehicles may be equipped with a Powertrain Control Module (PCM). This is similar to the original ECMs, but is designed to control additional systems as well. The PCM may control the manual transmission shift lamp or the shift functions of the electronically controlled automatic transmission.

Regardless of the name, all computer control modules are serviced in a similar manner. Care must be taken when handling these expensive components in order to protect them from damage. Carefully follow all instructions included with the replacement part. Avoid touching pins or connectors to prevent damage from static electricity.

All of these computer control modules contain a Programmable Read Only Memory (PROM) chip, MEM-CAL or EEPROM that contains calibration information which is particular to the vehicle application. For all applications except those equipped with an EEPROM, this chip is not supplied with a replacement module, and must be transferred to the new module before installation. If equipped with an Electronically Erasable Programmable Read Only Memory (EEPROM), it must be reprogrammed after installation. Some later model vehicles have a Knock Sensor (KS) module, mounted in the PCM. The KS module contains the circuitry that allows the PCM to utilize the Knock Sensor signal to diagnose the circuitry.

✻✻ WARNING

To prevent the possibility of permanent control module damage, the ignition switch MUST always be OFF when disconnecting power from or reconnecting power to the module. This includes unplugging the module connector, disconnecting the negative battery cable, removing the module fuse or even attempting to jump your dead battery using jumper cables.

In the event of an ECM failure, the system will default to a pre-programmed set of values. These are compromise values which allow the engine to operate, although at a reduced efficiency. This is variously known as the default, limp-in or back-up mode. Driveability is almost always affected when the ECM enters this mode.

REMOVAL & INSTALLATION

▶ See Figures 31, 32, 33, 34 and 35

For most applications, the computer control module is located in the engine compartment, in front of the right side shock tower. Some applications have the module mounted inside the passenger compartment under the instrument panel.

1. Make sure the ignition switch is turned **OFF**, then disconnect the negative battery cable.

✻✻ CAUTION

To prevent the possibility of permanent control module damage, the ignition switch MUST always be OFF when disconnecting power from or reconnecting power to the module. This includes unplugging the module connector, disconnecting the negative battery cable, removing the module fuse or even attempting to jump your dead battery using jumper cables.

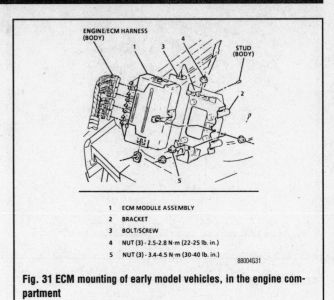

1	ECM MODULE ASSEMBLY
2	BRACKET
3	BOLT/SCREW
4	NUT (3) - 2.5-2.8 N·m (22-25 lb. in.)
5	NUT (3) - 3.4-4.5 N·m (30-40 lb. in.)

88004G31

Fig. 31 ECM mounting of early model vehicles, in the engine compartment

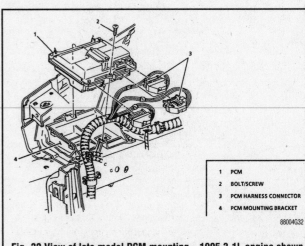

1	PCM
2	BOLT/SCREW
3	PCM HARNESS CONNECTOR
4	PCM MOUNTING BRACKET

88004G32

Fig. 32 View of late model PCM mounting—1995 3.1L engine shown

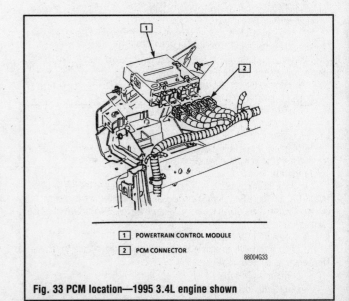

1	POWERTRAIN CONTROL MODULE
2	PCM CONNECTOR

88004G33

Fig. 33 PCM location—1995 3.4L engine shown

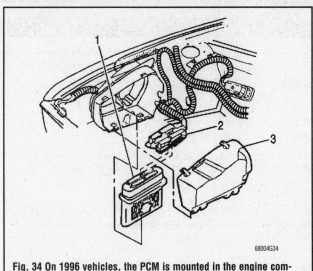

Fig. 34 On 1996 vehicles, the PCM is mounted in the engine compartment

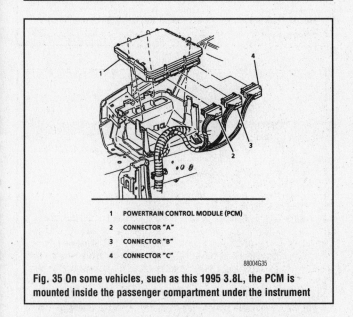

1	POWERTRAIN CONTROL MODULE (PCM)
2	CONNECTOR "A"
3	CONNECTOR "B"
4	CONNECTOR "C"

Fig. 35 On some vehicles, such as this 1995 3.8L, the PCM is mounted inside the passenger compartment under the instrument

2. Locate the computer control module. If not readily visible on the right side of the engine compartment, it is probably mounted inside the passenger compartment, under the dash.

3. If equipped with a passenger compartment mounted module, remove the interior access panel/right side hush panel.

4. If equipped with an engine compartment mounted module, one or all of the following steps may be necessary:
   a. Remove the coolant tank reservoir.
   b. Remove the air cleaner intake duct.
   c. Remove the right side splash shield.
   d. Remove the plastic ECM cover.

5. Carefully detach the harness connectors from the ECM.

6. Remove the ECM-to-bracket retaining screws and remove the ECM, then remove the ECM from the engine compartment.

To install:

7. If the module is being replaced, CAREFULLY replace the PROM chip, MEM-CAL or Knock Sensor (KS) module, as outlined later in this section.

8. Position the ECM in the vehicle and install the ECM-to-bracket retaining screws.

9. Attach the ECM harness connectors.

10. If equipped with an engine compartment mounted module, install the following components, as applicable.
   a. Plastic ECM cover.

b. Right side splash shield.
   c. Air cleaner intake duct.
   d. Coolant tank reservoir.

11. If equipped with a passenger compartment mounted module, install the hush panel/interior access panel.

12. Check that the ignition switch is **OFF**, then connect the negative battery cable.

13. If equipped with a computer control module that contains an EEPROM, it must be reprogrammed using a Tech 1® or equivalent scan tool and the latest available software. In all likelihood, the vehicle must be towed to a dealer or repair shop containing the suitable equipment for this service.

14. Perform the functional check, as outlined later in this section.

PROM/MEM-CAL/KS Module

REMOVAL & INSTALLATION

▶ **See Figures 36, 37 and 38**

As stated earlier, all computer control modules container information regarding the correct parameters for engine and system operation based on vehicle applications. In most modules, this information takes the form of a PROM chip or MEM-CAL, though some modules also store this information in an EEPROM. Some later model vehicles, also include a Knock Sensor (KS) module which is replaced like the PROM and MEM-CAL.

Replacement computers are normally not equipped with this PROM/MEM-CAL/KS module; you must transfer the chip from the old component. The EEPROM is a permanent memory that is physically soldered within the PCM. Unlike the PROM used in some earlier applications or the MEM-CAL, the EEPROM is not serviceable. If the PCM is replaced, the new PCM will have to programmed using a Tech 1® or equivalent scan tool.

✳✳ WARNING

The PROM/MEM-CAL chip, KS module and computer control module are EXTREMELY sensitive to electrical or mechanical damage. NEVER touch the connector pins or soldered components on the circuit board in order to prevent possible electrostatic damage to the components.

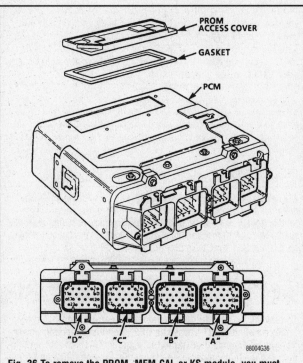

Fig. 36 To remove the PROM, MEM-CAL or KS module, you must remove the access cover on the control module

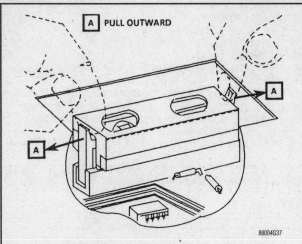

Fig. 37 The retaining tabs must be pushed back to release the unit—MEM-CAL shown, others similar

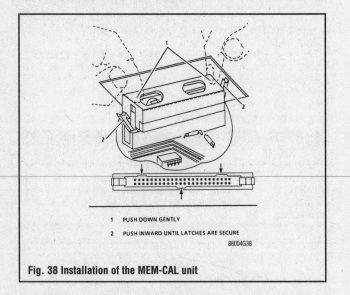

1 PUSH DOWN GENTLY
2 PUSH INWARD UNTIL LATCHES ARE SECURE

88004G38

Fig. 38 Installation of the MEM-CAL unit

1. Make sure the ignition switch is **OFF**, then remove the computer control module from the vehicle.
2. Remove the access panel. Note the position of the MEM-CAL/PROM/KS module for proper installation in the new ECM.
3. Using 2 fingers, carefully push both retaining clips back away from the MEM-CAL/PROM/KS module. At the same time, grasp it at both ends and lift it up out of the socket. Do not remove the cover of the MEM-CAL/PROM/KS module.

To install:
4. Fit the replacement MEM-CAL/PROM/KS module into the socket.

➥**The small notches in the MEM-CAL/PROM/KS module must be aligned with the small notches in the socket. Press only on the ends of the MEM-CAL/PROM/KS module until the retaining clips snap into the ends of the MEM-CAL/PROM/KS module. Do not press on the middle of the MEM-CAL/PROM/KS module, only the ends.**

5. Install the access cover and retaining screws.
6. Make sure the ignition switch is still **OFF**, then install the ECM, as outlined earlier in this section.

FUNCTIONAL CHECK

1988–94 Vehicles, Except 1994 3.4L Engine

1. Turn the ignition switch **ON**.
2. Enter diagnostics, as outlined later in this section.

a. Allow Code 12 to flash 4 times to verify no other codes are present. This indicates the PROM/MEM-CAL is installed properly and the ECM is functioning.
b. If trouble Codes 42, 43 or 51 occur, or if the Service Engine Soon light is ON constantly with no codes, the Mem-Cal is not fully seated or is defective.
c. If it is not fully seated, press firmly on the ends of the PROM/MEM-CAL.
3. If installed backwards, replace the PROM/MEM-CAL.

➥**Any time the PROM is installed backwards and the ignition switch is turned ON, the PROM is destroyed.**

4. If the pins are bent, remove the PROM/MEM-CAL, straighten the pins and reinstall the PROM/MEM-CAL. If the bent pins break or crack during straightening, discard the PROM/MEM-CAL and replace with a new PROM/MEM-CAL.

➥**To prevent possible electrostatic discharge damage to the PROM or MEM-CAL, do not touch the component leads and do not remove the integrated circuit from the carrier.**

1994 3.4L Engine and All 1995–96 Vehicles

1. Using a Tech 1® or equivalent scan tool, perform the on-board diagnostic system check.
2. Start the engine and run for one minute.
3. Scan for DTC's using the Tech 1® or equivalent scan tool, as outlined later in this section.
4. If trouble codes P0325, P1361, P1350, or P1623 occurs, or if the MIL (Service Engine Soon) is ON constantly with no diagnostic trouble codes, the PROM or KS module is not fully seated or is defective.
5. If it is not fully seated, press firmly on the ends of the PROM/KS module.

Oxygen Sensor

OPERATION

There are two types of oxygen sensor's used in these vehicles. They are the single wire oxygen sensor (02S) and the heated oxygen sensor (H02S). The oxygen sensor is a spark plug shaped device that is screwed into the exhaust manifold. It monitors the oxygen content of the exhaust gases and sends a voltage signal to the Electronic Control Module (ECM). The ECM monitors this voltage and, depending on the value of the received signal, issues a command to the mixture control solenoid on the carburetor to adjust for rich or lean conditions.

The heated oxygen sensor has a heating element incorporated into the sensor to aid in the warm up to the proper operating temperature and to maintain that temperature.

The proper operation of the oxygen sensor depends upon four basic conditions:
1. Good electrical connections. Since the sensor generates low currents, good clean electrical connections at the sensor are a must.
2. Outside air supply. Air must circulate to the internal portion of the sensor. When servicing the sensor, do not restrict the air passages.
3. Proper operating temperatures. The ECM will not recognize the sensor's signals until the sensor reaches approximately 600°F (316°C).
4. Non-leaded fuel. The use of leaded gasoline will damage the sensor very quickly.

Precautions:

• Careful handling of the oxygen sensor is essential.
• The electrical pigtail and connector are permanently attached and should not be removed from the oxygen sensor.
• The inline electrical connector and louvered end of the oxygen sensor must be kept free of grease, dirt and other contaminants.
• Avoid using cleaning solvents of any type on the oxygen sensor.
• Do not drop or roughly handle the oxygen sensor.
• The oxygen sensor may be difficult to remove if the engine temperature is below 120°F (48°C). Excessive force may damage the threads in the exhaust manifold or exhaust pipe.

TESTING

Single Wire Sensor

♦ See Figures 39 and 40

1. Start the engine and bring it to normal operating temperature, then run the engine above 1200 rpm for two minutes.

2. Backprobe with a high impedance averaging voltmeter (set to the DC voltage scale) between the oxygen sensor (02S) and battery ground.

3. Verify that the 02S voltage fluctuates rapidly between 0.35–0.55 volts.

4. If the 02S voltage is stabilized at the middle of the specified range (approximately 0.40–0.50 volts) or if the 02S voltage fluctuates very slowly between the specified range (02S signal crosses 0.5 volts less than 5 times in ten seconds), the 02S may be faulty.

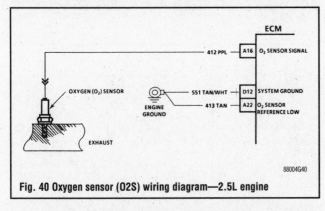

Fig. 39 Oxygen sensor (02S) wiring diagram, except 2.5L engine

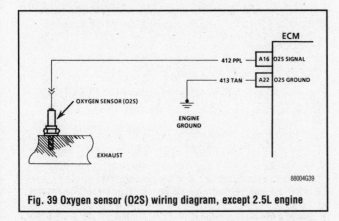

Fig. 40 Oxygen sensor (02S) wiring diagram—2.5L engine

5. If the 02S voltage stabilizes at either end of the specified range, the ECM is probably not able to compensate for a mechanical problem such as a vacuum leak or a faulty pressure regulator. These types of mechanical problems will cause the 02S to sense a constant lean or constant rich mixture. The mechanical problem will first have to be repaired and then the 02S test repeated.

6. Pull a vacuum hose located after the throttle plate. Voltage should drop to approximately 0.12 volts (while still fluctuating rapidly). This tests the ability of the 02S to detect a lean mixture condition. Reattach the vacuum hose.

7. Richen the mixture using a propane enrichment tool. Voltage should rise to approximately 0.90 volts (while still fluctuating rapidly). This tests the ability of the 02S to detect a rich mixture condition.

8. If the 02S voltage is above or below the specified range, the 02S and/or the 02S wiring may be faulty. Check the wiring for any breaks, repair as necessary and repeat the test.

Heated Oxygen Sensor

♦ See Figures 41, 42, 43 and 44

1. Start the engine and bring it to normal operating temperature, then run the engine above 1200 rpm for two minutes.

2. Turn the ignition **OFF**, then disengage the H02S harness connector.

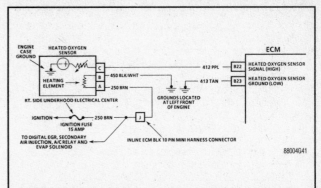

Fig. 41 Heated Oxygen Sensor (H02S) wiring diagram—1993 vehicles

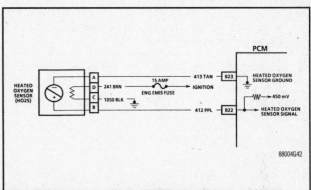

Fig. 42 Heated Oxygen Sensor (H02S) wiring diagram—1994–96 3.1L engines

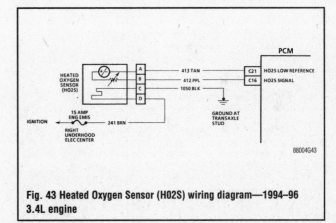

Fig. 43 Heated Oxygen Sensor (H02S) wiring diagram—1994–96 3.4L engine

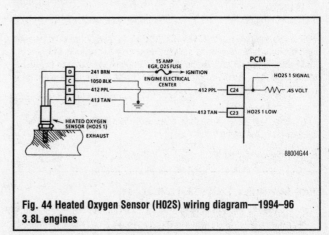

Fig. 44 Heated Oxygen Sensor (H02S) wiring diagram—1994–96 3.8L engines

3. Connect a test light between harness terminals A and B. With the ignition switch **ON** and the engine off, verify that the test light is lit. If the test light is not lit, either the supply voltage to the H02S heater or the ground circuit of the H02S heater is faulty. Check the H02S wiring and the fuse.

4. Next, connect a high impedance ohmmeter between the H02S terminals B and A and verify that the resistance is 3.5–14.0 ohms.

5. If the H02S heater resistance is not as specified, the H02S may be faulty.

6. Start the engine and bring it to normal operating temperature, then run the engine above 1200 rpm for two minutes.

7. Backprobe with a high impedance averaging voltmeter (set to the DC voltage scale) between the oxygen sensor (02S) and battery ground.

8. Verify that the 02S voltage fluctuates rapidly between 0.35–0.55 volts.

9. If the 02S voltage is stabilized at the middle of the specified range (approximately 0.40–0.50 volts) or if the 02S voltage fluctuates very slowly between the specified range (02S signal crosses 0.5 volts less than 5 times in ten seconds), the 02S may be faulty.

10. If the 02S voltage stabilizes at either end of the specified range, the ECM is probably not able to compensate for a mechanical problem such as a vacuum leak or a faulty fuel pressure regulator. These types of mechanical problems will cause the 02S to sense a constant lean or constant rich mixture. The mechanical problem will first have to be repaired and then the 02S test repeated.

11. Pull a vacuum hose located after the throttle plate. Voltage should drop to approximately 0.12 volts (while still fluctuating rapidly). This tests the ability of the 02S to detect a lean mixture condition. Reattach the vacuum hose.

12. Richen the mixture using a propane enrichment tool. Voltage should rise to approximately 0.90 volts (while still fluctuating rapidly). This tests the ability of the 02S to detect a rich mixture condition.

13. If the 02S voltage is above or below the specified range, the 02S and/or the 02S wiring may be faulty. Check the wiring for any breaks, repair as necessary and repeat the test.

REMOVAL & INSTALLATION

◆ **See Figures 45 thru 51**

✳✳ WARNING

The sensor uses a permanently attached pigtail and connector. This pigtail should not be removed from the sensor. Damage or removal of the pigtail or connector could affect the proper operation of the sensor. Keep the electrical connector and louvered end of the sensor clean and free of grease. NEVER use cleaning solvents of any type on the sensor!

➡The oxygen sensor may be difficult to remove when the temperature of the engine is below 120°F (49°C). Excessive force may damage the threads in the exhaust manifold or exhaust pipe.

1. Disconnect the negative battery cable.

2. For 3.1L engines, unbolt the coolant recovery reservoir (do not disconnect the hoses) and position aside. Unfasten the engine torque strut bolt, then rotate the engine forward.

3. If necessary for access, raise and safely support the vehicle, remove the intermediate pipe and heat shield.

4. Unplug the electrical connector and any attaching hardware.

➡Some late model vehicles utilize two oxygen sensors.

5. Remove the sensor from the vehicle. For some vehicles, it may be necessary to use tool J 29533/BT-8127 or equivalent to remove the sensor.

To install:

6. Coat the threads of the sensor with a GM anti-seize compound, part number 5613695, or its equivalent, before installation. New sensors are pre-coated with this compound.

➡The GM anti-seize compound is NOT a conventional anti-seize paste. The use of a regular paste may electrically insulate the sensor, rendering it useless. The threads MUST be coated with the proper electrically conductive anti-seize compound.

7. Install the sensor and tighten to 30 ft. lbs. (40 Nm). Use care in making

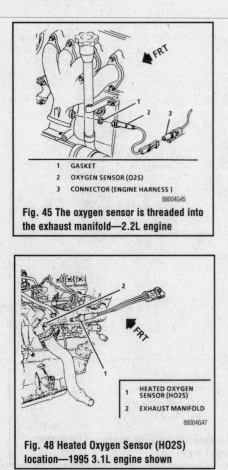

1 GASKET
2 OXYGEN SENSOR (02S)
3 CONNECTOR (ENGINE HARNESS)
88004G45

Fig. 45 The oxygen sensor is threaded into the exhaust manifold—2.2L engine

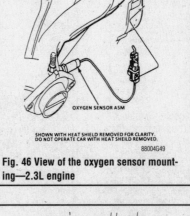

OXYGEN SENSOR ASM

SHOWN WITH HEAT SHIELD REMOVED FOR CLARITY.
DO NOT OPERATE CAR WITH HEAT SHIELD REMOVED.
88004G49

Fig. 46 View of the oxygen sensor mounting—2.3L engine

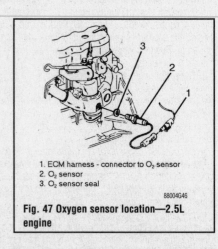

1. ECM harness - connector to O_2 sensor
2. O_2 sensor
3. O_2 sensor seal
88004G46

Fig. 47 Oxygen sensor location—2.5L engine

1 HEATED OXYGEN SENSOR (H02S)
2 EXHAUST MANIFOLD
88004G47

Fig. 48 Heated Oxygen Sensor (H02S) location—1995 3.1L engine shown

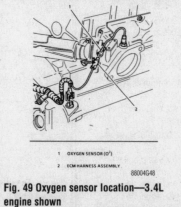

1 OXYGEN SENSOR (O^2)
2 ECM HARNESS ASSEMBLY
88004G48

Fig. 49 Oxygen sensor location—3.4L engine shown

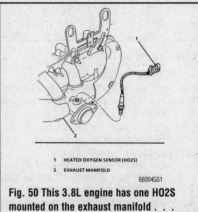

1 HEATED OXYGEN SENSOR (H02S)
2 EXHAUST MANIFOLD
88004G51

Fig. 50 This 3.8L engine has one H02S mounted on the exhaust manifold . . .

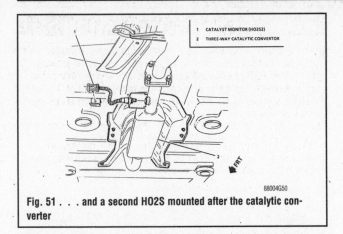

Fig. 51 . . . and a second HO2S mounted after the catalytic converter

sure the silicone boot is in the correct position to avoid melting it during operation.

8. Engage the electrical connector.

9. If necessary, install the heat shield, attach the intermediate pipe, then carefully lower the vehicle.

10. On 3.1L engines, rotate the engine back to its original position, then install the torque strut bolt. Position and fasten the coolant recovery reservoir.

11. Connect the negative battery cable.

Idle Air Control (IAC) Valve

OPERATION

Engine idle speeds are controlled by the ECM through the IAC valve mounted on the throttle body. The ECM sends voltage pulses to the IAC motor windings causing the IAC motor shaft and pintle to move in or out a given distance (number of steps) for each pulse (called counts). The movement of the pintle controls the airflow around the throttle plate, which in turn, controls engine idle speed. IAC valve pintle position counts can be observed using a scan tool. Zero (0) counts correspond to a fully closed passage, while 140 counts or more correspond to full flow.

Idle speed can be categorized in 2 ways: actual (controlled) idle speed and minimum idle speed. Controlled idle speed is obtained by the ECM positioning the IAC valve pintle. Resulting idle speed is determined by total air flow (IAC passage + PCV + throttle valve + calibrated vacuum leaks). Controlled idle speed is specified at normal operating conditions, which consists of engine coolant at normal operating temperature, air conditioning compressor off, manual transmission in Neutral or automatic transmission in **D**.

Minimum idle air speed is set at the factory with a stop screw. This setting allows enough air flow by the throttle valves to cause the IAC valve pintle to be positioned a calibrated number of steps (counts) from the seat during normal controlled idle operation.

The idle speed is controlled by the ECM through the IAC valve. No adjustment is required during routine maintenance. Tampering with the minimum idle speed adjustment is highly discouraged and may result in premature failure of the IAC valve.

TESTING

▶ **See Figures 52 and 53**

1. Disengage the IAC electrical connector.
2. Using an ohmmeter, measure the resistance between IAC terminals **A** and **B**. Next measure the resistance between terminals **C** and **D**.
3. Verify that the resistance between both sets of IAC terminals is 40–80 ohms. If the resistance is not as specified, the IAC may be faulty.
4. Measure the resistance between IAC terminals **B** and **C**. Next measure the resistance between terminals **A** and **D**.
5. Verify that the resistance between both sets of IAC terminals is infinite. If the resistance is not infinite, the IAC may be faulty.
6. Also, with a small mirror, inspect IAC air inlet passage and pintle for debris. Clean as necessary, as this can cause IAC malfunction.

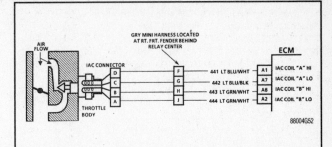

Fig. 52 Idle Air Control (IAC) valve wiring and terminal identification—1988–93 vehicles

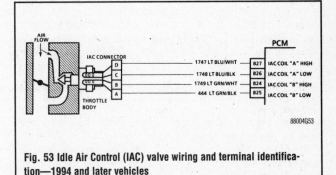

Fig. 53 Idle Air Control (IAC) valve wiring and terminal identification—1994 and later vehicles

REMOVAL & INSTALLATION

▶ **See Figures 54 and 55**

1. Disconnect the negative battery cable.
2. If necessary for access, remove the air cleaner.
3. Detach the electrical connector from the idle air control valve assembly.
4. Unfasten the retaining screws, then remove the IAC valve assembly from the throttle body. Clean the IAC valve O-ring sealing surface, pintle valve seat and air passage.

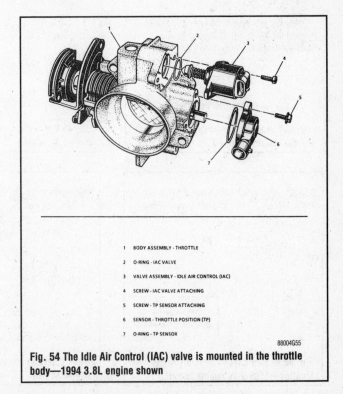

1	BODY ASSEMBLY - THROTTLE
2	O-RING - IAC VALVE
3	VALVE ASSEMBLY - IDLE AIR CONTROL (IAC)
4	SCREW - IAC VALVE ATTACHING
5	SCREW - TP SENSOR ATTACHING
6	SENSOR - THROTTLE POSITION (TP)
7	O-RING - TP SENSOR

Fig. 54 The Idle Air Control (IAC) valve is mounted in the throttle body—1994 3.8L engine shown

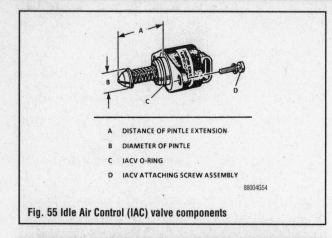

A   DISTANCE OF PINTLE EXTENSION
B   DIAMETER OF PINTLE
C   IACV O-RING
D   IACV ATTACHING SCREW ASSEMBLY

88004G54

Fig. 55 Idle Air Control (IAC) valve components

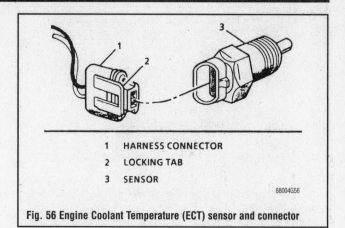

1   HARNESS CONNECTOR
2   LOCKING TAB
3   SENSOR

88004G56

Fig. 56 Engine Coolant Temperature (ECT) sensor and connector

※※ WARNING

If the IAC pintle has been in service, DO NOT push or pull in the valve pintle. The force required to move the pintle may damage the threads on the worm drive. Do not soak the valve in any liquid cleaner or solvent, as damage may result.

5. Use a suitable carburetor cleaner (be sure it is safe to use on systems equipped with a oxygen sensor) and a parts cleaning brush to remove the carbon deposits. Do not use a cleaner that contains methyl ethyl ketone. It is an extremely strong solvent and not necessary for this type of deposits. Shiny spots on the pintle or on the seat are normal and do not indicate a misalignment or a bent pintle shaft. If the air passage has heavy deposits, remove the throttle body for a complete cleaning.

To install:

➡ If you're installing a new IAC valve, you must replace if with an identical part. IAC valve pintle shape and diameter are designed for the specific application.

6. If you are installing a new IAC valve, measure the distance from the motor housing to end of the cone. If it is greater than 1⅛ in. (28mm), use finger pressure to slowly retract the pintle. The force required to retract the pintle of a NEW valve will not cause damage to the valve.

➡ The IAC valve pintle may also be retracted by using IAC/ISC Motor Tester J–37027/BT–8256K. Do not soak the IAC valve in any liquid cleaner or solvent as damage may result.

7. Install the new idle air control valve and tighten the retaining screws to 27 inch lbs. (3 Nm).
8. Attach the IAC valve electrical connections.
9. If removed, install the air cleaner assembly.
10. Connect the negative battery cable.
11. Reset the IAC valve as follows:
    a. Turn the ignition **ON** (engine off), for 5 seconds.
    b. Turn the ignition **OFF** for 10 seconds.
    c. Start the engine, then check for proper idle operation.

Coolant Temperature Sensor (CTS)

OPERATION

▶ See Figure 56

➡ On some vehicles, this may also be referred to as an Engine Coolant Temperature (ECT) sensor.

Most engine functions are affected by the coolant temperature. Determining whether the engine is hot or cold is largely dependent on the temperature of the coolant. An accurate temperature signal to the ECM is supplied by the coolant temperature sensor. The coolant temperature sensor is a thermistor mounted in the engine coolant stream. A thermistor is an electrical device that varies its resistance in relation to changes in temperature. Low coolant temperature pro-

duces a high resistance (100,000 ohms at 40°F/40°C) and high coolant temperature produces low resistance (70 ohms at 266°F/130°C). The ECM supplies a signal of 5 volts to the coolant temperature sensor through a resistor in the ECM and measures the voltage. The voltage will be high when the engine is cold and low when the engine is hot.

For 2.5L engines, the coolant temperature sensor is located on the left side of the cylinder head.

For MFI engines, the coolant temperature sensor is located on the intake manifold water jacket or near (or on) the thermostat housing.

TESTING

▶ See Figures 57 and 58

1. Remove the ECT sensor from the vehicle.
2. Immerse the tip of the sensor in container of water.
3. Connect a digital ohmmeter to the two terminals of the sensor.
4. Using a calibrated thermometer, compare the resistance of the sensor to the temperature of the water. Refer to the engine coolant sensor temperature vs. resistance illustration.
5. Repeat the test at two other temperature points, heating or cooling the water as necessary.
6. If the sensor does not met specification, it must be replaced.

REMOVAL & INSTALLATION

▶ See Figures 59, 60, 61 and 62

1. Relieve the cooling system pressure by removing the radiator cap.

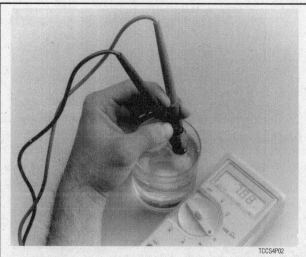

TCCS4P02

Fig. 57 Submerge the end of the coolant temperature sensor in cold or hot water and check the resistance

ENGINE COOLANT SENSOR		
TEMPERATURE VS. RESISTANCE VALUES (APPROXIMATE)		
°C	°F	OHMS
100	212	177
90	194	241
80	176	332
70	158	467
60	140	667
50	122	973
45	113	1188
40	104	1459
35	95	1802
30	86	2238
25	77	2796
20	68	3520
15	59	4450
10	50	5670
5	41	7280
0	32	9420
-5	23	12300
-10	14	16180
-15	5	21450
-20	-4	28680
-30	-22	52700
-40	-40	100700

88004G30

Fig. 58 Engine Coolant Temperature (ECT) sensor temperature vs. resistance values

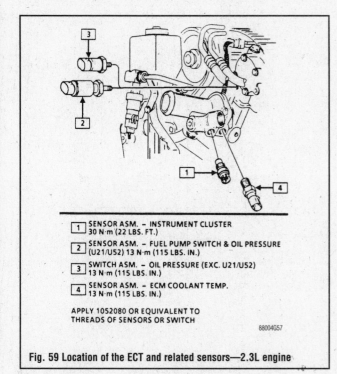

1 SENSOR ASM. – INSTRUMENT CLUSTER
30 N·m (22 LBS. FT.)

2 SENSOR ASM. – FUEL PUMP SWITCH & OIL PRESSURE
(U21/U52) 13 N·m (115 LBS. IN.)

3 SWITCH ASM. – OIL PRESSURE (EXC. U21/U52)
13 N·m (115 LBS. IN.)

4 SENSOR ASM. – ECM COOLANT TEMP.
13 N·m (115 LBS. IN.)

APPLY 1052080 OR EQUIVALENT TO
THREADS OF SENSORS OR SWITCH

88004G57

Fig. 59 Location of the ECT and related sensors—2.3L engine

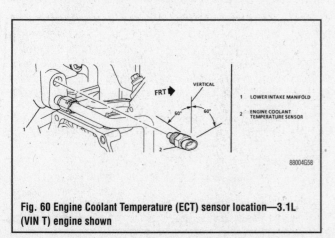

1 LOWER INTAKE MANIFOLD

2 ENGINE COOLANT TEMPERATURE SENSOR

88004G58

Fig. 60 Engine Coolant Temperature (ECT) sensor location—3.1L (VIN T) engine shown

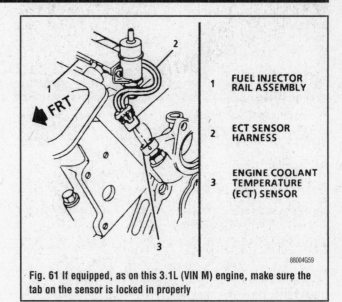

1 FUEL INJECTOR RAIL ASSEMBLY

2 ECT SENSOR HARNESS

3 ENGINE COOLANT TEMPERATURE (ECT) SENSOR

88004G59

Fig. 61 If equipped, as on this 3.1L (VIN M) engine, make sure the tab on the sensor is locked in properly

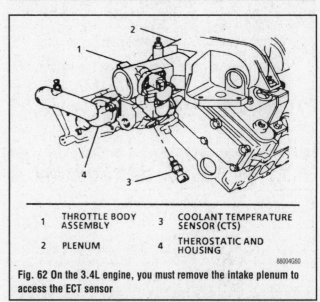

1	THROTTLE BODY ASSEMBLY	3	COOLANT TEMPERATURE SENSOR (CTS)
2	PLENUM	4	THEROSTATIC AND HOUSING

88004G60

Fig. 62 On the 3.4L engine, you must remove the intake plenum to access the ECT sensor

✳✳ CAUTION

Perform this procedure only on a cold engine. Attempting to remove any component that involves working with engine coolant can result in serious burns.

2. Disconnect the negative battery cable.
3. For 3.8L and 1994–96 3.4L engines, drain the engine coolant into a suitable container.

✳✳ CAUTION

When draining the coolant, keep in mind that cats and dogs are attracted by ethylene glycol antifreeze, and are quite likely to drink any that is left in an uncovered container or in puddles on the ground. This will prove fatal in sufficient quantity. Always drain the coolant into a sealable container. Coolant should be reused unless it is contaminated or several years old.

4. For 3.1L and 3.8L engines, remove the air intake duct or intercooler-to-intake manifold tube, as applicable.
5. For 1991–93 3.4L engines, remove the intake manifold plenum (upper manifold), as outlined in Section 3 of this manual.

6. For 1994–96 3.4L engines, perform the following
   a. Remove the air cleaner assembly.
   b. Remove the rear intake duct and MAF assembly.
   c. Remove the exhaust crossover pipe.
7. Detach the sensor electrical connector.

✳✳ WARNING

Be careful when handling the coolant temperature sensor. Damage to the sensor will affect proper operation of the fuel injection system.

8. Remove the threaded temperature sensor from the engine.

To install:

9. Coat the threads of the sensor with sealant 1052080, 9985253 or equivalent.

➡ If equipped, make sure the locking tab on the sensor is located within the area shown in the accompanying figure.

10. Install the sensor in the engine and tighten as follows:
    a. 2.2L engine: 18 ft. lbs. (25 Nm).
    b. 2.3L and 2.5L engines: 22 ft. lbs. (30 Nm).
    c. 3.1L (VIN T and V), 3.4L and 3.8L engines: 22 ft. lbs. (30 Nm).
    d. 3.1L (VIN M) engine: 10 ft. lbs. (14 Nm).
11. Attach the sensor electrical connector.
12. For 1994–96 3.4L engines, perform the following:
    a. Install the exhaust crossover pipe.
    b. Attach the rear intake duct and install the MAF sensor.
    c. Install the air cleaner assembly.
13. For 3.1L and 3.8L engines, install the air intake duct or intercooler-to-intake manifold tube, as applicable.
14. If any coolant was lost, fill the cooling system to the proper level with the correct type of coolant.
15. Connect the negative battery cable. Start the engine and check for leaks and proper operation.

Manifold Air Temperature (MAT)/Intake Air Temperature (IAT) Sensor

OPERATION

The Intake Air Temperature (IAT) sensor, also known as the Manifold Air Temperature (MAT) sensor, is a thermistor which supplies manifold air temperature information to the ECM. The MAT sensor produces high resistance (100,000 ohms at 40°F/40°C) at low temperatures and low resistance of 70 ohms at 266°F (130°C) at high temperatures. The ECM supplies a 5 volt signal to the MAT sensor and measures MAT sensor output voltage. The voltage signal will be high when the air is cold and low when the air is hot. By measuring the voltage, the ECM calculates the incoming air temperature.

The IAT sensor signal is used to adjust spark timing according to incoming air density. The IAT sensor is usually mounted in the air cleaner housing or in the air intake duct.

TESTING

▸ See Figures 63, 64, 65 and 66

1. Remove the Intake Air Temperature (IAT) sensor.
2. Connect a digital ohmmeter to the two terminals of the sensor.
3. Using a calibrated thermometer, compare the resistance of the sensor to the temperature of the ambient air. Refer to the temperature vs. resistance illustration.
4. Repeat the test at two other temperature points, heating or cooling the air as necessary with a hair dryer or other suitable tool.
5. If the sensor does not meet specification, it must be replaced.

REMOVAL & INSTALLATION

▸ See Figures 67, 68 and 69

1. Disconnect the negative battery cable.
2. If necessary for access, remove the air cleaner cover and filter element.

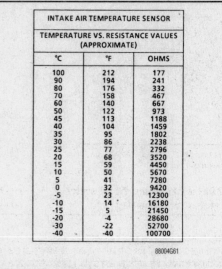

INTAKE AIR TEMPERATURE SENSOR		
TEMPERATURE VS. RESISTANCE VALUES (APPROXIMATE)		
°C	°F	OHMS
100	212	177
90	194	241
80	176	332
70	158	467
60	140	667
50	122	973
45	113	1188
40	104	1459
35	95	1802
30	86	2238
25	77	2796
20	68	3520
15	59	4450
10	50	5670
5	41	7280
0	32	9420
-5	23	12300
-10	14	16180
-15	5	21450
-20	-4	28680
-30	-22	52700
-40	-40	100700

88004G61

Fig. 63 MAT sensor temperature vs. resistance values

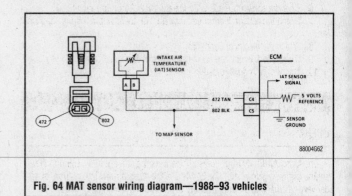

Fig. 64 MAT sensor wiring diagram—1988–93 vehicles

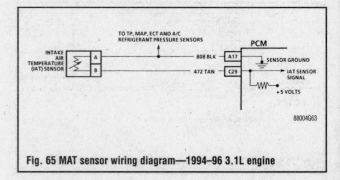

Fig. 65 MAT sensor wiring diagram—1994–96 3.1L engine

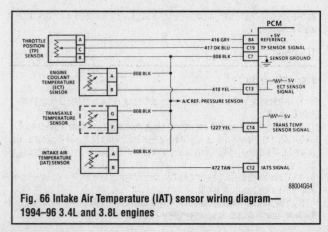

Fig. 66 Intake Air Temperature (IAT) sensor wiring diagram—1994–96 3.4L and 3.8L engines

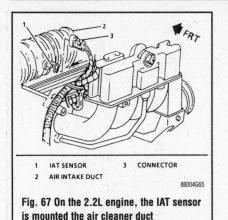

1 IAT SENSOR   3 CONNECTOR
2 AIR INTAKE DUCT

88004G65

Fig. 67 On the 2.2L engine, the IAT sensor is mounted the air cleaner duct

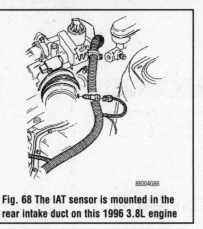

88004G66

Fig. 68 The IAT sensor is mounted in the rear intake duct on this 1996 3.8L engine

88004P06

Fig. 69 Detach the connector, then remove the IAT sensor—1992 3.1L engine shown

3. Detach the sensor electrical connector.
4. If equipped, unfasten the retaining clamp or clip from the sensor.
5. Carefully remove the sensor. The sensor is either threaded or snaps into place.

To install:

6. Coat the sensor threads with sealant 1052080 or equivalent.
7. Install the sensor. If equipped, secure with the clamp or clip, as applicable.
8. Attach the electrical connector.
9. If equipped, install the air cleaner filter element and cover.
10. Connect the negative battery cable.

Mass Air Flow (MAF) Sensor

OPERATION

The Mass Air Flow (MAF) sensor measures the amount of air entering the engine during a given time. The ECM uses the mass airflow information for fuel delivery calculations. A large quantity of air entering the engine indicates an

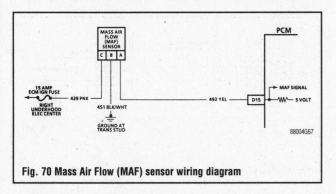

Fig. 70 Mass Air Flow (MAF) sensor wiring diagram

acceleration or high load situation, while a small quantity of air indicates deceleration or idle.

TESTING

▶ **See Figure 70**

1. Backprobe with a high impedance voltmeter between MAF sensor terminals **C** and **B**.
2. With the ignition **ON** engine off, verify that battery voltage is present.
3. If the voltage is not as specified, either the wiring to the MAF sensor, fuse or the ECM may be faulty. Correct any wiring or ECM faults before continuing the test.
4. Disconnect the voltmeter and backprobe with a frequency meter between MAF sensor terminals **A** and **B**.
5. Start the engine and wait until it reaches normal idle speed and verify that the MAF sensor output is approximately 2000 Hz.

6. Slowly raise engine speed up to maximum recommended rpm and verify that the MAF sensor output rises smoothly to approximately 8000 Hz.
7. If MAF sensor output is not as specified the sensor may be faulty.

REMOVAL & INSTALLATION

▶ **See Figures 71 and 72**

1. Disconnect the negative battery cable.
2. Detach the electrical connector from the MAF sensor.
3. For the 3.1L engine, remove the MAF sensor from the air cleaner housing.

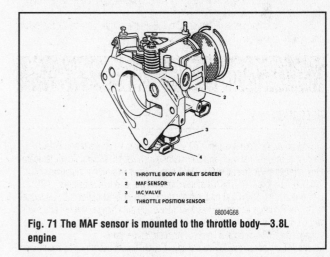

1   THROTTLE BODY AIR INLET SCREEN
2   MAF SENSOR
3   IAC VALVE
4   THROTTLE POSITION SENSOR

88004G68

Fig. 71 The MAF sensor is mounted to the throttle body—3.8L engine

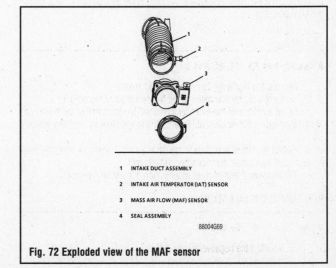

1   INTAKE DUCT ASSEMBLY
2   INTAKE AIR TEMPERATURE (IAT) SENSOR
3   MASS AIR FLOW (MAF) SENSOR
4   SEAL ASSEMBLY

88004G69

Fig. 72 Exploded view of the MAF sensor

4. For the 3.4L engine, remove the air cleaner and duct assembly. Loosen the sensor retaining clamp and remove the sensor.

5. For the 3.8L engine, remove the fresh air duct from the throttle body and air cleaner assembly. Remove the retaining screws, then remove the MAF sensor from the throttle body.

To install:

6. For the 3.8L engine, position the MAF sensor to the throttle body and secure with the 3 retaining screws.

7. For the 3.4L engine, position the sensor and fasten the retaining clamp. Install the air cleaner and duct assembly.

8. For the 3.1L engine, carefully install the MAF sensor to the air inlet grommet. Install the MAF sensor to the air inlet duct.

9. Attach the electrical connector, then connect the negative battery cable.

Manifold Absolute Pressure (MAP) Sensor

OPERATION

▶ See Figure 73

The Manifold Absolute Pressure (MAP) sensor measures the changes in intake manifold pressure, which result from the engine load and speed changes, and converts this to a voltage output.

A closed throttle on engine coastdown will produce a low MAP output, while a wide-open throttle will produce a high output. This high output is produced

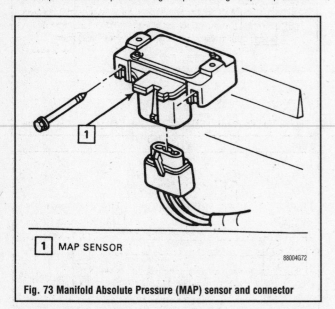

Fig. 73 Manifold Absolute Pressure (MAP) sensor and connector

because the pressure inside the manifold is the same as outside the manifold, so 100 percent of the outside air pressure is measured.

The MAP sensor reading is the opposite of what you would measure on a vacuum gauge. When manifold pressure is high, vacuum is low. The MAP sensor is also used to measure barometric pressure under certain conditions, which allows the ECM to automatically adjust for different altitudes.

The ECM sends a 5 volt reference signal to the MAP sensor. As the manifold pressure changes, the electrical resistance of the sensor also changes. By monitoring the sensor output voltage, the ECM knows the manifold pressure. A higher pressure, low vacuum (high voltage) requires more fuel, while a lower pressure, higher vacuum (low voltage) requires less fuel.

The ECM uses the MAP sensor to control fuel delivery and ignition timing.

TESTING

▶ See Figures 74 and 75

1. Backprobe with a high impedance voltmeter at MAP sensor terminals **A** and **C**.

2. With the key **ON** and engine off, the voltmeter reading should be approximately 5.0 volts.

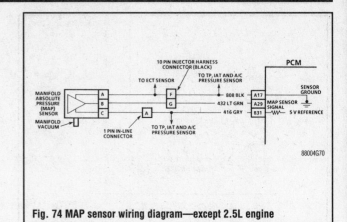

Fig. 74 MAP sensor wiring diagram—except 2.5L engine

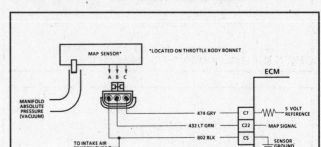

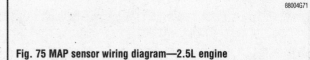

Fig. 75 MAP sensor wiring diagram—2.5L engine

3. If the voltage is not as specified, either the wiring to the MAP sensor or the ECM may be faulty. Correct any wiring or ECM faults before continuing test.

4. Backprobe with the high impedance voltmeter at MAP sensor terminals **B** and **A**.

5. Verify that the sensor voltage is approximately 0.5 volts with the engine not running (at sea level).

6. Record MAP sensor voltage with the key **ON** and engine off.

7. Start the vehicle.

8. Verify that the sensor voltage is greater than 1.5 volts (above the recorded reading) at idle.

9. Verify that the sensor voltage increases to approximately 4.5. volts (above the recorded reading) at Wide Open Throttle (WOT).

10. If the sensor voltage is as specified, the sensor is functioning properly.

11. If the sensor voltage is not as specified, check the sensor and the sensor vacuum source for a leak or a restriction. If no leaks or restrictions are found, the sensor may be defective and should be replaced.

REMOVAL & INSTALLATION

▶ See Figures 76 and 77

1. Disconnect the negative battery cable.

2. If equipped, unfasten the MAP sensor retaining clip from the engine bracket.

3. Detach the sensor electrical connector.

4. Disconnect the inlet vacuum hose, if equipped.

5. Unfasten the attaching screws or remove the retainer, then remove the MAP sensor.

6. If necessary, remove the retainer from the sensor.

To install:

7. For all engines except the 3.1L, lubricate the seal with a very thin film of clean engine oil, then position the seal into the manifold assembly halfway. Insert the MAP sensor nipple into the seal, then seat the sensor fully into the seal and onto the mounting surfaces.

8. Install the MAP sensor screws and tighten to 27 inch lbs. (3 Nm). Do NOT overtighten the screws.

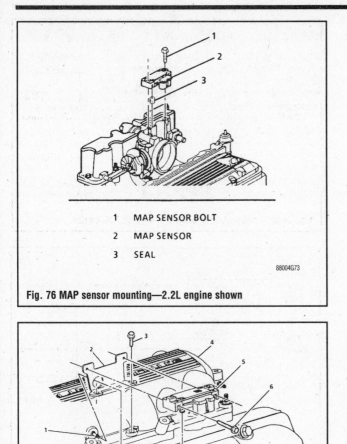

1   MAP SENSOR BOLT

2   MAP SENSOR

3   SEAL

88004G73

Fig. 76 MAP sensor mounting—2.2L engine shown

1   UPPER INTAKE MANIFOLD VACUUM TUBE   5   MAP SENSOR

2   MAP SENSOR BRACKET   6   BOLT/SCREW

3   BOLT/SCREW   7   VACUUM HARNESS ASSEMBLY

4   UPPER INTAKE MANIFOLD

88004G74

Fig. 77 View of the MAP sensor location—1994 3.1L engine shown

9. For the 3.1L engine, position the MAP sensor to the retainer.
10. Attach the sensor electrical connector.
11. If necessary, attach the inlet vacuum hose.
12. For 3.1L engines, fasten the MAP sensor and retainer to the engine bracket.
13. Connect the negative battery cable. If necessary, install the MAP sensor retaining clip.

Throttle Position Sensor (TPS)

OPERATION

The Throttle Position Sensor (TPS) is connected to the throttle shaft on the throttle body. It is a potentiometer with one end connected to 5 volts from the ECM and the other to ground.

A third wire is connected to the ECM to measure the voltage from the TPS. As the throttle valve angle is changed (accelerator pedal moved), the output of the TPS also changes. At a closed throttle position, the output of the TPS is low (approximately 0.5 volts). As the throttle valve opens, the output increases so that, at wide-open throttle, the output voltage should be approximately 4.5 volts.

By monitoring the output voltage from the TPS, the ECM can determine fuel delivery based on throttle valve angle (driver demand).

TESTING

◆ **See Figures 78, 79, 80, 81 and 82**

1. For all engines except the 3.8L, backprobe with a high impedance voltmeter at TPS terminals **A** and **B**.
2. For the 3.8L engine, backprobe with a high impedance voltmeter at TPS terminals **A** and **C**.
3. With the key **ON** and engine off, the voltmeter reading should be approximately 5.0 volts.
4. If the voltage is not as specified, either the wiring to the TPS or the ECM may be faulty. Correct any wiring or ECM faults before continuing test.
5. Backprobe with a high impedance voltmeter at terminals **C** and **B**.
6. With the key **ON** and engine off and the throttle closed, the TPS voltage should be approximately 0.5–1.2 volts.
7. Verify that the TPS voltage increases or decreases smoothly as the throttle is opened or closed. Make sure to open and close the throttle very slowly in order to detect any abnormalities in the TPS voltage reading.
8. If the sensor voltage is not as specified, replace the sensor.

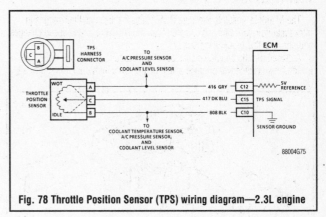

Fig. 78 Throttle Position Sensor (TPS) wiring diagram—2.3L engine

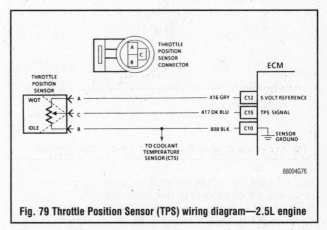

Fig. 79 Throttle Position Sensor (TPS) wiring diagram—2.5L engine

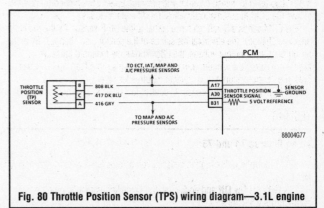

Fig. 80 Throttle Position Sensor (TPS) wiring diagram—3.1L engine

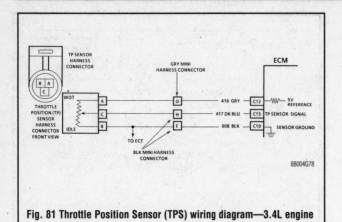

Fig. 81 Throttle Position Sensor (TPS) wiring diagram—3.4L engine

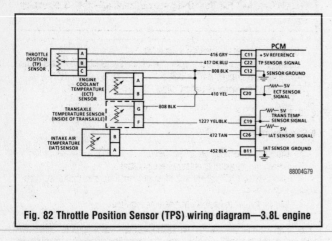

Fig. 82 Throttle Position Sensor (TPS) wiring diagram—3.8L engine

REMOVAL & INSTALLATION

▶ See Figure 83

1. Disconnect the negative battery cable.
2. If necessary, remove the air cleaner assembly along with the necessary duct work.
3. Unfasten the TPS attaching screws. If the TPS is riveted to the throttle body, it will be necessary to drill out the rivets.
4. Remove the TPS from the throttle body assembly. If equipped, inspect the TPS O-ring and replace if necessary.

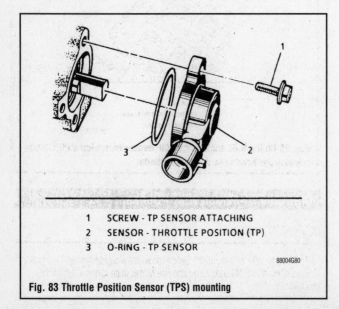

1	SCREW - TP SENSOR ATTACHING
2	SENSOR - THROTTLE POSITION (TP)
3	O-RING - TP SENSOR

Fig. 83 Throttle Position Sensor (TPS) mounting

⁑ WARNING

The throttle position sensor is an electrical component and should not be immersed in any type of liquid solvent or cleaner, as damage may result.

To install:
5. With the throttle valve closed, install the TPS onto the throttle shaft. Rotate the TPS counterclockwise to align the mounting holes. Install the retaining screws or rivets. Tighten the retaining screws to 18 inch lbs. (2.0 Nm).
6. Install the air cleaner assembly and connect the negative battery cable.

Camshaft Position (CMP) Sensor

OPERATION

The ECM uses the camshaft signal to determine the position of the No. 1 cylinder piston during its power stroke. The signal is used by the ECM to calculate fuel injection mode of operation.

If the cam signal is lost while the engine is running, the fuel injection system will shift to a calculated fuel injected mode based on the last fuel injection pulse, and the engine will continue to run.

TESTING

▶ See Figures 84, 85 and 86

1. Disconnect the CMP sensor wiring harness and connect an LED test light between CMP harness terminal **C** and battery ground.
2. With the ignition **ON** and the engine off, verify that the test light illuminates.

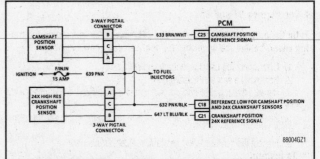

Fig. 84 Camshaft Position (CMP) and Crankshaft Position (CKP) sensor wiring diagram—3.1L (VIN M) engine

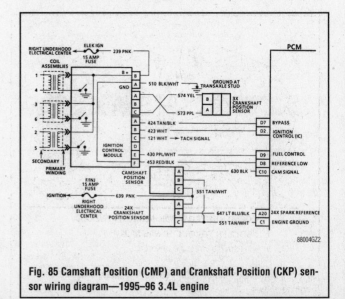

Fig. 85 Camshaft Position (CMP) and Crankshaft Position (CKP) sensor wiring diagram—1995–96 3.4L engine

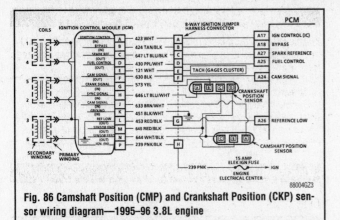

Fig. 86 Camshaft Position (CMP) and Crankshaft Position (CKP) sensor wiring diagram—1995–96 3.8L engine

3. If not as specified, repair or replace the fuse and/or wiring.

4. Carefully connect the test light between CMP harness terminal **A** and **C** and verify that the test light illuminates.

5. If not as specified, repair the CMP harness ground circuit (terminal **A**).

6. Turn the ignition **OFF** and disconnect the test light.

7. Next, connect suitable jumper wires between the CMP sensor and CMP sensor harness. Connect a DC volt meter to the jumper wire corresponding to CMP terminal **B** and battery ground.

8. Start the engine and verify that the voltage signal is 5–7 volts.

9. If it is not as specified, the CMP sensor may be faulty.

REMOVAL & INSTALLATION

3.1L and 3.8L Engines

▶ See Figures 87 and 88

➡ On the 3.1L and 3.8L engines, the CMP sensor is located on the timing cover, behind the water pump, near the camshaft sprocket.

1. Disconnect the negative battery cable.
2. Remove the serpentine drive belt.
3. Remove the power steering pump, as outlined in Section 8 of this manual.
4. Detach the sensor electrical connector.
5. Remove the CMP sensor mounting bolt, then remove the sensor from the engine.
6. Inspect the sensor O-ring seal and replace as required.

To install:
7. Position the CMP sensor and secure with the retaining bolt. Tighten the bolt to 8 ft. lbs. (10 Nm).

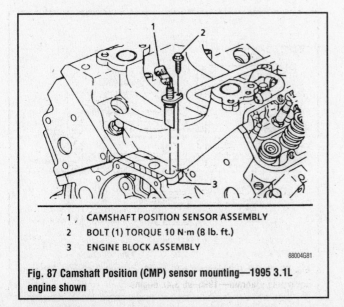

1	CAMSHAFT POSITION SENSOR ASSEMBLY
2	BOLT (1) TORQUE 10 N·m (8 lb. ft.)
3	ENGINE BLOCK ASSEMBLY

Fig. 87 Camshaft Position (CMP) sensor mounting—1995 3.1L engine shown

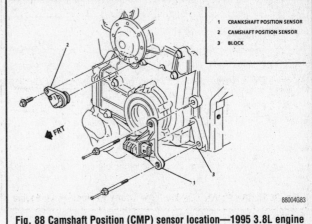

Fig. 88 Camshaft Position (CMP) sensor location—1995 3.8L engine shown

8. Attach the sensor electrical connector.
9. Install the power steering pump, as outlined in Section 8 of this manual.
10. Install the serpentine drive belt.
11. Connect the negative battery cable.

3.4L Engine

▶ See Figure 89

1. Disconnect the negative battery cable.
2. Detach the electrical connector from the sensor.
3. Unfasten the CMP sensor mounting bolt, then remove the sensor from the engine.
4. Inspect the O-ring seal and replace as required.

To install:
5. Position the CMP sensor and secure with the retaining bolt. Tighten the bolt to 8 ft. lbs. (10 Nm).
6. Attach the sensor electrical connector.
7. Connect the negative battery cable.

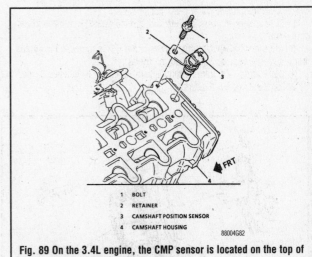

1	BOLT
2	RETAINER
3	CAMSHAFT POSITION SENSOR
4	CAMSHAFT HOUSING

Fig. 89 On the 3.4L engine, the CMP sensor is located on the top of the cylinder head towards the #3 cylinder

Crankshaft Position (CKP) Sensor

OPERATION

The Crankshaft Position (CKP) Sensor provides a signal through the ignition module which the ECM uses as a reference to calculate rpm and crankshaft position.

TESTING

▶ **See Figures 84, 85, 86, 90 thru 94**

1. Perform a visual inspection.
2. Detach the sensor connector and install jumper wires from the power and ground terminals of the sensor connector to the wiring harness. This permits the sensor to receive power and ground without signaling the ignition system during inspection.

➡ **Do not connect a jumper wire to the signal terminal on the sensor. This will cause the engine to start. Use extreme caution when performing this test.**

3. Using a multimeter set to the volts setting, check the voltage between the power and ground wires. This voltage may be either 4, 6, 8 or 12 volts depending on the system. Take note of this voltage reading.
4. Connect the multimeter between the signal terminal and the ground wire. Rotate the engine (by tapping the ignition key) with the starter motor. When the engine is rotated, the signal should fluctuate between 0 volts and the system voltage noted in the earlier step.
5. While rotating the engine, check for damaged shutter blades or any indication that the shutter blades are hitting the magnet.

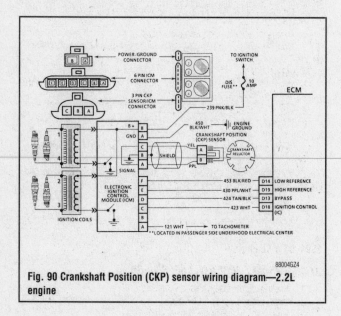

Fig. 90 Crankshaft Position (CKP) sensor wiring diagram—2.2L engine

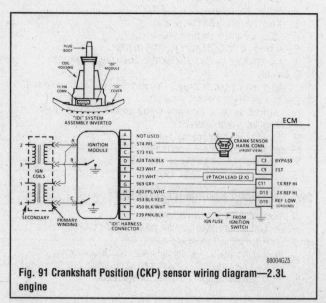

Fig. 91 Crankshaft Position (CKP) sensor wiring diagram—2.3L engine

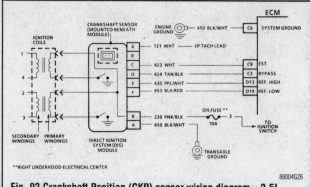

Fig. 92 Crankshaft Position (CKP) sensor wiring diagram—2.5L engine

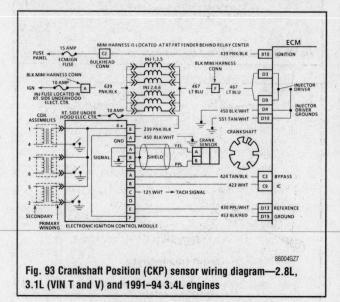

Fig. 93 Crankshaft Position (CKP) sensor wiring diagram—2.8L, 3.1L (VIN T and V) and 1991–94 3.4L engines

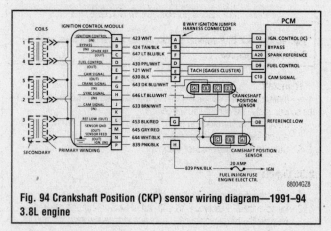

Fig. 94 Crankshaft Position (CKP) sensor wiring diagram—1991–94 3.8L engine

REMOVAL & INSTALLATION

▶ **See Figures 95 and 96**

2.2L, 2.3L, 3.1L (VIN T and V) and 1991–93 3.4L Engines

1. Disconnect the negative battery cable.
2. Detach the sensor harness connector from the sensor.
3. Unfasten the sensor retaining bolts, then remove the sensor from the engine.
4. Inspect the sensor O-ring for damage, and replace, if necessary.

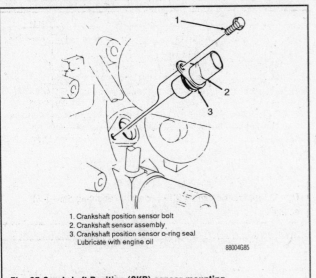

1. Crankshaft position sensor bolt
2. Crankshaft sensor assembly
3. Crankshaft position sensor o-ring seal
   Lubricate with engine oil

88004G85

Fig. 95 Crankshaft Position (CKP) sensor mounting

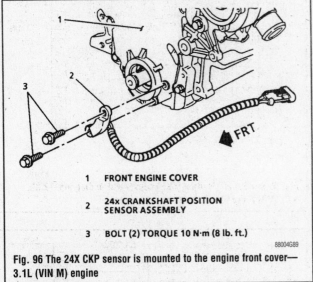

1 **FRONT ENGINE COVER**

2 **24x CRANKSHAFT POSITION SENSOR ASSEMBLY**

3 **BOLT (2) TORQUE 10 N·m (8 lb. ft.)**

88004G89

Fig. 96 The 24X CKP sensor is mounted to the engine front cover—3.1L (VIN M) engine

To install:
5. If necessary, lubricate a new O-ring with clean engine oil and install on the sensor. Install the sensor into the engine.
6. Install the sensor retaining bolt. Tighten to 88 inch lbs. (10 Nm).
7. Attach the sensor harness connector.
8. Connect the negative battery cable.

2.5L Engine

1. Disconnect the negative battery cable.
2. Remove the DIS assembly, as outlined in Section 2 of this manual.
3. Remove the sensor retaining screws and remove the sensor from DIS assembly.
4. Inspect the sensor O-ring for damage, and replace, if necessary.
   To install:
5. If necessary, lubricate a new O-ring with clean engine oil and install on the sensor.
6. Fit the sensor to the DIS assembly and install the retaining screws. Tighten the retaining screws to 20 inch lbs. (2.3 Nm).
7. Install the DIS assembly to the engine, as outlined in Section 2 of this manual.
8. Connect the negative battery cable.

3.1L (VIN M) Engines

3X CRANKSHAFT POSITION (CKP) SENSOR

1. Disconnect the negative battery cable.
2. Turn the steering wheel to the full left position.
3. Raise and safely support the vehicle.
4. Detach the sensor harness connector from the sensor.
5. Unfasten the sensor retaining bolts, then remove the sensor from the engine.
6. Inspect the sensor O-ring for damage, and replace, if necessary.
   To install:
7. If necessary, lubricate a new O-ring with clean engine oil and install on the sensor. Install the sensor into the engine.
8. Install the sensor retaining bolt. Tighten to 71 inch lbs. (8 Nm).
9. Attach the sensor harness connector.
10. Carefully lower the vehicle.
11. Turn the steering wheel to the straight ahead position, then connect the negative battery cable.

24X CRANKSHAFT POSITION (CKP) SENSOR

1. Disconnect the negative battery cable.
2. Remove the serpentine belt from the crankshaft pulley.
3. Raise and support the vehicle safely.
4. If necessary for access, remove the right front wheel and inner fender access cover.
5. Unfasten the crankshaft harmonic balancer retaining bolt, then remove the harmonic balancer using tool J 24420-B.
6. Detach the sensor electrical connector.
7. Unfasten the sensor retaining bolts, then remove the sensor from the vehicle.
   To install:
8. Install the CKP sensor and secure using the retaining bolts. Tighten the bolts to 8 ft. lbs. (10 Nm).
9. Attach the sensor electrical connector.
10. Install the balancer on the crankshaft using special tool J 29113, or equivalent.
11. Apply thread sealer 1052080 or equivalent to the bolt threads of the crankshaft balancer bolt. Tighten the bolt to 110 ft. lbs. (150 Nm).
12. If removed, install the inner fender shield and the right front wheel and tire assembly. Tighten the wheel lug nuts to 100 ft. lbs. (140 Nm).
13. Carefully lower the vehicle.
14. Install the serpentine belt.
15. Connect the negative battery cable.

1994–96 3.4L Engine

3X CRANKSHAFT POSITION (CKP) SENSOR

1. Disconnect the negative battery cable.
2. Raise and safely support the vehicle.
3. Remove the intermediate exhaust pipe.
4. Remove the rack and pinion heat shield.
5. Remove the alternator cooling duct.
6. Detach the sensor electric connector.
7. Remove the 3X CKP sensor from the engine.
8. Inspect the sensor O-ring for damage, and replace, if necessary.
   To install:
9. If necessary, lubricate a new O-ring with clean engine oil and install on the sensor. Install the sensor into the engine.
10. Install the sensor-to-block bolt and tighten to 71 inch lbs. (8 Nm).
11. Attach the sensor connector.
12. Install the alternator cooling duct.
13. Install the rack and pinion heat shield.
14. Install the intermediate exhaust pipe.
15. Connect the negative battery cable.

24X CRANKSHAFT POSITION (CKP) SENSOR

1. Disconnect the negative battery cable.
2. Remove the serpentine belt from the crankshaft pulley.
3. Raise and support the vehicle safely.
4. Remove the right front wheel and inner fender access cover.
5. Unfasten the crankshaft harmonic balancer retaining bolt, then remove the harmonic balancer using tool J 38197, or equivalent.

6. Detach the sensor electrical connector.

7. Unfasten the sensor retaining bolts, then remove the sensor from the vehicle.

To install:

8. Install the CKP sensor and secure using the retaining bolts. Tighten the bolts to 8 ft. lbs. (10 Nm).

9. Attach the sensor electrical connector.

10. Install the balancer on the crankshaft.

11. Apply thread sealer 1052080 or equivalent to the bolt threads of the crankshaft balancer bolt. Tighten the bolt to 110 ft. lbs. (150 Nm).

12. If removed, install the inner fender shield and the right front wheel and tire assembly. Tighten the wheel lug nuts to 100 ft. lbs. (140 Nm).

13. Carefully lower the vehicle.

14. Install the serpentine belt.

15. Connect the negative battery cable.

3.8L Engine

1. Disconnect the negative battery cable.

2. Remove the serpentine belt from the crankshaft pulley.

3. Raise and support the vehicle safely.

4. Remove the right front wheel and inner fender access cover.

5. Using a 28mm socket, unfasten the crankshaft harmonic balancer retaining bolt, then remove the harmonic balancer using tool J 38197, or equivalent.

6. Remove the CKP sensor shield. Do NOT use a prybar to remove the shield!

7. Detach the sensor electrical connector.

8. Unfasten the sensor retaining bolts, then remove the sensor from the block face.

To install:

9. Position the CKP sensor to the block face, then secure using the retaining bolts. Tighten the bolts to 14–28 ft. lbs. (20–40 Nm).

10. Install the CKP sensor shield.

11. Attach the sensor electrical connector.

12. Install the balancer on the crankshaft.

13. Apply thread sealer 1052080 or equivalent to the bolt threads of the crankshaft balancer bolt. Tighten the bolt to 110 ft. lbs. (150 Nm), plus an additional 76° turn.

14. Install the inner fender shield and the right front wheel and tire assembly. Tighten the wheel lug nuts to 100 ft. lbs. (140 Nm).

15. Carefully lower the vehicle.

16. Install the serpentine belt.

17. Connect the negative battery cable.

ESC Knock Sensor

OPERATION

The Knock Sensor (KS) is mounted to the engine block. When spark knock, or pinging is present, then sensor produces a voltage signal which is sent to the ECM. The ECM will then retard the ignition timing based on these signals.

When a Knock Sensor problem is suspected, first perform a visual inspection. Most problems can be found in wiring harnesses and connectors.

TESTING

Perform a basic knock sensor test as follows. To perform this test, you will need a timing light.

1. Connect a suitable timing light to the engine.

2. Start the engine and allow to warm up sufficiently.

3. Position the timing light near the timing marks on the harmonic balancer.

4. Locate the knock sensor.

5. Using a suitable metallic tool, tap on the intake manifold or side of the engine block; whichever is closer to the knock sensor. Do not strike hard or hit the sensor directly, light tapping should cause the knock sensor to react.

6. If the knock sensor is working, the ignition timing will begin to retard as you tap.

7. If the timing does not change, you will need to check voltage at the knock sensor harness connector. Also, make sure the connector is clean and making good connection.

REMOVAL & INSTALLATION

1. Disconnect the negative battery cable.

2. Raise and support the vehicle safely.

3. Detach the harness connector from the knock sensor.

4. Remove the sensor from the engine block.

To install:

➡**Do not apply thread sealant to sensor threads. Sensor is pre-coated at factory applying additional sealant will affect the sensors ability to detect detonation.**

5. Clean the threads on the engine block, where the sensor was installed. Install the sensor. Tighten to 11–16 ft. lbs. (15–22 Nm).

6. Attach the harness connector to the knock sensor.

7. Carefully lower the vehicle.

8. Connect the negative battery cable.

Torque Converter Clutch Solenoid

OPERATION

Most late model vehicles with an automatic transaxle use a Torque Converter Clutch (TCC) system. The ECM controls the torque converter by means of a solenoid mounted in the output drive housing of the transmission. When the vehicle speed reaches a certain point, the ECM sends a signal to the TCC solenoid, (energizing it), and allows the torque converter to mechanically couple the transaxle to the engine. When operating conditions, (according to various sensors), indicate that the transaxle should operate as a normal fluid coupled transaxle, then ECM will de-energize the solenoid. Depressing the brake pedal will also return the transaxle to normal automatic operation.

TESTING

Testing the TCC usually involves the use of special testing equipment. Here is a basic check that can be made to see if the TCC is functioning or not.

1. Connect a tachometer or special scan tool.

2. Drive the vehicle until the transmission is warmed up sufficiently.

3. Accelerate to 50–55 mph (80–88 kph).

4. Maintaining the throttle, lightly touch the brake pedal and check for release of the TCC. You will know if the torque converter clutch disengaged if the engine rpm increases.

5. Release the brake, slowly accelerate and check for a reapplication of the TCC. You will know if has engaged by a slight decrease in rpm.

REMOVAL & INSTALLATION

1. Remove the negative battery cable. Raise and support the vehicle safely.

2. Drain the transmission fluid into a suitable drain pan. Remove the transmission pan.

3. Remove the TCC solenoid retaining screws and then remove the electrical connector, solenoid and check ball.

4. Clean and inspect all parts. Replace defective parts as necessary.

To install:

5. Install the check ball, TCC solenoid and electrical connector. Install the solenoid retaining screws and torque them to 10 ft. lbs. (14 Nm).

6. Install the transmission pan with a new gasket and torque the pan retaining bolts to 10 ft. lbs. (14 Nm).

7. Lower the vehicle and refill the transmission with the proper amount of the automatic transmission fluid.

Vehicle Speed Sensor (VSS)

OPERATION

The VSS is located on the transmission and sends a pulsing voltage signal to the ECM which is converted to vehicle speed. This sensor mainly controls the operation of the TCC system, shift light, cruise control and activation of the EGR system.

TESTING

✳✳ CAUTION

The following test will require the vehicle to be raised off the ground, with the engine running and the transmission in D. Extreme caution must be used when raising and supporting the vehicle, otherwise personal and/or vehicle damage may occur.

1. Raise and safely support the vehicle.
2. Detach the VSS wire connector located on the transmission housing.
3. Connect an ohmmeter between the terminals of the speed sensor. Most sensors will usually be between 190–250 ohms.

4. Place the vehicle in Drive and allow the wheels to rotate. The ohmmeter should fluctuate. If it does not, or the ohmmeter reading is not within specification, replace the sensor.
5. Apply the brake, place the vehicle in Park, then turn the ignition **OFF**.
6. Attach the harness connector to the VSS.
7. Carefully lower the vehicle.

REMOVAL & INSTALLATION

1. Disconnect the negative battery cable.
2. Raise and safely support the vehicle.
3. Detach the electrical connector from the VSS, then remove the sensor.
4. Installation is the reverse of the removal procedure.

TROUBLE CODES

General Information

Since the computer control module is programmed to recognize the presence and value of electrical inputs, it will also note the lack of a signal or a radical change in values. It will, for example, react to the loss of signal from the vehicle speed sensor or note that engine coolant temperature has risen beyond acceptable (programmed) limits. Once a fault is recognized, a numeric code is assigned and held in memory. The dashboard warning lamp: CHECK ENGINE or SERVICE ENGINE SOON (SES), will illuminate to advise the operator that the system has detected a fault. This lamp is also known as the Malfunction Indicator Lamp (MIL).

More than one code may be stored. Keep in mind not every engine uses every code. Additionally, the same code may carry different meanings relative to each engine or engine family.

In the event of an computer control module failure, the system will default to a pre-programmed set of values. These are compromise values which allow the engine to operate, although possibly at reduced efficiency. This is variously known as the default, limp-in or back-up mode. Driveability is almost always affected when the ECM enters this mode.

SCAN TOOLS

On most models, the stored codes may be read with only the use of a small jumper wire, however the use of a hand-held scan tool such as GM's TECH-1® or equivalent is recommended. On 1994–95 3.4L and 3.8L engines, and all 1996 models, an OBD-II compliant scan tool must be used. There are many manufacturers of these tools; a purchaser must be certain that the tool is proper for the intended use. If you own a scan type tool, it probably came with comprehensive instructions on proper use. Be sure to follow the instructions that came with your unit if they differ from what is given here; this is a general guide with useful information included.

The scan tool allows any stored codes to be read from the ECM or PCM memory. The tool also allows the operator to view the data being sent to the computer control module while the engine is running. This ability has obvious diagnostic advantages; the use of the scan tool is frequently required for component testing. The scan tool makes collecting information easier; the data must be correctly interpreted by an operator familiar with the system.

An example of the usefulness of the scan tool may be seen in the case of a temperature sensor which has changed its electrical characteristics. The ECM is reacting to an apparently warmer engine (causing a driveability problem), but the sensor's voltage has not changed enough to set a fault code. Connecting the scan tool, the voltage signal being sent to the ECM may be viewed; comparison to normal values or a known good vehicle reveals the problem quickly.

ELECTRICAL TOOLS

The most commonly required electrical diagnostic tool is the digital multimeter, allowing voltage, ohmage (resistance) and amperage to be read by one instrument. The multimeter must be a high-impedance unit, with 10 megohms of impedance in the voltmeter. This type of meter will not place an additional load on the circuit it is testing; this is extremely important in low voltage circuits. The multimeter must be of high quality in all respects. It should be han-

dled carefully and protected from impact or damage. Replace batteries frequently in the unit.

Other necessary tools include an unpowered test light, a quality tachometer with an inductive (clip-on) pick up, and the proper tools for releasing GM's Metri-Pack, Weather Pack and Micro-Pack terminals as necessary. The Micro-Pack connectors are used at the ECM electrical connector. A vacuum pump/gauge may also be required for checking sensors, solenoids and valves.

Diagnosis and Testing

Diagnosis of a driveablility and/or emissions problems requires attention to detail and following the diagnostic procedures in the correct order. Resist the temptation to perform any repairs before performing the preliminary diagnostic steps. In many cases this will shorten diagnostic time and often cure the problem without electronic testing.

The proper troubleshooting procedure for these vehicles is as follows:

VISUAL/PHYSICAL INSPECTION

This is possibly the most critical step of diagnosis and should be performed immediately after retrieving any codes. A detailed examination of connectors, wiring and vacuum hoses can often lead to a repair without further diagnosis. Performance of this step relies on the skill of the technician performing it; a careful inspector will check the undersides of hoses as well as the integrity of hard-to-reach hoses blocked by the air cleaner or other component. Wiring should be checked carefully for any sign of strain, burning, crimping, or terminal pull-out from a connector. Checking connectors at components or in harnesses is required; usually, pushing them together will reveal a loose fit.

INTERMITTENTS

If a fault occurs intermittently, such as a loose connector pin breaking contact as the vehicle hits a bump, the ECM will note the fault as it occurs and energize the dash warning lamp. If the problem self-corrects, as with the terminal pin again making contact, the dash lamp will extinguish after 10 seconds but a code will remain stored in the computer control module's memory.

When an unexpected code appears during diagnostics, it may have been set during an intermittent failure that self-corrected; the codes are still useful in diagnosis and should not be discounted.

CIRCUIT/COMPONENT REPAIR

The fault codes and the scan tool data will lead to diagnosis and checking of a particular circuit. It is important to note that the fault code indicates a fault or loss of signal in an ECM-controlled system, not necessarily in the specific component.

Refer to the appropriate Diagnostic Code chart to determine the codes meaning. The component may then be tested following the appropriate component test procedures found in this section. If the component is OK, check the wiring for shorts or opens. Further diagnoses should be left to an experienced driveability technician.

If a code indicates the ECM to be faulty and the ECM is replaced, but does not correct the problem, one of the following may be the reason:

• There is a problem with the ECM terminal connections: The terminals may have to be removed from the connector in order to check them properly.

• The ECM or PROM is not correct for the application: The incorrect ECM or PROM may cause a malfunction and may or may not set a code.

• The problem is intermittent: This means that the problem is not present at the time the system is being checked. In this case, make a careful physical inspection of all portions of the system involved.

• Shorted solenoid, relay coil or harness: Solenoids and relays are turned on and off by the ECM using internal electronic switches called drivers. Each driver is part of a group of four called Quad-Drivers. A shorted solenoid, relay coil or harness may cause an ECM to fail, and a replacement ECM to fail when it is installed. Use a short tester, J34696, BT 8405, or equivalent, as a fast, accurate means of checking for a short circuit.

• The Programmable Read Only Memory (PROM) or MEM-CAL may be faulty: Although the PROM rarely fails, it operates as part of the ECM. Therefore, it could be the cause of the problem. Substitute a known good PROM/MEM-CAL.

• The replacement ECM may be faulty: After the ECM is replaced, the system should be rechecked for proper operation. If the diagnostic code again indicates the ECM is the problem, substitute a known good ECM. Although this is a very rare condition, it could happen.

Reading Codes

1988–95 VEHICLES EXCEPT 1994–95 3.4L AND 3.8L ENGINES

▶ See Figure 97

Listings of the trouble for the various engine control system covered in this manual are located in this section. Remember that a code only points to the faulty circuit NOT necessarily to a faulty component. Loose, damaged or corroded connections may contribute to a fault code on a circuit when the sensor or component is operating properly. Be sure that the components are faulty before replacing them, especially the expensive ones.

The Assembly Line Diagnostic Link (ALDL) connector or Data Link Connector (DLC) may be located under the dash and sometimes covered with a plastic cover labeled DIAGNOSTIC CONNECTOR.

1. The diagnostic trouble codes can be read by grounding test terminal **B**. The terminal is most easily grounded by connecting it to terminal **A** (internal ECM ground). This is the terminal to the right of terminal **B** on the top row of the ALDL connector.

2. Once the terminals have been connected, the ignition switch must be moved to the **ON** position with the engine not running.

3. The Service Engine Soon or Check Engine light should be flashing. If it isn't, turn the ignition **OFF** and remove the jumper wire. Turn the ignition **ON** and confirm that light is now on. If it is not, replace the bulb and try again. If the bulb still will not light, or if it does not flash with the test terminal grounded, the system should be diagnosed by an experienced driveability technician. If the light is OK, proceed as follows:

4. The code(s) stored in memory may be read through counting the flashes of the dashboard warning lamp. The dash warning lamp should begin to flash

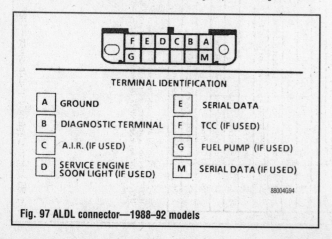

TERMINAL IDENTIFICATION

A	GROUND	E	SERIAL DATA
B	DIAGNOSTIC TERMINAL	F	TCC (IF USED)
C	A.I.R. (IF USED)	G	FUEL PUMP (IF USED)
D	SERVICE ENGINE SOON LIGHT (IF USED)	M	SERIAL DATA (IF USED)

88004G94

Fig. 97 ALDL connector—1988–92 models

Code 12. The code will display as one flash, a pause and two flashes. Code 12 is not a fault code. It is used as a system acknowledgment or handshake code; its presence indicates that the ECM can communicate as requested. Code 12 is used to begin every diagnostic sequence. Some vehicles also use Code 12 after all diagnostic codes have been sent.

5. After Code 12 has been transmitted 3 times, the fault codes, if any, will each be transmitted 3 times. The codes are stored and transmitted in numeric order from lowest to highest.

➡**The order of codes in the memory does not indicate the order of occurrence.**

6. If there are no codes stored, but a driveability or emissions problem is evident, the system should be diagnosed by an experienced driveability technician.

7. If one or more codes are stored, record them. Refer to the applicable Diagnostic Code chart in this section.

8. Switch the ignition **OFF** when finished with code retrieval or scan tool readings.

➡**After making repairs, clear the trouble codes and operate the vehicle to see if it will reset, indicating further problems.**

1994–95 3.4L AND 3.8L ENGINES AND ALL 1996 MODELS

▶ See Figure 98

On 1994–95 3.4L and 3.8L engines, and all 1996 models, an OBD-II compliant scan tool must be used to retrieve the trouble codes. Follow the scan tool manufacturer's instructions on how to connect the scan tool to the vehicle and how to retrieve the codes.

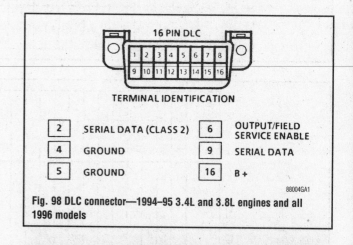

16 PIN DLC

TERMINAL IDENTIFICATION

2	SERIAL DATA (CLASS 2)	6	OUTPUT/FIELD SERVICE ENABLE
4	GROUND	9	SERIAL DATA
5	GROUND	16	B +

88004GA1

Fig. 98 DLC connector—1994–95 3.4L and 3.8L engines and all 1996 models

Clearing Codes

Stored fault codes may be erased from memory at any time by removing power from the ECM for at least 30 seconds. It may be necessary to clear stored codes during diagnosis to check for any recurrence during a test drive, but the stored codes must be written down when retrieved. The codes may still be required for subsequent troubleshooting. Whenever a repair is complete, the stored codes must be erased and the vehicle test driven to confirm correct operation and repair.

❊❊❊ WARNING

The ignition switch must be OFF any time power is disconnected or restored to the ECM. Severe damage may result if this precaution is not observed.

Depending on the electrical distribution of the particular vehicle, power to the ECM may be disconnected by removing the ECM fuse in the fusebox, disconnecting the in-line fuse holder near the positive battery terminal or disconnecting the ECM power lead at the battery terminal. Disconnecting the negative battery cable to clear codes is not recommended as this will also clear other memory data in the vehicle such as radio presets.

PCM DIAGNOSTIC TROUBLE CODES

DTC	DESCRIPTION	ILLUMINATE MIL
13	Oxygen Sensor (O2S) - open circuit	YES
14	Engine Coolant Temperature (ECT) Sensor - high temp. indicated	YES
15	Engine Coolant Temperature (ECT) Sensor - low temp. indicated	YES
16	System Voltage high or low	NO
17	Spark Reference Circuit	YES
18	Cam/Crank Error	YES
21	Throttle Position (TP) Sensor voltage high	YES
22	Throttle Position (TP) Sensor voltage low	NO
23	Intake Air Temperature (IAT) Sensor - low temp. indicated	YES
24	Vehicle Speed Sensor Circuit	NO
25	Intake Air Temperature (IAT) Sensor - high temp. indicated	YES
26	QDM "A" Circuit	NO
31	PRNDL Input Circuit	YES
34	Mass Air Flow (MAF) Sensor - low gm/sec indicated	NO
36	Transaxle Shift Problem	NO
38	Brake Input Circuit	NO
39	Torque Convertor Clutch (TCC) Problem	NO
41	Cam Sensor Circuit	YES
42	Ignition Control (IC) Circuit	YES
43	Knock Sensor (KS)	YES
44	Oxygen Sensor (O2S) - lean exhaust indicated	YES
45	Oxygen Sensor (O2S) - rich exhaust indicated	YES
51	PROM Error	YES
53, 54, 55	EGR Problem	YES
56	QDM "B" Circuit	YES
61	Cruise Vent Solenoid Circuit	NO
62	Cruise Vacuum Solenoid Circuit	NO
63	Cruise System Problem (SPS Indicated Low)	NO
65	Cruise Servo Position Sensor (SPS) Circuit (open/grounded)	NO
66	Excessive A/C Cycling (low refrigerant charge)	NO
67	Cruise Switches Circuit	NO
68	Cruise System Problem (SPS Indicated High)	NO
69	A/C Head Pressure Switch Circuit	NO
99	Power Management	NO

If a DTC not listed above appears on Tech 1, ground DLC Diagnostic Request Terminal "B" and observe flashed codes. If DTC does not reappear, Tech 1 data may be faulty. If DTC does reappear, check for incorrect or faulty PROM.

Fig. 100 Engine diagnostic trouble codes—1988–93 3.8L engines

88004G99

ECM DIAGNOSTIC TROUBLE CODES

DTC	DESCRIPTION	ILLUMINATE MIL
13	Oxygen Sensor - open circuit	YES
14	Engine Coolant Temperature Sensor - high temperature indicated	YES
15	Engine Coolant Temperature Sensor - low temperature indicated	YES
21	Throttle Position Sensor - voltage high	YES
22	Throttle Position Sensor - voltage low	YES
23	Intake Air Temperature Sensor - low temperature indicated	YES
24	Vehicle Speed Sensor Circuit	YES
25	Intake Air Temperature Sensor - high temperature indicated	YES
32	Exhaust Gas Recirculation Circuit	YES
33	MAP Sensor - High voltage, Low Vacuum indicated	YES
34	MAP Sensor - Low voltage, High Vacuum indicated	YES
35	IDLE Speed Control Circuit	YES
39	Transaxle Clutch Switch Circuit	YES
41	Cylinder Select Error	YES
42	Ignition Control (IC) Circuit	YES
43	Knock Sensor (KS) Circuit	YES
44	Oxygen Sensor - lean exhaust indicated	YES
45	Oxygen Sensor - rich exhaust indicated	YES
51	PROM Error	YES
53	System over voltage	YES
54	Fuel Pump Circuit - Low Voltage	YES
55	ECM Error	YES
61	Degraded Oxygen Sensor (O2S)	YES
66	A/C Pressure Sensor Circuit	NO

If a DTC not listed above appears on Tech 1, ground DLC diagnostic terminal "B" and observe flashed DTC(s).
If DTC does not reappear, refer to Tech 1 Operator's Guide.
If DTC does reappear, check for incorrect or faulty PROM.

88004G98

Fig. 99 Engine diagnostic trouble codes—1988–93 vehicles, except 3.8L engines

PCM DIAGNOSTIC TROUBLE CODES

DTC	DESCRIPTION	ILLUMINATE MIL
13	Heated Oxygen Sensor (HO2S) - open circuit	YES
14	Engine Coolant Temperature (ECT) Sensor Circuit (high temperature indicated)	YES
15	Engine Coolant Temperature (ECT) Sensor Circuit (low temperature indicated)	YES
16	System Low Voltage (low battery voltage)	YES
17	Camshaft Position Sensor Circuit Error	NO
21	Throttle Position (TP) Sensor Circuit (signal voltage high)	YES
22	Throttle Position (TP) Sensor Circuit (signal voltage low)	YES
23	Intake Air Temperature (IAT) Sensor Circuit (low temperature indicated)	YES
24	Vehicle Speed Sensor (VSS) Circuit (no signal voltage)	YES
25	Intake Air Temperature (IAT) Sensor Circuit (high temperature indicated)	YES
28	Transmission Range Switch Error	NO
33	Manifold Absolute Pressure (MAP) Sensor Circuit (signal voltage high - high MAP)	YES
34	Manifold Absolute Pressure (MAP) Sensor Circuit (signal voltage low - low MAP)	YES
35	Idle Speed Error	YES
36	Ignition Control 24X Signal Circuit Error	NO
37	TCC Brake Switch Error	NO
41	Ignition Control (EST) Error	NO
42	Ignition Control (EST) Bypass Error	YES
43	Knock Sensor (KS) Circuit Error	YES
44	Heated Oxygen Sensor (HO2S) Circuit (lean exhaust indicated)	YES
45	Heated Oxygen Sensor (HO2S) Circuit (rich exhaust indicated)	YES
46*	PASS Key II® Circuit (out of frequency range)	NO
51	PROM Error (faulty or incorrect calibration)	YES
53	System Voltage High	YES
54	Fuel Pump Circuit (low voltage)	YES
58	Trans Fluid Temperature (TFT) Sensor Circuit Low (high temperature)	NO
59	Trans Fluid Temperature (TFT) Sensor Circuit High (low temperature)	NO

* If Applicable

Fig. 101 Engine diagnostic trouble codes—1994–95 3.1L engines

PCM DIAGNOSTIC TROUBLE CODES

DTC	DESCRIPTION	ILLUMINATE MIL
66	A/C Refrigerant Pressure Sensor Circuit (low pressure)	NO
70	A/C Refrigerant Pressure Sensor Circuit (high pressure)	NO
72	Vehicle Speed Sensor (VSS) Circuit Signal Error	NO
75	Digital EGR #1 Solenoid (error)	YES
76	Digital EGR #2 Solenoid (error)	YES
77	Digital EGR #3 Solenoid (error)	YES
79	Transmission Fluid Overtemp	NO
80	Transmission Component Error	NO
82	Ignition Control 3X Signal Error	YES
85	PROM Error (faulty or incorrect calibration)	YES
86	Analog/Digital PCM Error	YES
87	Electrically Erasable Programmable Read Only Memory (EEPROM) Error	NO
90	TCC Error	NO
96	Trans System Voltage Low	NO
98	Invalid PCM Program	NO
99	Invalid PCM Program	NO

Fig. 102 Engine diagnostic trouble codes, continued—1994–95 3.1L engines

PCM DIAGNOSTIC TROUBLE CODES

DTC	FORMER DTC	DESCRIPTION	ILLUMINATE MIL
P0101	34	Mass Air Flow (MAF) Sensor - low gm/sec indicated	YES
P0112	23	Intake Air Temperature (IAT) Sensor - low temp. indicated	NO
P0113	25	Intake Air Temperature (IAT) Sensor - high temp. indicated	NO
P0117	15	Engine Coolant Temperature (ECT) Sensor - low temp. indicated	YES
P0118	14	Engine Coolant Temperature (ECT) Sensor - high temp. indicated	YES
P0122	22	Throttle Position (TP) Sensor voltage low	YES
P0123	21	Throttle Position (TP) Sensor voltage high	YES
P0125	-	Engine Coolant Temperature (ECT) Sensor - "Closed Loop" minimum temp not met in time	NO
P0131	44	Heated Oxygen Sensor (HO2S 1) - low signal voltage	YES
P0132	45	Heated Oxygen Sensor (HO2S 1) - high signal voltage	YES
P0134	13	Heated Oxygen Sensor (HO2S 1) - open circuit	YES
P0137	-	HO2S 2 (Catalyst Monitor) - low signal voltage	NO
P0138	-	HO2S 2 (Catalyst Monitor) - high signal voltage	NO
P0140	-	HO2S 2 (Catalyst Monitor) - open circuit	NO
P0171	-	Fuel Trim Lean	YES
P0172	-	Fuel Trim Rich	YES
P0300	-	Misfire Detected	YES
P0321	17	Spark Reference Circuit	NO
P0325	43	Knock Sensor (KS) Circuit	NO
P0341	18	Cam/Crank Error	YES
P0342	41	Cam Signal Circuit	YES
P1350	42	Ignition Control (IC) Circuit - open circuit	YES
P1361	42	Ignition Control (IC) Circuit - signal not toggling	YES
P0401	53/54/55	Exhaust Gas Recirculation (EGR) - flow failure	YES
P1406	-	Exhaust Gas Recirculation (EGR) - valve pintle position error	YES
P0420	-	Catalyst System - low oxygen storage capacity indicated	NO
P0501	24	Vehicle Speed Sensor (VSS) - intermittent signal	YES
P0502	24	Vehicle Speed Sensor (VSS) - no signal	YES
P1530	69	A/C Head Pressure Switch Circuit	NO
P1531	66	Excessive A/C Cycling (low refrigerant charge)	NO
P1550	-	Stepper Motor Cruise Control Problem	NO

Fig. 104 Engine diagnostic trouble codes—1994–95 3.8L engines

PCM DIAGNOSTIC TROUBLE CODES

DTC	DESCRIPTION	ILLUMINATE MIL
P0101	Mass Air Flow (MAF) Sensor Error - low gm/sec indicated	YES
P0112	Intake Air Temperature (IAT) Sensor - low temp. indicated	NO
P0113	Intake Air Temperature (IAT) Sensor - high temp. indicated	NO
P0117	Engine Coolant Temperature (ECT) Sensor - low temp. indicated	YES
P0118	Engine Coolant Temperature (ECT) Sensor - high temp. indicated	YES
P0122	Throttle Position (TP) Sensor voltage low	YES
P0123	Throttle Position (TP) Sensor voltage high	YES
P0131	Heated Oxygen Sensor (HO2S) - system lean	YES
P0132	Heated Oxygen Sensor (HO2S) - system rich	YES
P0134	Heated Oxygen Sensor (HO2S) - error	NO
P0321	IC 24X Signal Error	YES
P0325	Knock Sensor (KS) Circuit Error	YES
P0341	Cam Signal Error	YES
P0342	Cam Sensor Error	YES
P1350	Ignition Control Bypass Error	YES
P1361	Ignition Control Error	YES
P1403	EGR 1 Solenoid error	YES
P1404	EGR 2 Solenoid error	YES
P1405	EGR 3 Solenoid error	YES
P0501	Vehicle Speed Sensor (VSS) - intermittent signal	YES
P0502	Vehicle Speed Sensor (VSS) - no signal	YES
P1530	A/C Pressure Sensor Error	NO
P1550	Stepper Motor Cruise Control Engagement Error	NO
P1623	PROM Error	YES
P1626	PASS Key® II Error - invalid frequency seen after start-up	NO
P1629	PASS Key® II Signal Error - invalid frequency seen during crank	NO
P1630	System Voltage Error	YES
P1640	QDM A Error	YES
P1650	QDM B Error	NO
P0703	TCC Brake Switch Error	NO
P0705	Trans Range Switch Error	NO
P0712	Transaxle Fluid Temperature (TFT) Sensor - circuit high (low temp)	NO
P0713	Transaxle Fluid Temperature (TFT) Sensor - circuit high (high temp)	NO
P0740	Torque Convertor Clutch (TCC) Error	NO
P0755	Shift Solenoid "B" Error	NO

Fig. 103 Engine diagnostic trouble codes—1994–95 3.4L engines

Powertrain Control Module Diagnosis (PCM Diagnostic Trouble Codes)

Description	Illuminate MIL
DTC P0101 Mass Air Flow System Performance	Yes
DTC P0102 MAF Sensor Circuit Low Frequency	Yes
DTC P0103 MAF Sensor Circuit High Frequency	Yes
DTC P0106 MAP System Performance	Yes
DTC P0107 MAP Sensor Circuit Low Voltage	Yes
DTC P0108 MAP Sensor Circuit High Voltage	Yes
DTC P0112 IAT Sensor Circuit Low Voltage	Yes
DTC P0113 IAT Sensor Circuit High Voltage	Yes
DTC P0117 ECT Sensor Circuit Low Voltage	Yes
DTC P0118 ECT Sensor Circuit High Voltage	Yes
DTC P0121 TP Sensor Performance	Yes
DTC P0122 TP Sensor Circuit Low Voltage	Yes
DTC P0123 TP Sensor Circuit High Voltage	Yes
DTC P0125 ECT Excessive Time to Closed Loop	Yes
DTC P0131 HO2S Circuit Low Voltage Sensor1	Yes
DTC P0132 HO2S Circuit High Voltage Sensor1	Yes
DTC P0133 HO2S Circuit Slow Response Sensor1	Yes
DTC P0134 HO2S CKT Insufficient Activity Sensor1	Yes
DTC P0135 HO2S Heater Circuit Sensor1	Yes
DTC P0137 HO2S Circuit Low Voltage Sensor2	Yes
DTC P0138 HO2S Circuit High Voltage Sensor2	Yes
DTC P0140 HO2S CKT Insufficient Activity Sensor2	Yes
DTC P0141 HO2S Heater Circuit Sensor2	Yes
DTC P0171 Fuel Trim System Lean	Yes
DTC P0172 Fuel Trim System Rich	Yes
DTC P0300 Engine Misfire Detected	Yes
DTC P0325 Knock Sensor Module Circuit	No
DTC P0326 Knock Sensor Noise Channel High Voltage	No
DTC P0327 Knock Sensor Noise Channel Low Voltage	No
DTC P0336 18X Reference Signal Circuit	Yes
DTC P0341 CMP Sensor Circuit Performance	Yes
DTC P0401 EGR System Flow Insufficient	Yes
DTC P0420 TWC System Low Efficiency	Yes
DTC P0441 EVAP System No Flow During Purge	Yes
P0502 Vehicle Speed Sensor Circuit - Low Input	Yes
P0503 Vehicle Speed Sensor Circuit - Intermittent Input	Yes
DTC P0506 Idle Control System Low RPM	Yes
DTC P0507 Idle Control System High RPM	Yes

Fig. 106 Engine diagnostic trouble codes—1996 engines

PCM DIAGNOSTIC TROUBLE CODES

DTC	FORMER DTC	DESCRIPTION	ILLUMINATE MIL
P1623	51	PROM Error	YES
P1626	58	PASS Key ®II Fuel Enable Circuit - invalid frequency seen after start-up	NO
P1629	-	PASS Key ®II Fuel Enable Circuit - invalid frequency seen during crank	NO
P1630	16	System Voltage High or Low	YES
P1640	26/56	QDM 1 Circuit	YES
P1650	26/56	QDM 2 Circuit	NO
P1670	26/56	QDM 4 Circuit	NO
P0703	38	TCC Brake Input Circuit	NO
P0705	31	Trans Range Switch Circuit	NO
P0712	-	Transaxle Temperature Sensor - low temp. indicated	NO
P0713	-	Transaxle Temperature Sensor - high temp. indicated	NO
P0740	39	Torque Convertor Clutch (TCC) Problem	NO
P0755	36	Transaxle Shift B Solenoid Problem	NO

Fig. 105 Engine diagnostic trouble codes, continued—1994-95 3.8L engine

Powertrain Control Module Diagnosis (PCM Diagnostic Trouble Codes) (cont'd)

Description	Illuminate MIL
DTC P0530 A/C Refrigerant Pressure Sensor Circuit	No
DTC P0560 System Voltage	No
DTC P0601 PCM Memory	Yes
DTC P0602 PCM Not Programmed	No
DTC P0705 Trans Range Switch Circuit	No
DTC P0706 Transaxle Range Switch Performance	No
P0712 Transaxle Fluid Temperature (TFT) Sensor Circuit - Low Signal Voltage	Yes
P0713 Transaxle Fluid Temperature (TFT) Sensor Circuit - High Signal Voltage	Yes
P0719 Brake Switch Circuit Low	No
P0724 Brake Switch Circuit High	No
P0742 Torque Converter Clutch Circuit Stuck On	Yes
P0751 Shift Solenoid 1 - Performance/Stuck Off	Yes
P0753 Shift Solenoid 1 - Electrical	Yes
P0756 Shift Solenoid 2 - Performance/Stuck Off	Yes
P0758 Shift Solenoid 2 - Electrical	Yes
DTC P1106 MAP Sensor CKT Intermittent High Voltage	No
DTC P1107 MAP Sensor CKT Intermittent Low Voltage	No
DTC P1111 IAT Sensor CKT Intermittent High Voltage	No
DTC P1112 IAT Sensor CKT Intermittent Low Voltage	No
DTC P1114 ECT Sensor CKT Intermittent Low Voltage	No
DTC P1115 ECT Sensor CKT Intermittent High Voltage	No
DTC P1121 TP Sensor CKT Intermittent High Voltage	No
DTC P1122 TP Sensor CKT Intermittent Low Voltage	No
DTC P1133 HO2S Insufficient Switching Sensor1	Yes
DTC P1134 HO2S Transition Time Ratio Sensor1	Yes
DTC P1200 Injector Control Circuit	Yes
DTC P1350 Bypass Line Monitor	Yes
DTC P1361 IC Circuit Not Toggling	Yes
DTC P1374 3X Reference Circuit	Yes
DTC P1381 Misfire Detected No EBCM/PCM Serial Data	No
DTC P1406 EGR Valve Pintle Position Circuit	Yes
DTC P1441 EVAP System Flow During Non-Purge	Yes
DTC P1442 EVAP Vacuum Switch Circuit	Yes
DTC P1554 Cruise Control Status Circuit	No
DTC P1626 Theft Deterrent System Fuel Enable CKT	No

88004GC3

Fig. 107 Engine diagnostic trouble codes, continued—1996 engines

Powertrain Control Module Diagnosis (PCM Diagnostic Trouble Codes) (cont'd)

Description	Illuminate MIL
DTC P1629 Theft Deterrent Crank Signal Malfunction	No
DTC P1635 5 Volt Reference (A) Circuit	Yes
DTC P1639 5 Volt Reference (B) Circuit	No
DTC P1641 MIL Control Circuit	No
DTC P1651 Fan 1 Relay Control Circuit	Yes
DTC P1652 Fan 2 Relay Control Circuit	Yes
DTC P1654 A/C Relay Control Circuit	No
DTC P1655 EVAP Purge Solenoid Control Circuit	Yes
DTC P1662 Cruise Control Inhibit Control Circuit	No
DTC P1672 Low Engine Oil Level Lamp Control CKT	No
P1812 Transaxle Over Temperature Condition	Yes
P1860 Torque Converter Clutch PWM Solenoid Circuit	Yes
P1864 Torque Converter Clutch Enable Solenoid Circuit	Yes
P1870 Transaxle Component Slipping	Yes

88004GC4

Fig. 108 Engine diagnostic trouble codes, continued—1996 engines

VACUUM DIAGRAMS

Following is a listing of vacuum diagrams for many of the engine and emissions package combinations covered by this manual. Because vacuum circuits will vary based on various engine and vehicle options, always refer first to the vehicle emission control information label. Should the label be missing, or should the vehicle be equipped with a different engine from the original equipment, refer to the diagrams below for the same or similar configuration.

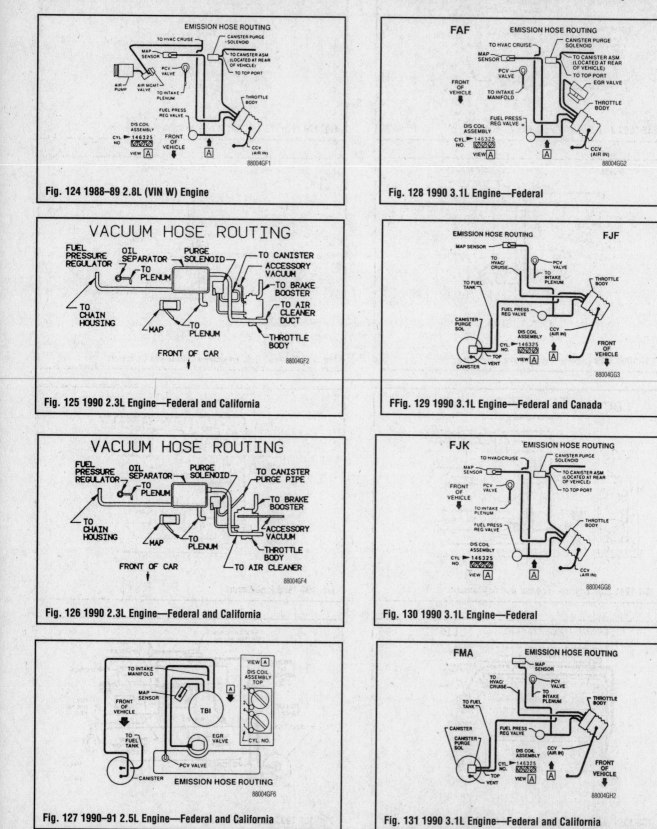

Fig. 124 1988–89 2.8L (VIN W) Engine

Fig. 125 1990 2.3L Engine—Federal and California

Fig. 126 1990 2.3L Engine—Federal and California

Fig. 127 1990–91 2.5L Engine—Federal and California

Fig. 128 1990 3.1L Engine—Federal

FFig. 129 1990 3.1L Engine—Federal and Canada

Fig. 130 1990 3.1L Engine—Federal

Fig. 131 1990 3.1L Engine—Federal and California

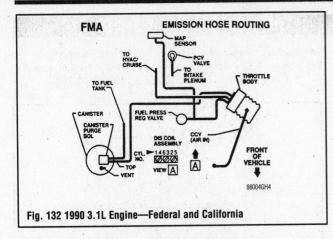

Fig. 132 1990 3.1L Engine—Federal and California

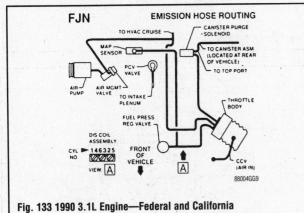

Fig. 133 1990 3.1L Engine—Federal and California

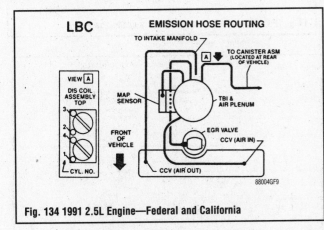

Fig. 134 1991 2.5L Engine—Federal and California

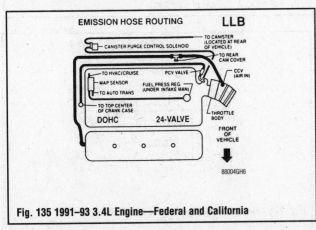

Fig. 135 1991–93 3.4L Engine—Federal and California

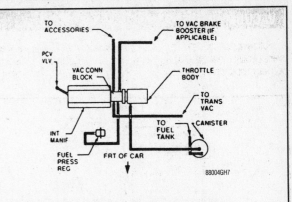

Fig. 136 1991–93 3.8L Engine—Federal and California

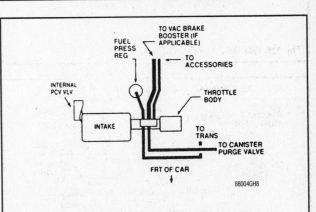

Fig. 137 1991–93 3.8L Engine—Federal and California

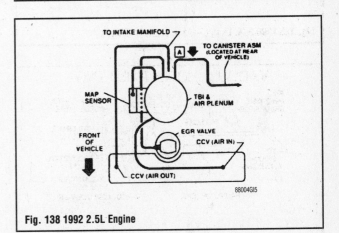

Fig. 138 1992 2.5L Engine

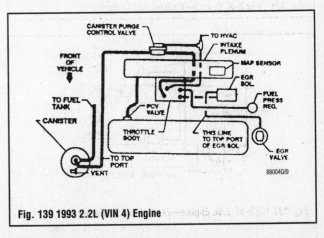

Fig. 139 1993 2.2L (VIN 4) Engine

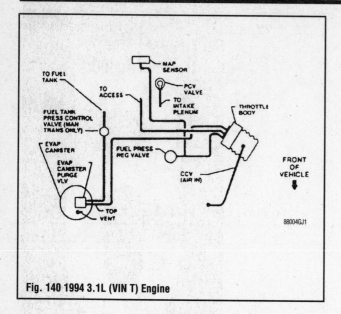

Fig. 140 1994 3.1L (VIN T) Engine

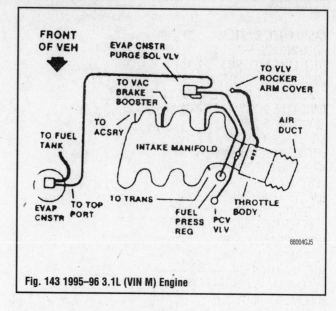

Fig. 143 1995–96 3.1L (VIN M) Engine

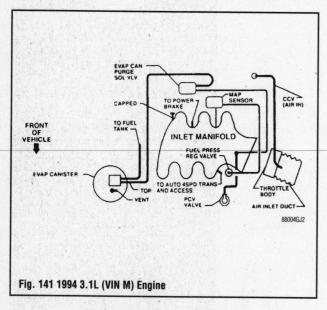

Fig. 141 1994 3.1L (VIN M) Engine

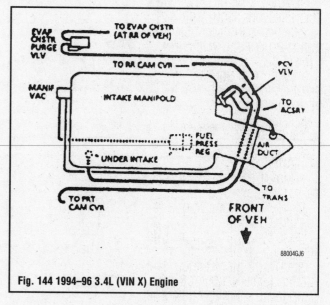

Fig. 144 1994–96 3.4L (VIN X) Engine

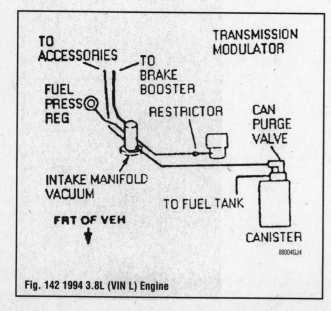

Fig. 142 1994 3.8L (VIN L) Engine

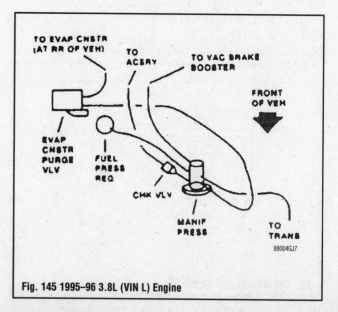

Fig. 145 1995–96 3.8L (VIN L) Engine

5

FUEL SYSTEMS

BASIC FUEL SYSTEM DIAGNOSIS

When there is a problem starting or driving a vehicle, two of the most important checks involve the ignition and the fuel systems. The questions most mechanics attempt to answer first, "is there spark?" and "is there fuel?" will often lead to solving most basic problems. For ignition system diagnosis and testing, please refer to the information on engine electrical components and ignition systems found earlier in this manual. If the ignition system checks out (there is spark), then you must determine if the fuel system is operating properly (is there fuel?).

FUEL LINE FITTINGS

Quick-Connect Fittings

REMOVAL & INSTALLATION

▶ **See Figure 1**

➡ **This procedure requires Tool Set J37088–A fuel line quick-connect separator.**

1. Grasp both sides of the fitting. Twist the female connector ¼ turn in each direction to loosen any dirt within the fittings. Using compressed air, blow out the dirt from the quick-connect fittings at the end of the fittings.

✳✳ CAUTION

Safety glasses MUST be worn when using compressed air to avoid eye injury due to flying dirt particles!

2. For plastic (hand releasable) fittings, squeeze the plastic retainer release tabs, then pull the connection apart.
3. For metal fittings, choose the correct tool from kit J37088–A for the size of the fitting to be disconnected. Insert the proper tool into the female connector, then push inward to release the locking tabs. Pull the connection apart.
4. If it is necessary to remove rust or burrs from the male tube end of a quick-connect fitting, use emery cloth in a radial motion with the tube end to prevent damage to the O-ring sealing surfaces. Using a clean shop towel, wipe off the male tube ends. Inspect all connectors for dirt and burrs. Clean and/or replace if required.

To install:

5. Apply a few drops of clean engine oil to the male tube end of the fitting.
6. Push the connectors together to cause the retaining tabs/fingers to snap into place.
7. Once installed, pull on both ends of each connection to make sure they are secure.

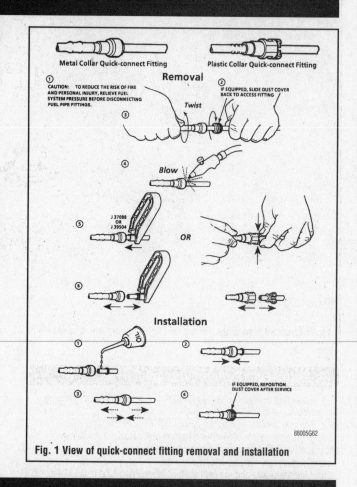

Fig. 1 View of quick-connect fitting removal and installation

THROTTLE BODY INJECTION (TBI) SYSTEM

System Description

▶ **See Figure 2**

The electronic Throttle Body Injection (TBI) system, used on 2.5L engines, is a fuel metering system with the amount of fuel delivered by the throttle body injector determined by an electronic signal supplied by the Electronic Control Module (ECM). The ECM monitors various engine and vehicle conditions to calculate the fuel delivery time (pulse width) of the injector. The fuel pulse may be modified by the ECM to account for special operating conditions, such as cranking, cold starting, altitude, acceleration, and deceleration.

The TBI system provides a means of fuel distribution for controlling exhaust emissions within legislated limits. The TBI system, by precisely controlling the air/fuel mixture under all operating conditions, provides as near as possible complete combustion.

This is accomplished by using an Electronic Control Module (ECM) (a small on-board microcomputer) that receives electrical inputs from various sensors about engine operating conditions. An oxygen sensor in the main exhaust stream functions to provide feedback information to the ECM as to the oxygen content, lean or rich, in the exhaust. The ECM uses this information from the oxygen sensor, and other sensors, to modify fuel delivery to achieve, as near as possible, an ideal air/fuel ratio of 14.7:1. This air/fuel ratio allows the 3-way catalytic converter to be more efficient in the conversion process of reducing exhaust emissions while at the same time providing acceptable levels of driveability and fuel economy.

The basic TBI model 700 is made up of 2 major casting assemblies: (1) a throttle body with a valve to control airflow and (2) a fuel body assembly with an integral pressure regulator and fuel injector to supply the required fuel. A device to control idle speed (Idle Air Control Valve) and a device to provide information about throttle valve position (Throttle Position Sensor) are included as part of the TBI unit.

Service Precautions

When working around any part of the fuel system, take precautionary steps to prevent fire and/or explosion:

• Disconnect negative terminal from battery (except when testing with battery voltage is required).
• When ever possible, use a flashlight instead of a drop light.
• Keep all open flame and smoking material out of the area.
• Use a shop cloth or similar to catch fuel when opening a fuel system.
• Relieve fuel system pressure before servicing.
• Use eye protection.
• Always keep a dry chemical (class B) fire extinguisher near the area.

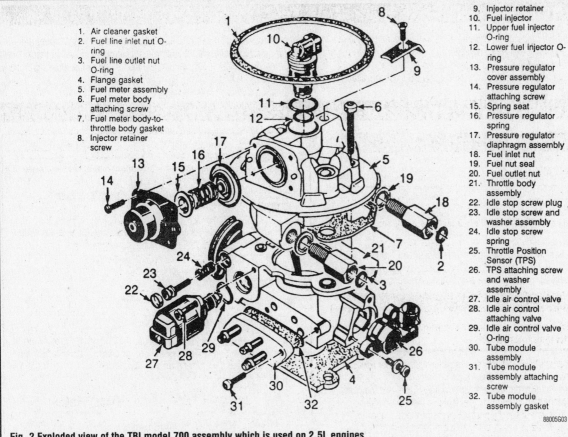

1. Air cleaner gasket
2. Fuel line inlet nut O-ring
3. Fuel line outlet nut O-ring
4. Flange gasket
5. Fuel meter assembly
6. Fuel meter body attaching screw
7. Fuel meter body-to-throttle body gasket
8. Injector retainer screw
9. Injector retainer
10. Fuel injector
11. Upper fuel injector O-ring
12. Lower fuel injector O-ring
13. Pressure regulator cover assembly
14. Pressure regulator attaching screw
15. Spring seat
16. Pressure regulator spring
17. Pressure regulator diaphragm assembly
18. Fuel inlet nut
19. Fuel nut seal
20. Fuel outlet nut
21. Throttle body assembly
22. Idle stop screw plug
23. Idle stop screw and washer assembly
24. Idle stop screw spring
25. Throttle Position Sensor (TPS)
26. TPS attaching screw and washer assembly
27. Idle air control valve
28. Idle air control attaching valve
29. Idle air control valve O-ring
30. Tube module assembly
31. Tube module assembly attaching screw
32. Tube module assembly gasket

88005G03

Fig. 2 Exploded view of the TBI model 700 assembly which is used on 2.5L engines

Relieving Fuel System Pressure

1. Loosen or remove the fuel filler cap to relieve fuel tank vapor pressure (do not tighten at this time).
2. Raise and safely support the vehicle.
3. From under the vehicle, detach the fuel pump electrical connector. It should be the only connector coming from the fuel tank.
4. Carefully lower the vehicle.
5. Start the engine and run until the fuel supply remaining in the fuel pipes is consumed (until the engine stalls). Crank the starter for an additional 3 seconds to assure relief of any remaining pressure.
6. Raise and safely support the vehicle, then attach the fuel pump electrical connector. Carefully lower the vehicle.
7. Install or tighten the fuel filler cap.
8. Disconnect the negative battery cable, to avoid possible fuel discharge if an accidental attempt is made to start the engine.

Electric Fuel Pump

TESTING

1. Relieve the fuel pressure from the fuel system.
2. Turn the ignition switch is **OFF**.
3. Uncouple the fuel supply flexible hose in the engine compartment and install fuel pressure gauge J29658/BT8205 or equivalent in the pressure line.
4. Be sure to tighten the fuel line to the gauge to ensure that there no leaks during testing.
5. Start the engine and observe the fuel pressure reading. The fuel pressure should be 26–32 psi (179–220 kPa).
6. Relieve the fuel pressure. Remove the fuel pressure gauge and reinstall the fuel line. Be sure to install a new O-ring on the fuel feed line.
7. Start the engine and check for fuel leaks.

REMOVAL & INSTALLATION

1990 Vehicles

◆ See Figure 3

1. Properly relieve the fuel system pressure, as outlined earlier in this section.
2. If not already done, disconnect the negative battery cable.
3. Raise and safely support the vehicle with jackstands.
4. Safely drain, then remove the fuel tank assembly as outlined later in this section.
5. Turn the fuel pump cam lockring counterclockwise and lift the assembly out of the tank.
6. Remove the fuel pump from the level sensor unit as follows:
   a. Pull the pump up into the attaching hose or pulsator while pulling outward away from the bottom support.
   b. Take care to prevent damage to the rubber insulator and strainer during removal.
   c. When the pump assembly is clear of the bottom support, pull the pump out of the rubber connector for removal.

To install:

7. Replace any attaching hoses or rubber sound insulator that show signs of deterioration.
8. Push the fuel pump into the attaching hoses and install the pump/sensor assembly into the tank. Always use a new O-ring seal.

➡**Be careful not to fold over or twist the strainer when installing the sensor unit. Also, make sure the strainer does not block full travel of the float arm.**

9. Install the camlock and turn clockwise to lock.
10. Install the fuel tank as outlined in this section.
11. Carefully lower the vehicle, then connect the negative battery cable.
12. Fill the tank with four gallons of gas and check for fuel leaks.

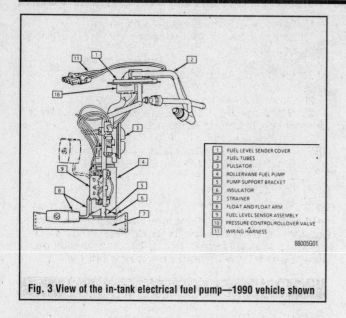

1	FUEL LEVEL SENDER COVER
2	FUEL TUBES
3	PULSATOR
4	ROLLERVANE FUEL PUMP
5	PUMP SUPPORT BRACKET
6	INSULATOR
7	STRAINER
8	FLOAT AND FLOAT ARM
9	FUEL LEVEL SENSOR ASSEMBLY
10	PRESSURE CONTROL/ROLLOVER VALVE
11	WIRING HARNESS

88005G01

Fig. 3 View of the in-tank electrical fuel pump—1990 vehicle shown

1991–92 Vehicles

▶ See Figure 4

1. Properly relieve the fuel system pressure, as outlined earlier in this section.
2. If not already done, disconnect the negative battery cable.
3. Raise and safely support the vehicle with jackstands.
4. Safely drain, then remove the fuel tank assembly as outlined later in this section.

➡**Clean all fuel pipe and hose connections and surrounding areas before disconnecting to avoid possible contamination of the fuel system.**

5. For 1991 vehicles, disconnect the rear fuel feed and return pipe assemblies from the fuel level meter.
6. For 1992 vehicles, disconnect the chassis-to-sender fuel feed and return pipes as follows:
    a. Grasp the fuel feed pipe and fuel sender quick-connect fitting. Twist the quick-connect fitting ¼ turn in each direction to loosen any dirt within the quick-connect fitting. Repeat for the other fitting

✳✳ CAUTION

Safely glasses MUST be worn when using compressed air, as flying dirt particles may cause eye injury.

b. Using compressed air, blow out the dirt from the quick-connect fitting.
    c. Squeeze the plastic tabs of the male end quick connector and pull the connection apart. Repeat for the other fitting.
7. Using tool J 35731 or equivalent, remove the fuel level meter assembly retaining cam, fuel level meter assembly and the O-ring from the fuel tank. Discard the fuel level meter O-ring and the fuel feed and return tube O-rings.
8. Support the pump with on hand and grasp the strainer with the other hand. Rotate the strainer in one direction and pull off of the pump. Discard the strainer after inspection.
9. Detach the fuel pump electrical connector.
10. Place the sender assembly, upside down, on a clean bench. Pull the fuel pump downward to remove the mounting bracket, then tilt the pump outward and remove from the fuel pulse dampener.
11. Inspect the fuel pump strainer. If the strainer is contaminated, then fuel tank should be cleaned. Check the fuel pump inlet for dirt and/or debris. If found, the fuel pump should be replaced. Clean any necessary mating surfaces.

To install:

12. Place the rubber bumper and rubber insulator on the fuel pump.
13. Position the fuel sender assembly upside down. Install the fuel pump between the fuel pulse dampener and mounting bracket.
14. Attach the fuel pump electrical connector.
15. Position a new pump strainer on the fuel pump and push on the outer edge of the ferrule until fully seated.

➡**Always install a new fuel pump strainer when installing the pump.**

16. Place a new fuel sender assembly O-ring on the fuel tank.

➡**Care should be taken not to fold over or twist the fuel pump strainer when installing the fuel sender assembly, as this will restrict fuel flow. Also, make sure the fuel pump strainer does not block full travel of the float arm.**

17. Install the fuel sender assembly and the fuel sender assembly retainer cam using tool J 35731.
18. For 1992 vehicles connect the fuel feed and return pipes, as follows:
    a. Apply a few drops of clean engine oil to the male tube ends.
    b. Push the connectors together to cause the retaining tabs/fingers to snap into place.
    c. Once installed, pull on both ends of each connection to make sure they are secure.
    d. Repeat for the other fitting.
19. For 1991 vehicles, position new O-rings on the fuel level meter fuel feed and return tubes. Attach the rear fuel feed and return pipe assemblies to the fuel level meter. Tighten the fittings to 16 ft. lbs. (22 Nm).
20. Install the fuel tank as outlined in this section.
21. Carefully lower the vehicle, then connect the negative battery cable.
22. Fill the tank with about four gallons of gas and check for fuel leaks. Turn the ignition switch to the **ON** position for 2 seconds, then turn **OFF** for 10 seconds. Again, turn the ignition to the **ON** position, and check for fuel leaks.

1	FUEL SENDER
2	FUEL PULSE DAMPENER
3	BUMPER
4	FUEL PUMP - ELECTRIC
5	INSULATOR
6	FUEL PUMP STRAINER
7	MOUNTING BRACKET
8	FUEL PUMP ELECTRICAL CONNECTOR
9	FUEL FEED TUBE
10	FUEL SENDER ASSEMBLY WIRING

88005G02

Fig. 4 Exploded view of the fuel pump and related components—1992 vehicle shown

Throttle Body

REMOVAL & INSTALLATION

▶ See Figure 5

1. Properly relieve the fuel system pressure, as outlined earlier in this section.
2. If not already done, disconnect the negative battery cable.
3. Remove the flexible air duct from the TBI bonnet.
4. Disconnect the crankcase vent hose.
5. Detach the electrical connector and vacuum hose at the MAP sensor.
6. Remove the air intake duct.
7. Detach the electrical connectors from the Idle Air Control (IAC) valve, Throttle Position Sensor (TPS), and fuel injector.
8. Remove the grommet, with the wires from the fuel meter body.
9. Disconnect the throttle cable, transmission control cable and, if equipped, the cruise control cable.
10. Tag and disconnect any necessary vacuum hoses.
11. Disconnect the fuel feed and return lines, using tool J 2968-A or equivalent back-up wrench, on the fuel nuts to prevent them from turning.
12. Remove and discard the fuel line O-rings.
13. Unfasten the TBI attaching bolts/studs, then remove the throttle body assembly from the vehicle. Remove and discard the throttle body flange gasket.
14. Thoroughly clean the gasket mating surfaces.

➡ Make sure to cover any openings to prevent and dirt or other contaminants from entering the engine while the throttle body is removed.

To install:
15. Position a new flange gasket, then position the TBI unit over the gasket. Install the attaching bolts/studs, then tighten to 18 ft. lbs. (25 Nm).
16. Place new O-rings on the fuel lines, then connect the feed and return lines. Tighten the fuel line nuts to 22 ft. lbs. (30 Nm), using tool J 29698-A or equivalent to prevent the nuts from turning.

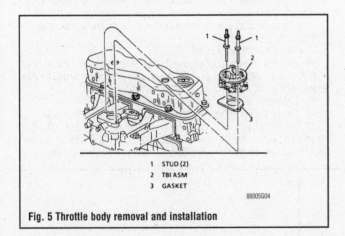

```
1  STUD (2)
2  TBI ASM
3  GASKET
                        88005G04
```

Fig. 5 Throttle body removal and installation

17. Connect the vacuum hoses, as tagged during removal.
18. Attach the throttle cable, transmission control cable and, if equipped, the cruise control cable.
19. Install the grommet with the wires to the fuel meter body.
20. Attach the electrical connectors, making sure they are fully seated and latched.
21. Connect the negative battery cable.
22. With the engine **OFF**, check to see that the accelerator pedal is free by depressing the pedal to the floor, then releasing it.
23. Turn the ignition switch to the **ON** position for 2 seconds, then turn **OFF** for 10 seconds. Again turn the switch **ON** and check for fuel leaks.
24. Install the air intake duct (TBI bonnet) with the gasket.
25. Attach the electrical connector and vacuum hose to the MAP sensor.
26. Connect the crankcase vent hose.
27. Attach the flexible air duct to the TBI bonnet.

➡ No physical adjustment of the IAC valve assembly is required after installation. The IAC valve is reset by the ECM when the vehicle is driven at a speed above 30 mph (48 kph), or when the diagnostic test terminal is grounded while the engine speed is above 2000 rpm.

Fuel Injector

REMOVAL & INSTALLATION

▶ See Figures 6, 7 and 8

➡ Use care in removing the injector to prevent damage to the electrical connector pins on top of the injector, the injector fuel filter and the nozzle. The fuel injector is serviced as a complete assembly only. The fuel injector is an electrical component and should not be immersed in any type of cleaner.

1. Properly relieve the fuel system pressure. If not done already, disconnect the negative battery cable.
2. Remove the air intake duct (TBI bonnet).
3. Detach the injector electrical connector by squeezing on the tabs and pulling straight up.
4. Remove the injector retainer screw and retainer.
5. Using a smooth object, such as a fulcrum, place a suitable prytool blade under the ridge opposite the electrical connector end of the fuel injector and carefully pry it out.
6. Remove the injector from the throttle body. Remove and discard the upper and lower O-rings from the injector cavity.

➡ Check the fuel injector filter for evidence of dirt and contamination. If present, check for presence of dirt in the fuel lines or fuel tank. Be sure to replace the injector with an identical part. Injectors from other models may fit in the TBI 700 unit, but are calibrated for different flow rates.

To install:
7. Lubricate the new upper and lower O-rings with clean engine oil, then place them on the injector. Make sure that the upper O-ring is in the groove and the lower one is flush up against the injector fuel filter.

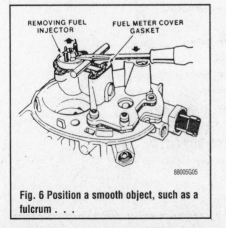

Fig. 6 Position a smooth object, such as a fulcrum . . .

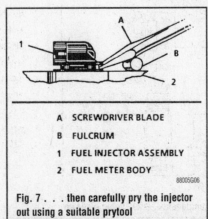

```
A  SCREWDRIVER BLADE
B  FULCRUM
1  FUEL INJECTOR ASSEMBLY
2  FUEL METER BODY
                        88005G06
```

Fig. 7 . . . then carefully pry the injector out using a suitable prytool

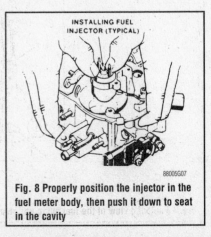

Fig. 8 Properly position the injector in the fuel meter body, then push it down to seat in the cavity

8. Install the injector assembly, pushing it straight into the fuel injector cavity. Be sure that the electrical connector end of the injector is parallel to the casting support rib and facing in the direction of the cut-out in the fuel meter body for the wire grommet.

9. Coat the threads of the injector retainer with Loctite® 262 or equivalent, then install the injector retainer and tighten the screw to 27 inch lbs. (3 Nm).

10. Connect the negative battery cable.

11. With the engine **OFF**, check to see that the accelerator pedal is free by depressing the pedal to the floor, then releasing it.

12. Turn the ignition switch to the **ON** position for 2 seconds, then turn **OFF** for 10 seconds. Again turn the switch **ON** and check for fuel leaks.

13. Install the air intake duct (TBI bonnet) with the gasket.

Fuel Meter Body

REMOVAL & INSTALLATION

▶ **See Figure 9**

1. Properly relieve the fuel system pressure. If not already done, disconnect the negative battery cable.

2. Remove the air intake duct (TBI bonnet).

3. Detach the electrical connector from the injector. Remove the grommet with wires from the fuel meter assembly.

4. Disconnect the fuel inlet and outlet lines and O-rings. Be sure to use tool J 28698-A, or equivalent back-up wrench, to keep the fuel nuts from turning. Discard the old fuel line O-rings.

5. Unfasten the TBI mounting bolts/studs. Remove the 2 fuel meter body attaching screws.

6. Remove the fuel meter assembly from the throttle body. Remove and discard the fuel meter-to-throttle body gasket.

To install:

7. Position a new throttle body-to-fuel meter body gasket. Make sure to match the cut portions in the gasket with the opening in the throttle body.

8. Place the fuel meter body assembly onto the throttle body assembly.

9. Coat the threads of the fuel meter body attaching screws with Loctite® 262 or equivalent, install the fuel meter body-to-throttle body attaching screws.

10. Tighten the screws to 31 inch lbs. (3.5 Nm). Install the fuel inlet and outlet nuts with new gaskets to the fuel meter body assembly. Tighten the inlet and outlet nuts to 18 ft. lbs. (25 Nm).

11. Place new O-rings on the fuel feed and return lines. Install the fuel inlet and return lines. Tighten the fuel line nuts to 22 ft. lbs. (30 Nm), making sure to use a back-up wrench to keep the TBI nuts from turning.

12. Install the grommet with wires to the fuel meter assembly. Attach the electrical connector to the injector.

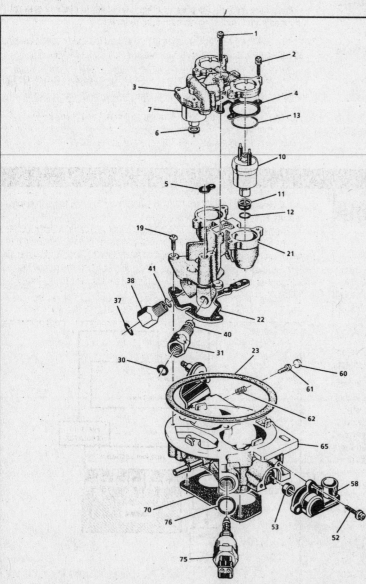

1	SCREW ASSEMBLY - FUEL METER COVER ATTACHING - LONG
2	SCREW ASSEMBLY - FUEL METER COVER ATTACHING - SHORT
3	FUEL METER COVER ASSEMBLY
4	GASKET - FUEL METER COVER
5	GASKET - FUEL METER OUTLET
6	SEAL - PRESSURE REGULATOR
7	PRESSURE REGULATOR
10	TBI FUEL INJECTOR ASSEMBLY
11	FILTER - FUEL INJECTOR INLET
12	O-RING - FUEL INJECTOR - LOWER
13	O-RING - FUEL INJECTOR - UPPER
19	SCREW - FUEL METER BODY - THROTTLE BODY ATTACHING
21	FUEL METER BODY ASSEMBLY
22	GASKET - THROTTLE BODY TO FUEL METER BODY
23	GASKET - AIR CLEANER
30	O-RING - FUEL RETURN LINE
31	NUT - FUEL INLET
37	O-RING - FUEL INLET NUT
38	NUT - FUEL INLET
40	GASKET - FUEL OUTLET NUT
41	GASKET - FUEL INLET NUT
52	SCREW ASSEMBLY - TPS ATTACHING
53	SEAL - THROTTLE POSITION SENSOR
58	SENSOR - THROTTLE POSITION (TPS)
60	PLUG - IDLE STOP SCREW
61	SCREW ASSEMBLY - IDLE STOP
62	SPRING - IDLE STOP SCREW
65	THROTTLE BODY ASSEMBLY
70	GASKET - FLANGE
75	IDLE AIR CONTROL VALVE ASSEMBLY
76	GASKET - IDLE AIR CONTROL VALVE ASSEMBLY

88005G08

Fig. 9 Exploded view of the fuel meter body and related TBI unit components

13. Connect the negative battery cable.

14. With the engine **OFF**, check to see that the accelerator pedal is free by depressing the pedal to the floor, then releasing it.

15. Turn the ignition switch to the **ON** position for 2 seconds, then turn **OFF** for 10 seconds. Again turn the switch **ON** and check for fuel leaks.

16. Install the air intake duct (TBI bonnet) with the gasket.

Fuel Pressure Regulator

REMOVAL & INSTALLATION

▶ See Figure 10

1. Properly relieve the fuel system pressure. If not already done, disconnect the negative battery cable.

2. Remove the air intake duct (TBI bonnet).

3. Unfasten the 4 pressure regulator retaining screws, while keeping the pressure regulator compressed by maintaining pressure on the regulator cover.

❋❋ CAUTION

The pressure regulator contains a large spring under heavy compression. Use care when removing the screws to prevent personal injury.

4. Carefully remove the pressure regulator cover, then remove the pressure regulator spring, spring seat and pressure regulator diaphragm assembly.

➡**To prevent leaks, the pressure regulator diaphragm assembly must be replaced whenever the cover is removed.**

5. Check the pressure regulator seat in the fuel meter body cavity for pitting, nicks or irregularities. Use a magnifying glass if necessary. If any of the above is present, the whole fuel body casting must be replaced.

To install:

6. Install the new pressure regulator diaphragm assembly making sure it is seated in the groove in the fuel meter body.

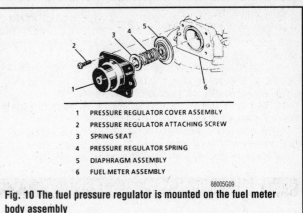

1	PRESSURE REGULATOR COVER ASSEMBLY
2	PRESSURE REGULATOR ATTACHING SCREW
3	SPRING SEAT
4	PRESSURE REGULATOR SPRING
5	DIAPHRAGM ASSEMBLY
6	FUEL METER ASSEMBLY

88005G09

Fig. 10 The fuel pressure regulator is mounted on the fuel meter body assembly

7. Install the regulator spring seat and spring into the cover assembly.

8. Position the cover assembly over the diaphragm, while aligning the mounting holes. Be sure to use care while installing the pressure regulator to prevent misalignment of the diaphragm and possible leaks.

➡**Make sure the hold the pressure regulator cover in place to prevent the diaphragm from slipping out of the groove.**

9. Coat the 4 regulator retaining bolts with Loctite® 262 or equivalent suitable thread sealer, then tighten the screws to 21 inch lbs. (2.4 Nm).

10. Connect the negative battery cable.

11. With the engine **OFF**, check to see that the accelerator pedal is free by depressing the pedal to the floor, then releasing it.

12. Turn the ignition switch to the **ON** position for 2 seconds, then turn **OFF** for 10 seconds. Again turn the switch **ON** and check for fuel leaks.

13. Install the air intake duct (TBI bonnet) with the gasket.

MULTI-PORT FUEL INJECTION (MFI)

System Description

▶ See Figure 11

The Multi-port Fuel Injection (MFI) system is controlled by an Electronic Control Module (ECM) which monitors engine operations and generates output signals to provide the correct air/fuel mixture, ignition timing and engine idle speed control. Input to the control unit is provided by an oxygen sensor, coolant temperature sensor, detonation sensor, hot film air mass sensor and throttle position sensor. The ECM also receives information concerning engine rpm, road speed, transmission gear position, power steering and air conditioning.

➡**Some later model vehicles are equipped with a Sequential Fuel Injection (SFI) system. This system operates basically the same and consists of the same components as the MFI system.**

With MFI, metered fuel is timed and injected sequentially through the injectors into individual cylinder ports. Each cylinder receives 1 injection per working cycle (every 2 revolutions), just prior to the opening of the intake valve. In addition, on V6 engines, the SFI system incorporates a Computer Controlled Coil Ignition (CI) system that uses an electronic coil module that replaced the conventional distributor and coil used on most engines. An Electronic Spark Control (ESC) is used to adjust the spark timing.

The injection system uses solenoid-type fuel injectors, 1 at each intake port, rather than the single injector found on the earlier throttle body system. The injectors are mounted on a fuel rail and are activated by a signal from the electronic control module. The injector is a solenoid-operated valve which remains open depending on the width of the electronic pulses (length of the signal) from the ECM; the longer the open time, the more fuel is injected. In this manner, the air/fuel mixture can be precisely controlled for maximum performance with minimum emissions.

Fuel is pumped from the tank by a high pressure fuel pump, located inside the fuel tank. It is a positive displacement roller vane pump. The impeller serves as a vapor separator and pre-charges the high pressure assembly. A pressure

regulator maintains 34–47 psi (240–315 kPa) in the fuel line to the injectors and the excess fuel is fed back to the tank.

Engine idle is controlled by an Idle Air Control (IAC) valve, which provides a bypass channel through which air can flow. It consists of an orifice and pintle which is controlled by the ECM through a stepper motor. The IAC provides air flow for idle and allows additional air during cold start until the engine reaches operating temperature. As the engine temperature rises, the opening through which air passes is slowly closed.

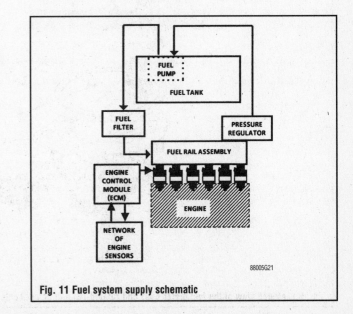

88005G21

Fig. 11 Fuel system supply schematic

Service Precautions

When working around any part of the fuel system, take precautionary steps to prevent fire and/or explosion:
- Disconnect negative terminal from battery (except when testing with battery voltage is required).
- When ever possible, use a flashlight instead of a drop light.
- Keep all open flame and smoking material out of the area.
- Use a shop cloth or similar to catch fuel when opening a fuel system.
- Relieve fuel system pressure before servicing.
- Use eye protection.
- Always keep a dry chemical (class B) fire extinguisher near the area.

Relieving Fuel System Pressure

PROCEDURE

2.2L Engine

1. Loosen or remove the fuel filler cap to relieve fuel tank vapor pressure (do not tighten at this time).
2. Raise and safely support the vehicle.
3. From under the vehicle, detach the fuel pump electrical connector. It should be the only connector coming from the fuel tank.
4. Carefully lower the vehicle.
5. Start the engine and run until the fuel supply remaining in the fuel pipes is consumed (until the engine stalls). Crank the starter for an additional 3 seconds to assure relief of any remaining pressure.
6. Raise and safely support the vehicle, then attach the fuel pump electrical connector. Carefully lower the vehicle.
7. Install or tighten the fuel filler cap.
8. Disconnect the negative battery cable, to avoid possible fuel discharge if an accidental attempt is made to start the engine.

Except 2.2L Engine

1. Disconnect the negative battery cable to avoid possible fuel discharge if an accidental attempt is made to start the engine.
2. Loosen the fuel filler cap to relieve fuel tank vapor pressure.
3. Connect fuel pressure valve J 34730-1 or equivalent to the fuel pressure relief connection at the fuel rail.
4. Wrap a shop towel around the fittings while connecting the tool to prevent fuel spillage.
5. Install a bleed hose into an approved container and open the valve to bleed the system pressure.
6. Install the fuel filler cap.

Electric Fuel Pump

TESTING

1. Connect pressure gauge J–34730–1, or equivalent, to fuel pressure test point on the fuel rail. Wrap a rag around the pressure tap to absorb any leakage that may occur when installing the gauge.
2. Turn the ignition **ON** and check that pump pressure is 24–40 psi. (165–276 kPa)
3. Start the engine and allow it to idle. The fuel pressure should drop to 28–32 psi (193–221 kPa) due to the lower manifold pressure.

➡**The idle pressure will vary somewhat depending on barometric pressure. Check for a drop in pressure indicating regulator control, rather than specific values.**

4. If the fuel pressure drops, check the operation of the check valve, the pump coupling connection, fuel pressure regulator valve and the injectors. A restricted fuel line or filter may also cause a pressure drip. To check the fuel pump output, restrict the fuel return line and run 12 volts to the pump. The fuel pressure should rise to approximately 75 psi (517 kPa) with the return line restricted.
5. Before attempting to remove or service any fuel system component, it is necessary to relieve the fuel system pressure.

REMOVAL & INSTALLATION

▶ **See Figure 12**

1. Properly relieve the fuel system pressure, as outlined earlier.

✳ CAUTION

Fuel injection systems remain under pressure, even after the engine has been turned OFF. The fuel system pressure must be relieved before disconnecting any fuel lines. Failure to do so may result in fire and/or personal injury.

2. If not already done, disconnect the negative battery cable.
3. Raise and safely support the vehicle with jackstands.
4. Safely drain and remove the fuel tank assembly as outlined later in this section.
5. Detach the quick-connects from the fuel sender assembly and remove the fuel lines.
6. Using tool J 35731, or an equivalent spanner wrench, remove the fuel sender lockring.
7. Lift the sender assembly carefully out of the fuel tank.
8. Remove the sender O-ring from the top of the sender and discard.

✳ WARNING

Do NOT run the fuel pump unless it is submerged in fuel. Running the pump dry will cause serious damage to the fuel pump and may cause the pump to explode due to the oxygen in the air.

9. Note the position of the fuel pump strainer on the fuel pump and, while supporting the pump assembly in one hand, twist the strainer off the pump and discard the strainer.
10. Detach the fuel pump electrical connector.
11. Remove the clamp from the fuel line at the top of the pump.
12. Hold the fuel sender upside down on a work bench and pull the fuel pump out of the lower mounting bracket. Once the pump is clear of the lower mounting bracket, tilt the pump outward and disconnect the pump from the sender assembly.

To install:
13. Replace any attaching hoses or rubber sound insulators that show signs of deterioration.
14. Install the rubber bumper and insulator on the fuel pump.
15. Hold the fuel sender upside down and install the fuel pump between the fuel pulse dampener and mounting bracket.
16. Attach the fuel pump electrical connector.
17. Install the retaining clamp on the fuel line.
18. Install a new fuel pump strainer on the outer edge of the ferrule until fully seated. The strainer must be facing the same direction as it was before removal.
19. Position a new O-ring on the top of the fuel tank and install the sender assembly.

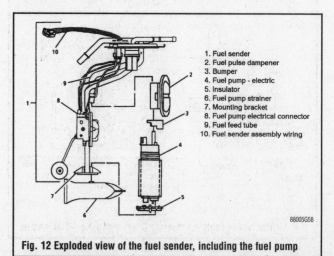

1. Fuel sender
2. Fuel pulse dampener
3. Bumper
4. Fuel pump - electric
5. Insulator
6. Fuel pump strainer
7. Mounting bracket
8. Fuel pump electrical connector
9. Fuel feed tube
10. Fuel sender assembly wiring

88005G58

Fig. 12 Exploded view of the fuel sender, including the fuel pump

20. Install the lockring using J-35731, or an equivalent spanner wrench.
21. Install the fuel tank as outlined later in this section.
22. Refill the gas tank.
23. Connect the negative battery cable.
24. Turn the ignition switch to the **ON** position to pressurize the fuel system and check for leaks.

Throttle Body

REMOVAL & INSTALLATION

2.2L Engine

On 2.2L engines, the fuel metering system is incorporated with the upper and lower intake manifolds. Please refer to Section 3 for intake manifold removal and installation procedures.

2.3L Engine

▶ **See Figures 13 and 14**

1. Disconnect the negative battery cable. Drain the top half of the engine coolant into a suitable drain pan.
2. Remove the air cleaner assembly/air inlet duct.
3. Detach the Idle Air Control (IAC) valve and Throttle Position (TP) sensor electrical connectors.
4. Tag and disconnect all necessary vacuum lines from the top of the throttle body.
5. Unfasten the nut attaching the accelerator cable bracket to the throttle body.
6. Remove the bolts attaching the bracket to engine strut.
7. Disconnect the power brake vacuum hose from the throttle body.
8. Unfasten the throttle body attaching bolt and stud. Loosen the throttle body from the manifold.
9. Disconnect the coolant lines from the coolant cavity cover.
10. Remove the throttle, T.V. and cruise control cables.
11. Remove the throttle body, gasket and coolant line O-rings. Discard the O-rings and thoroughly clean the gasket mating surfaces.

➥The TPS and IAC valve should **NOT** come into contact with solvent or cleaner, as they may be damaged.

To install:
12. Lubricate new coolant line O-rings with antifreeze, then install on the coolant lines.
13. Connect the throttle, cruise control and transmission control cables to the throttle body.
14. Fasten the coolant lines to the coolant cavity cover, with new O-rings.

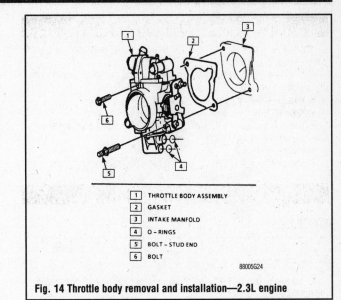

1	THROTTLE BODY ASSEMBLY
2	GASKET
3	INTAKE MANIFOLD
4	O – RINGS
5	BOLT – STUD END
6	BOLT

88005G24

Fig. 14 Throttle body removal and installation—2.3L engine

15. Position a new gasket, then install the throttle body. Tighten the retaining bolts to 19 ft. lbs. (26 Nm).
16. Connect the power brake vacuum hose to the throttle body.
17. Install the accelerator cable bracket nuts and bolts. Tighten to 19 ft. lbs. (25 Nm).
18. Connect the vacuum hoses to the top of the throttle body.
19. Attach the electrical connectors to the IAC valve and TPS.
20. Install the air cleaner assembly/air duct.
21. Connect the negative battery cable, then refill the cooling system.

2.8L. 3.1L and 3.8L Engines

EXCEPT 3.1L (VIN M) AND 1993–96 3.8L ENGINES

▶ **See Figures 15, 16 and 17**

1. Disconnect the negative battery cable. Drain the top half of the engine coolant into a suitable drain pan.
2. Remove the air inlet duct.
3. For 3.8L engines, remove the rear intake duct and remove the throttle cable bracket.

➥The TPS and IAC valve should **NOT** come into contact with solvent or cleaner, as they may be damaged.

4. Detach the Idle Air Control (IAC) valve and Throttle Position (TP) sensor electrical connectors.
5. Tag and disconnect all necessary vacuum lines from the top of the throttle body.
6. Disconnect the coolant hoses from the throttle body.
7. Remove the throttle, T.V. and cruise control cables.
8. Remove the throttle body, gasket and coolant line O-rings. Discard the O-rings and gasket, then thoroughly clean the gasket mating surfaces.
To install:
9. Position a new flange gasket, then place the throttle body on top. Install the retaining bolts and tighten to 18 ft. lbs. (25 Nm) for 2.8L and 3.1L engines. For 3.8L engines, tighten the retaining nuts to 11 ft. lbs. (15 Nm).
10. For 3.8L engines, install the throttle cable bracket.

➥Make sure the throttle and cruise control linkage does not hold the throttle open.

11. Connect the throttle, cruise control and transmission control cables to the throttle body.
12. Attach the coolant hoses to the throttle body.
13. Connect the vacuum hoses to the top of the throttle body.
14. Attach the electrical connectors to the IAC valve and TPS.
15. Install the air intake duct or rear duct, as applicable.
16. Connect the negative battery cable, then refill the cooling system.

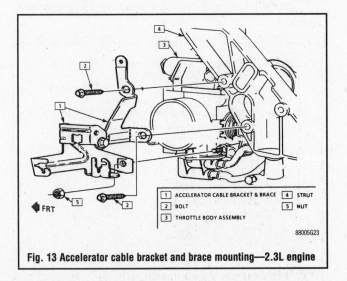

1	ACCELERATOR CABLE BRACKET & BRACE
2	BOLT
3	THROTTLE BODY ASSEMBLY
4	STRUT
5	NUT

◀ FRT

88005G23

Fig. 13 Accelerator cable bracket and brace mounting—2.3L engine

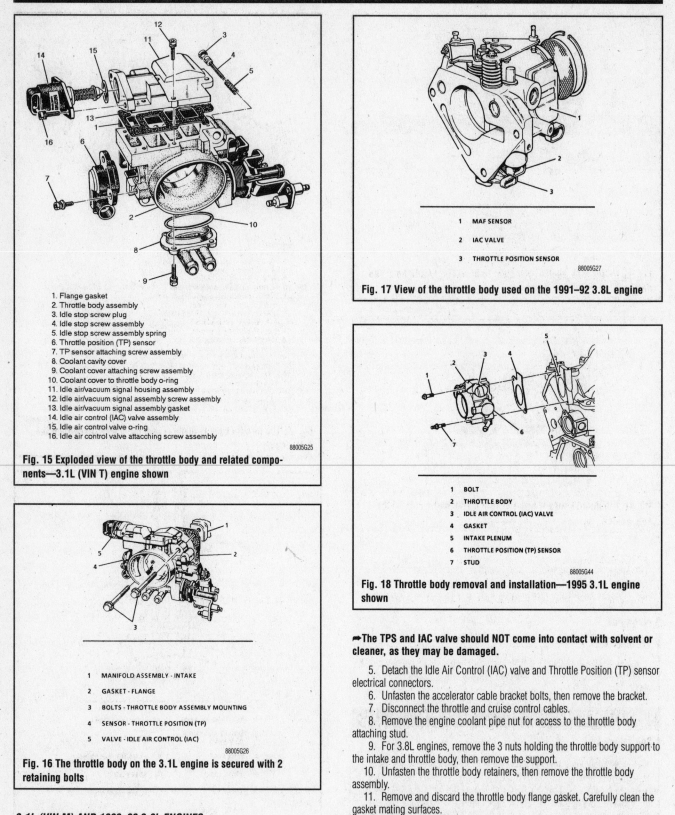

1. Flange gasket
2. Throttle body assembly
3. Idle stop screw plug
4. Idle stop screw assembly
5. Idle stop screw assembly spring
6. Throttle position (TP) sensor
7. TP sensor attaching screw assembly
8. Coolant cavity cover
9. Coolant cover attaching screw assembly
10. Coolant cover to throttle body o-ring
11. Idle air/vacuum signal housing assembly
12. Idle air/vacuum signal assembly screw assembly
13. Idle air/vacuum signal assembly gasket
14. Idle air control (IAC) valve assembly
15. Idle air control valve o-ring
16. Idle air control valve attacching screw assembly

88005G25

Fig. 15 Exploded view of the throttle body and related components—3.1L (VIN T) engine shown

1	MANIFOLD ASSEMBLY - INTAKE
2	GASKET - FLANGE
3	BOLTS - THROTTLE BODY ASSEMBLY MOUNTING
4	SENSOR - THROTTLE POSITION (TP)
5	VALVE - IDLE AIR CONTROL (IAC)

88005G26

Fig. 16 The throttle body on the 3.1L engine is secured with 2 retaining bolts

3.1L (VIN M) AND 1993–96 3.8L ENGINES

▶ See Figures 18, 19 and 20

1. Disconnect the negative battery cable.
2. For 3.8L engines, properly drain the coolant into a suitable container.
3. Remove the air inlet duct.
4. For 3.8L engines, remove the rear intake duct and remove the throttle cable bracket.

1	MAF SENSOR
2	IAC VALVE
3	THROTTLE POSITION SENSOR

88005G27

Fig. 17 View of the throttle body used on the 1991–92 3.8L engine

1	BOLT
2	THROTTLE BODY
3	IDLE AIR CONTROL (IAC) VALVE
4	GASKET
5	INTAKE PLENUM
6	THROTTLE POSITION (TP) SENSOR
7	STUD

88005G44

Fig. 18 Throttle body removal and installation—1995 3.1L engine shown

➡The TPS and IAC valve should NOT come into contact with solvent or cleaner, as they may be damaged.

5. Detach the Idle Air Control (IAC) valve and Throttle Position (TP) sensor electrical connectors.
6. Unfasten the accelerator cable bracket bolts, then remove the bracket.
7. Disconnect the throttle and cruise control cables.
8. Remove the engine coolant pipe nut for access to the throttle body attaching stud.
9. For 3.8L engines, remove the 3 nuts holding the throttle body support to the intake and throttle body, then remove the support.
10. Unfasten the throttle body retainers, then remove the throttle body assembly.
11. Remove and discard the throttle body flange gasket. Carefully clean the gasket mating surfaces.

To install:

12. Position a new flange gasket, then place the throttle body on top. Install the retaining bolts and tighten to 18 ft. lbs. (25 Nm) for 3.1L engines. For 3.8L engines, tighten the retaining nuts to 11 ft. lbs. (15 Nm).
13. For 3.8L engines, install the throttle cable bracket.

➡Make sure the throttle and cruise control linkage does not hold the throttle open.

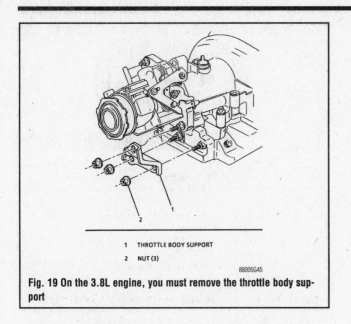

Fig. 19 On the 3.8L engine, you must remove the throttle body support

1	THROTTLE BODY SUPPORT
2	NUT (3)

88005G45

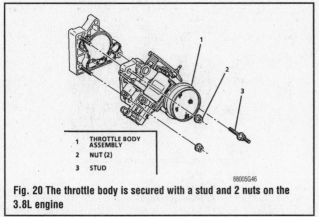

1	THROTTLE BODY ASSEMBLY
2	NUT (2)
3	STUD

88005G46

Fig. 20 The throttle body is secured with a stud and 2 nuts on the 3.8L engine

14. Connect the throttle and cruise control cables to the throttle body.
15. Attach the electrical connectors to the IAC valve and TPS.
16. Install the air intake duct or rear duct, as applicable.
17. Connect the negative battery cable, then refill the cooling system.

3.4L Engine

▶ See Figure 21

The 3.4L engine is equipped with an integrated throttle body/plenum assembly. For removal and installation procedures, please refer to Section 3 of this manual.

Fuel Injectors

▶ See Figure 22

Use care in removing the fuel injectors to prevent damage to the electrical connector pins on the injector and the nozzle. The fuel injector is serviced as a complete assembly only and should not be immersed in any kind of cleaner. Support the fuel rail to avoid damaging other components while removing the injector. Be sure to note that different injectors are calibrated for different flow rates. When ordering new fuel injectors, be sure to order the identical part number that is inscribed on the bottom of the old injector.

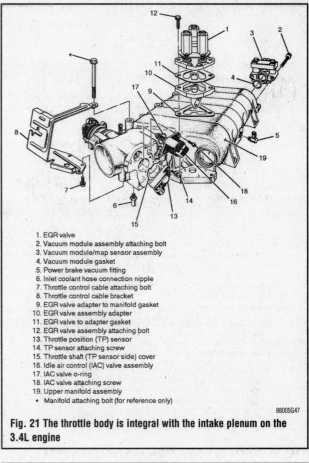

1. EGR valve
2. Vacuum module assembly attaching bolt
3. Vacuum module/map sensor assembly
4. Vacuum module gasket
5. Power brake vacuum fitting
6. Inlet coolant hose connection nipple
7. Throttle control cable attaching bolt
8. Throttle control cable bracket
9. EGR valve adapter to manifold gasket
10. EGR valve assembly adapter
11. EGR valve to adapter gasket
12. EGR valve assembly attaching bolt
13. Throttle position (TP) sensor
14. TP sensor attaching screw
15. Throttle shaft (TP sensor side) cover
16. Idle air control (IAC) valve assembly
17. IAC valve o-ring
18. IAC valve attaching screw
19. Upper manifold assembly
* Manifold attaching bolt (for reference only)

88005G47

Fig. 21 The throttle body is integral with the intake plenum on the 3.4L engine

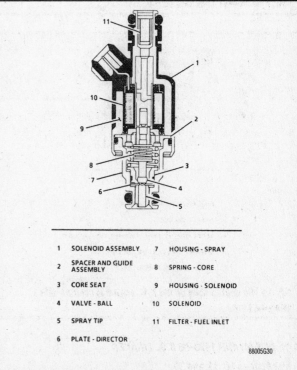

1	SOLENOID ASSEMBLY	7	HOUSING - SPRAY
2	SPACER AND GUIDE ASSEMBLY	8	SPRING - CORE
3	CORE SEAT	9	HOUSING - SOLENOID
4	VALVE - BALL	10	SOLENOID
5	SPRAY TIP	11	FILTER - FUEL INLET
6	PLATE - DIRECTOR		

88005G30

Fig. 22 Cross-section of a fuel injector

REMOVAL & INSTALLATION

2.2L Engine

> **※※ WARNING**
>
> Any time the injectors are removed for service, always remove the fuel pressure regulator to drain excess fuel, and prevent fuel from entering the engine cylinders. Flooded cylinders could result in engine damage.

1. Relieve the fuel system pressure as outlined earlier.
2. Disconnect the negative battery cable.
3. Remove the upper manifold assembly.

> **※※ CAUTION**
>
> To reduce the chance of personal injury, cover the fuel line connections with a shop towel, when disconnecting.

4. Disconnect the fuel return line retaining bracket nut and move the return line away from the regulator.
5. Remove the pressure regulator assembly.

> **※※ WARNING**
>
> Do not try to remove the injectors by lifting up on the injector retaining bracket while the injectors are still installed in the in the bracket slots or damage to the bracket and/or injectors could result. Do not attempt to remove the bracket without first removing the pressure regulator.

6. Remove the injector retainer bracket attaching screws and carefully slide the bracket off to clear the injector slots and regulator.
7. Detach the injector electrical connectors.
8. Remove the fuel injector(s), then remove and discard the O-ring seals.

> **※※ CAUTION**
>
> To reduce the risk fire and personal injury, make sure that the lower (small) O-ring of each injector does not remain in the lower manifold. If the O-ring is not removed with the injector, the replacement injector, with new O-rings, will not seat properly in the injector socket and could cause a fuel leak.

9. Cover the injector sockets to prevent dirt from entering the opening.

➡ Each injector is calibrated with a different flow rate so be sure to replace the injector with the identical part numbers.

To install:
10. Lubricate the new injector O-ring seals with clean engine oil and install on the injector assembly.
11. Install the injector assembly into the lower manifold injector socket, with the electrical connectors facing inward.

12. Carefully position the injector retainer bracket so that the injector retaining slots and regulator are aligned with the bracket slots.
13. Attach the injector electrical connectors.
14. Install the pressure regulator assembly.
15. Install the injector retainer bracket retaining screws, coated with thread locking material and tighten to 31 inch lbs. (3.5 Nm).
16. Install the accelerator cable bracket with the attaching bolts/nuts finger-tight at this time.

> **※※ WARNING**
>
> The accelerator bracket must be aligned with the accelerator cam to prevent cable wear, which could result in cable breakage.

17. Align the accelerator bracket as follows:
   a. Place a steel rule across the bore of the throttle body, with one end in contact with the accelerator bracket.
   b. Adjust the accelerator bracket to obtain a $^{25}/_{64}$ in. (9–11mm) gap between the bracket and the throttle body.
   c. Tighten the top bolt first and tighten all bolts/nuts to 18 ft. lbs. (25 Nm).
18. Tighten the fuel filer cap.
19. Connect the negative battery cable and turn the ignition **ON** for 2 seconds, **OFF** for 10 seconds, then **ON** and check for fuel leaks.
20. Install the air intake duct.

2.3L, 2.8L, 3.1L, 3.4L and 3.8L Engines

▶ See Figures 23, 24, 25, 26 and 27

1. Disconnect the negative battery cable.
2. Properly relieve the fuel system pressure.
3. If necessary for access, remove the intake manifold plenum, as outlined in Section 3 of this manual.
4. Detach the injector electrical connection(s).
5. Remove the fuel rail assembly, as outlined later in this section.

➡ It may be necessary to use a suitable prytool to carefully remove the fuel injector retaining clip.

6. Remove the injector retaining clip. Separate the injector from the fuel rail.
7. Remove both injector O-ring seals from the injector and discard.
To install:
8. Prior to installing the injectors, coat the new injector O-ring seals with clean engine oil. Install the seals on the injector assembly.
9. Use new injector retainer clips on the injector assembly. Position the open end of the clip facing the injector electrical connector.
10. Position the injector into the fuel rail injector socket with the electrical connectors facing outward. Push the injector in firmly until it engages with the retainer clip locking it in place.
11. Install the fuel rail and injector assembly, as outlined later in this section.
12. If removed, install the intake manifold plenum, as outlined in Section 3.
13. Connect the negative battery cable and turn the ignition **ON** for 2 seconds, **OFF** for 10 seconds, then **ON** and check for fuel leaks.

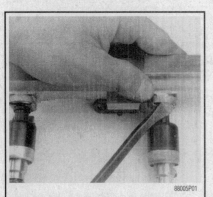

Fig. 23 Remove the fuel rail, then use a suitable prytool to . . .

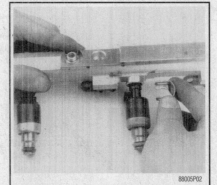

Fig. 24 . . . remove the fuel injector retaining clip

Fig. 25 Separate the fuel injector from the fuel rail

Fig. 26 Remove and discard the injector O-rings

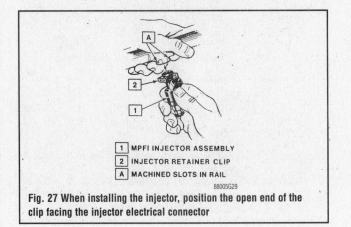

1	MPFI INJECTOR ASSEMBLY
2	INJECTOR RETAINER CLIP
A	MACHINED SLOTS IN RAIL

88005G29

Fig. 27 When installing the injector, position the open end of the clip facing the injector electrical connector

Fuel Rail Assembly

When servicing the fuel rail assembly, be careful to prevent dirt and other contaminants from entering the fuel passages. Fittings should be capped and holes plugged during servicing. At any time the fuel system is opened for service, the O-ring seals and retainers used with related components should be replaced.

Before removing the fuel rail, the fuel rail assembly may be cleaned with a spray type cleaner, GM–30A or equivalent, following package instructions. Do not immerse fuel rails in liquid cleaning solvent. Be sure to always use new O-rings and seals when reinstalling the fuel rail assemblies.

REMOVAL & INSTALLATION

2.3L Engine

▶ **See Figure 28**

1. Properly relieve the fuel system pressure.
2. If not already done, disconnect the negative battery cable.
3. Detach the hoses at the front and side of the crankcase ventilation oil/air separator. Leave the vacuum hoses connected to the canister purge solenoid.
4. Unfasten the bolts connecting the crankcase ventilation oil/air separator and canister purge solenoid.
5. Disconnect the hose to the bottom of the separator, then remove the separator.
6. Disconnect the fuel feed line and return line from the fuel rail assembly, be sure to use a backup wrench on the inlet fitting to prevent turning.
7. Remove the vacuum line at the pressure regulator. Remove the fuel rail assembly retaining bolts.
8. Push in the wire connector clip, while pulling the connector away from the injector.
9. Remove the fuel rail assembly and cover all openings with masking tape to prevent dirt entry.

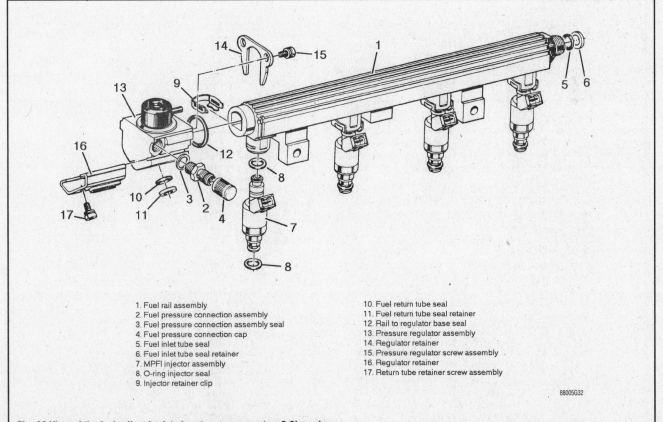

1. Fuel rail assembly
2. Fuel pressure connection assembly
3. Fuel pressure connection assembly seal
4. Fuel pressure connection cap
5. Fuel inlet tube seal
6. Fuel inlet tube seal retainer
7. MPFI injector assembly
8. O-ring injector seal
9. Injector retainer clip
10. Fuel return tube seal
11. Fuel return tube seal retainer
12. Rail to regulator base seal
13. Pressure regulator assembly
14. Regulator retainer
15. Pressure regulator screw assembly
16. Regulator retainer
17. Return tube retainer screw assembly

88005G32

Fig. 28 View of the fuel rail and related system components—2.3L engine

➡️ If any injectors become separated from the fuel rail and remain in the intake manifold, both O-ring seals and injector retaining clip must be replaced. Use care in removing the fuel rail assembly, to prevent damage to the injector electrical connector terminals and the injector spray tips. When removed, support the fuel rail to avoid damaging its components. The fuel injector is serviced as a complete unit only. Since it is an electrical component, it should not be immersed in any type of cleaner.

To install:

10. Be sure to lubricate all the O-rings and seals with clean engine oil. Carefully push the injectors into the cylinder head intake ports until the bolt holes on the fuel rail and manifold are aligned.

11. The remainder of the installation is the reverse order of the removal procedure.

12. Apply a coating of tread locking compound on the treads of the fittings. Tighten the fuel rail retaining bolts to 19 ft. lbs. (26 Nm), the fuel feed line nut to 22 ft. lbs. (30 Nm) and the fuel pipe fittings to 20 ft. lbs. (26 Nm).

13. Connect the negative battery cable.

14. Turn the ignition to the **ON** position for 2 seconds, then turn to the **OFF** position for 10 seconds. Again, turn to the **ON** position and check for fuel leaks.

2.8L, 3.1L, 3.4L and 3.8L Engines

▶ See Figures 29, 30, 31 and 32

1. Disconnect the negative battery cable.
2. Properly relieve fuel system pressure, as outlined earlier in this section.
3. For 3.1L and 3.4L engines, remove the intake manifold plenum.
4. If equipped, remove the engine fuel pipe bracket bolt.
5. Disconnect the fuel feed line and return lines from the fuel rail assembly; be sure to use a backup wrench on the inlet fitting to prevent turning or refer to the procedure for quick-connect fittings, located earlier in this section. Remove and discard the fuel feed and return pipe O-rings.
6. For the 3.4L and 3.8L engines, disconnect the vacuum line from the pressure regulator. Remove the return line from pressure regulator.
7. Detach the electrical connectors from each fuel injector.

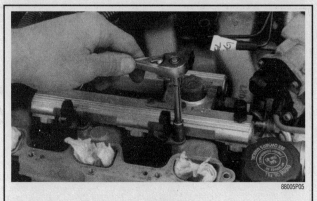
Fig. 29 Unfasten the fuel rail retaining bolts . . .

Fig. 30 . . . then remove the fuel rail from the engine

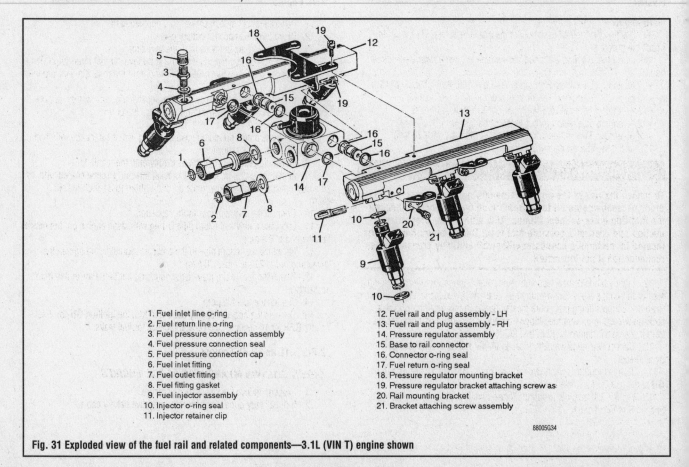

1. Fuel inlet line o-ring
2. Fuel return line o-ring
3. Fuel pressure connection assembly
4. Fuel pressure connection seal
5. Fuel pressure connection cap
6. Fuel inlet fitting
7. Fuel outlet fitting
8. Fuel fitting gasket
9. Fuel injector assembly
10. Injector o-ring seal
11. Injector retainer clip
12. Fuel rail and plug assembly - LH
13. Fuel rail and plug assembly - RH
14. Pressure regulator assembly
15. Base to rail connector
16. Connector o-ring seal
17. Fuel return o-ring seal
18. Pressure regulator mounting bracket
19. Pressure regulator bracket attaching screw as
20. Rail mounting bracket
21. Bracket attaching screw assembly

Fig. 31 Exploded view of the fuel rail and related components—3.1L (VIN T) engine shown

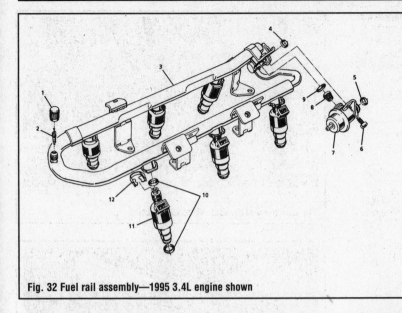

1	CAP - FUEL PRESSURE CONNECTION
2	VALVE CORE ASSEMBLY - FUEL PRESSURE CONNECTION
3	RAIL ASSEMBLY - FUEL
4	O-RING - FUEL INLET TUBE
5	O-RING - FUEL OUTLET TUBE
6	SCREW - PRESSURE REGULATOR ATTACHING
7	REGULATOR ASSEMBLY - FUEL PRESSURE
8	SCREEN - FILTER
9	O-RING - FUEL INLET FITTING
10	O-RING - FUEL INJECTOR
11	INJECTOR ASSEMBLY - FUEL
12	CLIP - INJECTOR RETAINER

88005G50

Fig. 32 Fuel rail assembly—1995 3.4L engine shown

8. Unfasten the bolts retaining the fuel rail assembly to the intake manifold. Remove the fuel rail assembly and cover all openings with masking tape to prevent dirt entry.

➡If any injectors become separated from the fuel rail and remain in the intake manifold, both O-ring seals and injector retaining clip must be replaced. Use care in removing the fuel rail assembly, to prevent damage to the injector electrical connector terminals and the injector spray tips. When removed, support the fuel rail to avoid damaging its components. The fuel injector is serviced as a complete unit only. Since it is an electrical component, it should not be immersed in any type of cleaner.

To install:
9. Position the fuel rail assembly to the intake manifold. Tilt the rail to install the injectors.
10. Install the retaining bolts and observe the following torque specifications:
- 2.8L and 3.1L engines: Fuel rail retaining nuts to 89 inch lbs. (10 Nm).
- 2.8L and 3.1L engines: Fuel feed line nut to 17 ft. lbs. (23 Nm).
- 3.4L engine: Fuel rail retaining nuts to 89 inch lbs. (10 Nm).
- 3.4L engine: Fuel feed line nut to 22 ft. lbs. (30 Nm).
- 3.8L engine: Fuel rail retaining bolts to 7–14 ft. lbs. (10–20 Nm).
11. Attach the injector electrical connectors.

✳✳ CAUTION

To reduce the risk of fire and/or personal injury, always apply a few drops of clean engine oil to the male tube ends before connecting the fuel line quick-connect fittings. This will ensure proper reconnection and prevent a possible fuel leak. During operation, O-rings located in the female connector will swell and may prevent proper reconnection if not lubricated.

12. Lightly lubricate new feed and return pipe O-rings with clean engine oil, then install on the pipes. Connect the fuel feed and return pipes, either following the quick-connect fitting procedure located earlier in this section or using a back-up wrench to prevent the fittings from turning, depending upon application. If necessary, tighten to 13 ft. lbs. (17 Nm).
13. Connect the negative battery cable, then install the fuel filler cap, if not done already.
14. Turn the ignition switch **ON** for 2 seconds, **OFF** for 10 seconds, then **ON** and check for fuel leaks.
15. For the 3.1L engine, install the intake manifold plenum, as outlined in Section 3 of this manual.

Fuel Pressure Regulator

REMOVAL & INSTALLATION

▶ **See Figures 28, 31 and 32**

➡**On some applications, the pressure regulator and fuel rail are only available as an assembly. Check with your local parts retailer for parts availability and compatibility.**

2.2L Engine

1. Relieve the fuel system pressure as outlined earlier.
2. Disconnect the negative battery cable.
3. Remove the vacuum hose from the regulator.
4. Place a rag under the connection and remove the fuel return pipe clamp.
5. Remove the fuel return pipe and O-ring from the regulator. Discard the O-ring.
6. Unfasten the pressure regulator bracket attaching screw, then remove the pressure regulator assembly and O-ring. Discard the O-ring.
To install:
7. Lubricate a new pressure regulator O-ring with clean engine oil, then install on the pressure regulator.
8. Install the pressure regulator assembly onto the manifold.
9. Install the pressure regulator bracket attaching screw coated with the appropriate thread locking material and tighten to 31 inch lbs. (3.5 Nm).
10. Connect the vacuum hose to the regulator.
11. Lubricate a new fuel return pipe O-ring with clean engine oil, then install on the end of the pipe.
12. Install the fuel return pipe to the pressure regulator and tighten the attaching nut to 22 inch lbs. (30 Nm).
13. Fasten the fuel return pipe clamp attaching nut to the lower manifold assembly.
14. Tighten the fuel filler cap.
15. Connect the negative battery cable and turn the ignition **ON** for 2 seconds, **OFF** for 10 seconds, then **ON** and check for fuel leaks.

2.8L, 3.1L and 3.4L Engines

EXCEPT 3.1L (VIN M) AND 1994–96 3.4L ENGINES

1. Properly relieve the fuel system pressure.
2. If not already done, disconnect the negative battery cable.

3. Disconnect the fuel feed line and return line from the fuel rail assembly; be sure to use a backup wrench on the inlet fitting to prevent turning.

4. Remove the fuel rail assembly from the engine.

➡**On some vehicles, it is possible to remove the pressure regulator with the fuel rail installed on the engine.**

5. With the fuel rail assembly removed from the engine, remove the pressure regulator mounting screw or retainer.

6. Remove the pressure regulator from the rail assembly by carefully twisting back and forth while pulling apart. Remove and discard the regulator O-rings.

To install:

7. Prior to assembling the pressure regulator to the fuel rail, lubricate the new rail-to-regulator O-ring seal with clean engine oil.

8. Place the O-ring on the pressure regulator and install the pressure regulator to the fuel rail.

9. Install the retainer or coat the regulator mounting screws with an approved tread locking compound and secure the pressure regulator in place. Tighten the mounting screws to 102 inch lbs. (11.5 Nm).

10. Install the fuel rail assembly to the engine, as outlined earlier.

11. Connect the fuel feed line and return line to the fuel rail assembly, use a backup wrench on the inlet fitting to prevent turning.

12. Connect the negative battery cable and turn the ignition **ON** for 2 seconds, **OFF** for 10 seconds, then **ON** and check for fuel leaks.

3.1L (VIN M) ENGINE

1. Disconnect the negative battery cable.
2. Properly relieve the fuel system pressure.
3. Remove the throttle body, as outlined earlier in this section.
4. Unfasten the fuel pressure regulator retaining screw.
5. Place a shop towel under the regulator to catch any fuel, then remove the pressure regulator from the rail using a twisting and pulling motion to remove it.
6. Remove the retainer and spacer from the fuel rail and discard.
7. Detach the fuel pressure regulator from the engine fuel return pipe.
8. Remove and discard the pressure regulator inlet O-ring.

To install:

9. Lubricate a new pressure regulator O-ring with clean engine oil and install on the regulator inlet.

✳✳ WARNING

The fuel return pipe must be connected before tightening the regulator attaching screw to prevent the regulator from rotating. Rotation of the regulator could damage the retainer and spacer bracket and lead to a fuel leak at the regulator inlet.

10. Place a new retainer and spacer bracket into the slot on the fuel rail.

11. Install the pressure regulator to the fuel rail.

12. Connect the fuel return line to the regulator. Tighten the engine fuel return pipe nut to 13 ft. lbs. (17 Nm).

13. Attach the vacuum line to the regulator.

14. Install the pressure regulator retaining screw and tighten to 80 inch lbs. (9 Nm). Make sure the retainer and spacer bracket is engaged in the slots in the fuel rail. Grasp and pull on the regulator to make sure it is properly seated.

15. Connect the negative battery cable, then install the fuel filler cap, if not done already.

16. Turn the ignition switch **ON** for 2 seconds, **OFF** for 10 seconds, then **ON** and check for fuel leaks.

1994–96 3.4L ENGINE

1. Disconnect the negative battery cable.
2. Properly relieve the fuel system pressure.
3. Remove the upper manifold assembly, as outlined in Section 3 of this manual.
4. Unfasten the fuel pressure regulator bracket attaching screw.
5. Remove the regulator assembly and O-rings. Discard the O-rings.

To install:

6. Lubricate new pressure regulator O-rings with clean engine oil and install on the regulator.

7. Install the regulator and attaching screw. Tighten to 84 inch lbs. (9.5 Nm).

8. Install the upper manifold assembly.

9. Connect the negative battery cable, then install the fuel filler cap, if not done already.

10. Turn the ignition switch **ON** for 2 seconds, **OFF** for 10 seconds, then **ON** and check for fuel leaks.

3.8L Engine

1. Disconnect the negative battery cable.
2. Properly relieve the fuel system pressure.
3. Clean the dirt and grease from the regulator retaining ring.
4. Disconnect the vacuum line from the regulator.
5. Remove the snapring from the regulator. Wrap a towel around the regulator to catch any fuel that may escape.
6. Lift and twist the regulator to remove it from the fuel rail assembly. Remove and discard the regulator O-rings.
7. Cover all openings with masking tape to prevent dirt entry.

To install:

8. Lubricate new O-ring seals with clean engine oil, then install on the regulator.

9. Install the regulator into the regulator housing and secure with the snapring.

10. Attach the vacuum line to the regulator.

11. Connect the negative battery cable, then install the fuel filler cap, if not done already.

12. Turn the ignition switch **ON** for 2 seconds, **OFF** for 10 seconds, then **ON** and check for fuel leaks.

Fuel Pressure Connection

REMOVAL & INSTALLATION

2.3L and 3.1L Engines

▶ **See Figure 33**

1. Clean the area around the connection with GM cleaner X-30A or equivalent.
2. Properly relieve the fuel system pressure.
3. If not already done, disconnect the negative battery cable.
4. Remove the fuel pressure connection and seal. Discard the seal.

To install:

5. Place a new seal on the pressure connection.

6. Install the fuel pressure connection assembly in the fuel rail. Tighten to the following specifications:
- 2.3L Engine: 115 inch lbs. (13 Nm)
- 3.1L Engine: 88 inch lbs. (10 Nm)

7. Connect the negative battery cable and turn the ignition **ON** for 2 seconds, **OFF** for 10 seconds, then **ON** and check for fuel leaks.

3.4L Engine

➡**The fuel pressure connection on these engines is non-replaceable, but it is serviceable.**

1. Clean the area around the connection with GM cleaner X-30A or equivalent.

1	PRESSURE REGULATOR ASSEMBLY
2	FUEL PRESSURE CONNECTION ASSEMBLY SEAL
3	FUEL PRESSURE CONNECTION ASSEMBLY
4	FUEL PRESSURE CONNECTION CAP

88005G42

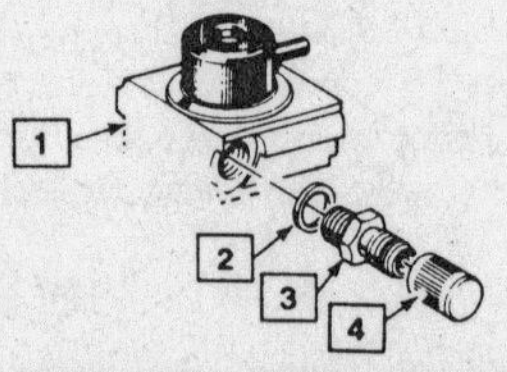

Fig. 33 Fuel pressure relief connection location—2.3L engine shown

2. Properly relieve the fuel system pressure.
3. If not already done, disconnect the negative battery cable.
4. Remove the fuel pressure connection cap.
5. Using a standard valve core removal tool, remove the and discard the valve core assembly.

To install:
6. Using the proper tool, install a new valve core assembly.
7. Install the fuel pressure connection cap.
8. Connect the negative battery cable and turn the ignition **ON** for 2 seconds, **OFF** for 10 seconds, then **ON** and check for fuel leaks.

FUEL TANK

Tank Assembly

REMOVAL & INSTALLATION

> ✳✳ **CAUTION**
>
> **The fuel system pressure must be relieved before disconnecting any fuel lines. Failure to do so may result in personal injury.**

1988 Vehicles

▶ **See Figures 34 and 35**

1. Disconnect the negative battery cable.
2. Properly relieve the fuel system pressure, as outlined earlier in this section.
3. Raise and safely support the vehicle.
4. Use a suitable hand operated pump device to drain the fuel through the filler tube into an approved container.

> ✳✳ **CAUTION**
>
> **Observe all applicable safety precautions when working around gasoline. Do not allow fuel spray or fuel vapors to come in contact with a spark or open flame. Keep a dry chemical (Class B) fire extinguisher near the work area. Never drain or store fuel in an open container due to the possibility of fire or explosion.**

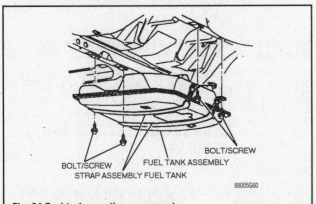

Fig. 34 Fuel tank mounting components

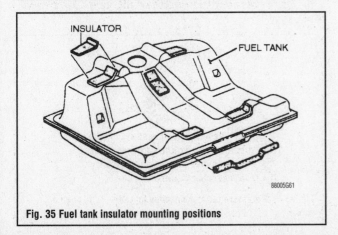

Fig. 35 Fuel tank insulator mounting positions

5. Support the fuel tank with a suitable jack.
6. Remove the 2 bolts securing the fuel tank straps, then swing the straps out of the way.
7. Lower the fuel tank enough to disconnect the vapor hose from the fuel sender assembly and the vapor hose from the vapor pipe at the rear of the fuel tank.
8. Detach the electrical connector from the fuel sender assembly and remove the two retaining clips. If equipped, disconnect the ground strap.
9. Disconnect the fuel filler and vent hoses from the fuel tank.
10. Remove the tank from the vehicle, slowly to ensure all connections and hoses have been disconnected.

To install:
11. Clean all parts well. Inspect the tank for dents, rust or other damage. On high-mileage vehicles, it may be good practice to remove the fuel pump module and replace the flexible strainer on the fuel pump.
12. Position the fuel tank under the vehicle and raise the tank with a suitable jack.
13. Connect the fuel feed and return lines to the sender assembly.
14. Attach the electrical connector to the fuel sender assembly. If equipped, connect the ground strap.
15. Raise the tank into position into the vehicle and swing the mounting straps under the tank.
16. Install the front fuel tank strap mounting bolts and tighten to 35 ft. lbs. (47 Nm).
17. Remove the jack.
18. Connect the fuel filler and vent hoses to the tank.
19. Carefully lower the vehicle, then refill the fuel system
20. Connect the negative battery cable, then install the fuel filler cap, if not done already.
21. Turn the ignition switch **ON** for 2 seconds, **OFF** for 10 seconds, then **ON** and check for fuel leaks.

1989–94 Vehicles

▶ **See Figures 34 and 35**

1. Disconnect the negative battery cable.
2. Properly relieve the fuel system pressure, as outlined earlier in this section.
3. Raise and safely support the vehicle.

> ✳✳ **CAUTION**
>
> **Observe all applicable safety precautions when working around gasoline. Do not allow fuel spray or fuel vapors to come in contact with a spark or open flame. Keep a dry chemical (Class B) fire extinguisher near the work area. Never drain or store fuel in an open container due to the possibility of fire or explosion.**

4. Use a suitable hand operated pump device to drain the fuel through the filler tube into an approved container.

➡ **Before disconnecting any fuel lines from the fuel tank, thoroughly clean around all hose connections.**

5. Disconnect the fuel filler vent hose from the fuel tank.
6. Detach the fuel filler hose from the fuel filler inlet tube on the fuel tank. Position the hose out of the way.
7. Disconnect the vapor hose from the front of the fuel tank.
8. Detach the fuel return pipe and position the hose out of the way.
9. Disconnect the two rear rubber exhaust hangers from the rear of the exhaust system and allow the exhaust system to hang down slightly.
10. Unfasten the exhaust shield mounting bolts, then remove the exhaust shield.
11. Support the fuel tank with a suitable jack.

12. Remove the two bolts securing the fuel tank straps, then swing the straps out of the way.

13. Lower the fuel tank enough to disconnect the vapor hose from the fuel sender assembly and the vapor hose from the vapor pipe at the rear of the fuel tank.

14. Detach the electrical connector from the fuel sender assembly and remove the two retaining clips.

15. Remove the tank from the vehicle, slowly to ensure all connections and hoses have been disconnected.

To install:

16. Clean all parts well. Inspect the tank for dents, rust or other damage. On high-mileage vehicles, it may be good practice to remove the fuel pump module and replace the flexible strainer on the fuel pump.

17. Position the fuel tank under the vehicle and raise the tank with a suitable jack.

18. Connect the vapor hose to the fuel tank at the vapor pipe at the rear of the tank and connect the vapor hose to the sender assembly.

19. Attach the electrical connector to the fuel sender assembly.

20. Connect the fuel feed and return lines to the sender assembly.

21. Raise the tank into position into the vehicle and swing the mounting straps under the tank.

22. Install the front fuel tank strap mounting bolts and tighten to 35 ft. lbs. (47 Nm).

23. Remove the jack.

24. Connect the fuel return pipe to the fuel feed pipe.

25. Attach the rear fuel feed pipe to the inlet side of the fuel filter.

26. Tighten the line fittings to 16 ft. lbs. (22 Nm). Make sure to use a back-up wrench to prevent the fuel filter from turning.

27. Connect the vapor hose to the vapor pipe at the front of the vehicle.

28. Attach the fuel filler vent hose to the tank. Connect the fuel filler hose to the fuel filler neck of the tank.

29. Install the exhaust heat shield and the mounting bolts.

30. Position the exhaust system and install the rubber hangers.

31. Carefully lower the vehicle, then refill the fuel system

32. Connect the negative battery cable, then install the fuel filler cap, if not done already.

33. Turn the ignition switch **ON** for 2 seconds, **OFF** for 10 seconds, then **ON** and check for fuel leaks.

1995–96 Vehicles

▶ **See Figure 35**

1. Disconnect the negative battery cable.
2. Properly relieve the fuel system pressure.
3. Raise and safely support the vehicle.

✳✳ CAUTION

Observe all applicable safety precautions when working around gasoline. Do not allow fuel spray or fuel vapors to come in contact with a spark or open flame. Keep a dry chemical (Class B) fire extinguisher near the work area. Never drain or store fuel in an open container due to the possibility of fire or explosion.

4. Drain the fuel tank using the following procedure:
   a. Make sure the negative battery cable has been disconnected.

➡ **Do NOT attempt to drain fuel through the filler neck, or damage to the filler neck check-ball may occur.**

b. Loosen the fuel filler cap to make sure there will be no pressure buildup in the tank.

c. With the vehicle raised and safely supported, remove the EVAP pipe from the restraints. Clean the fuel filler EVAP hose connection and surrounding area before disconnecting to avoid possible contamination of the fuel system.

d. Loosen the fuel filler EVAP hose clamp. Wrap a shop towel around the fuel filler EVAP hose and slowly remove the fuel filler EVAP hose from the fuel tank EVAP pipe.

e. Use an hand-operated fuel pump to drain the fuel through the EVAP pipe.

f. At this point, do not reconnect the filler EVAP hose to the filler EVAP pipe.

5. Disconnect the fuel tank filler neck from the filler neck hose.

6. Detach the quick-connecting fittings at the fuel tank.

7. Remove the EVAP hose from the connection at the front of the tank.

8. Disconnect the two rear rubber exhaust hangers from the rear of the exhaust system and allow the exhaust system to hang down slightly.

9. Unfasten the exhaust pipe heat shield bolts and remove the shield.

10. With the help of an assistant, support the tank and remove the fuel tank straps with attaching bolts retaining the fuel tank straps.

➡ **Do not bend the fuel tank straps, as this may damage the straps.**

11. Lower the fuel tank enough to disconnect the fuel sender electrical connector and remove the retaining clips.

12. Remove the EVAP hose from the sender assembly.

13. Remove the EVAP hose from the EVAP pipe at the rear of the fuel tank.

14. Remove the tank from the vehicle slowly to ensure all connections and hoses have been disconnected. Place the tank in a suitable work area.

To install:

15. Clean all parts well. Inspect the tank for dents, rust or other damage. On high-mileage vehicles, it may be good practice to remove the fuel pump module and replace the flexible strainer on the fuel pump.

16. With the help of an assistant, position and support the fuel tank. Position the fuel tank straps, loosely install the fuel tank strap attaching bolts and connect the following:
   a. EVAP hose to the vapor pipe at the rear of the tank.
   b. EVAP hose to the fuel sender assembly.
   c. Fuel sender electrical connector and install the retainer clips.
   d. Rear fuel tank strap attaching bolts. Tighten all retainer bolts to 35 ft. lbs. (47 Nm).

✳✳ CAUTION

To reduce the risk of fire and personal injury, always apply a few drops of clean engine oil to the quick-connect male tube ends. This will ensure proper connection and prevent a possible fuel leak. During normal operation, the O-rings located in the female connection will swell and may prevent proper connection if not lubricated.

17. Attach the quick-connect fittings.

18. Connect the EVAP hose to the EVAP pipe at the front of the tank.

19. Install the fuel filler hose to the fuel tank.

20. Install the heat shield and secure with the retaining screws.

21. Install the rubber pipe hangers.

22. Carefully lower the vehicle, then refill the fuel system

23. Connect the negative battery cable, then install the fuel filler cap, if not done already.

24. Turn the ignition switch **ON** for 2 seconds, **OFF** for 10 seconds, then **ON** and check for fuel leaks.

6

CHASSIS ELECTRICAL

UNDERSTANDING AND TROUBLESHOOTING ELECTRICAL SYSTEMS

Basic Electrical Theory

▶ **See Figure 1**

For any 12 volt, negative ground, electrical system to operate, the electricity must travel in a complete circuit. This simply means that current (power) from the positive (+) terminal of the battery must eventually return to the negative (-) terminal of the battery. Along the way, this current will travel through wires, fuses, switches and components. If, for any reason, the flow of current through the circuit is interrupted, the component fed by that circuit will cease to function properly.

Perhaps the easiest way to visualize a circuit is to think of connecting a light bulb (with two wires attached to it) to the battery—one wire attached to the negative (-) terminal of the battery and the other wire to the positive (+) terminal. With the two wires touching the battery terminals, the circuit would be complete and the light bulb would illuminate. Electricity would follow a path from the battery to the bulb and back to the battery. It's easy to see that with longer wires on our light bulb, it could be mounted anywhere. Further, one wire could be fitted with a switch so that the light could be turned on and off.

The normal automotive circuit differs from this simple example in two ways. First, instead of having a return wire from the bulb to the battery, the current travels through the frame of the vehicle. Since the negative (-) battery cable is attached to the frame (made of electrically conductive metal), the frame of the vehicle can serve as a ground wire to complete the circuit. Secondly, most automotive circuits contain multiple components which receive power from a single circuit. This lessens the amount of wire needed to power components on the vehicle.

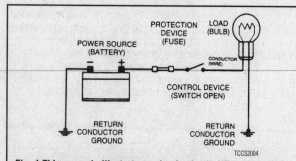

Fig. 1 This example illustrates a simple circuit. When the switch is closed, power from the positive (+) battery terminal flows through the fuse and the switch, and then to the light bulb. The light illuminates and the circuit is completed through the ground wire back to the negative (-) battery terminal. In reality, the two ground points shown in the illustration are attached to the metal frame of the vehicle, which completes the circuit back to the battery

HOW DOES ELECTRICITY WORK: THE WATER ANALOGY

Electricity is the flow of electrons—the subatomic particles that constitute the outer shell of an atom. Electrons spin in an orbit around the center core of an atom. The center core is comprised of protons (positive charge) and neutrons (neutral charge). Electrons have a negative charge and balance out the positive charge of the protons. When an outside force causes the number of electrons to unbalance the charge of the protons, the electrons will split off the atom and look for another atom to balance out. If this imbalance is kept up, electrons will continue to move and an electrical flow will exist.

Many people have been taught electrical theory using an analogy with water. In a comparison with water flowing through a pipe, the electrons would be the water and the wire is the pipe.

The flow of electricity can be measured much like the flow of water through a pipe. The unit of measurement used is amperes, frequently abbreviated as amps (a). You can compare amperage to the volume of water flowing through a pipe. When connected to a circuit, an ammeter will measure the actual amount of current flowing through the circuit. When relatively few electrons flow through a circuit, the amperage is low. When many electrons flow, the amperage is high.

Water pressure is measured in units such as pounds per square inch (psi); The electrical pressure is measured in units called volts (v). When a voltmeter is connected to a circuit, it is measuring the electrical pressure.

The actual flow of electricity depends not only on voltage and amperage, but also on the resistance of the circuit. The higher the resistance, the higher the force necessary to push the current through the circuit. The standard unit for measuring resistance is an ohm. Resistance in a circuit varies depending on the amount and type of components used in the circuit. The main factors which determine resistance are:

• Material—some materials have more resistance than others. Those with high resistance are said to be insulators. Rubber materials (or rubber-like plastics) are some of the most common insulators used in vehicles as they have a very high resistance to electricity. Very low resistance materials are said to be conductors. Copper wire is among the best conductors. Silver is actually a superior conductor to copper and is used in some relay contacts, but its high cost prohibits its use as common wiring. Most automotive wiring is made of copper.

• Size—the larger the wire size being used, the less resistance the wire will have. This is why components which use large amounts of electricity usually have large wires supplying current to them.

• Length—for a given thickness of wire, the longer the wire, the greater the resistance. The shorter the wire, the less the resistance. When determining the proper wire for a circuit, both size and length must be considered to design a circuit that can handle the current needs of the component.

• Temperature—with many materials, the higher the temperature, the greater the resistance (positive temperature coefficient). Some materials exhibit the opposite trait of lower resistance with higher temperatures (negative temperature coefficient). These principles are used in many of the sensors on the engine.

OHM'S LAW

There is a direct relationship between current, voltage and resistance. The relationship between current, voltage and resistance can be summed up by a statement known as Ohm's law.

Voltage (E) is equal to amperage (I) times resistance (R): $E = I \times R$

Other forms of the formula are $R = E/I$ and $I = E/R$

In each of these formulas, E is the voltage in volts, I is the current in amps and R is the resistance in ohms. The basic point to remember is that as the resistance of a circuit goes up, the amount of current that flows in the circuit will go down, if voltage remains the same.

The amount of work that the electricity can perform is expressed as power. The unit of power is the watt (w). The relationship between power, voltage and current is expressed as:

Power (w) is equal to amperage (I) times voltage (E): $W = I \times E$

This is only true for direct current (DC) circuits; The alternating current formula is a tad different, but since the electrical circuits in most vehicles are DC type, we need not get into AC circuit theory.

Electrical Components

POWER SOURCE

Power is supplied to the vehicle by two devices: The battery and the alternator. The battery supplies electrical power during starting or during periods when the current demand of the vehicle's electrical system exceeds the output capacity of the alternator. The alternator supplies electrical current when the engine is running. Just not does the alternator supply the current needs of the vehicle, but it recharges the battery.

The Battery

In most modern vehicles, the battery is a lead/acid electrochemical device consisting of six 2 volt subsections (cells) connected in series, so that the unit is capable of producing approximately 12 volts of electrical pressure. Each subsection consists of a series of positive and negative plates held a short distance apart in a solution of sulfuric acid and water.

The two types of plates are of dissimilar metals. This sets up a chemical reaction, and it is this reaction which produces current flow from the battery when its positive and negative terminals are conn___d to an electrical load. The power removed from the battery is replaced b y the alternator, restoring the battery to its original chemical state.

The Alternator

On some vehicles there isn't an alternator, but a generator. The difference is that an alternator supplies alternating current which is then changed to direct current for use on the vehicle, while a generator produces direct current. Alternators tend to be more efficient and that is why they are used.

Alternators and generators are devices that consist of coils of wires wound together making big electromagnets. One group of coils spins within another set and the interaction of the magnetic fields causes a current to flow. This current is then drawn off the coils and fed into the vehicles electrical system.

GROUND

Two types of grounds are used in automotive electric circuits. Direct ground components are grounded to the frame through their mounting points. All other components use some sort of ground wire which is attached to the frame or chassis of the vehicle. The electrical current runs through the chassis of the vehicle and returns to the battery through the ground (-) cable; if you look, you'll see that the battery ground cable connects between the battery and the frame or chassis of the vehicle.

➡It should be noted that a good percentage of electrical problems can be traced to bad grounds.

PROTECTIVE DEVICES

▶ See Figure 2

It is possible for large surges of current to pass through the electrical system of your vehicle. If this surge of current were to reach the load in the circuit, the surge could burn it out or severely damage it. It can also overload the wiring, causing the harness to get hot and melt the insulation. To prevent this, fuses, circuit breakers and/or fusible links are connected into the supply wires of the electrical system. These items are nothing more than a built-in weak spot in the system. When an abnormal amount of current flows through the system, these protective devices work as follows to protect the circuit:

• Fuse—when an excessive electrical current passes through a fuse, the fuse "blows" (the conductor melts) and opens the circuit, preventing the passage of current.

• Circuit Breaker—a circuit breaker is basically a self-repairing fuse. It will open the circuit in the same fashion as a fuse, but when the surge subsides, the circuit breaker can be reset and does not need replacement.

• Fusible Link—a fusible link (fuse link or main link) is a short length of special, high temperature insulated wire that acts as a fuse. When an excessive electrical current passes through a fusible link, the thin gauge wire inside the link melts, creating an intentional open to protect the circuit. To repair the circuit, the link must be replaced. Some newer type fusible links are housed in plug-in modules, which are simply replaced like a fuse, while older type fusible links must be cut and spliced if they melt. Since this link is very early in the electrical path, it's the first place to look if nothing on the vehicle works, yet the battery seems to be charged and is properly connected.

✱✱ CAUTION

Always replace fuses, circuit breakers and fusible links with identically rated components. Under no circumstances should a component of higher or lower amperage rating be substituted.

SWITCHES & RELAYS

▶ See Figures 3 and 4

Switches are used in electrical circuits to control the passage of current. The most common use is to open and close circuits between the battery and the various electric devices in the system. Switches are rated according to the amount of amperage they can handle. If a sufficient amperage rated switch is not used in a circuit, the switch could overload and cause damage.

Some electrical components which require a large amount of current to operate use a special switch called a relay. Since these circuits carry a large amount of current, the thickness of the wire in the circuit is also greater. If this large wire were connected from the load to the control switch, the switch would have to carry the high amperage load and the fairing or dash would be twice as large to accommodate the increased size of the wiring harness. To prevent these problems, a relay is used.

Relays are composed of a coil and a set of contacts. When the coil has a current passed though it, a magnetic field is formed and this field causes the contacts to move together, completing the circuit. Most relays are normally open, preventing current from passing through the circuit, but they can take any electrical form depending on the job they are intended to do. Relays can be considered "remote control switches." They allow a smaller current to operate devices that require higher amperages. When a small current operates the coil, a larger current is allowed to pass by the contacts. Some common circuits which may use relays are the horn, headlights, starter, electric fuel pump and other high draw circuits.

LOAD

Every electrical circuit must include a "load" (something to use the electricity coming from the source). Without this load, the battery would attempt to deliver its entire power supply from one pole to another. This is called a "short circuit." All this electricity would take a short cut to ground and cause a great amount of damage to other components in the circuit by developing a tremendous amount of heat. This condition could develop sufficient heat to melt the insulation on all the surrounding wires and reduce a multiple wire cable to a lump of plastic and copper.

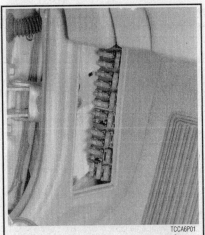

Fig. 2 Most vehicles use one or more fuse panels. This one is located on the driver's side kick panel

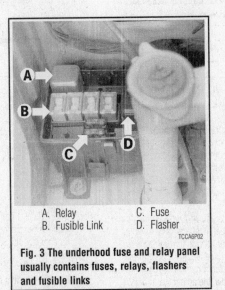

A. Relay   C. Fuse
B. Fusible Link   D. Flasher

Fig. 3 The underhood fuse and relay panel usually contains fuses, relays, flashers and fusible links

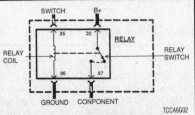

Fig. 4 Relays are composed of a coil and a switch. These two components are linked together so that when one operates, the other operates at the same time. The large wires in the circuit are connected from the battery to one side of the relay switch (B+) and from the opposite side of the relay switch to the load (component). Smaller wires are connected from the relay coil to the control switch for the circuit and from the opposite side of the relay coil to ground

WIRING & HARNESSES

The average vehicle contains meters and meters of wiring, with hundreds of individual connections. To protect the many wires from damage and to keep them from becoming a confusing tangle, they are organized into bundles, enclosed in plastic or taped together and called wiring harnesses. Different harnesses serve different parts of the vehicle. Individual wires are color coded to help trace them through a harness where sections are hidden from view.

Automotive wiring or circuit conductors can be either single strand wire, multi-strand wire or printed circuitry. Single strand wire has a solid metal core and is usually used inside such components as alternators, motors, relays and other devices. Multi-strand wire has a core made of many small strands of wire twisted together into a single conductor. Most of the wiring in an automotive electrical system is made up of multi-strand wire, either as a single conductor or grouped together in a harness. All wiring is color coded on the insulator, either as a solid color or as a colored wire with an identification stripe. A printed circuit is a thin film of copper or other conductor that is printed on an insulator backing. Occasionally, a printed circuit is sandwiched between two sheets of plastic for more protection and flexibility. A complete printed circuit, consisting of conductors, insulating material and connectors for lamps or other components is called a printed circuit board. Printed circuitry is used in place of individual wires or harnesses in places where space is limited, such as behind instrument panels.

Since automotive electrical systems are very sensitive to changes in resistance, the selection of properly sized wires is critical when systems are repaired. A loose or corroded connection or a replacement wire that is too small for the circuit will add extra resistance and an additional voltage drop to the circuit.

The wire gauge number is an expression of the cross-section area of the conductor. Vehicles from countries that use the metric system will typically describe the wire size as its cross-sectional area in square millimeters. In this method, the larger the wire, the greater the number. Another common system for expressing wire size is the American Wire Gauge (AWG) system. As gauge number increases, area decreases and the wire becomes smaller. An 18 gauge wire is smaller than a 4 gauge wire. A wire with a higher gauge number will carry less current than a wire with a lower gauge number. Gauge wire size refers to the size of the strands of the conductor, not the size of the complete wire with insulator. It is possible, therefore, to have two wires of the same gauge with different diameters because one may have thicker insulation than the other.

It is essential to understand how a circuit works before trying to figure out why it doesn't. An electrical schematic shows the electrical current paths when a circuit is operating properly. Schematics break the entire electrical system down into individual circuits. In a schematic, usually no attempt is made to represent wiring and components as they physically appear on the vehicle; switches and other components are shown as simply as possible. Face views of harness connectors show the cavity or terminal locations in all multi-pin connectors to help locate test points.

CONNECTORS

▶ See Figures 5 and 6

Three types of connectors are commonly used in automotive applications—weatherproof, molded and hard shell.

TCCA6P03

Fig. 5 Hard shell (left) and weatherproof (right) connectors have replaceable terminals

TCCA6P04

Fig. 6 Weatherproof connectors are most commonly used in the engine compartment or where the connector is exposed to the elements

• Weatherproof—these connectors are most commonly used where the connector is exposed to the elements. Terminals are protected against moisture and dirt by sealing rings which provide a weathertight seal. All repairs require the use of a special terminal and the tool required to service it. Unlike standard blade type terminals, these weatherproof terminals cannot be straightened once they are bent. Make certain that the connectors are properly seated and all of the sealing rings are in place when connecting leads.

• Molded—these connectors require complete replacement of the connector if found to be defective. This means splicing a new connector assembly into the harness. All splices should be soldered to insure proper contact. Use care when probing the connections or replacing terminals in them, as it is possible to create a short circuit between opposite terminals. If this happens to the wrong terminal pair, it is possible to damage certain components. Always use jumper wires between connectors for circuit checking and NEVER probe through weatherproof seals.

• Hard Shell—unlike molded connectors, the terminal contacts in hard-shell connectors can be replaced. Replacement usually involves the use of a special terminal removal tool that depresses the locking tangs (barbs) on the connector terminal and allows the connector to be removed from the rear of the shell. The connector shell should be replaced if it shows any evidence of burning, melting, cracks, or breaks. Replace individual terminals that are burnt, corroded, distorted or loose.

Test Equipment

Pinpointing the exact cause of trouble in an electrical circuit is most times accomplished by the use of special test equipment. The following describes different types of commonly used test equipment and briefly explains how to use them in diagnosis. In addition to the information covered below, the tool manufacturer's instructions booklet (provided with the tester) should be read and clearly understood before attempting any test procedures.

JUMPER WIRES

✳✳ CAUTION

Never use jumper wires made from a thinner gauge wire than the circuit being tested. If the jumper wire is of too small a gauge, it may overheat and possibly melt. Never use jumpers to bypass high resistance loads in a circuit. Bypassing resistances, in effect, creates a short circuit. This may, in turn, cause damage and fire. Jumper wires should only be used to bypass lengths of wire or to simulate switches.

Jumper wires are simple, yet extremely valuable, pieces of test equipment. They are basically test wires which are used to bypass sections of a circuit. Although jumper wires can be purchased, they are usually fabricated from lengths of standard automotive wire and whatever type of connector (alligator clip, spade connector or pin connector) that is required for the particular application being tested. In cramped, hard-to-reach areas, it is advisable to have insulated boots over the jumper wire terminals in order to prevent accidental grounding. It is also advisable to include a standard automotive fuse in any jumper wire. This is commonly referred to as a "fused jumper". By inserting an in-line fuse holder between a set of test leads, a fused jumper wire can be used for bypassing open circuits. Use a 5 amp fuse to provide protection against voltage spikes.

Jumper wires are used primarily to locate open electrical circuits, on either the ground (-) side of the circuit or on the power (+) side. If an electrical component fails to operate, connect the jumper wire between the component and a good ground. If the component operates only with the jumper installed, the ground circuit is open. If the ground circuit is good, but the component does not operate, the circuit between the power feed and component may be open. By moving the jumper wire successively back from the component toward the power source, you can isolate the area of the circuit where the open is located. When the component stops functioning, or the power is cut off, the open is in the segment of wire between the jumper and the point previously tested.

You can sometimes connect the jumper wire directly from the battery to the "hot" terminal of the component, but first make sure the component uses 12 volts in operation. Some electrical components, such as fuel injectors or sensors, are designed to operate on about 4 to 5 volts, and running 12 volts directly to these components will cause damage.

TEST LIGHTS

▶ **See Figure 7**

The test light is used to check circuits and components while electrical current is flowing through them. It is used for voltage and ground tests. To use a 12 volt test light, connect the ground clip to a good ground and probe wherever necessary with the pick. The test light will illuminate when voltage is detected. This does not necessarily mean that 12 volts (or any particular amount of voltage) is present; it only means that some voltage is present. It is advisable before using the test light to touch its ground clip and probe across the battery posts or terminals to make sure the light is operating properly.

✳✳ WARNING

Do not use a test light to probe electronic ignition, spark plug or coil wires. Never use a pick-type test light to probe wiring on computer controlled systems unless specifically instructed to do so. Any wire insulation that is pierced by the test light probe should be taped and sealed with silicone after testing.

Like the jumper wire, the 12 volt test light is used to isolate opens in circuits. But, whereas the jumper wire is used to bypass the open to operate the load, the 12 volt test light is used to locate the presence of voltage in a circuit. If the test light illuminates, there is power up to that point in the circuit; if the test light does not illuminate, there is an open circuit (no power). Move the test light in successive steps back toward the power source until the light in the handle illuminates. The open is between the probe and a point which was previously probed.

The self-powered test light is similar in design to the 12 volt test light, but contains a 1.5 volt penlight battery in the handle. It is most often used in place of a multimeter to check for open or short circuits when power is isolated from the circuit (continuity test).

The battery in a self-powered test light does not provide much current. A weak battery may not provide enough power to illuminate the test light even when a complete circuit is made (especially if there is high resistance in the circuit). Always make sure that the test battery is strong. To check the battery, briefly touch the ground clip to the probe; if the light glows brightly, the battery is strong enough for testing.

➡**A self-powered test light should not be used on any computer controlled system or component. The small amount of electricity transmitted by the test light is enough to damage many electronic automotive components.**

MULTIMETERS

Multimeters are an extremely useful tool for troubleshooting electrical problems. They can be purchased in either analog or digital form and have a price range to suit any budget. A multimeter is a voltmeter, ammeter and ohmmeter (along with other features) combined into one instrument. It is often used when testing solid state circuits because of its high input impedance (usually 10 megaohms or more). A brief description of the multimeter main test functions follows:

• Voltmeter—the voltmeter is used to measure voltage at any point in a circuit, or to measure the voltage drop across any part of a circuit. Voltmeters usually have various scales and a selector switch to allow the reading of different voltage ranges. The voltmeter has a positive and a negative lead. To avoid damage to the meter, always connect the negative lead to the negative (-) side of the circuit (to ground or nearest the ground side of the circuit) and connect the positive lead to the positive (+) side of the circuit (to the power source or the nearest power source). Note that the negative voltmeter lead will always be black and that the positive voltmeter will always be some color other than black (usually red).

• Ohmmeter—the ohmmeter is designed to read resistance (measured in ohms) in a circuit or component. Most ohmmeters will have a selector switch which permits the measurement of different ranges of resistance (usually the selector switch allows the multiplication of the meter reading by 10, 100, 1,000 and 10,000). Some ohmmeters are "auto-ranging" which means the meter itself will determine which scale to use. Since the meters are powered by an internal battery, the ohmmeter can be used like a self-powered test light. When the ohmmeter is connected, current from the ohmmeter flows through the circuit or component being tested. Since the ohmmeter's internal resistance and voltage are known values, the amount of current flow through the meter depends on the resistance of the circuit or component being tested. The ohmmeter can also be used to perform a continuity test for suspected open circuits. In using the meter for making continuity checks, do not be concerned with the actual resistance readings. Zero resistance, or any ohm reading, indicates continuity in the circuit. Infinite resistance indicates an opening in the circuit. A high resistance reading where there should be none indicates a problem in the circuit. Checks for short circuits are made in the same manner as checks for open circuits, except that the circuit must be isolated from both power and normal ground. Infinite resistance indicates no continuity, while zero resistance indicates a dead short.

✳✳ WARNING

Never use an ohmmeter to check the resistance of a component or wire while there is voltage applied to the circuit.

• Ammeter—an ammeter measures the amount of current flowing through a circuit in units called amperes or amps. At normal operating voltage, most circuits have a characteristic amount of amperes, called "current draw" which can be measured using an ammeter. By referring to a specified current draw rating, then measuring the amperes and comparing the two values, one can determine what is happening within the circuit to aid in diagnosis. An open circuit, for example, will not allow any current to flow, so the ammeter reading will be zero. A damaged component or circuit will have an increased current draw, so the reading will be high. The ammeter is always connected in series with the circuit being tested. All of the current that normally flows through the circuit must also flow through the ammeter; if there is any other path for the current to follow, the ammeter reading will not be accurate. The ammeter itself has very little resistance to current flow and, therefore, will not affect the circuit, but it will measure current draw only when the circuit is closed and electricity is flowing. Excessive current draw can blow fuses and drain the battery, while a reduced current draw can cause motors to run slowly, lights to dim and other components to not operate properly.

Troubleshooting Electrical Systems

When diagnosing a specific problem, organized troubleshooting is a must. The complexity of a modern automotive vehicle demands that you approach any

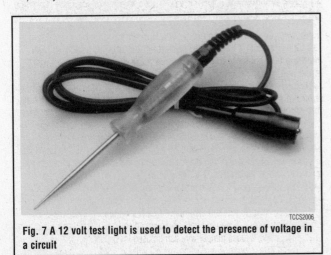

Fig. 7 A 12 volt test light is used to detect the presence of voltage in a circuit

TCCS2006

problem in a logical, organized manner. There are certain troubleshooting techniques, however, which are standard:

• Establish when the problem occurs. Does the problem appear only under certain conditions? Were there any noises, odors or other unusual symptoms? Isolate the problem area. To do this, make some simple tests and observations, then eliminate the systems that are working properly. Check for obvious problems, such as broken wires and loose or dirty connections. Always check the obvious before assuming something complicated is the cause.

• Test for problems systematically to determine the cause once the problem area is isolated. Are all the components functioning properly? Is there power going to electrical switches and motors. Performing careful, systematic checks will often turn up most causes on the first inspection, without wasting time checking components that have little or no relationship to the problem.

• Test all repairs after the work is done to make sure that the problem is fixed. Some causes can be traced to more than one component, so a careful verification of repair work is important in order to pick up additional malfunctions that may cause a problem to reappear or a different problem to arise. A blown fuse, for example, is a simple problem that may require more than another fuse to repair. If you don't look for a problem that caused a fuse to blow, a shorted wire (for example) may go undetected.

Experience has shown that most problems tend to be the result of a fairly simple and obvious cause, such as loose or corroded connectors, bad grounds or damaged wire insulation which causes a short. This makes careful visual inspection of components during testing essential to quick and accurate troubleshooting.

Testing

OPEN CIRCUITS

▶ See Figure 8

This test already assumes the existence of an open in the circuit and it is used to help locate the open portion.
1. Isolate the circuit from power and ground.
2. Connect the self-powered test light or ohmmeter ground clip to the ground side of the circuit and probe sections of the circuit sequentially.
3. If the light is out or there is infinite resistance, the open is between the probe and the circuit ground.
4. If the light is on or the meter shows continuity, the open is between the probe and the end of the circuit toward the power source.

SHORT CIRCUITS

➡ Never use a self-powered test light to perform checks for opens or shorts when power is applied to the circuit under test. The test light can be damaged by outside power.

1. Isolate the circuit from power and ground.
2. Connect the self-powered test light or ohmmeter ground clip to a good ground and probe any easy-to-reach point in the circuit.
3. If the light comes on or there is continuity, there is a short somewhere in the circuit.

4. To isolate the short, probe a test point at either end of the isolated circuit (the light should be on or the meter should indicate continuity).
5. Leave the test light probe engaged and sequentially open connectors or switches, remove parts, etc. until the light goes out or continuity is broken.
6. When the light goes out, the short is between the last two circuit components which were opened.

VOLTAGE

This test determines voltage available from the battery and should be the first step in any electrical troubleshooting procedure after visual inspection. Many electrical problems, especially on computer controlled systems, can be caused by a low state of charge in the battery. Excessive corrosion at the battery cable terminals can cause poor contact that will prevent proper charging and full battery current flow.
1. Set the voltmeter selector switch to the 20V position.
2. Connect the multimeter negative lead to the battery's negative (-) post or terminal and the positive lead to the battery's positive (+) post or terminal.
3. Turn the ignition switch **ON** to provide a load.
4. A well charged battery should register over 12 volts. If the meter reads below 11.5 volts, the battery power may be insufficient to operate the electrical system properly.

VOLTAGE DROP

▶ See Figure 9

When current flows through a load, the voltage beyond the load drops. This voltage drop is due to the resistance created by the load and also by small resistances created by corrosion at the connectors and damaged insulation on the wires. The maximum allowable voltage drop under load is critical, especially if there is more than one load in the circuit, since all voltage drops are cumulative.
1. Set the voltmeter selector switch to the 20 volt position.
2. Connect the multimeter negative lead to a good ground.
3. Operate the circuit and check the voltage prior to the first component (load).
4. There should be little or no voltage drop in the circuit prior to the first component. If a voltage drop exists, the wire or connectors in the circuit are suspect.
5. While operating the first component in the circuit, probe the ground side of the component with the positive meter lead and observe the voltage readings. A small voltage drop should be noticed. This voltage drop is caused by the resistance of the component.
6. Repeat the test for each component (load) down the circuit.
7. If a large voltage drop is noticed, the preceding component, wire or connector is suspect.

RESISTANCE

▶ See Figures 10 and 11

✱✱ WARNING

Never use an ohmmeter with power applied to the circuit. The ohmmeter is designed to operate on its own power supply. The normal 12 volt electrical system voltage could damage the meter!

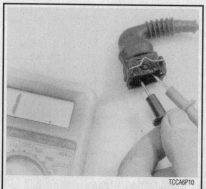

TCCA6P10

Fig. 8 The infinite reading on this multimeter indicates that the circuit is open

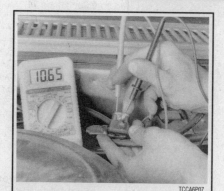

TCCA6P07

Fig. 9 This voltage drop test revealed high resistance (low voltage) in the circuit

TCCA6P08

Fig. 10 Checking the resistance of a coolant temperature sensor with an ohmmeter. Reading is 1.04 kilohms

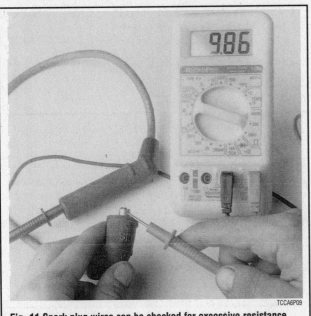

Fig. 11 Spark plug wires can be checked for excessive resistance using an ohmmeter

TCCA6P09

1. Isolate the circuit from the vehicle's power source.
2. Ensure that the ignition key is **OFF** when disconnecting any components or the battery.
3. Where necessary, also isolate at least one side of the circuit to be checked, in order to avoid reading parallel resistances. Parallel circuit resistances will always give a lower reading than the actual resistance of either of the branches.
4. Connect the meter leads to both sides of the circuit (wire or component) and read the actual measured ohms on the meter scale. Make sure the selector switch is set to the proper ohm scale for the circuit being tested, to avoid misreading the ohmmeter test value.

Wire and Connector Repair

Almost anyone can replace damaged wires, as long as the proper tools and parts are available. Wire and terminals are available to fit almost any need. Even the specialized weatherproof, molded and hard shell connectors are now available from aftermarket suppliers.

Be sure the ends of all the wires are fitted with the proper terminal hardware and connectors. Wrapping a wire around a stud is never a permanent solution and will only cause trouble later. Replace wires one at a time to avoid confusion. Always route wires exactly the same as the factory.

➡**If connector repair is necessary, only attempt it if you have the proper tools. Weatherproof and hard shell connectors require special tools to release the pins inside the connector. Attempting to repair these connectors with conventional hand tools will damage them.**

SUPPLEMENTAL INFLATABLE RESTRAINT (SIR) SYSTEM

General Information

▶ **See Figure 12**

Beginning in 1994, driver's side air bags became standard equipment for W-body vehicles. In 1995, passenger side air bags were implemented on some models. The Supplemental Inflatable Restraint (SIR) system offers protection in addition to that provided by the seat belt by deploying an air bag from the center of the steering wheel or dash panel. The air bag deploys when the vehicle is involved in a frontal crash of sufficient force up to 30° off the centerline of the vehicle. To further absorb the crash energy, there is also a knee bolster located beneath the instrument panel in the driver's area and the steering wheel is collapsible.

The system has an energy reserve, which can store a large enough electrical charge to deploy the air bag(s) for up to ten minutes after the battery has been disconnected or damaged. The system **MUST** be disabled before any service is performed on or around SIR components or SIR wiring.

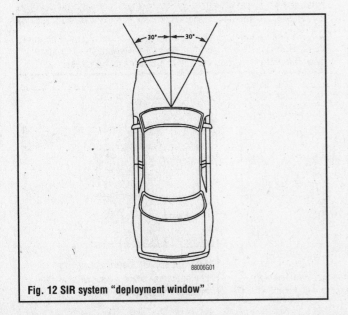

Fig. 12 SIR system "deployment window"

88006G01

SYSTEM COMPONENTS

▶ **See Figure 13**

Sensing and Diagnostic Module (SDM)

The SDM is designed to perform five main functions: energy reserve, malfunction detection, malfunction recording, driver notification and frontal crash recording.

The SDM maintains a reserve voltage supply to provide deployment energy for a few seconds when the vehicle voltage is low or lost in a frontal crash. The SDM performs diagnostic monitoring of the SIR system and records malfunctions in the form of diagnostic trouble codes, which can be obtained from a hand scan tool and/or on-board diagnostics. The SDM warns the driver of SIR system malfunctions by controlling the AIR BAG warning lamp and records SIR system status during a frontal crash.

Air Bag Warning Lamp

The AIR BAG warning/indicator lamp is used to verify lamp and SDM operation by flashing 7 times when the ignition is first turned **ON**. It is also used to warn the driver of an SIR system malfunction.

SIR Coil Assembly

▶ **See Figure 14**

The SIR coil assembly consists of two current carrying coils. They are attached to the steering column and allow rotation of the steering wheel while maintaining continuous deployment loop contact through the inflator module.

There is a shorting bar on the lower steering column connector that connects the SIR coil to the SIR wiring harness. The shorting bar shorts the circuit when the connector is disengaged. The circuit to the inflator module is shorted in this way to prevent unwanted air bag deployment when servicing the steering column or other SIR components.

Inflator Module

▶ **See Figure 15**

The inflator module consists of an inflatable bag and an inflator (a canister of gas-generating material and an initiating device). When the vehicle is in a frontal crash of sufficient force to close the arming sensor and at least one discriminating sensor simultaneously, current flows through the deployment loop.

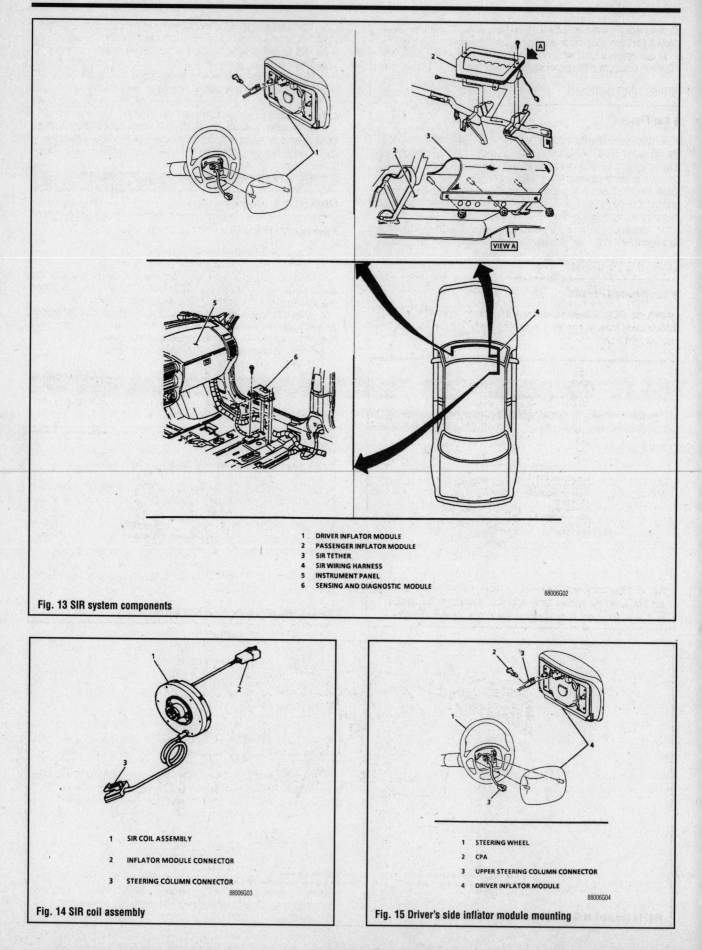

1   DRIVER INFLATOR MODULE
2   PASSENGER INFLATOR MODULE
3   SIR TETHER
4   SIR WIRING HARNESS
5   INSTRUMENT PANEL
6   SENSING AND DIAGNOSTIC MODULE

88006G02

Fig. 13 SIR system components

1   SIR COIL ASSEMBLY

2   INFLATOR MODULE CONNECTOR

3   STEERING COLUMN CONNECTOR

88006G03

Fig. 14 SIR coil assembly

1   STEERING WHEEL

2   CPA

3   UPPER STEERING COLUMN CONNECTOR

4   DRIVER INFLATOR MODULE

88006G04

Fig. 15 Driver's side inflator module mounting

Current passing through the initiator ignites the material in the inflator module, causing a reaction which produces a gas that rapidly inflates the air bag.

All vehicles are equipped with a driver's side inflator module located in the steering wheel. If equipped, a passenger side inflator module is located in the dash panel.

SERVICE PRECAUTIONS

▶ **See Figure 16**

• When performing service around the SIR system components or wiring, the SIR system **MUST** be disabled. Failure to do so could result in possible air bag deployment, personal injury or unneeded SIR system repairs.

• When carrying a live inflator module, make sure that the bag and trim cover are pointed away from you. Never carry the inflator module by the wires or connector on the underside of the module. In case of accidental deployment, the bag will then deploy with minimal chance of injury.

• When placing a live inflator module on a bench or other surface, always face the bag and trim cover up, away from the surface.

DISABLING THE SYSTEM

▶ **See Figures 17 and 18**

➡ **With the AIR BAG fuse removed and the ignition switch ON, the AIR BAG warning lamp will be on. The is normal and does not indicate any system malfunction.**

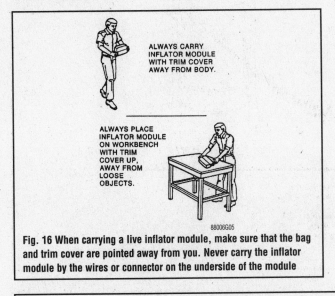

ALWAYS CARRY INFLATOR MODULE WITH TRIM COVER AWAY FROM BODY.

ALWAYS PLACE INFLATOR MODULE ON WORKBENCH WITH TRIM COVER UP, AWAY FROM LOOSE OBJECTS.

88006G05

Fig. 16 When carrying a live inflator module, make sure that the bag and trim cover are pointed away from you. Never carry the inflator module by the wires or connector on the underside of the module

1. Turn the steering wheel so that the vehicle's wheels are pointing straight ahead.

2. Turn the ignition switch to **LOCK**, remove the key, then disconnect the negative battery cable.

3. Remove the AIR BAG fuse from the fuse block.

4. Remove the steering column filler panel.

5. Disengage the Connector Position Assurance (CPA) and the yellow 2-way connector, located near the base of the steering column.

6. If equipped with a passenger side air bag, unfasten the instrument panel compartment door assembly, flip it down to access the connector. Detach the Connector Position Assurance (CPA) and yellow 2-way connector behind the instrument panel compartment door assembly.

7. Connect the negative battery cable.

ENABLING THE SYSTEM

▶ **See Figures 17 and 18**

1. Disconnect the negative battery cable.

2. Turn the ignition switch to **LOCK**, then remove the key.

3. If equipped with a passenger side air bag, attach the yellow 2-way connector and Connector Position Assurance (CPA) behind the instrument panel compartment door assembly. Secure the instrument panel compartment door assembly.

4. Engage the yellow SIR connector and corresponding CPA located near the base of the steering column.

5. Install the steering column filler panel/lower trim panel.

6. Install the AIR BAG fuse to the fuse block.

7. Connect the negative battery cable.

8. Turn the ignition switch to **RUN** and make sure that the AIR BAG warning lamp flashes seven times and then shuts off. If the warning lamp does not shut off, make sure that the wiring is properly connected. If the light remains on, take the vehicle to a reputable repair facility for service.

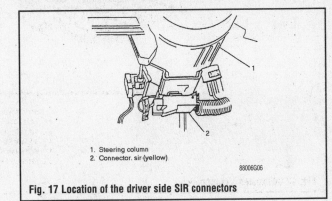

1. Steering column
2. Connector. sir (yellow)

88006G06

Fig. 17 Location of the driver side SIR connectors

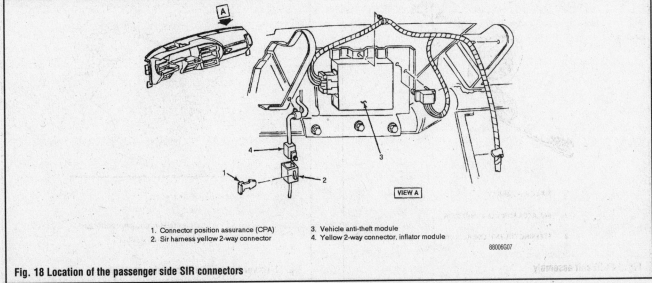

1. Connector position assurance (CPA)
2. Sir harness yellow 2-way connector
3. Vehicle anti-theft module
4. Yellow 2-way connector, inflator module

VIEW A

88006G07

Fig. 18 Location of the passenger side SIR connectors

HEATING AND AIR CONDITIONING

Blower Motor

REMOVAL & INSTALLATION

▶ See Figures 19 thru 25

1. Disconnect the negative battery cable.
2. Remove the right side sound insulator under the instrument panel.
3. Unfasten the convenience center rear screws. Loosen the front screw and slide the convenience center out.
4. Grasp the carpet at the top side of the cowl and pull forward.
5. Detach the blower motor electrical connection.
6. Disconnect the harness from the clip.

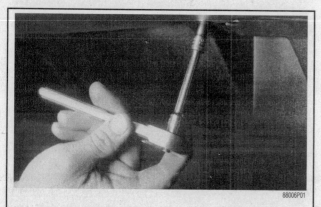

Fig. 19 Use a suitable socket and extension combination to . . .

7. Unfasten the blower motor mounting screws, then remove the blower motor from the vehicle.
8. Installation is the reverse of the removal procedure.
9. Connect the negative battery cable.

Heater Core

REMOVAL & INSTALLATION

1. Disconnect the negative battery cable.

✳✳ CAUTION

When draining the coolant, keep in mind that cats and dogs are attracted by ethylene glycol antifreeze, and are quite likely to drink any that is left in an uncovered container or in puddles on the ground. This will prove fatal in sufficient quantity. Always drain the coolant into a sealable container. Coolant should be reused unless it is contaminated or several years old.

1988–91 Vehicles

▶ See Figure 26

1. Disconnect the negative battery cable.
2. Properly drain the engine coolant into a suitable container.
3. Remove the upper weatherstrip from the body.
4. Remove the upper secondary cowl.
5. Remove the lower secondary cowl upper nut.
6. Disconnect the heater hoses from the heater core.

➡If you have access to an air compressor, blow out the residual coolant from the core. This will prevent coolant leakage into the passenger compartment.

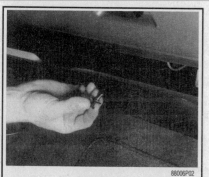

Fig. 20 . . . unfasten the right side insulator retaining screws, then remove the insulator

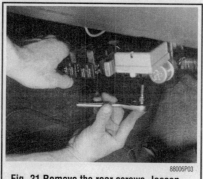

Fig. 21 Remove the rear screws, loosen the front screw, then slide the convenience center out

Fig. 22 If necessary, remove the retainer . . .

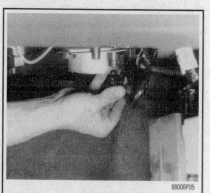

Fig. 23 . . . then detach the blower motor electrical connector(s)

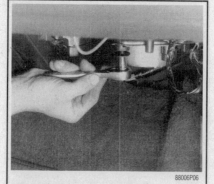

Fig. 24 Unfasten the retaining screws . . .

Fig. 25 . . . then remove the blower motor from the vehicle

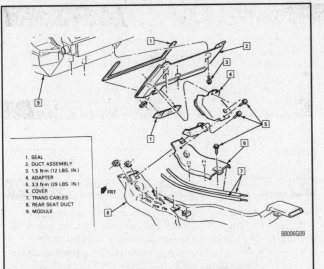

1. SEAL
2. DUCT ASSEMBLY
3. 1.5 N·m (12 LBS. IN.)
4. ADAPTER
5. 3.3 N·m (29 LBS. IN.)
6. COVER
7. TRANS CABLES
8. REAR SEAT DUCT
9. MODULE

88006G09

Fig. 26 Heater core cover mounting—1990 vehicle shown

7. Working inside the vehicle, remove the right and left side instrument panel sound insulators.

8. Remove the rear seat heater duct adapter.

9. Detach the lower heater duct.

10. Unfasten the heater core cover screws, then remove the heater core cover.

11. Remove the heater core from the vehicle.

12. Installation is the reverse of the removal procedure.

13. Connect the negative battery cable.

14. Fill cooling system and check for leaks. Start the engine and allow to come to normal operating temperature. Recheck for coolant leaks. Allow the engine to warm up sufficiently to confirm operation of the cooling fan.

1992–96 Vehicles

▶ See Figures 27, 28, 29 and 30

1. Relieve the fuel system pressure, as outlined in Section 5 of this manual.

2. Disconnect the negative battery cable.

3. Remove the air cleaner and duct assembly.

4. Properly drain the engine coolant into a suitable container.

5. For 2.2L and 3.1L engines, rotate the engine forward as outlined in Section 3 of this manual.

6. For 1994–96 3.4L engines, remove the upper intake manifold, as outlined in Section 3 of this manual.

7. If equipped with a 3.4L engine, perform the following:

   a. Disconnect and cap the fuel lines.

   b. Detach the upper radiator hose from the engine.

   c. Disconnect the exhaust crossover pipe.

   d. Remove the transmission dipstick tube.

8. Disconnect both hoses from the heater core by unfastening the clamps. It may be necessary to use tool J 38543 or equivalent clamp remover to unfasten the hose clamps.

9. Remove the right and left instrument panel sound insulators.

10. Remove the rear compartment heat duct adapter bolt/screw and the adapter.

11. Unfasten the heater outlet duct bolts, then remove the duct.

12. Remove the heater core cover screws, then remove the cover.

13. Remove the heater core from the vehicle.

To install:

14. Position the heater core, then install the core cover. Tighten the retaining screws to 27 inch lbs. (3 Nm).

15. Install the heater outlet duct and retaining bolts/screws. Tighten to 18 inch lbs. (2 Nm).

16. Install the rear compartment heat duct adapter and secure with the bolts/screws. Tighten to 27 inch lbs. (3 Nm).

17. Secure the right and left instrument panel sound insulators.

18. Connect both heater hoses to the heater core. Secure using the retaining clamps.

19. If equipped with a 1994–96 3.4L engine, perform the following:

   a. Install the transmission dipstick tube.

   b. Attach the exhaust crossover pipe.

   c. Connect the upper radiator hose to the engine assembly.

   d. Uncap and connect the fuel lines.

   e. Install the upper intake manifold.

20. For 2.2L and 3.1L engines, rotate the engine back to its original position, as outlined in Section 3 of this manual.

21. Properly refill the cooling system.

22. Install the air cleaner and duct assembly, then connect the negative battery cable. Start the engine and check for proper operation and/or leaks.

Temperature Control Cable

REMOVAL & INSTALLATION

1. Disconnect the negative battery cable.

2. Remove the right side sound insulator panel.

3. If necessary for access, remove the instrument panel compartment.

4. Disconnect the cable at the module.

5. Remove the control panel trim plate and control panel assembly, as outlined later in this section.

6. Disconnect the cable from the control assembly, then remove the cable.

7. Installation is the reverse of the removal procedure. Adjust temperature control cable, as outlined later in this section.

ADJUSTMENT

If the temperature control lever fails to move to full COLD or HOT, or a large amount of lever spring back is noticed when moving to either of the full positions, the cable clip may need adjustment. Failure to grip the clip in the correct manner will damage its ability to hold position on the cable. The temperature control cable must be replaced if clip retention fails.

88006P08

Fig. 27 Unfasten the retaining screws . . .

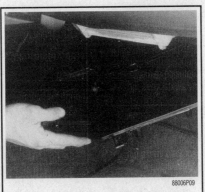

88006P09

Fig. 28 . . . then remove the heater core cover

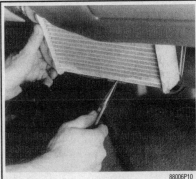

88006P10

Fig. 29 Removing the heater core from the vehicle—1992 Lumina shown

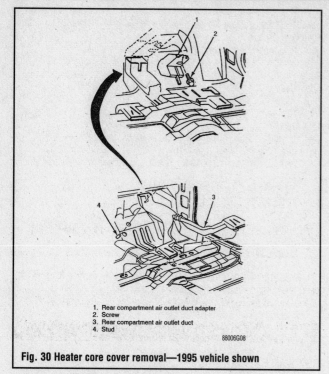

1. Rear compartment air outlet duct adapter
2. Screw
3. Rear compartment air outlet duct
4. Stud

88006G08

Fig. 30 Heater core cover removal—1995 vehicle shown

1. To adjust, grip the clip at the module end of the cable while pulling the temperature control lever to the correct full position (COLD or HOT) and connect.
2. Verify correct adjustment by observing for little or no spring back of the temperature control lever and listening for temperature door "slam" when the control lever is moved to full positions quickly.

Control Panel

REMOVAL & INSTALLATION

Cutlass Supreme

1988–94 VEHICLES

▶ **See Figure 31**

1. Disconnect the negative battery cable.
2. Remove the cluster trim plate-to-dash securing screws.

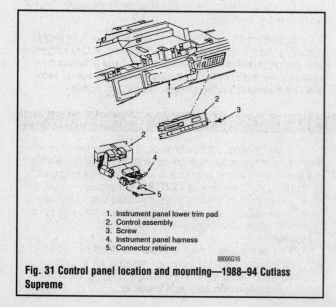

1. Instrument panel lower trim pad
2. Control assembly
3. Screw
4. Instrument panel harness
5. Connector retainer

88006G16

Fig. 31 Control panel location and mounting—1988–94 Cutlass Supreme

3. Tilt the top of the cluster trim plate downward releasing the clips that mount the bottom of the plate to the dash and remove the trim plate.
4. Remove the screws securing the accessory trim plate-to-dash.
5. Tilt the top of the accessory trim plate downward releasing the clips that mount the bottom of the plate-to-dash.
6. Remove the control assembly from the dash and unplug the electrical connectors.
7. Installation is the reverse of the removal procedure.
8. Connect the negative battery cable and check operation.

Grand Prix

1988–93 VEHICLES

▶ **See Figure 32**

1. Disconnect the negative battery cable.
2. Remove the lower left instrument panel pad.
3. Remove the control assembly trim plate.
4. Loosen the left securing screws, pull the assembly out and disconnect the electrical harness.
5. Installation is the reverse of the removal procedure.

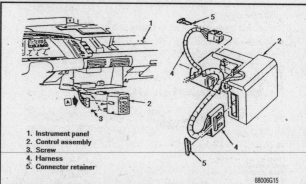

1. Instrument panel
2. Control assembly
3. Screw
4. Harness
5. Connector retainer

88006G15

Fig. 32 On 1988–93 Grand Prix, the control assembly is in the center of the panel, to the right of the radio controls

Regal

1988–94 VEHICLES

▶ **See Figure 33**

1. Disconnect the negative battery cable.
2. Remove the instrument panel trim plate.
3. Remove the control assembly securing screws, control assembly and disconnect the electrical harness.
4. Installation is the reverse of the removal procedure.
5. Connect the negative battery cable and check for proper operation.

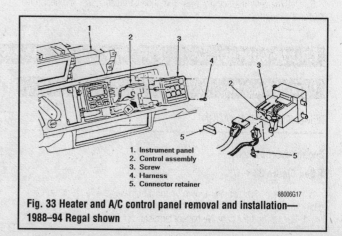

1. Instrument panel
2. Control assembly
3. Screw
4. Harness
5. Connector retainer

88006G17

Fig. 33 Heater and A/C control panel removal and installation—1988–94 Regal shown

Lumina and Monte Carlo

1990–94 VEHICLES

1. Disconnect the negative battery cable.
2. Remove the instrument cluster trim plate.
3. Remove the control assembly securing screws, then remove the control assembly and disconnect the electrical harness.
4. Installation is the reverse of the removal procedure.
5. Connect the negative battery cable and check for proper operation.

1995–96 VEHICLES

▶ See Figure 34

1. Disconnect the negative battery cable.
2. Remove the instrument cluster trim plate.
3. Unfasten the retaining bolt/screw, then remove the control assembly by unsnapping it.
4. Detach the electrical connectors.
5. Installation is the reverse of the removal procedure. Tighten the control panel retainers and tighten to 17 inch lbs. (2.0 Nm).

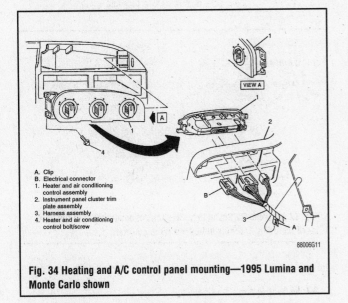

A. Clip
B. Electrical connector
1. Heater and air conditioning control assembly
2. Instrument panel cluster trim plate assembly
3. Harness assembly
4. Heater and air conditioning control bolt/screw

88006G11

Fig. 34 Heating and A/C control panel mounting—1995 Lumina and Monte Carlo shown

1994–96 Grand Prix and 1995–96 Cutlass Supreme and Regal

▶ See Figure 35

1. Disconnect the negative battery cable.
2. If equipped, remove the console assembly.
3. Remove the accessory trim plate.
4. Rotate the control assembly clockwise to unsnap.
5. Pull the control assembly away from the instrument panel and detach the electrical connectors.

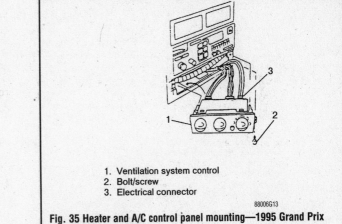

1. Ventilation system control
2. Bolt/screw
3. Electrical connector

88006G13

Fig. 35 Heater and A/C control panel mounting—1995 Grand Prix shown, others similar

6. Installation is the reverse of the removal procedure. Tighten the control panel retainers to 18 inch lbs. (2 Nm).
7. Connect the negative battery cable, then check for proper operation.

Blower Switch

REMOVAL & INSTALLATION

1. Disconnect the negative battery cable.
2. Remove the lower right side instrument panel sound insulator.
3. The blower switch is located behind the right hand side of the instrument panel mounted in the heater-A/C plenum.
4. Unfasten the retaining screws, then remove the resistor.
5. The installation is the reverse of the removal procedure.

Air Conditioning Components

REMOVAL & INSTALLATION

Repair or service of air conditioning components is not covered by this manual, because of the risk of personal injury or death, and because of the legal ramifications of servicing these components without the proper EPA certification and experience. Cost, personal injury or death, environmental damage, and legal considerations (such as the fact that it is a federal crime to vent refrigerant into the atmosphere), dictate that the A/C components on your vehicle should be serviced only by a Motor Vehicle Air Conditioning (MVAC) trained, and EPA certified automotive technician.

➡**If your vehicle's A/C system uses R-12 refrigerant and is in need of recharging, the A/C system can be converted over to R-134a refrigerant (less environmentally harmful and expensive). Refer to Section 1 for additional information on R-12 to R-134a conversions, and for additional considerations dealing with your vehicle's A/C system.**

CRUISE CONTROL

Control Switches

REMOVAL & INSTALLATION

Engagement Switch

▶ See Figure 36

The cruise control actuator switch on most of these vehicles is part of the multi-function lever located on the steering column.
1. Disconnect the negative battery terminal.

2. Detach the cruise control switch electrical connector. The connector may be located at the base of steering column or on the backside of the switch. It may be necessary to remove an under dash panel or trim piece for access.
3. Make sure the lever is in the **CENTER** or **OFF** position.
4. Pull lever straight out of retaining clip within the steering column.
5. Attach mechanic's wire or similar wire to the connector; gently pull the harness through the column, leaving the pull wire in place.
To install:
6. Place the transmission selector in **LOW** or **1**. Attach the mechanic's wire to the connector. Gently pull the harness into place, checking that the harness is completely clear of any moving or movable components such as tilt-column, telescoping column, brake pedal linkage, etc.

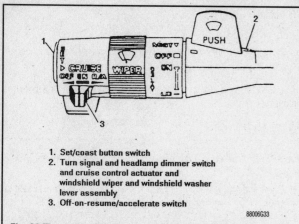

1. Set/coast button switch
2. Turn signal and headlamp dimmer switch and cruise control actuator and windshield wiper and windshield washer lever assembly
3. Off-on-resume/accelerate switch

88006G33

Fig. 36 The cruise control engagement switch is part of the multi-function lever assembly; the switch and lever must be replaced as an assembly

7. Position the lever and push it squarely into the retainer until it snaps in place.

8. Remove the mechanics' wire and attach the cruise control harness connector.

9. Reinstall any panels or insulation which were removed for access.

10. Connect the negative battery terminal.

Brake/Clutch Release Switches

All factory or dealer installed cruise control systems for these vehicles are equipped with either a brake or clutch release switch. The purpose of the switch is to deactivate the system when the driver begins to depress the pedal. Most of the switches found on earlier models are vacuum break switches (vacuum release valves) which will therefore have a vacuum line attached to rear of side of the switch. A vacuum break switch is used to quickly vent vacuum to the atmosphere so a vacuum controlled servo may return the throttle to the idle position. Later models may use a vacuum switch, an electric switch, or a combined vacuum and electric switch.

1. Disconnect the negative battery cable. At the brake switch, remove either the 2 electrical connectors or the electrical connector and the vacuum hose.

2. Remove the switch from the retainer.

3. Remove the tubular retainer from the brake pedal mounting bracket.

To install:

4. Install the tubular retainer to the brake pedal mounting bracket.

5. Press the brake pedal and install the release switch into the retainer until fully seated in the clips.

6. Connect the wiring and/or vacuum lines. Adjust the switch.

ADJUSTMENT

1. Depress the brake pedal and check that the release switch is fully seated in the clips.

2. Slowly pull the brake pedal back to the at-rest position; the switch and valve assembly will move within the clips to the adjusted position.

3. Measure pedal travel and check switch engagement. The electric brake release switch contacts must open at ⅛–½ in. (3–13mm) of pedal travel when measured at the centerline of the pedal pad. The brake lights should illuminate after another ⅛ in. (5mm) of travel. The vacuum release should engage at ⅝–1 in. (16–25mm) of pedal travel.

Cruise Control Module

REMOVAL & INSTALLATION

1988–93 Vehicles

1. Disconnect the negative battery cable.

2. Remove the driver side sound insulation panel.

3. Detach the connector from the module, located on a bracket on the brake pedal bracket/column support.

4. Unfasten the retaining screw and remove the module.

5. The installation is the reverse of the removal procedure.

6. Connect the negative battery cable and check the cruise control system for proper operation.

1994–96 Vehicles

▶ See Figures 37, 38 and 39

➡ The cruise control module is mounted on the left shock tower in the engine compartment.

1. Disconnect the negative battery cable.

2. Remove the cruise control cable at the engine bracket and throttle body cam.

3. Disconnect the cruise control cable from the module.

4. Detach the module electrical connector.

5. Unfasten the three nuts from the mounting studs, then remove the module.

To install:

6. Position the module on the mounting studs and install the three retaining nuts. Tighten the nuts to 18 inch lbs. (2 Nm).

7. Attach the electrical connector to the module.

8. Connect the cruise control cable to the module.

9. Fasten the cruise control cable to the engine bracket and throttle body cam.

10. Adjust the cruise control cable as follows:

a. Disengage the adjustment lock on the cruise control cable (the cable will move freely in and out of the adjuster when the lock is disengaged).

b. Hold the throttle at the closed position.

c. Engage the adjustment lock.

11. Connect the negative battery cable and check the cruise control system for proper operation.

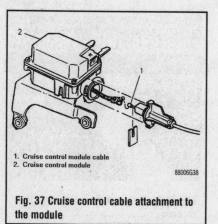

1. Cruise control module cable
2. Cruise control module

88006G38

Fig. 37 Cruise control cable attachment to the module

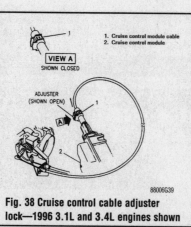

1. Cruise control module cable
2. Cruise control module

VIEW A
SHOWN CLOSED

ADJUSTER
(SHOWN OPEN)

88006G39

Fig. 38 Cruise control cable adjuster lock—1996 3.1L and 3.4L engines shown

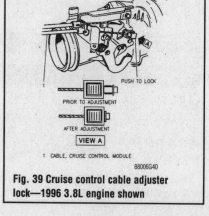

PUSH TO LOCK

PRIOR TO ADJUSTMENT

AFTER ADJUSTMENT

VIEW A

1 CABLE, CRUISE CONTROL MODULE

88006G40

Fig. 39 Cruise control cable adjuster lock—1996 3.8L engine shown

Cruise Control Servo

REMOVAL & INSTALLATION

▶ See Figure 40

➡A cruise control servo is utilized on 1988–93 vehicles.

1. Disconnect the negative battery cable.
2. Tag and detach the two vacuum lines and electrical connector from the servo.
3. Disconnect the cable by pushing the clip fastener.
4. Unfasten the retaining bolts, then remove the servo.

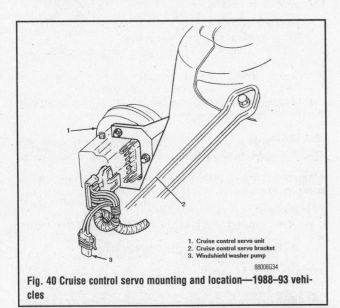

1. Cruise control servo unit
2. Cruise control servo bracket
3. Windshield washer pump

88006G34

Fig. 40 Cruise control servo mounting and location—1988–93 vehicles

ENTERTAINMENT SYSTEMS

Radio

REMOVAL & INSTALLATION

Lumina and Monte Carlo

▶ See Figures 41, 42, 43 and 44

1. Disconnect the negative battery cable.
2. Remove the instrument panel trim plate.

To install:
5. Position the servo, then secure using the retaining bolts. Tighten the bolts to 18 inch lbs. (2 Nm).
6. Connect the cable to the cruise control servo using the retainer. If necessary, adjust as outlined later in this section.
7. Attach the electrical connector and vacuum lines to the servo.
8. Connect the negative battery cable and check the cruise control system for proper operation.

LINKAGE ADJUSTMENT

➡Do not stretch cables or chains to make pins fit or holes align. This will prevent the engine from returning to idle.

1. Check that the cable is properly installed and that the throttle is closed to the idle position.
2. Pull the servo end of the cable toward the linkage bracket of the servo. Place the servo connector in one of the 6 holes in the bracket which allows the least amount of slack and does not move the throttle linkage.
3. Install the retainer clip. Check that the throttle linkage is still in the idle position.

Vacuum Tank

REMOVAL & INSTALLATION

➡A vacuum tank is utilized on 1988–93 vehicles.

1. Disconnect the negative battery cable.
2. Raise and safely support the vehicle.
3. Disconnect the vacuum hoses from the tank.
4. Unfasten the retaining nuts, then remove the tank from the vehicle.
To install:
5. The installation is the reverse of the removal procedure.
6. Tighten the vacuum tank retaining nuts to 27 inch lbs. (3 Nm).
7. Connect the negative battery cable, then check the cruise control system for proper operation.

3. Unfasten the radio retaining bolts, then while pulling the radio out, detach electrical harness and antenna lead.
4. Remove the radio from the vehicle.
To install:

✳✳ WARNING

When installing the radio, do not pinch the wires or a short circuit to ground may happen and damage the radio.

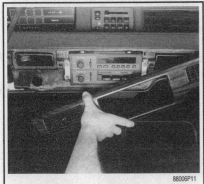

88006P11

Fig. 41 Remove the instrument panel trim plate—1992 Lumina shown

88006P12

Fig. 42 Unfasten the radio retaining bolts

88006P13

Fig. 43 Carefully pull the radio from its mounting . . .

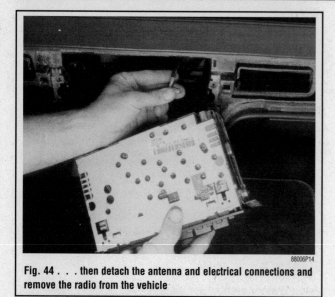

Fig. 44 . . . then detach the antenna and electrical connections and remove the radio from the vehicle

5. Attach the electrical harness and antenna lead to the back of the radio, then position the radio in the vehicle.
6. Install the retaining bolts.
7. Install the instrument panel trim plate.
8. Connect the negative battery cable.

Grand Prix, Cutlass Supreme and Regal

RADIO CONTROLS

The Grand Prix, Cutlass Supreme and Regal are equipped with a remote radio receiver with the controls mounted in the instrument panel.
1. Disconnect the negative battery cable.
2. Remove the cluster trim plate.
3. Remove the control retaining bolts, disconnect the electrical harness and remove the radio controls.
  To install:

❊❊ WARNING

When installing the radio controls, do not pinch the wires or a short circuit to ground may happen and damage the radio.

4. Connect the control electrical harness and tighten the control retaining bolts.
5. Install the cluster trim plate and reconnect the negative battery cable.

RADIO RECEIVER

▶ **See Figure 45**

1. Disconnect the negative battery cable.
2. Remove the right side sound insulator panel.
3. Remove the courtesy lamp and connector.
4. Remove the two receiver retaining bolts, disconnect the electrical harness and remove the receiver.
  To install:

❊❊ WARNING

When installing the receiver assembly, do not pinch the wires or a short circuit to ground may happen and damage the radio.

5. Connect the electrical harness, antenna cable and tighten the receiver retaining bolts.
6. Install the courtesy lamp and bolt.
7. Install the right side sound insulator panel and connect the negative battery cable.

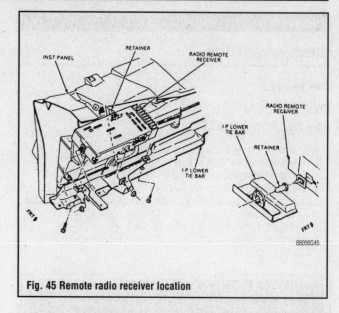

Fig. 45 Remote radio receiver location

Cassette/Equalizer/Compact Disc Player

REMOVAL & INSTALLATION

▶ **See Figure 46**

1. Disconnect the negative battery cable.
2. Remove any necessary instrument panel accessory trim plates.
3. Unfasten the retaining bolts, pull the unit out far enough to detach the electrical connector(s).
  To install:

❊❊ WARNING

When installing the assembly, do not pinch the wires or a short circuit to ground may happen and damage the radio.

4. Attach the electrical connector(s), then position the unit. Secure using the retaining bolts.
5. Install the instrument panel accessory plate(s).
6. Connect the negative battery cable, then check for proper operation.

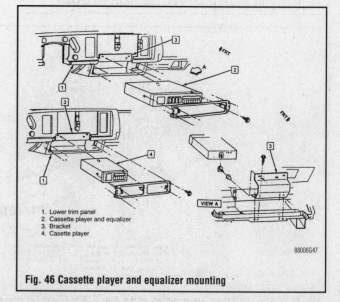

1. Lower trim panel
2. Cassette player and equalizer
3. Bracket
4. Cassette player

Fig. 46 Cassette player and equalizer mounting

Speakers

REMOVAL & INSTALLATION

Front Speakers

EXCEPT TWEETERS

▶ See Figures 47, 48 and 49

1. Disconnect the negative battery cable.
2. Remove the speaker grille or door trim panel, as applicable.
3. Unfasten the speaker housing retaining screws.
4. Detach the speaker electrical connector.
5. If necessary, unfasten the electrical connector clips from the speaker housing.
6. Unfasten the retaining screws, then remove the speaker from the housing.
7. Installation is the reverse of the removal procedure.
8. Connect the negative battery cable, then check the speakers for proper operation.

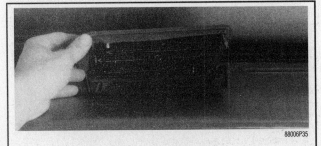

Fig. 47 Remove the speaker grille from the dash

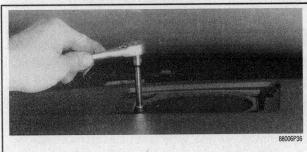

Fig. 48 Unfasten the retaining screws and remove the speaker

TWEETERS

1. Disconnect the negative battery cable.
2. Remove the door trim panel.
3. Unfasten the retainers from the tweeter, then detach the electrical connector.
4. Remove the tweeter from the vehicle.
5. Installation is the reverse of the removal procedure.
6. Connect the negative battery cable, then check the speakers for proper operation.

Rear Speakers

▶ See Figure 50

1. Disconnect the negative battery cable.
2. Remove the rear window trim panel.
3. Unfasten the retaining bolts/screws.
4. Pull the speaker up and detach the electrical connector.

➡ Some speakers are mounted in a speaker housing

5. If necessary, unfasten the retaining screws, then remove the speaker from the housing.

To install:

6. If necessary, install the speaker in the housing, and secure with the retaining screws. Tighten the screws to 18 inch lbs. (2 Nm).
7. Attach the speaker electrical connector.
8. Align the speaker with the mounting holes. Install the retaining screws and tighten to 18 inch lbs. (2 Nm).
9. Install the rear trim panel.
10. Connect the negative battery cable and check for proper speaker operation.

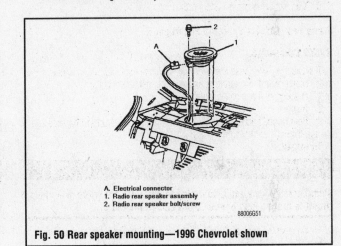

A. Electrical connector
1. Radio rear speaker assembly
2. Radio rear speaker bolt/screw

Fig. 50 Rear speaker mounting—1996 Chevrolet shown

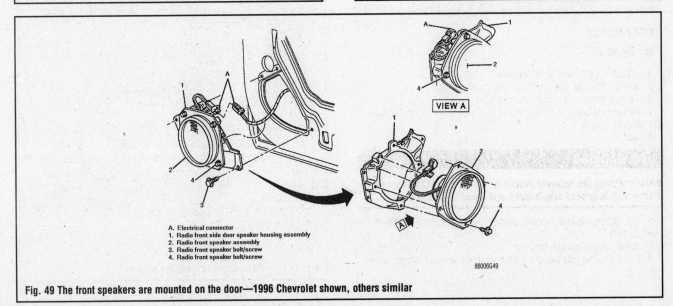

VIEW A

A. Electrical connector
1. Radio front side door speaker housing assembly
2. Radio front speaker assembly
3. Radio front speaker bolt/screw
4. Radio front speaker bolt/screw

Fig. 49 The front speakers are mounted on the door—1996 Chevrolet shown, others similar

WINDSHIELD WIPERS

Blade and Arm

REMOVAL & INSTALLATION

▶ See Figures 51, 52, 53, 54 and 55

1. Disconnect the negative battery cable.
2. Raise the hood and support.
3. Detach the washer nozzle hose from the arm.
4. Remove the protective cap and nut from the wiper arm.
5. Lift each wiper arm and insert a suitable pin or pop rivet completely through the two holes located next to the arm pivot.
6. Lift each arm off its transmission linkage shaft using a rocking motion. It may be necessary to use a battery terminal puller to remove the arm from the shaft.

To install:

7. Clean the metal shavings from the knurls of the shaft before installation.
8. Install the wiper arm onto the linkage shaft and adjust as follows:
    a. Left Arm: measure from the tip of the blade to the bottom edge of the glass. The measurement should be 2 in. (51mm).
    b. Right Arm: measure from the tip of the blade to the bottom edge of the glass. The measurement should be 9 in. (229mm).
9. Install the arm-to-shaft nut and tighten to 17–25 ft. lbs. (23–34 Nm) and install the protective cap.
10. Attach the washer hose, then close the hood.
11. Connect the negative battery cable and check for proper operation.

Wiper Module

REMOVAL & INSTALLATION

▶ See Figures 56 thru 66

1. Disconnect the negative battery cable.
2. Raise the hood and support.
3. Remove the wiper arm and blade assemblies, as outlined earlier in this section.
4. Remove the lower reveal molding screws, lower the hood and remove the lower reveal molding.
5. Remove the air inlet panel screws, underhood lamp switch and air inlet panel with the hood raised.
6. If the motor can run, place the crank arm in the inner wipe position as shown in the accompanying illustration.
7. If the motor cannot run, rotate the motor crank arm to the inner wipe position by applying suitable locking pliers against the top edge of the crank arm and lower jaw against the crank arm nut and turn the motor to the correct position before disassembly.
8. Remove the three bellcrank housing screws and lower the linkage from the module.
9. Unfasten the retaining screws, then remove the module assembly from the vehicle.

To install:

10. Install the module assembly into the vehicle.
11. Install the three bellcrank housing screws after lowering the linkage into the module.

Fig. 51 Disconnect the washer hose and remove the protective cap from the wiper arm

88006P15

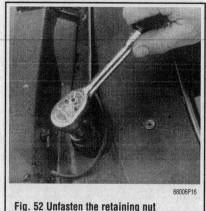

Fig. 52 Unfasten the retaining nut

88006P16

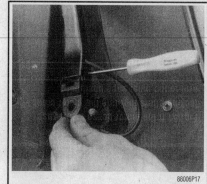

Fig. 53 Insert a suitable pin through the two holes located next to the arm pivot

88006P17

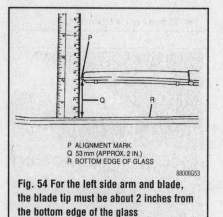

P ALIGNMENT MARK
Q 53 mm (APPROX. 2 IN.)
R BOTTOM EDGE OF GLASS

88006G53

Fig. 54 For the left side arm and blade, the blade tip must be about 2 inches from the bottom edge of the glass

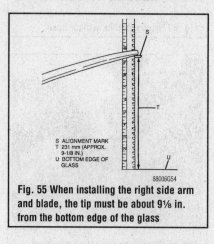

S ALIGNMENT MARK
T 231 mm (APPROX. 9-1/8 IN.)
U BOTTOM EDGE OF GLASS

88006G54

Fig. 55 When installing the right side arm and blade, the tip must be about 9⅛ in. from the bottom edge of the glass

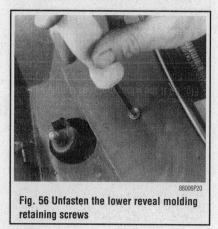

Fig. 56 Unfasten the lower reveal molding retaining screws

88006P20

Fig. 57 If necessary, remove any retaining clips using a suitable tool . . .

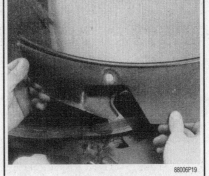

Fig. 58 . . . then remove the lower reveal molding

Fig. 59 Remove the air inlet panel

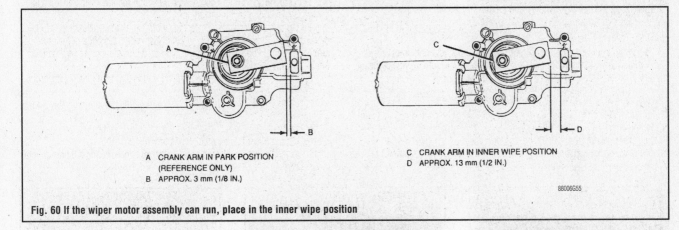

A CRANK ARM IN PARK POSITION
   (REFERENCE ONLY)
B APPROX. 3 mm (1/8 IN.)

C CRANK ARM IN INNER WIPE POSITION
D APPROX. 13 mm (1/2 IN.)

Fig. 60 If the wiper motor assembly can run, place in the inner wipe position

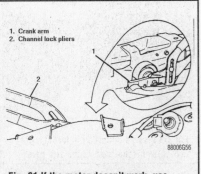

1. Crank arm
2. Channel lock pliers

Fig. 61 If the motor doesn't work, use locking pliers to rotate the motor crank arm to the inner wipe position

Fig. 62 Disconnect the washer hose

Fig. 63 Remove the retaining clip . . .

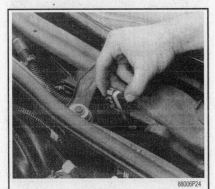

Fig. 64 . . . then detach the electrical connector

Fig. 65 Detach the remaining electrical connector

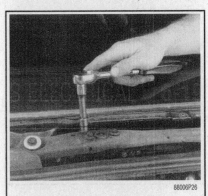

Fig. 66 Unfasten the retainers, then remove the module from the vehicle

12. Install the air inlet panel, underhood lamp switch and tighten the panel screws.

13. Install the lower reveal molding.

14. Install the wiper arm and blade, as outlined earlier in this section.

15. If not already done, connect the negative battery cable.

16. Adjust the wiper arm positioning as outlined earlier in the Wiper Arm procedure. Check each operation for proper installation.

Wiper Motor

REMOVAL & INSTALLATION

▶ **See Figures 67, 68, 69 and 70**

1. Disconnect the negative battery cable.

2. Remove the wiper module assembly from the vehicle as outlined earlier.

3. For 1995–96 Chevrolets, separate the wiper motor crank arm from the wiper transmission assembly using tool J 39232.

4. Unfasten the nut, then remove the crank arm from the motor.

➡ **For all vehicles except 1995–96 Chevrolets, the crank arm must be removed from the wiper motor only. Do NOT remove the crank arm from the transmission assembly because of a factory preset adjustment.**

5. Unfasten the 3 retaining screws and bracket, then remove the motor from the tube frame.

6. If necessary, remove the cover from the wiper motor assembly by removing the retaining screws.

To install:

7. If removed, attach the cover to the wiper motor and secure with the retaining screws.

8. Attach the motor and bracket (if equipped) to the module assembly and secure with the retaining screws. Tighten to 106 inch lbs. (12 Nm).

9. Fasten the wiper motor crank arm on the wiper motor assembly and secure with the retaining nut. Tighten the nut to 18 ft. lbs. (25 Nm).

10. For 1995–96 Chevrolets, attach the wiper transmission assembly on the wiper motor crank arm using tool J 39529 or equivalent.

11. Install the module assembly in the vehicle, as outlined earlier in this section.

12. Connect the negative battery cable and check for proper wiper operation.

Wiper Linkage (Transmission)

REMOVAL & INSTALLATION

▶ **See Figures 71, 72, 73, 74 and 75**

1. Disconnect the negative battery cable.

2. Remove the wiper arm and module as previously outlined in this section.

3. Remove the two linkage/transmission socket screws and disconnect the socket from the crank arm ball.

4. Unfasten the mounting screws, then remove the linkage/transmission from the module.

To install:

5. Position the linkage/transmission to the module and secure by tightening the mounting screws. The motor crank arm MUST be in the inner wiper position at this point. Refer to the accompanying illustration.

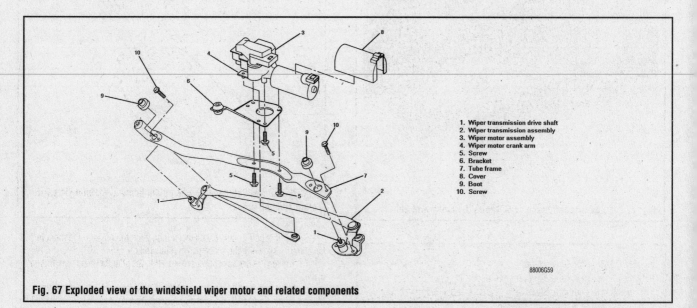

1. Wiper transmission drive shaft
2. Wiper transmission assembly
3. Wiper motor assembly
4. Wiper motor crank arm
5. Screw
6. Bracket
7. Tube frame
8. Cover
9. Boot
10. Screw

88006G59

Fig. 67 Exploded view of the windshield wiper motor and related components

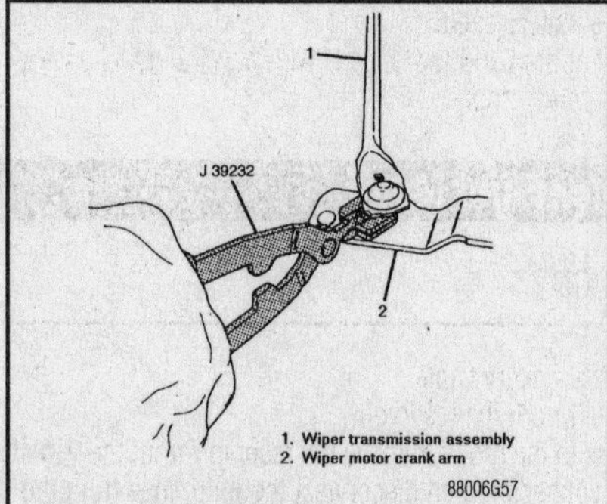

J 39232
1. Wiper transmission assembly
2. Wiper motor crank arm

88006G57

Fig. 68 For 1995–96 Chevrolets, detach the crank arm from the transmission assembly using the special tool as shown

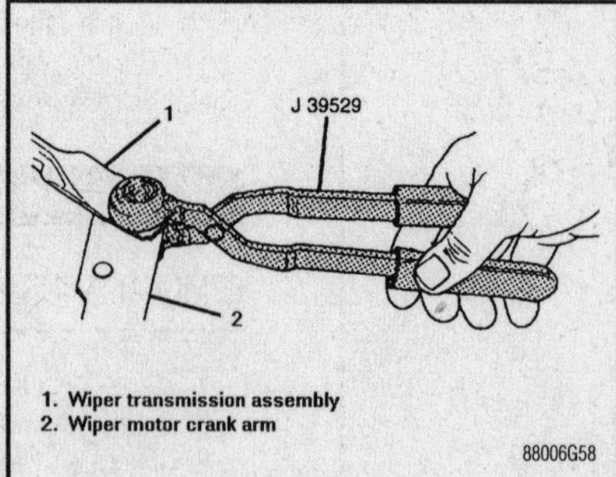

J 39529
1. Wiper transmission assembly
2. Wiper motor crank arm

88006G58

Fig. 69 For 1995–96 Chevrolets, attach the crank arm to the transmission

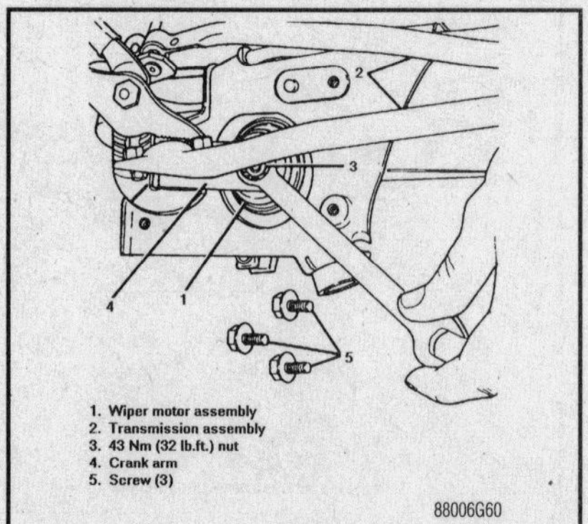

1. Wiper motor assembly
2. Transmission assembly
3. 43 Nm (32 lb.ft.) nut
4. Crank arm
5. Screw (3)

88006G60

Fig. 70 Unfasten the retaining nuts, then detach the crank arm from the motor

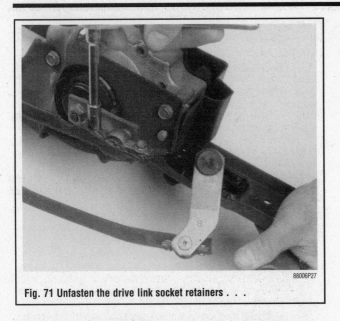
Fig. 71 Unfasten the drive link socket retainers . . .

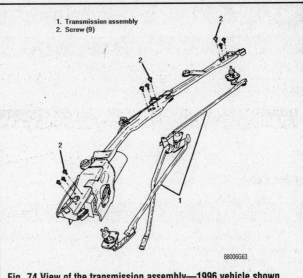
1. Transmission assembly
2. Screw (9)

Fig. 74 View of the transmission assembly—1996 vehicle shown

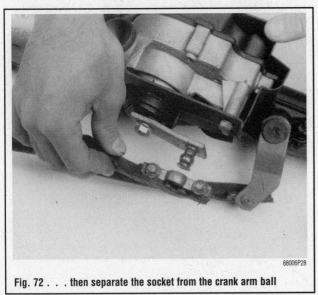
Fig. 72 . . . then separate the socket from the crank arm ball

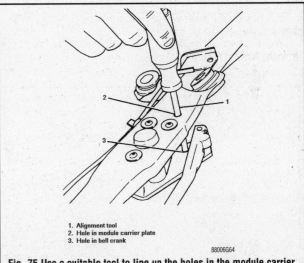
1. Alignment tool
2. Hole in module carrier plate
3. Hole in bell crank

Fig. 75 Use a suitable tool to line up the holes in the module carrier plate and bell crank

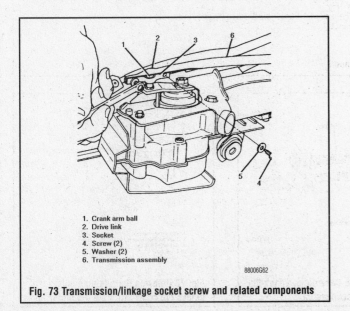
1. Crank arm ball
2. Drive link
3. Socket
4. Screw (2)
5. Washer (2)
6. Transmission assembly

Fig. 73 Transmission/linkage socket screw and related components

6. Using a bolt or suitable diameter tool, align the holes in the module and bellcrank as shown in the accompanying illustration.

7. Tighten the linkage socket screws while the alignment tool remains in place.

8. Install the module into the vehicle, as outlined earlier in this section. Make sure the body seals are in the proper position.

9. Install the wiper arms and blades, as outlined earlier in this section.

10. Connect the negative battery cable.

11. Run the wiper motor at high and low speeds with a wet and tacky windshield. Make sure the wiper parks properly.

Windshield Washer Fluid Motor

REMOVAL & INSTALLATION

1. Disconnect the negative battery cable.
2. Siphon the washer fluid from the reservoir.
3. If necessary for access to the motor, remove the reservoir from the vehicle.
4. Detach the electrical connector, then disconnect the fluid hose from the pump motor.
5. Remove the motor from the reservoir.
6. Installation is the reverse of the removal procedure.

INSTRUMENTS AND SWITCHES

Precautions

When handling a part that has an "ESD-sensitive" sticker warning of Electrostatic Discharge (it looks like a hand inside a black triangle with a white stripe through it), follow these guidelines to reduce any possible buildup of electrostatic charge:
- If replacing a part that has the sticker, do not open the package until just prior to installation. Before removing the part from its package, ground the package to a good ground on the car.
- Avoid touching the electrical terminals of the component.
- Always touch a good ground before handling a part with the sticker. This should be repeated while handling the part; do it more often when sliding across the seat, sitting from the standing position, or after walking.

Instrument Cluster

Individual gauges may not be replaceable on these clusters. If one has failed, cluster assembly replacement may be necessary, depending on application and parts availability.

Conventional speedometer cables are not used; the speedometer is a fully electronic unit.

REMOVAL & INSTALLATION

Cutlass Supreme

1988–94 VEHICLES

▶ See Figure 76

1. If necessary for access to the battery, remove the air cleaner assembly.
2. Disconnect the negative battery cable.
3. Remove the instrument cluster trim plate.
4. Unfasten the bolts securing the cluster to the carrier.
5. If equipped, remove the automatic transaxle control indicator cable.
6. Pull the cluster forward, detach the electrical connector, then remove the instrument cluster from the vehicle.
7. Installation is the reverse of the removal procedure. Tighten the cluster retaining bolts to 18 inch lbs. (2 Nm).

Grand Prix

1988–93 VEHICLES

▶ See Figure 77

1. If necessary for access to the battery, remove the air cleaner assembly.
2. Disconnect the negative battery cable.

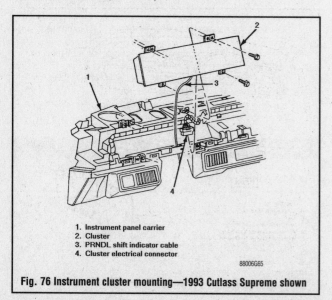

1. Instrument panel carrier
2. Cluster
3. PRNDL shift indicator cable
4. Cluster electrical connector

88006G65

Fig. 76 Instrument cluster mounting—1993 Cutlass Supreme shown

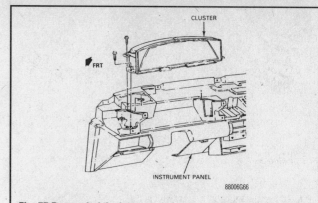

Fig. 77 Removal of the instrument cluster—1993 Grand Prix shown

3. Remove the instrument panel pad cover from the vehicle.
4. If equipped, remove the Head Up Display (HUD) mounting bracket bolts/screws and bracket.
5. If necessary, remove the trim panel.
6. Unfasten the screws retaining the instrument cluster.
7. Pull the cluster forward, detach the electrical connector(s) and the PRNDL cable (if necessary).
8. Remove the cluster from the vehicle.
9. Installation is the reverse of the removal procedure. Tighten the cluster retaining bolts to 18 inch lbs. (2 Nm).

Regal

1988–94 VEHICLES

1. If necessary for access to the battery, remove the air cleaner assembly.
2. Disconnect the negative battery cable.
3. Remove the instrument panel pad cover from the vehicle.
4. Remove the cluster trim plate.
5. For 1992–94 vehicles, remove the left sound insulator and steering column knee bolster trim panel.
6. Detach the shift control cable at the bracket and lever.
7. Remove the shift indicator cable.
8. Detach the electrical connectors, then remove the instrument cluster.
9. Installation is the reverse of the removal procedure. Tighten the cluster retaining bolts to 18 inch lbs. (2 Nm).

1994–96 Grand Prix and 1995–96 Cutlass Supreme and Regal

▶ See Figures 78 and 79

1. Disconnect the negative battery cable.
2. Remove the instrument panel cluster trim plate, as follows:
   a. If equipped, remove the front console, as outlined in Section 10 of this manual.
   b. Remove the instrument panel accessory trim plate.
   c. Remove the ventilation (heater and A/C) control.
   d. Set the parking brake.
   e. If equipped with column shift, move the shift lever to **L1**.
   f. Tilt the steering to the lowest position and remove the tilt lever.
   g. Insert a suitable prytool into the slot in the trim plate directly below the headlamp switch.
   h. Pull the prytool handle down, releasing the tab and pull the plate rearward.
   i. Grasp the trim plate at the right end below the right center A/C outlet and carefully pull to release the clip.
   j. Remove the screw.
   k. Grasp the trim plate bottom edge on both sides of the steering column and pull to release 2 additional steel clips.
   l. Detach the connector from the lighter.
   m. Insert a suitable prytool into the slot at the left upper corner and raise the handle.

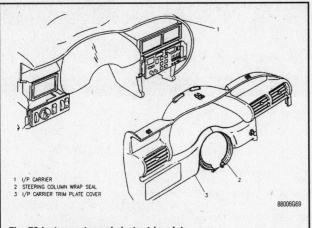

1 I/P CARRIER
2 STEERING COLUMN WRAP SEAL
3 I/P CARRIER TRIM PLATE COVER

88006G69

Fig. 78 Instrument panel cluster trim plate

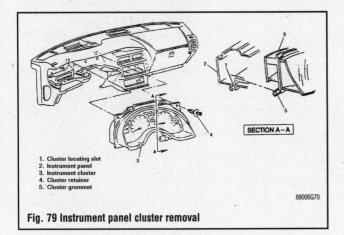

SECTION A–A

1. Cluster locating slot
2. Instrument panel
3. Instrument cluster
4. Cluster retainer
5. Cluster grommet

88006G70

Fig. 79 Instrument panel cluster removal

n. Pull rearward at the center of the top edge to disengage the plastic clip on the trim plate, then remove the trim plate.

3. Remove the two push-pin retainers at the top of the clusters.

4. Rotate the top of the cluster rearward and disengage the locating pins on the bottom of the cluster at the instrument panel.

5. Detach the electrical connector.

To install:

6. Attach the cluster electrical connector(s).

7. Position the locating pines on the bottom of the cluster to the pin receivers in the instrument panel.

8. Install the cluster retaining bolts/screws and tighten to 18 inch lbs. (2 Nm).

9. Install the instrument cluster trim plate, as follows:

a. Fasten the trim plate upper plastic clip to the instrument panel.

b. Move the upper left corner into place.

c. Attach the connector to the lighter.

d. Push the clips on both sides of the steering column into place.

e. Push the metal clip at the bottom right corner of the trim plate into place.

f. Install the retaining screw and tighten to 18 inch lbs. (2 Nm).

g. Push the left corner of the trim plate below the headlamp switch into place.

h. Install the tilt lever and raise the steering column.

i. Move the shift lever to the **P** position.

j. Install the ventilation control.

k. Fasten the instrument panel accessory trim plate.

l. If equipped, install the front console.

10. Connect the negative battery cable.

Lumina and Monte Carlo

1990–94 VEHICLES

1. Remove the air cleaner assembly.

2. Disconnect the negative battery cable.

3. Remove the instrument panel pad from the vehicle.

4. Unfasten the screws retaining the instrument cluster.

5. Pull the cluster forward, detach the electrical connector(s) and the PRNDL cable (if equipped), then remove the cluster from the vehicle.

6. Installation is the reverse of the removal procedure. Tighten the cluster retaining bolts to 18 inch lbs. (2 Nm).

1995–96 VEHICLES

▶ See Figures 80 and 81

1. Disconnect the negative battery cable.

2. Remove the instrument panel cluster trim plate, as follows:

a. If equipped with a column shift, move the shift lever to the L1 position.

b. Tilt the steering column to its lowest position.

c. Remove the trim plate by unsnapping the clips from the instrument panel.

3. Unfasten the cluster retaining bolts/screws.

4. Rotate the top of the cluster rearward and disengage the locating pins on the bottom of the cluster at the instrument panel.

5. Detach the cluster electrical connector(s).

To install:

6. Attach the cluster electrical connector(s).

7. Position the locating pins on the bottom of the cluster to the pin receivers in the instrument panel.

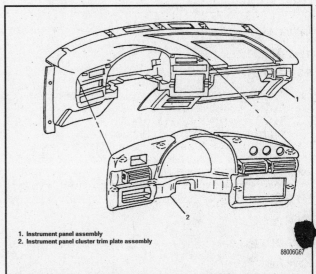

1. Instrument panel assembly
2. Instrument panel cluster trim plate assembly

88006G67

Fig. 80 Instrument panel cluster trim plate—1996 Chevrolet shown

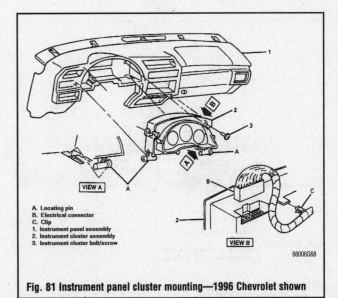

VIEW A

VIEW B

A. Locating pin
B. Electrical connector
C. Clip
1. Instrument panel assembly
2. Instrument cluster assembly
3. Instrument cluster bolt/screw

88006G68

Fig. 81 Instrument panel cluster mounting—1996 Chevrolet shown

8. Install the cluster retaining bolts/screws and tighten to 18 inch lbs. (2 Nm).
9. Install the trim plate by snapping it in the clips to the instrument panel.
10. Move the shift lever to the **P** position, if equipped with a column shifter.
11. Connect the negative battery cable.

Windshield Wiper Switch

REMOVAL & INSTALLATION

Dash Mounted Switches

1. Disconnect the negative battery cable.
2. Unfasten the screw from the instrument panel, under the switch.
3. Remove the assembly by carefully pulling the switch out to release the two spring clips at the top.
To install:
4. Carefully push the switch into place, making sure the spring clips line up with the holes and the connector attaches securely.
5. Install the retaining screw and tighten to 18 inch lbs. (2 Nm).
6. Connect the negative battery cable.

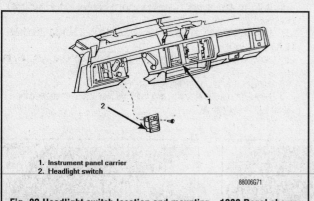

1. Instrument panel carrier
2. Headlight switch

88006G71

Fig. 82 Headlight switch location and mounting—1988 Regal shown

Column Mounted Switches

The wiper switch is located inside the steering column. To gain access to the switch, the steering wheel, multi-function (turn signal) and ignition lock will have to be removed. Please refer to Section 8 for these procedures.

Headlight Switch

REMOVAL & INSTALLATION

Except With Head Up Display (HUD)

▶ **See Figures 82, 83, 84 and 85**

1. Disconnect the negative battery cable.
2. Remove the instrument cluster trim plate by unfastening the retaining screws or simply unsnapping it.
3. If necessary, remove the air outlet trim plate. If may be secured with screws/bolts or clips.
4. If accessible at this time, detach the switch electrical connector.
5. Remove the switch, using one of the following procedures:
   a. Unfasten the retaining bolts/screws from the switch, then remove the switch from the instrument panel.
   b. Unsnap the headlight switch from the instrument panel.
6. If not already done, detach the electrical connector from the switch at this time.
To install:
7. Attach the switch electrical connector and fasten the switch to the instrument panel. If the switch is secured with screws, tighten to 18 inch lbs. (2 Nm).
8. Install the air outlet and cluster trim plates.
9. Connect the negative battery cable.

With Head Up Display (HUD)

1. Disconnect the negative battery cable.
2. Remove the steering column opening filler panel.
3. Remove the instrument cluster, as outlined earlier in this section.
4. Depress the locking tabs, then pull the switch out.
5. Detach the HUD electrical connectors.
6. Installation is the reverse of the removal procedure.

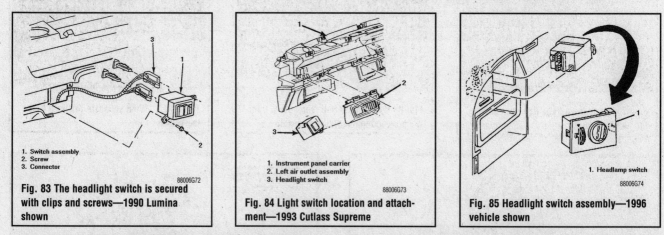

1. Switch assembly
2. Screw
3. Connector

88006G72

Fig. 83 The headlight switch is secured with clips and screws—1990 Lumina shown

1. Instrument panel carrier
2. Left air outlet assembly
3. Headlight switch

88006G73

Fig. 84 Light switch location and attachment—1993 Cutlass Supreme

1. Headlamp switch

88006G74

Fig. 85 Headlight switch assembly—1996 vehicle shown

LIGHTING

Headlights

REMOVAL & INSTALLATION

Sealed Beam

▶ **See Figure 86**

1. Open the hood.
2. Disconnect the negative battery cable.

3. Remove the headlight bezel retainers and bezel.
4. Remove the spring from the bottom edge of the headlight assembly.

➡ **Do NOT apply pressure to the plastic bubble of the vertical aim indicator.**

5. Detach the electrical connector from the assembly.
6. Unfasten the two screws from the headlight retaining ring.
7. Rotate the retaining ring away from the headlight.
8. Remove the headlight from the vehicle.
To install:
9. Position the headlight and retaining ring and secure with the two retaining screws. Tighten the screws to 18 inch lbs. (2 Nm).

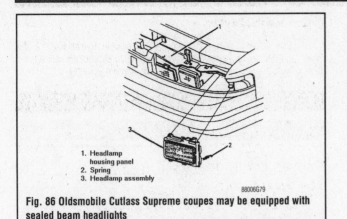

1. Headlamp housing panel
2. Spring
3. Headlamp assembly

Fig. 86 Oldsmobile Cutlass Supreme coupes may be equipped with sealed beam headlights

10. Attach the electrical connector to the assembly.
11. Install the spring to the bottom of the headlight assembly
12. Install the headlamp bezel and retainers.
13. Connect the negative battery cable, then close the hood.
14. Check for proper headlight operation.

Composite

▶ See Figures 87, 88, 89, 90 and 91

Most of the later model vehicles covered by this manual are equipped with composite headlight assemblies. Due to space constraints, no access may be provided to withdraw the bulbs, so the replacement usually requires removal of the composite assembly.

⁕⁕ **CAUTION**

Halogen bulbs contain gas under pressure. Handling the bulbs incorrectly could cause it to shatter into flying glass fragments. Do NOT leave the light switch ON. Always allow the bulb to cool before removal. Handle the bulb only by the base; avoid touching the glass itself. Whenever handling a halogen bulb, ALWAYS follow these precautions:

• Turn the headlight switch **OFF** and allow the bulb to cool before changing it. Leave the switch **OFF** until the change is complete.
• ALWAYS wear eye protection when changing a halogen bulb.
• Handle the bulb only by its base. Avoid touching the glass.
• DO NOT drop or scratch the bulb.
• Keep dirt and moisture off the bulb.
• Place the used bulb in the new bulb's carton and dispose of it properly.
  1. Raise the hood and disconnect the negative battery cable.
  2. Locate the bulb mounting location at the rear of the composite headlamp body.
  3. If necessary for access to the bulb, perform one or more of the following steps:
     a. Remove the radiator upper air baffle.
     b. Raise the access cover/plastic flap covering the rear of the headlight assembly.
     c. Remove the headlight cover by turning the knob to release, then folding the cover back.
  4. If necessary for Pontiac sedans, remove the center light bar assembly as follows:
     a. Remove the light bar retaining wing nuts.
     b. Detach the electrical connectors from the light bar, then remove the light bar from the vehicle.

Fig. 87 Lift up the plastic flap to access the headlight bulb

Fig. 88 Remove the bulb and socket from the back of the headlight assembly . . .

Fig. 89 . . . then separate the bulb from the socket

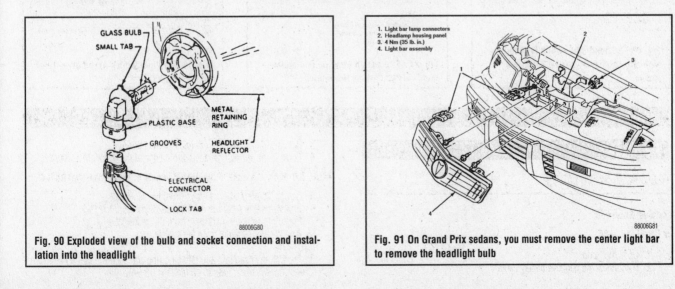

GLASS BULB
SMALL TAB
METAL RETAINING RING
PLASTIC BASE
GROOVES
HEADLIGHT REFLECTOR
ELECTRICAL CONNECTOR
LOCK TAB

Fig. 90 Exploded view of the bulb and socket connection and installation into the headlight

1. Light bar lamp connectors
2. Headlamp housing panel
3. 4 Nm (35 lb. in.)
4. Light bar assembly

Fig. 91 On Grand Prix sedans, you must remove the center light bar to remove the headlight bulb

5. For Pontiac sedans, perform the following:

   a. Unfasten the four headlight bolts, there are two at the bottom rear of the assembly and two at the top rear, behind the assembly.

   b. Cover the fender front cover, sidemarker lamp and fascia under the headlamp to protect from damage.

   c. Rotate the inboard side of the headlight assemblies forward to rest on the fascia.

   d. Tilt the headlight assembly rearward to access the peanut bulb socket from the bottom of the assembly.

6. Remove the socket with the bulb, then remove the bulb. It may be necessary to detach the connector by carefully opening the tabs.

To install:

7. Install the bulb in the socket, then secure the socket in the headlight assembly.

8. For Pontiac sedans, position the headlight assembly, then install the four retaining bolts and tighten to 18 inch lbs. (2 Nm).

9. If necessary for Pontiac sedans, install the center light bar, as follows:

   a. Position the light bar and attach the electrical connectors.

   b. Instal the light bar retaining wing nuts, and tighten to 35 inch lbs. (4 Nm).

10. As necessary, perform the following:

   a. Install the headlight cover.

   b. Fasten the bulb access cover or lower the flap covering the headlight assembly.

11. Connect the negative battery cable, then lower the hood assembly.

12. Check the headlights for proper operation, then, if necessary, have the headlights aimed by a qualified repair shop.

HEADLIGHT AIMING

The headlights must be properly aimed to provide the best, safest road illumination. The lights should be checked for proper aim and adjusted as necessary. Certain state and local authorities have requirements for headlight aiming; these should be checked before adjustment is made.

Headlight adjustment may be temporarily made using a wall, as described below, or on the rear of another vehicle. When adjusted, the lights should not glare in oncoming car or truck windshields, nor should they illuminate the passenger compartment of vehicles driving in front of you. These adjustments are rough and should always be fine-tuned by a repair shop which is equipped with headlight aiming tools. Improper adjustments may be both dangerous and illegal.

For most of the vehicles covered by this manual, horizontal and vertical aiming of each sealed beam unit is provided by two adjusting screws which move the retaining ring and adjusting plate against the tension of a coil spring. There is no adjustment for focus; this is done during headlight manufacturing.

➡ **Because the composite headlight assembly is bolted into position, no adjustment should be necessary or possible. Some applications, however, may be bolted to an adjuster plate or may be retained used adjusting screws. If so, follow this procedure when adjusting the lights, BUT always have the adjustment checked by a reputable shop.**

Before removing the headlight bulb or disturbing the headlamp in any way, note the current settings in order to ease headlight adjustment upon reassembly. If the high or low beam setting of the old lamp still works, this can be done using the wall of a garage or a building:

1. Park the car on a level surface, with the fuel tank about ½ full and with the vehicle empty of all extra cargo (unless normally carried). The vehicle should be facing a wall which is no less than 6 feet (1.8m) high and 12 feet (3.7m) wide. The front of the vehicle should be about 25 feet from the wall.

2. If aiming is to be performed outdoors, it is advisable to wait until dusk in order to properly see the headlight beams on the wall. If done in a garage, darken the area around the wall as much as possible by closing shades or hanging cloth over the windows.

3. Turn the headlights **ON** and mark the wall at the center of each light's low beam, then switch on the brights and mark the center of each light's high beam. A short length of masking tape which is visible from the front of the truck may be used. Although marking all four positions is advisable, marking one position from each light should be sufficient.

4. If neither beam on one side of the vehicle is working, and if another like-sized car is available, park the second car in the exact spot where the vehicle was and mark the beams using the same-side light on that truck. Then switch

the cars so the one to be aimed is back in the original spot. The car must be parked no closer to or farther away from the wall than the second vehicle.

5. Perform any necessary repairs, but make sure the car is not moved, or is returned to the exact spot from which the lights were marked. Turn the headlights **ON** and adjust the beams to match the marks on the wall.

6. Have the headlight adjustment checked as soon as possible by a reputable repair shop.

Signal and Marker Lights

REMOVAL & INSTALLATION

Front Turn Signal and Parking Lights

LUMINA AND MONTE CARLO

▶ **See Figure 92**

1. Raise the hood and disconnect the negative battery cable.

2. If necessary, remove the grille assembly as outlined in Section 10 of this manual.

3. Remove the retaining screw and assembly lens.

4. Remove the bulb and socket, then separate the bulb from the socket.

To install:

5. Install a new bulb into the socket assembly.

6. Place the bulb and socket assembly into position.

7. Install the signal assembly and secure with the retaining screws.

8. If removed, install the grille.

9. Connect the negative battery cable, then lower the hood. Check for proper lighting operation

REGAL

▶ **See Figure 93**

1. Raise the hood and support safely.

2. Disconnect the negative battery cable.

3. For coupes, remove the cover over the headlights by turning the knob and folding back.

4. Remove the light housing nuts and remove the sockets from the housing.

5. If replacing, separate the bulb from the sockets.

To install:

6. If necessary, install a new bulb in the socket.

7. Install the sockets, and housing. Secure the housing using the retaining nuts.

8. If removed, install the headlight cover.

9. Connect the negative battery cable and lower the hood.

10. Check for proper operation.

GRAND PRIX AND CUTLASS SUPREME

▶ **See Figures 94 and 95**

1. Disconnect the negative battery cable.

2. Remove the two screws at the top of the assembly and pull the assembly forward.

3. Disconnect the electrical connector by opening the tab.

4. Remove the bulb and socket assembly.

To install:

5. Install a new bulb in the socket.

6. Position the socket assembly into the housing and tighten the two retaining screws.

7. Connect the negative battery cable and check for proper operation.

Side Marker Lights

▶ **See Figures 96 and 97**

1. Disconnect the negative battery cable.

2. Unfasten the side marker light cover assembly retaining screws, then remove the light.

3. Remove the light socket from the assembly.

4. If replacing, separate the bulb from the socket.

To install:

5. Install a new bulb into the light socket.

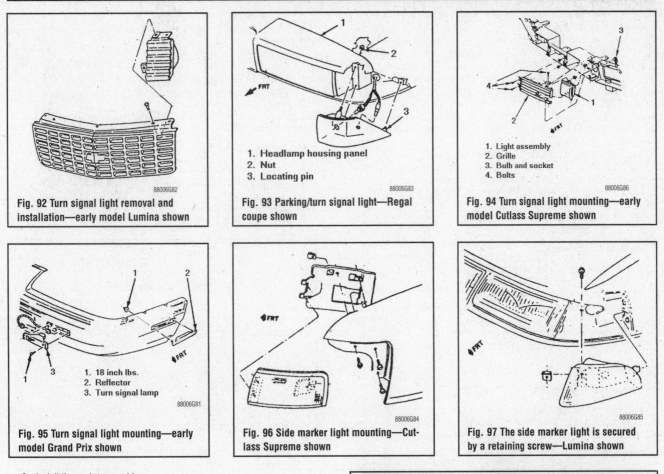

Fig. 92 Turn signal light removal and installation—early model Lumina shown

1. Headlamp housing panel
2. Nut
3. Locating pin

Fig. 93 Parking/turn signal light—Regal coupe shown

1. Light assembly
2. Grille
3. Bulb and socket
4. Bolts

Fig. 94 Turn signal light mounting—early model Cutlass Supreme shown

1. 18 inch lbs.
2. Reflector
3. Turn signal lamp

Fig. 95 Turn signal light mounting—early model Grand Prix shown

Fig. 96 Side marker light mounting—Cutlass Supreme shown

Fig. 97 The side marker light is secured by a retaining screw—Lumina shown

6. Install the socket assembly.
7. Position the side marker light cover, then the retaining screws.
8. Connect the negative battery cable, then check for proper operation.

Rear Turn Signal/Brake/Reverse Lights

▶ See Figures 98, 99, 100 and 101

➡Take care to prevent water leaks if the sealing surfaces around the tail light assembly is disturbed. Damaged gaskets must be replaced by using body caulking compound or equivalent in the critical areas.

1. Disconnect the negative battery cable.
2. Open the rear luggage compartment.
3. Either remove the carpet retaining clips and fold the carpet forward or remove the trunk trim panel(s).
4. If accessible at this time, remove the bulb sockets from the light assembly.

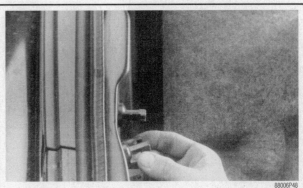

Fig. 98 Remove the trunk compartment trim panel(s)

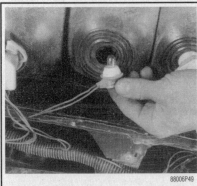

Fig. 99 Remove the bulb and socket from the rear light assembly . . .

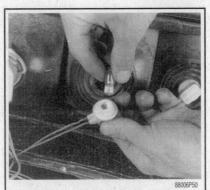

Fig. 100 . . . then remove the bulb from the socket by carefully pulling it out

Fig. 101 If necessary, remove the rear light assembly by unfastening the retainers

5. Remove the back light assembly retaining nuts/screws and remove the assembly. If the light assembly does not come right out, it may be because the gasket is holding it in place. Pry very gently on all corners equally and push the assembly out of the rear light cavity. When the assembly starts to move, cut the gasket with a knife.

6. If not already done, remove the bulb sockets from the light assembly.

7. If replacing, separate the bulb from the socket.

To install:

8. If necessary, install a new bulb in the back light socket.

9. Using a new gasket, install the light assembly and secure by tightening the retaining nuts/screws.

10. Install the light sockets into their proper location.

11. Install the carpeting and retaining clips or trim panels, as applicable.

12. Close the luggage compartment (trunk) lid.

13. Connect the negative battery cable and, with the help of an assistant, check for proper light operation.

Center High Mounted Brake Light

▶ **See Figures 102 and 103**

1. Disconnect the negative battery cable.

2. Remove the lamp cover. It may be held on by screws or clips.

3. Detach the electric connector.

4. Remove the nuts or screws that retain the lamp assembly to the roof or window trim panel, and remove the bulb.

5. Installation is the reverse of the removal procedure.

6. Connect the negative battery cable and check for proper operation.

Courtesy and Dome Light

▶ **See Figures 104 and 105**

1. Disconnect the negative battery cable.

2. Remove the lamp lens/cover from the housing by prying carefully. Press inward and down to disengage the retaining tabs. If the lens is cold, heat up the lens or interior of the car before prying the lens.

3. Remove the bulb from the terminal clips.

4. If necessary, remove the retaining nut(s), if equipped, then remove the lamp assembly.

To install:

5. If removed, install the lamp assembly and secure with the retaining nuts.

6. Fasten the bulb to the clips.

7. Install the lens.

8. Connect the negative battery cable.

License Plate Lights

▶ **See Figures 106 and 107**

1. Disconnect the negative battery cable.

2. Unfasten the mounting screws/bolts and remove the lamp assembly.

3. Pull the socket and bulb assembly down, then remove the bulb from the socket, if replacement is necessary.

4. The installation is the reverse of the removal procedure.

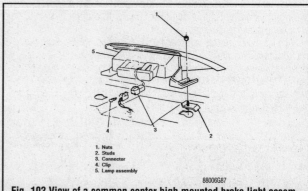

1. Nuts
2. Studs
3. Connector
4. Clip
5. Lamp assembly

88006G87

Fig. 102 View of a common center high mounted brake light assembly—coupe shown

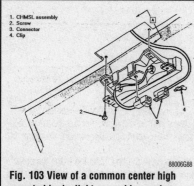

1. CHMSL assembly
2. Screw
3. Connector
4. Clip

88006G88

Fig. 103 View of a common center high mounted brake light assembly—sedan shown

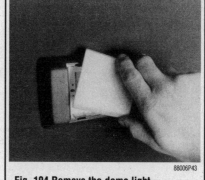

88006P43

Fig. 104 Remove the dome light cover . . .

88006P44

Fig. 105 . . . then pull the bulb from the terminal clips

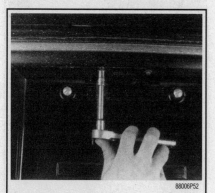

88006P52

Fig. 106 Unfasten the retaining bolts/screws

88006P53

Fig. 107 Pull the socket and bulb assembly down

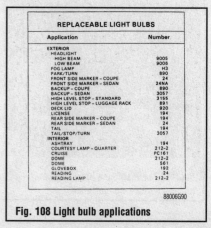

REPLACEABLE LIGHT BULBS	
Application	Number
EXTERIOR	
HEADLIGHT	
HIGH BEAM	9005
LOW BEAM	9006
FOG LAMP	H3
PARK/TURN	890
FRONT SIDE MARKER – COUPE	24
FRONT SIDE MARKER – SEDAN	24NA
BACKUP – COUPE	890
BACKUP – SEDAN	3057
HIGH LEVEL STOP – STANDARD	3155
HIGH LEVEL STOP – LUGGAGE RACK	891
DECK LID	920
LICENSE	194
REAR SIDE MARKER – COUPE	194
REAR SIDE MARKER – SEDAN	24
TAIL	194
TAIL/STOP/TURN	3057
INTERIOR	
ASHTRAY	194
COURTESY LAMP – QUARTER	212-2
CRUISE	PC161
DOME	212-2
DOME	561
GLOVEBOX	192
READING	24
READING LAMP	212-2

88006G90

Fig. 108 Light bulb applications

CIRCUIT PROTECTION

Fuses Block and Fuses

Fuses protect all the major electrical systems in the car. In case of an electrical overload, the fuse melts, breaking the circuit and stopping the flow of electricity.

If a fuse blows, the cause should be investigated and corrected before the installation of a new fuse. This, however, is easier to say than to do. Because each fuse protects a limited number of components, your job is narrowed down somewhat. Begin your investigation by looking for obvious fraying, loose connections, breaks in insulation, etc. Use the techniques outlined at the beginning of this section. Electrical problems are almost always a real headache to solve, but if you are patient and persistent, and approach the problem logically (that is, don't start replacing electrical components randomly), you will eventually find the solution.

Each fuse block uses miniature fuses (normally plug-in blade terminal-type for these vehicles) which are designed for increased circuit protection and greater reliability. The compact plug-in or blade terminal design allows for fingertip removal and replacement.

Although most fuses are interchangeable in size, the amperage values are not. Should you install a fuse with too high a value, damaging current could be allowed to destroy the component you were attempting to protect by using a fuse in the first place. The plug-in type fuses have a volt number molded on them and are color coded for easy identification. Be sure to only replace a fuse with the proper amperage rated substitute.

Fig. 109 On some vehicles, you may have to remove a cover for access to the main fuse block

A blown fuse can easily be checked by visual inspection or by continuity checking.

FUSE LOCATIONS

Main Fuse Block

◗ See Figures 109 and 110

The main fuse block is located in the underside of the instrument panel, in or behind the glove compartment. Remove the access cover in the glove compartment to access the fuse block. Spare fuses and a fuse puller should always be kept here. Various convenience connectors, which snap-lock into the fuse block, add to the serviceability of this unit.

Convenience Center

The convenience center is located under the instrument panel, on the right side next to the fuse block. This unit houses circuit breakers, relays, chime module and hazard flasher.

Underhood Electrical Centers

◗ See Figures 111, 112 and 113

The right side electrical center is located on the right side inner fender in the engine compartment. The left side electrical center is located on the left inner fender behind the battery. These centers house a variety of fuses, fusible links and relays, all of which are identified on the cover. The center can be serviced by unfastening the cover and remove the appropriate component.

Some vehicles may use a forward lamp center, which is located on the front right inner fender in front of the ECM unit.

Some vehicles with ABS utilize an ABS electrical center. The center is located between the shock tower and the battery.

REPLACEMENT

◗ See Figures 114 and 115

1. Locate the fuse for the circuit in question.

➡When replacing the fuse, DO NOT use one with a higher amperage rating.

2. Check the fuse by pulling it from the fuse block and observing the element. If it is broken, install a replacement fuse the same amperage rating. If the fuse blows again, check the circuit for a short to ground or faulty device in the circuit protected by the fuse.

3. Continuity can also be checked with the fuse installed in the fuse block with the use of a test light connected across the 2 test points on the end of the

Fig. 110 The main fuse block is in or under the glove compartment

Fig. 111 Various underhood electrical centers contain fuses and relays

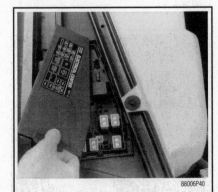

Fig. 112 To access the fuses and relays . . .

Fig. 113 . . . remove the electrical center covers

Fig. 114 Pull the fuse from the block and check the element

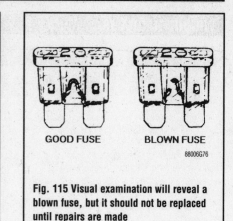

Fig. 115 Visual examination will reveal a blown fuse, but it should not be replaced until repairs are made

fuse. If the test light lights, replace the fuse. Check the circuit for a short to ground or faulty device in the circuit protected by the fuse.

Fusible Links

A fusible link is a protective device used in an electrical circuit. When the current increases beyond a certain amperage, the fusible metal of the wire link melts, thus breaking the electrical circuit and preventing further damage to other components and wiring. Whenever a fusible link is melted because of a short circuit, correct the cause before installing a new one. There are four different gauge sizes commonly used and they are usually color coded so that they may be easily installed in their original positions.

Circuit Breakers

REPLACEMENT

Circuit breakers differ from fuses in that they are reusable. Circuit breakers open when the flow of current exceeds specified value and will close after a few seconds when current flow returns to normal. Some of the circuits protected by circuit breakers include electric windows and power accessories. Circuits breakers are used in these applications due to the fact that they must operated at times under prolonged high current flow due to demand even though there is not malfunction in the circuit.

There are 2 types of circuit breakers. The first type opens when high current flow is detected. A few seconds after the excessive current flow has been removed, the circuit breaker will close. If the high current flow is experienced again, the circuit will open again.

The second type is referred to as the Positive Temperature Coefficient (PTC) circuit breaker. When excessive current flow passes through the PTC circuit breaker, the circuit is not opened but its resistance increases. As the device heats ups with the increase in current flow, the resistance increases to the point where the circuit is effectively open. Unlike other circuit breakers, the PTC circuit breaker will not reset until the circuit is opened, removing voltage from the terminals. Once the voltage is removed, the circuit breaker will re-close within a few seconds.

Replace the circuit breaker by unplugging the old one and plugging in the new one. Confirm proper circuit operation.

Flashers

The turn signal flasher is mounted in a clip on the right side of the steering column support bracket. The hazard flasher is located in the component center, under the instrument panel, on the right side. Replace the flasher by unplugging the old one and plugging in the new one.

WIRING DIAGRAMS

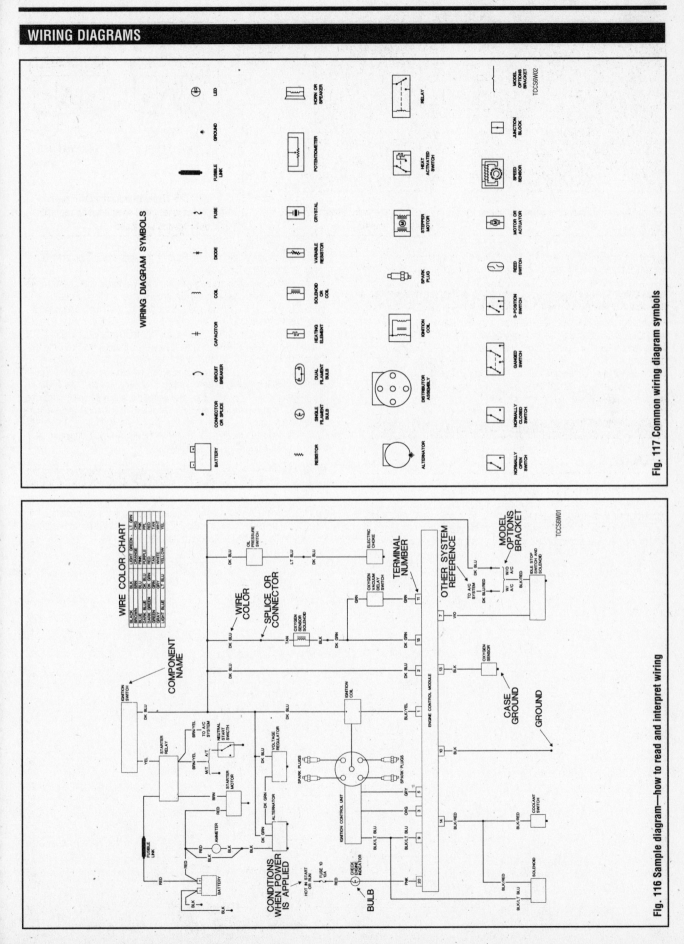

Fig. 117 Common wiring diagram symbols

Fig. 116 Sample diagram—how to read and interpret wiring

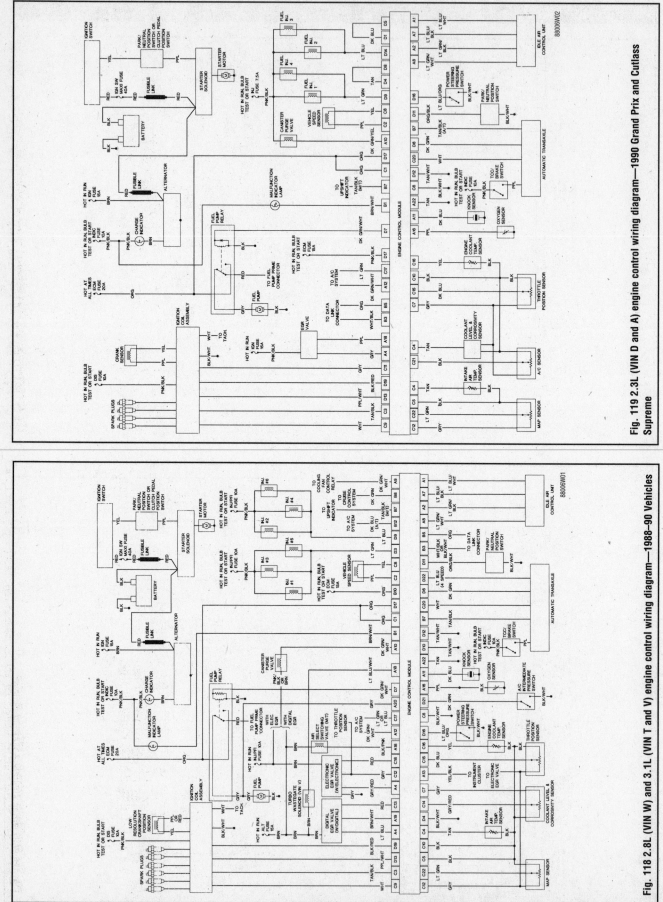

Fig. 119 2.3L (VIN D and A) engine control wiring diagram—1990 Grand Prix and Cutlass Supreme

Fig. 118 2.8L (VIN W) and 3.1L (VIN T and V) engine control wiring diagram—1988-90 Vehicles

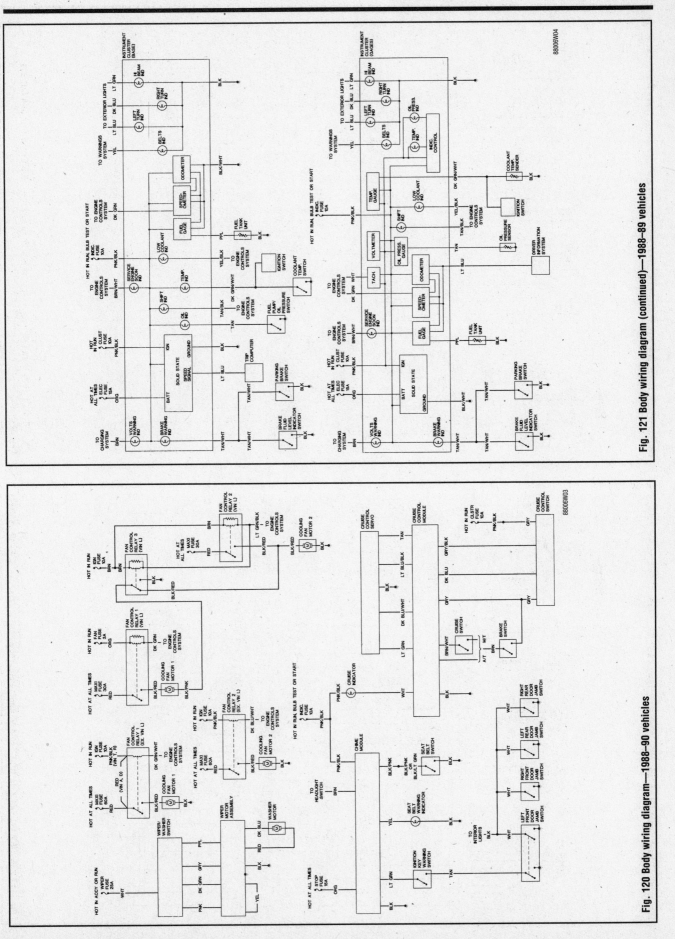

Fig. 121 Body wiring diagram (continued)—1988–89 vehicles

Fig. 120 Body wiring diagram—1988–90 vehicles

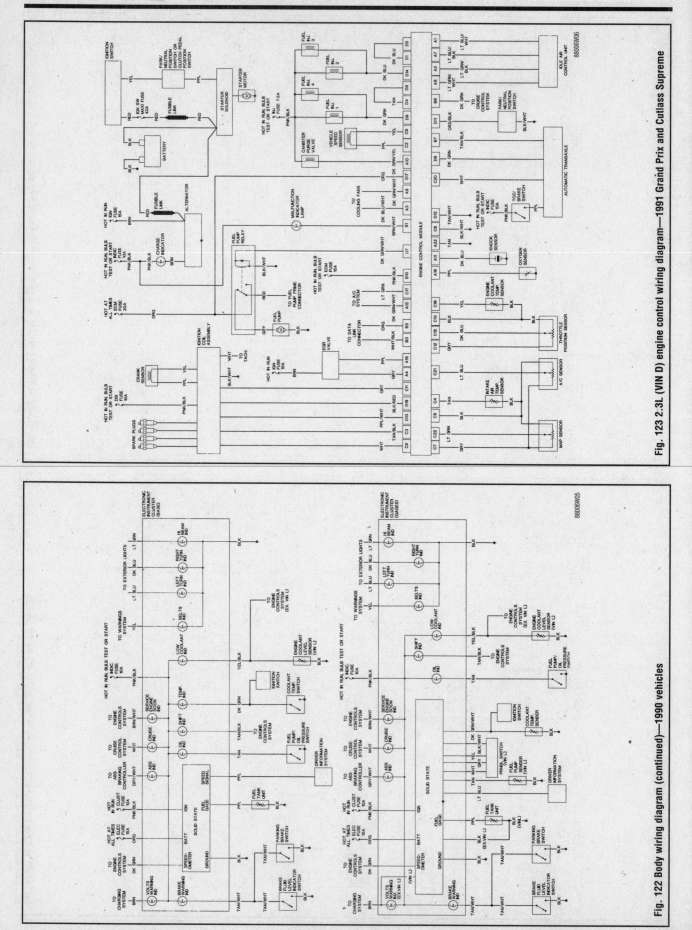

Fig. 123 2.3L (VIN D) engine control wiring diagram—1991 Grand Prix and Cutlass Supreme

Fig. 122 Body wiring diagram (continued)—1990 vehicles

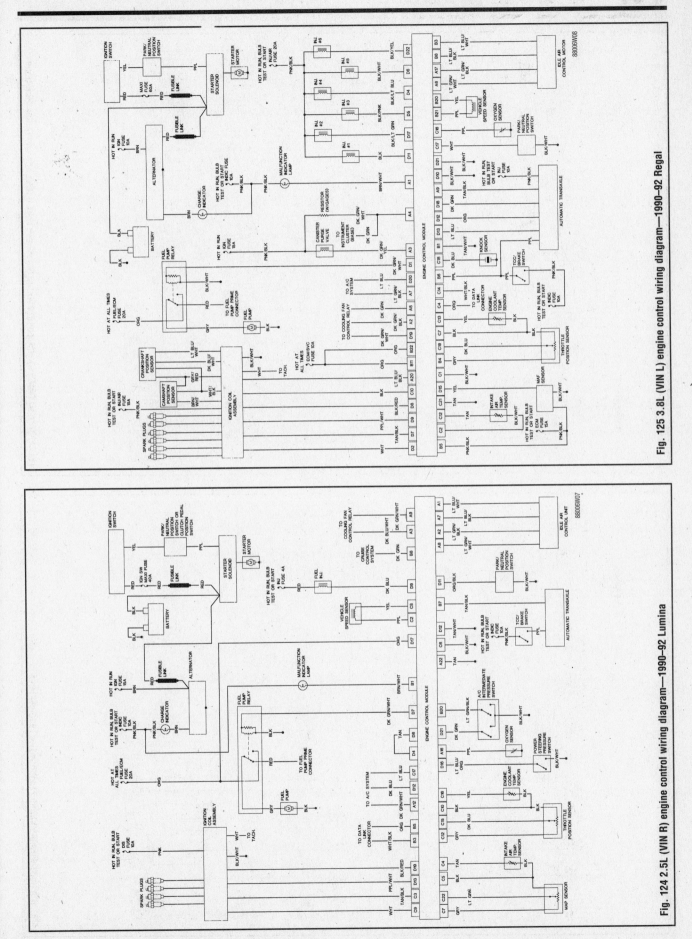

Fig. 125 3.8L (VIN L) engine control wiring diagram—1990-92 Regal

Fig. 124 2.5L (VIN R) engine control wiring diagram—1990-92 Lumina

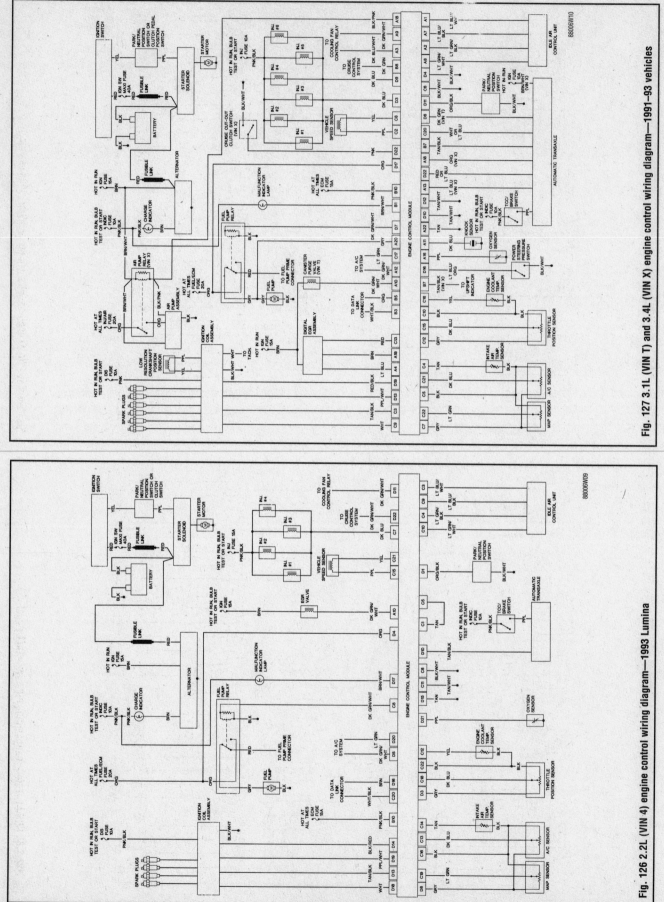

Fig. 127 3.1L (VIN T) and 3.4L (VIN X) engine control wiring diagram—1991-93 vehicles

Fig. 126 2.2L (VIN 4) engine control wiring diagram—1993 Lumina

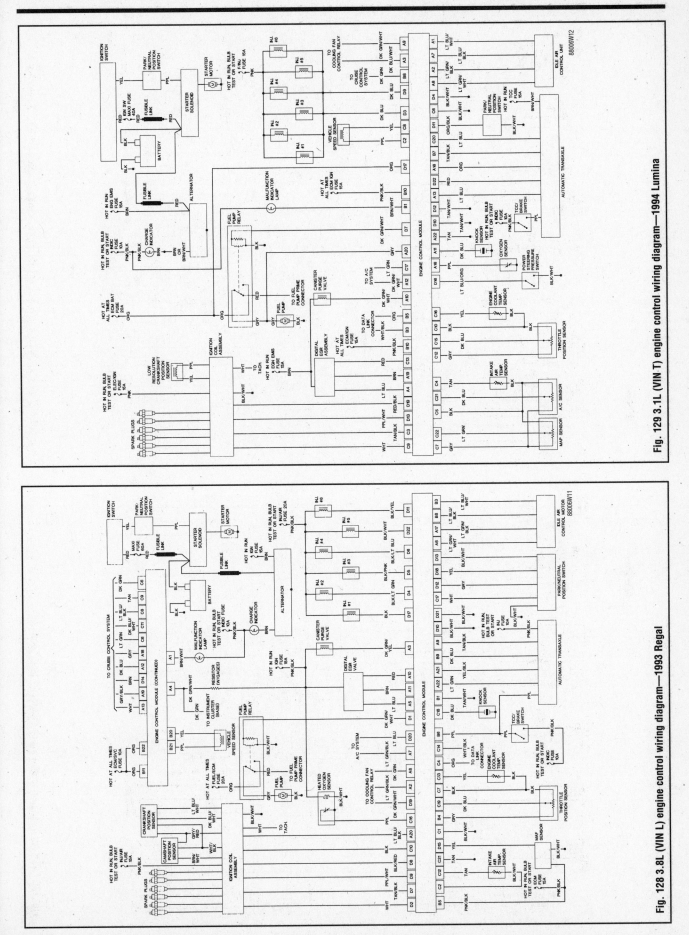

Fig. 129 3.1L (VIN T) engine control wiring diagram—1994 Lumina

Fig. 128 3.8L (VIN L) engine control wiring diagram—1993 Regal

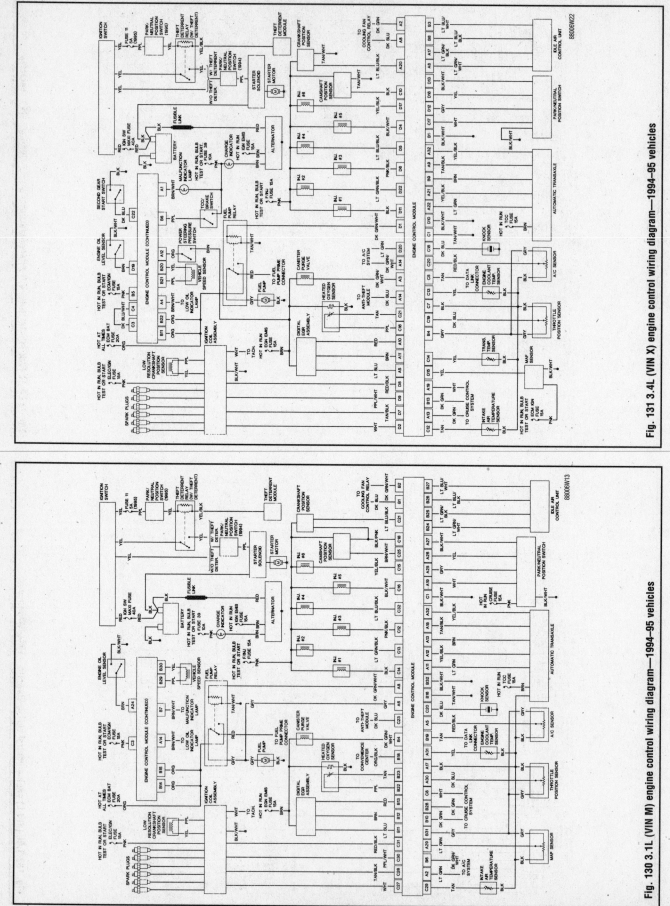

Fig. 131 3.4L (VIN X) engine control wiring diagram—1994–95 vehicles

Fig. 130 3.1L (VIN M) engine control wiring diagram—1994–95 vehicles

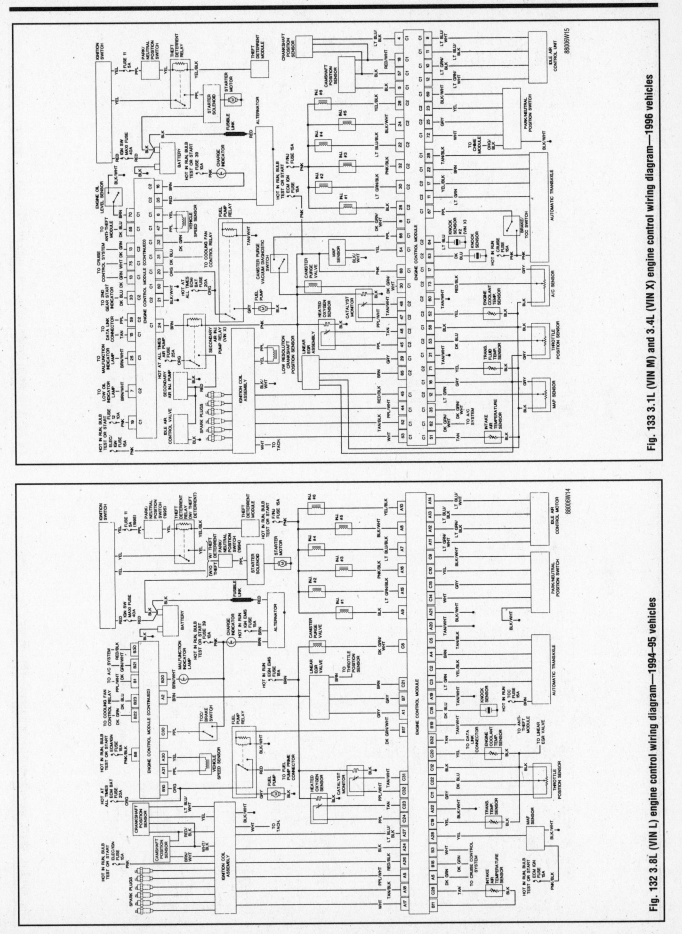

Fig. 133 3.1L (VIN M) and 3.4L (VIN X) engine control wiring diagram—1996 vehicles

Fig. 132 3.8L (VIN L) engine control wiring diagram—1994–95 vehicles

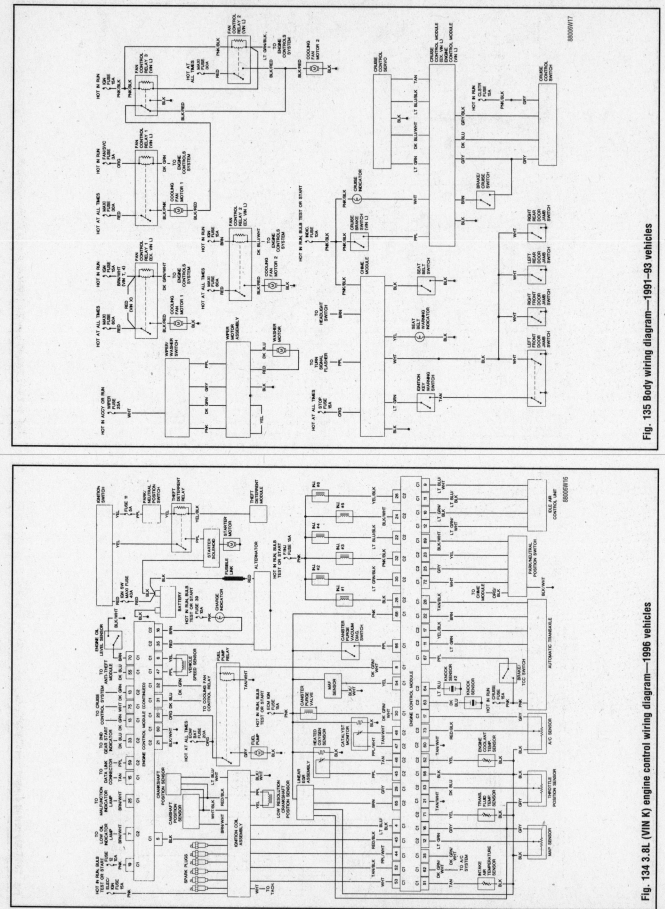

Fig. 135 Body wiring diagram—1991–93 vehicles

Fig. 134 3.8L (VIN K) engine control wiring diagram—1996 vehicles

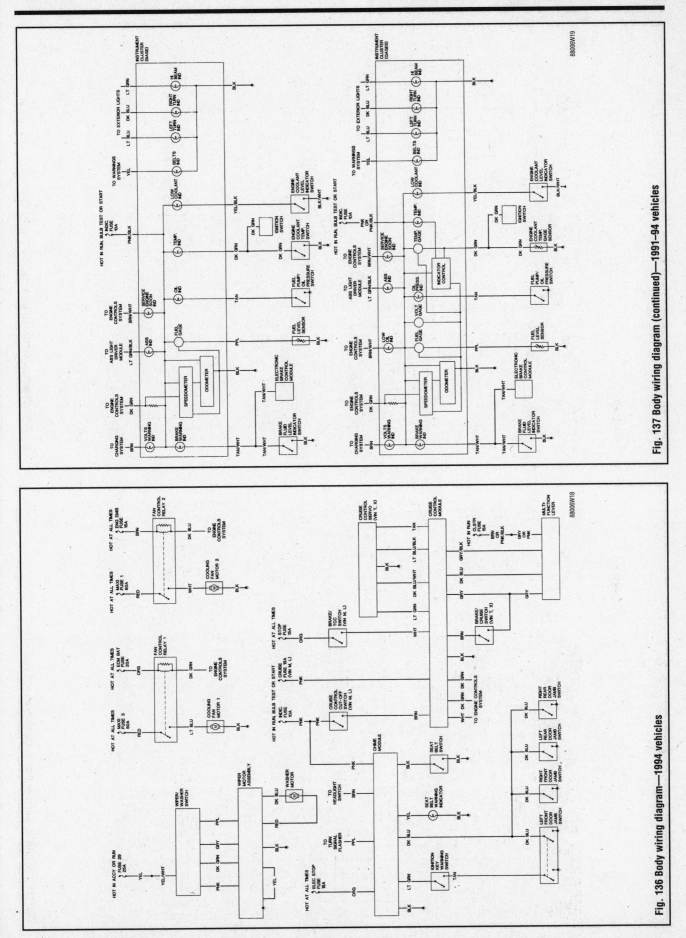

Fig. 137 Body wiring diagram (continued)—1991–94 vehicles

Fig. 136 Body wiring diagram—1994 vehicles

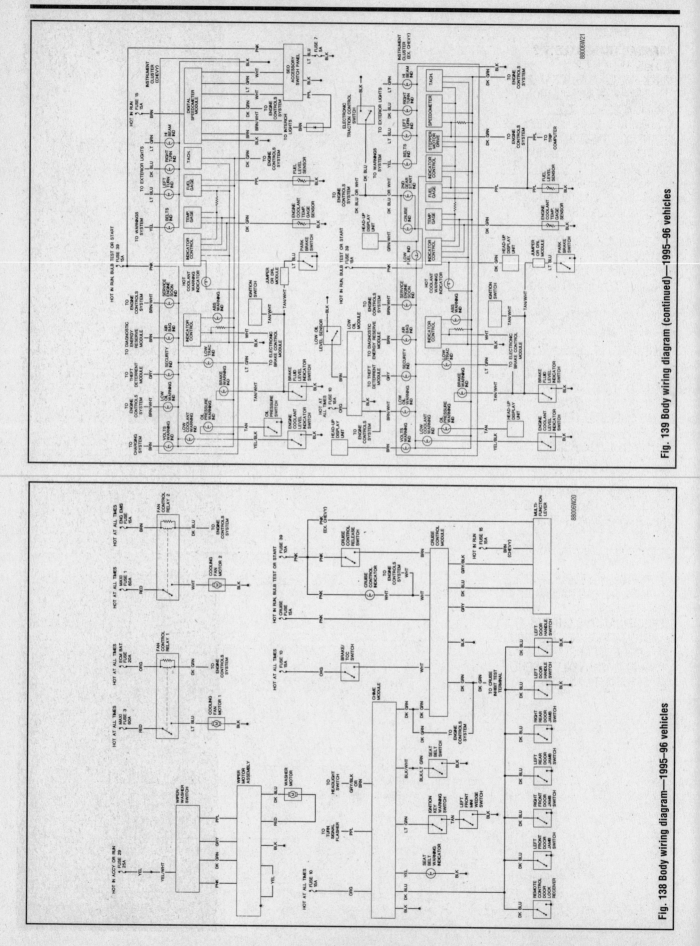

Fig. 139 Body wiring diagram (continued)—1995-96 vehicles

Fig. 138 Body wiring diagram—1995-96 vehicles

7

DRIVETRAIN

MANUAL TRANSAXLE

Adjustments

The shift linkage and cables are preset at the factory, requiring no adjustments. The clutch is a hydraulically-actuated system that is self-adjusting. No periodic adjustments are needed.

Back-up Light Switch

REMOVAL & INSTALLATION

1. Disconnect the negative battery cable. Remove the air cleaner assembly if necessary to gain access to the switch, which is located on top of the transaxle.
2. Disconnect the back-up light switch connector and remove the switch using the proper-size box wrench.
   To install:
3. Apply thread locking compound to the switch threads when installing.
4. Install the switch and tighten to 25 ft. lbs. (34 Nm).
5. Connect the negative battery cable and make sure the back-up lights illuminate when in Reverse.

Frame Assembly

REMOVAL & INSTALLATION

▶ See Figures 1 and 2

1. Disconnect the negative battery cable and remove the air cleaner assembly.
2. Install the engine support fixture J28467–A.
3. Raise the vehicle and support with jackstands.
4. Position jackstands under the engine for support.
5. Remove the front wheel assemblies.
6. Disconnect the intermediate shaft from the steering gear stub shaft.
7. Remove the power steering hose bracket from the frame.
8. Remove the steering gear from the frame and support.
9. Remove the lower ball joints from the lower control arms.
10. Disconnect the engine and transaxle mounts.
11. Support the frame assembly and remove the frame-to-body mounting bolts.
12. Remove the frame assembly with the lower control arms and stabilizer shaft attached. Work the frame downward toward the rear of the vehicle.
13. Remove all loose frame hardware from the body.
    To install:
14. Lubricate the frame insulators with rubber lubricant before installation.
15. Install the lower and upper insulators, retainers and spacers.
16. Install the transaxle mounting bracket, lower control arms and stabilizer shaft, if removed.
17. With an assistant, position the frame to the body, and hand-tighten the retaining bolts.

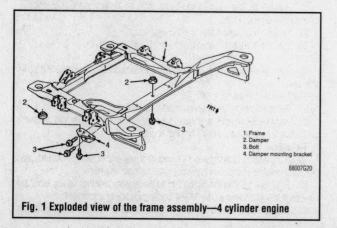

1. Frame
2. Damper
3. Bolt
4. Damper mounting bracket

88007G20

Fig. 1 Exploded view of the frame assembly—4 cylinder engine

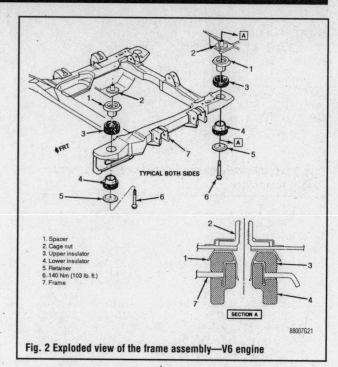

1. Spacer
2. Cage nut
3. Upper insulator
4. Lower insulator
5. Retainer
6. 140 Nm (103 lb. ft.)
7. Frame

TYPICAL BOTH SIDES

SECTION A

88007G21

Fig. 2 Exploded view of the frame assembly—V6 engine

18. Align the frame-to-body by inserting two 0.74 in. (19mm) x 8.0 in. (203mm) long pins in the alignment holes on the right side of the frame.
19. Tighten the frame-to-body retaining bolts to 103 ft. lbs. (140 Nm).
20. Reconnect the engine and transaxle mounts.
21. Install the lower ball joints and steering gear.
22. Install the hoses and brackets.
23. Install the intermediate shaft-to-steering stub shaft.
24. Install the front wheels.
25. Lower the vehicle and remove the engine support fixture.
26. Install the air cleaner and connect the negative battery cable.
27. Have a qualified alignment technician check the front end alignment.

Transaxle Assembly

REMOVAL & INSTALLATION

▶ See Figures 3, 4, 5, 6 and 7

➡ Before performing any manual transaxle removal procedures, the clutch master cylinder pushrod MUST be disconnected from the clutch pedal and the connection in the hydraulic line must be separated using tool No. J–36221. Permanent damage may occur to the actuator if the clutch pedal is depressed while the system is not resisted by clutch loads. Also, the pushrod bushing should be replaced once it has been disconnected from the master cylinder.

1. Disconnect the negative battery cable and remove the air cleaner assembly.
2. Disconnect the master cylinder pushrod from the clutch pedal.
3. Remove the shift and selector cables from the transaxle case.
4. Remove the clutch actuator from the transaxle.
5. Remove the clutch release lever access plug from the clutch housing.
6. Pull the clutch fork lever off the release bearing flanges.
7. Install a wire through the hole in the end of the fork lever. Hold lever out as far as possible and back towards the transaxle side of the access hole. Wrap one end of the wire around the bottom attaching stud for the actuator.
8. Remove the transaxle vent hose.
9. Remove the two upper transaxle-to-engine bolts and studs. Leave one lower mounting stud attached to hold the assembly in place.
10. Install the engine support fixture tool J28467–A along with the support leg.

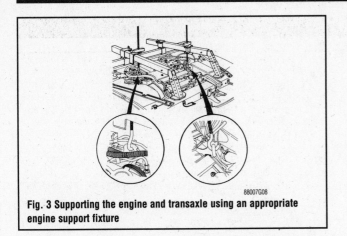

Fig. 3 Supporting the engine and transaxle using an appropriate engine support fixture

88007G08

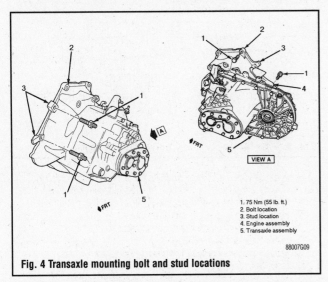

1. 75 Nm (55 lb. ft.)
2. Bolt location
3. Stud location
4. Engine assembly
5. Transaxle assembly

88007G09

Fig. 4 Transaxle mounting bolt and stud locations

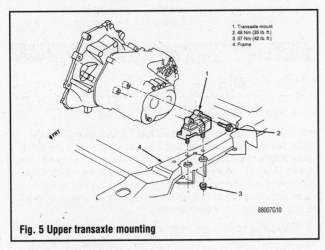

1. Transaxle mount
2. 48 Nm (35 lb. ft.)
3. 57 Nm (42 lb. ft.)
4. Frame

88007G10

Fig. 5 Upper transaxle mounting

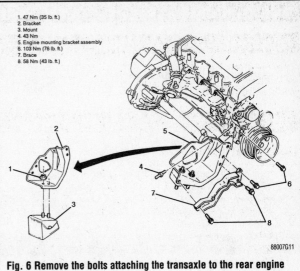

1. 47 Nm (35 lb. ft.)
2. Bracket
3. Mount
4. 43 Nm
5. Engine mounting bracket assembly
6. 103 Nm (76 lb. ft.)
7. Brace
8. 58 Nm (43 lb. ft.)

88007G11

Fig. 6 Remove the bolts attaching the transaxle to the rear engine mount bracket brace

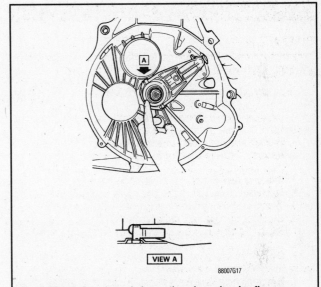

88007G17

Fig. 7 Sliding the release fork over the release bearing flanges

11. Remove the electrical connectors from the back-up switch and vehicle speed sensor.

12. Remove the exhaust crossover pipe at the left exhaust manifold.

13. Remove the EGR tube from the crossover.

14. Loosen the bolts and swing the crossover upward to gain clearance to the top transaxle bolts.

15. Raise the vehicle and support with jackstands.

16. Drain the transaxle fluid into a pan.

17. Remove the four clutch housing cover screws.

18. Remove the front wheels and both wheelhouse splash shields.

19. Remove the power steering lines from the frame, rack and pinion heat shield and rack and pinion from the frame. The power steering hoses should remain connected throughout this procedure.

20. Remove the right and left ball joints from the steering knuckle.

21. Remove the intermediate shaft bracket bolts and remove intermediates shaft.

22. Remove the transaxle upper mount retaining bolts and lower engine mount bracket brace bolts.

23. Remove the frame-to-body retaining bolts.

24. Remove the frame from the vehicle as outlined previously in this section.

25. Disconnect both drive axles from the transaxle and support to the body with wire.

26. Remove the starter motor.

27. Securely support the transaxle case for removal.

28. Remove the remaining transaxle-to-engine retaining bolts and remove the transaxle by pulling it away from the engine.

To install:

29. If the release bearing was removed or a new one is being installed, place the clutch release bearing on the input shaft bearing retainer.

30. Prior to engaging the clutch fork to the release bearing, lightly lubricate the clutch fork ends with a GM-01344 bearing grease or equivalent.

31. Slide the fork toward the center of the transaxle over the bearing flanges.

➡The clutch lever must not be moved toward the flywheel until the transaxle is bolted to the engine, or damage to the transaxle may result.

32. Align the transaxle to the engine and work the input shaft through the clutch disc. Slide the assembly forward and install. Install the lower retaining bolts.

33. Install the starter motor and drive axles.

34. Install the frame assembly and retaining bolts as previously outlined in this section.

35. Install the engine mount retaining nuts and upper transaxle retaining bolt. Tighten the transaxle-to-engine bolts to 55 ft. lbs. (75 Nm).

36. Install the remaining components in the reverse of the removal procedure. Tighten the two upper transaxle mounting bolts and studs to 55 ft. lbs. (75 Nm).

37. Refill the transaxle to the proper fluid level. Refer to Section 1 of this manual.

38. Check each procedure for proper installation and completion of repair, then connect the negative battery cable and road test the vehicle.

Halfshaft

The halfshaft assemblies used on these cars are flexible units consisting of an inner Tri-Pot joint and an outer Constant Velocity (CV) joint. The inner joint is completely flexible, capable of up and down, in and out movement. The outer joint is only capable of up and down movement.

NOISE DIAGNOSIS

1. Clicking noise in turn: inspect for worn or damaged outer CV-joint and outer dust boots.

2. Clunk when accelerating from coast to drive: inspect for worn or damaged outer CV-joint.

3. Shudder or vibration during acceleration: inspect for excessive joint angle, excessive toe, incorrect trim height, worn or damaged outer CV-joint and sticking spider assembly.

4. Vibration at highway speeds: inspect for out of balance rear tires or wheels, out of round tires or wheels, worn outer CV-joint and binding or tight joint.

REMOVAL & INSTALLATION

➡Use care when removing the halfshaft. Tri-pot joints can be damaged if the drive axle is over-extended. It is important to handle the halfshaft in a manner to prevent over-extending.

1. Disconnect the negative battery cable.
2. Raise the car and support with jackstands. Remove the wheel and tire.
3. Remove the brake calipers, bracket assemblies and hang out of the way with wire.
4. Remove the brake rotors.
5. Remove the four hub/bearing retaining bolts and hub.
6. If equipped with ABS brakes, remove the ABS sensor mounting bolt and position the sensor out of the way.

7. Place a drain pan under the transaxle.
8. RIGHT: using a axle shaft removing tool J–33008 or equivalent, separate the halfshaft from the transaxle.
9. LEFT: using a suitable prybar, separate the halfshaft from the transaxle. Pry on the frame and the groove provided on the inner joint.
10. Separate the halfshaft from the bearing assembly, if not removed.

To install:

11. Install the halfshaft/bearing assembly through the knuckle and into the transaxle until the retaining clip engages. Do NOT overextend the inner joint.
12. Install the ABS sensor.
13. Tighten the bearing assembly retaining bolts to 52 ft. lbs. (70 Nm).
14. Remove the drain pan and install a new halfshaft nut and washer.
15. Install the rotor, brake caliper and wheels.
16. Lower the vehicle and tighten the halfshaft axle nut to 184 ft. lbs. (250 Nm).
17. Add the necessary amount of transaxle fluid. Refer to Section 1 of this manual.
18. Connect the negative battery cable.

CV-JOINT OVERHAUL

♦ **See Figures 8 thru 21**

Outer Joint Boot

1. Cut and remove the boot retaining clamps with wire cutters.
2. Remove the race retaining ring with snapring pliers. Remove the joint and boot assembly from the axle shaft. Refer to Step 1 of the CV-joint procedures.
3. Flush the grease from the joint and repack the boot with half of the grease provided with the new boot.
4. Install the new boot and clamps first. Second, install the joint and snap the race retaining ring into place. Put the remainder of the grease into the joint.
5. Using an axle seal clamp tool J–35910 and a torque wrench, tighten the small clamp to 100 ft. lbs. (136 Nm). Tighten the large clamp to 130 ft. lbs. (176 Nm).

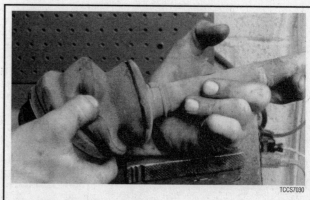

Fig. 8 Check the CV-boot for wear

Fig. 9 Removing the outer band from the CV-boot

Fig. 10 Removing the inner band from the CV-boot

Fig. 11 Removing the CV-boot from the joint housing

Fig. 12 Clean the CV-joint housing prior to removing boot

Fig. 13 Removing the CV-joint housing assembly

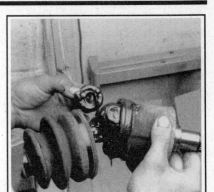
Fig. 14 Removing the CV-joint

Fig. 15 Inspecting the CV-joint housing

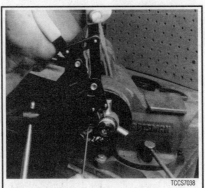
Fig. 16 Removing the CV-joint outer snapring

Fig. 17 Checking the CV-joint snapring for wear

Fig. 18 CV-joint snapring (typical)

Fig. 19 Removing the CV-joint assembly

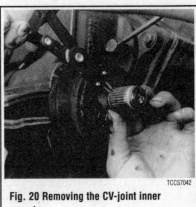
Fig. 20 Removing the CV-joint inner snapring

Fig. 21 Installing the CV-joint assembly (typical)

Outer Joint Assembly

1. Remove the large boot clamp and joint assembly from the axle as previously mentioned. Clean out the grease from the joint to aid in disassembly.

2. Use a brass drift to gently tap on the cage until tilted enough to remove the first ball. Remove the other balls in a similar manner.

3. Pivot the cage and inner race at 90 to the center line of the outer race with the cage windows aligned with the lands of the outer race. Lift the cage out with the inner race. Refer to Step 2 of the CV-joint procedures.

4. Rotate the inner race up and out of the cage as in Step 2. Clean all parts with solvent and blow dry with compressed air.

To install:

5. Lightly coat the ball grooves with the provided grease.

6. Install the inner race into the cage, cage into the outer race and balls into the cage as removed.

7. Refill the joint with half the grease provided. Install the boot and clamps.

Install the joint onto the axle. Fill the joint with the remaining grease and tighten the clamps as in the outer joint boot procedure.

Inner Tri-Pot Boot

1. Cut the clamps from the boot.
2. Remove the spider assembly from the axle by removing the shaft retaining snaprings.
3. Clean all metal parts with solvent and blow dry with compressed air.

To install:

4. Refill the housing with half of the grease provided with the new boot. Install the boot and clamps first, then the spider and snapring assembly onto the axle.
5. Position the axle into the Tri-Pot housing. Install the remaining grease into the joint.
6. Using a seal clamp tool J-35910 or equivalent, tighten the small clamp to 100 ft. lbs. (136 Nm) and tighten the large clamp to 130 ft. lbs. (176 Nm). Side cutters can be used the tighten the boot clamps, but care must be used so not to cut the new clamps.

Intermediate Shaft

REMOVAL & INSTALLATION

♦ **See Figure 22**

➡ **The intermediate shaft is found on manual transaxle models only.**

1. Disconnect the negative battery cable.
2. Raise the car and support with jackstands. Remove the right wheel and tire.
3. Position a drain pan under the transaxle.

➡ **Use care when removing the halfshaft. Tri-pot joints can be damaged if the drive axle is over-extended. It is important to handle the halfshaft in a manner to prevent over-extending.**

4. Remove the right halfshaft assembly as previously outlined in this section.
5. Remove the housing-to-bracket bolts, bracket and housing-to-transaxle bolts.
6. Carefully disengage the intermediate axle shaft from the transaxle and remove the shaft.

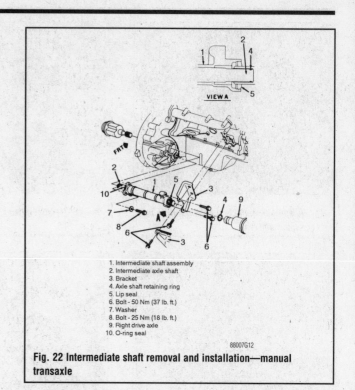

1. Intermediate shaft assembly
2. Intermediate axle shaft
3. Bracket
4. Axle shaft retaining ring
5. Lip seal
6. Bolt - 50 Nm (37 lb. ft.)
7. Washer
8. Bolt - 25 Nm (18 lb. ft.)
9. Right drive axle
10. O-ring seal

Fig. 22 Intermediate shaft removal and installation—manual transaxle

To install:

7. Install the intermediate shaft into position and lock the shaft into the transaxle.
8. Install the housing-to-transaxle bolts and tighten to 18 ft. lbs. (25 Nm).
9. Install the bracket-to-engine block bolts and tighten to 37 ft. lbs. (50 Nm).
10. Install the housing-to-bracket bolts and tighten to 37 ft. lbs. (50 Nm).
11. Coat the splines of the intermediate shaft with chassis grease and install the right halfshaft assembly as previously outlined in this section.
12. Install the front wheels.
13. Lower the vehicle and refill the transaxle to the proper level. Refer to Section 1 of this manual.
14. Connect the negative battery cable and recheck all procedures to ensure complete repair.

CLUTCH

The clutch system consists of a driving member (flywheel and clutch cover), a driven member (clutch disc and input shaft) and a operating member (hydraulic system and release bearing).

Adjustments

The clutch operating system consists of a hydraulic master cylinder, slave cylinder (actuator) and fluid lines. This system is adjusted automatically, requiring no periodic service.

Driven Disc and Pressure Plate

REMOVAL & INSTALLATION

♦ **See Figures 23 thru 32**

➡ **Before performing any manual transaxle removal procedures, the clutch master cylinder pushrod MUST be disconnected from the clutch pedal and the actuator must be separated from the transaxle. Permanent damage may occur to the actuator if the clutch pedal is depressed while the system is not resisted by clutch loads. Also, the pushrod bushing must be replaced once it has been disconnected from the master cylinder.**

1. Disconnect the negative battery cable.

2. Remove the sound insulator from inside the vehicle and disconnect the clutch master cylinder pushrod from the clutch pedal.

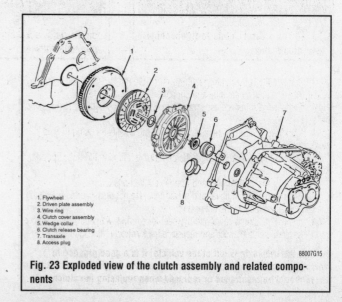

1. Flywheel
2. Driven plate assembly
3. Wire ring
4. Clutch cover assembly
5. Wedge collar
6. Clutch release bearing
7. Transaxle
8. Access plug

Fig. 23 Exploded view of the clutch assembly and related components

Fig. 24 Remove the pressure plate bolts in a crisscross pattern

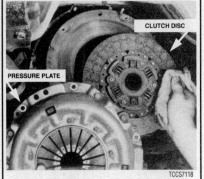

Fig. 25 Removing the clutch and pressure plate

Fig. 26 Be sure that the flywheel surface is clean, before installing the clutch

Fig. 27 Check across the flywheel surface, it should be flat

Fig. 28 Checking the pressure plate for excessive wear

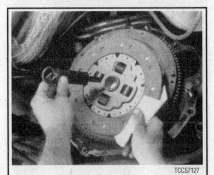

Fig. 29 Install a clutch alignment arbor, to align the clutch assembly during installation

Fig. 30 The pressure plate-to-flywheel bolt hole should align

Fig. 31 Apply a locking agent to the clutch assembly bolts

Fig. 32 Be sure to use a torque wrench to tighten all bolts

3. Remove the two actuator retaining nuts from the transaxle and remove the actuator. Position to the side and support.

4. Remove the transaxle assembly from the vehicle as outlined earlier in this section.

5. Mark the position of the clutch cover to the flywheel if using the old clutch cover.

6. Loosen the cover retaining bolts one turn at a time until all the spring pressure is released.

7. Support the clutch cover and remove all the bolts.

8. Remove the clutch cover and driven disc. Do not disassemble the clutch cover; if damaged replace the entire unit.

9. Inspect the clutch cover and flywheel for scoring, warpage and excessive wear. Replace the clutch cover and resurface the flywheel if damaged.

➡ While the transaxle is out of the vehicle, it is a good practice to replace the clutch cover, driven disc and release bearing. Also, the flywheel should be resurfaced or replaced when replacing the clutch assembly. Removing the transaxle is not an easy job, especially if it has to be done twice.

10. Clean the clutch cover and flywheel surfaces with solvent and low-grit sandpaper if installing the used parts.

To install:

11. Position the clutch disc and cover onto the flywheel mating surface. The raised hub and springs should face away from the flywheel. The disc may be marked "Flywheel Side", meaning the stamp faces the flywheel.

12. Loosely install the clutch cover retaining bolts. Do NOT tighten at this time.

13. Support the clutch disc using a clutch alignment tool J–35822 or equivalent. This tool is needed to align the clutch disc to the flywheel so when the transaxle is installed, the input splines will align with the flywheel pilot bearing.

14. With the clutch alignment tool installed, tighten the clutch cover-to-flywheel bolts to 6 ft. lbs. (21 Nm). Remove the alignment tool.

15. Replace the release bearing if needed. Lightly lubricate the clutch fork

ends which contact the bearing and the inner recess of the release bearing with chassis grease.

16. Make sure the release bearing and fork move freely on the fork shaft.

17. Tie the actuator lever to the studs to hold the release bearing in place.

➡**The clutch actuator lever must NOT move toward the flywheel until the transaxle is bolted to the engine, otherwise damage to the transaxle could result.**

18. Install the transaxle assembly.

19. Remove the actuator lever tie. Inspect the actuator pushrod for the bushing and replace if missing.

20. Install the actuator to the transaxle, making sure the bushing is centered in the pocket of the internal lever in the housing.

21. Install the actuator retaining nuts and tighten evenly to draw the actuator to the transaxle. Tighten the nuts to 18 ft. lbs. (25 Nm).

22. Install a new bushing in the master cylinder pushrod and lubricate before installation.

23. Install the master cylinder pushrod to the clutch pedal.

24. Press the clutch pedal down several times to assure normal operation.

25. Install the sound insulator and negative battery cable.

Release Bearing

REMOVAL & INSTALLATION

The clutch release bearing used with the 5TM40 manual transaxle is a conventional type bearing. It is snapped into a clutch release forkshaft and held in place. This type bearing is generally used with a push type clutch assembly.

The release bearing used with the Getrag 284 is snapped into the clutch pressure plate. This type bearing is used with a pull type clutch assembly and may be held in place by one of two methods. The first method is a wedge collar and wire ring. The second is a simple snapring retainer. Both retainer methods allow the release bearing to be snapped onto the clutch fingers and held in place during clutch operation. If any of the collar legs are broken or bent, or if the wire ring is distorted, the wedge collar/wire ring or snapring should be replaced.

Conventional Type

▶ **See Figures 33 and 34**

1. With the transaxle removed, the bearing is located on the clutch release shaft located in the bell housing of the transaxle.

2. The bearing is held in place by retaining clips. Simply pull the bearing from the forkshaft.

To install:

➡**Do not place the bearing in degreaser, or damage to the seals will result. If the bearing is going to be reused, clean by wiping with a clean cloth. Inspect it for galling or other signs of wear.**

3. Lightly lubricate the clutch fork ends with a suitable bearing grease.

4. If the bearing is not a seal type bearing, pack the bearing with a suitable grease.

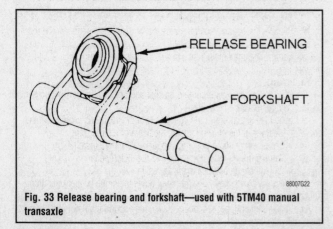

Fig. 33 Release bearing and forkshaft—used with 5TM40 manual transaxle

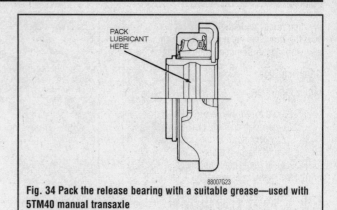

Fig. 34 Pack the release bearing with a suitable grease—used with 5TM40 manual transaxle

5. Install the release bearing onto the clutch fork. Levers on the forkshaft must bear on the large ears of the release bearing. The levers fit between the 2 large ears and small tangs of the bearing. The fork shaft must move freely with the bearing in place.

6. Position the release fork and bearing back toward the transaxle and tie shaft actuator lever to prevent it from moving out of position.

➡**The clutch lever must NOT move toward the flywheel until the transaxle is bolted to the engine, otherwise damage to the transaxle could result.**

Wedge Collar Type

▶ **See Figure 35**

1. Remove the clutch pressure plate and disc from the flywheel.

2. Hold the wedge collar in towards the pressure plate. Working from the engine side of the pressure plate, use a prytool to remove the wire ring from the wedge collar legs.

3. Pry the wedge collar from the pressure plate assembly.

➡**Take care not to deform the wire ring as a deformed wire ring will allow the bearing to pull out of the clutch during operation. Also take note of the bearing condition. Heavy galling on either bearing or sleeve indicates replacement is necessary.**

To install:

4. Push the wedge collar (without the wire ring) in to the clutch pressure plate assembly.

5. Hold the wedge collar in towards the pressure plate assembly.

6. Working from the engine side of the clutch pressure plate, install the wire ring onto the V-bend in the wedge collar legs.

7. Install the clutch drive disc and pressure plate to the flywheel.

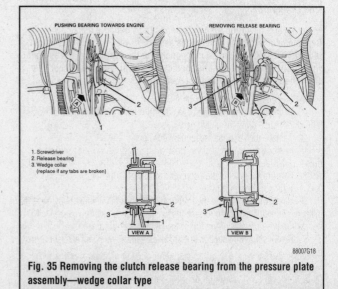

Fig. 35 Removing the clutch release bearing from the pressure plate assembly—wedge collar type

➡When removing installing the transaxle, care must be taken to prevent the transaxle input shaft from contacting the clutch wedge collar and wire ring or damage to the wedge collar and wire ring may result.

Snaping Type

♦ **See Figure 36**

1. Remove the clutch pressure plate and disc from the flywheel.
2. Lay the clutch pressure plate assembly up on a flat surface.
3. Lightly push down on the clutch cover assembly to partially open the release bearing attaching snapring.
4. Use a snapring pliers to open the snapring. Lift the pressure plate assembly up to allow the release bearing to slide out.

➡**Inspect the bearing. Heavy galling on either bearing or sleeve indicates replacement is necessary.**

To install:

5. Insure that the bearing sleeve outer surface is free of any oil or grease deposits.
6. From engine side of the clutch pressure plate, spread the snapring open.
7. Push the release bearing in place far enough to seat the snapring. Release the snapring.
8. Install the clutch drive disc and pressure plate to the flywheel.

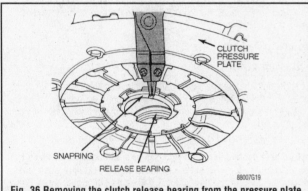

CLUTCH PRESSURE PLATE

SNAPRING

RELEASE BEARING

88007G19

Fig. 36 Removing the clutch release bearing from the pressure plate assembly—snapring type

Master Cylinder

REMOVAL & INSTALLATION

♦ **See Figure 37**

➡**The factory hydraulic system is serviced as a single assembly. Replacement hydraulic assemblies are pre-filled with fluid and do not require bleeding. Individual components of the system are not available separately. Check with an aftermarket parts supplier to see if individual components can be purchased separately.**

1. Disconnect the negative battery cable.
2. Remove the sound insulator inside the vehicle and disconnect the master cylinder pushrod at the clutch pedal.
3. Remove the left upper secondary cowl panel.
4. Remove the two master cylinder reservoir-to-strut tower retaining nuts.
5. Remove the anti-rotation screw located next to the master cylinder flange at the pedal support plate.
6. Using wrench flats on the front end of the master cylinder body, twist the cylinder counterclockwise to release the twist lock attachment-to-plate. Do NOT tighten the hose connection on top of the cylinder body, damage may occur.
7. Remove the two actuator-to-transaxle retaining nuts and actuator assembly.
8. Pull the master cylinder with the pushrod attached forward out of the pedal plate. Lift the reservoir off the strut tower studs and remove the three components as a complete assembly.

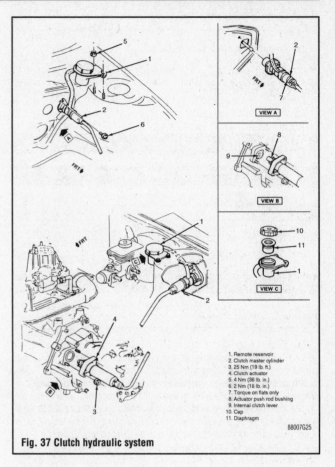

1. Remote reservoir
2. Clutch master cylinder
3. 25 Nm (19 lb. ft.)
4. Clutch actuator
5. 4 Nm (36 lb. in.)
6. 2 Nm (18 lb. in.)
7. Torque on flats only
8. Actuator push rod bushing
9. Internal clutch lever
10. Cap
11. Diaphragm

88007G25

Fig. 37 Clutch hydraulic system

To install:

9. Install the master cylinder into the opening in the pedal plate and rotate 45 degrees by applying torque on the wrench flats only.
10. Install the anti-rotation screw.
11. Install the fluid reservoir to the strut tower and tighten the retaining nuts to 36 inch lbs. (4 Nm).
12. Install a new pushrod bushing and lubricate before installation.
13. Install the master cylinder pushrod to the clutch pedal.
14. Install the clutch actuator to the transaxle.
15. Press the clutch pedal down several times to ensure proper operation.
16. Install the left upper secondary cowl panel, sound insulator and connect the negative battery cable.

Clutch Slave Cylinder

REMOVAL & INSTALLATION

1. Disconnect the negative battery cable.
2. Remove the sound insulator inside the vehicle and disconnect the master cylinder pushrod at the clutch pedal.
3. Remove 2 bolts holding the canister to transaxle. Remove the 2 actuator retainer nuts and remove the actuator from transaxle housing.

To install:

4. Position the canister mounting bracket and bolts to the transaxle assembly and secure the retaining bolts.
5. Install the actuator-to-housing studs with the pushrods centered in the pocket of the lever in the housing. Install the actuator retainer nuts.
6. Install a new pushrod bushing and lubricate before installation.
7. Install the master cylinder pushrod to the clutch pedal.
8. Install the clutch actuator to the transaxle.
9. Press the clutch pedal down several times to ensure proper operation. Adjust cruise control switch if equipped.
10. Install the left upper secondary cowl panel, sound insulator and connect the negative battery cable.

HYDRAULIC SYSTEM BLEEDING

1. Disconnect the negative battery cable.
2. Disengage the quick connect fittings in the clutch hydraulic line. Insert J–36221 or equivalent hydraulic line separator tool and depress the plastic sleeve to separate the connection.
3. Remove the cap and diaphragm, then fill reservoir with DOT 3 brake fluid.

4. Remove the left hand upper secondary cowl.
5. Remove air from supply hose by squeezing it until no more air bubbles are seen in reservoir.
6. Pump the clutch pedal slowly until slight pressure is observed. Hold pressure on pedal and depress the internal valve on quick connect fitting.
7. Repeat Step 6 until pedal is firm and no bubbles are seen.
8. Reconnect the clutch hydraulic line. Refill the clutch system and install the reservoir cap. Reconnect battery cable.

AUTOMATIC TRANSAXLE

Adjustments

RANGE SELECTOR CABLE

♦ See Figure 38

1. Disconnect the negative battery cable.
2. Apply the parking brake and block the rear wheels.
3. From inside the passenger compartment; place the steering column or floor shifter in the **N** position.
4. From under the hood; lift up the range selector cable locking button at the transaxle and cable bracket.
5. Remove the range selector cable end from the transaxle range selector lever.
6. Place the transaxle range selector lever in the **N** position. This position can be found by rotating the selector shaft/shift lever clockwise from **P** through **R** to **N** positions. (**P** position is toward the rear of the vehicle, **N** is 2 detents forward of **P**).
7. If not previously done, place the shift control inside the vehicle to the **N** position.
8. Snap the range selector cable end onto the range selector lever.
9. Push down the locking button at the cable bracket and connect the negative battery cable.
10. Check the selector positions in each range.
11. Remove the blocks from the wheels.

3. With the key in the **RUN** position and the shifter in the **N** position, the key should NOT turn to the **LOCK** position.
4. Adjust the cable by pulling up the cable connector lock at the shifter.
5. If the key cannot be removed in the **P** position, snap the connector lock button to the up position and move the cable connector nose rearward until the key can be removed from the ignition.
6. Snap the lock button down and recheck operation. Connect the negative battery cable.

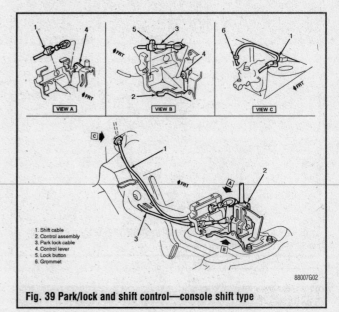

1. Shift cable
2. Control assembly
3. Park lock cable
4. Control lever
5. Lock button
6. Grommet

88007G02

Fig. 39 Park/lock and shift control—console shift type

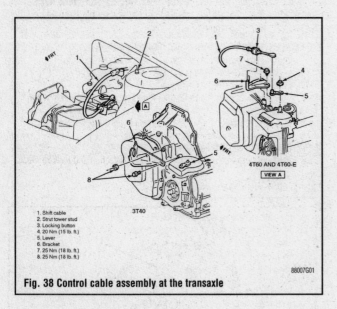

1. Shift cable
2. Strut tower stud
3. Locking button
4. 20 Nm (15 lb. ft.)
5. Lever
6. Bracket
7. 25 Nm (18 lb. ft.)
8. 25 Nm (18 lb. ft.)

3T40

4T60 AND 4T60-E
VIEW A

88007G01

Fig. 38 Control cable assembly at the transaxle

PARK/LOCK CONTROL CABLE

♦ See Figures 39 and 40

1. Disconnect the negative battery cable.
2. With the shift lever in the **P** position and the key in the **LOCK** position, make sure that the shifter cannot be moved to another position. The key should be removable from the column.

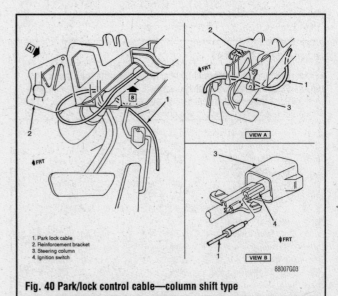

1. Park lock cable
2. Reinforcement bracket
3. Steering column
4. Ignition switch

VIEW A

VIEW B

88007G03

Fig. 40 Park/lock control cable—column shift type

THROTTLE VALVE (TV) CABLE

♦ **See Figure 41**

1. Disconnect the negative battery cable.
2. Pull on the upper end of the TV cable. It should travel a short distance with light resistance caused by a small spring on the TV lever.
3. The cable should go to the zero position when the upper end of the cable is released.
4. Verify that the TV cable is installed properly in the throttle lever and the slider is in the non-adjusted position as shown in the illustration.
5. With the engine NOT running, rotate the throttle lever to the full travel position (throttle body stop).
6. Depress and hold the adjustment button, pull the cable conduit out until the slider hits against the adjustment and release the button.
7. Repeat steps to ensure proper adjustment.

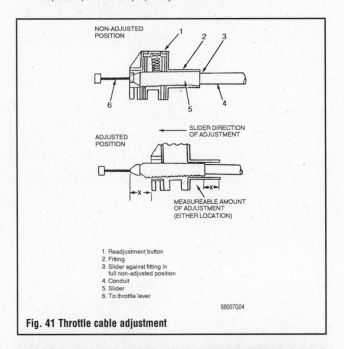

1. Readjustment button
2. Fitting
3. Slider against fitting in full non-adjusted position
4. Conduit
5. Slider
6. To throttle lever

88007G04

Fig. 41 Throttle cable adjustment

Reverse/Neutral Safety Switch

The Neutral Safety Switch and Back-up light switch is combined as one unit.

REMOVAL & INSTALLATION

♦ **See Figures 42 and 43**

1. Disconnect the negative battery cable. Apply the parking brake.
2. Place the transaxle in the **N** position.
3. Raise the vehicle and support with jackstands.

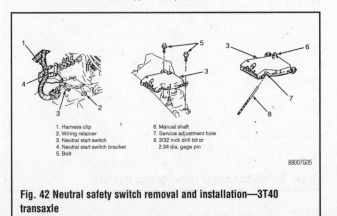

1. Harness clip
2. Wiring retainer
3. Neutral start switch
4. Neutral start switch bracket
5. Bolt
6. Manual shaft
7. Service adjustment hole
8. 3/32 inch drill bit or 2.34 dia. gage pin

88007G05

Fig. 42 Neutral safety switch removal and installation—3T40 transaxle

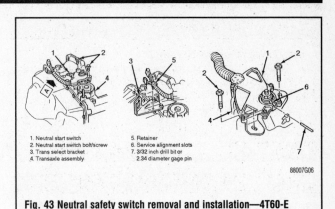

1. Neutral start switch
2. Neutral start switch bolt/screw
3. Trans select bracket
4. Transaxle assembly
5. Retainer
6. Service alignment slots
7. 3/32 inch drill bit or 2.34 diameter gage pin

88007G06

Fig. 43 Neutral safety switch removal and installation—4T60-E transaxle

4. Unplug the switch electrical connector and remove the retaining clips.
5. Lower the vehicle and remove the vacuum hoses and electrical connectors from the cruise control servo, if so equipped.
6. Remove the shift lever at the transaxle. Do NOT disconnect the lever from the cable. Remove the two retaining bolts and switch.

To install:

7. Align the notch (groove) on the inner sleeve with the notch on the switch body. Install the switch and tighten the retaining bolts to 18 ft. lbs. (25 Nm).
8. Install the shift lever and tighten the nut to 15 ft. lbs. (20 Nm).
9. Raise the vehicle and support with jackstands.
10. Engage the switch connector, harness clips and lower the vehicle.
11. Install the cruise control servo, if removed.
12. Connect the negative battery cable and check for proper operation.

ADJUSTMENT

♦ **See Figure 44**

➥**Replacement switches are pinned in the Neutral position to ease installation. If the switch has been rotated or the switch is broken, adjustment may be performed as follows.**

1. Apply the parking brake and block the wheels.
2. Place the shift control lever in **N**.
3. Disconnect the negative battery cable.
4. Loosen the switch mounting bolts.
5. Rotate the switch on the shifter to align the service adjustment hole with the carrier tang hole.
6. Insert a small drill bit into the adjustment holes to align the switch. Tighten the mounting screws to 18 ft. lbs. (25 Nm).
7. Connect the negative battery cable.
8. Verify proper switch operation for gear start selection and back-up light operation.

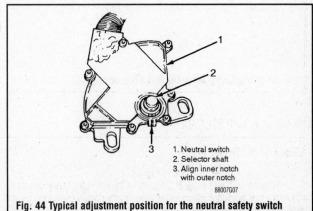

1. Neutral switch
2. Selector shaft
3. Align inner notch with outer notch

88007G07

Fig. 44 Typical adjustment position for the neutral safety switch

Transaxle Assembly

REMOVAL & INSTALLATION

3-Speed Unit

▶ **See Figures 45, 46, 47 and 48**

1. Disconnect the negative battery cable and remove the air cleaner assembly.

2. Remove the shift control and throttle valve (TV) cables at the transaxle.

3. Remove the throttle cable bracket and brake booster hose.

4. Remove the engine torque struts, left torque strut bracket and oil cooler lines at the transaxle.

5. Install the engine support fixture tool J28467–A and J–36462.

6. Raise the vehicle and support with jackstands.

7. Remove the front wheels, splash shields, calipers and rotors. Support the caliper to the frame with wire.

8. Remove the front halfshafts (axle) assemblies as outlined in this section.

9. Disconnect both ball joints and tie rod ends from the strut assemblies. For further assistance, refer to Section 8.

10. Remove the engine oil filter.

11. Remove the A/C compressor and support out of the way. Do NOT disconnect the refrigerant lines.

12. Remove the rack and pinion heat shield and electrical connector.

13. Remove the rack and pinion assembly and secure it to the exhaust for support.

14. Remove the power steering hoses bracket.

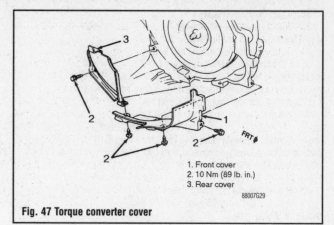

1. Front cover
2. 10 Nm (89 lb. in.)
3. Rear cover

88007G29

Fig. 47 Torque converter cover

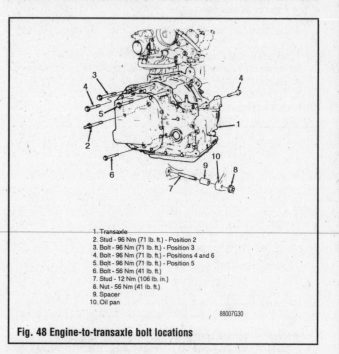

1. Transaxle
2. Stud - 96 Nm (71 lb. ft.) - Position 2
3. Bolt - 96 Nm (71 lb. ft.) - Position 3
4. Bolt - 96 Nm (71 lb. ft.) - Positions 4 and 6
5. Bolt - 96 Nm (71 lb. ft.) - Position 5
6. Bolt - 56 Nm (41 lb. ft.)
7. Stud - 12 Nm (106 lb. in.)
8. Nut - 56 Nm (41 lb. ft.)
9. Spacer
10. Oil pan

88007G30

Fig. 48 Engine-to-transaxle bolt locations

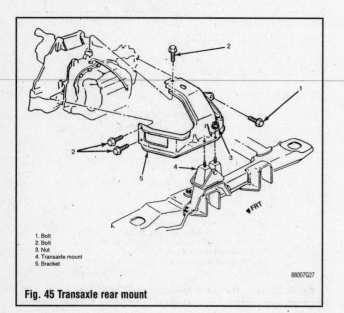

1. Bolt
2. Bolt
3. Nut
4. Transaxle mount
5. Bracket

88007G27

Fig. 45 Transaxle rear mount

15. Remove the engine and transaxle mounts at the frame.

16. Support the frame with jackstands at each end, remove the frame bolts and frame. Refer to the Frame removal and installation procedure in this section.

17. Remove the torque converter cover.

18. Turn the crankshaft to expose the converter bolts. Remove the torque converter to flywheel bolts.

19. Remove the starter bolts and support out of the way.

20. Remove the ground cable from the transaxle case.

21. Remove the fluid fill tube bolt and transaxle mount bracket.

22. Lower the vehicle.

23. Remove the fill tube.

24. Using the engine support fixture, lower the left side of the engine about 4 in. (102mm).

25. Raise the vehicle, support with jackstands and install a transaxle jack.

26. Remove the transaxle-to-engine bolts and transaxle.

To install:

27. The transaxle oil cooler lines should be flushed with a converter flush kit J–35944 or equivalent.

28. Lubricate the torque converter pilot hub with chassis grease. Make sure the torque converter is properly seated in the oil pump drive. Damage to the transaxle may occur if converter is not seated completely.

29. Position the transaxle into the vehicle and tighten the transaxle-to-engine bolts to 55 ft. lbs. (75 Nm).

30. Install the transaxle mount bracket and lower the vehicle.

31. Using the engine support fixture, raise the engine into the proper position.

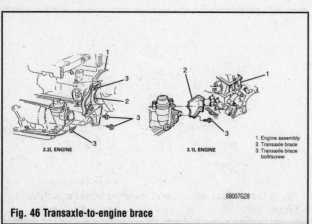

2.2L ENGINE

3.1L ENGINE

1. Engine assembly
2. Transaxle brace
3. Transaxle brace bolt/screw

88007G28

Fig. 46 Transaxle-to-engine brace

32. Install the fluid fill tube.
33. With an assistant, position and support the frame under the vehicle. Install the frame bolts and tighten to 103 ft. lbs. (140 Nm).
34. Remove the frame supports and lower the vehicle.
35. Position the engine and transaxle into the frame mounts. Remove the engine support fixture.
36. Raise the vehicle, install the torque converter-to-flywheel bolts and tighten to 44 ft. lbs. (60 Nm). Install the torque converter cover.
37. Install the remaining components in the reverse of the removal procedure.
38. Connect the negative battery cable, install the air cleaner and recheck each operation to ensure completion of repair.
39. Adjust the shift linkage and TV cable. Check the engine and transaxle oil levels.
40. Start the engine and check for fluid leaks.

4-Speed Units

▶ See Figures 49 thru 54

1. Disconnect the negative battery cable and remove the air cleaner assembly.
2. Install the engine support fixture tool J28467–A and J–36462.
3. Remove the shift control and Throttle Valve (TV) cables at the transaxle.
4. Remove the throttle cable bracket and brake booster hose.
5. Remove the crossover pipe-to-left exhaust manifold, EGR tube at crossover and crossover-to-exhaust pipe bolts.

6. Loosen the crossover-to-right manifold and swing the crossover upward to gain clearance to the top bell housing bolts.
7. Remove the four upper bell housing bolts.
8. Remove the TCC electrical connector, neutral start switch electrical connector and vacuum modulator hose at the transaxle.
9. Raise the vehicle and support with jackstands.
10. Remove the vehicle speed sensor electrical connector.
11. Remove the front wheels, splash shields, calipers and rotors. Support the caliper to the frame with wire.
12. Remove the front halfshafts (axle) assemblies as outlined in this section.

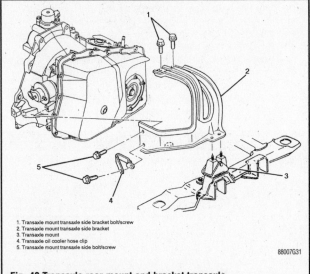
Fig. 49 Transaxle rear mount and bracket transaxle

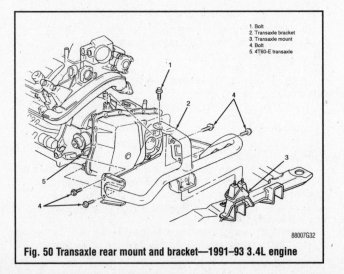
Fig. 50 Transaxle rear mount and bracket—1991–93 3.4L engine

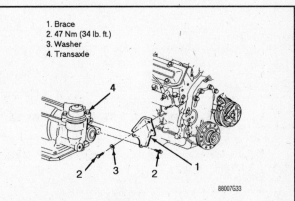
Fig. 51 Transaxle to-engine-brace

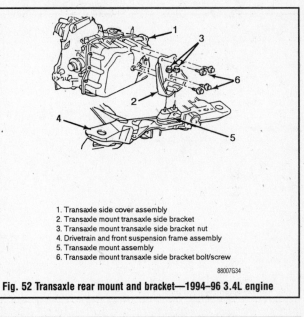
Fig. 52 Transaxle rear mount and bracket—1994–96 3.4L engine

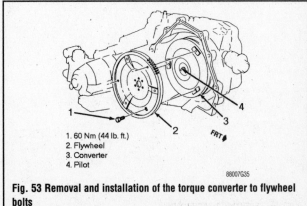
Fig. 53 Removal and installation of the torque converter to flywheel bolts

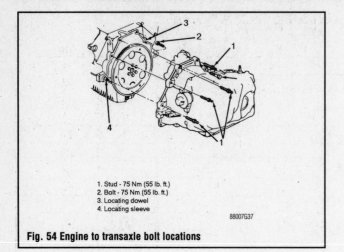

1. Stud - 75 Nm (55 lb. ft.)
2. Bolt - 75 Nm (55 lb. ft.)
3. Locating dowel
4. Locating sleeve

88007G37

Fig. 54 Engine to transaxle bolt locations

13. Disconnect both ball joints and tie rod ends from the strut assemblies. For further assistance, refer to Section 8.

14. Remove the rack and pinion heat shield and electrical connector.

15. Remove the rack and pinion assembly and secure it to the exhaust for support.

16. Remove the power steering hoses, bracket, if so equipped.

17. Remove the engine and transaxle mounts at the frame.

18. Support the frame with jackstands at each end, remove the frame bolts and frame. Refer to the Frame removal and installation procedure in this section.

19. Remove the torque converter cover and bolts.

20. Remove the transaxle oil cooler lines, support bracket and torque converter cover.

21. Remove the starter bolts and support it out of the way.

22. Remove the ground cable from the transaxle case.

23. Support the transaxle with jackstands.

24. Remove the fluid fill tube bolt and transaxle mount bracket.

25. Remove the transaxle-to-engine bolts and transaxle.

To install:

26. The transaxle oil cooler lines should be flushed with a converter flush kit J–35944 or equivalent.

27. Lubricate the torque converter pilot hub with chassis grease.

Make sure the torque converter is properly seated in the oil pump drive. Damage to the transaxle may occur if converter is not seated completely.

28. Position the transaxle into the vehicle and tighten the transaxle-to-engine bolts to 55 ft. lbs. (75 Nm).

29. Install the transaxle mount bracket.

30. Install the torque converter-to-flywheel bolts and tighten to 44 ft. lbs. (60 Nm).

31. Install the starter motor, halfshafts (axles) and torque converter cover.

32. Connect the oil cooler lines and support bracket.

33. Install the frame assembly and retaining bolts. Tighten the bolts to 103 ft. lbs. (140 Nm).

34. Install the lower engine mount retaining nuts and upper transaxle mount retaining nuts.

35. Install the ball joints-to-steering knuckle and rack and pinion assembly-to-frame.

36. Install the power steering heat shield and cooler lines-to-frame.

37. Install the wheel house splash shields.

38. Install the rotor, calipers and front wheels.

39. Install the vehicle speed sensor and lower the vehicle.

40. Connect the back-up/neutral switch.

41. Engage the modulator hose and TCC electrical connector.

42. Install the four upper bell housing bolts and tighten to 55 ft. lbs. (75 Nm).

43. Install the crossover pipe to its proper position.

44. Install the crossover pipe-to-right and left manifolds.

45. Install the EGR tube-to-crossover.

46. Connect the TV and shift control cables.

47. Remove the engine support fixture J28467–A and J–36462.

48. Connect the negative battery cable and install the air cleaner.

49. Adjust the fluid level, TV and shift cables.

50. Recheck all procedures for completion of repair. Start the engine and check for fluid leaks.

Halfshafts

Refer to the Halfshaft procedures under Manual Transaxles in this section.

AUTOMATIC TRANSAXLE TORQUE SPECIFICATIONS

Component	ft. lbs.	inch lbs.	Nm
Accumulator bolt/screw - 4 spd.	-	97	11
Case Extention Housing bolt/screw	32	-	43
Case Side cover bolt/screw (up to 1991)	-	125	14
Case Side cover bolt/screw (after 1991)	-	97	11
Case Side cover nut - 4 spd.	-	71	71
Channel plate bolt/screw	18	-	24
Console Shift Control nut	18	-	24
Converter Shield bolt/screw	-	89	10
Filler tube bracket			
Nut - 3 spd. (2.2L engine)	-	124	14
Bolt/screw - 3 spd (3.1L engine)	18	-	25
Bolt/screw - 4 spd.	-	115	13
Flywheel access cover bolt/screw - 3 spd.	-	89	10
Flywheel-to-Torque converter bolt/screw	46	-	63
Inside detent lever nut	24	-	32
Manual detent roller bolt/screw	-	97	11
Neutral start switch bolt/screw	18	-	25
Oil pan bolt/screw			
3 spd.	-	97	11
4 spd.	13	-	17
Oil scoop bolt/screw - 4 spd.	-	116	13
Oil scoop bolt/screw - 4 spd.	-	71	8
Pump bolt/screw	-	97	11
Pump bolt/screw	18	-	24
Servo cover bolt/screw - 4 spd.	-	89	10
Shift control cable bracket bolt/screw	18	-	25
Shift control cable bracket nut	18	-	25
Shift control cable lever nut	15	-	20
Speed sensor bolt/screw - 4 spd.	-	97	11
Transaxle auxiliary oil cooler			
Bolt/screw	18	-	25
Bracket bolt/screw	-	9	1
Clip bolt/screw	-	35	4
Fitting	18	-	25
Hose clamp	-	18	2
Nut	-	89	10
Transaxle bracket-to-transaxle bolt/screw			
3 Spd. Transaxle			
Rear	63	-	85
Front	35	-	48
Top	35	-	48
4 Spd. Transaxle (1991-94 except 1994 3.4L engine)			
Rear	35	-	48
Front	35	-	48
Top	63	-	85
4 spd. (1994-96 3.4L engine)	70		95
Transaxle bracket -to-mount nut	39	-	53
Transaxle mount support bolt/screw	43		58

88007C01

AUTOMATIC TRANSAXLE TORQUE SPECIFICATIONS

Component	ft. lbs.	inch lbs.	Nm
Transaxle mount support nut	43	-	58
Transaxle mount-to-support nut			
3.1L engine	35	-	47
3.4L engine	39	-	53
Transaxle oil cooler fitting -to-radiator			
3 spd.	16	-	22
4 spd	17	-	23
Transaxle oil cooler fitting -to-transaxle	-	-	-
3 spd.	16	-	22
4 spd	17	-	23
Transaxle oil cooler hose clamp	-	18	2
Transaxle oil cooler retainer bolt/screw	-	53	6
Transaxle-to-engine bolt/screw	55	-	75
Transaxle-to-engine brace bolt/screw	35	-	47
Throttle valve cable bolt/screw	-	89	10
Vacuum modulator clamp bolt/screw - 4 spd.	20	-	27
Vacuum modulator line nut	18	-	25
Valve body bolt/screw	-	97	11
Valve body-to-case bolt/screw	18	-	24

88007C02

MANUAL TRANSAXLE TORQUE SPECIFICATIONS

Component	ft. lbs.	Inch lbs.	Nm
Backup light switch	25	-	34
Cable retaining clamp nut	-	89	10
Clutch housing cover screw	-	116	13
Control assembly bolt	18	-	25
Shift lever nut	61	-	83
Shift linkage bracket bolt	17	-	23
Speedometer signal assembly bolt	-	80	9
Transaxle mount-to-frame nut	42	-	57
Transaxle mount-to-transaxle bolt	35	-	48
Transaxle-to-engine mounting bolt	55	-	75
Speed sensor	-	80	9

88007C03

8

SUSPENSION AND STEERING

WHEELS

Front and Rear Wheels

REMOVAL & INSTALLATION

▶ **See Figure 1**

1. If equipped, remove the hub cap/wheel cover.
2. Loosen, but do not remove the lug nuts.
3. Raise and safely support vehicle so the tire is clear of the ground.

➡**Always use a suitable floor jack for raising the vehicle to be serviced. Never use the jacking device supplied with the vehicle for vehicle service. That jacking device is designed for emergency use only to change a flat tire.**

4. Remove the lug nuts, then remove the wheel from the vehicle.

To install:

5. Install the wheel.
6. Install the lug nuts, then hand-tighten in a star pattern.
7. Carefully lower the vehicle.
8. Final tighten the lug nuts, in a star pattern, to 100 ft. lbs. (140 Nm).

INSPECTION

Inspect the tread for abnormal wear, check for nails or other foreign material embedded into the tire. To check for leaks, submerse the wheel assembly into a tub of water and watch for air bubbles.

Wheels must be replaced if they are bent, dented, leak air through welds, have elongated bolt holes, if wheel nuts won't stay tight, or if the wheels are heavily rusted. Replacement wheels must be equivalent to the original equipment wheels in load capacity, diameter, rim width, offset, and mounting configuration.

A wheel of improper size may affect wheel bearing life, brake cooling, speedometer/odometer calibration, vehicle ground clearance and tire clearance to the body and/or chassis.

➡**Replacement with used wheels is not recommended as their service history may have included severe treatment or very high mileage and they could fail without warning.**

Check runout in all directions (up and down, in and out) using a dial indicator. For aluminum wheels, maximum runout is 0.030 in. (0.762mm) For steel wheels, the specification is 0.045 in. (1.143mm). If the wheel causes a vibration and tire balance does not solve the problem, replace the wheel.

Wheel Lug Studs

All models use metric wheel nuts and studs. The nut will have the word "metric" stamped on the face and the stud will have the letter "M" into the threaded end.

The thread size of the metric wheel nuts and wheel studs are M12 X 1.5, this signifies:

- M = Metric
- 12 = Diameter in millimeters
- 1.5 = Millimeters per thread

REPLACEMENT

▶ **See Figures 2 and 3**

➡**Never try to reuse a wheel stud. Once a wheel stud has been removed, discard it and replace it with a new one.**

1. Raise the vehicle and support safely.
2. Remove the wheel, brake caliper, bracket and rotor.
3. Cut about ½ in. (13mm) off of the outer end of the stud.
4. Position the stud at the 6 o'clock position. Use tool J 6627–A or equivalent to extract the stud from the hub. Do not hammer on the studs to remove, as this could damage the bearing.

To install:

5. Clean the hub and place the replacement stud in the hub.
6. Add enough washers to draw the stud into the hub.
7. Install the lug nut flat side to the washers and tighten until the stud head seats in the hub flange.
8. Remove the nut and washers.
9. Repeat for other studs as required.
10. Install the brake parts and wheel. Tighten the lug nuts to 100 ft. lbs. (140 Nm).
11. Lower the vehicle and recheck the wheel nut torque.

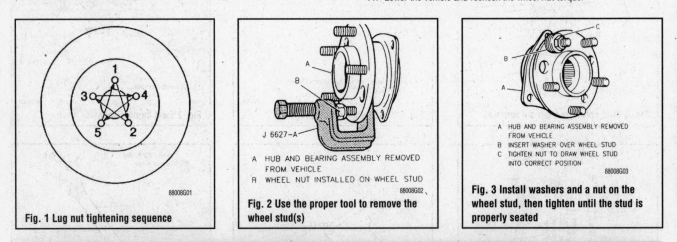

Fig. 1 Lug nut tightening sequence

A HUB AND BEARING ASSEMBLY REMOVED FROM VEHICLE
B WHEEL NUT INSTALLED ON WHEEL STUD

Fig. 2 Use the proper tool to remove the wheel stud(s)

A HUB AND BEARING ASSEMBLY REMOVED FROM VEHICLE
B INSERT WASHER OVER WHEEL STUD
C TIGHTEN NUT TO DRAW WHEEL STUD INTO CORRECT POSITION

Fig. 3 Install washers and a nut on the wheel stud, then tighten until the stud is properly seated

FRONT SUSPENSION

Strut Cartridge

REMOVAL & INSTALLATION

▶ **See Figures 4 thru 10**

➡**During this procedure, the vehicle's weight is used to keep the coil spring from expanding. The front MacPherson strut assembly does**

NOT have to be removed from the vehicle to remove the strut cartridge.

1. Disconnect the negative battery cable.
2. Scribe the strut mount cover plate-to-body to ensure proper camber adjustment when installing.
3. Unfasten the three strut mount cover plate retaining nuts, then remove the cover.
4. Remove the strut shaft nut using a No. 50 Torx® bit and tool J 35669, or equivalent.

5. Remove the strut mount bushing by prying with a suitable prybar. Use tool J 35668 to apply pressure on the strut as necessary to relieve side load (compression) on the bushing.

6. For 1988–92 vehicles, perform the following:

a. Remove the jounce bumper retainer using a jounce bumper spanner wrench tool J35670. Remove the jounce bumper by attaching the strut extension rod J–35668.

b. Install tool J 38844, or equivalent. Use the information shown on the label of the tool to install in the correct position.

c. Compress the shaft down into the cartridge. Remove the extension rod and pull out the jounce bumper.

d. Remove the strut cartridge closure nut by attaching the strut extension rod and re-extending the shaft. Remove the extension rod and unscrew the closure nut using a strut cap nut wrench J–35671 or equivalent.

7. For 1993–96 vehicles, perform the following:

a. Remove the bumper by attaching tool J 35668 or equivalent to the strut and pulling out the bumper.

b. Install tool J 38844, or equivalent. Use the information shown on the label of the tool to install in the correct position.

c. Compress the strut shaft down into the cartridge.

d. Remove the strut cartridge closure nut by unscrewing the closure nut using tool J 35671 or equivalent.

8. Remove the strut cartridge, then remove the oil from the strut tube using a suitable suction device.

To install:

9. Install the self contained replacement cartridge. Secure the closure nut using strut cap nut wrench J–35671, or equivalent. Tighten to 82 ft. lbs. (110 Nm). The cartridge does not need oil added unless specified. If oil is not supplied with the cartridge, add the specified amount of hydraulic jack oil.

10. Install tool J 35668 or equivalent.

11. Remove tool J 38844, or equivalent.

12. Install the jounce bumper and retainer.

13. Raise the strut shaft, then remove tool J 35668.

14. Install the strut mount bushing. Use a soap solution to lubricate the bushing during installation. If necessary, install J 35668 after the bushing is partially installed and position the strut as required to assist in bushing installation.

15. Install the strut shaft nut, using a No. 50 Torx® bit and tool J 35669, then tighten to 72 ft. lbs. (98 Nm) for vehicles through 1994. For 1995–96 vehicles, tighten the shaft nut to 81 ft. lbs. (110 Nm).

16. Align the scribed marks from the strut cover-to-body. Install the strut cover plate and nuts. Tighten the nuts to 18 ft. lbs. (24 Nm) for vehicles through 1994. For 1995–96 vehicles tighten the cover bolts/nuts to 24 ft. lbs. (33 Nm).

17. Connect the negative battery cable and check for proper suspension operation.

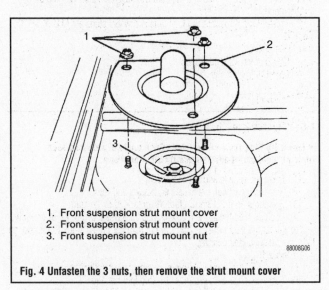

1. Front suspension strut mount cover
2. Front suspension strut mount cover
3. Front suspension strut mount nut

88008G06

Fig. 4 Unfasten the 3 nuts, then remove the strut mount cover

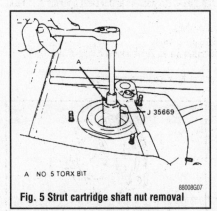

A NO 5 TORX BIT

88008G07

Fig. 5 Strut cartridge shaft nut removal

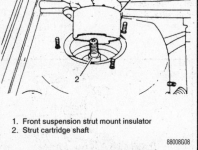

1. Front suspension strut mount insulator
2. Strut cartridge shaft

88008G08

Fig. 6 Strut mount bushing removal

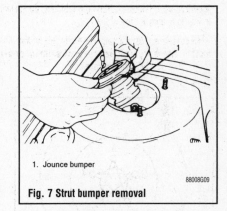

1. Jounce bumper

88008G09

Fig. 7 Strut bumper removal

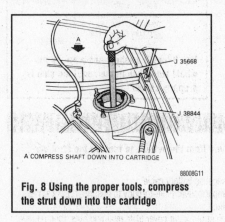

A COMPRESS SHAFT DOWN INTO CARTRIDGE

88008G11

Fig. 8 Using the proper tools, compress the strut down into the cartridge

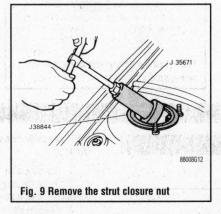

88008G12

Fig. 9 Remove the strut closure nut

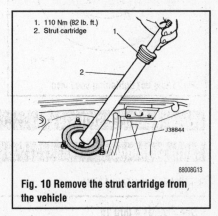

1. 110 Nm (82 lb. ft.)
2. Strut cartridge

88008G13

Fig. 10 Remove the strut cartridge from the vehicle

MacPherson Strut/Knuckle Assembly

REMOVAL & INSTALLATION

▶ See Figures 11, 12 and 13

✷✷ CAUTION

Do NOT remove the strut cartridge nut without compressing the coil spring first. This procedure MUST be followed because it keeps the coil spring compressed. Use care to support the strut assembly adequately because the coil spring is under heavy load; if released too quickly, serious personal injury could result. Never remove the center strut nut unless the spring is compressed with a compressor tool J–26584 or equivalent.

1. Disconnect the negative battery cable.
2. Loosen the strut cover plate bolts.
3. Loosen the wheel nuts. Raise and safely support the vehicle.
4. Remove the wheel assembly and tire assembly. Remove the brake caliper and bracket; hang the caliper aside using a suitable piece of wire. DO NOT hang the caliper by the brake lines.
5. Remove the brake rotor. Remove the hub and bearing-to-knuckle attaching bolts.
6. If equipped with ABS, remove the sensor and position aside.
7. Remove the halfshaft, as outlined in Section 7 of this manual.

✷✷ CAUTION

Use ONLY the recommended tools for separating ball joints. Failure to use the proper tools may cause damage to the ball joint and seal.

8. Unfasten the tie rod attaching nut, then separate the tie rod from the steering knuckle using tool J 35917, or equivalent.
9. Unfasten the lower ball joint attaching nut, then, using tool J 35917 or equivalent, separate the lower ball joint from the lower control arm.
10. Remove the ball joint heat shield retaining bolts and shield.
11. Remove the cover plate bolts/nuts, then remove the strut/knuckle assembly from the vehicle.
To install:
12. Install the strut mount cover plate and upper strut mount-to-body attaching nuts. Do not tighten the nuts at this time; tighten the nuts after lowering the vehicle.
13. Install the ball joint heat shield and retaining bolts. Tighten to 62 inch lbs. (7 Nm).
14. Install the lower ball joint.
15. For 1988–91 vehicles, tighten the new ball joint nut to 15 ft. lbs. (20 Nm) plus at least an additional 90° (1½ flats), plus enough to align the cotter pin hole. Do NOT overtighten!
16. For 1992–96 vehicles, tighten the lower ball joint nut to 63 ft. lbs. (85 Nm). Tighten to align the next slot in the nut with the cotter pin hole in the stud. Do NOT tighten more than 60° (1 flat) to align with the hole.
17. Install a new cotter pin, then bend the ends of the pin over to secure.
18. Install the tie rod to the knuckle, install the nut and tighten to 40 ft. lbs. (54 Nm) for 1988–93 vehicles. For 1994–96 vehicles, tighten the nut to 63 ft. lbs. (85 Nm). Install a new cotter pin.
19. Carefully install the halfshaft through the opening in the knuckle.
20. Install the hub and bearing-to-knuckle attaching bolts. Tighten to 52 ft. lbs. (70 Nm).
21. If equipped, properly position the ABS sensor and install the retaining bolt.
22. Install the brake rotor and caliper/bracket assembly, as outlined in Section 9 of this manual.
23. Install the wheel and tire assembly, then tighten the wheel lug nuts hand-tight.
24. Carefully lower the vehicle.
25. Tighten the strut cover bolts/nuts to 18 ft. lbs. (24 Nm) for 1988–94 vehicles. For 1995–96 vehicles tighten the cover bolts/nuts to 24 ft. lbs. (33 Nm).
26. Final-tighten the wheel lug nuts to 100 ft. lbs. (140 Nm).
27. Connect the negative battery cable.

OVERHAUL

▶ See Figures 11 and 12

✷✷ CAUTION

Do NOT remove the strut cartridge nut without compressing the coil spring first. This procedure MUST be followed because it keeps the coil spring compressed. Use care to support the strut assembly adequately because the coil spring is under heavy load; if released too quickly, serious personal injury could result. Never remove the center strut nut unless the spring is compressed with a compressor tool J–26584 or equivalent.

1. Remove the MacPherson strut assembly as outlined in this section.
2. Mount the strut assembly in a strut compressing tool J–34013–A and J–34013–88. Compress the spring using the forcing screw. Release the spring tension enough to remove the spring insulator.
3. Using a Torx® bit and a strut shaft nut remover tool J–35669, remove the strut shaft nut. Make sure there is no spring tension on the shaft.
4. Release all spring tension and remove the coil spring and insulator. Remove any component needed to perform repair.
To assemble:
5. Inspect all components for wear and damage.
6. Install the spring seat and bearing.
7. Install the lower spring insulator. The lower spring coil end must be visible between the step and the first retention tab of the insulator.
8. Install the spring, dust shield, and jounce bumper.
9. Install the upper spring insulator. The upper spring coil end must be between the step and location mark on the insulator.
10. Install the jounce bumper retainer-to-strut mount using a jounce bumper spanner tool J–35670 or equivalent.
11. Align the strut cartridge shaft with a strut extension rod tool J–35668.
12. Install the strut mount and the upper strut mount bushing.
13. Compress the strut assembly using the strut spring compressor tool J–34013–A and J34013–88.
14. Install the shaft nut using the strut rod installer and Torx® bit. Tighten the shaft nut to 72 ft. lbs. (98 Nm) for 1988–94 vehicles. For 1995–96 vehicles, tighten the shaft nut to 81 ft. lbs. (110 Nm).
15. Install the strut/knuckle assembly into the vehicle as outlined earlier in this section.

Coil Spring

REMOVAL & INSTALLATION

Refer to the strut overhaul procedure for coil spring removal and installation.

Lower Ball Joint

INSPECTION

1. Raise and safely support the vehicle on jackstands. Allow the suspension to hang free.
2. Grasp the tire at the top and the bottom and move the top of the tire in and out.
3. Check for any horizontal movement of the steering knuckle relative to the front lower control arm. If any movement is detected, replace the lower ball joint.
4. If the ball stud is disconnected from the steering knuckle and any looseness is detected, or if the ball stud can be twisted in its socket using finger pressure, replace the ball joint.

REMOVAL & INSTALLATION

▶ See Figure 13

1. Disconnect the negative battery cable.
2. Raise and safely support the vehicle with jackstands.

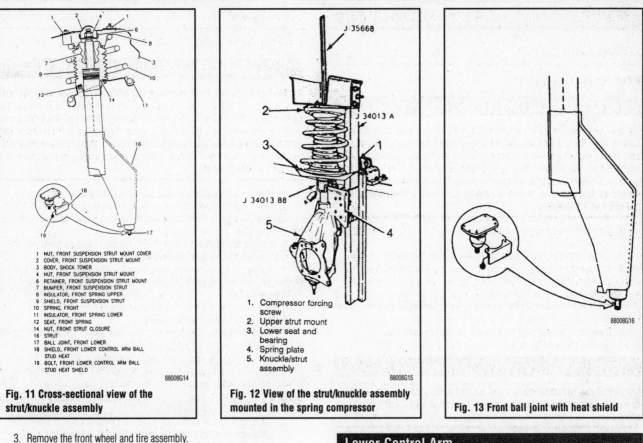

1   NUT, FRONT SUSPENSION STRUT MOUNT COVER
2   COVER, FRONT SUSPENSION STRUT MOUNT
3   BODY, SHOCK TOWER
4   NUT, FRONT SUSPENSION STRUT MOUNT
6   RETAINER, FRONT SUSPENSION STRUT MOUNT
7   BUMPER, FRONT SUSPENSION STRUT
8   INSULATOR, FRONT SPRING UPPER
9   SHIELD, FRONT SUSPENSION STRUT
10 SPRING, FRONT
11 INSULATOR, FRONT SPRING LOWER
12 SEAT, FRONT SPRING
14 NUT, FRONT STRUT CLOSURE
16 STRUT
17 BALL JOINT, FRONT LOWER
18 SHIELD, FRONT LOWER CONTROL ARM BALL
      STUD HEAT
19 BOLT, FRONT LOWER CONTROL ARM BALL
      STUD HEAT SHIELD

88008G14

Fig. 11 Cross-sectional view of the strut/knuckle assembly

1. Compressor forcing screw
2. Upper strut mount
3. Lower seat and bearing
4. Spring plate
5. Knuckle/strut assembly

88008G15

Fig. 12 View of the strut/knuckle assembly mounted in the spring compressor

88008G16

Fig. 13 Front ball joint with heat shield

3. Remove the front wheel and tire assembly.
4. Unfasten the retaining bolts, then remove the ball joint heat shield.
5. Remove and discard the lower ball joint cotter pin.
6. Remove the ball joint nut.
7. Loosen, but do NOT remove, the stabilizer shaft bushing assembly bolts.
8. Separate the ball joint from the strut/knuckle assembly using ball joint/tie rod puller J–35917 or equivalent.

➡**Do NOT damage the halfshaft boots when drilling out the ball joint rivets.**

9. Drill out the rivets retaining the ball joint to the knuckle strut assembly and remove the ball joint from the knuckle. Use a ⅛ in. drill bit to make a pilot hole through the rivets. Finish drilling the rivets with a ½ in. drill bit. Refer to the instructions in the ball joint replacement kit.

To install:

10. Position the lower ball joint in the strut/knuckle assembly.
11. Install the four ball joint bolts and nuts, as shown in the ball joint kit and tighten to specifications.
12. Install the ball joint-to-lower control arm. Install a new ball joint-to-lower control arm nut.
13. Tighten the stabilizer shaft bolts to 35 ft. lbs. (48 Nm).
14. For 1988–91 vehicles, tighten the ball joint-to-lower control arm nut 15 ft. lbs. (20 Nm) plus at least an additional 90° (1½ flats), plus enough to align the cotter pin hole. Do NOT overtighten.
15. For 1992–96 vehicles, tighten the lower ball joint nut to 63 ft. lbs. (85 Nm). Tighten to align the next slot in the nut with the cotter pin hole in the stud. Do NOT tighten more than 60° (1 flat) to align with the hole.
16. Install a new cotter pin.
17. Position the ball joint heat shield and secure with the retaining bolts. Tighten to 62 inch lbs. (7 Nm).
18. Install the front wheel and tire assembly, then carefully lower the vehicle.
19. Connect the negative battery cable and check for proper suspension operation.

Lower Control Arm

REMOVAL & INSTALLATION

▶ **See Figure 14**

1. Disconnect the negative battery cable.
2. Raise and safely support the vehicle with jackstands.
3. Remove the front wheel and tire assembly.
4. For vehicles equipped with 3.4L engines, remove the engine splash shields.
5. Remove the stabilizer shaft-to-lower control arm insulator clamp/bracket bolts.
6. Remove the lower ball joint cotter pin and nut. Discard the cotter pin.
7. Using a ball joint/tie rod puller J–35917 or equivalent, separate the ball joint from the control arm.
8. Unfasten the lower control arm-to-frame bolts and nuts, then remove the control arm. Be careful not to damage the halfshaft boots.

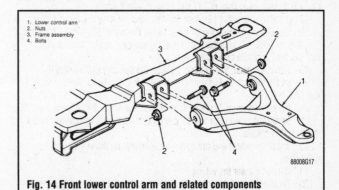

1. Lower control arm
2. Nuts
3. Frame assembly
4. Bolts

88008G17

Fig. 14 Front lower control arm and related components

To install:

9. Install the lower control arm and bolts as shown in the illustration. Do NOT tighten at this time.

10. Install the ball joint to the control arm and install the nut.

11. Tighten the lower control arm-to-frame bolts to 52–56 ft. lbs. (70–75 Nm).

12. For 1988–91 vehicles, tighten the new ball joint nut to 15 ft. lbs. (20 Nm) plus at least an additional 90° (1½ flats), plus enough to align the cotter pin hole. Do NOT overtighten!

13. For 1992–96 vehicles, tighten the lower ball joint nut to 63 ft. lbs. (85 Nm). Tighten to align the next slot in the nut with the cotter pin hole in the stud. Do NOT tighten more than 60° (1 flat) to align with the hole.

14. Install a new cotter pin.

15. Install the stabilizer shaft-to-lower control arm bracket and tighten to 35 ft. lbs. (48 Nm).

16. If removed, install the engine splash shields.

17. Install the front wheel and tire assembly and hand-tighten the lug nuts.

18. Carefully lower the vehicle, then tighten the lug nuts to 100 ft. lbs. (136 Nm).

19. Connect the negative battery cable. Check for proper suspension operation before moving the vehicle.

Front Hub and Bearing

All W-body cars are equipped with sealed hub and bearing assemblies. The hub and bearing assemblies are not serviceable. If the assembly is damaged, the complete unit must be replaced.

REMOVAL & INSTALLATION

▶ **See Figure 15**

1. Disconnect the negative battery cable.

2. Loosen the halfshaft/driveaxle nut and washer one turn. Do NOT remove the nut at this time.

✳✳ WARNING

Do NOT remove the nut at this time. Failure to follow proper removal sequence may cause permanent bearing damage.

3. Raise and safely support the vehicle with jackstands.

4. Remove the front wheel and tire assembly.

5. Remove the brake caliper, bracket and rotor. For details, please refer to

6. Remove the halfshaft/driveaxle nut and washer.

7. Loosen the four hub/bearing-to-knuckle attaching bolts.

➡ **Protect the halfshaft boots from damage during removal.**

8. Using front hub spindle removing tool J-28733–A or equivalent, push the halfshaft splines back out of the hub/bearing assembly.

9. Remove the hub/bearing-to-knuckle attaching bolts.

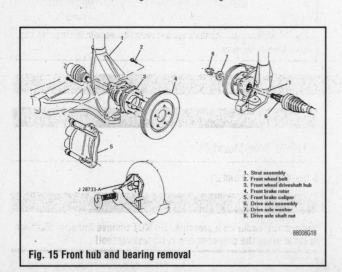

J 28733-A-

1. Strut assembly
2. Front wheel bolt
3. Front wheel driveshaft hub
4. Front brake rotor
5. Front brake caliper
6. Drive axle assembly
7. Drive axle washer
8. Drive axle shaft nut

88008G18

Fig. 15 Front hub and bearing removal

10. If equipped, remove the ABS sensor mounting bolt and position the sensor aside to prevent damage.

11. Remove the hub/bearing assembly from the vehicle. Inspect all components for damage, and replace as necessary.

To install:

12. Position the hub/bearing assembly onto the halfshaft splines.

13. Install the knuckle-to-hub/bearing assembly attaching bolts and tighten to 52 ft. lbs. (70 Nm).

14. If equipped, properly position the ABS sensor and install the mounting bolt.

15. Install the rotor, caliper and bracket assembly, as outlined in Section 9 of this manual.

16. Install a new halfshaft nut and washer. Do NOT tighten the nut at this time.

17. Install the front wheel and tire assembly and hand-tighten the lug nuts.

18. Carefully lower the vehicle.

19. Install a new halfshaft/driveaxle nut and washer and tighten to 184 ft. lbs. (250 Nm).

20. Tighten the wheel lug nuts to 100 ft. lbs. (136 Nm).

21. Connect the negative battery cable.

Stabilizer Shaft and Insulators

REMOVAL & INSTALLATION

1. Disconnect the negative battery cable.

2. Raise and safely support the vehicle with jackstands.

3. Remove the front wheel and tire assembly.

4. If equipped with a 3.4L engine, remove the engine splash shields.

✳✳ CAUTION

Failure to disconnect the intermediate shaft from the rack and pinion stub shaft can result in damage to the steering gear and/or intermediate shaft. This damage can cause loss of steering control which could result in personal injury.

5. Move the steering shaft dust seal for access to the pinch bolt. Refer to the Rack and Pinion procedure in this section.

6. Remove the pinch bolt from the lower intermediate steering shaft.

7. Loosen all the stabilizer insulator clamp attaching nuts and bolts.

8. Place a jackstand under the center of the rear frame crossmember.

9. Loosen the two front frame-to-body bolts (four turns only).

10. Remove the two rear frame-to-body bolts.

11. Carefully lower the rear of the frame just enough to gain access to remove the stabilizer shaft.

12. Remove the insulators and clamps or bracket from the frame and control arms.

13. Pull the stabilizer shaft rearward, swing down and remove from the left side of the vehicle.

To install:

14. Install the stabilizer shaft through the left side of the vehicle.

15. Coat the new insulators with rubber lubricant and install.

16. Loosely install the clamp to the control arm

17. Loosely install the clamp and bracket or bolts to the frame.

18. Tighten the frame nuts to 35 ft. lbs. (47 Nm) on the 28mm and 30mm shafts. Tighten the bracket-to-frame nuts to 27 ft. lbs. (37 Nm) on the 34mm shaft. Tighten the clamp-to-lower control arm bolts to 35 ft. lbs. (47 Nm).

19. Raise the frame into position while guiding the steering gear into place.

20. Install new frame-to-body bolts and tighten to 103 ft. lbs. (140 Nm).

21. Remove the frame jackstand.

➡ **When installing the intermediate shaft, make sure the shaft is seated before pinch bolt installation. If the pinch bolt is inserted into the coupling before shaft installation, the two mating shafts may disengage.**

22. Install the steering gear pinch bolt and the dust seal onto the steering gear.

23. For 3.4L engines, install the engine splash shields.

24. Install the front wheel and tire assembly and hand-tighten the lug nuts.

25. Carefully lower the vehicle, then connect the negative battery cable.

Wheel Alignment

If the tires are worn unevenly, if the vehicle is not stable on the highway or if the handling seems uneven in spirited driving, the wheel alignment should be checked. If an alignment problem is suspected, first check for improper tire inflation and other possible causes. These can be worn suspension or steering components, accident damage or even unmatched tires. If any worn or damaged components are found, they must be replaced before the wheels can be properly aligned. Wheel alignment requires very expensive equipment and involves minute adjustments which must be accurate; it should only be performed by a trained technician. Take your vehicle to a properly equipped shop.

Following is a description of the alignment angles which are adjustable on most vehicles and how they affect vehicle handling. Although these angles can apply to both the front and rear wheels, usually only the front suspension is adjustable.

CASTER

▶ See Figure 16

Looking at a vehicle from the side, caster angle describes the steering axis rather than a wheel angle. The steering knuckle is attached to a control arm or strut at the top and a control arm at the bottom. The wheel pivots around the line between these points to steer the vehicle. When the upper point is tilted back, this is described as positive caster. Having a positive caster tends to make the wheels self-centering, increasing directional stability. Excessive positive caster makes the wheels hard to steer, while an uneven caster will cause a pull to one side. Overloading the vehicle or sagging rear springs will affect caster, as will raising the rear of the vehicle. If the rear of the vehicle is lower than normal, the caster becomes more positive.

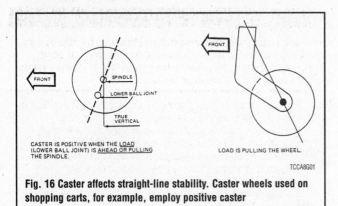

Fig. 16 Caster affects straight-line stability. Caster wheels used on shopping carts, for example, employ positive caster

CAMBER

▶ See Figure 17

Looking from the front of the vehicle, camber is the inward or outward tilt of the top of wheels. When the tops of the wheels are tilted in, this is negative camber; if they are tilted out, it is positive. In a turn, a slight amount of negative

REAR SUSPENSION

▶ See Figure 19

The rear suspension features a lightweight composite fiberglass mono-leaf transverse spring. Each wheel is mounted to a tri-link independent suspension system. The three links consist of an inverted U-channel trailing arm and tubular front and rear rods. Some late model vehicles may also utilize a coil spring.

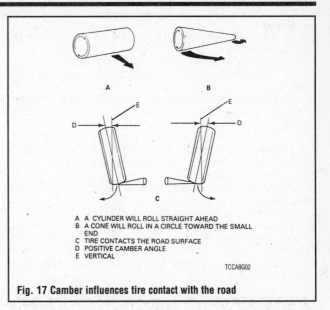

A A CYLINDER WILL ROLL STRAIGHT AHEAD
B A CONE WILL ROLL IN A CIRCLE TOWARD THE SMALL END
C TIRE CONTACTS THE ROAD SURFACE
D POSITIVE CAMBER ANGLE
E VERTICAL

Fig. 17 Camber influences tire contact with the road

camber helps maximize contact of the tire with the road. However, too much negative camber compromises straight-line stability, increases bump steer and torque steer.

TOE

▶ See Figure 18

Looking down at the wheels from above the vehicle, toe angle is the distance between the front of the wheels, relative to the distance between the back of the wheels. If the wheels are closer at the front, they are said to be toed-in or to have negative toe. A small amount of negative toe enhances directional stability and provides a smoother ride on the highway.

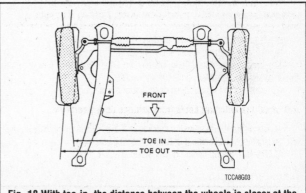

Fig. 18 With toe-in, the distance between the wheels is closer at the front than at the rear

Coil Spring

REMOVAL & INSTALLATION

▶ See Figures 20 and 21

✳ CAUTION

Springs are under high pressure. DO NOT remove the strut shaft nut without using the proper spring compressing tool!

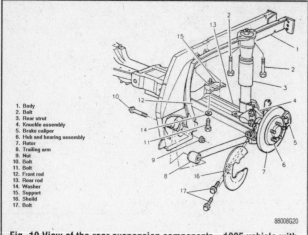

1. Body
2. Bolt
3. Rear strut
4. Knuckle assembly
5. Brake caliper
6. Hub and bearing assembly
7. Rotor
8. Trailing arm
9. Nut
10. Bolt
11. Bolt
12. Front rod
13. Rear rod
14. Washer
15. Support
16. Sheild
17. Bolt

88008G20

Fig. 19 View of the rear suspension components—1995 vehicle with rear disc brakes shown

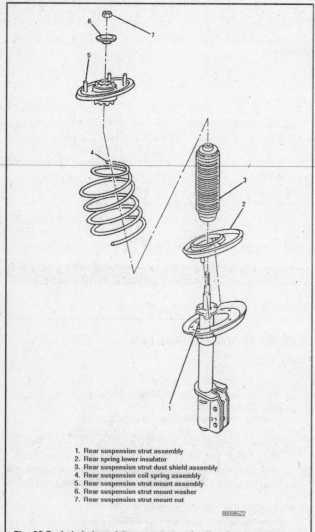

1. Rear suspension strut assembly
2. Rear spring lower insulator
3. Rear suspension strut dust shield assembly
4. Rear suspension coil spring assembly
5. Rear suspension strut mount assembly
6. Rear suspension strut mount washer
7. Rear suspension strut mount nut

88008G22

Fig. 20 Exploded view of the rear strut and coil spring assembly

1. Disconnect the negative battery cable.
2. Remove the strut assembly from the vehicle, as outlined in this section.
3. Mount the strut in spring compressing tools J 34013-B and J 34013-88 or equivalents. Compress the spring using the forcing screw just enough to release the tension from the strut mount.

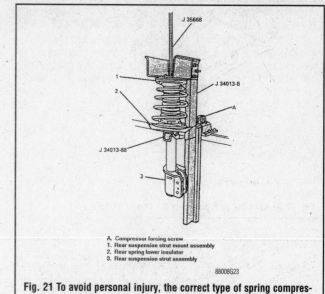

A. Compressor forcing screw
1. Rear suspension strut mount assembly
2. Rear spring lower insulator
3. Rear suspension strut assembly

88008G23

Fig. 21 To avoid personal injury, the correct type of spring compressor MUST be used

4. Remove the strut shaft nut using the proper size Torx® bit and tool J 35669, or equivalent.
5. Relieve all spring tension.
6. Remove the spring and strut components.
7. Inspect all components for wear and/or damage and replace, as necessary.

To install:

8. Assembly the rear spring insulator. The lower spring coil end must be visible between the step and the first retention tab of the insulator.
9. Install the rear suspension coil spring.
10. Fasten the dust shield to the lower insulator.
11. Install the jounce bumper.
12. Install the strut mount. The upper spring coil end must be between the step and location mark on the strut mount.
13. Align the strut shaft with tool J 35668 or equivalent.
14. Compress the strut assembly with tools J 34013-B and J 34018-88 or equivalent.
15. Pull the strut shaft through the strut mount and remove tool J 35668.
16. Install the strut mount washer and strut mount using tool J 35669 and the proper size Torx® bit. Tighten the strut mount nut to 72 ft. lbs. (98 Nm).
17. Install the strut assembly in the vehicle.
18. Connect the negative battery cable.

Transverse Spring Assembly

REMOVAL & INSTALLATION

▶ **See Figures 22, 23, 24, 25 and 26**

※ CAUTION

Do NOT disconnect any rear suspension components until the transverse spring has been compressed using a rear spring compressor tool J–35778 or equivalent. Failure to follow this procedure may result in personal injury. Wear protective eye equipment when working on the suspension.

➡ Do not use any corrosive cleaning agents, silicone lubricants, engine degreasers, solvents, etc. on or near the rear transverse fiberglass spring. These materials may cause spring strength depletion and consequent damage.

1. Disconnect the negative battery cable.
2. Raise and safely support the vehicle with jackstands.
3. Remove the jack pad from the middle of the spring.

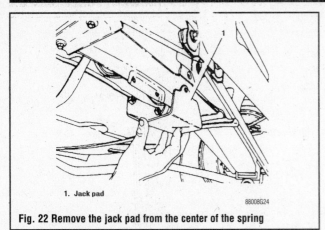

1. Jack pad

88008G24

Fig. 22 Remove the jack pad from the center of the spring

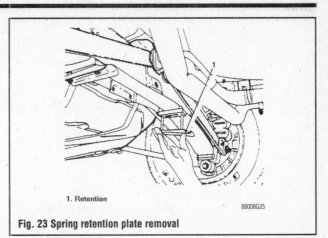

1. Retention

88008G25

Fig. 23 Spring retention plate removal

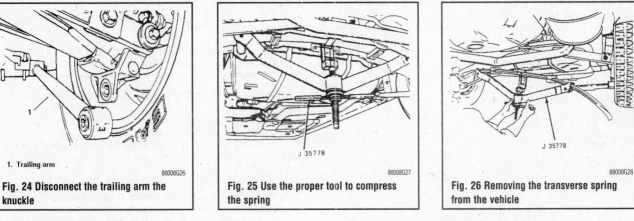

1. Trailing arm

88008G26

Fig. 24 Disconnect the trailing arm the knuckle

J 35778

88008G27

Fig. 25 Use the proper tool to compress the spring

J 35778

88008G28

Fig. 26 Removing the transverse spring from the vehicle

4. If equipped with dual exhaust, remove the exhaust system.
5. Remove the spring retention plates.
6. Disconnect the right trailing arm from the knuckle.
7. If equipped, detach the ABS electrical harness.
8. Separate the rear leaf spring compressor tool J–35778 from the center shank and hang the center shank of the tool at the spring center.

✳✳ CAUTION

Attach the center shank of the compressor from the front side of the vehicle only.

9. Install the compressor body to the center shank and spring. Center the spring on the rollers of the spring compressor only.
10. Fully compress the spring using the spring compressor tool J–35778.
11. Slide the spring to the left side. It may be necessary to pry the spring to the left using a prybar against the right knuckle. When prying, be careful not to damage any components.
12. Relax the spring to provide removal clearance from the right side, then remove the spring.

To install:

13. Using the spring compressor tool, compress the spring and install it through the left knuckle. Slide towards the left side as far as possible and raise the right side of the spring as far as possible.
14. Compress the spring fully and install it into right knuckle.

➡ **The rear spring retention plates are designed with tabs on one end. The tabs must be aligned with the support assembly to prevent damage to the fuel tank.**

15. Center the spring to align the holes for the spring retention plate bolts.
16. Install the spring retention plates and bolts. Do NOT tighten at this time.
17. Position the trailing arm and install the bolt. Tighten the bolt to 192 ft. lbs. (260 Nm) for vehicles through 1994. For 1995–96, tighten the bolt to 177 ft. lbs. (240 Nm).
18. Remove the spring compressor tool J35778.

19. Tighten the spring retention plate bolts to 15 ft. lbs. (20 Nm) for 1988–94 vehicles or to 22 ft. lbs. (30 Nm) for 1995–96 vehicles.
20. Install the jack pads and tighten the bolts to 18 ft. lbs. (25 Nm).
21. Carefully lower the vehicle, then tighten the lug nuts to 100 ft. lbs. (136 Nm).
22. Connect the negative battery cable.

Rear Strut Assembly

REMOVAL & INSTALLATION

Except 1995–96 Lumina and Monte Carlo

▶ **See Figure 27**

1. Disconnect the negative battery cable.
2. Raise and safely support the vehicle with jackstands.
3. Remove the rear wheel and tire assembly.
4. Scribe the strut-to-knuckle for proper installation.
5. If equipped, remove the auxiliary spring, as outlined in this section.
6. Remove the jack pad.
7. Install rear leaf spring compressor tool J–35778, or equivalent. Refer to the Transverse Spring Assembly procedures in this section for installation details.
8. Fully compress the spring, but do NOT remove the retention plates or the spring.
9. Unfasten the two strut-to-body bolts.
10. Remove the brake hose bracket from the strut.
11. Remove the strut and auxiliary spring upper bracket from the knuckle.

To install:

12. Position the strut to the body and knuckle bracket.
13. Install the strut-to-body bolts and tighten to 34 ft. lbs. (46 Nm).
14. Install the strut to the knuckle, aligning the scribe marks and tighten the bolts to 133 ft. lbs. (180 Nm) for 1988–94 vehicles. For 1995–96 vehicles, tighten the bolts to 122 ft. lbs. (165 Nm).

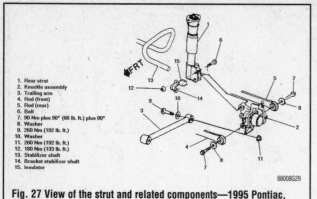

1. Rear strut
2. Knuckle assembly
3. Trailing arm
4. Rod (front)
5. Rod (rear)
6. Bolt
7. 90 Nm plus 90° (66 lb. ft.) plus 90°
8. Washer
9. 260 Nm (192 lb. ft.)
10. Washer
11. 260 Nm (192 lb. ft.)
12. 180 Nm (133 lb. ft.)
13. Stabilizer shaft
14. Bracket stabilizer shaft
15. Insulator

88008G29

Fig. 27 View of the strut and related components—1995 Pontiac, Oldsmobile and Buick shown

15. Install the brake hose bracket.
16. Remove the spring compressing tool.
17. Install the jack pad and tighten the retaining bolts to 18 ft. lbs. (25 Nm).
18. If equipped, install the auxiliary spring.
19. Install the wheel and tire assembly and install the lug nuts finger-tighten
20. Carefully lower the vehicle, then tighten the lug nuts to 100 ft. lbs. (136 Nm).
21. Connect the negative battery cable.

1995–96 Lumina and Monte Carlo

▶ See Figure 28

1. Disconnect the negative battery cable.
2. Raise and safely support the vehicle with jackstands.
3. Remove the rear wheel and tire assembly.
4. Scribe the strut-to-knuckle for proper installation.
5. Remove the brake hose bracket from the strut.
6. Unfasten the strut mount-to-body nuts.
7. Remove the strut/stabilizer shaft bracket from the knuckle.

To install:

8. Position the strut assembly in the vehicle and tighten the strut mount-to-body nuts. Tighten to 37 ft. lbs. (50 Nm).
9. Fasten the strut/stabilizer shaft bracket to the knuckle. Align the scribe marks to ensure proper alignment. Tighten the nuts to 122 ft. lbs. (165 Nm).
10. Install the brake hose bracket.
11. Install the wheel and tire assembly and install the lug nuts finger-tight.
12. Carefully lower the vehicle, then tighten the lug nuts to 100 ft. lbs. (136 Nm).
13. Connect the negative battery cable.

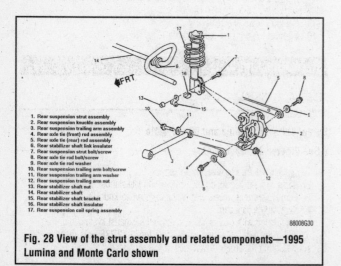

1. Rear suspension strut assembly
2. Rear suspension knuckle assembly
3. Rear suspension trailing arm assembly
4. Rear axle tie (front) rod assembly
5. Rear axle tie (rear) rod assembly
6. Rear stabilizer shaft link insulator
7. Rear suspension strut bolt/screw
8. Rear axle tie rod bolt/screw
9. Rear axle tie rod washer
10. Rear suspension trailing arm bolt/screw
11. Rear suspension trailing arm washer
12. Rear suspension trailing arm nut
13. Rear stabilizer shaft nut
14. Rear stabilizer shaft
15. Rear stabilizer shaft bracket
16. Rear stabilizer shaft insulator
17. Rear suspension coil spring assembly

88008G30

Fig. 28 View of the strut assembly and related components—1995 Lumina and Monte Carlo shown

OVERHAUL

Except 1995–96 Lumina and Monte Carlo

The rear strut assembly is not serviceable. The assembly is replaced as a complete unit.

1995–96 Lumina and Monte Carlo

▶ See Figures 29 and 30

This procedure requires the following tools:
- J 34013-B Strut Spring Compressor
- J 34013-20 Damper Rod Clamp
- J 34013-38 Alignment Rod
- J 34013-88 Strut Compressor Adapter
- J 34013-125 Mounting Adapter
- J 34013-218 Module Shock Support
- J 35669 Strut Rod Nut Remover and Installer

1. Remove the strut assembly from the vehicle, as outlined earlier.
2. Install tool J 34013-125 mounting adapter to tool J 34013-B spring compressor. Use the wing nuts to secure the tool to mounting holes C and E/K. The wide end of the adapter should be positioned outboard.

➡ **Be sure tools J 34013-125 and J 34013-88 are aligned so they can open and close together. If the tools are not aligned properly, they will not open.**

3. Install module shock support J 34013-218 and strut compressor adapter J 34013-88.
4. Install the strut assembly to the top of spring compressor J 34013-B. The angle of the upper strut should match the angle of tool J 34013-125.
5. Close tool J 34013-218 and J 34013-88 and install the locking pin through the lower hole of J 34013-B and lower knuckle mounting hole of the strut.

➡ **Only one pin can be used for mounting.**

6. Turn the screw on J 34013-B counterclockwise to raise the strut assembly up to J 34013-125. Be sure the studs go through the guide holes in J 34013-125 and the top of the strut assembly is flat against the tool.
7. Compress the spring approximately 0.50 in. (13mm) or 3 or 4 complete turns of the operating screw on tool J 34013-125.

✳✳ CAUTION

Do NOT over compress the spring assembly. Severe overloading may cause tool failure which could result in bodily injury.

8. Insert strut rod nut remover and installer J 35699 on the nuts, then insert J 34013-38 or a No. 50 Torx® bit into the end of the shaft.
9. Remove the nut with J 35669 while holding the rod from rotating with J 34013-38 or a Torx® bit.
10. Discard the strut nut.
11. Turn the operating screw on J 34013-B clockwise to fully relieve spring assembly compression.

To assemble:

12. Install J 34013-125 to J 34013-B. Use the wing nuts to secure the tool to the mounting holes C and E/K. The wide end of the adapter should be positioned outboard.

➡ **Be sure tools J 34013-125 and J 34013-88 are aligned so they can open and close together. If the tools are not aligned properly, they will not open.**

13. Install J 34013-218 and J 34013-88.
14. Install the strut assembly to tools J 34013-218 and J 34013-88.
15. Close tool J 34013-218 and J 34013-88 and install the locking pin through the lower hole of J 34013-B and lower knuckle mounting hole of the strut.

➡ **Only one pin can be used for mounting.**

16. Install the strut assembly on top of J 34013-B. The angle of the upper strut should match the angle of J 34013-125. Be sure the top of the shock absorber assembly is flat tool J 34013-125. The shock absorber assembly will not be aligned correctly if it does not lay flat against the tool.
17. Install the spring and all other components to the strut. Make sure the upper and lower spring seats are positioned correctly.

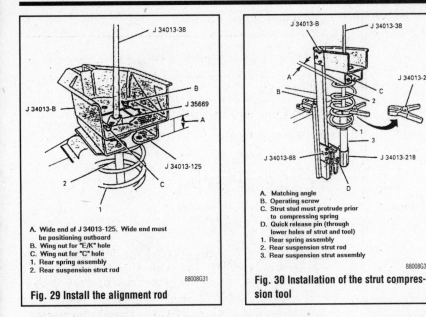

A. Wide end of J 34013-125. Wide end must
   be positioning outboard
B. Wing nut for "E/K" hole
C. Wing nut for "C" hole
1. Rear spring assembly
2. Rear suspension strut rod

88008G31

Fig. 29 Install the alignment rod

A. Matching angle
B. Operating screw
C. Strut stud must protrude prior
   to compressing spring
D. Quick release pin (through
   lower holes of strut and tool)
1. Rear spring assembly
2. Rear suspension strut rod
3. Rear suspension strut assembly

88008G32

Fig. 30 Installation of the strut compression tool

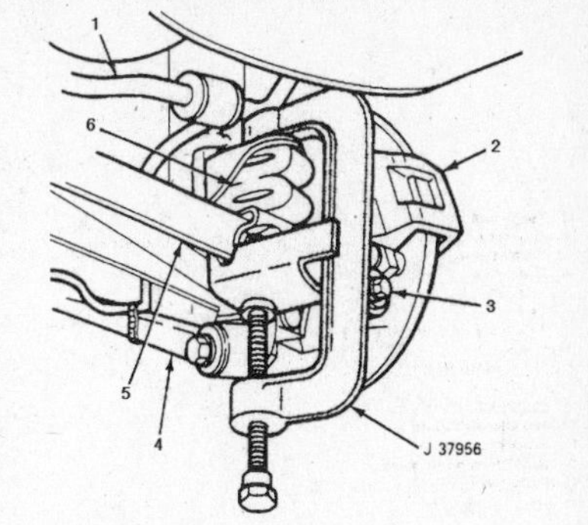

1. Stabilizer shaft
2. Caliper assembly
3. 90 Nm + 90o (66 lb. ft.)
4. Trailing arm
5. Spindle rod (rear)
6. Auxiliary spring

88008G33

Fig. 31 Some vehicles, such as 1995 Oldsmobiles and Buicks, utilize an auxiliary spring

18. Rotate the spring and spring seats together until the angled top matches the angle of the bottom surfaces of tool J 34013-125.

➡ **Be sure the top of the strut assembly is flat against tool J 34013-125. The strut assembly will not be aligned properly if it does not lay flat against the tool.**

19. Turn the operating screw to J 34013-B counterclockwise to raise the strut assembly up to J 34013-125 without compressing the spring assembly. Be sure the studs on the strut assembly go through the guide holes in J 34013-125.

20. Fully extend the strut shaft and attach tool J 34013-20. this prevents the shaft from retracting during compression.

21. Place J 34013-38 down through the top of J 34013-B through the top of the strut assembly and onto the shaft.

➡ **Make sure tool J 34013-38 is straight with the strut assembly. If J 34013-38 is angled, repeat steps 19–21 until the tool is straight.**

22. Slowly turn the operating screw clockwise to compress the spring assembly until the threaded portion of the strut shaft is through the top of the strut assembly.

✳✳ CAUTION

Do NOT over compress the spring assembly. Severe overloading may cause tool failure which could result in bodily injury.

23. Install a new strut nut on the strut rod. Do not turn the strut rod when tightening the strut nut or the strut assembly could be damaged. Keep the strut rod in a stationary position when tightening the strut nut.

24. Place tool J 35669 on the shock absorber nut.

25. Insert tool J 34013-38 through J 35669 and tighten the shock absorber nut.

26. Tighten the shock absorber nut while holding onto tool J 35669. Tighten to 55 ft. lbs. (75 Nm).

27. Remove tools J34013-20, J 34013-38, and J 35669 from J 34013-B.

28. Remove the strut assembly from tool J 34013-B.

29. Install the strut assembly in the vehicle.

Auxiliary Spring

REMOVAL & INSTALLATION

Oldsmobile and Buick Only

▶ **See Figure 31**

1. Disconnect the negative battery cable.
2. Raise and safely support the vehicle with jackstands.

3. Unfasten the leaf spring rear retention plate bolt.

4. Loosen the leaf spring front retention plate bolt just enough to rotate the plate clear of the rod.

➡ **Do not use silicone lubricants on or near the auxiliary spring. These materials may damage or deteriorate rubber components.**

5. Install tool J 37956 or equivalent, making sure the pin in the stationary end of the clamp is inserted in the hole of the upper auxiliary spring bracket. Remove the plug from the upper bracket.

6. Seat the rod in the tool channel and hand-tighten.

7. Remove the rod-to-knuckle bolt.

8. Loosen tool J 37956 forcing screw to allow the spring to expand.

➡ **When removing the auxiliary spring, make sure that the rod/bushing clears the transverse spring and boss on the knuckle.**

9. Remove the auxiliary spring and the spring compressor tool.

To install:

10. Install the auxiliary spring and the spring compressor tool.

11. Compress the auxiliary spring using J 37956 enough to install the rod-to-knuckle bolt. Make sure the pin in the stationary end of the clamp is inserted in the hole of the upper auxiliary spring bracket and the rod is seated in the tool channel. When compressing the auxiliary spring, make sure that the rod/bushing clears the transverse spring and boss on the knuckle.

12. Coat the threads of the rod-to-knuckle bolt with GM sealer 1052624 or equivalent, then install the bolt. Tighten the bolt to 177 ft. lbs. (240 Nm).

13. Remove tool J 37956 and install the plug.

14. Properly position the retention plate and install the retaining bolt. Tighten the bolt to 15 ft. lbs. (20 Nm).

15. Carefully lower the vehicle.

16. Connect the negative battery cable.

Rear Knuckle

REMOVAL & INSTALLATION

Except 1995–96 Lumina and Monte Carlo

▶ **See Figures 27, 32 and 33**

1. Disconnect the negative battery cable.
2. Raise and safely support the vehicle with jackstands.
3. Remove the rear wheels and scribe the strut-to-knuckle.
4. Remove the jack pad.
5. If equipped with dual exhaust, remove the exhaust system.
6. Install the rear leaf spring compressor tool J–35778 as outlined in the Transverse Spring Assembly procedures in this section.

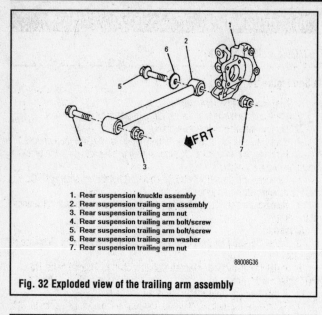

1. Rear suspension knuckle assembly
2. Rear suspension trailing arm assembly
3. Rear suspension trailing arm nut
4. Rear suspension trailing arm bolt/screw
5. Rear suspension trailing arm bolt/screw
6. Rear suspension trailing arm washer
7. Rear suspension trailing arm nut

88008G36

Fig. 32 Exploded view of the trailing arm assembly

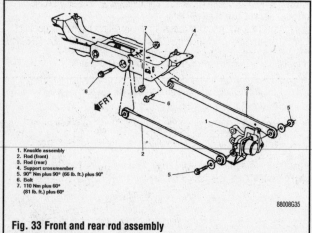

1. Knuckle assembly
2. Rod (front)
3. Rod (rear)
4. Support crossmember
5. 90° Nm plus 90° (66 lb. ft.) plus 90°
6. Bolt
7. 110 Nm plus 60° (81 lb. ft.) plus 60°

88008G35

Fig. 33 Front and rear rod assembly

7. Fully compress the spring but do not remove the spring or retention plates.

8. Remove the auxiliary spring, if so equipped. If not equipped, remove the rod-to-knuckle bolt.

9. Remove the front rod from the knuckle.

10. Remove the brake hose bracket, caliper and rotor. Do not allow the caliper to hang by the brake hose.

11. If equipped, detach the ABS electrical harness.

12. Remove the hub and bearing assembly.

13. Separate the trailing arm from the knuckle.

14. Remove the strut/upper auxiliary spring bracket from the knuckle.

15. Remove the knuckle.

To install:

16. Install the knuckle and position it to the strut/upper auxiliary spring bracket.

17. Hand-start the bolts, but do not tighten.

18. Coat the threads of the rod-to-knuckle bolt with GM 1052624 or equivalent. Install the front rod to the knuckle and snug the bolt.

19. Attach the trailing arm to the knuckle. Tighten the trailing arm bolt and nut to 192 ft. lbs. (260 Nm) for 1988–94 vehicles. For 1995–96 vehicles tighten the bolts and/or nut to 66 ft. lbs. (90 Nm) plus a 75° rotation.

20. Install the hub/bearing assembly and tighten the bolts to 52 ft. lbs. (70 Nm).

21. If equipped, attach the ABS electrical harness.

22. Install the rotor and caliper.

23. Align the scribe marks to ensure proper alignment. Tighten the strut-to-knuckle attaching bolts to 133 ft. lbs. (180 Nm) for vehicles through 1994. For 1995–96 vehicles, tighten the bolts to 122 ft. lbs. (165 Nm).

24. Install the brake hose bracket.

25. Remove the rear leaf spring compressor.

26. If removed, install the exhaust system.

27. Install the jack pad. Tighten the retaining bolt to 18 ft. lbs. (25 Nm).

28. Install the auxiliary spring (if equipped) and rod-to-knuckle bolt. Apply thread locking compound to the knuckle bolts.

29. Tighten the rod-to-knuckle bolts to 66 ft. lbs. (90 Nm) plus 90° for 1988–94 vehicles. For 1995–96 vehicles, tighten the bolts to 177 ft. lbs. (240 Nm).

30. Install the wheel and tire assembly and install the lug nuts finger-tight.

31. Carefully lower the vehicle, then tighten the lug nuts to 100 ft. lbs. (136 Nm).

32. Connect the negative battery cable.

1995–96 Lumina and Monte Carlo

▶ **See Figures 28, 32 and 34**

1. Disconnect the negative battery cable.

2. Raise and safely support the vehicle with jackstands.

3. Remove the rear wheels and scribe the strut-to-knuckle.

4. Remove the rear rod-to-knuckle bolt/screw.

5. Detach the front rod at the knuckle bolt/screw.

6. Remove the brake hose bracket and drum.

7. On vehicles with the police package only, remove the brake hose bracket, caliper and rotor.

8. If equipped, detach the ABS electrical harness.

9. Remove the hub and bearing assembly and the brake assembly,.

10. Disconnect the trailing arm from the knuckle.

11. Remove the strut/stabilizer shaft bracket from the knuckle.

12. Remove the knuckle from the vehicle.

To install:

13. Install the knuckle.

14. Fasten the strut/stabilizer shaft bracket to the knuckle and hand-start the nuts.

15. Coat the threads of the rod-to-knuckle bolt with GM 1052624 or equivalent. Install the front rod to the knuckle and snug the bolt.

16. Attach the trailing arm to the knuckle. Tighten the bolts/screws to 66 ft. lbs. (90 Nm) plus an additional 75° rotation.

17. Install the hub and bearing assembly and the brake assembly. Tighten the bolts/screws to 52 ft. lbs. (70 Nm).

18. If equipped, attach the ABS electrical harness.

19. On vehicles with the police package only, install the rotor and caliper. Install the brake drum for all other vehicles.

20. Align the scribe marks to ensure proper alignment. Tighten the strut-to-stabilizer shaft attaching bolts to 122 ft. lbs. (165 Nm).

21. Install the brake hose bracket.

22. Coat the threads of the rod-to-knuckle bolt/screw using thread locker 1052624 or equivalent. Tighten to 177 ft. lbs. (240 Nm).

23. Install the wheel and tire assembly and install the lug nuts finger-tight.

24. Carefully lower the vehicle, then tighten the lug nuts to 100 ft. lbs. (136 Nm).

25. Connect the negative battery cable.

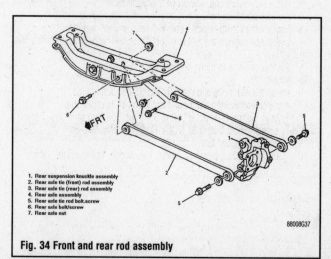

1. Rear suspension knuckle assembly
2. Rear axle tie (front) rod assembly
3. Rear axle tie (rear) rod assembly
4. Rear axle assembly
5. Rear axle tie rod bolt.screw
6. Rear axle bolt/screw
7. Rear axle nut

88008G37

Fig. 34 Front and rear rod assembly

Tri-Link Suspension Assembly

REMOVAL & INSTALLATION

Trailing Arm

▶ **See Figures 28 and 32**

1. Raise and safely support the vehicle with jackstands.
2. If equipped, detach the ABS electrical harness.
3. Unfasten the trailing arm-to-knuckle nut and bolt/screw.
4. Remove the trailing arm-to-body nut, bolt, then remove the arm itself.

To install:

5. Install the trailing arm to the underbody.
6. Install the trailing arm-to-body nut and bolt/screw Do NOT tighten at this time.
7. Install the trailing arm-to-knuckle nut and bolt/screw.
8. Tighten the arm-to-knuckle bolt to 192 ft. lbs. (260 Nm) for 1988–94 vehicles. For 1995–96 vehicles, tighten the bolt to 66 ft. lbs. (90 Nm) plus an additional 75° rotation.
9. Tighten the arm-to-body bolt to 48 ft. lbs. (65 Nm) for 1988–94 vehicles. For 1995–96 vehicles, tighten the bolt to 44 ft. lbs. (60 Nm), plus an additional 90° rotation.
10. If equipped, attach the ABS electrical harness.
11. Carefully lower the vehicle and recheck all repair procedures.

Rear Rod

▶ **See Figures 28 and 34**

1. Raise and safely support the vehicle with jackstands.
2. Remove the rear wheel and tire assembly.
3. Remove the auxiliary spring, if so equipped. If not equipped, remove the rod-to-knuckle bolt.
4. Remove the lower auxiliary spring bracket at the rod, if so equipped.
5. Scribe the toe adjusting cam, remove the rod-to-crossmember bolt and the rod itself.

To install:

6. Install the rod, push the bolt through the rod bushing and install the adjusting cam in its original location. Do not tighten at this time.
7. Install the lower auxiliary spring bracket-to-rod, if so equipped. Tighten the nut to 133 ft. lbs. (180 Nm).
8. Install the rod-to-knuckle with thread locking compound. Do not tighten.
9. Install the rear wheels and lower the vehicle.
10. Tighten the rod-to-knuckle bolt to 66 ft. lbs. (90 Nm) plus 90°. Tighten the rod-to-crossmember bolt to 81 ft. lbs. (110 Nm) plus 60°.
11. Have a qualified alignment technician adjust the rear toe.

Front Rod

▶ **See Figures 28 and 34**

1. Raise the vehicle and support with jackstands.
2. Remove the rear wheels.
3. Remove the rod-to-knuckle bolt and exhaust pipe heat shield.
4. Lower and support the fuel tank just enough for access to the bolt at the frame.
5. Remove the rod-to-frame bolt and the rod itself.

To install:

6. Install the rod, bolts and nuts. Do not tighten at this time.
7. Apply thread locking compound to the rod-to-knuckle bolt.
8. Tighten the rod-to-knuckle bolt to 66 ft. lbs. (90 Nm) plus 90°. Tighten the rod-to-crossmember bolt to 81 ft. lbs. (110 Nm) plus 60°.
9. Reposition the fuel tank.
10. Install the exhaust pipe heat shield, rear wheels and lower the vehicle.

Stabilizer Shaft

REMOVAL & INSTALLATION

▶ **See Figure 35**

1. Disconnect the negative battery cable.
2. Raise and safely support the vehicle with jackstands.
3. Remove the wheel and tire assembly.
4. Scribe the relation of the strut to the knuckle for installation purposes.
5. Remove the right and left stabilizer shaft link bolts and open the brackets to remove the insulators.
6. Remove the right and left strut-to-knuckle-to-stabilizer shaft nuts. Do NOT remove the strut-to-knuckle bolts.
7. Remove the stabilizer shaft by prying the shaft on one side for clearance at the strut.

To install:

8. Install the stabilizer shaft by prying the shaft on one side for clearance at the strut.
9. Install the insulator brackets-to-stabilizer shaft-to-knuckle bolts. Do NOT tighten at this time.
10. Install the right and left stabilizer shaft link bolts.
11. Tighten the link bolts to 40 ft. lbs. (54 Nm) and the knuckle bolts to 133 ft. lbs. (180 Nm) for 1988–94 vehicles. For 1995–96 vehicles, tighten the knuckle bolts to 122 ft. lbs. (165 Nm).
12. Install the wheel and tire assembly and install the lug nuts finger-tight.
13. Carefully lower the vehicle, then tighten the lug nuts to 100 ft. lbs. (136 Nm).
14. Connect the negative battery cable.

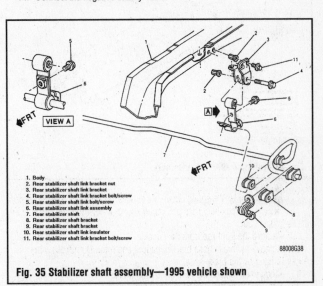

1. Body
2. Rear stabilizer shaft link bracket nut
3. Rear stabilizer shaft link bracket
4. Rear stabilizer shaft link bracket bolt/screw
5. Rear stabilizer shaft link bolt/screw
6. Rear stabilizer shaft link assembly
7. Rear stabilizer shaft
8. Rear stabilizer shaft bracket
9. Rear stabilizer shaft bracket
10. Rear stabilizer shaft link insulator
11. Rear stabilizer shaft link bracket bolt/screw

88008G38

Fig. 35 Stabilizer shaft assembly—1995 vehicle shown

Hub/Bearing Assembly

▶ **See Figure 36**

All W-body cars are equipped with sealed hub and bearing assemblies. The hub and bearing assemblies are not serviceable. If the assembly is damaged, the complete unit must be replaced.

REMOVAL & INSTALLATION

1. Disconnect the negative battery cable.
2. Raise and safely support the vehicle with jackstands.

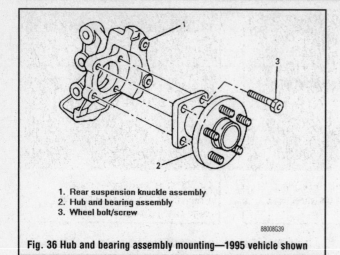

1. Rear suspension knuckle assembly
2. Hub and bearing assembly
3. Wheel bolt/screw

88008G39

Fig. 36 Hub and bearing assembly mounting—1995 vehicle shown

3. Remove the rear wheel and tire assembly.
4. If equipped with rear disc brakes, remove the caliper, bracket and rotor.
5. If equipped with rear drum brakes, remove the brake hose bracket and drum.
6. If equipped, detach the ABS electrical harness.
7. Unfasten the four hub/bearing-to-knuckle attaching bolts, then remove the hub/bearing assembly.
To install:
8. Install the hub/bearing assembly onto the knuckle. Install the four attaching bolts and tighten to 52 ft. lbs. (70 Nm).
9. If equipped attach the ABS electrical harness.
10. Install the rotor, caliper and bracket or drum and bracket, as applicable.
11. Install the wheel and tire assembly and install the lug nuts finger-tight.
12. Carefully lower the vehicle, then tighten the lug nuts to 100 ft. lbs. (136 Nm).
13. Connect the negative battery cable.

Rear Wheel Alignment

Refer to Wheel Alignment earlier in this section for precautions and explanations of important alignment angles, which also pertain to the rear wheels.

STEERING

Steering Wheel

REMOVAL & INSTALLATION

Vehicles Without Air Bags

▶ **See Figures 37 thru 44**

1. If necessary to access the battery, remove the air cleaner assembly.
2. Disconnect the negative battery cable.
3. Remove the horn pad and retainer along with any other switches that are mounted to the steering wheel.
4. Disconnect the horn electrical lead from the canceling cam tower.
5. Turn the ignition switch to the **ON** position.
6. Scribe an alignment mark on the steering wheel hub in line with the slash mark on the steering shaft.
7. Remove the retainer.
8. Loosen the steering shaft nut, positioning it flush with the end of the shaft.
9. Assemble steering wheel puller J 1859-03 or equivalent, on the steering wheel hub with two 5/16–18x4 in. bolts. Break the steering wheel loose from the shaft.
10. Remove the steering wheel puller.
11. Remove the steering shaft nut.
12. For 2.5L engines, remove the steering wheel vibration diameter.
13. Remove the steering wheel from the vehicle.
To install:
14. Align the matchmarks on the wheel hub and shaft and install the steering wheel.
15. For 2.5L engines, install the steering wheel vibration damper.

16. Tighten the steering wheel retaining nut to 30 ft. lbs. (41 Nm). Install the retainer
17. Attach the horn electrical lead.
18. Install the horn pad and/or any controls located on the steering wheel.
19. Connect the negative battery cable.
20. If removed, install the air cleaner assembly.

88008P01

Fig. 37 Steering wheel assembly—1992 Lumina shown

88008P02

Fig. 38 Remove the horn pad by gently pulling it off

88008P03

Fig. 39 Gently push down on the horn lead and turn left to remove the wire and spring

88008P04

Fig. 40 Remove the retaining circlip

Fig. 41 Unfasten the steering wheel nut, until it is flush with the end of the shaft

Fig. 42 Assemble a suitable steering wheel puller and break the wheel loose from the shaft

Fig. 43 When installing the steering wheel, make sure the align the marks made during removal

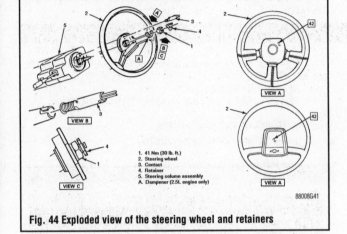

1. 41 Nm (30 lb. ft.)
2. Steering wheel
3. Contact
4. Retainer
5. Steering column assembly
A. Dampener (2.5L engine only)

Fig. 44 Exploded view of the steering wheel and retainers

Vehicles With Air Bags

♦ See Figures 45 and 46

✳✳ WARNING

On vehicles with air bags, disable the SIR system. The vehicles wheels must be in the straight ahead position and the key must be in the LOCK position when removing or installing the steering column. Failure to do so may cause the SIR coil assembly to become uncentered and may result in otherwise unneeded SIR repairs.

1. Disconnect the negative battery cable.
2. Properly disable the SIR system, as outlined in Section 6 of this manual.

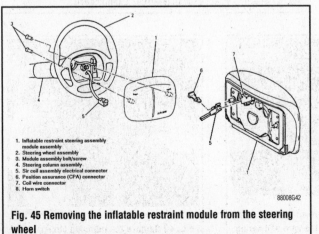

1. Inflatable restraint steering assembly module assembly
2. Steering wheel assembly
3. Module assembly bolt/screw
4. Steering column assembly
5. Sir coil assembly electrical connector
6. Position assurance (CPA) connector
7. Coil wire connector
8. Horn switch

Fig. 45 Removing the inflatable restraint module from the steering wheel

3. Make sure the ignition is in the OFF position.

✳✳ CAUTION

When carrying a live air bag, make sure the bag and trim cover are pointed away from the body. In the unlikely event of an accidental deployment, the bag will then deploy with minimal chance of injury. In addition, when placing a live air bag on a bench or other surface. always face the bag and the trim cover up, away from the surface. This will reduce the chance of personal injury if it is accidentally deployed.

4. Remove the air bag inflator module, as follows:
   a. Loosen the bolts or screws from the back of the steering wheel, using the proper Torx® driver, until the inflatable restraint module can be released from the steering wheel.
   b. While pulling the module away from the steering wheel, detach the SIR coil electrical connector and remove the retainer from the module.
   c. Remove the horn and ground lead from the steering column.
5. Scribe an alignment mark on the steering wheel hub in line with the slash mark on the steering shaft.
6. Loosen the steering wheel nut, positioning it flush with the end of the shaft.

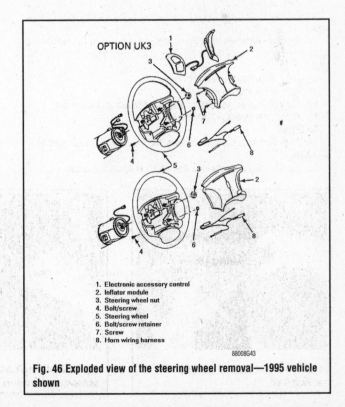

OPTION UK3

1. Electronic accessory control
2. Inflator module
3. Steering wheel nut
4. Bolt/screw
5. Steering wheel
6. Bolt/screw retainer
7. Screw
8. Horn wiring harness

Fig. 46 Exploded view of the steering wheel removal—1995 vehicle shown

7. Assemble steering wheel puller J 1859-03 or equivalent, on the steering wheel hub with two ⁵⁄₁₆–18x4 in. bolts. Break the steering wheel loose from the shaft.

8. Remove the steering wheel puller.

9. Remove the steering shaft nut.

10. Remove the steering wheel from the vehicle.

To install:

11. Route the SIR connector through the steering wheel.

12. Align the scribe mark on the steering wheel with the slash mark on the steering shaft and install the steering wheel.

13. Install the steering shaft nut and tighten to 30 ft. lbs. (41 Nm).

14. Install the air bag inflator module, as follows:

   a. Connect the horn and ground lead to the column assembly.

   b. Attach the SIR coil assembly-electrical connector and retainer to the module.

   c. Secure the SIR coil assembly electrical connector to the steering wheel assembly by inserting the thick section of wire into the existing retainer.

   d. Position the air bag inflator module to the steering wheel. Make sure the wiring is not exposed or trapped between the inflatable restraint module and the steering wheel assembly.

   e. Install the retaining bolts/screws. Tighten to 25 inch lbs. (2.8 Nm).

15. Connect the negative battery cable, then enable the SIR system, as outlined in Section 6 of this manual.

Turn Signal Switch

REMOVAL & INSTALLATION

1988–93 Buick, Oldsmobile and Pontiac and 1988–94 Chevrolet

▶ See Figures 47 and 48

➡ Tool No. J35689A or equivalent, is required to remove the terminals from the connector on the turn signal switch.

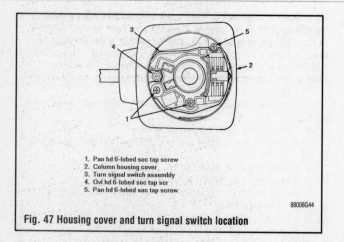

1. Pan hd 6-lobed soc tap screw
2. Column housing cover
3. Turn signal switch assembly
4. Ovl hd 6-lobed soc tap scr
5. Pan hd 6-lobed soc tap screw

88008G44

Fig. 47 Housing cover and turn signal switch location

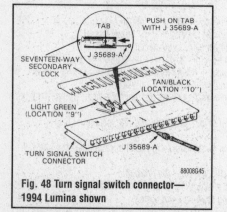

88008G45

Fig. 48 Turn signal switch connector—1994 Lumina shown

1. Disconnect the negative battery cable.

2. Remove the steering wheel, as outlined earlier in this section.

3. Pull the turn signal canceling cam assembly from the steering shaft.

4. Remove the hazard warning knob-to-steering column screw and the knob.

➡ **Before removing the turn signal assembly, position the turn signal lever so the turn signal assembly to steering column screws can all be removed.**

5. Remove the column housing cover-to-column housing bowl screw and the cover. If equipped with cruise control, unplug the cruise control electrical connector.

6. Remove the turn signal lever-to-pivot assembly screw and the lever; one screw is in the front and one is in the rear.

7. Using the terminal remover tool No. J 35689A or equivalent, label and unplug the wires **F** and **G** on the connector at the buzzer switch assembly from the turn signal switch electrical harness connector.

8. Remove the turn signal switch-to-steering column screws and remove the switch.

To install:

9. Install the turn signal switch to the steering column, and tighten the turn signal switch-to-steering column screws.

10. Attach the electrical connectors, and install the turn signal lever to the pivot assembly.

11. Install the hazard flasher knob. Install the canceling cam.

12. Install the steering wheel and column cover.

13. Connect the negative battery cable and check for proper operation.

1994–96 Vehicles, Except 1994 Lumina

▶ See Figures 49, 50, 51, 52 and 53

✳✳ WARNING

On vehicles with air bags, disable the SIR system. The vehicles wheels must be in the straight ahead position and the key must be in the LOCK position when removing or installing the steering column. Failure to do so may cause the SIR coil assembly to become uncentered and may result in otherwise unneeded SIR repairs.

1. Disconnect the negative battery cable.

2. If equipped, disable the SIR system, as outlined in Section 6 of this manual.

3. Remove the steering wheel, as outlined earlier in this section.

4. Remove the SIR coil assembly retaining ring.

5. Remove the SIR coil assembly. Let the coil hang freely if removal is not needed.

6. Remove the wave washer.

7. Remove the shaft lock retaining ring using tool J 23653-SIR to push down the shaft lock. Discard the ring.

8. Remove the shaft lock, turn signal canceling cam assembly and upper bearing spring.

9. Remove the upper bearing inner race seat, then remove the inner race.

10. Remove the multi-function lever, as follows:

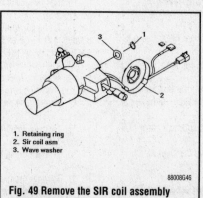

1. Retaining ring
2. Sir coil asm
3. Wave washer

88008G46

Fig. 49 Remove the SIR coil assembly from the shaft

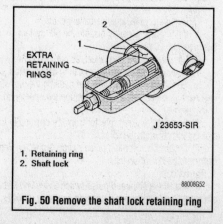

J 23653-SIR

1. Retaining ring
2. Shaft lock

88008G52

Fig. 50 Remove the shaft lock retaining ring

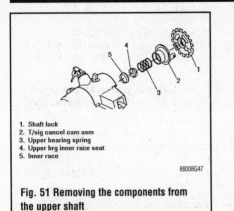

1. Shaft lock
2. T/sig cancel cam asm
3. Upper bearing spring
4. Upper brg inner race seat
5. Inner race

88008G47

Fig. 51 Removing the components from the upper shaft

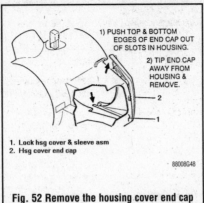

1) PUSH TOP & BOTTOM EDGES OF END CAP OUT OF SLOTS IN HOUSING.

2) TIP END CAP AWAY FROM HOUSING & REMOVE.

1. Lock hsg cover & sleeve asm
2. Hsg cover end cap

88008G48

Fig. 52 Remove the housing cover end cap

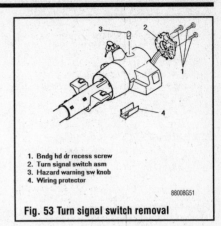

1. Bndg hd dr recess screw
2. Turn signal switch asm
3. Hazard warning sw knob
4. Wiring protector

88008G51

Fig. 53 Turn signal switch removal

a. Make sure the lever is in the center or **OFF** position.
b. Detach the electrical connection behind the lever.
c. Pull the lever straight out.

11. Remove the housing cover end cap. Using fingers, pry up and out at the location shown in the accompanying figure. Tilt the end cap away from the lock housing cover and sleeve assembly then remove.

12. Unfasten the round washer head screw and the flat head screw.

13. Remove the pivot and pulse dimmer switch assembly. Let the switch hang freely if removal is not needed.

14. Using a suitable prytool, carefully pry off the hazard warning switch knob.

15. Place the turn signal in the right turn position (up).

16. Unfasten the three binding head cross recess screws.

17. Remove the turn signal switch, as follows:
a. Detach the turn signal connector from the bulkhead.
b. Remove the wiring protector.
c. Gently pull the wire harness through the column and remove the switch.

18. Installation is the reverse of the removal procedure.

19. Connect the negative battery cable, then enable the SIR system, as outlined in Section 6 of this manual.

Windshield Wiper Switch

REMOVAL & INSTALLATION

The wiper switch is controlled by the multi-function turn signal lever but the actual switch is located in the steering column. For dash-mounted switch removal, please refer to Section 6 of this manual.

❈❈ WARNING

On vehicles with air bags, disable the SIR system. The vehicles wheels must be in the straight ahead position and the key must be in the LOCK position when removing or installing the steering column. Failure to do so may cause the SIR coil assembly to become uncentered and may result in otherwise unneeded SIR repairs.

1. Disconnect the negative battery cable.
2. If equipped, properly disable the SIR system, as outlined in Section 6 of this manual.
3. Remove the steering wheel, as outlined earlier in this section.
4. Remove the turn signal canceling cam assembly.
5. Remove the hazard knob and position the turn signal lever so the housing cover screw can be removed through the opening in the switch. Remove the housing cover.
6. Remove the wire protector from the opening in the instrument panel bracket and separate the wires.
7. Detach the pivot and pulse switch connector. Remove the pivot switch connector and pivot switch.

To install:
8. Install the pivot and pulse switch assembly. Install the wiring protector around the instrument panel opening, covering all wires.

9. Install the steering column housing cover and tighten the screws to 35 inch lbs. (4 Nm).

10. Install the hazard knob and lubricate the bottom side of the canceling cam with lithium grease.

11. Install the steering wheel, as outlined earlier in this section.

12. Connect the negative battery cable.

13. If equipped, properly enable the SIR system, as outlined in Section 6 of this manual.

14. Check steering column operations.

Ignition Switch/Lock Cylinder

REMOVAL & INSTALLATION

♦ **See Figures 54, 55 and 56**

❈❈ WARNING

On vehicles with air bags, disable the SIR system. The vehicles wheels must be in the straight ahead position and the key must be in the LOCK position when removing or installing the steering column. Failure to do so may cause the SIR coil assembly to become uncentered and may result in otherwise unneeded SIR repairs.

1. Disconnect the negative battery cable.
2. If equipped, properly disable the SIR system, as outlined in Section 6 of this manual.
3. Remove the left side lower trim panel.
4. Remove the steering column-to-support screws and lower the steering column.
5. Unplug the dimmer switch and turn signal switch connectors.
6. Remove the wiring harness-to-firewall nuts.
7. Remove the steering column-to-steering gear bolt and remove the steering column from the vehicle.
8. Remove the combination switch.
9. Place the lock cylinder in the **RUN** position.
10. Remove the steering shaft assembly and turn signal switch housing as an assembly.
11. Using the terminal remover tool No. J 35689A or equivalent, label and unplug the wires **F** and **G** on the connector at the buzzer switch assembly from the turn signal switch electrical harness connector.
12. With the lock cylinder in the **RUN** position, remove the buzzer switch.
13. Place the lock cylinder in the **ACCESSORY** position, remove the lock cylinder retaining screw, and remove the lock cylinder.
14. Remove the dimmer switch nut/bolt, the dimmer switch, and the actuator rod.
15. Remove the dimmer switch mounting stud (the mounting nut was attached to it).
16. Remove the ignition switch-to-steering column screws and the ignition switch.
17. Remove the lockbolt screws and the lockbolt.
18. Remove the switch actuator rack and ignition switch.
19. Remove the steering shaft lock and spring.

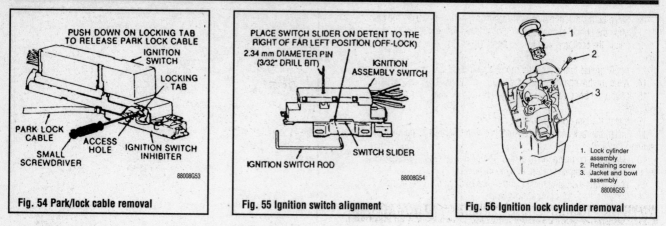

Fig. 54 Park/lock cable removal

Fig. 55 Ignition switch alignment

Fig. 56 Ignition lock cylinder removal

To install:

20. To install the lockbolt, lubricate it with lithium grease and install the lockbolt, spring and retaining plate.

21. Lubricate the teeth on the switch actuator rack, install the rack and the ignition switch through the opening in the steering bolt until it rests on the retaining plate.

22. Install the steering column lock cylinder set by holding the barrel of the lock cylinder, inserting the key and turning the key to the **ACCESSORY** position.

23. Install the lock set in the steering column while holding the rack against the lockplate.

24. Install the lock retaining screw. Insert the key in the lock cylinder and turn the lock cylinder to the **START** position and the rack will extend.

25. Center the slotted holes on the ignition switch mounting plate and install the ignition switch mounting screw and nut.

26. Install the dimmer switch and actuator rod into the center slot on the switch mounting plate.

27. Install the buzzer switch and turn the lock cylinder to the **RUN** position. Push the switch in until it is bottomed out with the plastic tab that covers the lock retaining screw.

28. Install the steering shaft and turn signal housing as an assembly.

29. Install the turn signal switch. Install the steering wheel to the column, and tighten the steering shaft nut to 30 ft. lbs. (41 Nm).

30. Install the steering column in the vehicle. Connect all electrical leads. Install the lower trim panels.

31. Connect the negative battery cable.

32. If equipped, properly enable the SIR system, as outlined in Section 6 of this manual.

33. Check steering column operations.

Steering Linkage

REMOVAL & INSTALLATION

Outer Tie Rod Ends

▶ **See Figure 57**

1. Disconnect the negative battery cable.

2. Remove the cotter pin and hex slotted nut from the outer tie rod assembly. Discard the cotter pin.

3. Loosen the jam nut and remove the tie rod from the steering knuckle using a steering linkage removing tool J–35917 or equivalent.

4. Holding the inner tie rod stationary, count the amount of turns to remove the outer tie rod.

To install:

5. Lubricate the inner rod threads with anti-seize compound and install the outer tie rod the same amount of turns that it took to remove.

6. Install the outer tie rod-to-knuckle and install the slotted nut. Tighten the nut to 40 ft. lbs. (54 Nm); 45 ft. lbs. (60 Nm) maximum to align the cotter pin slot. Do NOT back off to align the cotter pin.

7. Install a new cotter pin.

8. Tighten the jam nut to 50 ft. lbs. (70 Nm) and connect the negative battery cable.

9. Have a qualified alignment technician adjust the toe angle.

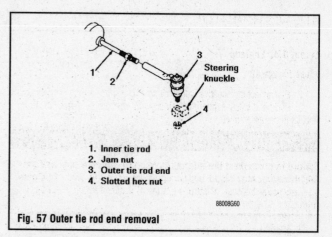

1. Inner tie rod
2. Jam nut
3. Outer tie rod end
4. Slotted hex nut

Fig. 57 Outer tie rod end removal

Inner Tie Rod

▶ **See Figure 58**

1. Disconnect the negative battery cable.

2. Remove the rack and pinion assembly from the vehicle as outlined in this section.

3. Remove the outer tie rod end as previously outlined.

4. Remove the jam nut, boot clamps and boot. Use side cutters to cut the boot clamps.

5. Remove the shock dampener from the inner tie rod and slide back on the rack. Do not let the rack slide out of the rack housing while the tie rods are moved.

6. Place suitable wrenches on the flats of the rack and inner tie rod assemblies.

7. Rotate the housing counterclockwise until the inner rod separates from the rack.

To install:

8. Install the inner tie rod end onto the rack and tighten to 70 ft. lbs. (95 Nm) with suitable wrenches.

9. Support the rack assembly in a vise.

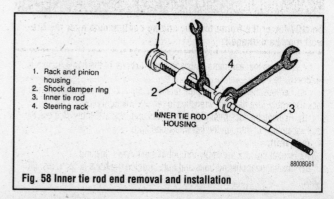

1. Rack and pinion housing
2. Shock damper ring
3. Inner tie rod
4. Steering rack

Fig. 58 Inner tie rod end removal and installation

10. Stake both sides of the inner tie rod housing to the flats on the rack.

11. Slide the shock dampener over the housing until it engages.

12. Install the boot and new boot clamps. Do NOT tighten the clamps at this time.

13. Apply grease to the inner tie rod, housing and boot.

14. Align the breather tube with the boot, making sure it is not twisted.

15. Crimp the boot clamps with a keystone clamp pliers tool J-22610 or equivalent.

16. Install the jam nut and outer tie rod end.

17. Install the rack and pinion assembly into the vehicle as outlined in this section.

18. Recheck each operation to ensure completion of repair. Make sure all fasteners have been tighten before moving the vehicle.

19. Have a qualified alignment technician adjust the front toe angle.

Power Rack and Pinion Steering Gear

REMOVAL & INSTALLATION

Except 3.4L Engines

♦ See Figure 59

1. Disconnect the negative battery cable.

2. Raise and safely support the vehicle with jackstands. Remove the front wheel and tire assemblies.

> ✳✳ **CAUTION**
>
> **Failure to disconnect the intermediate shaft from the rack and pinion stub shaft may result in damage to the steering gear. This damage may cause a loss of steering control and may cause personal injury.**

3. Remove the intermediate shaft lower pinch bolt at the steering gear (end of the steering column shaft).

> ✳✳ **WARNING**
>
> **Set the steering shaft so the block tooth on the upper steering shaft is at the 12 o'clock position, wheels on the vehicle are straight ahead and set the ignition switch to the LOCK position. Failure to follow these procedures could result in damage to the coil assembly.**

4. Remove the intermediate shaft from the stub shaft.

> ✳✳ **WARNING**
>
> **Use only the recommended tools for separating the tie rod ends from the knuckle/strut assembly. Failure to use the recommended tools may cause damage to the tie rod and seal.**

5. Remove both tie rod ends from the knuckle using a tie rod puller tool J–35917 or equivalent.

6. Support the vehicle body with jackstands so that the frame assembly can be lowered.

> ✳✳ **WARNING**
>
> **Do NOT lower the frame too far; engine components near the fire-wall may be damaged.**

7. Remove the rear frame bolts and lower the rear of the frame up to 5 in. (128mm).

8. Remove the heat shield, pipe retaining clip and the fluid pipes from the rack assembly. Use flare nut wrenches to remove the fluid pipes.

9. Remove the rack mounting bolts, nuts and rack assembly. Remove the rack assembly out through the left wheel opening.

To install:

10. Install the rack assembly through the left wheel opening.

11. Install the mounting bolts and nuts. Tighten the bolts to 59 ft. lbs. (80 Nm).

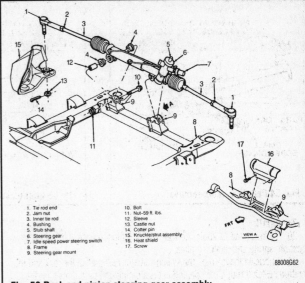

1. Tie rod end
2. Jam nut
3. Inner tie rod
4. Bushing
5. Stub shaft
6. Steering gear
7. Idle speed power steering switch
8. Frame
9. Steering gear mount
10. Bolt
11. Nut–59 ft. lbs.
12. Sleeve
13. Castle nut
14. Cotter pin
15. Knuckle/strut assembly
16. Heat shield
17. Screw

88008G62

Fig. 59 Rack and pinion steering gear assembly

12. Install the fluid pipes with new O-rings using flare nut wrenches. Tighten the fittings to 20 ft. lbs. (27 Nm).

13. Install the pipe retaining clips and heat shield. Tighten the heat shield screws to 54 inch lbs. (6 Nm).

14. Raise the frame and install the rear bolts. Tighten the rear bolts to 103 ft. lbs. (140 Nm).

15. Install the tie rod ends and retaining nut. Tighten the nuts to 40 ft. lbs. (54 Nm). Install a new cotter pin.

> ✳✳ **WARNING**
>
> **When installing the steering column to the intermediate shaft, make sure that the shaft is seated before pinch bolt installation. If the bolt is inserted into the coupling before shaft installation, the two mating shafts may disengage. Set the steering shaft so the block tooth on the upper steering shaft is at the 12 o'clock position, wheels on the vehicle are straight ahead and set the ignition switch to the LOCK position. Failure to follow these procedures could result in damage to the coil assembly.**

16. Install the intermediate shaft-to-stub shaft. Tighten the lower pinch bolt to 40 ft. lbs. (54 Nm).

17. Install the front wheel and tire assemblies, then carefully lower the vehicle.

18. Fill the power steering pump with GM steering fluid or its equivalent.

19. Bleed the power steering system as outlined later in this section.

20. Connect the negative battery cable.

21. Inspect the system for leaks.

22. Have a qualified alignment technician adjust the front toe angle.

3.4L Engines

1. Remove the air cleaner and duct assembly.

2. Disconnect the negative battery cable.

3. Install tools J 28467-A, J 28467-90 and J 36462, or equivalent engine support fixtures.

4. Raise and safely support the vehicle.

5. Remove the left wheel and tire assembly.

6. Loosen the right side engine splash shield.

7. Remove both tie rod ends from the knuckle using a tie rod puller tool J–35917 or equivalent.

> ✳✳ **CAUTION**
>
> **Failure to disconnect the intermediate shaft from the rack and pinion stub shaft may result in damage to the steering gear. This damage may cause a loss of steering control and may cause personal injury.**

8. Remove the intermediate shaft lower pinch bolt at the steering gear (end of the steering column shaft).

❊❊ WARNING

Set the steering shaft so the block tooth on the upper steering shaft is at the 12 o'clock position, wheels on the vehicle are straight ahead and set the ignition switch to the LOCK position. Failure to follow these procedures could result in damage to the coil assembly.

9. Detach the electrical connection from the steering gear pressure switch.
10. Remove the exhaust pipe and catalytic converter assembly.
11. Using jackstands, securely support the frame. Unfasten the frame retaining bolts, then carefully lower the frame 3 in. (76mm).
12. Unfasten the steering gear heat shield screws, then remove the heat shield.
13. Remove the power steering line clamp from the steering gear.
14. Unfasten the steering gear bolts.
15. Disconnect and plug the pressure and return lines from the steering gear.
16. Remove the steering gear through the left wheel opening.
17. Replace the stud shaft shields.

To install:
18. Install the rack assembly through the left wheel opening.
19. Unplug and connect the pressure and return lines to the steering gear.
20. Install the steering gear bolts and tighten to 59 ft. lbs. (80 Nm).
21. Fasten the power steering line clamp at the steering gear.
22. Install the steering gear heat shield and secure with the retaining screws. Tighten the screws to 54 inch lbs. (6 Nm).
23. Raise the frame assembly and align the steering gear stub shaft to the intermediate steering shaft.
24. Install the frame retaining bolts and tighten to 125 ft. lbs. (170 Nm). Remove the jackstands supporting the frame.
25. Install the exhaust pipe and catalytic converter assembly.
26. Attach the electrical connection to the steering gear pressure switch.

❊❊ WARNING

When installing the steering column to the intermediate shaft, make sure that the shaft is seated before pinch bolt installation. If the bolt is inserted into the coupling before shaft installation, the two mating shafts may disengage. Set the steering shaft so the block tooth on the upper steering shaft is at the 12 o'clock position, wheels on the vehicle are straight ahead and set the ignition switch to the LOCK position. Failure to follow these procedures could result in damage to the coil assembly.

27. Install the intermediate steering shaft pinch bolt at the steering gear. Tighten the bolt to 35 ft. lbs. (47 Nm).
28. Install the both tie rod ends, as outlined earlier in this section.
29. Tighten the right side engine splash shield.
30. Install the left tire and wheel assembly.
31. Carefully lower the vehicle.
32. Remove the engine support fixtures. Connect the negative battery cable, then install the air cleaner and duct assembly.
33. Bleed the power steering system, as outlined later in this section.

ADJUSTMENT

Rack Bearing Preload

▶ See Figure 60

➡ Make the adjustment with the front wheels raised and centered. Make sure to check the returnability of the steering wheel to center after the adjustment.

1. Loosen the adjuster plug locknut and turn the adjuster plug clockwise until it bottoms in the housing, then back off 50 to 70 degrees (about one flat).
2. Tighten the locknut on the adjuster plug. Hold the adjuster plug in place while tightening.

Power Steering Pump

REMOVAL & INSTALLATION

2.2L Engine

▶ See Figures 61 and 62

1. Disconnect the negative battery cable.
2. Remove the serpentine drive belt.
3. Place a suitable drain pan under the pump, then disconnect the pressure pipe from the pump.
4. Unfasten the hose clamp, then disconnect the return hose from the reservoir.
5. Remove the pump mounting bolts. They are accessible through the holes in the pulley.
6. Unfasten the pump mounting bolt from the rear of the pump, then remove the pump from the vehicle.
7. If installing a new pump, transfer the pulley from the old pump to the new one.

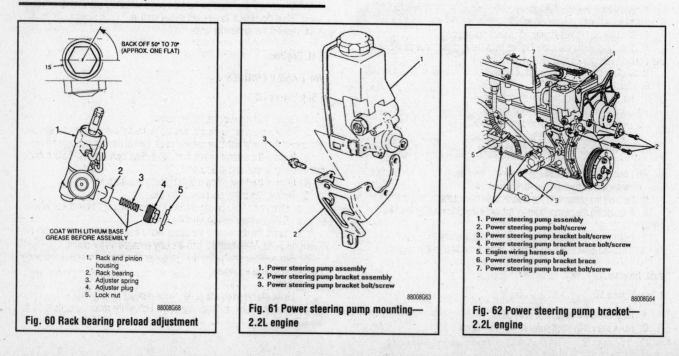

Fig. 60 Rack bearing preload adjustment

Fig. 61 Power steering pump mounting— 2.2L engine

Fig. 62 Power steering pump bracket— 2.2L engine

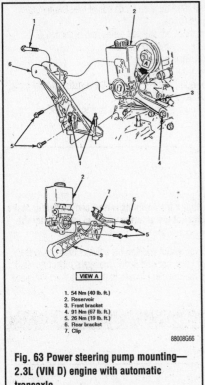

Fig. 63 Power steering pump mounting—
2.3L (VIN D) engine with automatic
transaxle

VIEW A

1. 54 Nm (40 lb. ft.)
2. Reservoir
3. Front bracket
4. 91 Nm (67 lb. ft.)
5. 26 Nm (19 lb. ft.)
6. Rear bracket
7. Clip

88008G66

Fig. 64 Power steering pump mounting—
2.3L (VIN A) engine with manual transaxle

VIEW A

1. 54 Nm (40 lb. ft.)
2. Reservoir
3. Front bracket
4. 91 Nm (67 lb. ft.)
5. 26 Nm (19 lb. ft.)
6. Rear bracket
7. Clip

88008G67

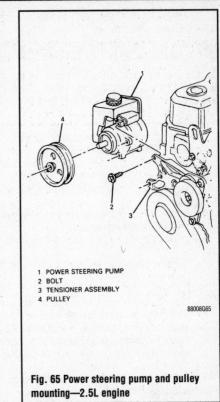

1. POWER STEERING PUMP
2. BOLT
3. TENSIONER ASSEMBLY
4. PULLEY

88008G65

Fig. 65 Power steering pump and pulley
mounting—2.5L engine

To install:
8. Position the pump to the vehicle.
9. Install the front pump mounting bolt and tighten to 25 ft. lbs. (34 Nm).
10. Install the rear pump mounting bolt and tighten to 22 ft. lbs. (30 Nm).
11. Connect the return hose to the reservoir and secure with the clamp.
12. Attach the pressure pipe to the pump.
13. Install the serpentine drive belt.
14. Connect the negative battery cable.
15. Fill and bleed the power steering system. Check for fluid leaks.

2.3L Engine

♦ **See Figures 63 and 64**

1. Disconnect the negative battery cable.
2. Remove the air cleaner assembly.
3. Remove the left side tighten strut from the engine.
4. Separate the throttle cable bracket from the engine torque strut bracket and position it aside. Do NOT remove the cables.
5. Remove the engine torque strut bracket.
6. Disconnect the lines.
7. For VIN D engines, perform the following:
   a. Unfasten the rear bracket-to-pump bolts.
   b. Remove the drive belt and position aside.
   c. remove the rear bracket-to-transaxle bolts.
8. For VIN A engines, perform the following:
   a. Loosen the drive belt.
   b. Remove the rear bracket.
   c. Remove the front bracket-to-engine bolt.
9. Remove the pump with the bracket from the vehicle.
10. If replacing the pump, transfer the pulley and bracket to the new pump.
11. Installation is the reverse of the removal procedure.
12. Bleed the power steering system, as outlined later in this section.

2.5L Engine

♦ **See Figure 65**

1. Disconnect the negative battery cable.
2. Raise the vehicle and support with jackstands.

3. Place a drain pan under the pump and remove the inlet and outlet lines from the pump.
4. Lower the vehicle.
5. Remove the ECM heat shield cover.
6. Remove the serpentine belt by loosening the automatic tensioner as outlined in Section 1.
7. Remove the three pump retaining bolts and pump.

To install:
8. If required, transfer the pulley using the proper tools. Install the pump and bolts. Tighten the retaining bolts to 20 ft. lbs. (27 Nm).
9. Install the serpentine belt and ECM heat shield.
10. Raise the vehicle and support with jackstands.
11. Install the inlet and outlet hoses to the pump.
12. Lower the vehicle and connect the negative battery cable.
13. Bleed the system as outlined in this section.
14. Inspect the system for leaks.

3.1L Engines

VIN T AND V ENGINES

♦ **See Figure 66**

1. Disconnect the negative battery cable.
2. Place a drain pan under the steering pump and remove the inlet and outlet hoses at the pump with flare nut wrenches. Do not damage the hose fittings.
3. Remove the serpentine belt from the pulleys by loosening the automatic belt tensioner as outlined in Section 1.
4. Remove the three pump mounting bolts and the pump.
5. Remove the pump reservoir as follows.
   a. Using a suitable prybar, remove the retaining clips from the reservoir.
   b. Separate the reservoir from the pump.
   c. Install the reservoir to the pump with a new O-ring seal and install the retaining clip. Make sure the tabs are fully engaged on the pump.
6. Remove the pump pulley using a power steering pump pulley removing tool J–25034–B or equivalent.
   To install:
7. Install the reservoir and pulley to the pump.
8. Install the pump and retaining bolts. Tighten the retaining bolts to 20 ft. lbs. (27 Nm).

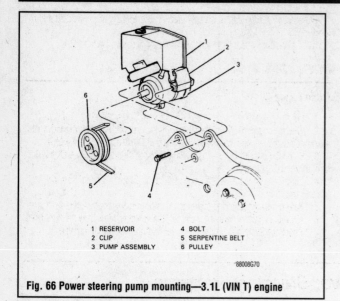

1 RESERVOIR	4 BOLT
2 CLIP	5 SERPENTINE BELT
3 PUMP ASSEMBLY	6 PULLEY

88008G70

Fig. 66 Power steering pump mounting—3.1L (VIN T) engine

9. Install the serpentine belt and ECM heat shield.
10. Install the inlet and outlet hoses using new O-rings, if so equipped.
11. Connect the negative battery cable.
12. Fill and bleed the power steering system as outlined later in this section.

VIN M ENGINES

▶ See Figure 67

1. Disconnect the negative battery cable.
2. Remove the coolant recovery reservoir and position it aside.
3. Remove the serpentine drive belt from the power steering pump assembly.
4. Detach the ignition control wiring harness near the pump assembly.
5. Disconnect the inlet and outlet hoses from the pump assembly.
6. Unfasten the pump retaining bolts/screws.
7. Remove the pump assembly from the vehicle.
8. Remove the power steering pump pulley from the pump assembly.
9. Remove the reservoir assembly from the pump.

To install:

10. Attach the reservoir to the pump assembly.
11. Install the pulley to the pump.
12. Position the pump to the engine and secure with the retaining bolts/screws. Tighten the bolts/screws to 25 ft. lbs. (34 Nm).

13. Connect the inlet and outlet hoses to the power steering pump.
14. Attach the ignition control wiring harness at the pump assembly.
15. Install the serpentine drive belt over the power steering pump pulley.
16. Install the coolant recovery reservoir.
17. Connect the negative battery cable.
18. Fill and bleed the power steering system.

3.4L Engines

▶ See Figure 68

1. Remove the air cleaner and duct assembly.
2. Disconnect the negative battery cable.
3. Remove the coolant recovery tank.
4. Remove the serpentine drive belt.

➡Siphon the power steering fluid from the reservoir before disconnecting the lines to avoid spilling fluid on the secondary timing belt cover. Use shop rags when disconnecting the lines to ensure any remaining fluid does NOT contact the secondary timing belt cover. Power steering fluid can damage the timing belt.

5. Siphon as much fluid as possible from the reservoir.
6. Remove the power steering pump from the bracket.
7. Disconnect the power steering lines. Plug the lines or drain the fluid into a container if changing fluid at this time.
8. If installing a new pump, transfer the pulley from the old pump to the new one.

To install:

9. Connect the power steering fluid lines.
10. Position the power steering pump in the bracket and secure with the retaining bolts. Tighten the bolts to 25 ft. lbs. (34 Nm).
11. Install the serpentine belt.
12. Install the coolant recovery tank.
13. Connect the negative battery cable.
14. Install the air cleaner and duct assembly.
15. Fill and bleed the power steering system.
16. Check the system for leaks, road test and recheck the fluid level.

3.8L Engine

▶ See Figure 69

1. Disconnect the negative battery cable.
2. Remove the coolant recovery reservoir and bracket.
3. Unfasten the ECM retaining nuts, then remove the cover.
4. Remove the serpentine belt from the pulleys by loosening the automatic belt tensioner as outlined in Section 1 of this manual.

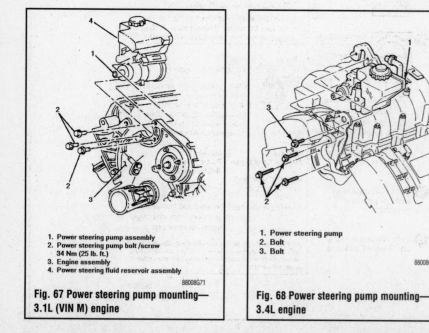

1. Power steering pump assembly
2. Power steering pump bolt /screw
   34 Nm (25 lb. ft.)
3. Engine assembly
4. Power steering fluid reservoir assembly

88008G71

Fig. 67 Power steering pump mounting—3.1L (VIN M) engine

1. Power steering pump
2. Bolt
3. Bolt

88008G69

Fig. 68 Power steering pump mounting—3.4L engine

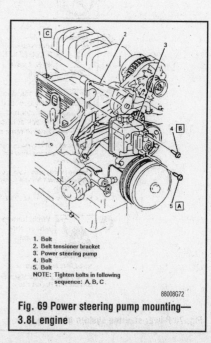

1. Bolt
2. Belt tensioner bracket
3. Power steering pump
4. Bolt
5. Bolt
NOTE: Tighten bolts in following
sequence: A, B, C

88008G72

Fig. 69 Power steering pump mounting—3.8L engine

5. Disconnect the inlet and outlet hoses from the pump.

6. Unfasten the pump mounting bolts, then remove the pump and reservoir.

7. Using a suitable prybar, remove the retaining clips from the reservoir, then separate the reservoir from the pump.

8. Remove the pump pulley using a power steering pump pulley removing tool J–25034–B or equivalent.

To install:

9. Install the reservoir to the pump with a new O-ring seal and install the retaining clip. Make sure the tabs are fully engaged on the pump.

10. Install the pulley to the power steering pump.

11. Install the pump and retaining bolts. Tighten the retaining bolts to 25 ft. lbs. (34 Nm).

12. Connect the inlet and outlet hoses to the pump.

13. Install the serpentine drive belt.

14. Install the ECM cover and secure with the retaining nuts.

15. Connect the negative battery cable.

16. Fill and bleed the power steering system as outlined later in this section.

17. Allow the engine to warm up, road test the vehicle and recheck the fluid level.

18. Check the system for leaks, road test and recheck the fluid level.

BLEEDING

▶ See Figure 70

1. Fill the power steering pump reservoir with power steering fluid.

2. With the engine **OFF** and the wheels off the ground. Turn the steering wheel all the way to the left, add steering fluid to the **COLD** mark on the level indicator.

3. Bleed the system by turning the wheels from side to side. Keep the fluid level at the **COLD** mark.

4. Start the engine and add fluid if necessary. Turn the wheels from right to left and add fluid if necessary.

5. Return the wheels to the center position and lower the vehicle.

6. Allow the engine to warn up, road test the vehicle and recheck the fluid level.

7. Check the system for leaks, road test and recheck the fluid level.

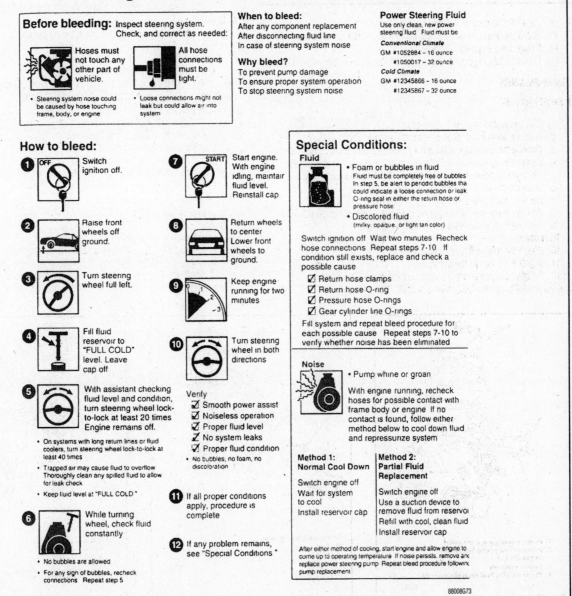

Fig. 70 Power steering system bleeding

TORQUE SPECIFICATIONS

Component	ft. lbs.	inch lbs.	Nm
Front ball joint heat shield	-	62	7
Front ball joint nut			
1988-91 vehicles	15	-	20
1992-96 vehicles	63	-	85
Front frame-to-body bolt	103	-	140
Front rod-to-crossmember bolt	81	-	110
Front rod-to-knuckle bolt	66	-	90
Front stabilizer shaft bolts			
28mm and 30mm	35	-	47
34mm	27	-	37
Front strut cartridge closure nut	80	-	110
Front strut cover nut			
1988-94 vehicles	18	-	24
1995-96 vehicles	24	-	33
Front strut shaft nut	72	-	98
Front tie rod-to-knuckle nut			
1988-93 vehicles	40	-	54
1994-96 vehicles	63	-	85
Halfshaft/driveaxle nut	184	-	250
Hub and bearing bolts	52	-	70
Inner tie rod end nut	70	-	95
Jack pad bolt	18	-	25
Jam nut	50	-	70
Link bolt	40	-	54
Lower auxiliary spring bracket-to-rod nut	133	-	180
Lug nuts	100	-	140
Outer tie rod end nut	40-45	-	54-60
Power steering fluid line fitting	20	-	27
Power steering pump bolt			
2.2L engine			
front	25	-	34
rear	22	-	30
2.3L engine	19	-	26
2.5L and 3.1L (VIN T and V) engines	20	-	27
3.1L (VIN M), 3.4L and 3.8L engines	25	-	34

88008C03

TORQUE SPECIFICATIONS

Component	ft. lbs.	inch lbs.	Nm
Rack and pinion bolts	59	-	80
Rear frame bolts			
Except 3.4L engine	103	-	140
3.4L Engine	125	-	170
Rear knuckle bolt			
1988-94 vehicles	133	-	180
1995-96 vehicles	122	-	165
Rear shock absorber nut			
1995-96 Lumina and Monte Carlo	55	-	75
Rear spring retention plate bolt			
1988-94 vehicles	15	-	20
1995-96 vehicles	22	-	30
Rear strut mount nut	72	-	98
Rear strut mount-to-body nut			
1995-96 Lumina and Monte Carlo	37	-	50
Rear strut/stabilizer shaft bracket to knuckle bolt			
1995-96 Lumina and Monte Carlo	122	-	165
Rear strut-to-body bolt			
Except 1995-96 Lumina and Monte Carlo	34	-	46
Rear strut-to-knuckle bolt			
Except 1995-96 Lumina and Monte Carlo	-	-	-
1988-94 Vehicles	133	-	180
1995-96 Vehicles	122	-	165
Rear trailing arm bolt			
1988-94 vehicles	192	-	260
1995-96 vehicles	177	-	244
SIR inflator module screw	-	25	2.8
Steering column bolts	18	-	25
Steering column housing cover screw	-	35	4
Steering wheel nut	30	-	41
Upper intermediate shaft pinch bolt	35	-	48

88008C04

9

BRAKES

BRAKE OPERATING SYSTEM

Basic Operating Principles

Hydraulic systems are used to actuate the brakes of all modern automobiles. The system transports the power required to force the frictional surfaces of the braking system together from the pedal to the individual brake units at each wheel. A hydraulic system is used for two reasons.

First, fluid under pressure can be carried to all parts of an automobile by small pipes and flexible hoses without taking up a significant amount of room or posing routing problems.

Second, a great mechanical advantage can be given to the brake pedal end of the system, and the foot pressure required to actuate the brakes can be reduced by making the surface area of the master cylinder pistons smaller than that of any of the pistons in the wheel cylinders or calipers.

The master cylinder consists of a fluid reservoir along with a double cylinder and piston assembly. Double type master cylinders are designed to separate the front and rear braking systems hydraulically in case of a leak. The master cylinder coverts mechanical motion from the pedal into hydraulic pressure within the lines. This pressure is translated back into mechanical motion at the wheels by either the wheel cylinder (drum brakes) or the caliper (disc brakes).

Steel lines carry the brake fluid to a point on the vehicle's frame near each of the vehicle's wheels. The fluid is then carried to the calipers and wheel cylinders by flexible tubes in order to allow for suspension and steering movements.

In drum brake systems, each wheel cylinder contains two pistons, one at either end, which push outward in opposite directions and force the brake shoe into contact with the drum.

In disc brake systems, the cylinders are part of the calipers. At least one cylinder in each caliper is used to force the brake pads against the disc.

All pistons employ some type of seal, usually made of rubber, to minimize fluid leakage. A rubber dust boot seals the outer end of the cylinder against dust and dirt. The boot fits around the outer end of the piston on disc brake calipers, and around the brake actuating rod on wheel cylinders.

The hydraulic system operates as follows: When at rest, the entire system, from the piston(s) in the master cylinder to those in the wheel cylinders or calipers, is full of brake fluid. Upon application of the brake pedal, fluid trapped in front of the master cylinder piston(s) is forced through the lines to the wheel cylinders. Here, it forces the pistons outward, in the case of drum brakes, and inward toward the disc, in the case of disc brakes. The motion of the pistons is opposed by return springs mounted outside the cylinders in drum brakes, and by spring seals, in disc brakes.

Upon release of the brake pedal, a spring located inside the master cylinder immediately returns the master cylinder pistons to the normal position. The pistons contain check valves and the master cylinder has compensating ports drilled in it. These are uncovered as the pistons reach their normal position. The piston check valves allow fluid to flow toward the wheel cylinders or calipers as the pistons withdraw. Then, as the return springs force the brake pads or shoes into the released position, the excess fluid reservoir through the compensating ports. It is during the time the pedal is in the released position that any fluid that has leaked out of the system will be replaced through the compensating ports.

Dual circuit master cylinders employ two pistons, located one behind the other, in the same cylinder. The primary piston is actuated directly by mechanical linkage from the brake pedal through the power booster. The secondary piston is actuated by fluid trapped between the two pistons. If a leak develops in front of the secondary piston, it moves forward until it bottoms against the front of the master cylinder, and the fluid trapped between the pistons will operate the rear brakes. If the rear brakes develop a leak, the primary piston will move forward until direct contact with the secondary piston takes place, and it will force the secondary piston to actuate the front brakes. In either case, the brake pedal moves farther when the brakes are applied, and less braking power is available.

All dual circuit systems use a switch to warn the driver when only half of the brake system is operational. This switch is usually located in a valve body which is mounted on the firewall or the frame below the master cylinder. A hydraulic piston receives pressure from both circuits, each circuit's pressure being applied to one end of the piston. When the pressures are in balance, the piston remains stationary. When one circuit has a leak, however, the greater pressure in that circuit during application of the brakes will push the piston to one side, closing the switch and activating the brake warning light.

In disc brake systems, this valve body also contains a metering valve and, in some cases, a proportioning valve. The metering valve keeps pressure from

traveling to the disc brakes on the front wheels until the brake shoes on the rear wheels have contacted the drums, ensuring that the front brakes will never be used alone. The proportioning valve controls the pressure to the rear brakes to lessen the chance of rear wheel lock-up during very hard braking.

Warning lights may be tested by depressing the brake pedal and holding it while opening one of the wheel cylinder bleeder screws. If this does not cause the light to go on, substitute a new lamp, make continuity checks, and, finally, replace the switch as necessary.

The hydraulic system may be checked for leaks by applying pressure to the pedal gradually and steadily. If the pedal sinks very slowly to the floor, the system has a leak. This is not to be confused with a springy or spongy feel due to the compression of air within the lines. If the system leaks, there will be a gradual change in the position of the pedal with a constant pressure.

Check for leaks along all lines and at wheel cylinders. If no external leaks are apparent, the problem is inside the master cylinder.

DISC BRAKES

Instead of the traditional expanding brakes that press outward against a circular drum, disc brake systems utilize a disc (rotor) with brake pads positioned on either side of it. An easily-seen analogy is the hand brake arrangement on a bicycle. The pads squeeze onto the rim of the bike wheel, slowing its motion. Automobile disc brakes use the identical principle but apply the braking effort to a separate disc instead of the wheel.

The disc (rotor) is a casting, usually equipped with cooling fins between the two braking surfaces. This enables air to circulate between the braking surfaces making them less sensitive to heat buildup and more resistant to fade. Dirt and water do not drastically affect braking action since contaminants are thrown off by the centrifugal action of the rotor or scraped off the by the pads. Also, the equal clamping action of the two brake pads tends to ensure uniform, straight line stops. Disc brakes are inherently self-adjusting. There are three general types of disc brake:

1. A fixed caliper.
2. A floating caliper.
3. A sliding caliper.

The fixed caliper design uses two pistons mounted on either side of the rotor (in each side of the caliper). The caliper is mounted rigidly and does not move.

The sliding and floating designs are quite similar. In fact, these two types are often lumped together. In both designs, the pad on the inside of the rotor is moved into contact with the rotor by hydraulic force. The caliper, which is not held in a fixed position, moves slightly, bringing the outside pad into contact with the rotor. There are various methods of attaching floating calipers. Some pivot at the bottom or top, and some slide on mounting bolts. In any event, the end result is the same.

DRUM BRAKES

Drum brakes employ two brake shoes mounted on a stationary backing plate. These shoes are positioned inside a circular drum which rotates with the wheel assembly. The shoes are held in place by springs. This allows them to slide toward the drums (when they are applied) while keeping the linings and drums in alignment. The shoes are actuated by a wheel cylinder which is mounted at the top of the backing plate. When the brakes are applied, hydraulic pressure forces the wheel cylinder's actuating links outward. Since these links bear directly against the top of the brake shoes, the tops of the shoes are then forced against the inner side of the drum. This action forces the bottoms of the two shoes to contact the brake drum by rotating the entire assembly slightly (known as servo action). When pressure within the wheel cylinder is relaxed, return springs pull the shoes back away from the drum.

Most modern drum brakes are designed to self-adjust themselves during application when the vehicle is moving in reverse. This motion causes both shoes to rotate very slightly with the drum, rocking an adjusting lever, thereby causing rotation of the adjusting screw. Some drum brake systems are designed to self-adjust during application whenever the brakes are applied. This on-board adjustment system reduces the need for maintenance adjustments and keeps both the brake function and pedal feel satisfactory.

⁂ WARNING

Clean, high quality brake fluid is essential to the safe and proper operation of the brake system. You should always buy the highest quality brake fluid that is available. If the brake fluid becomes contaminated, drain and flush the system and fill the master cylinder with new fluid. Never reuse any brake fluid. Any brake fluid that is removed from the system should be discarded.

Adjustment

DISC BRAKES

The front disc brakes are inherently self-adjusting. No adjustments are either necessary or possible.

DRUM BRAKES

The drum brakes are designed to self-adjust when applied with the car moving in reverse. However, they can also be adjusted manually. This manual adjustment should also be performed whenever the linings are replaced.

1. Raise and safely support the vehicle with jackstands.
2. Matchmark the relationship between the wheel to the axle flange to insure proper balance upon reassembly, then remove the tire and wheel assembly.
3. Matchmark the relationship of the drum to the axle flange, then remove the brake drum.
4. Make sure the stops on both parking brake levers are against the edges of the webs on the parking brake shoes. If the parking brake cable is holding the stops off the edge of the shoe webs, loosen the parking brake cable adjustment.
5. Measure the drum inside diameter, using tool J 21177-A or equivalent tool.
6. Turning the star wheel on the adjusting bolt/screw assembly, adjust the shoe and lining diameter to be 0.05 in. (1.27mm) less that the drum inside diameter at each wheel.
7. Apply and release the brake pedal 30–35 times, with a one second pause between each brake application.
8. Install the drums and wheels, aligning the previous marks.
9. Carefully lower the vehicle.
10. Tighten the wheel nuts to 100 ft. lbs. (136 Nm).
11. Make several alternate forward and reserve stops applying firm force to the brake pedal until ample pedal reserve is built up.

Brake Light Switch

REMOVAL & INSTALLATION

1988–92 Vehicles

▶ See Figure 1

1. Disconnect the negative battery cable.
2. Remove the three fasteners from the left side insulator panel.
3. Slide the steering shaft protective cover towards the cowl.
4. Remove the vacuum hose at the cruise control cut off switch, if so equipped.
5. Remove the stoplamp switch-to-steering column bracket retaining pin.
6. Unplug the electrical connector.
7. Push the switch arm to the left and towards the cowl to disconnect switch-to-pedal arm. Release the snap clip and remove the switch.
To install:
8. Install the switch and push up until it is seated into the top snap clip.
9. Attach the electrical connectors.
10. Connect the switch to the pedal.
11. Install the switch-to-steering column retaining pin.
12. Connect the vacuum hose if equipped with cruise control.
13. Install the steering shaft protective sleeve.

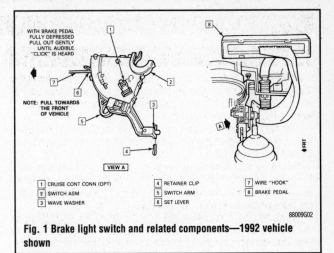

1 CRUISE CONT CONN (OPT)	4 RETAINER CLIP	7 WIRE "HOOK"
2 SWITCH ASM	5 SWITCH ARM	8 BRAKE PEDAL
3 WAVE WASHER	6 SET LEVER	

88009G02

Fig. 1 Brake light switch and related components—1992 vehicle shown

14. Adjust the stoplamp switch.
15. Install the left sound insulator, connect the negative battery cable and check switch operation.

1993–96 Vehicles

▶ See Figure 2

1. Disconnect the negative battery cable.
2. For 1995–96 vehicles, remove the driver's side instrument panel sound insulator panel.
3. Detach the switch electrical connectors.
4. Remove the switch from the brake pedal bracket.
To install:
5. Position the switch to the brake pedal bracket.
6. Attach the electrical connectors.
7. If removed, install the driver's side instrument panel sound insulator panel.
8. Connect the negative battery cable.

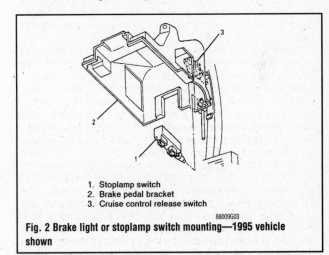

1. Stoplamp switch
2. Brake pedal bracket
3. Cruise control release switch

88009G03

Fig. 2 Brake light or stoplamp switch mounting—1995 vehicle shown

ADJUSTMENT

1988–92 Vehicles

▶ See Figures 3 and 4

1. Depress the brake pedal (push down), as far as possible and hold.
2. Using a stiff wire with a hooked end, gently pull the switch set lever forward (toward the front of the vehicle), and listen for an audible click that indicates release of the automatic adjuster.

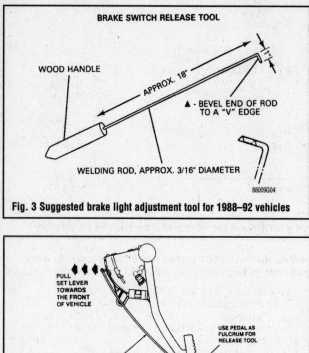

Fig. 3 Suggested brake light adjustment tool for 1988–92 vehicles

Fig. 4 Adjusting the brake light switch—1992 vehicle shown

➡️If no click is heard, release the brake pedal and repeat the above procedure.

3. After release of the automatic adjuster, slowly pull the brake pedal all the way rearward. Listen for the switch to ratchet into the set position (setting the brake light switch). At least three clicks of the ratchet should be heard.
4. Inspect the operation of the brake lights, as follows:
   a. The brake lights should light at maximum brake pedal travel of 1 ¼ in. (32mm) and throughout the remainder of the pedal travel.
   b. If the brake lights do not light, repeat the switch adjuster procedure one more time.

1993–96 Vehicles

With the brake pedal in the fully released position, the brake light plunger should be fully depressed against the brake pedal switch.
1. Insert the brake light switch into the brake pedal bracket.
2. Push the brake pedal forward to set the brake pushrod into the booster.
3. Pull the brake pedal to the rear, against the internal pedal stop. The brake light switch will be adjusted.
4. Check the brake lights for proper operation.

Master Cylinder

REMOVAL & INSTALLATION

Vehicles Without ABS

◆ See Figures 5, 6, 7, 8 and 9

➡️Always use a proper size flare nut wrench when removing and installing the brake lines. Failure to use the proper wrench may cause damage to the line fittings.

1. Disconnect the negative battery cable.
2. Detach the electrical connector from the fluid level sensor at the master cylinder.
3. Using a flare nut wrench, remove and plug the brake lines from the master cylinder. Plugging the lines will prevent fluid loss and contamination.
4. Unfasten the two master cylinder-to-brake power booster retaining nuts and remove the master cylinder.

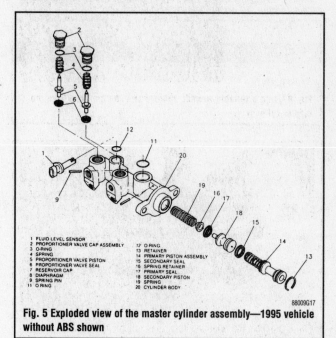

Fig. 5 Exploded view of the master cylinder assembly—1995 vehicle without ABS shown

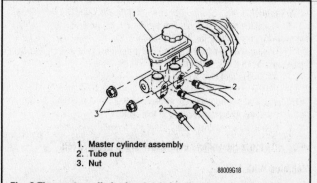

Fig. 6 The master cylinder is mounted to the power booster with two retaining nuts

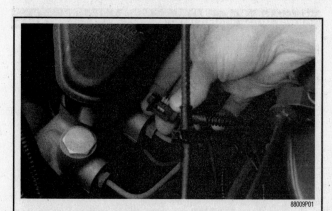

Fig. 7 Detach the fluid lever sensor electrical connector

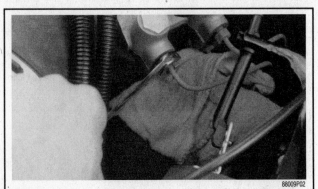

Fig. 8 Using a suitable wrench, remove and cap the lines from the master cylinder

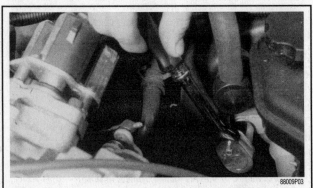

Fig. 9 Unfasten the retaining nuts, then remove the master cylinder assembly

To install:

5. Install the master cylinder and secure with the retaining nuts. Tighten the retaining nuts to 20 ft. lbs. (27 Nm).

6. Unplug and connect the brake lines using a flare nut wrench. Tighten the brake pipes to 15 ft. lbs. (20 Nm).

7. Attach the fluid level sensor electrical connector.

8. Fill the master cylinder to the proper level with NEW brake fluid meeting DOT 3 specifications from a clean, sealed container.

9. Bleed the system as outlined in this section.

10. Connect the negative battery cable and recheck the fluid level.

➡Do NOT move the vehicle until a firm brake pedal is felt.

Vehicles With ABS

For vehicles equipped with ABS, please refer to the Hydraulic Modulator/Master Cylinder removal and installation procedure, located later in this section.

Power Brake Booster

REMOVAL & INSTALLATION

◆ **See Figure 10**

1. Disconnect the negative battery cable.

2. For 3.4L engines, remove the upper intake manifold, as outlined in Section 3 of this manual.

3. For 1988–89 vehicles, perform the following:

a. From inside the engine compartment, remove the panels around the booster assembly.

b. Remove the booster grommet bolt and grommet.

4. Remove the master cylinder or hydraulic modulator/master cylinder assembly, as applicable from the power booster.

5. Scribe a mark on the front and rear booster covers in case the two covers get separated during removal.

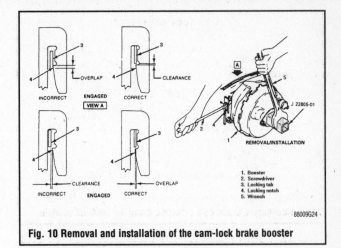

Fig. 10 Removal and installation of the cam-lock brake booster

➡When disconnecting the pushrod from the brake pedal, the brake pedal must be kept stationary or damage to the brake switch may result.

6. Disconnect the brake pushrod from the brake pedal.

7. Unlock the booster from the front of the dash as follows:

a. Attach booster holding tool J 22805-01, or equivalent, to the master cylinder mounting studs with the nuts. Tighten the stud nuts to 18–20 ft. lbs. (25–27 Nm).

b. Use a suitable prybar to pry the locking tab on the booster out of the locking notch on the mounting flange.

c. At the same time, turn the booster counterclockwise with a large wrench on the booster holding tool.

➡Do NOT attempt to remove the booster until the pushrod has been disconnected from the brake pedal.

8. Disconnect the booster pushrod from the brake pedal.

9. Remove the brake booster from the vehicle. Be careful not to damage the insulator boot mounted on the front of the dash when pulling the pushrod end through the hole.

To install:

10. Lubricate the inside and outside diameters of the grommet and front housing seal with silicone grease before installation.

11. Attach tool J 22805-01, or equivalent, to the booster with the nuts. Tighten the nuts to 20 ft. lbs. (27 Nm).

12. Position the booster on the cowl, slightly counterclockwise from the final installation position, so that the locking flanges on the booster and mounted plate engage.

➡Be careful not to damage or dislodge the insulation boot when passing the pushrod through the hole.

13. Connect the booster pushrod to the brake pedal.

14. Turn the booster clockwise with a wrench on tool J 22805-01, until the locking flanges are engaged. Make sure the locking tab is fully seated to prevent rotation of the booster. It is not necessary to use a prytool on the locking tab to install the booster. When correctly installed, the locking tab will slide up the flange and snap in the locking notch.

15. Install the master cylinder or hydraulic modulator/master cylinder assembly, as applicable.

16. If removed, install the booster grommet and secondary dash panel.

17. Connect the negative battery cable and bleed the system if the fluid pipes were disconnected from the master cylinder.

Proportioning Valves

REMOVAL & INSTALLATION

◆ **See Figure 11**

1. Disconnect the negative battery cable.

➡In order to remove the proportioning valve caps, it may be necessary to remove the reservoir assembly from the master cylinder.

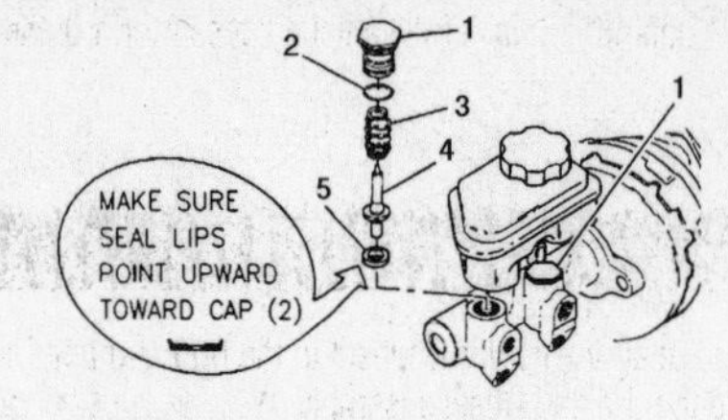

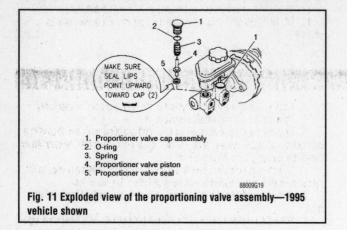

1. Proportioner valve cap assembly
2. O-ring
3. Spring
4. Proportioner valve piston
5. Proportioner valve seal

88009G19

Fig. 11 Exploded view of the proportioning valve assembly—1995 vehicle shown

2. Remove the proportioning valve cap assemblies.
3. Remove and discard the O-rings.
4. Remove the springs.
5. Using needle-nosed pliers, remove the proportioning valve pistons. Be very careful not to scratch or damage the piston stems.
6. Remove the proportioning valve seals from the pistons.
7. Inspect the pistons for corrosion or other damage, and replace, if necessary.

To install:

8. Lubricate new O-rings and proportioning valve seals with the silicone grease supplied in the repair kit. Also lubricate the stem of the proportioning valve pistons.
9. Place the new seals on the proportioning valve pistons with the seal lips facing upward toward the cap assembly.
10. Position the proportioning valve pistons and seals into the master cylinder body.
11. Install the springs in the master cylinder body.
12. Place new O-rings in the grooves in the proportioning valve cap assemblies.
13. Install the proportioning valve caps on the master cylinder body. Tighten the caps to 20 ft. lbs. (27 Nm).
14. If removed, install the reservoir assembly to the master cylinder.
15. Connect the negative battery cable.

Bleeding the Brake System

⁂ WARNING

The brake system MUST be bled after the hydraulic system has been serviced. Air enters the system when components are removed, and this air has to be removed to prevent a spongy pedal resulting in poor system performance.

The time required to bleed the system can be reduced by removing as much air as possible before installing the master cylinder onto the vehicle. This is called bench bleeding the master cylinder. Place the master cylinder in a vise or holding fixture, run tubing from the fluid pipe fittings to the reservoir, fill the cylinder with DOT 3 brake fluid and pump the brake pushrod until most of the air is removed from the master cylinder. Install the master cylinder onto the vehicle and bleed all four wheels.

➡Care MUST be taken to prevent brake fluid from contacting any automotive paint surface. Brake fluid can stain or dissolve paint finishes if not removed immediately. Clean the surface with soap and water immediately after the fluid has contacted the painted surface.

MANUAL BLEEDING

➡The procedure for bleeding the ABS system differs from this one. Refer to the section on Bleeding under ANTI-LOCK BRAKING SYSTEM head later in this section if working with on a vehicle equipped with ABS.

For those of us who are not fortunate enough to have access to a power bleeding tool, the manual brake bleeding procedure will quite adequately remove air from the hydraulic system. The major difference between the pressure and manual bleeding procedures is that the manual method takes more time and will require help from an assistant. One person must depress the brake pedal, while another opens and closes the bleeder screws.

1. Fill the master cylinder reservoir with brake fluid and keep the reservoir at least half full during the bleeding operation.
2. If the master cylinder has air in the bore, it must be removed before bleeding the calipers. Bleed the master cylinder as follows.
   a. Disconnect the forward brake pipe at the master cylinder.
   b. Fill the reservoir until fluid begins to flow from the forward pipe connector port.
   c. Reconnect the forward brake pipe and tighten.
   d. Depress the brake pedal slowly one time and hold. Loosen the forward brake pipe and purge the air from the bore. Tighten the brake pipe, wait 15 seconds and repeat until all air is removed.
   e. When the air is removed from the forward brake pipe, repeat the same procedures for the rear brake pipe.
3. Bleed the calipers in the following order, (right front, right rear, left rear, left front).
4. Install a box end wrench over the bleeder valve and connect a clear tube onto the valve. Place the other end of the tube into a container of new brake fluid. The end of the tube must be submerged in brake fluid.
5. Depress the brake pedal slowly one time and hold. Loosen the bleeder valve to purge the air from the caliper. Close the valve and release the pedal. Repeat the procedure until all air is removed from the brake fluid.
6. Do NOT pump the brake pedal rapidly; this causes the air to churn and make bleeding difficult.
7. After the calipers have been bled, check the brake pedal for sponginess and the BRAKE warning lamp for low fluid level.
8. Repeat the bleeding operation if a spongy pedal is felt.
9. Fill the reservoir to the MAX line.

PRESSURE BLEEDING

➡The procedure for bleeding the ABS system differs from this one. Refer to the section on Bleeding under ANTI-LOCK BRAKING SYSTEM head later in this section if working with on a vehicle equipped with ABS.

For the lucky ones with access to a pressure bleeding tool, this procedure may be used to quickly and efficiently remove air from the brake system. This procedure may be used as a guide, but be careful to follow the tool manufacturer's directions closely. Any pressure bleeding tool MUST be of the diaphragm-type. A proper pressure bleeder tool will utilize a rubber diaphragm between the air source and brake fluid in order to prevent air, moisture oil and other contaminants from entering the hydraulic system.

1. Install Pressure Bleeder Adapter Cap J 35589 or equivalent, to the master cylinder.
2. Charge Diaphragm Type Brake Bleeder J 29532 or equivalent, to 20–25 psi (140–172 kPa).
3. Connect the line to the pressure bleeder adapter cap, then open the line valve.
4. Raise and safely support the vehicle.
5. If it is necessary to bleed all of the calipers/cylinders, the following sequence should be used:
   - Right rear
   - Left front
   - Left rear
   - Right front
6. Place a proper size box end wrench (or tool J 21472) over the caliper/cylinder bleeder valve.
7. Attach a clear tube over the bleeder screw, then submerge the other end of the tube in a clear container partially filled with clean brake fluid.
8. Open the bleeder screw at least ¾ of a turn and allow flow to continue until no air is seen in the fluid.
9. Close the bleeder screw. Tighten the rear bleeder screws to 62 inch lbs. (7 Nm) and the front bleeder screws to 115 inch lbs. (13 Nm).
10. Repeat Steps 6–9 until all of the calipers and/or cylinders have been bled.

11. Carefully lower the vehicle.

12. Check the brake pedal for sponginess. If the condition is found, the entire bleeding procedure must be repeated.

13. Remove tools J 35589 and J 29532.

FRONT DISC BRAKES

▶ See Figure 12

✳✳ CAUTION

Brake pads may contain asbestos, which has been determined to be a cancer causing agent. Never clean the brake surfaces with compressed air! Avoid inhaling any dust from any brake surface! When cleaning brake surfaces, use a commercially available brake cleaning fluid.

Fig. 12 View of the front disc brake system—1992 Lumina shown

Brake Pads

REMOVAL & INSTALLATION

▶ See Figures 13, 14 and 15

✳✳ CAUTION

Always replace all pads on both front wheels at the same time. Failure to do so will result in uneven braking action.

1. Disconnect the negative battery cable.

2. Remove ⅔ of the brake fluid from the brake reservoir using a clean syringe or equivalent.

3. Raise and safely support the vehicle with jackstands.

4. Mark the relationship of the wheel to the hub and bearing assembly.

5. Remove the tire and wheel assembly.

6. Remove the caliper, as outlined later, and suspend from the strut with a wire hook or suitable piece of wire. Do NOT disconnect the brake hose or allow the caliper to hang from the brake line!

7. Remove the outboard shoe and lining by using a suitable prybar to lift up the outboard pad retaining spring so it will clear the center lug.

8. Remove the inboard pad by unsnapping the pad springs from the pistons.

9. Wipe the outside surface of the caliper boots clean with denatured alcohol.

To install:

10. Bottom the pistons into the caliper bores if new shoe and linings are being installed, as follows:

a. Using a C-clamp, clamp both pistons at the same time with a metal plate or wooden block across the face of both pistons. Be careful not to damage the pistons or caliper boots.

b. After bottoming the pistons, lift the inner edge of each caliper boot next to the piston and press out any trapped air. The boots must lay flat.

c. Make sure the convolutions are tucked back into place.

11. Install the inboard shoe and lining/pad by snapping the shoe retainer springs into the pistons. The shoe retainer springs are already staked to the inboard shoe. Make sure both tangs of the retainer spring are installed inside the piston ID. The shoe must lay flat against the pistons.

12. After installing the shoe and lining, check that the caliper boots are not touching the shoe. If there is contact, remove the shoe and lining and re-seat or re-position the boots.

13. Install the outboard shoe and lining/pad by snapping the pad retainer spring over the caliper center lug and into the housing slot.

14. Make sure both pads remain free of grease or oil. The wear sensor should be at the trailing edge of the pad during rotation. The back of the shoe should lay flat against the caliper.

15. Install the caliper assembly, as outlined later in this section.

16. Install the tire and wheel assembly, then carefully lower the vehicle.

17. Fill the master cylinder to the FULL mark, then firmly apply the brake pedal three times to seat the pads.

18. Connect the negative battery cable.

14. Refill the master cylinder to the proper level with brake fluid.

15. DO NOT attempt to move the vehicle unless a firm brake pedal is obtained.

INSPECTION

The pad thickness should be inspected every time that the wheels are removed. Pad thickness can be checked by looking down through the inspection hole in the top of the caliper. If the thickness of the pad is worn to within 0.030 inch (0.76mm) (if the pads are the riveted type, be sure not to include the thickness of the rivets when measuring pad thickness), all the pads should be

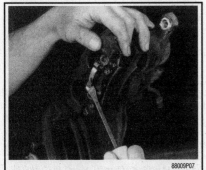

Fig. 13 Remove the outboard pad by using a prytool to lift up the retaining spring so it will clear the center lug

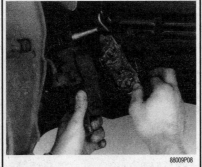

Fig. 14 Remove the inboard pad by unsnapping the pad springs from the pistons

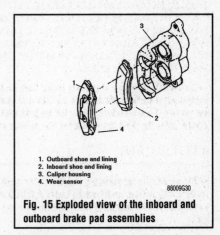

1. Outboard shoe and lining
2. Inboard shoe and lining
3. Caliper housing
4. Wear sensor

Fig. 15 Exploded view of the inboard and outboard brake pad assemblies

replaced. A thermal material is sandwiched between the lining and backing. Don't include this material when determining the lining thickness. This is the factory-recommended measurement. Your state's automobile inspection laws may be different.

Brake Caliper

REMOVAL & INSTALLATION

▶ **See Figures 16, 17, 18 and 19**

1. Disconnect the negative battery cable.
2. Remove ⅔ of the brake fluid from the brake reservoir using a clean syringe or equivalent.
3. Raise and safely support the vehicle with jackstands.
4. Mark the relationship of the wheel to the hub and bearing assembly.
5. Remove the tire and wheel assembly.
6. Reinstall two lug nuts to retain the rotor.
7. Push the pistons into the caliper bore to provide clearance between the linings and the rotor, as follows:

   a. Install a large C-clamp over the top of the caliper housing and against the back of the outboard shoe.

➡ **If the C-clamp is tightening too far, the outboard shoe retaining spring will be deformed and require replacement.**

   b. Slowly tighten the C-clamp until the pistons are pushed into the caliper bore enough to slide the caliper assembly off the rotor.

8. If the caliper is going to be replaced or removed for overhaul, disconnect and plug the brake hose.

✳✳ WARNING

Do NOT allow the caliper to hang from the brake hose!

9. Unfasten the caliper mounting/slide bolts, then pull the caliper from the mounting bracket and rotor. Support the caliper with a suitable piece wire from the strut, if not removing.
10. Inspect the bolt boots and support bushings for cuts or damage, replace if necessary.

To install:

➡ **Each caliper is marked with a "L" (left side) or "R" (right side) for proper installation. Also, proper caliper position also required that the bleeder valve is on top.**

11. Install the caliper over the rotor into the mounting bracket. Make sure the bolt boots/bushings are in place.
12. Lubricate the entire shaft of the mounting/sliding bolts and cavities with silicone grease.
13. Install the mounting or slide bolts and tighten them to 80 ft. lbs. (108 Nm).
14. If removed, unplug and connect the brake hose, using new copper washers and a new inlet fitting bolt. Tighten the fitting bolt to 24 ft. lbs. (32 Nm).
15. Remove the two wheel lugs, and install the wheel and tire assembly.
16. Carefully lower the vehicle.
17. Fill the master cylinder and bleed the brake system as outlined in this section.
18. Check for hydraulic leaks. Pump the brake pedal a few times before moving the vehicle.

OVERHAUL

▶ **See Figures 20 thru 26**

1. Remove the caliper assembly from the vehicle as outlined earlier in this section.

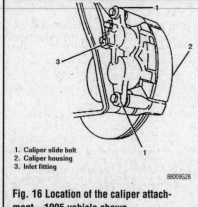

1. Caliper slide bolt
2. Caliper housing
3. Inlet fitting

88009G28

Fig. 16 Location of the caliper attachment—1995 vehicle shown

88009P05

Fig. 17 Use the proper size socket to unfasten . . .

88009P06

Fig. 18 . . . then remove the caliper sliding bolts

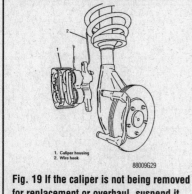

1. Caliper housing
2. Wire hook

88009G29

Fig. 19 If the caliper is not being removed for replacement or overhaul, suspend it from the strut with a piece of wire

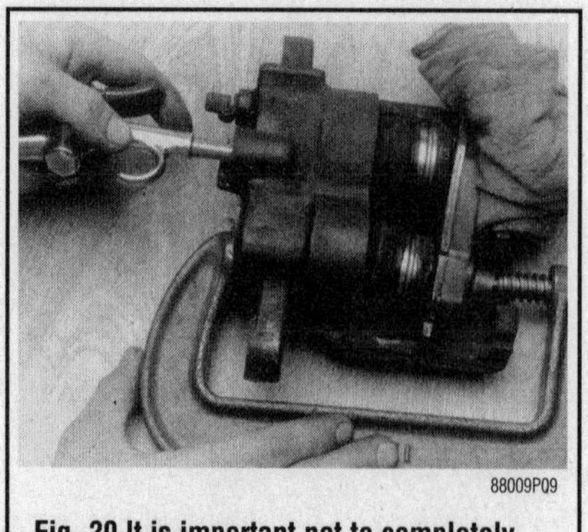

88009P09

Fig. 20 It is important not to completely remove one piston before the other one is freed

88009P10

Fig. 21 Do NOT put your fingers in front of the pistons when blowing them out with compressed air!

Fig. 22 Remove the pistons from the bores

Fig. 23 When removing the caliper boots, be careful not to scratch the bores

Fig. 24 Never use a metal tool to remove the piston seals!

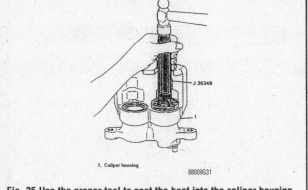

1. Caliper housing

Fig. 25 Use the proper tool to seat the boot into the caliper housing

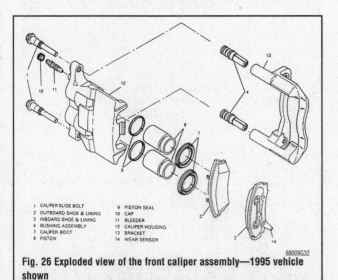

1 CALIPER SLIDE BOLT
2 OUTBOARD SHOE & LINING
3 INBOARD SHOE & LINING
4 BUSHING ASSEMBLY
7 CALIPER BOOT
8 PISTON
9 PISTON SEAL
10 CAP
11 BLEEDER
12 CALIPER HOUSING
13 BRACKET
14 WEAR SENSOR

Fig. 26 Exploded view of the front caliper assembly—1995 vehicle shown

✳✳ CAUTION

Do NOT place fingers in front of the pistons in an attempt to catch or protect them when applying compressed air. This could result in personal injury!

➡It is critical that one piston is not completely removed before the other is freed. A pad or spacer may be used to prevent this situation. In the event one piston is frozen and will not break free, is may be necessary to block the other piston with a piece of wood or C-clamp until the frozen piston can be freed.

2. Remove the caliper pistons with compressed air applied into the caliper inlet hole. Inspect the pistons for scoring, nicks corrosion, and/or worn or damaged chrome plating. Replace the piston, if any of these conditions are found.

3. Remove the caliper boots, being careful not to scratch the housing bore.

✳✳ WARNING

Do not use a metal tool to remove the piston seals. Metal tools may damage the caliper bores or piston seal grooves.

4. Remove the piston seals from the groove in the caliper bore, using a small wood or plastic tool.

5. Carefully loosen the brake bleeder valve cap and valve from the caliper housing. If the valve breaks off, the caliper should be replaced.

6. Inspect the caliper bores, pistons and mounting threads for scoring or excessive wear.

7. Use crocus cloth to polish out light corrosion from the piston and bore.

8. Clean all parts with denatured alcohol and dry with compressed air.

9. Lubricate and install the bleeder valve and cap. Tighten the cap to 11 ft. lbs. (15 Nm).

10. Lubricate the new piston seals and bore with clean brake fluid or brake assembly fluid.

11. Install the new seals into the caliper bore grooves, making sure they are not twisted.

12. Lubricate the piston bore.

13. Install the pistons and boots into the bores of the calipers and push to the bottom of the bores.

14. Seat the boots in the housing using tool J 36349, or equivalent.

15. Install the caliper onto the vehicle, as outlined earlier.

16. Install the front wheel and tire assembly, then carefully lower the vehicle.

17. Properly bleed the brake system as outlined in this section.

Brake Rotor

REMOVAL & INSTALLATION

1. Disconnect the negative battery cable.

2. Remove ⅔ of the brake fluid from the brake reservoir using a clean syringe or equivalent.

3. Raise and safely support the vehicle with jackstands.

4. Mark the relationship of the wheel to the hub and bearing assembly.

5. Remove the tire and wheel assembly.

6. Remove the caliper and suspend it from the strut with a wire hook or suitable piece of wire. Do NOT disconnect the brake hose or allow the caliper to hang from the brake line!

7. Remove the rotor assembly.

To install:

8. Install the brake rotor over the hub assembly.

9. Install the brake caliper as outlined in this section.

10. Install the wheel and tire assembly.

11. Carefully lower the vehicle, then fill the master cylinder reservoir to the FULL level with the correct type of DOT 3 brake fluid from a clean, unsealed container.

12. Firmly depress the brake pedal three times before moving the vehicle.

INSPECTION

Thickness Variation Check

The thickness variation can be checked by measuring the thickness of the rotor at four or more points. All of the measurements must be made at the same distance from the edge of the rotor. A rotor the varies by more than 0.0005 inch (0.0127mm) can cause a pulsation in the brake pedal. If these measurement are excessive, the rotor should be refinished or replaced.

Lateral Runout Check

1. Remove the caliper and hang from the body with a piece of wire. Install two inverted lug nuts to retain the rotor.

2. Install a dial indicator to the steering knuckle so that the indicator button contacts the rotor about 1 in. (25mm) from the rotor edge.

3. Zero the dial indicator.

4. Move the rotor one complete revolution and observe the total indicated runout.

5. If the rotor runout exceeds 0.0015 inch (0.040mm) have the rotor refinished or replaced.

Refinishing Brake Rotors

All brake rotors have a minimum thickness dimension cast onto them. Do NOT use a brake rotor that will not meet minimum thickness specifications in the "Brake Specifications" chart at the end of this section.

Accurate control of rotor tolerances is necessary for proper brake performance and safety. Machining of the rotor should be done by a qualified machine shop with the proper machining equipment.

The optimum speed for refinishing the rotor surface is a spindle speed of 200 rpm. Crossfeed for rough cutting should range from 0.006–0.010 in. (0.152–0.254mm) per revolution. The finish cuts should be made at crossfeeds no greater than 0.002 in. (0.05mm) per revolution.

REAR DRUM BRAKES

▶ See Figure 27

☀☀ CAUTION

Some brake shoes contain asbestos, which has been determined to be a cancer causing agent. Never clean the brake surfaces with compressed air! Avoid inhaling any dust from any brake surface! When cleaning brake surfaces, use a commercially available brake cleaning fluid.

Some 1995–96 Luminas and Monte Carlos utilize a leading/trailing shoe design rear drum brake system. This brake assembly design operates with less total parts and is supposed to be easier to service. It uses a single universal spring to hold both the shoe and lining assemblies to the backing plate and also acts as a retractor spring for the shoes. Use care when servicing this brake assembly as the large spring can pinch fingers.

Brake Drums

REMOVAL & INSTALLATION

▶ See Figure 28

1. Raise and safely support the vehicle with jackstands.

2. Mark the relationship of the wheel to the axle flange to help maintain wheel balance after assembly.

3. Remove the tire and wheel assembly.

4. Mark the relationship of the brake drum to the axle flange.

➡**Do not pry against the splash shield that surrounds the backing plate in an attempt to free the drum. This will bend the splash shield.**

5. If difficulty is encountered in removing the brake drum, the following steps may be of assistance.

   a. Make sure the parking brake is released.

   b. Back off the parking brake cable adjustment.

   c. Remove the access hole plug from the backing plate.

   d. Using a screwdriver, back off the adjusting screw.

   e. Re–install the access hole plug to prevent dirt or contamination from entering the drum brake assembly.

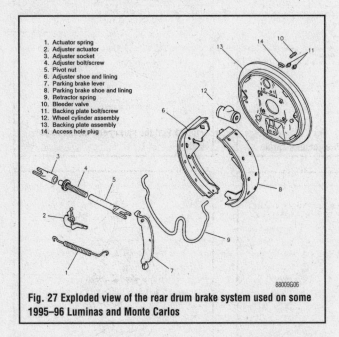

1. Actuator spring
2. Adjuster actuator
3. Adjuster socket
4. Adjuster bolt/screw
5. Pivot nut
6. Adjuster shoe and lining
7. Parking brake lever
8. Parking brake shoe and lining
9. Retractor spring
10. Bleeder valve
11. Backing plate bolt/screw
12. Wheel cylinder assembly
13. Backing plate assembly
14. Access hole plug

88009G06

Fig. 27 Exploded view of the rear drum brake system used on some 1995–96 Luminas and Monte Carlos

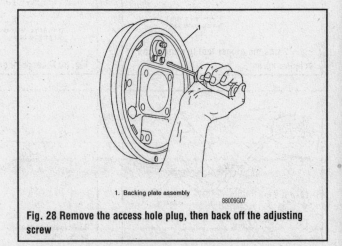

1. Backing plate assembly

88009G07

Fig. 28 Remove the access hole plug, then back off the adjusting screw

f. Use a small amount of penetrating oil applied around the brake drum pilot hole.

g. Carefully remove the brake drum from the vehicle.

6. After removing the brake drum it should be checked for the following:

a. Inspecting for cracks and deep grooves.

b. Inspect for out of round and taper.

c. Inspecting for hot spots (black in color).

To install:

7. Install the brake drum onto the vehicle aligning the reference marks on the axle flange.

8. Install the tire and wheel assembly and hand-tighten the lug nuts.

9. Carefully lower the vehicle, then tighten the lug nuts to 100 ft. lbs. (140 Nm).

10. Road test the vehicle for proper brake operation.

INSPECTION

1. Inspect the brake drum for scoring, cracking or grooving. Light scoring of the drum not exceeding 0.020 in. (0.51mm) in depth will not affect brake operation.

2. Inspect the brake drum for excessive taper and out-of-round. When measuring a drum for out-of-round, taper and wear, take measurements at the open and closed edges of the machined surfaces and at right angles to each other.

Brake Shoes

INSPECTION

1. Remove the wheel and drum.

2. Inspect the shoes for proper thickness. The lining should be at least $\frac{1}{32}$ in. (0.8mm) above the rivet head for riveted brakes and $\frac{1}{16}$ in. (1.6mm) above the mounting surface for bonded brake linings.

3. Inspect the linings for even wear, cracking and scoring. Replace as necessary.

REMOVAL & INSTALLATION

▶ **See Figures 29 thru 34**

1. Raise and safely support the vehicle with jackstands.

2. Mark the relationship of the wheel to the axle flange to help maintain wheel balance after assembly.

3. Remove the tire and wheel assembly.

4. Remove the brake drum, as outlined earlier in this section.

5. Using tool J-38400, or an equivalent brake spanner and remover, remove the actuator spring from the adjuster lever. Use care not to distort the spring when removing it.

✳✳ CAUTION

During the following steps when removing the retractor spring from either shoe and lining assembly, do not over stretch the spring. This will reduce its effectiveness. Keep fingers away from retractor spring to prevent fingers from being pinched between the spring and shoe web or spring and the backing plate.

6. Lift the end of the retractor spring from the adjuster shoe assembly. Insert the hook end of the J-38400 between the retractor spring and the shoe. Pry slightly to remove the spring end from the hole in the shoe.

7. Pry the end of the retractor spring toward the axle with the flat end of the tool until the spring snaps down off the shoe web onto the backing plate.

8. Remove the adjuster shoe and lining assembly, adjuster actuator and adjusting bolt/screw assembly.

9. Disconnect the parking brake lever from the shoe. DO NOT remove the parking brake lever from the cable end unless it is being replaced.

10. Using J-38400 or the equivalent, lift the end of the retractor spring from the adjuster shoe assembly.

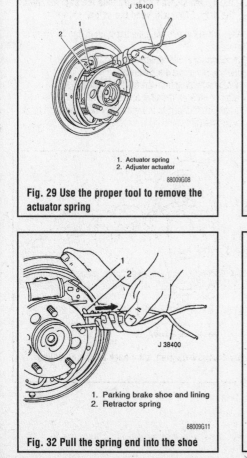

1. Actuator spring
2. Adjuster actuator

88009G08

Fig. 29 Use the proper tool to remove the actuator spring

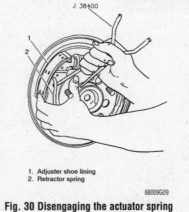

1. Adjuster shoe lining
2. Retractor spring

88009G09

Fig. 30 Disengaging the actuator spring

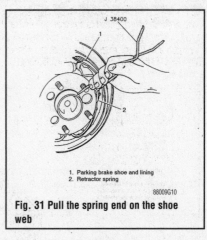

1. Parking brake shoe and lining
2. Retractor spring

88009G10

Fig. 31 Pull the spring end on the shoe web

1. Parking brake shoe and lining
2. Retractor spring

88009G11

Fig. 32 Pull the spring end into the shoe

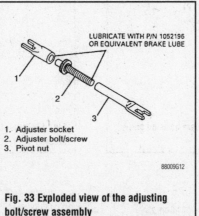

LUBRICATE WITH P/N 1052196 OR EQUIVALENT BRAKE LUBE

1. Adjuster socket
2. Adjuster bolt/screw
3. Pivot nut

88009G12

Fig. 33 Exploded view of the adjusting bolt/screw assembly

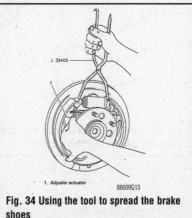

1. Adjuster actuator

88009G13

Fig. 34 Using the tool to spread the brake shoes

11. Insert the hook end of the J-38400 or the equivalent between the retractor spring and the shoe. Pry slightly to remove the spring end from the hole in the shoe. Pry the end of the retractor spring toward the axle with the flat end of the tool until the spring snaps down off the shoe web onto the backing plate.

12. Remove the parking brake shoe and lining assembly.

13. If necessary, remove the retractor spring from the anchor plate. If only the shoe and linings are being replaced, it is not necessary to remove the retractor spring.

To install:

14. Clean all the brake spring completely with brake solvent and allow to air dry.

15. Disassemble, clean and lubricate the adjuster screw. Once lubricated, reassemble.

16. Clean the backing plate and after it is dry apply a thin coat of brake grease to the brake shoe contact points on the backing plate.

17. Position the brake shoe, that connects to the parking brake lever, on the backing plate.

18. Using J-38400 or the equivalent, pull the end of the retractor spring up to rest on the web of the shoe. Pull the end of the retractor spring up until it snaps into the slot in the brake shoe.

19. Connect the parking brake lever.

20. Install the remaining shoe and the adjuster screw assembly.

21. Position the brake shoe, using J-38400 or the equivalent, pull the end of the retractor spring up to rest on the web of the shoe. Pull the end of the retractor spring up until it snaps into the slot in the brake shoe.

22. Using J-38400 or the equivalent, spread the brake shoes and work the adjuster screw into position.

23. Install the actuator spring with the U-shaped end going through the web.

24. Install the brake drum, as outlined earlier in this section.

25. Install the tire and wheel assembly and hand-tighten the lug nuts.

26. Adjust the brakes.

27. Carefully lower the vehicle, then tighten the lug nuts to 100 ft. lbs. (140 Nm).

28. Road test the vehicle for proper brake operation.

Wheel Cylinder

REMOVAL & INSTALLATION

▶ **See Figures 35 and 36**

1. Raise and safely support the vehicle.

2. Remove the tire and wheel assembly.

3. Mark the relationship of the wheel to the axle flange to help maintain wheel balance after assembly.

4. Remove the tire and wheel assembly.

5. Remove the brake drum, as outlined earlier in this section.

6. Using tool J-38400, or an equivalent brake spanner and remover, remove the actuator spring from the adjuster lever. Use care not to distort the spring when removing it.

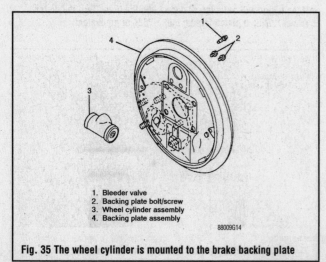

1. Bleeder valve
2. Backing plate bolt/screw
3. Wheel cylinder assembly
4. Backing plate assembly

88009G14

Fig. 35 The wheel cylinder is mounted to the brake backing plate

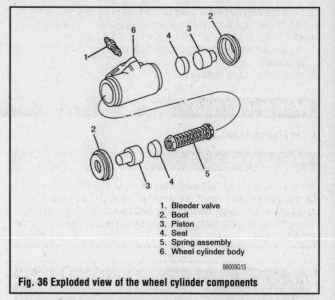

1. Bleeder valve
2. Boot
3. Piston
4. Seal
5. Spring assembly
6. Wheel cylinder body

88009G15

Fig. 36 Exploded view of the wheel cylinder components

➡ **During the following steps when removing the retractor spring from either shoe and lining assembly, do not over stretch the spring. This will reduce its effectiveness.**

✳✳ CAUTION

Keep fingers away from retractor spring to prevent fingers from being pinched between the spring and shoe web or spring and the backing plate.

7. Remove the bleeder screw to gain access to the brake line.

8. Disconnect and cap or plug the wheel cylinder brake line to prevent fluid loss and/or brake system contamination.

9. Spread the upper half of the brake shoes and remove the wheel cylinder retaining bolts and remove the wheel cylinder.

To install:

10. Apply Loctite® Master Gasket Maker or equivalent sealer to the wheel cylinder shoulder face that contacts the backing plate.

11. Position the wheel cylinder assembly on the backing plate and hold into place.

12. Install attaching bolts and tighten to 110 inch lbs. (12 Nm).

13. Connect the brake line to the wheel cylinder torquing to 12 ft. lbs. (17 Nm).

14. Bleed the wheel cylinder using the recommended procedure.

15. Install the bleeder valve and tighten to 62 inch lbs. (7 Nm).

16. Clean all the brake spring completely with brake solvent and allow to air dry.

17. Install the actuator spring and adjust the brake shoes.

18. Install the brake drum and wheel assembly, torquing the wheel to specifications.

19. Add DOT 3 brake fluid to the master cylinder if needed and road test to verify proper brake system performance.

Brake Backing Plate

REMOVAL & INSTALLATION

▶ **See Figure 35**

1. Raise and safely support the vehicle.

2. Remove the tire and wheel assembly.

3. Mark the relationship of the wheel to the axle flange to help maintain wheel balance after assembly.

4. Remove the tire and wheel assembly.

5. Remove the brake drum, as outlined earlier in this section.

6. Remove the wheel cylinder, as outlined earlier in this section.

7. Disconnect the parking brake cable from the backing plate.
8. Remove the hub and bearing assembly, as outlined in Section 8 of this vehicle.
9. Remove the brake backing plate from the vehicle.
To install:
10. Install the brake backing plate.

11. Install the hub and bearing assembly, as outlined in Section 8 of this manual.
12. Connect the parking brake cable to the backing plate.
13. Install the wheel cylinder, as outlined earlier in this section.
14. Properly bleed the brake hydraulic system, as outlined later in this section.

REAR DISC BRAKES

▶ See Figures 37 and 38

✳✳ CAUTION

Some brake pads contain asbestos, which has been determined to be a cancer causing agent. Never clean the brake surfaces with compressed air! Avoid inhaling any dust from any brake surface! When cleaning brake surfaces, use a commercially available brake cleaning fluid.

Fig. 37 View of the rear disc brake assembly—1992 Lumina shown

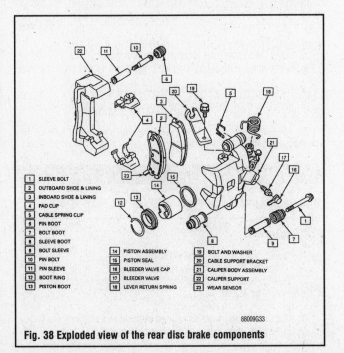

Fig. 38 Exploded view of the rear disc brake components

Brake Pads

REMOVAL & INSTALLATION

✳✳ CAUTION

Always replace all pads on both rear wheels at the same time. Failure to do so will result in uneven braking action and premature wear.

1988–92 Vehicles

▶ See Figures 39, 40, 41 and 42

1. Raise the vehicle and support with jackstands.
2. Remove the rear wheel and tire assemblies.
3. Remove the rear caliper and hang by the suspension with a piece of wire to prevent brake hose damage. Refer to the Caliper removal procedures in this section for assistance.
4. Using a suitable prybar, disengage the buttons on the outboard pad from the holes in the caliper housing, then remove the outboard pad.
5. Press in on the edge of the inboard pad and tilt outward to release the pad from the pad retainer.
6. Remove the two way check valve from the end of the caliper piston using a small prybar.
To install:

➡Do NOT allow pliers to contact the actuator screw. Protect the piston so the contact surface does not get damaged.

7. Bottom the piston into the caliper bore by positioning 12 in. (305mm) adjustable pliers over the caliper housing and piston surface.
8. Lubricate a new two way check valve and install it into the end of the piston.
9. Install the inboard brake pad. Engage the pad edge in the retainer tabs closest to the caliper bridge. Press down and snap the tabs at the open side of the caliper. The wear sensor should be at the leading edge of the pad during wheel rotation. The back of the pad must lay flat against the piston. The button on the back of the pad must engage the D-shaped notch in the piston.

➡If the piston will not align or retract into the bore. Turn the piston clockwise using a piston turning tool J-7624 or equivalent.

Fig. 39 Use a suitable prybar to detach the buttons . . .

Fig. 40 . . . then remove the outboard pad from the caliper

Fig. 41 Remove the inboard pad and pad retainer (if necessary

Fig. 42 Before installing the pad, use a pair of pliers to bottom out the caliper piston

10. Install the outboard brake pad. Snap the pad retainer spring into the slots in the caliper housing. The back of the pad must lay flat against the caliper.

11. Install the caliper onto the mounting bracket as outlined in this section.

12. Apply force at least three times to the brake pedal to seat the brake pads before moving the vehicle.

13. Install the rear wheels.

14. Lower the vehicle and check for fluid leaks.

1993–96 Vehicles

1. Remove about ⅔ of the brake fluid from the reservoir with a clean syringe or baster type utensil.

2. Raise and safely support the vehicle.

3. Matchmark the relationship of the wheel to the axle flange. Remove the wheel and tire assembly.

4. Reinstall two lug nuts to retain the rotor.

5. Unfasten the bolt and washer attaching the cable support bracket to the caliper body assembly. It is not necessary to disconnect the parking brake cable from the caliper parking brake lever or disconnect the brake hose unless the caliper is to be completely removed from the vehicle. Freeing the cable support bracket allows enough flexibility in the cable to pivot the caliper up and down and remove the shoe and lining.

6. Remove the sleeve bolt.

7. Pivot the caliper body assembly up. Do not completely remove the caliper assembly body.

8. Remove the outboard and inboard shoe and linings (pads) from the caliper support.

9. Remove the two pad clips from the caliper support.

To install:

10. Bottom the piston assembly into the caliper bore. Use a suitable spanner-type tool in the piston slot to turn the piston assembly and thread it into the caliper body assembly.

11. After bottoming the piston, lift the inner edge of the boot next to the piston assembly and press out any trapped air. The boot must lie flat. Make sure the slots in the end of the piston are positioned correctly before pivoting the caliper body assembly down over the shoe and lining in the caliper support. Use a suitable spanner-type tool in the piston slots to turn the piston as necessary.

➡ **Whenever installing new pads, install new pad clips. These should be provided in the disc pad kit.**

12. Install the two pad clips in the caliper support.

13. Install the outboard and inboard shoe and lining in the caliper support. The wear sensor is on the outboard pad. The sensor is positioned downward at the leading edge of the rotor during forward wheel rotation. Hold the metal shoe edge against the spring end of the clips in the caliper support. Push the shoe in toward the hub, bending the spring ends slightly, and engage the shoe notches with the support abutments.

14. Pivot the caliper body assembly down over the shoe and lining assembly. Be careful not to damage the piston boot on the inboard. Compress the sleeve boot by hand as the caliper body moves into position to prevent boot damage.

15. After the caliper body is in position, recheck the installation of the pad clips. If necessary, use a small prytool to re-seat or center the pad clips on the support abutments.

16. Install the sleeve bolt and tighten to 20 ft. lbs. (27 Nm).

17. Install the cable support bracket (with the cable attached) with the bolt and washer. Tighten the bolt to 32 ft. lbs. (43 Nm).

18. Remove the two lug nuts retaining the rotor.

19. Install the wheel and tire assembly, aligning the marks made during removal.

20. Carefully lower the vehicle, then firmly depress the brake pedal 3 times to seat the pads against the rotors.

INSPECTION

The pad thickness should be inspected every time that the wheels are removed. Pad thickness can be checked by looking down through the inspection hole in the top of the caliper. If the thickness of the pad is worn to within 0.030 inch (0.76mm) (if the pads are the riveted type, be sure not to include the thickness of the rivets when measuring pad thickness), all the pads should be replaced. A thermal material is sandwiched between the lining and backing. Don't include this material when determining the lining thickness.

This is the factory-recommended measurement. Your state's automobile inspection laws may be different.

Brake Caliper

REMOVAL & INSTALLATION

1988–93 Vehicles

▶ **See Figure 43**

1. Remove about ⅔ of the brake fluid from the reservoir with a clean syringe or baster type utensil.

2. Raise and safely support the vehicle with jackstands.

Fig. 43 If the caliper is not being removed, suspend it from the body with a piece of wire

3. Remove the rear wheel and tire assembly, then reinstall two lug nuts to retain the rotor.

4. Remove the brake shield assembly.

5. Loosen the tension on the parking brake cable at the equalizer.

6. Remove the parking cable and return spring from the lever.

7. Hold the cable lever and remove the locknut, lever and seal.

8. Push the piston into the caliper bore using two adjustable pliers over the inboard pad tabs.

➡**Do NOT allow pliers to contact the actuator screw. Protect the piston so the contact surface does not get damaged.**

9. Reinstall the lever seal with the sealing bead against the caliper housing, lever and locknut.

10. Remove and plug the brake hose inlet fitting only if the caliper is going to be removed from the vehicle.

11. Remove the bolt and bracket to gain access to the upper mounting bolt.

12. Unfasten the caliper mounting bolts, then pull the caliper from the rotor and suspend from the strut with a suitable piece of wire to prevent brake hose damage. Do NOT allow the caliper to hang from the brake hose.

To install:

13. Inspect all brake parts for damage and deterioration. Replace any parts if necessary.

14. Push the caliper sleeves inward.

15. Install the caliper to the mounting bracket. Tighten the mounting bolts to 92 ft. lbs. (125 Nm).

16. Install the bracket and bolt after the mounting bolts have been torqued.

17. Install the brake hose inlet with new copper washers if removed.

18. Remove the locknut, lever and seal. Lubricate the lever seal and lever shift.

19. Install the seal and lever with the lever facing down.

20. Hold the lever back against the stop and tighten the locknut to 35 ft. lbs. (47 Nm).

21. Install the return spring and parking brake cable. Adjust the cable as outlined in the Parking Brake Cable Adjustment procedures in this section.

22. Install the brake shield and rear wheel assembly.

23. Lower the vehicle.

24. Fill the brake reservoir with DOT 3 brake fluid.

25. Bleed the caliper, if it was removed from the vehicle. Refer to the Brake System Bleeding procedures in this section.

26. Inspect the brake system for fluid leaks.

27. Apply the brake pedal three times to seat the brake pads before moving the vehicle.

1994–96 Vehicles

▶ **See Figures 44 and 45**

1. Raise and safely support the vehicle.

2. Matchmark the relationship of the wheel to the axle flange. Remove the wheel and tire assembly.

3. Reinstall two lug nuts to retain the rotor.

4. If the caliper is being removed from the vehicle for replacement or overhaul, perform the following:

   a. Disconnect the brake hose from the caliper. Plug the opening in the caliper and the brake hose to prevent fluid loss and system contamination.

   b. Detach the parking brake cable by lifting up on one end of the cable spring clip to free the end of the cable from the lever.

5. Remove the bolt and washer attaching the cable support brake to the caliper body assembly.

6. Remove the sleeve bolt, then remove the caliper body assembly. Pivot the caliper body up to clear the rotor and then slide it inboard off the pin sleeve.

7. If the caliper is being removed for shoe and lining replacement or to provide access to the support bracket, rotor of wheel brake components, hang the caliper from suspension using a suitable wire hook so as not to stretch or damage the brake hose or brake cable.

8. Inspect the pin boot, bolt boot and sleeve for cuts, tears or deterioration. If damaged, replace the boots.

To install:

9. Install the caliper assembly, as follows:

   a. If not replaced, remove the pin boot from the caliper body assembly and install the small end over the pint sleeve (installed on the caliper sup-

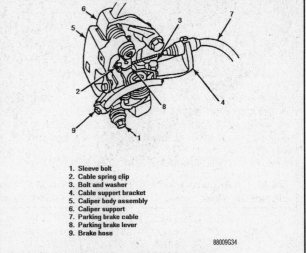

1. Sleeve bolt
2. Cable spring clip
3. Bolt and washer
4. Cable support bracket
5. Caliper body assembly
6. Caliper support
7. Parking brake cable
8. Parking brake lever
9. Brake hose

88009G34

Fig. 44 Caliper installation—1995 vehicle shown

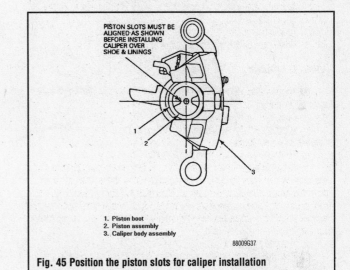

PISTON SLOTS MUST BE ALIGNED AS SHOWN BEFORE INSTALLING CALIPER OVER SHOE & LININGS

1. Piston boot
2. Piston assembly
3. Caliper body assembly

88009G37

Fig. 45 Position the piston slots for caliper installation

port) until the boot seats in the pin groove. This is to prevent cutting the pin boot when the sliding body assembly onto the pin sleeve.

   b. Hold the caliper body assembly in position it was removed and start over the end of the pin sleeve. As the caliper body assembly approaches the pin boot, work the large end of the pin boot in the caliper body groove. Then push the caliper body fully onto the pin.

   c. Pivot the caliper body assembly down, using care not to damage the piston boot on the inboard shoe. Compress the sleeve boot by hand as the caliper body move into position to prevent boot damage.

   d. After the caliper body assembly is in position, recheck the installation of the pad clips. If necessary, use a small prytool to re-seat or center the pad clips on the support abutments.

10. Install the sleeve bolt and tighten to 20 ft. lbs. (27 Nm).

11. Fasten the cable support bracket (with the cable attached) with the retaining bolts and washer. Tighten to 32 ft. lbs. (43 Nm).

12. If disconnected, attach the end of the parking brake cable to the parking brake lever by lifting up on the end of the cable spring clip and work the end of the parking brake cable into the notch in the lever.

13. Unplug and attach the brake hose, if it was disconnected.

14. Remove the two lug nuts retaining the rotor.

15. Install the wheel and tire assembly, aligning the marks made during removal.

16. Carefully lower the vehicle, then bleed the brake system if the brake hose was disconnected.

17. Firmly depress the brake pedal 3 times to seat the pads against the rotors.

OVERHAUL

1988–93 Vehicles

▶ **See Figures 46 thru 59**

1. Remove the caliper assembly from the vehicle as previously outlined.
2. Remove the sleeve and bolt boots. Check the boots and bolts for damage and corrosion.
3. Remove the brake pad retainer from the end of the piston by rotating the retainer until the inside tabs line up with the notches in the piston.
4. Remove the locknut, lever, lever seal and anti-friction washer (if installed) from the caliper.
5. Remove the piston by using a wrench to rotate the actuator screw to work the piston out of the caliper bore.
6. Remove the balance spring and actuator screw.
7. Remove the shaft seal, thrust washer and boot.
8. Remove the retainer using ring pliers and a piston locator.
9. Remove the piston seal using a non-metallic seal pick.
10. Carefully remove the bleeder valve. If the valve breaks, the caliper should be replaced.
11. Inspect all parts for damage and replace if necessary.
12. Clean all parts in denatured alcohol and dry with compressed air.
13. Install the bleeder valve.
14. Install the bracket and bolt.
15. Lubricate the new piston seals with clean brake fluid and install into the caliper bore. Make sure they are not twisted.
16. Lubricate the piston locating tool J36627, do NOT install the piston.
17. Install the thrust washer on the actuator screw with the copper side towards the piston.
18. Lubricate the shaft seal and install it on the actuator screw.
19. Install the actuator into the piston assembly.
20. Install the balance spring and retainer into the piston.
21. After all the components are lubricated and installed into the piston, install the piston into the bore. Push the piston into the bore so that the locator is past the retainer groove in the caliper bore.

Fig. 46 Unfasten the nut . . .

Fig. 47 . . . then remove the lever

Fig. 48 Remove the lever seal and . . .

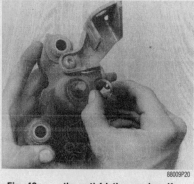

Fig. 49 . . . the anti-friction washer, if used

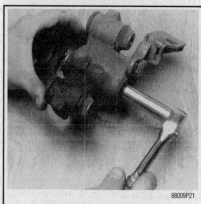

Fig. 50 Rotate the actuator screw . . .

Fig. 51 . . . then remove the piston from the bore

Fig. 52 Remove the balance spring

Fig. 53 Remove the actuator screw by pressing on the thread end

Fig. 54 Remove the shaft seal and thrust washer from the screw

Fig. 55 Remove the boot, being careful not to scratch the caliper bore

Fig. 56 Use ring pliers to compress the retainer . . .

Fig. 57 . . . then withdraw the retainer from the bore

Fig. 58 Remove the piston locator . . .

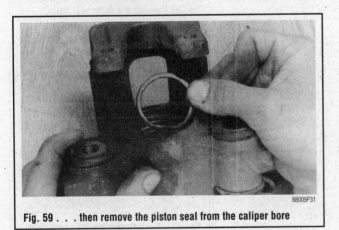

Fig. 59 . . . then remove the piston seal from the caliper bore

22. Install the retainer using retainer ring pliers.
23. Install the boot onto the piston with the inside lip of the boot in the piston groove and the boot fold is towards the end of the piston. Push the piston to the bottom of the bore.
24. Lubricate and install the lever seal over the end of the actuator screw.
25. Install the lever and rotate away from the stop slightly. Hold the lever while tightening the locknut to 32 ft. lbs. (44 Nm).
26. Install the pad retainer in the groove at the end of the piston.
27. Align the inside retainer tabs with the piston notches. Rotate the retainer so that the tabs enter the piston groove.
28. Lubricate with silicone grease and install the sleeve and bolt boots.
29. Install the caliper assembly and tighten the retaining bolts to 92 ft. lbs. (125 Nm).
30. Bleed the brake system as outlined in this section.

1994–96 Vehicles

▶ See Figure 60

1. Remove the caliper from the vehicle, as outlined earlier, then place on a clean workbench.

➡Pad the interior of the caliper assembly with clean shop towels to prevent damage to the piston assembly as it is removed.

✸✸ CAUTION

Do NOT place fingers in front of the piston in an attempt to catch or protect it when applying compressed air. This could result in serious personal injury.

2. Remove the piston from the caliper using compressed air into the caliper inlet hole. The piston will come out through the piston boots.

➡Another method for piston removal is to use a spanner-type tool in the slots in the end of the piston to thread the piston assembly off the caliper.

3. Remove the boot ring and piston boot. Use a small prytool to carefully pry up one end of the boot ring. Work the boot ring out of the caliper groove.
4. Use a small wooden or plastic tool to start the piston seal out of the caliper groove, then remove the seal.
5. Remove the bleeder valve cap and the bleeder valve.
6. If replacement is required, remove the lever return spring. Use a suitable prytool to disengage the return spring from the parking brake lever. Then unhook the spring from the stopper pin.
7. Remove the pin boot and the bolt boot from the caliper body.
8. Remove the bolt sleeve and sleeve boot from the caliper support.

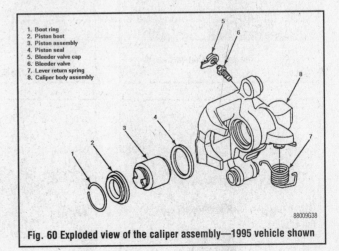

1. Boot ring
2. Piston boot
3. Piston assembly
4. Piston seal
5. Bleeder valve cap
6. Bleeder valve
7. Lever return spring
8. Caliper body assembly

Fig. 60 Exploded view of the caliper assembly—1995 vehicle shown

9. Remove the pin bolt and pin sleeve from the caliper support.

10. Inspect all parts for damage, and replace as necessary. Clean all parts in denatured alcohol, then allow to dry thoroughly.

11. Lubricate the pin sleeve with silicone grease. Install the pin bolt and pin sleeve to the caliper support. Tighten the bolt to 20 ft. lbs. (27 Nm).

12. Lubricate the sleeve boot with silicone grease to ease installation. Compress the lip sleeve boot and push it all the way through the caliper body until the lip emerges and seats on the inboard face of the caliper ear.

13. Lubricate the sleeve with silicone grease to ease assembly. Push the bolt sleeve in through the lip end of the boot until the boot seats in the sleeve groove at the other end.

14. Install the bolt boot onto the caliper body.

15. Install the pin boot over the pin sleeve (installed on the caliper support).

16. If removed, install a new lever return spring. Position the spring with the hook end around the stopper pin, then pry the other end of the spring over the lever.

17. Install the bleeder valve and tighten to 97 inch lbs. (11 Nm), then install the valve cap.

18. Lubricate a new piston seal with clean brake fluid, then install the seal. Make sure the seal is not twisted.

19. Install the piston boot onto the piston assembly.

20. Lubricate the piston assembly with clean brake fluid, then install the piston and boot into the bore of the caliper body assembly. Start the piston in by hand, then thread it into the bottom of the caliper bore using a suitable spanner-type tool into the slots in the end of the piston assembly.

21. Install the boot ring. Make sure the outside edge of the piston boot is smoothly seated in the counterbore or the caliper body assembly. Work the boot ring into the groove near the open end of the caliper bore, being careful not to pinch the piston boot between the boot ring and the caliper body.

22. After installing the ring, lift the inner edge of the boot next to the piston assembly and press out any trapped air. The boot must lie flat.

23. Install the caliper as outlined earlier in this section. Make sure to properly bleed the brake system.

Brake Rotor

REMOVAL & INSTALLATION

♦ **See Figures 61 and 62**

❊❊ CAUTION

Some brake pads may contain asbestos, which has been determined to be a cancer causing agent. Never clean the brake surfaces with compressed air! Avoid inhaling any dust from any brake surface! When cleaning brake surfaces, use a commercially available brake cleaning fluid.

Fig. 61 Clean the rotor using a commercially available brake cleaner

Fig. 62 Remove the rotor from the hub and bearing assembly

1. Raise and safely support the vehicle with jackstands.
2. Remove the wheel and tire assembly.

➡**Do NOT allow the caliper to hang from the brake hose!**

3. Remove the brake caliper, as outlined earlier in this section, and support with a wire to the surrounding body.
4. If equipped, remove the caliper support.
5. Remove the rotor assembly.

To install:

6. Install the brake rotor over the hub assembly.
7. If equipped, install the caliper support.
8. Install the brake caliper as outlined in this section.
9. Install the wheel and tire assembly.
10. Carefully lower the vehicle, then firmly pump the brake pedal 3 time before moving the vehicle.

INSPECTION

Thickness Variation Check

The thickness variation can be checked by measuring the thickness of the rotor at four or more points. All of the measurements must be made at the same distance from the edge of the rotor. A rotor the varies by more than 0.0005 in. (0.0127mm) can cause a pulsation in the brake pedal. If these measurement are excessive, the rotor should be refinished or replaced.

Lateral Runout Check

1. Remove the caliper and hang from the body with a piece of wire. Install two inverted lug nuts to retain the rotor.
2. Install a dial indicator to the steering knuckle so that the indicator button contacts the rotor about 1 in. (25mm) from the rotor edge.
3. Zero the dial indicator.
4. Move the rotor one complete revolution and observe the total indicated runout.
5. If the rotor runout exceeds 0.0015 in. (0.040mm) have the rotor refinished or replaced.

Refinishing Brake Rotors

All brake rotors have a minimum thickness dimension cast onto them. Do NOT use a brake rotor that will not meet minimum thickness specifications in the "Brake Specifications" chart at the end of this section.

Accurate control of rotor tolerances is necessary for proper brake performance and safety. Machining of the rotor should be done by a qualified machine shop with the proper machining equipment.

The optimum speed for refinishing the rotor surface is a spindle speed of 200 rpm. Crossfeed for rough cutting should range from 0.006–0.010 in. (0.152–0.254mm) per revolution. The finish cuts should be made at crossfeeds no greater than 0.002 in. (0.051mm) per revolution.

PARKING BRAKE

Cables

REMOVAL & INSTALLATION

1988–93 Vehicles

▶ See Figures 63 and 64

FRONT CABLE

1. Raise the vehicle and support with jackstands.
2. Loosen the equalizer under the drivers side door.
3. Remove the front cable from the left rear cable at the retainer.
4. Remove the nut at the underbody bracket.
5. Remove the clip from underbody.
6. Lower the vehicle.
7. Remove the cable from the parking brake lever assembly using a brake cable release tool J-37043 or equivalent.

To install:

8. Install the cable to the parking brake lever assembly.
9. Raise the vehicle and support with jackstands.
10. Install the clip to the underbody and the nut at the underbody bracket.
11. Install the front cable to the left rear cable at the retainer.
12. Adjust the cable as outlined in this section.
13. Lower the vehicle and check operation.

LEFT REAR CABLE

1. Raise the vehicle and support with jackstands.
2. Remove the spring from the equalizer under the drivers door and equalizer.
3. Remove the left rear cable from the front cable at the retainer.
4. Remove the cable retainer and cable from the caliper parking lever bracket using a cable release tool J-37043 or equivalent.

To install:

5. Install the cable to the bracket and cable support.
6. Install the cable to the brake lever and cable retainer.
7. Install the left rear cable to the front cable with the retainer.
8. Install the equalizer and spring.
9. Adjust the parking brake as outlined in this section.
10. Lower the vehicle and check operation.

RIGHT REAR CABLE

1. Raise the vehicle and support with jackstands.
2. Remove the spring from the equalizer under the driver's door and equalizer.
3. Remove the cable from the underbody bracket using a cable release tool J-37043 or equivalent.
4. Remove the bolts from the clips above the fuel tank.
5. Remove the cable retainer and cable from the caliper parking lever bracket using a cable release tool J-37043 or equivalent.

To install:

6. Position the cable above the fuel tank.
7. Install the cable to the bracket and cable support.
8. Install the cable to the brake lever and cable retainer.
9. Install the clips above the fuel tank.
10. Install the cable to the underbody brackets.
11. Install the equalizer and spring.
12. Adjust the parking brake as outlined in this section.
13. Lower the vehicle and check operation.

1995–96 Vehicles

▶ See Figures 65, 66 and 67

This vehicle is equipped with coated parking brake cable assemblies. The wire strand is coated with a clear plastic material which slides over plastic seals

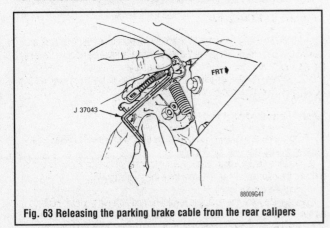

Fig. 63 Releasing the parking brake cable from the rear calipers

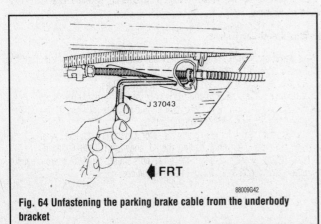

Fig. 64 Unfastening the parking brake cable from the underbody bracket

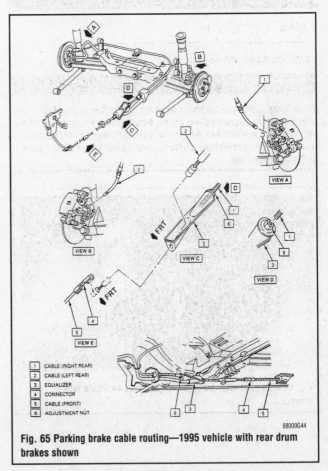

Fig. 65 Parking brake cable routing—1995 vehicle with rear drum brakes shown

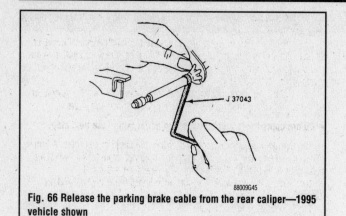

Fig. 66 Release the parking brake cable from the rear caliper—1995 vehicle shown

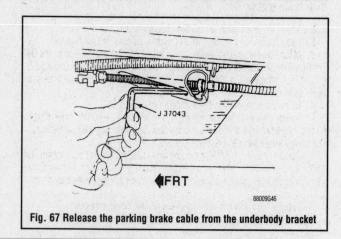

Fig. 67 Release the parking brake cable from the underbody bracket

inside the conduit end fittings. This is for corrosion protection and reduced parking brake effort.

Handling of these cables during servicing of the parking brake system requires extra care. Damage to the plastic coating will reduce corrosion protection and if the damaged area passes through the seal, increased parking brake effort could result. Contact of the coating with sharp-edged tools, or with sharp surfaces of the vehicle underbody should be avoided.

To prevent damage to the threaded parking brake adjusting rod when servicing the parking brake, the following is recommended: before attempting to turn the adjusting nut, clean the exposed threads on each side of the nut; lubricate the threads of the adjusting rod before turning the nut.

If any one of the parking brake cables has been replaced, it is necessary to pre-stretch the new cable before adjusting the parking brake. To do this, apply the parking brake pedal several times. Fully release it each time. The parking brake pedal assembly, located on the dash panel left of the service brake pedal, is a push-to-release type mechanism which is APPLIED by depressing the pedal once and RELEASED by depressing the pedal again. No release handle is used.

➡This is a parking brake NOT a emergency brake. It is designed to hold the vehicle on a flat or an incline and will not stop a vehicle in motion.

FRONT CABLE

1. Remove the lower door sill trim plate.
2. Remove the driver's side sound insulator panel.
3. Fold back the carpeting to expose the parking brake cable.
4. Raise and safely support the vehicle.
5. Loosen the parking brake cable at the equalizer.
6. Pull the front cable at the connector clip and attach loop of the shear strap to hook of the parking brake ratcheting.
7. Remove the parking brake front cable at the connector clip.
8. Remove the parking brake front cable clip from the underbody bracket using special tool J 37043 Brake Cable Release Tool or equivalent.
9. Remove the cable button end from the lever clevis.

10. Remove the parking brake cable from the parking brake assembly using special tool J 37043 or equivalent.

To install:

11. Install the cable into the vehicle and from inside the vehicle connect the parking brake cable housing to the parking brake lever assembly and fully seat the locking fingers.
12. Install the parking brake cable end to the lever clevis.
13. Feed the parking brake cable and snap clip to the underbody.
14. Install the carpeting.
15. Install the driver's side sound insulator.
16. Install the lower door sill trim plate.
17. From under the vehicle, connect the front cable to the left rear cable at the connector clip. Tighten the nut on the equalizer to remove cable slack.
18. Adjust the parking brake cable.
19. Lower the vehicle.

LEFT REAR CABLE

1. Raise and safely support the vehicle.
2. Loosen the cable at the equalizer assembly.
3. Disconnect the left rear cable from the front cable at the connector clip.
4. Disconnect the cable from the bracket.
5. Compress the locking fingers to disconnect the parking brake cable housing from the equalizer assembly using special tool J 37043 or the equivalent Brake Cable Release Tool.
6. Disconnect the parking brake cable end from the parking brake lever on the caliper, if equipped with rear disc brakes. If equipped with rear drum brakes, remove the rear wheel and brake drum. Disconnect the cable end from the brake shoe lever and disengage from the backing plate.
7. Disconnect the cable from the rear bracket and cable support and remove the cable from the vehicle.

To install:

8. Route the cable through the rear cable bracket and cable support.
9. Feed the cable through the equalizer and front cable bracket.
10. Fully seat the cable housing locking fingers into the equalizer assembly.
11. Connect the parking brake cable to the parking brake lever on the caliper, if equipped with rear disc brakes. If equipped with rear drum brakes, thread the cable end through the opening in the backing plate and then connect the cable end to the brake shoe lever.
12. Connect the left rear cable to the front cable at the connector clip.
13. Tighten nut on the equalizer to remove the parking cable slack.
14. Lower the vehicle.
15. Adjust the parking brakes.

RIGHT REAR CABLE

1. Raise and safely support the vehicle.
2. Remove the parking brake cable at the equalizer.
3. Remove the parking brake cable from the brake cable support assembly.
4. Remove the parking brake cable from the rear underbody bracket using special tool J 37043 or the equivalent.
5. Remove the two bolts from clips on the underbody rail.
6. Remove the parking brake cable from the backing plate and parking brake lever for vehicle equipped with drum brakes.
7. Remove the caliper parking brake lever and bracket using special tool J 37043 or the equivalent on vehicles equipped with rear disc brakes.

To install:

8. Install the parking brake cable in position on the underbody rail.
9. Install the two bolts to support clips above the knuckle hub support.
10. Install the parking brake cable to the backing plate and the parking brake lever on vehicle equipped with drum brakes.
11. Install the parking brake cable to the caliper parking brake lever and bracket on vehicles equipped with disc brakes. Tighten the bolts to 36 inch lbs. (4 Nm).
12. Feed the parking brake cable through the underbody bracket and snap conduit to the bracket.
13. Install the parking brake cable threaded rod to the equalizer.
14. Tighten the nut on the equalizer to remove the cable slack.
15. Safely lower the vehicle.
16. Adjust the parking brakes as required.

ADJUSTMENT

> See Figure 68

Rear Disc Brakes

1. Apply the parking brake pedal three times with heavy force of about 175 lbs. (778 N).

➡ **Do not apply the main/service brake pedal during the next step.**

2. Fully apply and release the parking brake three times.
3. Raise the vehicle and support with jackstands.
4. Matchmark the position of the wheel to the hub and bearing assembly.
5. Make sure the parking brake is fully released. Turn the ignition to the **ON** position. The BRAKE warning lamp should be off. If the BRAKE warning light is still on, pull downward on the front parking brake to remove the slack from the pedal assembly.

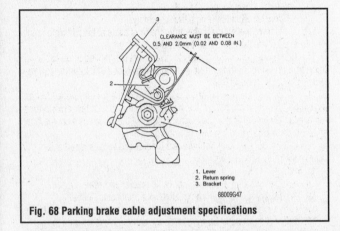

Fig. 68 Parking brake cable adjustment specifications

6. Remove the rear wheel and tire assemblies, then reinstall two lug nuts to retain the rotors.
7. The parking brake levers on both calipers should be against the lever stops on the caliper housing. If not against the stops, check for binding in the rear cables and/or loosen the cables at the adjuster until both left and right levers are against their stops.
8. Tighten the parking brake cable at the adjuster until either the right or left lever reaches the dimensions shown in the accompanying figure.

➡ **Do not apply the main/service brake pedal during the next step.**

9. Operate the parking brake several times to check adjustments. A firm pedal should be present. The rear wheels should not rotate forward when the parking brake is fully applies. If necessary, repeat steps 8 and 9.
10. Remove the two wheel lug nuts, then install the rear wheel and tire assemblies.
11. Carefully lower the vehicle.

Rear Drum Brakes

1. Adjust the rear brakes, as outlined earlier in this section.
2. Apply the parking brake to 10 clicks, then release. Repeat 5 times.
3. Make sure the parking brake is fully released. Turn the ignition to the **ON** position. The BRAKE warning lamp should be off. If the BRAKE warning light is still on, pull downward on the front parking brake to remove the slack from the pedal assembly.
4. Raise and safely support the vehicle with jackstands.
5. Adjust the parking brake by turning the nut on the equalizer while spinning both rear wheels. When either rear wheel develops drag, stop adjusting and back off the equalizer 1 full turn.
6. Apply the parking brake to 4 clicks and check the rear wheel rotation. The wheel should not move when you attempt to rotate it, by hand, in a forward rotation. The wheel should drag or not move when attempting to rotate it in a rearward direction.
7. Release the parking brake and check for free wheel rotation.
8. Carefully lower the vehicle.

DELCO MORAINE ANTI-LOCK BRAKE SYSTEM (ABS) III

Description and Operation

> See Figure 69

The Delco Moraine Anti-Lock Brake System (DM ABS-III) was used on 1988–91 vehicles. This system operates on all 4 wheels. The system is designed to reduce the tendency of 1 or more wheels to lock while braking. In most cases, the conventional power brake system of the vehicle performs the braking function; anti-lock braking occurs only when a combination of wheel speed sensors and a microprocessor determines a wheel (or wheels) is about to lose traction during braking. The DM ABS-III then adjusts the brake pressure to both front wheels independently and/or both rear wheels to reduce the tendency of the wheel(s) to lock-up. This system helps the driver maintain control during hard braking on a wide range of road surfaces and driving conditions. The driver can minimize stopping distance and bring the vehicle to a controlled stop. The DM ABS-III cannot increase the brake pressure above the master cylinder pressure and can never apply the brakes by itself.

The DM-ABS III system provides improved braking by regulating the amount of force at any wheel to a value which will prevent locking and by keeping all 4 wheels at or near the same speed during braking. These 2 functions combine to provide the driver with the shortest possible stop while maintaining control of the vehicle.

When the ignition switch is turned **ON**, the system enters its initial cycle. At this time, a clicking noise may be heard; this is normal and results from the controller cycling the relays and solenoids to check circuitry. While the vehicle is operating, the controller is constantly monitoring the system as well as reacting to brake inputs. If any faults are found, the controller assigns a fault code and stores the code for future retrieval. The amber warning light on the dash will be illuminated when a fault is detected.

The amber ABS dash light will inform the driver of system status. If the light is flashing, the controller has detected a fault but is still allowing the ABS system to operate. If the light is on constantly (no flash) the controller has detected a fault and disabled part or all of the ABS system. The front and rear wheel portions may be individually disabled by the controller. The amber warning light refers only to the ABS system; with ABS disabled, the vehicle will still have conventional braking capabilities if that system is not damaged.

➡ **The red brake warning lamp can indicate conditions damaging to the ABS system, such as low fluid. If the red lamp is on with the amber lamp, attend to the conventional brake system before diagnosing ABS. The brake system must be operating properly before ABS diagnosis.**

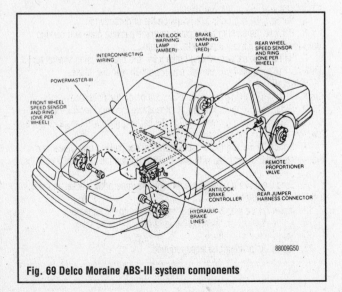

Fig. 69 Delco Moraine ABS-III system components

When the brake pedal is depressed, the controller is alerted that the brakes have been applied and monitors the speed of each wheel. If impending lock-up or uneven wheel speeds are detected, the controller cycles the solenoids on and off rapidly. This can occur independently on each front wheel or on the rear wheel which begins to lock first. When the solenoids are turned on or off, brake hydraulic pressure is applied or released at the each wheel in an attempt to equalize the deceleration rate.

During ABS operation, the system is varying the line pressures very quickly. The driver should not try to assist the system by pumping the brake pedal; hard, firm and continuous application is recommended for best ABS response. During ABS operation, the driver will feel a pulsing in the brake pedal as the line pressures change rapidly. Additionally, the clicking of the solenoids may be heard as well as momentary tire noise (screech or chirp). Both noises are normal for the system. Rapid speed change at a wheel may result in the wheel appearing to lock momentarily, resulting in road noise. Any wheel which locks and stays locked for more than 1 second is not normal; the system should be inspected immediately.

The DM ABS-III is designed only as a skid prevention system. It cannot operate properly if the base power brake system is defective. Dragging brakes, defective wheel bearings, etc. will not allow proper ABS operation.

SYSTEM COMPONENTS

Anti-lock Brake Controller

Located below the right front seat, the brake controller monitors the speed of each wheel to determine impending lock-up and, when necessary, activates the appropriate solenoid(s) to adjust brake pressures. The controller also monitors the complete system for malfunctions, provides diagnostic information and shuts the system down if a serious fault is detected. The control unit is not serviceable and must be replaced as a complete assembly.

Powermaster III Unit

The Powermaster III is an integral power booster and modulator designed to provide both normal power assist and anti-lock braking. Brake fluid pressure for both normal and ABS braking is created and maintained by a combination of an electric motor/pump and an accumulator. The accumulator is pre-charged to approximately 1200 psi (8274 kPa) with nitrogen gas.

The electric pump maintains system pressure between 2200 psi (15,169 kPa) and 2700 psi (18,616.5 kPa). During an ABS stop, fluid to the wheel units is modulated by 3 solenoid assemblies. One solenoid is assigned to each front brake; both rear brakes are controlled by 1 solenoid.

Control Solenoids

Each solenoid assembly can apply, hold or release fluid pressure in the line it controls. The left and right front brakes can be controlled individually since each is controlled by its own solenoid. However, since there is a single solenoid for both rear brakes, they are modulated together when either rear wheel approaches lock-up. (Since the rear brake modulation is based on the lowest wheel speed, this type of system is known as a Select Low 3-channel System.) The solenoids are located on the Powermaster III and are controlled by electrical signals from the Brake Controller.

Wheel Speed Sensors

The wheel speed sensors generate an AC voltage as a magnetic toothed ring passes a stationary coil. The frequency of this voltage, which increases with wheel speed, is used by the Brake Controller to determine wheel speed. By comparing wheel speeds during braking, the Anti-lock Brake Controller determines impending wheel lock.

At the front, the speed sensor rings are located on the outer CV-joints, directly below the wheel speed sensor. No repair or air gap adjustment to the speed sensor units is possible or permissible.

The rear wheel speed sensors and rings are integral parts of the rear wheel hub and bearing assemblies. Each sensor and ring is self-contained and sealed from the environment. If a sensor or ring requires is damaged or malfunctioning, the entire rear hub and bearing assembly for that side must be replaced. No repair or air gap adjustment is possible or permissible.

Proportioner Valve

Proportional control of brake line pressure to the rear brakes takes place only after a preset input pressure has been reached. Above this preset pressure, the valve limits outlet pressure to the rear wheel brakes at a set percentage of the total system output. If malfunctioning, the proportioner valve must be replaced; the separate components of the valve cannot be serviced.

Interconnecting Wiring

The interconnecting wiring is made up of 3 specific harnesses:
- The main ABS harness
- The Powermaster III harness
- The rear harness from the controller to the rear wheel speed sensor jumper harness.

Two separate jumper harnesses extend from each rear wheel speed sensor to the rear harness through underbody connectors. Additionally, 2 separate jumper harnesses extend from each front wheel speed sensor to the main ABS wiring harness.

➡**The wiring in these jumper harnesses cannot be repaired. If the wiring is damaged, the entire jumper harness must be replaced.**

The Powermaster wiring harness can be serviced separately. The main ABS wiring harness also contains and ABS power center. This power center includes the front and rear solenoid enable relays, a 10 amp fuse for the brake controller, a 15 amp fuse for the power feed to the rear wheel control solenoid, a 30 amp fusible link for the front solenoid power feed and a 30 amp fusible link for the Powermaster III pump motor.

The Powermaster III is equipped with connectors using Connector Position Assurance (CPA) locking pins. These pins assure correct alignment and retention when snapped securely. The pin must be removed before separating the connector and always reinstalled after re-connection. Make certain the rubber connector seals are in place on each connector before assembly.

Front and Rear Enable Relays

▶ **See Figure 70**

Located on the ABS power center, these relays are grounded by the brake controller when the system contains no detectable faults. Once the enable relays are grounded, voltage is applied to the solenoids. If the brake controller detects a fault, loses power or loses ground, the controller de-energizes the ground to the front enable relay. The amber light on the dash will come on to indicate loss of ABS function. The controller may detect a fault in the rear circuits and disable only the rear; if this occurs the amber light will not come on.

Brake Switch

The brake pedal switch signals the brake controller that the brakes are in use. The switch must be functioning and properly adjusted for the ABS to perform correctly.

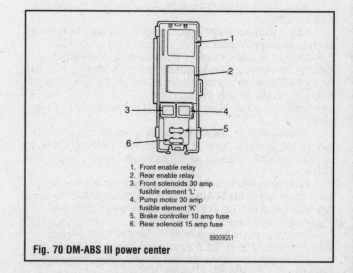

1. Front enable relay
2. Rear enable relay
3. Front solenoids 30 amp fusible element 'L'
4. Pump motor 30 amp fusible element 'K'
5. Brake controller 10 amp fuse
6. Rear solenoid 15 amp fuse

88009G51

Fig. 70 DM-ABS III power center

Brake Warning Indicator

The red brake warning lamp will light after the ignition switch is in the **RUN** position to indicate that any or all of the following conditions exist:
- Parking brake applied.
- Brake fluid level is low.
- Accumulator pressure is below 1800 psi (12,411 kPa).

Each of these conditions can damage the brake and ABS systems or reduce there efficiency. If the red light remains on after starting, the vehicle should be checked as soon as possible.

The amber Anti-lock warning lamp will light after the ignition switch is in the **RUN** position to indicate that either of the following conditions exist:
- A solid light indicates the controller has detected a fault and disabled part or all of the ABS system. It will not disable the normal power brake system.
- A flashing light indicates detection of a fault by the controller, but the controller is allowing full operation of the ABS. If the warning light is flashing, prolonged operation may result in further damage to the ABS system and may cause complete ABS failure.

Both the red and amber lights can be tested for bulb function; they should be lit when the ignition switch is turned to **START**. Additionally, the amber anti-lock warning lamp should light for approximately 3 seconds after the ignition switch is turned to **RUN** while the system undergoes initialization.

Testing

SERVICE PRECAUTIONS

✳✳ CAUTION

This brake system uses a hydraulic accumulator which, when fully charged, contains brake fluid at very high pressure. Before disconnecting any hydraulic lines, hoses or fittings be certain that the accumulator pressure is completely relieved. Failure to depressurize the accumulator may result in personal injury and/or vehicle damage.

- Certain components within the ABS system are not intended to be serviced or repaired individually. Only those components with removal and installation procedures should be serviced.
- Do not use rubber hoses or other parts not specifically specified for the DM ABS-III system. When using repair kits, replace all parts included in the kit. Partial or incorrect repair may lead to functional problems and require the replacement of the Powermaster III.
- Lubricate rubber parts with clean, fresh brake fluid to ease assembly. Do not use lubricated shop air to clean parts; damage to rubber components may result.
- Use only DOT 3 brake fluid from an unopened container. Use of DOT 5 silicone brake fluid is not recommended; reduced system performance or durability may result.
- If any hydraulic component or line is removed or replaced, it may be necessary to bleed the entire system.
- A clean repair area is essential. Perform repairs after components have been thoroughly cleaned; use only denatured alcohol to clean components. Do not allow ABS components to come into contact with any substance containing mineral oil; this includes used shop rags.
- Remove the lock pin before disconnecting CPA connectors at the Powermaster III.
- The Anti-lock brake controller is a microprocessor similar to other computer units in the vehicle. Insure that the ignition switch is **OFF** before removing or installing controller harnesses. Avoid static electricity discharge at or near the Controller.
- Fault codes stored within the system can only be read with a bi-directional scanner such as GM 9400100-A (Tech 1 Diagnostic Computer) or equivalent. Some scanners will require an additional cartridge (GM 9400008-A or equivalent) to read the system.
- The brake controller is equipped with on-board diagnostic programs beyond the setting of codes. Not all scanners are capable of using these other features. Consult the scanner manufacturer's manual for directions and capabilities.

PRE-DIAGNOSIS INSPECTION

A visual check of specific system components may reveal problems creating an apparent ABS malfunction. Performing this inspection may reveal a simple failure, thus eliminating extended diagnostic time. The steps should be performed in order.
1. Depressurize the Powermaster III.
2. Inspect the brake fluid level in the reservoir.
3. Inspect brake lines, hoses, Powermaster III and brake calipers for leakage.
4. Visually check brake lines and hoses for excessive wear, heat damage, punctures, contact with other parts, missing clips or holders, blockage or crimping.
5. Check the calipers and pins for rust or corrosion. Check for proper sliding action.
6. Check the caliper pistons for freedom of motion during application and release.
7. Inspect the front wheel speed sensors for proper mounting and connections.
8. Inspect the front speed sensor rings for broken teeth or poor mounting.
9. Measure front wheel speed sensor to ring air gap. Air gap is not adjustable but should be 0.019–0.068 in. (0.5–0.17mm).
10. Inspect rear wheel speed sensors for proper installation or damage. Inspect rear speed sensor wiring connections.
11. Brake pedal travel should not bottom near the floor after Powermaster III is depressurized.
12. Check for worn or missing isolator bushings on Powermaster III which may cause or amplify pump motor noise.
13. Inspect the high pressure line on Powermaster III which may be contacting other engine compartment components.

TROUBLE CODES

▶ **See Figures 71 and 72**

The Anti-lock Brake Controller contains diagnostic capabilities which can identify faults specifically including whether or not the fault is intermittent. The diagnostics must be read with a bi-directional scanner.

There are 58 possible 4-digit fault codes. The first 5 codes generated are stored in the order in which they occurred from least to most recent. Fault codes will not disappear when the ignition is turned **OFF** or the battery cable is disconnected. If no further fault codes occur within 50 driving cycles (Ignition switch **ON** and vehicle speed over 10 mph) the controller will clear the memory.

In order to access the trouble codes, connect a bi-directional scan tool to the ALDL connector and follow the scan tool manufacturer's instructions to read the codes. The ALDL connector is located behind the instrument panel to the right of the steering column.

A current code indicates that the malfunction occurred during the current ignition cycle. After all current codes have been displayed, the history codes will be displayed. History codes are malfunctions which do not currently exist, but could possibly aid in determining the cause of an intermittent condition.

➡**Always turn the ignition switch OFF prior to initial troubleshooting to ensure all diagnostic data is preserved. If the ignition is not turned OFF prior to reading fault codes, any information stored for a fault in the last drive cycle will be lost.**

The hand scanner must be used to clear trouble codes from the memory after repairs are completed.

ADDITIONAL DIAGNOSTIC CAPABILITIES

➡**Not all scanners can use the additional diagnostics within the controller. Consult tool manufacturer's instructions for correct application and use.**

ABS Data List: allows data parameters for many circuits to be monitored. This feature can be particularly helpful in tracking intermittent problems.

ABS Snapshot: will store the ABS data list parameters for a period of time before, during and after a fault triggers a code. Snapshot may be set for a specific code, any ABS code or at operator's command.

TROUBLE CODE	DESCRIPTION
A011	ABS Warning Light Circuit Open or Shorted to Ground
A013	ABS Warning Light Circuit Shorted to Battery
A014	Enable Relay Contacts or Fuse Open
A015	Enable Relay Contacts Shorted to Battery
A016	Enable Relay Coil Circuit Open
A017	Enable Relay Coil Circuit Shorted to Ground
A018	Enable Relay Coil Circuit Shorted to Battery
A021	Left Front Wheel Speed = 0 (1 of 2)
A022	Right Front Wheel Speed = 0 (1 of 2)
A023	Left Rear Wheel Speed = 0 (1 of 2)
A024	Right Rear Wheel Speed = 0 (1 of 2)
A025	Left Front Excessive Wheel Speed Variation (1 of 2)
A026	Right Front Excessive Wheel Speed Variation (1 of 2)
A027	Left Rear Excessive Wheel Speed Variation (1 of 2)
A028	Right Rear Excessive Wheel Speed Variation (1 of 2)
A031	Two Wheel Speeds = 0 (1 of 2)
A032	Left Front Wheel Sensor Shorted to Battery or Ground
A033	Right Front Wheel Sensor Shorted to Battery or Ground
A034	Left Rear Wheel Sensor Shorted to Battery or Ground
A035	Right Rear Wheel Sensor Shorted to Battery or Ground
A036	Low System Voltage
A037	High System Voltage
A038	Left Front ESB Will Not Hold Motor
A041	Right Front ESB Will Not Hold Motor
A042	Rear Axle ESB Will Not Hold Motor
A044	Left Front Channel Will Not Move
A045	Right Front Channel Will Not Move
A046	Rear Axle Channel Will Not Move
A047	Left Front Motor Free Spins
A048	Right Front Motor Free Spins
A051	Rear Axle Motor Free Spins
A052	Left Front Channel In Release Too Long
A053	Right Front Channel In Release Too Long
A054	Rear Axle Channel in Release Too Long
A055	Motor Driver Fault Detected
A056	Left Front Motor Circuit Open
A057	Left Front Motor Circuit Shorted to Ground

Fig. 71 List of ABS Diagnostic Trouble Codes (DTCs)—1988–91 vehicles

88009G21

TROUBLE CODE	DESCRIPTION
A058	Left Front Motor Circuit Shorted to Battery or Motor Shorted
A061	Right Front Motor Circuit Open
A062	Right Front Motor Circuit Shorted to Ground
A063	Right Front Motor Circuit Shorted to Battery or Motor Shorted
A064	Rear Axle Motor Circuit Open
A065	Rear Axle Motor Circuit Shorted to Ground
A066	Rear Axle Motor Circuit Shorted to Battery or Motor Shorted
A076	Left Front Solenoid Circuit Shorted to Battery or Open
A077	Left Front Solenoid Circuit Shorted to Ground or Driver Open
A078	Right Front Solenoid Circuit Shorted to Battery or Open
A081	Right Front Solenoid Circuit Shorted to Ground or Driver Open
A082	Calibration Memory Failure
A086	Red Brake Warning Light Activated by ABS
A087	Red Brake Warning Light Circuit Open
A088	Red Brake Warning Light Circuit Shorted to Battery
A091	Open Brake Switch Contacts During Deceleration
A092	Open Brake Switch Contacts When ABS Was Required
A093	Code A091 or A092 Set in Current or Previous Ignition Cycle
A094	Brake Switch Contacts Always Closed
A095	Brake Switch Circuit Open
A096	Brake Lights Circuit Open

Fig. 72 List of ABS Diagnostic Trouble Codes (DTCs)—1988–91 vehicles, continued

88009G22

Manual Relay and Solenoid Control: allows the front and rear enable relays and the individual hold and release solenoids to be commanded ON or OFF. Feature will display actual output or voltage (HIGH or LOW) at that particular terminal on the controller. Solenoids can only be energized for about 40 seconds; they will then be turned off for purposes of cooling.

Enhanced Diagnostics: used to determine if a trouble code is intermittent, identify how intermittent it is and give information regarding vehicle operating conditions when the most recent trouble code was set. The following data can be displayed:

• How often each of the 5 stored codes occurred. Example: A code which set once in the last 35 driving cycles might indicate a one-time occurrence such as a severe pot-hole.

• The speed the ABS controller sensed the vehicle traveling when the last fault occurred.

• State of the brake switch (ON, OFF or OPEN) at time of the last fault occurrence. Only the state of the switch is known; no information on braking or deceleration is given.

• Brake system fluid pressure.

• Whether or not brake pedal had been applied during this driving cycle. If no application is seen, fault may have been detected when ignition was turned **ON**.

• Whether or not ABS stop was in progress when fault occurred.

• How many drive cycles have occurred since last code was set.

INTERMITTENTS

The diagnostic procedures may or may not be helpful in determining the cause of intermittent problems in the system electrical components. In most cases, the fault must be present to locate.

Most intermittent problems are caused by faulty electrical connections or wiring. When an intermittent failure is encountered:

1. Check for history codes which may be stored in the anti-lock brake controller. If a history code is stored, this may indicate the circuitry which has the intermittent condition. Move the related connectors, harness and components in an effort to induce the failure.

2. Enter the Enhanced Diagnostic feature. This feature will help determine how intermittent the fault is and may help determine certain conditions that cause the fault.

3. Set the ABS snapshot to trigger on the intermittent trouble code and use the enhanced diagnostic feature to recreate the conditions that cause the intermittent code to set.

4. Check for poor mating of connector halves or terminals not fully seated in the connector body.

5. Inspect for improperly formed or damaged terminals. All connector terminals in a problem circuit should be carefully reformed to increase contact tension.

6. Check for poor terminal-to-wire connection. This requires removing the terminal from the connector body to inspect.

HYDRAULIC DIAGNOSIS

The Anti-lock Brake Controller must be scanned for trouble codes before attempting any of the following diagnostic procedures.

If no codes have been set, the tests must be performed in the alphabetical order given. Always perform the pre-diagnosis inspection before any other testing is begun.

Test A—ABS System Functional Check

1. Properly connect a scanner to ALDL connector.

➥**An assistant must sit in the driver's seat and operate the brakes and hand scanner during testing.**

2. Raise and safely support the vehicle.

3. Turn ignition switch **ON** and put transmission in **P**. Do not apply the brakes. Attempt to rotate each wheel by hand. If any wheel does not rotate, inspect for correct operation of parking brake or calipers.

➥**The rear wheels should turn with little or no resistance. The front wheels will have some resistance caused by driveline and differential drag. This is normal. If the wheel can be turned with normal hand force, the condition is acceptable.**

4. Apply medium pressure to the brake pedal. Attempt to rotate each wheel again; no rotation should be possible.

5. If either of the front wheel rotate, replace the Powermaster III; the front master cylinder portion is malfunctioning. If either of the rear wheels rotate, a Low or No Boost Pressure condition exists; refer to Test C.

6. Apply the service brakes with moderate effort and use the hand scanner to energize the hold and release solenoids for a specific wheel. Check the wheel for rotation. While some drag may be present due to residual line pressure, the wheel should rotate with hand force. Repeat this step for other wheels.

7. While the solenoids are energized, the brake pedal should not sink steadily to the floor, the pump should not run constantly or frequently, and the sound of fluid being forcefully sprayed in the reservoir should not be heard.

If any of these conditions occur, check the wiring and connections to the appropriate solenoid. If any wires or connectors are found damaged, replace the Powermaster III wiring harness.

8. If the any condition in the previous step recurs after replacing the wiring harness, replace the Powermaster III unit.

Test B—ABS Hold Function Check

1. Properly connect hand scanner to ALDL connector.

➥**An assistant must sit in the driver's seat and operate the brakes a scanner during testing.**

2. Raise and safely support the vehicle.

3. Turn ignition switch **ON** and put transmission in **N**. Keep transmission in **N** throughout testing. Allow ABS unit to pressurize before proceeding.

4. Use the scanner to energize only the rear hold solenoid, then apply the brakes moderately.

5. Attempt to turn a rear wheel; it should turn freely for 6 or more seconds before the brakes apply.

6. While the solenoid is energized, the brake pedal should not sink steadily to the floor, the pump should not run constantly or frequently, and the sound of fluid being forcefully sprayed in the reservoir should not be heard. If any of these conditions occur, or if the brakes apply in 5 seconds or less, replace the rear solenoid assembly in the Powermaster III and retest the system. If similar conditions still exist, replace the Powermaster III unit.

7. Moderately apply the brakes and use the hand scanner to energize the hold function of 1 of the front wheels.

8. Attempt to turn the appropriate front wheel; it should turn freely for 6 or more seconds before the brakes apply.

9. While the solenoid is energized, the brake pedal should not sink steadily to the floor, the pump should not run constantly or frequently, and the sound of fluid being forcefully sprayed in the reservoir should not be heard. If any of these conditions occur, or if the brakes apply in 5 seconds or less, replace the proper solenoid assembly in the Powermaster III and retest the system. If similar conditions still exist, replace the Powermaster III unit.

10. Repeat the testing procedure for the other front wheel.

Test C—Low or No Boost Pressure Check

1. With ignition **OFF**, depressurize the Powermaster III unit completely.

2. Properly connect a scanner to the ALDL connector.

3. Use the hand scanner to activate the pump. Note the total pump running time; this is the amount of time between ignition on and pump shut-off.

4. If the total time is 40 seconds or less, the Powermaster III is developing satisfactory boost pressure. If the running time is greater than 40 seconds, perform Test D.

5. Determine the pump off time by moderately applying the brakes and holding the brake pedal down. Use a stopwatch to measure the time between brake application and pump engagement.

➥**Some a scanners can compute this time using the bleed-down check function.**

6. If the pump off time is 50 seconds or less, a problem may exist within the Powermaster III. Refer to Test E. If the pump off time is greater than 50 seconds, the Powermaster III is holding boost pressure satisfactorily.

Test D—Pump Run Time Too Long

1. With ignition **OFF**, disconnect the wiring harness at pump connector. Turn the ignition switch **ON**.

2. Use a digital volt/ohmmeter (DVOM) to check voltage of Pin A to ground. If less than 12 volts, check the battery, charging system and non-ABS circuits for damage.

3. Turn the ignition switch to **OFF** and reconnect the pump harness to the connector. Depressurize the Powermaster III unit.

4. Remove the accumulator and install pressure gauge J-37118 or equivalent. Install the accumulator on the pressure gauge adapter.

5. Bleed the Powermaster III at the bleeder valves or use the hand scanner to perform ABS Solenoid Bleed and Checkout Test.

6. Observe the pressure gauge while turning ignition **ON**. The system should pressurize from 0–500 psi (0–3448 kPa) or greater almost immediately after the ignition is switched on.

7. If the correct pressure is not reached, the accumulator is not holding sufficient precharge and must be replaced.

8. Allow the pump motor to run and note the pressure at which it either stops or reaches the high-pressure limit. If the indicated pressure is greater than 2900 psi (19,995.5 kPa), the pressure switch is faulty.

9. Using the hand scanner, monitor the pump state while applying the brakes slowly 1–3 times. Note the low pressure at which the pump engages. The pump should turn on at or above 2000 psi (13,790 kPa). If it turns on at a lower pressure, the pressure valve must be replaced.

10. If the pressure switch functions properly, depressurize the Powermaster III completely. Remove the reservoir cover. Do not apply the brakes with the reservoir cover removed.

11. Visually check the pump outlet in the reservoir to be sure it is not clogged. If the outlet is clear, attach 1 end of a clear plastic hose over the relief valve in the reservoir.

12. Hold the other end of the tube pointed downward into the rear reservoir chamber. Turn the ignition switch **ON**.

13. If fluid flows through the tube into the reservoir, replace the relief valve. If fluid does not flow through the tube, replace the Powermaster III unit.

Test E—Pump Off Time Too Short

1. Turn the ignition switch to **OFF** and depressurize the Powermaster III unit.

2. Remove the accumulator and install pressure gauge J-37118 or equivalent. Install the accumulator on the pressure gauge adapter.

3. Bleed the Powermaster III at the bleeder valves or use a scanner to perform ABS Solenoid Bleed and Checkout Test.

4. Observe the pressure gauge while turning ignition **ON**. The system should pressurize from 0–500 psi (0–3448 kPa) or greater almost immediately after the ignition is switched on.

5. If the correct pressure is not reached, the accumulator is not holding sufficient precharge and must be replaced.

6. Allow the system to pressurize until the pump shuts off. With the ignition still on, moderately apply and hold the brakes on. Measure the time between brake application and pump start-up.

7. If the pump off time is less than 50 seconds, check the accumulator precharge. If the accumulator precharge is less than 600 psi (4137 kPa), replace the accumulator. If precharge is 600 psi (4137 kPa) or greater and the pump off time is less than the correct value shown below, replace the Powermaster III unit.

Test F—External Leakage Check

1. Depressurize the Powermaster III unit.

2. Clean and remove the reservoir cover and diaphragm assembly. Inspect the fluid levels.

3. If the front chamber level is high, drain or siphon fluid to restore the correct level.

4. If the rear chamber level is too high, drain or siphon fluid to restore the correct level. High level in the rear chamber may be caused by filling the reservoir without depressurizing the system.

5. Clean and dry the Powermaster III unit so that any leaks or seepage may be easily detected. Install the reservoir cover and diaphragm.

6. Turn the ignition **ON** and pump the brakes. Check for leaks on the Powermaster III and throughout the system, including lines, fittings and calipers.

7. Depressurize the Powermaster III, remove the cover and diaphragm and inspect the fluid levels. If the rear fluid level is too high, the Powermaster III must be replaced.

8. If the level in the front reservoir is too high:

a. Drain or siphon the brake fluid in the front reservoir to a point below the divider wall for the left front and right front circuits.

b. Install the reservoir cover and diaphragm. Turn the ignition switch **ON** and pump the brakes several times.

c. Depressurize the Powermaster III. Remove the reservoir cover and the diaphragm.

d. Note the level of fluid in the front reservoirs. If the fluid level has risen in either front chamber, the Powermaster III must be replaced. If the fluid level has dropped or remained constant, replace the reservoir, cover and diaphragm assembly.

ABS System Depressurizing

PROCEDURE

✳✳ WARNING

The Powermaster III Unit MUST be depressurized before performing any service operations!

1. Turn the ignition to the **OFF** position.

2. Firmly apply and release the brake pedal up to 40 times. A noticeable change in brake feel (to a hard pedal) will occur when the accumulator is completely discharged.

3. Do NOT turn the ignition **ON** after depressurizing the system unless instructed by service procedures or until all service operations have been performed.

Accumulator

REMOVAL & INSTALLATION

▶ **See Figure 73**

➡**The accumulator is a nitrogen-charged pressure vessel which holds brake fluid under high pressure. It can not be repaired and must be serviced as an assembly.**

1. Depressurize the Powermaster III completely.

2. Remove the air cleaner, duct and stud if present.

3. Disconnect the negative battery cable.

4. Remove the 30 amp fusible element K from the ABS power center.

5. Remove the accumulator by turning the hex nut on the end of the accumulator with a 17mm socket. Remove from the vehicle by sliding out from underneath the hydraulic unit, towards the left front wheel well.

6. Remove the O-ring from the accumulator.

To install:

7. Lightly lubricate a new O-ring with clean brake fluid and install on the accumulator.

8. Install the accumulator and tighten to 24 ft. lbs. (33 Nm).

9. Install the 30 amp fusible element.

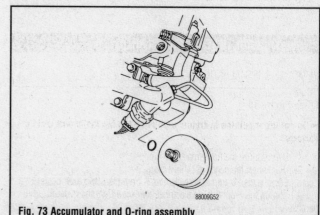

88009G52

Fig. 73 Accumulator and O-ring assembly

10. Connect the negative battery cable.
11. Install the air cleaner, duct and stud.
12. Properly bleed the ABS brakes, as outlined in this section.

Solenoid Assemblies

REMOVAL & INSTALLATION

▶ See Figure 74

➡ Wipe the reservoir cover assembly and surrounding area clean before removing. A clean work area is essential to completing this procedure without damaging the hydraulic unit.

1. Depressurize the Powermaster III unit.
2. Disconnect the negative battery cable.
3. Remove the reservoir cover assembly and reservoir assembly.
4. Unplug the 3-pin electrical connector from the solenoid assembly.
5. Remove the screws attaching the solenoid assembly.
6. Remove the solenoid assembly. Make sure both lower solenoid O-rings (2 per solenoid) are removed from the hydraulic unit.

To install:
7. Install the solenoid assembly into position; make sure the lower solenoid O-rings are in place and in good condition before installing.
8. Install the screws holding the solenoid assembly and tighten to 45 inch lbs. (5 Nm).
9. Engage the electrical connector to the solenoid. Make sure all connector position assurance locking pins are installed.
10. Install the reservoir cover and reservoir assembly.
11. Connect the negative battery cable.
12. Properly bleed the ABS brakes, as outlined in this section.

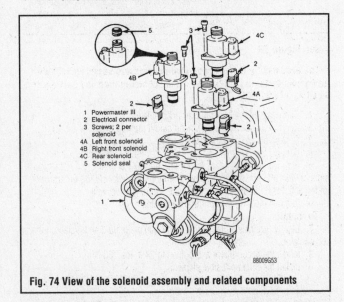

1 Powermaster III
2 Electrical connector
3 Screws; 2 per solenoid
4A Left front solenoid
4B Right front solenoid
4C Rear solenoid
5 Solenoid seal

88009G53

Fig. 74 View of the solenoid assembly and related components

Powermaster III (Hydraulic Unit)

REMOVAL & INSTALLATION

▶ See Figure 75

➡ Do not lift or pull the hydraulic unit using the hydraulic unit wiring harness.

1. Depressurize the Powermaster III completely.
2. Disconnect the negative battery cable.
3. Remove the 30 amp fusible element K from the ABS power center.
4. Unplug the 7-pin vehicle electrical connector from the hydraulic unit harness.

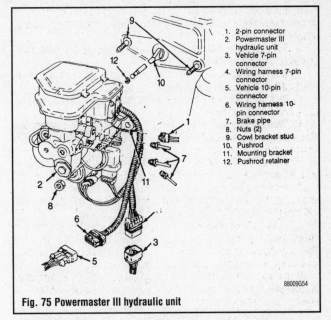

1. 2-pin connector
2. Powermaster III hydraulic unit
3. Vehicle 7-pin connector
4. Wiring harness 7-pin connector
5. Vehicle 10-pin connector
6. Wiring harness 10-pin connector
7. Brake pipe
8. Nuts (2)
9. Cowl bracket stud
10. Pushrod
11. Mounting bracket
12. Pushrod retainer

88009G54

Fig. 75 Powermaster III hydraulic unit

5. Detach the vehicle 10-pin electrical connector from the hydraulic unit harness.
6. Unplug the 2-pin connector from the fluid level sensor.
7. Disconnect the 3 brake pipes from the hydraulic unit. Plug the open lines to prevent fluid loss and contamination.
8. Inside the vehicle, remove the hair pin clip and pushrod from the brake pedal.
9. Remove the 2 attaching nuts from the cowl bracket studs.

➡ To avoid damage to the protruding hydraulic unit parts, install unit on J–37116 (or equivalent) holding fixture.

10. Remove the hydraulic unit.
To install:
11. Lightly lubricate the entire outer surface of the pushrod with silicone grease. Position the hydraulic unit in the vehicle. Guide the pushrod through the grommet.
12. Position the mounting bracket on the cowl bracket studs. Loosely install the attaching nuts.
13. Install the pushrod on the brake pedal mounting pin and install the hair pin clip.
14. Install the 2 attaching nuts. Tighten the nuts to 20 ft. lbs. (27 Nm).
15. Install the 3 brake pipes to the hydraulic unit and tighten to 15 ft. lbs. (17 Nm).
16. Attach the 3 electrical connectors to the hydraulic unit or its harness. Make sure all CPA locking pins are installed.
17. Install the 30 amp fusible element.
18. Adjust the brakelight switch.
19. Connect the negative battery cable.
20. Properly bleed the ABS brakes, as outlined in this section.

Proportioner Valve

REMOVAL & INSTALLATION

➡ The proportioner valve is not repairable; if any fault is present, it must be replaced as a complete assembly. The use of rubber hoses or hydraulic lines not specifically listed for use with DM ABS-III may lead to system problems requiring major repairs.

1. Depressurize the Powermaster III unit.
2. Disconnect the negative battery cable.
3. Raise and safely support vehicle.
4. Disconnect the input brake line (12mm) and the 2 output brake lines (10mm) from the proportioner valve.
5. Remove the proportioner valve.

To install:

6. When reinstalling, place the proportioner valve so that the rub pad is against vehicle body.

7. Connect the input and output brake lines to the valve. Tighten the nuts to 15 ft. lbs. (17 Nm).

8. Lower the vehicle.

9. Connect the negative battery cable.

10. Properly bleed the system. Only the rear brake circuits require bleeding.

Front Wheel Speed Sensors

REMOVAL & INSTALLATION

1. Raise the vehicle and support it safely.

2. Detach the sensor connector from the wiring harness.

3. Remove the 2 front wheel speed sensor bolts and remove the connector bracket bolt.

4. Remove the front wheel speed sensor.

To install:

5. Install the front wheel speed sensor in place. Install the sensor retaining bolts and tighten the sensor retaining bolts to 59 ft. lbs. (80 Nm). Tighten the connector bracket bolt.

6. Inspect for proper air gap between the sensor and the signal ring. While not adjustable, gap should be 0.019–0.068 in. (0.5–0.17mm). If the gap is not correct, the damaged or misaligned component must be corrected.

7. Attach the sensor connector to the wiring harness, making sure the CPA locking pin is in place.

8. Inspect and route the wiring to avoid contact with the suspension components.

9. Lower the vehicle.

Rear Wheel Speed Sensors

REMOVAL & INSTALLATION

The rear wheel speed sensors are integral with the hub and bearing assemblies. Should a speed sensor require replacement, the entire hub and bearing assembly must be replaced. Refer to Section 8 for hub and bearing replacement.

Wheel Tone Rings

REMOVAL & INSTALLATION

The front wheel speed sensor rings are integral with the outer CV-joint housing. Should a front wheel speed sensor ring require replacement, the entire CV-joint must be replaced. Refer to Section 7 for CV-joint replacement.

The rear wheel speed sensors rings are integral with the hub and bearing assemblies. Should a ring require replacement, the entire hub and bearing assembly must be replaced. Refer to Section 8 for hub and bearing replacement.

Anti-Lock Brake Controller

REMOVAL & INSTALLATION

➡**The controller can be removed from the vehicle without removing the front passenger seat.**

1. Turn the ignition switch to the **OFF** position.

2. Slide the front passenger seat forward.

3. If applicable, tip the passenger seat forward.

4. Remove the bolts holding the case cover.

5. Remove the controller. It is not necessary to remove the harness connectors to slide the controller out of the case.

6. Disconnect the wiring harnesses from the controller.

➡**The anti-lock brake controller should be protected from extremes of temperature, shock or impact and the discharge of static electricity.**

To install:

7. Attach the wiring connectors to the controller. Make certain the CPA locking pins are correctly installed.

8. Install the controller into its case. Install the case cover and tighten the retaining bolts hand tight.

9. Return the front passenger seat to the correct position.

System Filling

1. Park the vehicle on a level surface.

2. Depressurize the Powermaster III system.

3. Clean the reservoir cover and remove the cover and diaphragm assembly from the hydraulic unit.

4. Note the fluid level in the hydraulic reservoir chambers.

5. If any reservoir chamber is underfilled, look for signs of leakage. Make repairs as necessary. Fill the reservoir chambers with clean, DOT 3 brake fluid until the levels reach the full marks. Install the reservoir cover and diaphragm assembly.

6. If a reservoir chamber is overfilled, correct the fluid level and install the cover and diaphragm assembly. Turn the ignition switch **ON** and allow the system to pressurize.

7. Again, depressurize the hydraulic unit and check the fluid level.

System Bleeding

➡**If the hydraulic unit has been replaced, or if air has entered the brake lines, the entire brake system (hydraulic unit, lines and calipers) must be bled at each wheel.**

If only a hydraulic part of the hydraulic unit has been replaced (bleeder valve, tube and nut assembly, accumulator, reservoir, solenoid, or pressure switch), and no air has entered the brake lines, it may only be necessary to bleed the hydraulic unit by performing an ABS solenoid bleed and checkout test using a hand scanner tool or by bleeding the booster section of the hydraulic unit at its bleeder valves. Neither performing an ABS solenoid bleed and checkout test nor bleeding the hydraulic unit at its bleeder valves will remove air from the brake lines.

PRESSURE BLEEDING

➡**The pressure bleeding equipment must be of the diaphragm type. It must have a rubber diaphragm between the air supply and the brake fluid to prevent air, moisture and other contaminants from entering the hydraulic system.**

Use only DOT 3 brake fluid from a sealed container. Do not use any suspect or contaminated fluid. Do not use DOT 5 silicone fluid.

1. Depressurize the hydraulic unit before pressure bleeding.

➡**Make sure the vehicle ignition switch is OFF, unless otherwise noted. This will prevent the hydraulic unit pump from starting during the bleeding procedure.**

2. Clean the reservoir cover and diaphragm assembly, then remove the cover.

3. Check the fluid level in both the reservoir sections and fill to the correct level using clean brake fluid, if necessary.

4. Install the bleeder adapter J–37115 or equivalent and secure with attachment cable. Make sure attachment cable does not interfere with access to the bleeder valves on the hydraulic unit.

5. Attach the adapter to the pressure bleed equipment and charge to 5–10 psi (34.5–69 kPa) for approximately 30 seconds. If no leaks exist, slowly increase the pressure to 30–35 psi (207–241 kPa). 20–25 psi (138–241 kPa) is acceptable but not preferred.

6. Bleed the adapter; place a rag over the valve to absorb vented fluid. Depress ball to open the bleeder valve; continue until fluid flows without air.

7. Raise and safely support the vehicle.

8. Bleed individual wheel brakes in this sequence: right rear, left rear, right front and left front.

   a. Attach the bleeder hose to the bleeder valve and submerge the opposite end in a clean container partially filled with fresh brake fluid.

   b. Slowly open the bleeder valve and allow the fluid to flow until no air is seen in the fluid.

c. Allow the brake fluid to flow for at least 20–30 seconds at each wheel when checking for trapped air.

d. To assist in freeing trapped air, tap lightly on the caliper castings with a rubber mallet.

e. Close the valve when the fluid begins to flow without any air bubbles.

9. Lower the vehicle.

10. Bleed the Powermaster III isolation valves.

a. Attach the bleeder hose to the bleeder valve on the inboard side of the Powermaster III and submerge the opposite end in a container partially filled with fresh brake fluid.

b. Slowly open the bleeder valve and allow the fluid to flow until no air is seen in the fluid.

c. Close the valve when the fluid begins to flow without any air bubbles.

d. Repeat the procedure on the outboard side of the bleeder valve.

11. Remove the bleeder adapter J–37115 from the hydraulic unit.

12. Check the fluid level in both the reservoir chambers. Using clean brake fluid, fill the reservoirs to the proper level, if necessary.

13. Replace the reservoir cover and snap all 4 cover tabs in place on the reservoir.

14. Apply brake pedal 3 times with sharp, jabbing applications.

15. Bleed the booster section of the Powermaster III.

a. If scanner 094-00101 or equivalent, is available connect it. Turn the ignition to **ON** and allow the pump to pressurize the accumulator. When the pump stops, use the scanner to perform the "Solenoid Bleed and Check Test".

b. If a scanner is not available, depress the brake pedal with moderate pressure and turn the key to **ON** without starting the motor for 3 seconds. Repeat this **OFF/ON** cycle 10 times to cycle the solenoids.

16. Bleed the accumulator. Do not check brake fluid level without depressurizing the Powermaster III; overfilling may result. After depressurizing, wait 2 minutes before checking level; this will allow air to clear from the brake fluid.

17. Turn the ignition to **ON** without starting the engine; allow the system to pressurize. Check brake pedal for correct feel and travel.

18. Road test the vehicle.

MANUAL BLEEDING

1. Depressurize the hydraulic unit before pressure bleeding.

➡**Make sure the vehicle ignition switch is OFF, unless otherwise noted. This will prevent the hydraulic unit pump from starting during the bleeding procedure.**

2. Clean the reservoir cover and diaphragm assembly; then remove the assembly.

3. Check the fluid level in both the reservoir sections and fill to the correct level using clean brake fluid, if necessary.

4. Raise the vehicle and support safely.

5. Bleed the right front wheel brake.

a. Attach a bleeder hose to the bleeder valve and submerge the opposite end in a clean container partially filled with brake fluid.

b. Open the bleeder valve.

c. Slowly depress the brake pedal.

d. To assist in freeing entrapped air, tap lightly on the caliper with a rubber mallet.

e. Close the valve and release the brake pedal.

f. Check the fluid level and add new brake fluid, if necessary.

6. Repeat Step 5 until the brake pedal feels firm at half travel and no air bubbles are observed in the bleeder hose.

7. Repeat Steps 5 and 6 on the left front wheel brake.

8. Turn the ignition switch **ON** and allow the pump motor to run. (Shut ignition switch **OFF** if the pump runs for more than 60 seconds; check the hydraulic system.)

9. Bleed the right rear wheel brake.

a. Attach a bleeder hose to the bleeder valve and submerge the opposite end in a clean container partially filled with brake fluid.

b. Open the bleeder valve.

c. With the ignition switch **ON**, slowly depress the brake pedal part way, until the brake fluid begins to flow from the bleeder hose. Hold for 15 seconds. Do NOT fully depress the brake pedal.

d. To assist in freeing entrapped air, tap lightly on the caliper castings with a rubber mallet.

e. Close the valve and release the brake pedal.

f. Repeat these steps until no air bubbles are observed in the bleeder hose.

g. Check the fluid level and add new brake fluid, if necessary. Turn the ignition **OFF** and depressurize the hydraulic unit before checking the fluid level.

10. Repeat Steps 8 and 9 on the left rear wheel brake.

11. Lower the vehicle.

12. Bleed the Powermaster III isolation valves.

a. Attach the bleeder hose to the bleeder valve on the inboard side of the Powermaster III and submerge the opposite end in a container partially filled with fresh brake fluid.

b. Slowly open the bleeder valve and allow the fluid to flow until no air is seen in the fluid.

c. Close the valve when the fluid begins to flow without any air bubbles.

d. Repeat the procedure on the outboard side of the bleeder valve.

➡**This step can also be performed using a scanner.**

13. Bleed the hydraulic unit solenoids. This step will insure that the brake pedal applies firmly and smoothly.

a. Apply moderate force on the brake pedal.

b. With the pedal applied, turn the ignition switch **ON** for 3 seconds, then turn **OFF**. Do this 10 times in succession to cycle the solenoids Do not start the engine.

14. Depressurize the hydraulic unit and wait 2 minutes for the air to clear from within the reservoir.

15. Bleed the hydraulic unit of air accumulated from the solenoids.

a. Attach the bleeder hose to the bleeder valve on the inboard side of the hydraulic unit and submerge the opposite end in a clean container partially filled with fresh brake fluid.

b. With the ignition switch **ON**, apply light force to the brake pedal.

c. With the pedal applied, slowly open the bleeder valve and allow the fluid to flow until no air is seen in the fluid.

d. Close the valve when the fluid begins to flow without any air bubbles.

e. Repeat the procedure on the outboard side of the hydraulic unit.

16. Turn the ignition switch **OFF**, depressurize the hydraulic unit.

17. Remove the reservoir cover and diaphragm assembly.

18. Check the fluid level in both reservoir sections. Using clean brake fluid, fill the reservoirs to their proper level, if necessary.

19. Install the reservoir cover and snap all 4 tabs in place on the reservoir.

20. Turn the ignition switch **ON** and allow the pump motor to run. Shut the ignition switch **OFF** if the pump motor runs for more than 60 seconds; check the hydraulic system.

21. Apply the brake pedal noting feel and travel. If feel is firm, smooth and without excess pedal travel, vehicle is ready for road testing. If pedal feel is soft, spongy or has excessive pedal travel re-bleed the front brakes. If conditions still exist, perform Preliminary Inspection. Depressurize Powermaster III and recheck fluid level.

DELCO ANTI-LOCK BRAKING SYSTEM (ABS) VI

General Information

The Delco Anti-lock Braking System (ABS) VI was first introduced on W-body cars in 1992. ABS provides the driver with 3 important benefits over standard braking systems: increased vehicle stability, improved vehicle steerability, and potentially reduced stopping distances during braking. It should be noted that although the ABS-VI system offers definite advantages, the system cannot increase brake pressure above master cylinder pressure applied by the driver and cannot apply the brakes itself.

The ABS-VI Anti-lock Braking System consists of a conventional braking system with vacuum power booster, compact master cylinder, front disc brakes, rear drum brakes and interconnecting hydraulic brake lines augmented with the ABS components. The ABS-VI system includes a hydraulic modulator assembly, Electronic Brake Control Module (EBCM), a system relay, 4 wheel speed sensors, interconnecting wiring and an amber ABS warning light.

The EBCM monitors inputs from the individual wheel speed sensors and determines when a wheel or wheels is/are about to lock up. The EBCM controls the motors on the hydraulic modulator assembly to reduce brake pressure to the wheel about to lock up. When the wheel regains traction, the brake pressure is increased until the wheel again approaches lock-up. The cycle repeats until either the vehicle comes to a stop, the brake pedal is released, or no wheels are about to lock up. The EBCM also has the ability to monitor itself and can store diagnostic codes in a non-volatile (will not be erased if the battery is disconnected) memory. The EBCM is serviced as an assembly.

The ABS-VI braking system employs 2 modes: base (conventional) braking and anti-lock braking. Under normal braking, the conventional part of the system stops the vehicle. When in the ABS mode, the Electromagnetic Brakes (EMB) action of the ABS system controls the two front wheels individually and the rear wheels together. If the one rear wheel is about to lock up, the hydraulic pressure to both wheels is reduced, controlling both wheels together.

BASIC KNOWLEDGE REQUIRED

Before using this section, it is important that you have a basic knowledge of the following items. Without this basic knowledge, it will be difficult to use the diagnostic procedures contained in this section.

Basic Electrical Circuits—You should understand the basic theory of electricity and know the meaning of voltage, current (amps) and resistance (ohms). You should understand what happens in a circuit with an open or shorted wire. You should be able to read and understand a wiring diagram.

Use Of Circuit Testing Tools—You should know how to use a test light and how to use jumper wires to bypass components to test circuits. You should be familiar with the High Impedance Multimeter (DVM) such as J 34029–A. You should be able to measure voltage, resistance and current and be familiar with the meter controls and how to use them correctly.

ONBOARD DIAGNOSTICS

The ABS-VI contains sophisticated onboard diagnostics that, when accessed with a bidirectional scan tool, are designed to identify the source of any system fault as specifically as possible, including whether or not the fault is intermittent. There are over 58 diagnostic fault codes to assist with diagnosis.

The last diagnostic fault code to occur is identified, specific ABS data is stored at the time of this fault, and the first five codes set are stored. Additionally, using a bidirectional scan tool, each input and output can be monitored, thus enabling fault confirmation and repair verification. Manual control of components and automated functional tests are also available when using a GM approved scan tool. Details of many of these functions are contained in the following sections.

ENHANCED DIAGNOSTICS

Enhanced Diagnostic Information, found in the CODE HISTORY function of the bidirectional scan tool, is designed to provide specific fault occurrence information. For each of the first five (5) and the very last diagnostic fault codes stored, data is stored to identify the specific fault code number, the number of failure occurrences, and the number of drive cycles since the failure first and last occurred (a drive cycle occurs when the ignition is turned **ON** and the vehicle is driven faster than 10 mph). However, if a fault is present, the drive cycle counter will increment by turning the ignition **ON** and **OFF**. These first five (5) diagnostic fault codes are also stored in the order of occurrence. The order in which the first 5 faults occurred can be useful in determining if a previous fault is linked to the most recent faults, such as an intermittent wheel speed sensor which later becomes completely open.

During difficult diagnosis situations, this information can be used to identify fault occurrence trends. Does the fault occur more frequently now than it did during the last time when it only failed 1 out of 35 drive cycles? Did the fault only occur once over a large number of drive cycles, indication an unusual condition present when the fault occurred? Does the fault occur infrequently over a large number of drive cycles, indication special diagnosis techniques may be required to identify the source of the fault?

If a fault occurred 1 out of 20 drive cycles, the fault is intermittent and has not reoccurred for 19 drive cycles. This fault may be difficult or impossible to duplicate and may have been caused by a severe vehicle impact (large pot hole, speed bump at high speed, etc.) that momentarily opened an electrical connec-

tor or caused unusual vehicle suspension movement. Problem resolution is unlikely, and the problem may never reoccur (check diagnostic aids proved for that code). If the fault occurred 3 out of 15 drive cycles, the odds of finding the cause are still not good, but you know how often it occurs and you can determine whether or not the fault is becoming more frequent based on an additional or past occurrences visit if the source of the problem can not or could not be found. If the fault occurred 10 out of 20 drive cycles, the odds of finding the cause are very good, as the fault may be easily reproduced.

By using the additional fault data, you can also determine if a failure is randomly intermittent or if it has not reoccurred for long periods of time due to weather changes or a repair prior to this visit. Say a diagnostic fault code occurred 10 of 20 drive cycles but has not reoccurred for 10 drive cycles. This means the failure occurred 10 of 10 drive cycles but has not reoccurred since. A significant environmental change or a repair occurred 10 drive cycles ago. A repair may not be necessary if a recent repair can be confirmed. If no repair was made, the service can focus on diagnosis techniques used to locate difficult to recreate problems.

Diagnostic Procedures

When servicing the ABS-VI, the following steps should be followed in order. Failure to follow these steps may result in the loss of important diagnostic data and may lead to difficult and time consuming diagnosis procedures.

1. Connect a bidirectional scan tool, as instructed by the tool manufacturer, then read all current and historical diagnostic codes. Be certain to note which codes are current diagnostic code failures. DO NOT CLEAR CODES unless directed to do so.

2. Using a bidirectional scan tool, read the CODE HISTORY data. Note the diagnostic fault codes stored and their frequency of failure. Specifically note the last failure that occurred and the conditions present when this failure occurred. This last failure should be the starting point for diagnosis and repair.

3. Perform a vehicle preliminary diagnosis inspection. This should include:
   a. Inspection of the compact master cylinder for proper brake fluid level.
   b. Inspection of the ABS hydraulic modulator for any leaks or wiring damage.
   c. Inspection of brake components at all four (4) wheels. Verify no drag exists. Also verify proper brake apply operation.
   d. Inspection for worn or damaged wheel bearings that allow a wheel to wobble.
   e. Inspection of the wheel speed sensors and their wiring. Verify correct air gap range, solid sensor attachment, undamaged sensor toothed ring, and undamaged wiring, especially at vehicle attachment points.
   f. Verify proper outer CV-joint alignment and operation.
   g. Verify tires meet legal tread depth requirements.

4. If no codes are present, or mechanical component failure codes are present, perform the automated modulator test using the Tech 1® or T-100® to isolate the cause of the problem. If the failure is intermittent and not reproducible, test drive the vehicle while using the automatic snapshot feature of the bidirectional scan tool.

Perform normal acceleration, stopping, and turning maneuvers. If this does not reproduce the failure, perform an ABS stop, on a low coefficient surface such as gravel, from approximately 30–50 mph (48–80 km/h) while triggering any ABS code. If the failure is still not reproducible, use the enhanced diagnostic information found in CODE HISTORY to determine whether or not this failure should be further diagnosed.

5. Once all system failures have been corrected, clear the ABS codes. The Tech 1® and T-100®, when plugged into the ALDL connector, becomes part of the vehicle's electronic system. The Tech 1® and T-100® can also perform the following functions on components linked by the Serial Data Link (SDL):
   • Display ABS data
   • Display and clear ABS trouble codes
   • Control ABS components
   • Perform extensive ABS diagnosis
   • Provide diagnostic testing for intermittent ABS conditions

Each test mode has specific diagnosis capabilities which depend upon various keystrokes. In general, five (5) keys control sequencing: YES, NO, EXIT, UP arrow and DOWN arrow. The F0 through F9 keys select operating modes, perform functions within an operating mode, or enter trouble code or model year designations.

In general, the Tech 1® has five (5) test modes for diagnosing the anti-lock brake system. The five (5) test modes are as follows:

MODE F0: DATA LIST—In this test mode, the Tech 1® continuously monitors wheel speed data, brake switch status and other inputs and outputs.

MODE F1: CODE HISTORY—In this mode, fault code history data is displayed. This data includes how many ignition cycles since the fault code occurred, along with other ABS information. The first five (5) and last fault codes set are included in the ABS history data.

MODE F2: TROUBLE CODES—In this test mode, trouble codes stored by the EBCM, both current ignition cycle and history, may be displayed or cleared.

MODE F3: ABS SNAPSHOT—In this test mode, the Tech 1® captures ABS data before and after a fault occurrence or a forced manual trigger.

MODE F4: ABS TESTS—In this test mode, the Tech 1® performs hydraulic modulator functional tests to assist in problem isolation during troubleshooting. Included here is manual control of the motors which is used prior to bleeding the brake system.

Press F7 to covert from English to metric.

INTERMITTENT FAILURES

As with most electronic systems, intermittent failures may be difficult to accurately diagnose. The following is a method to try to isolate an intermittent failure especially wheel speed circuitry failures.

If an ABS fault occurs, the ABS warning light indicator will be on during the ignition cycle in which the fault was detected. If it is an intermittent problem which seems to have corrected itself (ABS warning light off), a history trouble code will be stored. Also stored will be the history data of the code at the time the fault occurred. The Tech 1® must be used to read ABS history data.

INTERMITTENTS AND POOR CONNECTIONS

Most intermittents are caused by faulty electrical connections or wiring, although occasionally a sticking relay or solenoid can be a problem. Some items to check are:

1. Poor mating of connector halves, or terminals not fully seated in the connector body (backed out).

2. Dirt or corrosion on the terminals. The terminals must be clean and free of any foreign material which could impede proper terminal contact.

3. Damaged connector body, exposing the terminals to moisture and dirt, as well as not maintaining proper terminal orientation with the component or mating connector.

4. Improperly formed or damaged terminals. All connector terminals in problem circuits should be checked carefully to ensure good contact tension. Use a corresponding mating terminal to check for proper tension. Refer to "Checking Terminal Contact" later in this section for the specific procedure.

5. The J 35616–A Connector Test Adapter Kit must be used whenever a diagnostic procedure requests checking or probing a terminal. Using the adapter will ensure that no damage to the terminal will occur, as well as giving an idea of whether contact tension is sufficient. If contact tension seems incorrect, refer to "Checking Terminal Contact" later in this section for specifics.

6. Poor terminal-to-wire connection. Checking this requires removing the terminal from the connector body. Some conditions which fall under this description are poor crimps, poor solder joints, crimping over wire insulation rather than the wire itself, corrosion in the wire-to-terminal contact area, etc.

7. Wire insulation which is rubbed through, causing an intermittent short as the bare area touches other wiring or parts of the vehicle.

8. Wiring broken inside the insulation. This condition could cause a continuity check to show a good circuit, but if only 1 or 2 strands of a multi-strand type wire are intact, resistance could be far too high.

Checking Terminal Contact

When diagnosing an electrical system that uses Metri-Pack 150/280/480/630 series terminals (refer to Terminal Repair Kit J 38125–A for terminal identification), it is important to check terminal contact between a connector and component, or between inline connectors, before replacing a suspect component.

Mating terminals must be inspected to ensure good terminal contact. A poor connection between the male and female terminal at a connector may be the result of contamination or deformation.

Contamination is caused by the connector halves being improperly connected, a missing or damaged connector seal, or damage to the connector itself, exposing the terminals to moisture and dirt. Contamination, usually in under-

hood or underbody connectors, leads to terminal corrosion, causing an open circuit or an intermittently open circuit.

Deformation is caused by probing the mating side of a connector terminal without the proper adapter, improperly joining the connector halves or repeatedly separating and joining the connector halves. Deformation, usually to the female terminal contact tang, can result in poor terminal contact causing an open or intermittently open circuit.

Follow the procedure below to check terminal contact.

1. Separate the connector halves. Refer to Terminal Repair Kit J 38125–A, if available.

2. Inspect the connector halves for contamination. Contamination will result in a white or green buildup within the connector body or between terminals, causing high terminal resistance, intermittent contact or an open circuit. An underhood or underbody connector that shows signs of contamination should be replaced in its entirety: terminals, seals, and connector body.

3. Using an equivalent male terminal from the Terminal Repair Kit J 38125–A, check the retention force of the female terminal in question by inserting and removing the male terminal to the female terminal in the connector body. Good terminal contact will require a certain amount of force to separate the terminals.

4. Using an equivalent female terminal from the Terminal Repair Kit J 38125–A, compare the retention force of this terminal to the female terminal in question by joining and separating the male terminal to the female terminal in question. If the retention force is significantly different between the two female terminals, replace the female terminal in question, using a terminal from Terminal Repair Kit J 38125–A.

Reading Codes

▶ **See Figures 76 and 77**

Diagnostic fault codes can only be read through the use of a bidirectional scan tool. There are no provisions for "Flash Code" diagnostics. Follow the scan tool manufacturer's instructions.

Clearing Codes

The trouble codes in EBCM memory are erased in one of two ways:
1. Tech 1®. "Clear Codes" selection.
2. Ignition cycle default.

These two methods are detailed below. Be sure to verify proper system operation and absence of codes when clearing procedure is completed. The EBCM will not permit code clearing until all of the codes have been displayed. Also, codes cannot be cleared by unplugging the EBCM, disconnecting the battery cables, or turning the ignition **OFF** (except on an ignition cycle default).

TECH 1® METHOD

Select F2 for trouble codes. After codes have been viewed completely, Tech 1® will ask, "CLEAR ABS CODES"; ANSWER "YES." Tech 1® will then read, "DISPLAY CODE HIST. DATA?" "LOST" if the codes have been cleared or "NO" to clear the codes. Answer "NO" and codes will be cleared.

IGNITION CYCLE DEFAULT

If no diagnostic fault code occurs for 100 drive cycles (a drive cycle occurs when the ignition is turned **ON** and the vehicle is driven faster than 10 mph or 16 km/h), any existing fault codes are cleared from the EBCM memory.

ABS Service

PRECAUTIONS

Failure to observe the following precautions may result in system damage.
• Performing diagnostic work on the ABS-VI requires the use of a Tech 1® Scan diagnostic tool or equivalent. If unavailable, please refer diagnostic work to a qualified technician.
• Before performing electric arc welding on the vehicle, disconnect the Electronic Brake Control Module (EBCM) and the hydraulic modulator connectors.

DIAGNOSTIC TROUBLE CODE	DESCRIPTION
56	Left Front ABS Motor Circuit Open
57	Left Front ABS Motor Circuit Shorted to Ground
58	Left Front ABS Motor Circuit Shorted to Battery
61	Right Front ABS Motor Circuit Open
62	Right Front ABS Motor Circuit Shorted to Gnd
63	Right Front ABS Motor Circuit Shorted to Batt
64	Rear ABS Motor Circuit Open
65	Rear ABS Motor Circuit Shorted to Ground
66	Rear ABS Motor Circuit Shorted to Battery
76	Left Front Sol Circuit Open or Shorted to Batt
77	Left Front Solenoid Circuit Shorted to Gnd
78	Right Front Sol Circuit Open or Shorted to Batt
81	Right Front Solenoid Circuit Shorted to Gnd
82	Calibration Malfunction
86	EBCM Turned "ON" the Red "BRAKE" Warning Lamp
87	Red "BRAKE" Warning Lamp Circuit Open
88	Red "BRAKE" Warning Lamp Ckt Shorted to Batt
91	Open Brake Switch During Deceleration
92	Open Brake Switch When ABS Was Required
93	DTC 91 or 92 Set in Current or Prev. Ign Cycle
94	Brake Switch Contacts Always Closed
95	Brake Switch Circuit Open
96	Brake Lamps Circuit Open

Fig. 77 ABS Diagnostic Trouble Codes—continued

DIAGNOSTIC TROUBLE CODE	DESCRIPTION
11	ABS Warning Lamp Circuit Malfunction
14	ABS Enable Relay Contact Circuit Open (1 of 3)
15	ABS Rly Contact Ckt Short to Batt or Always Closed
16	ABS Enable Relay Coil Circuit Open
17	ABS Enable Relay Coil Circuit Shorted to Gnd
18	ABS Enable Relay Coil Circuit Shorted to Batt
21	Left Front Wheel Speed = 0
22	Right Front Wheel Speed = 0
23	Left Rear Wheel Speed = 0
24	Right Rear Wheel Speed = 0
25	Left Front Excessive Wheel Speed Variation
26	Right Front Excessive Wheel Speed Variation
27	Left Rear Excessive Wheel Speed Variation
28	Right Rear Excessive Wheel Speed Variation
32	LF Wheel Speed Snr Ckt Open or Short to Gnd/Batt (1 of 3)
33	RF Wheel Speed Snr Ckt Open or Short to Gnd/Batt (1 of 3)
34	LR Wheel Speed Snr Ckt Open or Short to Gnd/Batt (1 of 3)
35	RR Wheel Speed Snr Ckt Open or Short to Gnd/Batt (1 of 3)
36	Low System Voltage (1 of 2)
37	High System Voltage
38	Left Front ESB Will Not Hold Motor
41	Right Front ESB Will Not Hold Motor
42	Rear ESB Will Not Hold Motor
44	Left Front Channel Will Not Move
45	Right Front Channel Will Not Move
46	Rear Channel Will Not Move
47	Left Front ABS Motor Free Spins (1 of 2)
48	Right Front ABS Motor Free Spins (1 of 2)
51	Rear ABS Motor Free Spins (1 of 2)
52	Left Front Channel in Release Too Long
53	Right Front Channel in Release Too Long
54	Rear Channel in Release Too Long
55	EBCM Malfunction

Fig. 76 ABS Diagnostic Trouble Codes

• When performing painting work on the vehicle, do not expose the Electronic Brake Control Module (EBCM) to temperatures in excess of 185°F (85°C) for longer than 2 hours. The system may be exposed to temperatures up to 200°F (95°C) for less than 15 minutes.

• Never disconnect or connect the Electronic Brake Control Module (EBCM) or hydraulic modulator connectors with the ignition switch **ON** or damage to the system will occur.

• Never disassemble any component of the Anti-Lock Brake System (ABS) which is designated non-serviceable; the component must be replaced as an assembly.

• When filling the master cylinder, always use Delco Supreme 11 brake fluid or equivalent, which meets DOT-3 specifications; petroleum-base fluid will destroy the rubber parts.

Fluid Level Sensor

REMOVAL & INSTALLATION

▶ **See Figure 78**

1. Disconnect the negative battery cable.
2. Detach the electrical connection from the fluid level sensor.
3. Remove the fluid level sensor, using needle-nose pliers to compress the switch locking tabs at the inboard side of the master cylinder.
   To install:
4. Insert the fluid level sensor unit until the locking tabs snap in place.
5. Attach the sensor electrical connector.
6. Connect the negative battery cable.

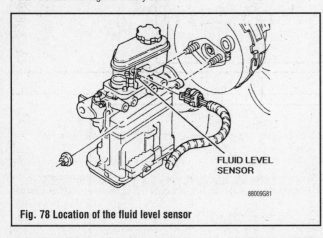

Fig. 78 Location of the fluid level sensor

Enable Relay

REMOVAL & INSTALLATION

1. Disconnect the negative battery cable.
2. Detach the electrical connection.
3. Unfasten the retainer on the bracket, then slide the relay off the bracket.
   To install:
4. Slide the relay onto the bracket and make sure the retainer locks the relay to the bracket. Fasten the retainer.
5. Attach the electrical connection.
6. Connect the negative battery cable.

ABS Lamp Driver Module

REMOVAL & INSTALLATION

▶ **See Figure 79**

1. Disconnect the negative battery cable.

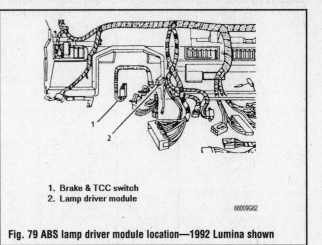

1. Brake & TCC switch
2. Lamp driver module

Fig. 79 ABS lamp driver module location—1992 Lumina shown

2. Remove the fasteners from the lower sound insulator panel under the steering column.
3. Remove the lamp driver module from the instrument panel harness on the right side of the steering column.
   To install:
4. Position the lamp driver module to the instrument panel wiring harness. Make sure the lamp driver is taped back in the same position.
5. Install the fasteners on the lower sound insulator to the instrument panel.
6. Connect the negative battery cable.

ABS Hydraulic Modulator/Master Cylinder Assembly

REMOVAL & INSTALLATION

▶ **See Figure 80**

➡ **To avoid personal injury, use the Tech 1® scan tool to relieve the gear tension in the hydraulic modulator. This procedure must be performed prior to removal of the brake control and motor assembly.**

1. Disconnect the negative battery cable.
2. For 1992–93 vehicles, perform the following:
   a. Properly relieve the fuel system pressure, as outlined in Section 5 of this manual.
   b. Remove the air cleaner assembly.

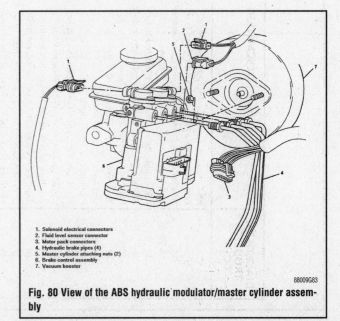

1. Solenoid electrical connectors
2. Fluid level sensor connector
3. Motor pack connectors
4. Hydraulic brake pipes (4)
5. Master cylinder attaching nuts (2)
6. Brake control assembly
7. Vacuum booster

Fig. 80 View of the ABS hydraulic modulator/master cylinder assembly

c. For 3.1L and 3.4L engines, disconnect and plug the upper fuel lines and position aside.

3. Disengage the two solenoid electrical connectors and the fluid level sensor connector.

4. Detach the 6-pin and 3-pin motor pack electrical connectors.

5. Wrap a shop towel around the hydraulic brake lines, then disconnect the four brake lines from the modulator.

➡**Cap the disconnected lines to prevent the loss of fluid and the entry of moisture and contaminants.**

6. Unfasten the 2 nuts attaching the ABS hydraulic modulator/master cylinder assembly to the vacuum booster.

7. Remove the ABS hydraulic modulator assembly from the vehicle.

To install:

8. Install the ABS hydraulic modulator assembly to the vehicle. Secure using the two attaching nuts and tighten to 20 ft. lbs. (27 Nm).

9. Uncap and connect the 4 brake pipes to the modulator assembly. Tighten to 13 ft. lbs. (17 Nm).

10. Attach the 6-pin and 3-pin electrical connectors.

11. Engage the fluid level sensor connector and the two solenoid electrical connections.

12. For 1992–93 vehicles, perform the following:

a. Unplug and connect the fuel lines for 3.1L and 3.4L engines.

b. Install the air cleaner assembly.

13. Properly bleed the system, as outlined later in this section.

14. Connect the negative battery cable.

Electronic Brake Control Module (EBCM)

REMOVAL & INSTALLATION

1992–93 Vehicles

▶ **See Figure 81**

1. Disconnect the negative battery cable.

2. Raise and safely support the vehicle.

3. Remove the left front wheel and tire assembly.

4. Remove the screws retaining the inner fender shield.

5. Unfasten the screw retaining the Electromagnetic Compatibility (EMC) shield. Slide the EMC shield back on the harness, making sure not to damage it.

6. Remove the screws retaining the EBCM, then slide the EBCM from the bracket.

7. Detach the connectors from the EBCM.

To install:

8. Attach the electrical connectors to the EBCM.

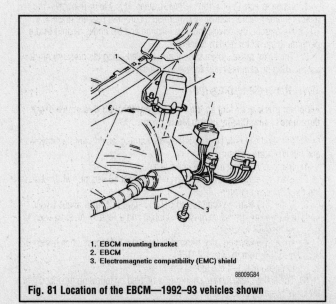

1. EBCM mounting bracket
2. EBCM
3. Electromagnetic compatibility (EMC) shield

88009G84

Fig. 81 Location of the EBCM—1992–93 vehicles shown

9. Slide the EBCM into the bracket, making sure the back guide pin is in its groove.

10. Install the hex-head screws securing the EBCM and tighten to 14 inch lbs. (2 Nm).

11. Inspect the EMC shield, and replace if damaged or torn. Slide the EMC shield over the harness and install the retaining screw. Tighten the screw to 13 inch lbs. (1.5 Nm).

12. Install the inner fender shield and secure with the retaining screws.

13. Install the left front wheel and tire assembly, then carefully lower the vehicle.

14. Connect the negative battery cable.

1994–96 Vehicles

▶ **See Figure 82**

1. Disconnect the negative battery cable.

2. Remove the glove compartment.

3. Remove the EBCM from the EBCM bracket, using the pressure tabs to release the EBCM.

4. Detach the EBCM electrical connectors.

To install:

5. Attach the EBCM electrical connector.

6. Install the EBCM into the bracket. Slide the EBCM into the bracket until secured by the pressure tabs.

7. Install the glove compartment assembly.

8. Connect the negative battery cable.

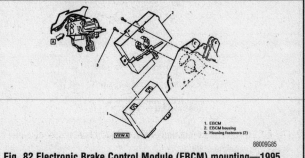

1. EBCM
2. EBCM housing
3. Housing fasteners (2)

VIEW A

88009G85

Fig. 82 Electronic Brake Control Module (EBCM) mounting—1995 vehicle shown

Speed Sensors

REMOVAL & INSTALLATION

Front Wheels

▶ **See Figures 83 and 84**

➡**The front wheel speed sensor is serviceable only as an assembly. Do not attempt to service the sensor harness pigtail is it is part of the sensor.**

1. Disconnect the negative battery cable.

2. Raise and safely support the vehicle.

3. Detach the front sensor electrical connector.

4. Remove the bolt retaining the sensor pigtail.

5. Unfasten the 2 bolts retaining the sensor, then remove the sensor from the vehicle.

To install:

6. Position the front wheel speed sensor, making sure the sensor guide pins are properly aligned and the sensor is seated.

7. Install the sensor retaining bolts and tighten to 52 ft. lbs. (70 Nm).

8. Attach the front sensor electrical connector.

9. Carefully lower the vehicle.

10. Connect the negative battery cable.

Rear Wheels

The rear integral wheel hub/bearing and sensor assembly must be replaced as a unit. Refer to Section 8 for hub and bearing removal and installation procedures.

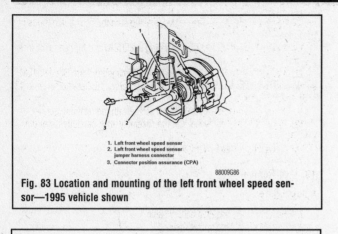

Fig. 83 Location and mounting of the left front wheel speed sensor—1995 vehicle shown

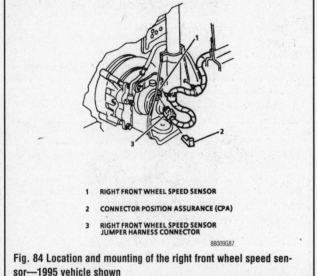

1 RIGHT FRONT WHEEL SPEED SENSOR

2 CONNECTOR POSITION ASSURANCE (CPA)

3 RIGHT FRONT WHEEL SPEED SENSOR
   JUMPER HARNESS CONNECTOR

88009G87

Fig. 84 Location and mounting of the right front wheel speed sensor—1995 vehicle shown

ABS Hydraulic Modulator Solenoid

REMOVAL & INSTALLATION

▶ See Figure 85

1. Disconnect the negative battery cable.
2. Detach the solenoid electrical connector.
3. Unfasten the Torx® head bolts, then remove the solenoid assembly.

To install:

4. Lubricate the O-rings on the new solenoid with clean brake fluid.
5. Position the solenoid so the connectors face each other.
6. Press down firmly by hand until the solenoid assembly flange seats on the modulator assembly.
7. Install the Torx® head bolts. Tighten to 40 inch lbs. (4.5 Nm).
8. Attach the solenoid electrical connector. Make sure the connectors are installed on the correct solenoids.
9. Properly bleed the brake system.
10. Connect the negative battery cable.

Filling and Bleeding

✳✳ WARNING

Do NOT allow brake fluid to spill on or come in contact with the vehicle's finish as it will remove the paint. In case of a spill, immediately flush the area with water.

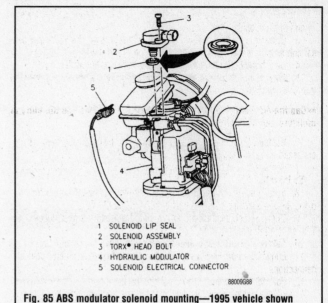

1 SOLENOID LIP SEAL
2 SOLENOID ASSEMBLY
3 TORX® HEAD BOLT
4 HYDRAULIC MODULATOR
5 SOLENOID ELECTRICAL CONNECTOR

88009G88

Fig. 85 ABS modulator solenoid mounting—1995 vehicle shown

SYSTEM FILLING

The master cylinder reservoirs must be kept properly filled to prevent air from entering the system. No special filling procedures are required because of the anti-lock system.

When adding fluid, use only DOT 3 fluid; the use of DOT 5 or silicone fluids is specifically prohibited. Use of improper or contaminated fluid may cause the fluid to boil or cause the rubber components in the system to deteriorate. Never use any fluid with a petroleum base or any fluid which has been exposed to water or moisture.

SYSTEM BLEEDING

Before bleeding the ABS brake system, the front and rear displacement cylinder pistons must be returned to the topmost position. The preferred method uses a Tech 1® or T-100® scan tool to perform the rehoming procedure. If a Tech 1® is not available, the second procedure may be used, but it must be followed EXACTLY.

Rehome Procedure

WITH TECH 1® OR T-100®

1. Using a Tech 1® or T-100® (CAMS), select "F5: Motor Rehome." The motor rehome function cannot be performed if current DTC's are present. If DTC's are present, the vehicle must be repaired and the codes cleared before performing the motor rehome function.
2. The entire brake system should now be bled using the pressure or manual bleeding procedures outlined later in this section.

WITHOUT TECH 1® OR T-100®

➡Do not place your foot on the brake pedal through this entire procedure unless specifically instructed to do so.

This method can only be used if the ABS warning lamp is not illuminated and not DTC's are present.

1. Remove your foot from the brake pedal.
2. Start the engine and allow it to run for at least 10 seconds while observing the ABS warning lamp.
3. If the ABS warning lamp turned ON and stayed ON after about 10 seconds, the bleeding procedure must be stopped and a Tech 1® must be used to diagnose the ABS function.
4. If the ABS warning lamp turned ON for about 3 seconds, then turned OFF and stayed OFF, turn the ignition OFF.
5. Repeat Steps 1–4 one more time.
6. The entire brake system should now be bled by following the manual or pressure bleeding procedure.

Pressure Bleeding

▶ See Figures 86 and 87

➡The pressure bleeding equipment must be of the diaphragm type. It must have a rubber diaphragm between the air supply and the brake fluid to prevent air, moisture and other contaminants from entering the hydraulic system.

1. Clean the master cylinder fluid reservoir cover and surrounding area, then remove the cover.
2. Add fluid, if necessary to obtain a proper fluid level.
3. Connect bleeder adapter J 35589, or equivalent, to the brake fluid reservoir, then connect the bleeder adapter to the pressure bleeding equipment.
4. Adjust the pressure bleed equipment to 5–10 psi (35–70 kPa) and wait about 30 seconds to be sure there is no leakage.
5. Adjust the pressure bleed equipment to 30–35 psi (205–240 kPa).

✱✱ WARNING

Use a shop rag to catch the escaping brake fluid. Be careful not to let any fluid run down the motor pack base or into the electrical connector.

6. With the pressure bleeding equipment connected and pressurized, proceed as follows:
   a. Attach a clear plastic bleeder hose to the rearward bleeder valve on the hydraulic modulator.
   b. Slowly open the bleeder valve and allow fluid to flow until no air is seen in the fluid.
   c. Close the valve when fluid flows out without any air bubbles.
   d. Repeat Steps 6b and 6c until no air bubbles are present.
   e. Relocate the bleeder hose on the forward hydraulic modulator bleed valve and repeat Steps 6a through 6d.
7. Tighten the bleeder valve to 80 inch lbs. (9 Nm).
8. Proceed to bleed the hydraulic modulator brake pipe connections as follows with the pressure bleeding equipment connected and pressurized:

   a. Slowly open the forward brake pipe tube nut on the hydraulic modulator and check for air in the escaping fluid.
   b. When the air flow ceases, immediately tighten the tube nut. Tighten the tube nut to 18 ft. lbs. (24 Nm).
9. Repeat Steps 8a and 8b for the remaining three brake pipe connections moving from the front to the rear.
10. Raise and safely support the vehicle.
11. Proceed, as outlined in the following steps, to bleed the wheel brakes in the following sequence: right rear, left rear, right front, then left front.
    a. Attach a clear plastic bleeder hose to the bleeder valve at the wheel, then submerge the opposite hose end in a clean container partially filled with clean brake fluid.
    b. Slowly open the bleeder valve and allow the fluid to flow.
    c. Close the valve when fluid begins to flow without any air bubbles. Tap lightly on the caliper or backing plate to dislodge any trapped air bubbles.
12. Repeat Step 11 on the other brakes using the earlier sequence.
13. Remove the pressure bleeding equipment, including bleeder adapter J 35589.
14. Carefully lower the vehicle, then check the brake fluid and add if necessary. Don't forget to put the reservoir cap back on.
15. With the ignition turned to the **RUN** position, apply the brake pedal with moderate force and hold it. Note the pedal travel and feel. If the pedal feels firm and constant and the pedal travel is not excessive, start the engine. With the engine running, recheck the pedal travel. If it's still firm and constant and pedal travel is not excessive, go to Step 17.
16. If the pedal feels soft or has excessive travel either initially or after the engine is started, the following procedure may be used:
    a. With the Tech 1® scan tool, "release" then "apply" each motor 2–3 times and cycle each solenoid 5–10 times. When finished, be sure to "apply" the front and rear motors to ensure the pistons are in the upmost position. DO NOT DRIVE THE VEHICLE.
    b. If a Tech 1® is not available, remove your foot from the brake pedal, start the engine and allow it run for at least 10 seconds to initialize the ABS. DO NOT DRIVE THE VEHICLE. After 10 seconds, turn the ignition **OFF**. The initialization procedure most be repeated 5 times to ensure any trapped air has been dislodged.
    c. Repeat the bleeding procedure, starting with Step 1.
17. Road test the vehicle, and make sure the brakes are operating properly.

Manual Bleeding

▶ See Figure 88

1. Clean the master cylinder fluid reservoir cover and surrounding area, then remove the cover.
2. Add fluid, if necessary to obtain a proper fluid level, then put the reservoir cover back on.
3. Prime the ABS hydraulic modulator/master cylinder assembly as follows:
   a. Attach a bleeder hose to the rearward bleeder valve, then submerge the opposite hose end in a clean container partially filled with clean brake fluid.
   b. Slowly open the rearward bleeder valve.
   c. Depress and hold the brake pedal until the fluid begins to flow.
   d. Close the valve, then release the brake pedal.
   e. Repeat Steps 3b–3d until no air bubbles are present.

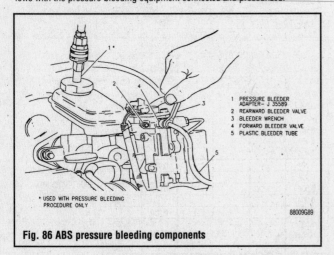

1 PRESSURE BLEEDER ADAPTER– J 35589
2 REARWARD BLEEDER VALVE
3 BLEEDER WRENCH
4 FORWARD BLEEDER VALVE
5 PLASTIC BLEEDER TUBE

* USED WITH PRESSURE BLEEDING PROCEDURE ONLY

88009G89

Fig. 86 ABS pressure bleeding components

88009G90

Fig. 87 Position a shop rag to catch escaping brake fluid

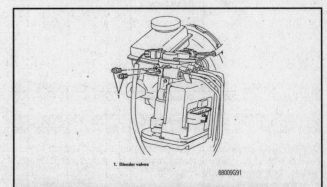

1. Bleeder valves

88009G91

Fig. 88 ABS hydraulic modulator/master cylinder bleeder locations

f. Relocate the bleeder hose to the forward hydraulic modulator bleeder valve, then repeat Steps 3a–3e.

4. Once the fluid is seen to flow from both modulator bleeder valves, the ABS modulator/master cylinder assembly is sufficiently full of fluid. However, it may not be completely purged of air. At this point, move to the wheel brakes and bleed them. This ensures that the lowest points in the system are completely free of air and then the assembly can purged of any remaining air.

5. Remove the fluid reservoir cover. Fill to the correct level, if necessary, then fasten the cover.

6. Raise and safely support the vehicle.

7. Proceed, as outlined in the following steps, to bleed the wheel brakes in the following sequence: right rear, left rear, right front, then left front.

a. Attach a clear plastic bleeder hose to the bleeder valve at the wheel, then submerge the opposite hose end in a clean container partially filled with clean brake fluid.

b. Open the bleeder valve.

c. Have an assistant slowly depress the brake pedal.

d. Close the valve and slowly release the release the brake pedal.

e. Wait 5 seconds.

f. Repeat Steps 7a–7e until the brake pedal feels firm at half travel and no air bubbles are observed in the bleeder hose. To assist in freeing the entrapped air, tap lightly on the caliper or braking plate to dislodge any trapped air bubbles.

8. Repeat Step 7 for the remaining brakes in the sequence given earlier.

9. Carefully lower the vehicle.

10. Remove the reservoir cover, then fill to the correct level with brake fluid and replace the cap.

11. Bleed the ABS hydraulic modulator/master cylinder assembly as follows:

a. Attach a clear plastic bleeder hose to the rearward bleeder valve on the modulator, then submerge the opposite hose end in a clean container partially filled with clean brake fluid.

b. Have an assistant depress the brake pedal with moderate force.

c. Slowly open the rearward bleeder valve and allow the fluid to flow.

d. Close the valve, then release the brake pedal.

e. Wait 5 seconds.

f. Repeat Steps 11a–11e until no air bubbles are present.

g. Relocate the bleeder hose to the forward hydraulic modulator bleeder valve, then repeat Steps 11a–11f.

12. Carefully lower the vehicle, then check the brake fluid and add if necessary. Don't forget to put the reservoir cap back on.

13. With the ignition turned to the **RUN** position, apply the brake pedal with moderate force and hold it. Note the pedal travel and feel. If the pedal feels firm and constant and the pedal travel is not excessive, start the engine. With the engine running, recheck the pedal travel. If it's still firm and constant and pedal travel is not excessive, road test the vehicle and make sure the brakes are operating properly.

14. If the pedal feels soft or has excessive travel either initially or after the engine is started, the following procedure may be used:

a. With the Tech 1® scan tool, "Release" then "Apply" each motor 2–3 times and cycle each solenoid 5–10 times. When finished, be sure to "Apply" the front and rear motors to ensure the pistons are in the upmost position. DO NOT DRIVE THE VEHICLE.

b. If a Tech 1® scan tool is not available, remove your foot from the brake pedal, start the engine and allow it run for at least 10 seconds to initialize the ABS. DO NOT DRIVE THE VEHICLE. After 10 seconds, turn the ignition **OFF**. The initialization procedure most be repeated 5 times to ensure any trapped air has been dislodged.

c. Repeat the bleeding procedure, starting with Step 1.

15. Road test the vehicle, and make sure the brakes are operating properly.

BRAKE SPECIFICATIONS
All measurements in inches unless noted

Year	Model		Master Cylinder Bore	Brake Disc Original Thickness	Brake Disc Minimum Thickness	Brake Disc Maximum Runout	Brake Drum Diameter Original Inside Diameter	Brake Drum Diameter Max. Wear Limit	Brake Drum Diameter Maximum Machine Diameter	Minimum Lining Thickness Front	Minimum Lining Thickness Rear
1988	Cutlass Supreme	F	0.945	1.043	0.972	0.004	-	-	-	0.030	-
		R	0.945	0.492	0.429	0.004	-	-	-	-	0.030
	Grand Prix	F	0.945	1.039	0.972	0.004	-	-	-	0.030	-
		R	0.945	0.492	0.429	0.004	-	-	-	-	0.030
	Regal	F	0.945	1.040	0.972	0.004	-	-	-	0.030	-
		R	0.945	0.492	0.429	0.004	-	-	-	-	0.030
1989	Cutlass Supreme	F	0.945	1.043	0.972	0.004	-	-	-	0.030	-
		R	0.945	0.492	0.429	0.004	-	-	-	-	0.030
	Grand Prix	F	0.945	1.039	0.972	0.004	-	-	-	0.030	-
		R	0.945	0.492	0.429	0.004	-	-	-	-	0.030
	Regal	F	0.945	1.040	0.972	0.004	-	-	-	0.030	-
		R	0.945	0.492	0.429	0.004	-	-	-	-	0.030
1990	Cutlass Supreme	F	0.945	1.043	0.972	0.004	-	-	-	0.030	-
		R	0.945	0.492	0.429	0.004	-	-	-	-	0.030
	Grand Prix	F	0.945	1.039	0.972	0.004	-	-	-	0.030	-
		R	0.945	0.492	0.429	0.004	-	-	-	-	0.030
	Lumina	F	0.945	1.040	0.972	0.004	-	-	-	0.030	-
		R	0.945	0.492	0.429	0.004	-	-	-	-	0.030
	Regal	F	0.945	1.040	0.972	0.004	-	-	-	0.030	-
		R	0.945	0.492	0.429	0.004	-	-	-	-	0.030
1991	Cutlass Supreme	F	0.945	1.043	0.972	0.004	-	-	-	0.030	-
		R	0.945	0.492	0.429	0.004	-	-	-	-	0.030
	Grand Prix	F	0.945	1.039	0.972	0.004	-	-	-	0.030	-
		R	0.945	0.492	0.429	0.004	-	-	-	-	0.030
	Lumina	F	0.945	1.040	0.972	0.004	-	-	-	0.030	-
		R	0.945	0.492	0.429	0.004	-	-	-	-	0.030
	Regal	F	0.945	1.040	0.972	0.004	-	-	-	0.030	-
		R	0.945	0.492	0.429	0.004	-	-	-	-	0.030
1992	Cutlass Supreme	F	0.945	1.040	0.972	0.004	-	-	-	0.030	-
		R	0.945	0.492	0.429	0.004	-	-	-	-	0.030
	Grand Prix	F	0.945	1.039	0.972	0.004	-	-	-	0.030	-
		R	0.945	0.492	0.429	0.004	-	-	-	-	0.030
	Lumina	F	0.945	1.040	0.972	0.004	-	-	-	0.030	-
		R	0.945	0.492	0.429	0.004	-	-	-	-	0.030
	Regal	F	0.945	1.040	0.972	0.004	-	-	-	0.030	-
		R	0.945	0.492	0.429	0.004	-	-	-	-	0.030

88009C02

BRAKE SPECIFICATIONS
All measurements in inches unless noted

Year	Model		Master Cylinder Bore	Brake Disc Original Thickness	Brake Disc Minimum Thickness	Brake Disc Maximum Runout	Brake Drum Diameter Original Inside Diameter	Brake Drum Diameter Max. Wear Limit	Brake Drum Diameter Maximum Machine Diameter	Minimum Lining Thickness Front	Minimum Lining Thickness Rear
1993	Cutlass Supreme	F	0.945	1.040	0.972	0.003	-	-	-	0.030	-
		R	0.945	0.492	0.429	0.003	-	-	-	-	0.030
	Grand Prix	F	0.945	1.039	0.972	0.003	-	-	-	0.030	-
		R	0.945	0.492	0.429	0.003	-	-	-	-	0.030
	Lumina	F	0.945	1.040	0.972	0.003	-	-	-	0.030	-
		R	0.945	0.492	0.429	0.003	-	-	-	-	0.030
	Regal	F	0.945	1.040	0.972	0.003	-	-	-	0.030	-
		R	0.945	0.492	0.429	0.003	-	-	-	-	0.030
1994	Cutlass Supreme	F	0.945	1.039	0.972	0.003	-	-	-	0.030	-
		R	0.945	0.433	0.370	0.003	-	-	-	-	0.030
	Grand Prix	F	0.945	1.039	0.972	0.003	-	-	-	0.030	-
		R	0.945	0.433	0.370	0.003	-	-	-	-	0.030
	Lumina	F	0.945	1.039	0.972	0.003	-	-	-	0.030	-
		R	0.945	0.492	0.429	0.003	-	-	-	-	0.030
	Regal	F	0.945	1.039	0.972	0.003	-	-	-	0.030	-
		R	0.945	0.433	0.370	0.003	-	-	-	-	0.030
1995	Cutlass Supreme	F	1.000	1.039	0.972	0.003	-	-	-	0.030	-
		R	1.000	0.433	0.370	0.003	-	-	-	-	0.030
	Grand Prix	F	1.000	1.039	0.972	0.003	-	-	-	0.030	-
		R	1.000	0.433	0.370	0.003	-	-	-	-	0.030
	Lumina	F	1.000	1.039	0.972	0.003	-	-	-	0.030	-
		R	1.000	0.433	0.370	0.003	8.863	NA	8.880	-	0.030
	Monte Carlo	F	1.000	1.039	0.972	0.003	-	-	-	0.030	-
		R	1.000	0.433	0.370	0.003	8.863	NA	8.880	-	0.030
	Regal	F	1.000	1.039	0.972	0.003	-	-	-	0.030	-
		R	1.000	0.433	0.370	0.003	-	-	-	-	0.030
1996	Cutlass Supreme	F	0.945	1.039	0.956	0.003	-	-	-	0.030	-
		R	0.945	0.433	0.370	0.003	-	-	-	-	0.030
	Grand Prix	F	0.945	1.039	0.956	0.003	-	-	-	0.030	-
		R	0.945	0.433	0.370	0.003	-	-	-	-	0.030
	Lumina	F	0.945	1.039	0.956	0.003	-	-	-	0.030	-
		R	0.945	0.433	0.370	0.003	8.863	NA	8.880	-	0.030
	Monte Carlo	F	0.945	1.039	0.956	0.003	-	-	-	0.030	-
		R	0.945	0.433	0.370	0.003	8.863	NA	8.880	-	0.030
	Regal	F	0.945	1.039	0.956	0.003	-	-	-	0.030	-
		R	0.945	0.433	0.370	0.003	-	-	-	-	0.030

88009C01

10

BODY AND TRIM

EXTERIOR

Doors

DOOR ALIGNMENT

▶ **See Figures 1, 2, 3 and 4**

Adjust the up and down, and in and out by loosening the four hinge-to-door retaining bolts and move to the desired position. An assistant is recommended to perform this procedure. Tighten the bolts to 18–21 ft. lbs. (24–27 Nm).

Hood

REMOVAL & INSTALLATION

▶ **See Figures 5 and 6**

➡Always remove the hood assembly with an assistant present. Cover the entire area with well padded blankets to prevent damage to the painted surfaces. The hood is heavy and may cause severe damage if not removed carefully.

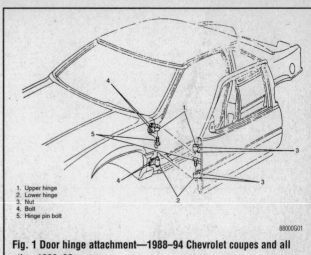

1. Upper hinge
2. Lower hinge
3. Nut
4. Bolt
5. Hinge pin bolt

88000G01

Fig. 1 Door hinge attachment—1988–94 Chevrolet coupes and all other 1988–96 coupes

1. Front side door upper hinge assembly
2. Front side door hinge nut
3. Front side door hinge bolt/screw
4. Front side door lower hinge assembly

88000G02

Fig. 2 Door hinge attachment—1988–94 Chevrolet sedans and all other 1988–96 sedans

1. Front side door upper hinge assembly
2. Front side door upper body side hinge bolt/screw
3. Front side door lower hinge assembly
4. Front side door lower body side hinge bolt/screw
5. Rear side door upper door side hinge bolt/screw
6. Rear side door lower door side hinge bolt/screw

88000G03

Fig. 3 Door hinge attachment—all 1995–96 Chevrolet models

1. Check link assembly
2. Screw
3. Door
4. Sealing grommet

88000G04

Fig. 4 Door check link-to-body installation—1988–94 Chevrolet and all other 1988–96 models

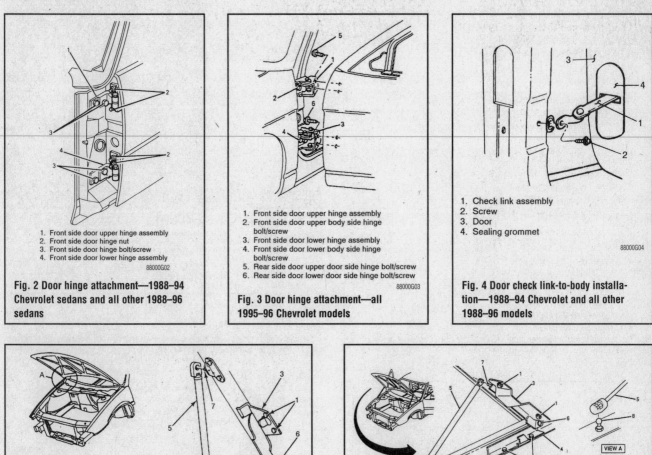

1. Bolt/screw
2. Bolt/screw
3. Hood side hinge
4. Fender side hinge
5. Support cylinder
6. Bolt/screw
7. Support cylinder upper support pin
8. Support cylinder lower support pin

VIEW A

88000G07

Fig. 5 Hood hinge and support cylinder—1988–94 Chevrolet and all other 1988–96 models

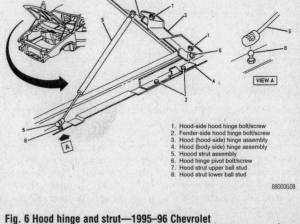

1. Hood-side hood hinge bolt/screw
2. Fender-side hood hinge bolt/screw
3. Hood (hood-side) hinge assembly
4. Hood (body-side) hinge assembly
5. Hood strut assembly
6. Hood hinge pivot bolt/screw
7. Hood strut upper ball stud
8. Hood strut lower ball stud

VIEW A

88000G08

Fig. 6 Hood hinge and strut—1995–96 Chevrolet

1. Place covers over the front fenders and lower windshield to prevent damage.
2. Disconnect the underhood lamp, if applicable.
3. With an assistant, remove the hinge-to-hood pivot bolts.
4. Disconnect the strut or support cylinders from the hood and lift the hood clear of the vehicle.

To install:

5. Position the hood onto the hinges and loosely install the hinge bolts.
6. Install the support cylinders or struts to the hood.
7. Align the hood to the body and tighten the hinge pivot bolts to 18–20 ft. lbs. (25–27 Nm).
8. Connect the underhood lamp, if applicable.

Front Bumpers

REMOVAL & INSTALLATION

Cutlass Supreme

1. Disconnect the negative battery cable.
2. Raise the vehicle and support with jackstands.
3. Remove the air deflector.
4. Remove the fascia-to-wheelwell screws.
5. Remove the fascia-to-body retaining nuts.
6. Remove the upper and lower fascia-to-body retainers.
7. Remove the bumper-to-body retaining bolts.
8. Remove the bumper and fascia as an assembly.
9. Installation is the reverse of the removal procedure.

Regal

1. Disconnect the negative battery cable.
2. Raise the vehicle and support with jackstands.
3. Remove the chrome strip bracket, air deflector and center push retainers.
4. Remove the fascia-to-wheelwell screws.
5. Remove the upper and lower fascia-to-body retaining nuts (right and left).
6. Remove the bumper guards.
7. Remove the lower fascia-to-bumper nuts (center).
8. Unplug the top fascia retaining tabs.
9. Remove the bumper-to-body bolts and bumper assembly.
10. Installation is the reverse of the removal procedure.

Lumina

1990–94 MODELS

▶ See Figure 7

1. Disconnect the negative battery cable.
2. Raise the vehicle and support with jackstands.
3. Remove the valance panels.
4. Remove the fascia-to-fender nuts.
5. Remove the bumper-to-body nuts.

6. Remove the assembly from the vehicle.

To install:

7. Position the bumper assembly onto the body and install the bumper-to-body nuts. Tighten the nuts to 18 ft. lbs. (24 Nm).
8. Install the remaining components in the reverse of the removal procedure.

1995–96 MODELS

▶ See Figure 8

1. Disconnect the negative battery cable.
2. Disconnect the front side marker lamps.
3. Remove the fascia-to-fender liner screws.
4. Disconnect the upper retainers from the headlamp brackets.
5. On coupes, disconnect the top center front fascia retainers from the energy absorber.
6. On sedan and the base coupe, remove the lower support bolt/screw from the hood latch support bracket.
7. Raise the vehicle and support with jackstands.
8. Remove the nuts from the fender.
9. Remove the fascia lower retainers from the bumper bar.
10. Remove the bolts/screws from the impact bar to the body.
11. Remove the bumper from the vehicle.

To install:

12. Position the bumper assembly onto the body and install the bumper-to-body bolts/screws. Tighten to 18 ft. lbs. (24 Nm).
13. Install the remaining components in the reverse of the removal procedure.

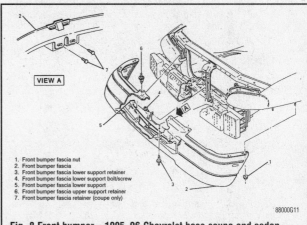

VIEW A

1. Front bumper fascia nut
2. Front bumper fascia
3. Front bumper fascia lower support retainer
4. Front bumper fascia lower support bolt/screw
5. Front bumper fascia lower support
6. Front bumper fascia upper support retainer
7. Front bumper fascia retainer (coupe only)

88000G11

Fig. 8 Front bumper—1995–96 Chevrolet base coupe and sedan models

Grand Prix

1. Disconnect the negative battery cable.
2. Raise the hood and remove the top fascia bolts.
3. Raise the vehicle and support with jackstands.
4. Remove the turn signal lamps.
5. Remove the front valance-to-fascia bolts.
6. Remove the fender-to-fascia screws on both sides.
7. Remove the right and left reinforcement and fascia-to-fender bolts.
8. Remove the vacuum tank if in the way.
9. Remove the fascia from the vehicle.
10. Installation is the reverse of the removal procedure.

Rear Bumper

REMOVAL & INSTALLATION

Cutlass Supreme

1. Disconnect the negative battery cable.
2. Raise the vehicle and support with jackstands.

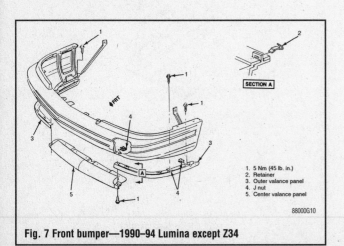

SECTION A

1. 5 Nm (45 lb. in.)
2. Retainer
3. Outer valance panel
4. J nut
5. Center valance panel

88000G10

Fig. 7 Front bumper—1990–94 Lumina except Z34

3. Remove the splash shield-to-upper and lower fascia screws.
4. From underneath the vehicle, remove the fascia-to-body nuts.
5. Remove the bumper-to-body nuts.
6. Disconnect the side marker lamp connections and lower the vehicle.
7. Remove the luggage compartment liner.
8. From inside the luggage compartment, remove the fascia-to-body nuts and bumper-to-body nuts.
9. Remove the bumper assembly from the vehicle.
10. Installation is the reverse of the removal procedure.

Regal

1. Disconnect the negative battery cable.
2. Remove the splash shield screws on both sides.
3. Remove the fascia-to-body screws from inside the luggage compartment.
4. Remove the bumper-to-body nuts and bumper.
5. Installation is the reverse of the removal procedure.

Lumina

1990–94 MODELS

1. Disconnect the negative battery cable.
2. Raise the vehicle and support with jackstands.
3. Remove the fascia-to-quarter panel nuts from underneath the vehicle.
4. Remove the bumper-to-body nuts from underneath the vehicle.
5. Lower the vehicle.
6. Remove the luggage compartment trim panel.
7. Remove the fascia-to-body screws from inside the luggage compartment.
8. Remove the bumper-to-body nuts from inside the luggage compartment and bumper.
9. Installation is the reverse of the removal procedure.

1995–96 MODELS

1. Remove the rear fascia.
2. Remove the rear energy absorber.
3. Remove the bolts/screws or retainers and disconnect the exhaust hangers.
4. Remove the rear impact bar.
5. Installation is the reverse of the removal procedure. Tighten the rear impact bar bolts/screws to 18 ft. lbs. (25 Nm).

Grand Prix

1. Disconnect the negative battery cable.
2. Remove luggage compartment liner.
3. Remove the two right side and one left side fascia-to-body nuts from inside the luggage compartment.
4. Raise the vehicle and support with jackstands.
5. Remove the right and left inner fenders.
6. Remove the two left and one right fascia-to-body nuts from underneath the vehicle.
7. Remove the lower reinforcement and fascia-to-body bolts.
8. Remove the retainers.
9. Remove the license plate lamp electrical connector and bumper from the vehicle.
10. Installation is the reverse of the removal procedure.

Grille

REMOVAL & INSTALLATION

 See Figures 9, 10, 11 and 12

1. Disconnect the negative battery cable.
2. Remove the grille retaining screws at the fascia.
3. Remove the grille assembly from the vehicle.
4. Installation is the reverse of the removal procedure.

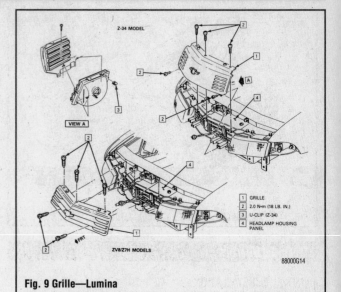

1 GRILLE
2 2.0 N·m (18 LB. IN.)
3 U-CLIP (Z-34)
4 HEADLAMP HOUSING PANEL

88000G14

Fig. 9 Grille—Lumina

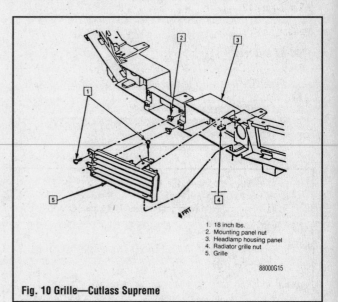

1. 18 inch lbs.
2. Mounting panel nut
3. Headlamp housing panel
4. Radiator grille nut
5. Grille

88000G15

Fig. 10 Grille—Cutlass Supreme

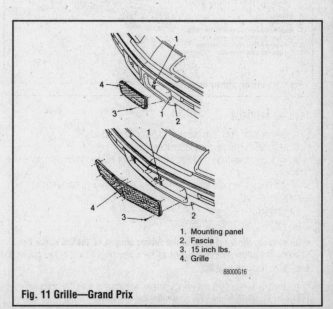

1. Mounting panel
2. Fascia
3. 15 inch lbs.
4. Grille

88000G16

Fig. 11 Grille—Grand Prix

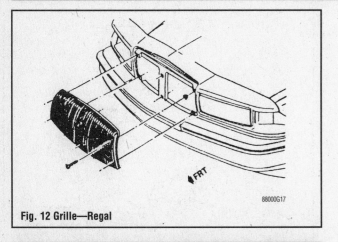

Fig. 12 Grille—Regal

Outside Mirrors

REMOVAL & INSTALLATION

▶ **See Figure 13**

Manual

1988–94 MODELS

1. Remove the door trim panel as outlined in this section.
2. Remove the three mirror-to-door retaining nuts, mirror and filler.
To install:
3. Install the filler, mirror and retaining nuts.
4. Tighten the retaining nuts in sequence to 80 inch lbs. (9 Nm). Tighten sequence is center, top, then bottom.
5. Install the door trim panel as outlined in this section.

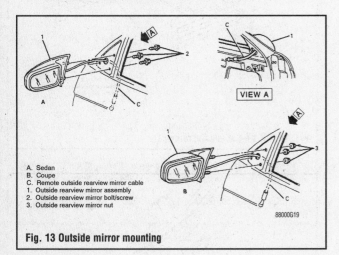

A. Sedan
B. Coupe
C. Remote outside rearview mirror cable
1. Outside rearview mirror assembly
2. Outside rearview mirror bolt/screw
3. Outside rearview mirror nut

Fig. 13 Outside mirror mounting

1995–96 MODELS

1. Remove the door trim panel as outlined in this section.
2. Remove the mirror reinforcement cover.
3. On coupes, remove the three mirror-to-door retaining nuts, and remove the mirror.
4. On sedans, remove the three mirror-to-door retaining bolts/screws, and remove the mirror.
To install:
5. Position the mirror to the door.

➡ **On sedans, the front edge of the mirror should be tucked under the channel. Slide the mirror forward as far as possible so that the mirror is flush with the belt molding.**

6. Install the retaining nuts/bolts/screws and staring with the lower left, tighten in a clockwise direction to 89 inch lbs. (10 Nm).

7. Install the mirror reinforcement cover.
8. Install the door trim panel as outlined in this section.

Electric and Remote

1988–94 MODELS

1. Remove the door trim panel as outlined in this section.
2. Remove the water deflector.
3. Remove the remote control cable or electrical connector from the inner panel.
4. Remove the three mirror-to-door retaining nuts, mirror and filler.
To install:
5. Install the filler, mirror and retaining nuts.
6. Install the control cable or electrical connector to the inner panel.
7. Tighten the retaining nuts in sequence to 80 inch lbs. (9 Nm). Tighten sequence; center, top then bottom.
8. Install the water deflector and door trim panel as outlined in this section.

1995–96 MODELS

1. Remove the door trim panel as outlined in this section.
2. Unplug the electrical connectors.
3. Remove the mirror reinforcement cover.
4. On coupes, remove the three mirror-to-door retaining nuts, and remove the mirror.
5. On sedans, remove the three mirror-to-door retaining bolts/screws, and remove the mirror.
To install:
6. Route the cable through the hole in the door panel at the mirror reinforcement.
7. Position the mirror to the door.

➡ **On sedans, the front edge of the mirror should be tucked under the channel. Slide the mirror forward as far as possible so that the mirror is flush with the belt molding.**

8. Install the retaining nuts/bolts/screws and staring with the lower left, tighten in a clockwise direction to 89 inch lbs. (10 Nm).
9. Install the mirror reinforcement cover.
10. Engage the electrical connectors.
11. Install the door trim panel as outlined in this section.

MIRROR GLASS REPLACEMENT

✳✳ CAUTION

Wear gloves and safety glasses to prevent personal injury when removing broken mirror glass.

1. Place masking or duct tape over the entire mirror glass.
2. Cover the painted surfaces of the vehicle to prevent damage to the paint surfaces.
3. Break the mirror face with a small hammer.
4. Remove all pieces of mirror glass from the frame.
5. Clean all adhesive from the mirror frame with solvent.
To install:
6. Remove the paper backing from the back side of the new mirror to expose the adhesive.
7. Center the mirror in the frame and press firmly to ensure the adhesion of the mirror glass-to-frame.

Antenna

REMOVAL & INSTALLATION

Fixed

▶ **See Figure 14**

1. Remove the antenna mast from the antenna lead.
2. Remove the nut from the top of the quarter panel.
3. Remove the luggage compartment side trim panel.

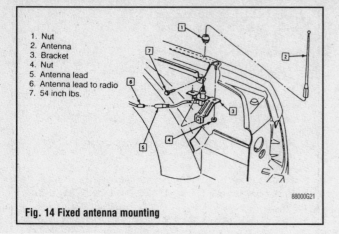

1. Nut
2. Antenna
3. Bracket
4. Nut
5. Antenna lead
6. Antenna lead to radio
7. 54 inch lbs.

88000G21

Fig. 14 Fixed antenna mounting

4. Remove the antenna securing bracket from the quarter panel.
5. Disconnect the antenna lead and remove the antenna assembly.
To install:
6. Install the bracket, nut and bolt.
7. Install the antenna and lead.
8. Install the nut to the top of the quarter panel.
9. Install the mast-to-antenna lead.

Power

▶ See Figure 15

➡The power antenna may be replaced separately from the motor. The mast should be cleaned when it becomes dirty, but do not lubricate.

1. With the antenna in the down position, remove the antenna mast nut.

➡Do NOT pull the antenna mast up by hand. Clean the bottom the contact spring with contact cleaner and set aside to be reused.

2. With the ignition key in the **ON** position, turn the radio **ON** to raise the antenna out of the motor.
To install:
3. Insert the plastic cable into the housing and stop when about 12 in. (305mm) of resistance if felt.
4. The serrated side of the cable MUST face the antenna motor. Activate the motor to the down position until the plastic cable retracts into the housing.
5. If the cable does NOT retract into the housing, rotate the cable until the cable is pulled into the housing while the motor is operating.
6. Install the contact spring to the antenna. Make sure the flanged end of the contact spring faces upward.

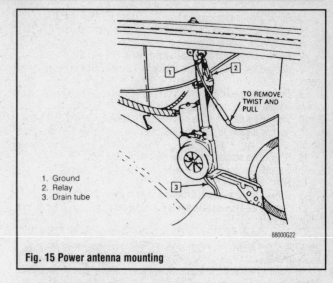

1. Ground
2. Relay
3. Drain tube

TO REMOVE, TWIST AND PULL

88000G22

Fig. 15 Power antenna mounting

7. Install the antenna nut and cycle the antenna several times to check operation.
8. Remove the luggage compartment side trim panel if the entire antenna assembly has to be replaced.

Power Sunroof

MOTOR REPLACEMENT

1. Disconnect the negative battery cable.
2. Remove the sunvisor, sunroof switch, rear view mirror and passenger assist handle.
3. Remove the headliner lace from retainers and lower the headliner.
4. Disconnect the sunroof actuator connector and remove the motor-to-support retaining bolts.
5. Pull the sunroof actuator downward and remove the actuator.
To install:
6. Check that the sunroof is at its maximum vent position by pushing the mechanism forward on both sides. This procedure aligns the drive cables.
7. Fit the sunroof actuator into position. Install the motor-to-support retaining bolts and reconnect the electrical connector.
8. Secure the headliner assembly.
9. Install the passenger assist handle, rear view mirror, switch and sunvisor.
10. Reconnect the negative battery cable.

INTERIOR

Instrument Panel and Pad

PRECAUTIONS

When handling a part that has an "ESD-sensitive" sticker warning of Electrostatic Discharge (it looks like a hand inside a black triangle with a white stripe through it), follow these guidelines to reduce any possible buildup of electrostatic charge:
• If replacing a part that has the sticker, do not open the package until just prior to installation. Before removing the part from its package, ground the package to a good ground on the car.
• Avoid touching the electrical terminals of the component.
• Always touch a good ground before handling a part with the sticker. This should be repeated while handling the part; do it more often when sliding across the seat, sitting from the standing position, or after walking.

✳✳ CAUTION

Properly disarm the air bag on vehicles equipped with the Supplemental Restraint System (SRS). Failure to do so can cause

serious injury. The procedure can be found in Section 6 of this manual.

REMOVAL & INSTALLATION

Cutlass Supreme

1988–94 MODELS

1. Disconnect the negative battery cable.
2. Remove the instrument panel pad:
   a. Open the glove box door, remove the lower storage compartment, remove the revealed screws, and remove the defroster grille and deflector.
   b. Remove the screws inside the defroster opening and remove the instrument cluster trim plate.
   c. Remove the screws at the sides of the cluster opening and remove the cluster. Remove the Head-Up Display retaining screws behind the cluster.
   d. Lift the pad and disconnect the Daytime Running Lamps connector, speaker wiring and glovebox lamp switch.
   e. Remove the upper pad from the instrument panel.

3. Remove the speakers and radio.

4. Remove the air outlet trim plates and climate control system switch panel.

5. Remove the ashtray or sport pod housing on International Series.

6. Remove the left and right side sound insulators.

7. Remove the ALDL connector and allow it to dangle below the instrument panel.

8. Remove the steering column trim plate and lower the steering column.

9. Remove the courtesy lights.

10. Remove the parking brake release handle and allow it to dangle below.

11. Remove the screws fastening the fuse block and position the fuse block aside.

12. Remove the screws holding the main ventilation duct.

13. Remove the nut holding the wiring harness clip.

14. Remove the glove box lamp.

15. Remove the screws at both bottom ends of the instrument panel.

16. Remove the screws at the top of the instrument panel and at the steering column support.

17. Have a helper assist you, and remove the instrument panel assembly from the vehicle.

To install:

18. Carefully install the instrument panel to the vehicle. Be sure to clear all wiring, etc.

19. Install the screws at the steering column support, the top of the instrument panel, and at the bottom of both sides of the instrument panel.

20. Install the remaining components in the reverse of the removal procedure.

21. Connect the negative battery cable and check all items in the instrument panel for proper operation.

1995–96 MODELS

▶ **See Figure 16**

※※ CAUTION

Properly disarm the air bag on vehicles equipped with the Supplemental Restraint System (SRS). Failure to do so can cause serious injury. The procedure can be found in Section 6 of this manual.

---

1. Disconnect the front door inside carpet retainers.

2. Remove the sound insulators.

3. Disable the air bag system as outlined in Section 6.

4. Remove the windshield side upper garnish moldings.

5. Remove the instrument panel upper trim panel as follows:

   a. Insert a flat bladed tool, downward at the rearmost edge of the upper trim panel.

   b. Carefully pry the panel up to release the 10 panel tabs.

   c. Lift the rear edge approximately 2 inches and pull the panel rearward to remove.

6. Remove the instrument panel lower compartment.

7. Disconnect the theft deterrent module.

8. Disconnect the passenger side air bag inflator module.

9. Remove the steering column opening filler.

10. Remove the instrument panel cluster trim plate.

11. Remove the console, if equipped.

12. Remove the audio system as outlined in Section 6.

13. Remove the ventilation control system.

14. Remove the instrument panel cluster.

15. Disconnect the headlamp switch, foglamp, HUD switch and trip calculator, if equipped.

16. Disconnect the fuse block.

17. Remove the knee bolster deflector.

18. Remove the steering column nuts and lower the steering column.

19. Remove the instrument panel carrier mounting bolts and screws.

20. Disconnect the data link connector, lower compartment light and trunk release switch.

21. Remove the instrument panel carrier clips.

22. Reposition the instrument panel wiring harness and remove the carrier assembly.

To install:

23. Reposition the instrument panel carrier assembly and route the instrument panel wiring.

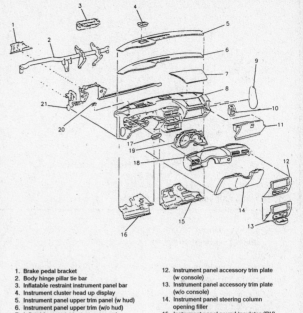

1. Brake pedal bracket
2. Body hinge pillar tie bar
3. Inflatable restraint instrument panel bar
4. Instrument cluster head up display
5. Instrument panel upper trim panel (w hud)
6. Instrument panel upper trim (w/o hud)
7. Inflatable restraint instrument panel module trim cover
8. Instrument panel
9. Instrument panel fuse block accessory cover door
10. Instrument panel outer air outlet
11. Instrument panel compartment
12. Instrument panel accessory trim plate (w console)
13. Instrument panel accessory trim plate (w/o console)
14. Instrument panel steering column opening filler
15. Instrument panel sound insulator (RH)
16. Instrument panel sound insulator (LH)
17. Trip calculator
18. Instrument panel cluster trim plate
19. Instrument cluster
20. Side window defogger outlet
21. Instrument panel lower tie bar

88000G36

Fig. 16 Exploded view of the instrument panel assembly—1994–96 Grand Prix and 1995–96 Regal and Cutlass Supreme

24. Install the instrument panel carrier clips.

25. Connect the data link connector, lower compartment light and trunk release switch.

26. Install the instrument panel carrier mounting bolts and screws and tighten the bolts to 89 inch lbs. (10 Nm).

27. Raise the steering column and install the retaining nuts.

28. Install the remaining components in the reverse of the removal procedure.

29. Enable the air bag system as outlined in Section 6.

Grand Prix

1988–93 MODELS

▶ **See Figure 17**

1. Disconnect the negative battery cable.

2. Remove the instrument panel pad:

   a. Remove the 2 screws at the top of the instrument panel trim plate.

   b. Remove the glove box and the screw above it.

   c. Lift the front of the pad and pull toward you to release the clips.

   d. Disconnect the speaker connectors and Daytime Running Lights connector, and remove the pad.

3. Remove the lights switches assembly and wiper/washer switch assembly.

4. Remove the instrument cluster trim plate.

5. Remove the parking brake release handle and allow it to dangle below.

6. Remove the ALDL connector and allow it to dangle below the instrument panel.

7. Remove the left and right side sound insulators.

8. Remove the steering column trim plate.

9. Lower the steering column.

10. Remove the screws fastening the fuse block and position the fuse block aside.

11. Disconnect the HVAC connector and remove the remote radio amplifier.

12. Remove the radio controls trim cover and climate control switch panel trim cover. Then remove the radio and climate control switch panel.

13. Remove the ashtray and cassette deck or compartment that replaces it if not equipped. Remove the remote radio receiver.

14. Remove the instrument cluster.

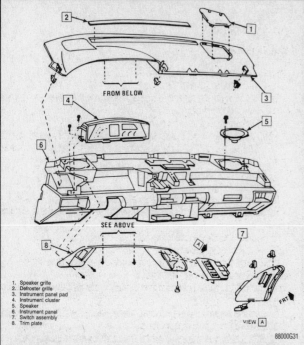

1. Speaker grille
2. Defroster grille
3. Instrument panel pad
4. Instrument cluster
5. Speaker
6. Instrument panel
7. Switch assembly
8. Trim plate

88000G31

Fig. 17 Exploded view of the instrument panel assembly—1988–93 Grand Prix

15. Remove both speakers.
16. Remove 7 screws holding ventilation duct to instrument panel.
17. Remove 3 nuts holding wiring harness carrier.
18. Have a helper assist you, and remove the instrument panel assembly from the vehicle.

To install:

19. Carefully install the instrument panel to the vehicle. Be sure to clear all wiring, etc.
20. Install the nuts holding wiring harness carrier.
21. Install the remaining components in the reverse of the removal procedure.
22. Connect the negative battery cable and check all items in the instrument panel for proper operation.

1994–96 MODELS

▶ See Figure 16

✳✳ CAUTION

Properly disarm the air bag on vehicles equipped with the Supplemental Restraint System (SRS). Failure to do so can cause serious injury. The procedure can be found in Section 6 of this manual.

1. Disconnect the front door inside carpet retainers.
2. Remove the sound insulators.
3. Disable the air bag system as outlined in Section 6.
4. Remove the windshield side upper garnish moldings.
5. Remove the instrument panel upper trim panel as follows:
   a. Insert a flat bladed tool, downward at the rearmost edge of the upper trim panel.
   b. Carefully pry the panel up to release the 10 panel tabs.
   c. Lift the rear edge approximately 2 inches and pull the panel rearward to remove.
6. Remove the instrument panel lower compartment.
7. Disconnect the theft deterrent module.
8. Disconnect the passenger side air bag inflator module.
9. Remove the steering column opening filler.
10. Remove the instrument panel cluster trim plate.
11. Remove the console, if equipped.
12. Remove the audio system as outlined in Section 6.

13. Remove the ventilation control system.
14. Remove the instrument panel cluster.
15. Disconnect the headlamp switch, foglamp, HUD switch and trip calculator, if equipped.
16. Disconnect the fuse block.
17. Remove the knee bolster deflector.
18. Remove the steering column nuts and lower the steering column.
19. Remove the instrument panel carrier mounting bolts and screws.
20. Disconnect the data link connector, lower compartment light and trunk release switch.
21. Remove the instrument panel carrier clips.
22. Reposition the instrument panel wiring harness and remove the carrier assembly.

To install:

23. Reposition the instrument panel carrier assembly and route the instrument panel wiring.
24. Install the instrument panel carrier clips.
25. Connect the data link connector, lower compartment light and trunk release switch.
26. Install the instrument panel carrier mounting bolts and screws and tighten the bolts to 89 inch lbs. (10 Nm).
27. Raise the steering column and install the retaining nuts.
28. Install the remaining components in the reverse of the removal procedure.
29. Enable the air bag system as outlined in Section 6.

Lumina and Monte Carlo

1990–94 MODELS

▶ See Figure 18

1. Disconnect the negative battery cable.
2. Disconnect the Daytime Running Lamp sensor if equipped.
3. Remove the screws under the edge of the instrument panel pad, and remove the pad by pulling up to release and out.
4. Remove the speakers.
5. Remove the instrument cluster.
6. Remove the glovebox.
7. Remove the right side sound insulator.
8. Remove the climate control system switch panel.
9. Remove the radio.
10. Remove the lamps switches.
11. Remove the ashtray and bracket.
12. Remove the ALDL connector and allow it to dangle below the instrument panel.

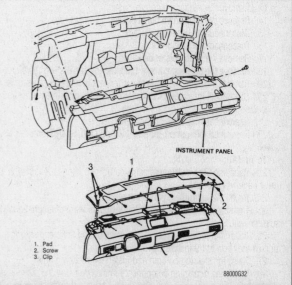

INSTRUMENT PANEL

1. Pad
2. Screw
3. Clip

88000G32

Fig. 18 Exploded view of the instrument panel assembly—1990–94 Lumina

13. Remove the parking brake release handle and allow it to dangle below.
14. Remove the screws fastening the fuse block and position the fuse block aside.
15. Remove the steering column trim plate and lower the steering column.
16. Remove 7 bolts holding the carrier (5 at the top and 2 at the bottom).
17. Remove the 5 screws holding the main air duct.
18. Disengage 9 clips holding the wiring harness.
19. Have a helper assist you, and remove the instrument panel assembly from the vehicle.

To install:

20. Carefully install the instrument panel to the vehicle. Be sure to clear all wiring, etc.
21. Engage the clips holding the wiring harness.
22. Install the 5 screws holding the main air duct and the bolts holding the carrier.
23. Install the remaining components in the reverse of the removal procedure.
24. Connect the negative battery cable and check all items in the instrument panel for proper operation.

1995–96 MODELS

▶ See Figure 19

⁕⁕ CAUTION

Properly disarm the air bag on vehicles equipped with the Supplemental Restraint System (SRS). Failure to do so can cause serious injury. The procedure can be found in Section 6 of this manual.

1. Disconnect the front door inside carpet retainers.
2. Remove the sound insulators.
3. Disable the air bag system as outlined in Section 6.
4. Remove the windshield side upper garnish moldings.
5. Remove the instrument panel upper trim panel as follows:
    a. Insert a flat bladed tool, downward at the rearmost edge of the upper trim panel.
    b. Carefully pry the panel up to release the 10 panel tabs.
    c. Lift the rear edge approximately 2 in. (50.8mm) and pull the panel rearward to remove.
6. Remove the instrument panel lower compartment.
7. Disconnect the theft deterrent module.
8. Disconnect the passenger side air bag inflator module.
9. Remove the steering column opening filler.
10. Remove the instrument panel cluster trim plate.
11. Remove the console, if equipped.
12. Remove the audio system as outlined in Section 6.
13. Remove the ventilation control system.
14. Remove the instrument panel cluster.
15. Disconnect the headlamp switch.
16. Disconnect the fuse block.
17. Remove the knee bolster deflector.
18. Remove the steering column nuts and lower the steering column.
19. Remove the instrument panel carrier mounting bolts and screws.
20. Disconnect the data link connector, lower compartment light and trunk release switch.
21. Remove the instrument panel carrier clips.
22. Reposition the instrument panel wiring harness and remove the carrier assembly.

To install:

23. Reposition the instrument panel carrier assembly and route the instrument panel wiring.
24. Install the instrument panel carrier clips.
25. Connect the data link connector, lower compartment light and trunk release switch.
26. Install the instrument panel carrier mounting bolts and screws and tighten the bolts to 89 inch lbs. (10 Nm).
27. Raise the steering column and install the retaining nuts.
28. Install the remaining components in the reverse of the removal procedure.
29. Enable the air bag system as outlined in Section 6.

Regal

1988–94 MODELS

▶ See Figure 20

1. Disconnect the negative battery cable.
2. Remove the instrument panel pad:
    a. Carefully pry the speaker grilles and disconnect the Daytime Running Lamp sensor if equipped.
    b. Remove the screw under each speaker grille.
    c. Remove the screws at the lower edge of the instrument panel pad.
    d. Remove the pad by lifting the front and pulling toward you to release it.
3. Remove the speakers.
4. Remove the instrument cluster.
5. Remove the glovebox.
6. Remove the right side sound insulator.
7. Remove the climate control system switch panel and sound system controls.
8. Remove the English/Metric switch.
9. Remove the lights switches.
10. Remove the cassette deck or compartment that replaces it if not equipped. Remove the ashtray and bracket.
11. Remove the ALDL connector and allow it to dangle below the instrument panel.
12. Remove the parking brake release handle and allow it to dangle below.
13. Remove the remote radio receiver.
14. Remove the steering column trim plate and lower the steering column.
15. Remove 7 bolts holding the carrier (5 at the top and 2 at the bottom). Remove the 2 bolts above the steering column.
16. Remove the 5 screws holding the main air duct.
17. Remove the 3 nuts holding the conduit. Two are above the glovebox and the other is through the cassette/compartment opening.
18. Disengage 9 clips holding the wiring harness.
19. Have a helper assist you, and remove the instrument panel assembly from the vehicle.

To install:

20. Carefully install the instrument panel to the vehicle. Be sure to clear all wiring, etc.
21. Engage the clips holding the wiring harness.
22. Install the 3 nuts holding the conduit.
23. Install the screws holding the main air duct.
24. Install the bolts holding the carrier.
25. Secure the steering column and install the trim plate.
26. Install the remaining components in the reverse of the removal procedure.
27. Connect the negative battery cable and check all items in the instrument panel for proper operation.

1995–96 MODELS

▶ See Figure 16

⁕⁕ CAUTION

Properly disarm the air bag on vehicles equipped with the Supplemental Restraint System (SRS). Failure to do so can cause serious injury. The procedure can be found in Section 6 of this manual.

1. Disconnect the front door inside carpet retainers.
2. Remove the sound insulators.
3. Disable the air bag system as outlined in Section 6.
4. Remove the windshield side upper garnish moldings.
5. Remove the instrument panel upper trim panel as follows:
    a. Insert a flat bladed tool, downward at the rearmost edge of the upper trim panel.
    b. Carefully pry the panel up to release the 10 panel tabs.
    c. Lift the rear edge approximately 2 in. (50.8mm) and pull the panel rearward to remove.
6. Remove the instrument panel lower compartment.
7. Disconnect the theft deterrent module.
8. Disconnect the passenger side air bag inflator module.
9. Remove the steering column opening filler.

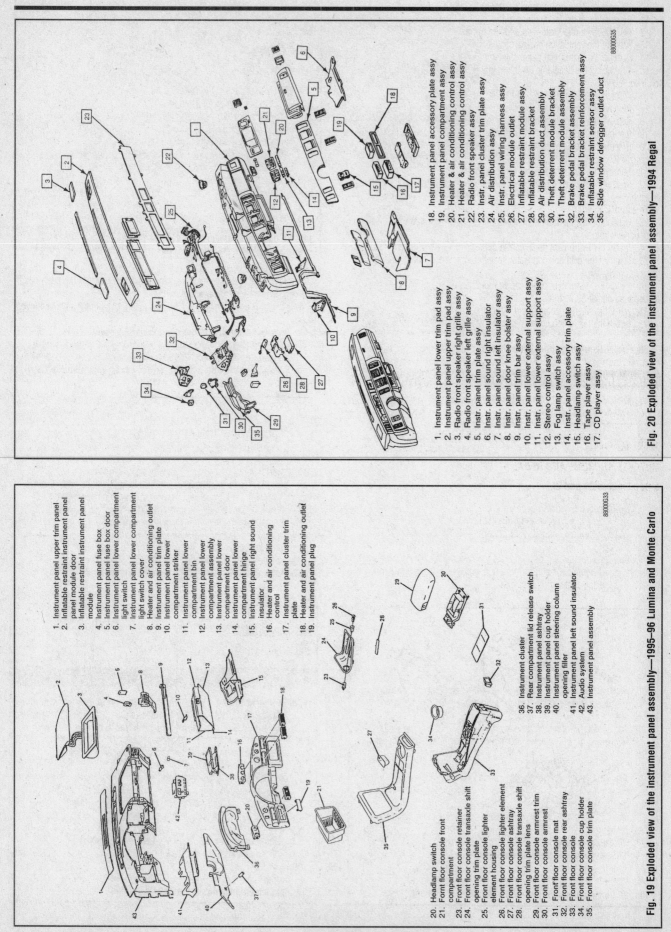

88000635

1. Instrument panel lower trim pad assy
2. Instrument panel upper trim pad assy
3. Radio front speaker right grille assy
4. Radio front speaker left grille assy
5. Instr. panel trim plate assy
6. Instr. panel sound right insulator
7. Instr. panel sound left insulator assy
8. Instr. panel door knee bolster assy
9. Instr. panel trim bar assy
10. Instr. panel lower external support assy
11. Instr. panel lower external support assy
12. Stereo control assy
13. Fog lamp switch assy
14. Instr. panel accessory trim plate
15. Headlamp switch assy
16. Tape player assy
17. CD player assy
18. Instrument panel accessory plate assy
19. Instrument panel compartment assy
20. Heater & air conditioning control assy
21. Heater & air conditioning control assy
22. Radio front speaker assy
23. Instr. panel cluster trim plate assy
24. Air distribution assy
25. Instr. panel wiring harness assy
26. Electrical module outlet
27. Inflatable restraint module assy.
28. Inflatable restraint bracket
29. Air distribution duct assembly
30. Theft deterrent module bracket
31. Theft deterrent module assembly
32. Brake pedal bracket assembly
33. Brake pedal bracket reinforcement assy
34. Inflatable restraint sensor assy
35. Side window defogger outlet duct

Fig. 20 Exploded view of the instrument panel assembly—1994 Regal

88000633

1. Instrument panel upper trim panel
2. Inflatable restraint instrument panel panel module door
3. Inflatable restraint instrument panel module
4. Instrument panel fuse box
5. Instrument panel fuse box door
6. Instrument panel lower compartment light switch
7. Instrument panel lower compartment light switch cover
8. Heater and air conditioning outlet
9. Instrument panel trim plate
10. Instrument panel lower compartment striker
11. Instrument panel lower compartment bin
12. Instrument panel lower compartment assembly
13. Instrument panel lower compartment door
14. Instrument panel lower compartment hinge
15. Instrument panel right sound insulator
16. Heater and air conditioning control
17. Instrument panel cluster trim plate
18. Heater and air conditioning outlet
19. Instrument panel plug
20. Headlamp switch
21. Front floor console front compartment
23. Front floor console retainer
24. Front floor console transaxle shift opening trim plate
25. Front floor console lighter element housing
26. Front floor console lighter element lens
27. Front floor console ashtray
28. Front floor console transaxle shift opening trim plate
29. Front floor console armrest trim
30. Front floor console armrest
31. Front floor console mat
32. Front floor console rear ashtray
33. Front floor console
34. Front floor console cup holder
35. Front floor console trim plate
36. Instrument cluster
37. Rear compartment lid release switch
38. Instrument panel ashtray
39. Instrument panel cup holder
40. Instrument panel steering column opening filler
41. Instrument panel left sound insulator
42. Audio system
43. Instrument panel assembly

Fig. 19 Exploded view of the instrument panel assembly—1995-96 Lumina and Monte Carlo

10. Remove the instrument panel cluster tri   ate.
11. Remove the console, if equipped.
12. Remove the audio system as outlined in Section 6.
13. Remove the ventilation control system.
14. Remove the instrument panel cluster.
15. Disconnect the headlamp switch, foglamp, HUD switch and trip calculator, if equipped.
16. Disconnect the fuse block.
17. Remove the knee bolster deflector.
18. Remove the steering column nuts and lower the steering column.
19. Remove the instrument panel carrier mounting bolts and screws.
20. Disconnect the data link connector, lower compartment light and trunk release switch.
21. Remove the instrument panel carrier clips.
22. Reposition the instrument panel wiring harness and remove the carrier assembly.

To install:

23. Reposition the instrument panel carrier assembly and route the instrument panel wiring.
24. Install the instrument panel carrier clips.
25. Connect the data link connector, lower compartment light and trunk release switch.
26. Install the instrument panel carrier mounting bolts and screws and tighten the bolts to 89 inch lbs. (10 Nm).
27. Raise the steering column and install the retaining nuts.
28. Install the remaining components in the reverse of the removal procedure.
29. Enable the air bag system as outlined in Section 6.

Console

REMOVAL & INSTALLATION

1988–94 Models

CUTLASS SUPREME AND REGAL

▶ **See Figures 21 and 22**

1. Disconnect the negative battery cable.
2. Apply the parking brake and place the transaxle in Neutral.
3. Remove the front compartment, cassette tape holder, or coin holder by lifting up and out.
4. On Regal, remove the retaining clip and remove the shifter knob. On Cutlass Supreme, remove the retaining screw and remove the shifter knob.
5. Remove the shifter trim or cover plate.

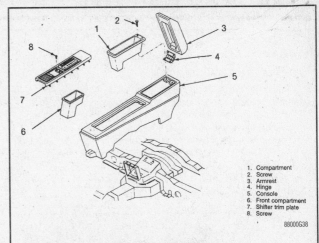

1. Compartment
2. Screw
3. Armrest
4. Hinge
5. Console
6. Front compartment
7. Shifter trim plate
8. Screw

88000G38

Fig. 22 Console installation—1988–94 Regal

6. Remove the armrest and armrest compartment.
7. On Cutlass Supreme, disconnect the lamp at the light at the rear of the upper console.
8. Remove the upper console assembly slowly; disconnect any remaining connectors.
9. On Regal, disconnect the light on the lower console.
10. Remove the retaining bolts and remove the lower console assembly.
11. Installation is the reverse of the removal procedure.
12. Connect the negative battery cable and make sure all lamps, etc. work properly.

GRAND PRIX AND LUMINA

▶ **See Figure 23**

1. Disconnect the negative battery cable.
2. Apply the parking brake and place the transaxle in Neutral.
3. Remove the retaining clip and remove the shifter knob.
4. Remove the front compartments and/or ashtray by lifting up and out.
5. Remove the armrest and cassette holder/armrest compartment.
6. Remove the shifter trim or cover plate assembly. If equipped with trip calculator, lift the rear edge of the trim plate, then pull rear ward to release the clips at the front of the plate. Then remove the trip calculator.
7. Disconnect any remaining wiring, remove the retaining bolts and remove the console assembly.
8. Installation is the reverse of the removal procedure.

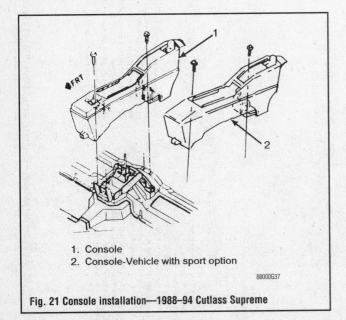

1. Console
2. Console-Vehicle with sport option

88000G37

Fig. 21 Console installation—1988–94 Cutlass Supreme

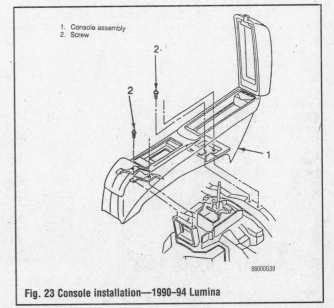

1. Console assembly
2. Screw

88000G39

Fig. 23 Console installation—1990–94 Lumina

1995–96 Models

LUMINA AND MONTE CARLO

▶ **See Figure 24**

1. Disconnect the negative battery cable.
2. Remove the front floor console trim plate.
3. Unsnap the CD storage bin at the front of the console.
4. Raise the armrest and remove the armrest compartment mat.
5. Remove the console retaining bolts/screws.
6. Unplug the electrical connector and remove the console from the vehicle.
7. Installation is the reverse of the removal procedure. Start with the front right and install the console retaining bolts/screws in a clockwise rotation. Tighten the bolts to 106 inch lbs. (12 Nm).
8. Connect the negative battery cable.

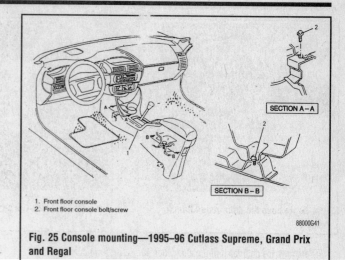

1. Front floor console
2. Front floor console bolt/screw

88000G41

Fig. 25 Console mounting—1995–96 Cutlass Supreme, Grand Prix and Regal

9. Installation is the reverse of the removal procedure.
10. Position the console, install the bolts to the front and rear of the console and tighten to 44 inch lbs. (5 Nm).
11. Connect the negative battery cable.

Door Trim Panels

REMOVAL & INSTALLATION

▶ **See Figures 26 thru 32**

➡ Use a door trim panel and garnish clip remover tool J–24595–C or equivalent to remove the door trim panel. Failure to use this tool may cause damage to the retaining clips, panel backing and door.

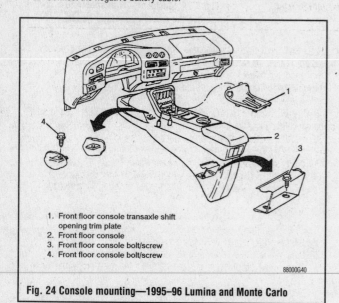

1. Front floor console transaxle shift opening trim plate
2. Front floor console
3. Front floor console bolt/screw
4. Front floor console bolt/screw

88000G40

Fig. 24 Console mounting—1995–96 Lumina and Monte Carlo

CUTLASS SUPREME, GRAND PRIX AND REGAL

▶ **See Figure 25**

1. Disconnect the negative battery cable.
2. Remove the snap ring holding the shift handle by using a suitable prying tool.
3. Remove the shift handle.
4. Remove the screws in the rear compartment.
5. Remove the front floor console transaxle shift opening trim by carefully prying. Pry the two rear tabs last.
6. Remove the armrest.
7. Disconnect the console wiring electrical connectors.
8. Remove the bolts from the front and rear of the console and remove the console from the vehicle.

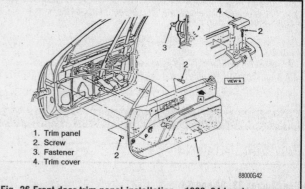

1. Trim panel
2. Screw
3. Fastener
4. Trim cover

88000G42

Fig. 26 Front door trim panel installation—1990–94 Lumina coupe shown, others similar

88000P44

Fig. 27 Remove the upper trim cover

88000P45

Fig. 28 Remove the door inside handle trim plate retaining screw . . .

88000P46

Fig. 29 . . . then remove the door inside handle trim plate

Fig. 30 Remove the door inside handle bezel . . .

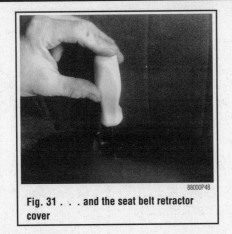

Fig. 31 . . . and the seat belt retractor cover

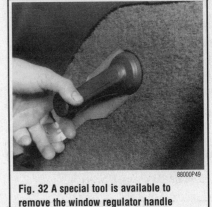

Fig. 32 A special tool is available to remove the window regulator handle

1. Remove the door latch trim plate (coupe and sedan front doors).
2. Remove the ashtray (sedan rear doors).
3. Remove the seat belt retractor cover (coupe and sedan front doors). Use the door trim panel removing tool J–24595–C to release the clip retainers.
4. Remove the door lock trim plate and the power window switch, if so equipped.
5. Remove the window regulator handle by removing the inner retaining clip, A common special tool is available for this purpose which is designed to slide between the handle and trim panel and release the spring clip.
6. Remove the remote mirror control, if so equipped.
7. Remove the trim panel retaining screws.
8. Remove the door trim panel using the door trim panel removing tool J–24595–C or equivalent.
9. Disconnect all electrical and remote mirror controls.

To install:

10. Install the wiring harnesses through the openings in the panel, if so equipped.
11. Position the trim panel to the door and align the clips. Press the trim panel to the door until all the clips are fully engaged. Align all the holes before engaging the clips.
12. Install the screws, remote mirror control and inside door handle bezel, if so equipped.
13. Install the window regulator handle or power window switch.
14. Install the door trim plate, seat belt retractor cover or ashtray.
15. Check each operation for completion of repair.

Door Locks

REMOVAL & INSTALLATION

▶ See Figures 33, 34 and 35

Lock Module

2-DOOR COUPE

1. Disconnect the negative battery cable.
2. Remove the door trim panel as outlined in this section.
3. Remove the energy absorber, if equipped.
4. Loosen the water deflector to gain access to the lock module.
5. Remove the screw and nut securing the cover assembly to the door.
6. Remove the door handle cover assembly.
7. Remove the lock cylinder-to-lock rod and outside handle-to-lock rod.
8. Remove the screws securing the lock assembly to the door.
9. Using a ³⁄₁₆ in. (5mm) drill bit, drill out the rivets securing the lock module to the door.
10. Disconnect the power lock electrical connector and remove the lock module.

To install:

11. Install the lock module through the access hole in the door inner panel.

12. Install the lock assembly screws at a 90 degree angle to prevent cross threading. Tighten the screws to 62 inch lbs. (7 Nm).
13. Install the power lock connector, if so equipped.
14. Install the rivets securing the lock module-to-door. Use a ³⁄₁₆ in. by ¼ in. peel type rivets.
15. Install the outside handle and lock cylinder lock rods. Check the locking operation before going any further.
16. Install the door handle cover, retaining screws and nuts.
17. Install the energy absorber, if equipped.
18. Install the water deflector and door trim panel.
19. Connect the negative battery cable and check all door operations for completion of repair.

4-DOOR SEDAN

1. Disconnect the negative battery cable.
2. Remove the door trim panel and water deflector.
3. Remove the lock cylinder lock rod.
4. Remove the retaining screws and rivets. Drill the rivets out with a ³⁄₁₆ in. (5mm) drill bit.
5. Disconnect the power lock connector, if so equipped.
6. Remove the lock module and disconnect the handle lock rod.

To install:

7. Position the lock module onto the door and connect the handle lock rod.
8. Install the screws at a 90 degree angle to prevent cross threading.
9. Connect the power lock connector, if so equipped.
10. Install the lock module rivets. Use ³⁄₁₆ in. by ¼ in. peel type rivets.
11. Check the door operations at this time.
12. Install the water deflector and door trim panel.
13. Connect the negative battery cable and recheck door operations.

Lock Cylinder

2-DOOR COUPE EXCEPT 1995–96 MONTE CARLO

1. Disconnect the negative battery cable.
2. Remove the door handle cover.
3. Remove the lock cylinder-to-lock rod.
4. Remove the anti-theft shield.
5. Remove the lock cylinder from the door.

To install:

6. Install the lock cylinder, anti-theft shield and shield retaining screw.
7. Connect the cylinder lock rod and handle cover assembly.
8. Check all door operations.
9. Connect the negative battery cable.

1995–96 MONTE CARLO

1. Remove the door trim panel.
2. Remove the energy absorber pad.
3. Remove the water deflector.
4. Remove the lock cylinder lock rod from the cylinder.
5. Remove the lock cylinder rod retainer.
6. Remove the lock cylinder and gasket.

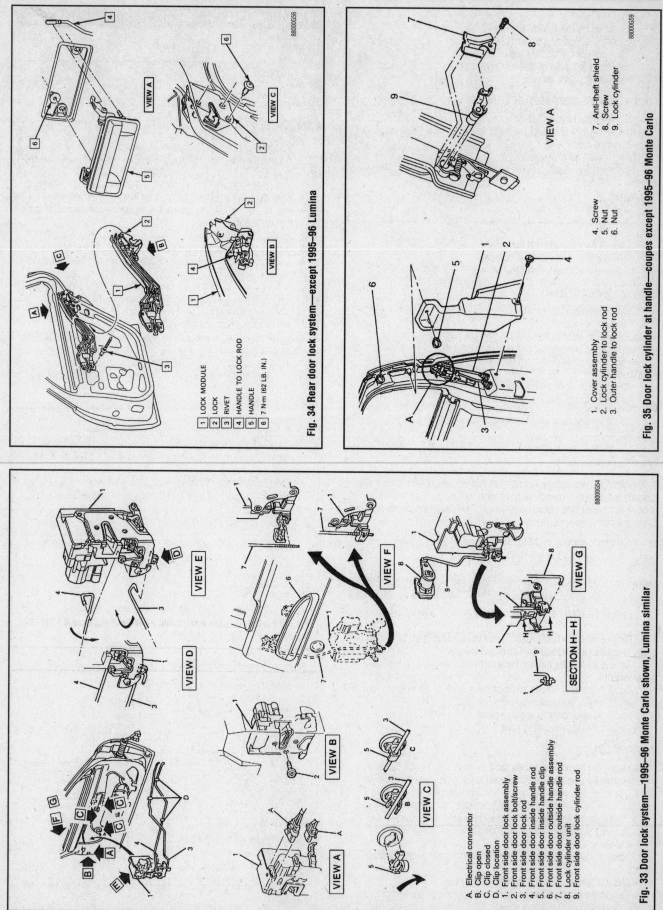

88000G56

1 LOCK MODULE
2 LOCK
3 RIVET
4 HANDLE TO LOCK ROD
5 HANDLE
6 7 N·m (62 LB. IN.)

Fig. 34 Rear door lock system—except 1995–96 Lumina

88000G59

1. Cover assembly
2. Lock cylinder to lock rod
3. Outer handle to lock rod
4. Screw
5. Nut
6. Nut
7. Anti-theft shield
8. Screw
9. Lock cylinder

Fig. 35 Door lock cylinder at handle—coupes except 1995–96 Monte Carlo

88000G54

A. Electrical connector
B. Clip open
C. Clip closed
D. Clip location
1. Front side door lock assembly
2. Front side door lock bolt/screw
3. Front side door lock rod
4. Front side door inside handle rod
5. Front side door inside handle clip
6. Front side door outside handle assembly
7. Front side door outside handle rod
8. Lock cylinder unit
9. Front side door lock cylinder rod

Fig. 33 Door lock system—1995–96 Monte Carlo shown, Lumina similar

To install:

7. Reposition the lock cylinder and gasket.
8. Install the lock cylinder rod retainer.
9. Install the lock cylinder lock rod to the cylinder.
10. Install the water deflector and energy absorber pad.
11. Install the door trim panel.

4-DOOR SEDAN EXCEPT 1995–96 LUMINA

1. Disconnect the negative battery cable.
2. Remove the door trim panel and water deflector. Refer to the appropriate section in this section.
3. Using a small flat prybar, remove the lock cylinder retainer.
4. Disconnect the cylinder lock rod and remove the lock cylinder and gasket.

To install:

5. Install the cylinder and gasket.
6. Connect the cylinder lock rod and install the retainer with a small flat prybar.
7. Check all door operations at this time.
8. Install the trim panel and water deflector.
9. Connect the negative battery cable.

1995–96 LUMINA SEDAN

1. Remove the door trim panel.
2. Remove the water deflector.
3. Remove the lock cylinder lock rod from the cylinder.
4. Remove the lock cylinder rod retainer.
5. Remove the lock cylinder and gasket.

To install:

6. Reposition the lock cylinder and gasket.
7. Install the lock cylinder rod retainer.
8. Install the lock cylinder lock rod to the cylinder.
9. Install the water deflector.
10. Install the door trim panel.

Power Lock Actuator

The optional power door lock system has motor actuators in each door. The system is activated by a control switch on each front door. All locks are activated when any switch is pushed up or down. Each actuator has an internal circuit breaker which may require one to three minutes to reset after service.

➡ The door lock actuator on 1995–96 Chevrolet models is part of the door lock and cannot be serviced separately.

2-DOOR COUPE

1. Disconnect the negative battery cable.
2. Remove the door trim panel and water deflector as outlined in this section.
3. Remove the two actuator retaining screws located at opposite corners.
4. Disconnect the electrical connector and linkage.
5. Remove the actuator through the access hole.

To install:

6. Install the actuator linkage, electrical connector and retaining screws.
7. Check for proper operation by cycling the system.
8. Install the water deflector and trim panel.
9. Connect the negative battery cable.

4-DOOR SEDAN

1. Disconnect the negative battery cable.
2. Remove the door trim panel and water deflector as outlined in this section.
3. Using a ³⁄₁₆ in. (5mm) drill bit, drill out the actuator retaining rivets.
4. Disconnect the electrical connector and linkage rod.
5. Remove the actuator through the access hole.

To install:

6. Install the actuator linkage, electrical connector and retaining rivets or screws.
7. Check for proper operation by cycling the system.
8. Install the water deflector and trim panel.
9. Connect the negative battery cable.

Door Glass

REMOVAL & INSTALLATION

Front

EXCEPT 1995–96 CHEVROLET

♦ See Figures 36 and 37

1. Disconnect the negative battery cable.
2. Remove the door trim panel and water deflector as outlined in this section.
3. Remove the inner belt sealing strip and front window guide retainer.
4. Raise the window half way and push on the rear guide retainer with a flat prybar to disengage the rear run channel. Lift the glass up and to the inboard side of the door frame.

To install:

5. Install the glass into the regulator arm roller and sash channel.
6. Lower the glass half way and pull rearward to engage the rear guide retainer-to-run channel.
7. Install the front window guide retainer by lowering the glass to about 3 in. (76mm) above the belt line and locate the retainer on the door.
8. Check for proper window and door operation at this time.
9. Adjust the door glass as follows.
   a. With the trim panel and water deflector removed, loosen the front window guide retainer bolts.
   b. Cycle the glass to the full down position.
   c. Finger tighten the top retainer bolt and tighten the bottom bolt to 53 inch lbs. (6 Nm).

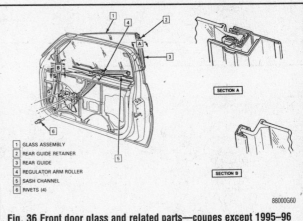

1	GLASS ASSEMBLY
2	REAR GUIDE RETAINER
3	REAR GUIDE
4	REGULATOR ARM ROLLER
5	SASH CHANNEL
6	RIVETS (4)

88000G60

Fig. 36 Front door glass and related parts—coupes except 1995–96 Monte Carlo

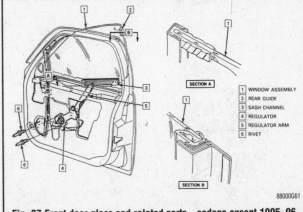

1	WINDOW ASSEMBLY
2	REAR GUIDE
3	SASH CHANNEL
4	REGULATOR
5	REGULATOR ARM
6	RIVET

88000G61

Fig. 37 Front door glass and related parts—sedans except 1995–96 Lumina

d. Run the glass up to 1 in. (25mm) from the full-up position and tighten the top bolt to 53 inch lbs. (6 Nm).

e. Recheck the glass for proper operation without binding.

10. Install the inner belt sealing strip, water deflector and trim panel.

11. Connect the negative battery cable and check for proper door operation.

1995–96 CHEVROLET

▶ See Figure 38

1. Disconnect the negative battery cable.
2. Remove the door trim panel as outlined in this section.
3. On the Monte Carlo, remove the energy absorber pad.
4. Remove the water deflector.
5. Remove the inner and outer belt sealing strip.
6. Remove the window run channel.
7. Remove the rivets and remove the window from the regulator sash.
8. Remove the sash insulators, if necessary.

To install:

9. Securely snap the sash insulators to the bottom edge of the window.

10. Position the window between the inner and outer panels. Point the lower front corner of the window down and pass through the belt opening, aligning the edges with the door window channel. Turn the window to a horizontal position and align the holes in the window with the holes in the regulator sash.

11. Install the rivets.
12. Install the window run channel.
13. Install the inner and outer belt sealing strip.
14. Install the water deflector.
15. On the Monte Carlo, install the energy absorber pad.
16. Install the door trim panel as outlined in this section.

Rear

EXCEPT 1995–96 LUMINA

▶ See Figure 39

1. Disconnect the negative battery cable.
2. Remove the door trim panel and water deflector as outlined in this section.

3. Remove the inner and outer belt sealing strip.

4. Remove the nuts securing the regulator sash-to-glass and place a wedge between the division channel and door outer panel.

5. Mask the outboard side of the division channel with protective tape and lower the glass to the bottom of the door.

6. Remove the front portion of the glass channel from the front door frame.

7. Make sure the glass is disengaged from the division channel and lift the glass upward and outboard of the door frame.

To install:

8. Install the glass to the door from the outboard side.

9. Install the front portion of the window channel-to-door frame by lowering the glass to the bottom.

10. Install the rear guide-to-division channel. Tighten the nuts to 80 inch lbs. (9 Nm).

11. Remove the wedge and masking tape.

12. Check the window for proper operation.

13. Install the outer and inner belt sealing strips.

14. Install the water deflector and trim panel.

15. Connect the negative battery cable.

1995–96 LUMINA

▶ See Figure 40

1. Disconnect the negative battery cable.
2. Remove the door trim panel as outlined in this section.
3. Remove the water deflector.
4. Remove the inner and outer belt sealing strip.
5. Remove the window run channel.
6. Remove the rivets and remove the window from the regulator sash.
7. Remove the sash insulators, if necessary.

To install:

8. Securely snap the sash insulators to the bottom edge of the window.

9. Position the window between the inner and outer panels. Point the lower front corner of the window down and pass through the belt opening, aligning the edges with the door window channel. Turn the window to a horizontal position and align the holes in the window with the holes in the regulator sash.

10. Install the rivets.

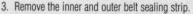

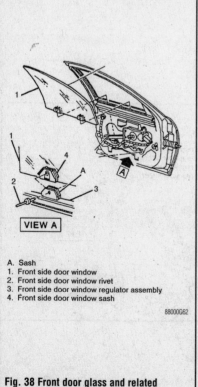

A. Sash
1. Front side door window
2. Front side door window rivet
3. Front side door window regulator assembly
4. Front side door window sash

88000G62

Fig. 38 Front door glass and related parts—1995–96 Chevrolets

VIEW A

SECTION B

1. Window assembly
2. Rear guide
3. Regulator sash
4. 9 Nm (80 lb. in.)
5. Division channel
6. Regulator
7. Rivet

88000G63

Fig. 39 Rear door glass and related parts—except 1995–96 Lumina

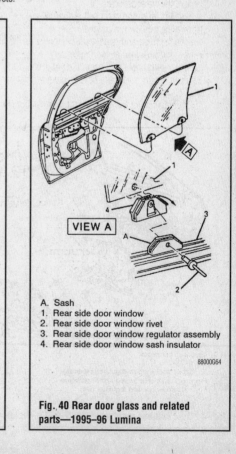

VIEW A

A. Sash
1. Rear side door window
2. Rear side door window rivet
3. Rear side door window regulator assembly
4. Rear side door window sash insulator

88000G64

Fig. 40 Rear door glass and related parts—1995–96 Lumina

11. Install the window run channel.
12. Install the inner and outer belt sealing strip.
13. Install the water deflector.
14. Install the door trim panel as outlined in this section.

Window Regulator

REMOVAL & INSTALLATION

Front

EXCEPT 1995–96 CHEVROLET

▶ See Figures 36 and 37

1. Disconnect the negative battery cable.
2. Tape the window in the full-up position.
3. Remove the door trim panel and water deflector.
4. Using a ¼ in. (6mm) drill bit, drill out the regulator rivets.
5. Remove the regulator by disengaging the regulator arm from the sash channel.
6. Unplug the electrical connectors, if so equipped.

To install:

7. Install the regulator through the access hole and attach the regulator arm-to-sash channel.
8. Engage the electrical connectors.
9. Install ¼ in. by ½ in. rivets to retain the regulator. Check for proper operation.
10. Install the water deflector and trim panel.
11. Connect the negative battery cable and remove the tape.

1995–96 CHEVROLET

▶ See Figure 41

1. Disconnect the negative battery cable.
2. Remove the door trim panel as outlined in this section.
3. On the Monte Carlo, remove the energy absorber pad.
4. Remove the water deflector.
5. Remove the inner and outer belt sealing strip.
6. Remove the window run channel.
7. Remove the rivets and remove the window from the regulator sash.
8. Remove the sash insulators, if necessary.
9. Remove the electrical connector, if equipped.
10. Remove the nuts, rivets and bolts/screws and remove the regulator.

To install:

11. Insert the bottom of the regulator through the access opening, then rotate the top through the opening while lowering the regulator to clear the top of the access opening and align with the holes in the door inner panel.
12. Install the upper right base plate bolt/screw, followed by the lower base plate bolt/screw. Tighten to 89 inch lbs. (10 Nm).
13. Install the upper left rivet, followed by the lower right rivet.
14. Install the cam nut and tighten to 89 inch lbs. (10 Nm).
15. Install the electrical connector, if equipped.
16. Securely snap the sash insulators to the bottom edge of the window.
17. Position the window between the inner and outer panels. Point the lower front corner of the window down and pass through the belt opening, aligning the edges with the door window channel. Turn the window to a horizontal position and align the holes in the window with the holes in the regulator sash.
18. Install the rivets.
19. Install the window run channel.
20. Install the inner and outer belt sealing strip.
21. Install the water deflector.
22. On the Monte Carlo, install the energy absorber pad.
23. Install the door trim panel as outlined in this section.

Rear

EXCEPT 1995–96 LUMINA

▶ See Figure 39

1. Disconnect the negative battery cable.
2. Tape the window in the full-up position.
3. Remove the door trim panel and water deflector.
4. Remove the nuts securing the regulator sash-to-glass.
5. Using a ¼ in. (6mm) drill bit, drill out the regulator rivets.
6. Unplug the electrical connectors, if so equipped.
7. Remove the regulator through the access hole.

To install:

8. Install the regulator through the access hole.
9. Engage the electrical connectors.
10. Install ¼ in. by ½ in. rivets to retain the regulator. Check for proper operation.
11. Install the retaining nuts and tighten to 80 inch lbs. (9 Nm).
12. Install the water deflector and trim panel.
13. Connect the negative battery cable and remove the tape.

1995–96 LUMINA

▶ See Figure 42

1. Disconnect the negative battery cable.
2. Remove the door trim panel as outlined in this section.
3. Remove the water deflector.

A. With power windows (sedan and coupe)
B. Without power windows (sedan only)
C. Electrical connector
D. Nut
1. Front side door window regulator assembly
2. Front side door window regulator bolt/screw
3. Front side door window regulator rivet

VEIW A

88000G65

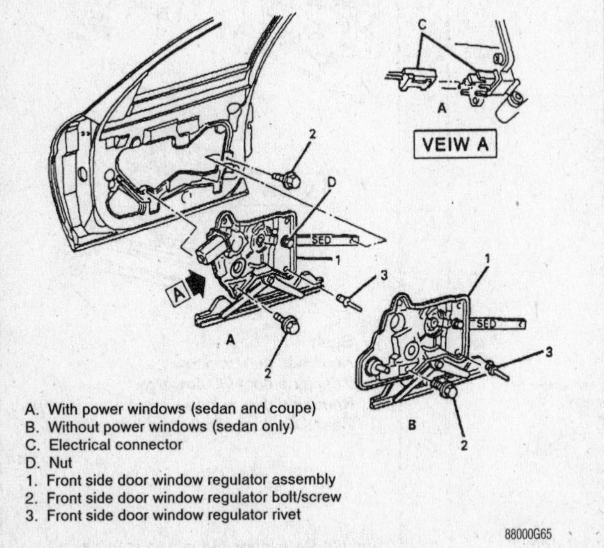

Fig. 41 Door window regulator—1995–96 Chevrolet

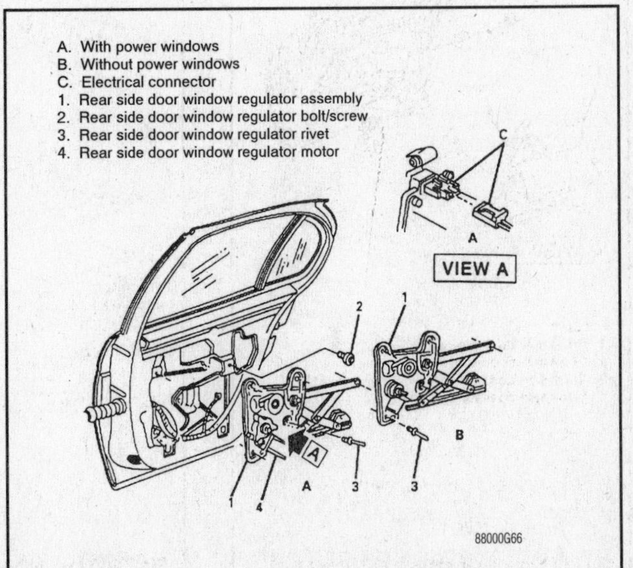

A. With power windows
B. Without power windows
C. Electrical connector
1. Rear side door window regulator assembly
2. Rear side door window regulator bolt/screw
3. Rear side door window regulator rivet
4. Rear side door window regulator motor

VIEW A

88000G66

Fig. 42 Rear door window regulator—1995–96 Lumina

4. Remove the inner and outer belt sealing strip.
5. Remove the window run channel.
6. Remove the rivets and remove the window from the regulator sash.
7. Remove the sash insulators, if necessary.
8. Remove the electrical connector, if equipped.
9. Remove the nuts, rivets and bolts/screws and remove the regulator.

To install:

10. Install the regulator with the rivets and bolts/screws. Tighten the bolts to 89 inch lbs. (10 Nm).
11. Install the electrical connector, if equipped.
12. Securely snap the sash insulators to the bottom edge of the window.
13. Position the window between the inner and outer panels. Point the lower front corner of the window down and pass through the belt opening, aligning the edges with the door window channel. Turn the window to a horizontal position and align the holes in the window with the holes in the regulator sash.
14. Install the rivets.
15. Install the window run channel.
16. Install the inner and outer belt sealing strip.
17. Install the water deflector.
18. Install the door trim panel as outlined in this section.

Window Regulator Motor

REMOVAL & INSTALLATION

Front

EXCEPT 1995–96 CHEVROLET

▶ See Figures 43 and 44

1. Disconnect the negative battery cable.
2. Remove the regulator as outlined in this section.

✳✳ CAUTION

The regulator lift arm is under tension from the counterbalance spring and can cause personal injury if the motor is removed without locking the sector gear in position.

3. With the regulator removed, drill a hole through the regulator sector gear and the backplate. Do not drill closer than ½ inch to the edge of the sector gear or backplate.
4. Install a bolt and nut to lock the sector gear in position.
5. Drill out the ends of the three rivets using a ¼ inch drill bit.
6. Remove the motor.

To install:

7. Install the motor to the backplate.
8. Rivet the motor at the bottom location using a ball peen hammer.
9. Clamp the motor to the backplate using locking pliers.

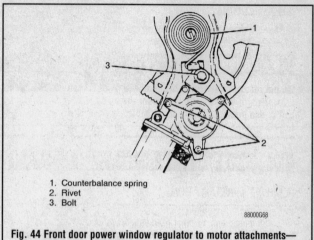

1. Counterbalance spring
2. Rivet
3. Bolt

88000G68

Fig. 44 Front door power window regulator to motor attachments— except 1995–96 Chevrolet

10. Remove the bolt and nut locking the sector gear in position.
11. Supply power to the regulator to gain access for the remaining 2 motor rivets.
12. Remove the locking pliers.
13. Install the regulator as outlined in this section.

1995–96 CHEVROLET

The door window regulator motor on these vehicles cannot be serviced separately. Replace the regulator and motor as an assembly.

✳✳ CAUTION

Do not attempt to service the regulator motor separately. The regulator lift arm is under tension from the counterbalance spring and can cause personal injury if the motor is removed from the regulator.

Rear

EXCEPT 1995–96 LUMINA

▶ See Figure 45

1. Disconnect the negative battery cable.
2. Remove the regulator as outlined in this section.
3. Drill out the ends of the rivets holding the motor to the regulator using a ¼ inch drill bit.

To install:

4. Install the motor to the regulator using a ¼ x 0.968 inch rivet.
5. Install the regulator as outlined in this section.
6. Connect the negative battery cable.

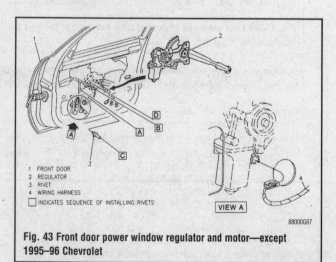

1 FRONT DOOR
2 REGULATOR
3 RIVET
4 WIRING HARNESS
☐ INDICATES SEQUENCE OF INSTALLING RIVETS

VIEW A

88000G67

Fig. 43 Front door power window regulator and motor—except 1995–96 Chevrolet

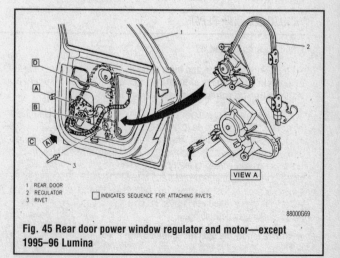

1 REAR DOOR
2 REGULATOR
3 RIVET
☐ INDICATES SEQUENCE FOR ATTACHING RIVETS

VIEW A

88000G69

Fig. 45 Rear door power window regulator and motor—except 1995–96 Lumina

1995–96 LUMINA

The door window regulator motor on these vehicles cannot be serviced separately. Replace the regulator and motor as an assembly.

❋❋ CAUTION

Do not attempt to service the regulator motor separately. The regulator lift arm is under tension from the counterbalance spring and can cause personal injury if the motor is removed from the regulator.

Windshield and Fixed Glass

REMOVAL & INSTALLATION

If your windshield, or other fixed window, is cracked or chipped, you may decide to replace it with a new one yourself. However, there are two main reasons why replacement windshields and other window glass should be installed only by a professional automotive glass technician: safety and cost.

The most important reason a professional should install automotive glass is for safety. The glass in the vehicle, especially the windshield, is designed with safety in mind in case of a collision. The windshield is specially manufactured from two panes of specially-tempered glass with a thin layer of transparent plastic between them. This construction allows the glass to "give" in the event that a part of your body hits the windshield during the collision, and prevents the glass from shattering, which could cause lacerations, blinding and other harm to passengers of the vehicle. The other fixed windows are designed to be tempered so that if they break during a collision, they shatter in such a way that there are no large pointed glass pieces. The professional automotive glass technician knows how to install the glass in a vehicle so that it will function optimally during a collision. Without the proper experience, knowledge and tools, installing a piece of automotive glass yourself could lead to additional harm if an accident should ever occur.

Cost is also a factor when deciding to install automotive glass yourself. Performing this could cost you much more than a professional may charge for the same job. Since the windshield is designed to break under stress, an often life saving characteristic, windshields tend to break VERY easily when an inexperienced person attempts to install one. Do-it-yourselfers buying two, three or even four windshields from a salvage yard because they have broken them during installation are common stories. Also, since the automotive glass is designed to prevent the outside elements from entering your vehicle, improper installation can lead to water and air leaks. Annoying whining noises at highway speeds from air leaks or inside body panel rusting from water leaks can add to your stress level and subtract from your wallet. After buying two or three windshields, installing them and ending up with a leak that produces a noise while driving and water damage during rainstorms, the cost of having a professional do it correctly the first time may be much more alluring. We here at Chilton, therefore, advise that you have a professional automotive glass technician service any broken glass on your vehicle.

WINDSHIELD CHIP REPAIR

▶ **See Figures 46 and 47**

➥Check with your state and local authorities on the laws for state safety inspection. Some states or municipalities may not allow chip repair as a viable option for correcting stone damage to your windshield.

Although severely cracked or damaged windshields must be replaced, there is something that you can do to prolong or even prevent the need for replacement of a chipped windshield. There are many companies which offer windshield chip repair products, such as Loctite's® Bullseye™ windshield repair kit. These kits usually consist of a syringe, pedestal and a sealing adhesive. The syringe is mounted on the pedestal and is used to create a vacuum which pulls the plastic layer against the glass. This helps make the chip transparent. The adhesive is then injected which seals the chip and helps to prevent further stress cracks from developing

➥**Always follow the specific manufacturer's instructions.**

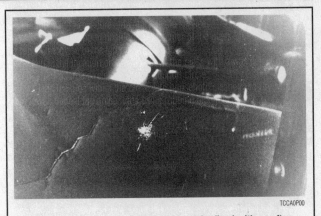

Fig. 46 Small chips on your windshield can be fixed with an aftermarket repair kit, such as the one from Loctite®

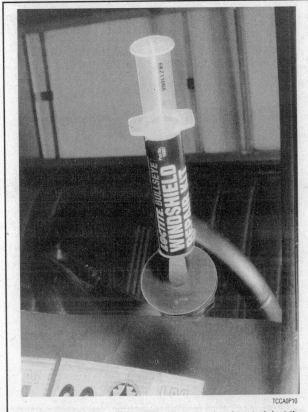

Fig. 47 Most kits use a self-stick applicator and syringe to inject the adhesive into the chip or crack

Inside Rear View Mirror

REMOVAL & INSTALLATION

The rearview mirror is attached to a support which is secured to the windshield glass. A service replacement windshield glass has the support bonded to the glass assembly. To install a detached mirror support or install a new part, use the following procedures to complete the service.

1. Locate the support position at the center of the glass 3 in. (76mm) from the top of the glass to the top of the support.
2. Circle the location on the outside of the glass with a wax pencil or crayon. Draw a large circle around the support circle.
3. Clean the area within the circle with household cleaner and dry with a clean towel. Repeat the procedures using rubbing alcohol.

4. Sand the bonding surface of the support with fine grit (320360) emery cloth or sandpaper. If the original support is being used, remove the old adhesive with rubbing alcohol and a clean towel.
5. Apply the adhesive as outlined in the kit instructions.
6. Position the support to the marked location with the rounded end UP.

✳✳ CAUTION

Do NOT apply excessive pressure to the windshield glass. The glass may break, causing personal injury.

7. Press the support to the glass for 30–60 seconds. Excessive adhesive can be removed after five minutes with rubbing alcohol.

Seats

REMOVAL & INSTALLATION

Front

▶ **See Figure 48**

1. Operate the seat to the full-forward position (full-forward and full-up if six way power seat).
2. Remove the track covers and front anchor bolts.

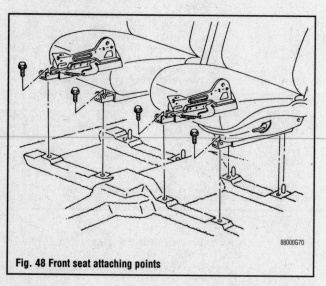

Fig. 48 Front seat attaching points

3. Operate the seat to the full-rearward position.
4. Remove the rear anchor bolts.
5. Unplug the electrical connectors (six way power seats).
6. With an assistant, lift the seat out of the vehicle making sure the spacer washers remain in place.

➡**Be careful not to damage the interior and painted surfaces when removing the seat assemblies.**

To install:
7. With an assistant, install the seat assembly into place and make sure the spacer washers are located between the floor pan and seat tracks.
8. Engage the electrical connectors (six way power seats).
9. Install the rear anchor bolts and tighten to 18 ft. lbs. (24 Nm).
10. Operate the seat to the full-forward position.
11. Install the front anchor bolts and tighten to 18 ft. lbs. (24 Nm).
12. Install the track covers and check for proper operation.

Rear

▶ **See Figures 49 and 50**

1. Remove the two bolts at the base of the seat bottom (one bolt for buckets).
2. Remove the seat bottom by lifting up and pulling out.
3. At the bottom of the seatback, remove the two or four anchor nuts.
4. Grasp the bottom of the seatback and swing upward to disengage the offsets on the upper frame bar. Then lift the seat and remove.
To install:
5. Slide the seatback into place and make sure the offsets are engaged to the seatback.
6. Install the retaining nuts and tighten to 89 inch lbs. (10 Nm).
7. Install the seat bottom into position and tighten the retaining bolts to 18–19 ft. lbs. (25–27 Nm).

Head Rest

REMOVAL & INSTALLATION

1. Raise the head rest to the full-up position.
2. Insert the spring clip release tool down into the left head rest shaft.
3. Push the head rest and tool down at the same time to disengage the detent from the tab.
4. Lift the head rest out after the detent has been released.
To install:
5. Install the shafts into the guides.
6. Push the head rest into the full-down position.
7. Raise the head rest to ensure the detent is properly seated.

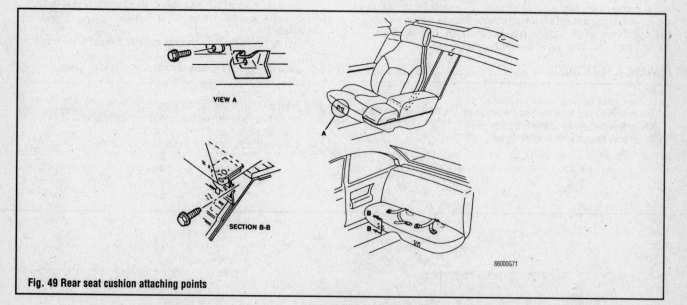

Fig. 49 Rear seat cushion attaching points

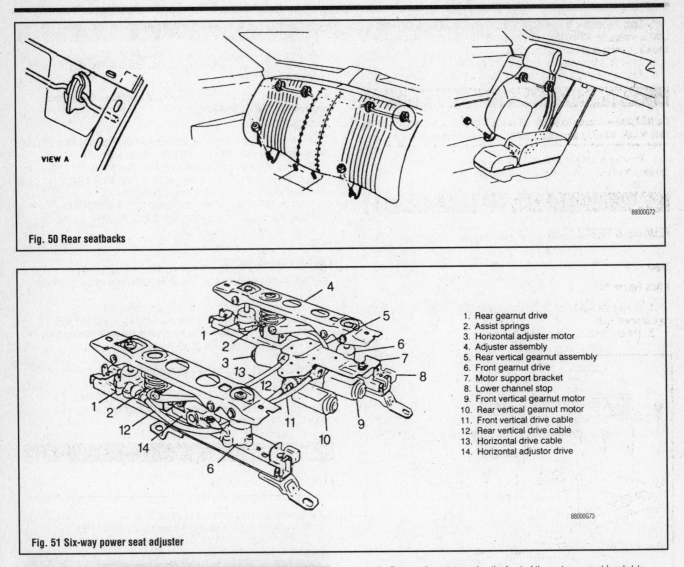

Fig. 50 Rear seatbacks

Fig. 51 Six-way power seat adjuster

1. Rear gearnut drive
2. Assist springs
3. Horizontal adjuster motor
4. Adjuster assembly
5. Rear vertical gearnut assembly
6. Front gearnut drive
7. Motor support bracket
8. Lower channel stop
9. Front vertical gearnut motor
10. Rear vertical gearnut motor
11. Front vertical drive cable
12. Rear vertical drive cable
13. Horizontal drive cable
14. Horizontal adjustor drive

Power Seat Motors

♦ See Figure 51

The six-way power seat adjusters are actuated by three 12V, reversible permanent magnet motors with built in circuit breakers. The motors drive the front and rear vertical gearnuts and a horizontal actuator. When the adjusters are at their limit of travel, an overload relay provides stall tighten so the motors are not overloaded. Each motor can be serviced as a separate unit.

REMOVAL & INSTALLATION

1. Disconnect the negative battery cable.
2. Remove the seat assembly from the vehicle as outlined in this section.
3. Remove the adjuster assembly from the seat.
4. Remove the feed wires from the motor.

5. Remove the nuts securing the front of the motor support bracket-to-inboard adjuster. Partially withdraw the assembly from the adjuster and gearnut drives.
6. Remove the drive cables from the motor. Completely disassemble the support bracket with the motors attached.
7. Grind off the peened over ends of the grommet assembly securing the motor-to-support. Separate the motor from the support.

To install:

8. Drill out the top end of the grommet assembly using a ³⁄₁₆ in. (5mm) drill bit.
9. Install the grommet assembly-to-motor support bracket. Secure the motor with a ³⁄₁₆ in. (5mm) rivet.
10. Install the drive cables.
11. Install the motor-to-inboard adjuster.
12. Connect the motor feed wires and negative battery cable.
13. Install the adjuster assembly-to-seat bottom.
14. With an assistant, install the seat and check for proper operation.

GLOSSARY

AIR/FUEL RATIO: The ratio of air-to-gasoline by weight in the fuel mixture drawn into the engine.

AIR INJECTION: One method of reducing harmful exhaust emissions by injecting air into each of the exhaust ports of an engine. The fresh air entering the hot exhaust manifold causes any remaining fuel to be burned before it can exit the tailpipe.

ALTERNATOR: A device used for converting mechanical energy into electrical energy.

AMMETER: An instrument, calibrated in amperes, used to measure the flow of an electrical current in a circuit. Ammeters are always connected in series with the circuit being tested.

AMPERE: The rate of flow of electrical current present when one volt of electrical pressure is applied against one ohm of electrical resistance.

ANALOG COMPUTER: Any microprocessor that uses similar (analogous) electrical signals to make its calculations.

ARMATURE: A laminated, soft iron core wrapped by a wire that converts electrical energy to mechanical energy as in a motor or relay. When rotated in a magnetic field, it changes mechanical energy into electrical energy as in a generator.

ATMOSPHERIC PRESSURE: The pressure on the Earth's surface caused by the weight of the air in the atmosphere. At sea level, this pressure is 14.7 psi at 32°F (101 kPa at 0°C).

ATOMIZATION: The breaking down of a liquid into a fine mist that can be suspended in air.

AXIAL PLAY: Movement parallel to a shaft or bearing bore.

BACKFIRE: The sudden combustion of gases in the intake or exhaust system that results in a loud explosion.

BACKLASH: The clearance or play between two parts, such as meshed gears.

BACKPRESSURE: Restrictions in the exhaust system that slow the exit of exhaust gases from the combustion chamber.

BAKELITE: A heat resistant, plastic insulator material commonly used in printed circuit boards and transistorized components.

BALL BEARING: A bearing made up of hardened inner and outer races between which hardened steel balls roll.

BALLAST RESISTOR: A resistor in the primary ignition circuit that lowers voltage after the engine is started to reduce wear on ignition components.

BEARING: A friction reducing, supportive device usually located between a stationary part and a moving part.

BIMETAL TEMPERATURE SENSOR: Any sensor or switch made of two dissimilar types of metal that bend when heated or cooled due to the different expansion rates of the alloys. These types of sensors usually function as an on/off switch.

BLOWBY: Combustion gases, composed of water vapor and unburned fuel, that leak past the piston rings into the crankcase during normal engine operation. These gases are removed by the PCV system to prevent the buildup of harmful acids in the crankcase.

BRAKE PAD: A brake shoe and lining assembly used with disc brakes.

BRAKE SHOE: The backing for the brake lining. The term is, however, usually applied to the assembly of the brake backing and lining.

BUSHING: A liner, usually removable, for a bearing; an anti-friction liner used in place of a bearing.

CALIPER: A hydraulically activated device in a disc brake system, which is mounted straddling the brake rotor (disc). The caliper contains at least one piston and two brake pads. Hydraulic pressure on the piston(s) forces the pads against the rotor.

CAMSHAFT: A shaft in the engine on which are the lobes (cams) which operate the valves. The camshaft is driven by the crankshaft, via a belt, chain or gears, at one half the crankshaft speed.

CAPACITOR: A device which stores an electrical charge.

CARBON MONOXIDE (CO): A colorless, odorless gas given off as a normal byproduct of combustion. It is poisonous and extremely dangerous in confined areas, building up slowly to toxic levels without warning if adequate ventilation is not available.

CARBURETOR: A device, usually mounted on the intake manifold of an engine, which mixes the air and fuel in the proper proportion to allow even combustion.

CATALYTIC CONVERTER: A device installed in the exhaust system, like a muffler, that converts harmful byproducts of combustion into carbon dioxide and water vapor by means of a heat-producing chemical reaction.

CENTRIFUGAL ADVANCE: A mechanical method of advancing the spark timing by using flyweights in the distributor that react to centrifugal force generated by the distributor shaft rotation.

CHECK VALVE: Any one-way valve installed to permit the flow of air, fuel or vacuum in one direction only.

CHOKE: A device, usually a moveable valve, placed in the intake path of a carburetor to restrict the flow of air.

CIRCUIT: Any unbroken path through which an electrical current can flow. Also used to describe fuel flow in some instances.

CIRCUIT BREAKER: A switch which protects an electrical circuit from overload by opening the circuit when the current flow exceeds a predetermined level. Some circuit breakers must be reset manually, while most reset automatically.

COIL (IGNITION): A transformer in the ignition circuit which steps up the voltage provided to the spark plugs.

COMBINATION MANIFOLD: An assembly which includes both the intake and exhaust manifolds in one casting.

COMBINATION VALVE: A device used in some fuel systems that routes fuel vapors to a charcoal storage canister instead of venting them into the atmosphere. The valve relieves fuel tank pressure and allows fresh air into the tank as the fuel level drops to prevent a vapor lock situation.

COMPRESSION RATIO: The comparison of the total volume of the cylinder and combustion chamber with the piston at BDC and the piston at TDC.

CONDENSER: 1. An electrical device which acts to store an electrical charge, preventing voltage surges. 2. A radiator-like device in the air conditioning system in which refrigerant gas condenses into a liquid, giving off heat.

CONDUCTOR: Any material through which an electrical current can be transmitted easily.

CONTINUITY: Continuous or complete circuit. Can be checked with an ohmmeter.

COUNTERSHAFT: An intermediate shaft which is rotated by a mainshaft and transmits, in turn, that rotation to a working part.

CRANKCASE: The lower part of an engine in which the crankshaft and related parts operate.

CRANKSHAFT: The main driving shaft of an engine which receives reciprocating motion from the pistons and converts it to rotary motion.

CYLINDER: In an engine, the round hole in the engine block in which the piston(s) ride.

CYLINDER BLOCK: The main structural member of an engine in which is found the cylinders, crankshaft and other principal parts.

CYLINDER HEAD: The detachable portion of the engine, usually fastened to the top of the cylinder block and containing all or most of the combustion chambers. On overhead valve engines, it contains the valves and their operating parts. On overhead cam engines, it contains the camshaft as well.

DEAD CENTER: The extreme top or bottom of the piston stroke.

DETONATION: An unwanted explosion of the air/fuel mixture in the combustion chamber caused by excess heat and compression, advanced timing, or an overly lean mixture. Also referred to as "ping".

DIAPHRAGM: A thin, flexible wall separating two cavities, such as in a vacuum advance unit.

DIESELING: A condition in which hot spots in the combustion chamber cause the engine to run on after the key is turned off.

DIFFERENTIAL: A geared assembly which allows the transmission of motion between drive axles, giving one axle the ability to turn faster than the other.

DIODE: An electrical device that will allow current to flow in one direction only.

DISC BRAKE: A hydraulic braking assembly consisting of a brake disc, or rotor, mounted on an axle, and a caliper assembly containing, usually two brake pads which are activated by hydraulic pressure. The pads are forced against the sides of the disc, creating friction which slows the vehicle.

DISTRIBUTOR: A mechanically driven device on an engine which is responsible for electrically firing the spark plug at a predetermined point of the piston stroke.

DOWEL PIN: A pin, inserted in mating holes in two different parts allowing those parts to maintain a fixed relationship.

DRUM BRAKE: A braking system which consists of two brake shoes and one or two wheel cylinders, mounted on a fixed backing plate, and a brake drum, mounted on an axle, which revolves around the assembly.

DWELL: The rate, measured in degrees of shaft rotation, at which an electrical circuit cycles on and off.

ELECTRONIC CONTROL UNIT (ECU): Ignition module, module, amplifier or igniter. See Module for definition.

ELECTRONIC IGNITION: A system in which the timing and firing of the spark plugs is controlled by an electronic control unit, usually called a module. These systems have no points or condenser.

END-PLAY: The measured amount of axial movement in a shaft.

ENGINE: A device that converts heat into mechanical energy.

EXHAUST MANIFOLD: A set of cast passages or pipes which conduct exhaust gases from the engine.

FEELER GAUGE: A blade, usually metal, or precisely predetermined thickness, used to measure the clearance between two parts.

FIRING ORDER: The order in which combustion occurs in the cylinders of an engine. Also the order in which spark is distributed to the plugs by the distributor.

FLOODING: The presence of too much fuel in the intake manifold and combustion chamber which prevents the air/fuel mixture from firing, thereby causing a no-start situation.

FLYWHEEL: A disc shaped part bolted to the rear end of the crankshaft. Around the outer perimeter is affixed the ring gear. The starter drive engages the ring gear, turning the flywheel, which rotates the crankshaft, imparting the initial starting motion to the engine.

FOOT POUND (ft. lbs. or sometimes, ft.lb.): The amount of energy or work needed to raise an item weighing one pound, a distance of one foot.

FUSE: A protective device in a circuit which prevents circuit overload by breaking the circuit when a specific amperage is present. The device is constructed around a strip or wire of a lower amperage rating than the circuit it is designed to protect. When an amperage higher than that stamped on the fuse is present in the circuit, the strip or wire melts, opening the circuit.

GEAR RATIO: The ratio between the number of teeth on meshing gears.

GENERATOR: A device which converts mechanical energy into electrical energy.

HEAT RANGE: The measure of a spark plug's ability to dissipate heat from its firing end. The higher the heat range, the hotter the plug fires.

HUB: The center part of a wheel or gear.

HYDROCARBON (HC): Any chemical compound made up of hydrogen and carbon. A major pollutant formed by the engine as a byproduct of combustion.

HYDROMETER: An instrument used to measure the specific gravity of a solution.

INCH POUND (inch lbs.; sometimes in.lb. or in. lbs.): One twelfth of a foot pound.

INDUCTION: A means of transferring electrical energy in the form of a magnetic field. Principle used in the ignition coil to increase voltage.

INJECTOR: A device which receives metered fuel under relatively low pressure and is activated to inject the fuel into the engine under relatively high pressure at a predetermined time.

INPUT SHAFT: The shaft to which torque is applied, usually carrying the driving gear or gears.

INTAKE MANIFOLD: A casting of passages or pipes used to conduct air or a fuel/air mixture to the cylinders.

JOURNAL: The bearing surface within which a shaft operates.

KEY: A small block usually fitted in a notch between a shaft and a hub to prevent slippage of the two parts.

MANIFOLD: A casting of passages or set of pipes which connect the cylinders to an inlet or outlet source.

MANIFOLD VACUUM: Low pressure in an engine intake manifold formed just below the throttle plates. Manifold vacuum is highest at idle and drops under acceleration.

MASTER CYLINDER: The primary fluid pressurizing device in a hydraulic system. In automotive use, it is found in brake and hydraulic clutch systems and is pedal activated, either directly or, in a power brake system, through the power booster.

MODULE: Electronic control unit, amplifier or igniter of solid state or integrated design which controls the current flow in the ignition primary circuit based on input from the pick-up coil. When the module opens the primary circuit, high secondary voltage is induced in the coil.

NEEDLE BEARING: A bearing which consists of a number (usually a large number) of long, thin rollers.

OHM: (Ω) The unit used to measure the resistance of conductor-to-electrical flow. One ohm is the amount of resistance that limits current flow to one ampere in a circuit with one volt of pressure.

OHMMETER: An instrument used for measuring the resistance, in ohms, in an electrical circuit.

OUTPUT SHAFT: The shaft which transmits torque from a device, such as a transmission.

OVERDRIVE: A gear assembly which produces more shaft revolutions than that transmitted to it.

OVERHEAD CAMSHAFT (OHC): An engine configuration in which the camshaft is mounted on top of the cylinder head and operates the valve either directly or by means of rocker arms.

OVERHEAD VALVE (OHV): An engine configuration in which all of the valves are located in the cylinder head and the camshaft is located in the cylinder block. The camshaft operates the valves via lifters and pushrods.

OXIDES OF NITROGEN (NOx): Chemical compounds of nitrogen produced as a byproduct of combustion. They combine with hydrocarbons to produce smog.

OXYGEN SENSOR: Use with the feedback system to sense the presence of oxygen in the exhaust gas and signal the computer which can reference the voltage signal to an air/fuel ratio.

PINION: The smaller of two meshing gears.

PISTON RING: An open-ended ring with fits into a groove on the outer diameter of the piston. Its chief function is to form a seal between the piston and cylinder wall. Most automotive pistons have three rings: two for compression sealing; one for oil sealing.

PRELOAD: A predetermined load placed on a bearing during assembly or by adjustment.

PRIMARY CIRCUIT: the low voltage side of the ignition system which consists of the ignition switch, ballast resistor or resistance wire, bypass, coil, electronic control unit and pick-up coil as well as the connecting wires and harnesses.

PRESS FIT: The mating of two parts under pressure, due to the inner diameter of one being smaller than the outer diameter of the other, or vice versa; an interference fit.

RACE: The surface on the inner or outer ring of a bearing on which the balls, needles or rollers move.

REGULATOR: A device which maintains the amperage and/or voltage levels of a circuit at predetermined values.

RELAY: A switch which automatically opens and/or closes a circuit.

RESISTANCE: The opposition to the flow of current through a circuit or electrical device, and is measured in ohms. Resistance is equal to the voltage divided by the amperage.

RESISTOR: A device, usually made of wire, which offers a preset amount of resistance in an electrical circuit.

RING GEAR: The name given to a ring-shaped gear attached to a differential case, or affixed to a flywheel or as part of a planetary gear set.

ROLLER BEARING: A bearing made up of hardened inner and outer races between which hardened steel rollers move.

ROTOR: 1. The disc-shaped part of a disc brake assembly, upon which the brake pads bear; also called, brake disc. 2. The device mounted atop the distributor shaft, which passes current to the distributor cap tower contacts.

SECONDARY CIRCUIT: The high voltage side of the ignition system, usually above 20,000 volts. The secondary includes the ignition coil, coil wire, distributor cap and rotor, spark plug wires and spark plugs.

SENDING UNIT: A mechanical, electrical, hydraulic or electro-magnetic device which transmits information to a gauge.

SENSOR: Any device designed to measure engine operating conditions or ambient pressures and temperatures. Usually electronic in nature and designed to send a voltage signal to an on-board computer, some sensors may operate as a simple on/off switch or they may provide a variable voltage signal (like a potentiometer) as conditions or measured parameters change.

SHIM: Spacers of precise, predetermined thickness used between parts to establish a proper working relationship.

SLAVE CYLINDER: In automotive use, a device in the hydraulic clutch system which is activated by hydraulic force, disengaging the clutch.

SOLENOID: A coil used to produce a magnetic field, the effect of which is to produce work.

SPARK PLUG: A device screwed into the combustion chamber of a spark ignition engine. The basic construction is a conductive core inside of a ceramic insulator, mounted in an outer conductive base. An electrical charge from the spark plug wire travels along the conductive core and jumps a preset air gap to a grounding point or points at the end of the conductive base. The resultant spark ignites the fuel/air mixture in the combustion chamber.

SPLINES: Ridges machined or cast onto the outer diameter of a shaft or inner diameter of a bore to enable parts to mate without rotation.

TACHOMETER: A device used to measure the rotary speed of an engine, shaft, gear, etc., usually in rotations per minute.

THERMOSTAT: A valve, located in the cooling system of an engine, which is closed when cold and opens gradually in response to engine heating, controlling the temperature of the coolant and rate of coolant flow.

TOP DEAD CENTER (TDC): The point at which the piston reaches the top of its travel on the compression stroke.

TORQUE: The twisting force applied to an object.

TORQUE CONVERTER: A turbine used to transmit power from a driving member to a driven member via hydraulic action, providing changes in drive ratio and torque. In automotive use, it links the driveplate at the rear of the engine to the automatic transmission.

TRANSDUCER: A device used to change a force into an electrical signal.

TRANSISTOR: A semi-conductor component which can be actuated by a small voltage to perform an electrical switching function.

TUNE-UP: A regular maintenance function, usually associated with the replacement and adjustment of parts and components in the electrical and fuel systems of a vehicle for the purpose of attaining optimum performance.

TURBOCHARGER: An exhaust driven pump which compresses intake air and forces it into the combustion chambers at higher than atmospheric pressures. The increased air pressure allows more fuel to be burned and results in increased horsepower being produced.

VACUUM ADVANCE: A device which advances the ignition timing in response to increased engine vacuum.

VACUUM GAUGE: An instrument used to measure the presence of vacuum in a chamber.

VALVE: A device which control the pressure, direction of flow or rate of flow of a liquid or gas.

VALVE CLEARANCE: The measured gap between the end of the valve stem and the rocker arm, cam lobe or follower that activates the valve.

VISCOSITY: The rating of a liquid's internal resistance to flow.

VOLTMETER: An instrument used for measuring electrical force in units called volts. Voltmeters are always connected parallel with the circuit being tested.

WHEEL CYLINDER: Found in the automotive drum brake assembly, it is a device, actuated by hydraulic pressure, which, through internal pistons, pushes the brake shoes outward against the drums.

MASTER
INDEX